Praise for *Graphics Programming with GDI+*

"This is the most comprehensive book about graphics programming using GDI+ so far. A lot of useful sample code inside this book reveals that Mr. Chand apparently has done a fair amount of research on GDI+. This book will be a very useful handbook for everyone who does graphics programming for Windows."

> —*Min Liu, Software Design Engineer of GDI+, Microsoft Corporation*

"*Graphics Programming with GDI+* explores and exploits a wonderful range of GDI+ programming concepts, techniques, and applications for programmers of beginner to intermediate abilities. Being a prolific contributor to the Internet community of developers, Mahesh Chand is offering what seems to be a natural extension of what he does best—sharing his programming skills with other talented programmers. Each chapter compels to the next."

> —*Jason Hattingh, Director, Greystone Digital FX*

"Mahesh does a very good job getting .NET developers up to speed using the GDI+ features supported in the .NET Framework. There is good coverage of graphics fundamentals that helps the reader better understand the concepts of graphics programming with GDI+, and there are some excellent sample applications that demonstrate the graphics topics covered to reinforce the concepts presented."

> —*Charles G. Parker, President, Parallel Consulting, Inc.*

"*Graphics Programming with GDI+* is a comprehensive reference for anyone who wants to leverage this technology. It presents a clear discussion of the topics in such a manner that is comprehensible to the beginner, but sufficiently in-depth to challenge seasoned programmers."

> —*Deborah J. Bechtold, MCSD, MCDBA*

Graphics Programming
with GDI+

Microsoft .NET Development Series

John Montgomery, *Series Advisor*
Don Box, *Series Advisor*
Martin Heller, *Series Editor*

The **Microsoft .NET Development Series** is supported and developed by the leaders and experts of Microsoft development technologies including Microsoft architects and DevelopMentor instructors. The books in this series provide a core resource of information and understanding every developer needs in order to write effective applications and managed code. Learn from the leaders how to maximize your use of the .NET Framework and its programming languages.

Titles in the Series

Brad Abrams, *.NET Framework Standard Library Annotated Reference Volume 1*, 0-321-15489-4

Keith Ballinger, *.NET Web Services: Architecture and Implementation*, 0-321-11359-4

Bob Beauchemin, Niels Berglund, Dan Sullivan, *A First Look at SQL Server 2005 for Developers*, 0-321-18059-3

Don Box with Chris Sells, *Essential .NET, Volume 1: The Common Language Runtime*, 0-201-73411-7

Mahesh Chand, *Graphics Programming with GDI+*, 0-321-16077-0

Anders Hejlsberg, Scott Wiltamuth, Peter Golde, *The C# Programming Language*, 0-321-15491-6

Alex Homer, Dave Sussman, Mark Fussell, *A First Look at ADO.NET and System.Xml v. 2.0*, 0-321-22839-1

Alex Homer, Dave Sussman, Rob Howard, *A First Look at ASP.NET v. 2.0*, 0-321-22896-0

James S. Miller and Susann Ragsdale, *The Common Language Infrastructure Annotated Standard*, 0-321-15493-2

Fritz Onion, *Essential ASP.NET with Examples in C#*, 0-201-76040-1

Fritz Onion, *Essential ASP.NET with Examples in Visual Basic .NET*, 0-201-76039-8

Ted Pattison and Dr. Joe Hummel, *Building Applications and Components with Visual Basic .NET*, 0-201-73495-8

Chris Sells, *Windows Forms Programming in C#*, 0-321-11620-8

Chris Sells and Justin Gehtland, *Windows Forms Programming in Visual Basic .NET*, 0-321-12519-3

Paul Vick, *The Visual Basic .NET Programming Language*, 0-321-16951-4

Damien Watkins, Mark Hammond, Brad Abrams, *Programming in the .NET Environment*, 0-201-77018-0

Shawn Wildermuth, *Pragmatic ADO.NET: Data Access for the Internet World*, 0-201-74568-2

Paul Yao and David Durant, *.NET Compact Framework Programming with C#*, 0-321-17403-8

Paul Yao and David Durant, *.NET Compact Framework Programming with Visual Basic .NET*, 0-321-17404-6

For more information go to www.awprofessional.com/msdotnetseries/

Graphics Programming with GDI+

■ Mahesh Chand

✦✦ Addison-Wesley

Boston • San Francisco • New York • Toronto • Montreal
London • Munich • Paris • Madrid
Capetown • Sydney • Tokyo • Singapore • Mexico City

Many of the designations used by manufacturers and sellers to distinguish their products are claimed as trademarks. Where those designations appear in this book, and Addison-Wesley was aware of a trademark claim, the designations have been printed with initial capital letters or in all capitals.

The .NET logo is either a registered trademark or trademark of Microsoft Corporation in the United States and/or other countries and is used under license from Microsoft.

The author and publisher have taken care in the preparation of this book, but make no expressed or implied warranty of any kind and assume no responsibility for errors or omissions. No liability is assumed for incidental or consequential damages in connection with or arising out of the use of the information or programs contained herein.

The publisher offers discounts on this book when ordered in quantity for bulk purchases and special sales. For more information, please contact:

U.S. Corporate and Government Sales
(800) 382-3419
corpsales@pearsontechgroup.com

For sales outside of the U.S., please contact:

International Sales
(317) 581-3793
international@pearsontechgroup.com

Visit Addison-Wesley on the Web:
www.awprofessional.com

Library of Congress Cataloging-in-Publication Data

Chand, Mahesh
  Graphics programming with GDI+ / Mahesh
  Chand.
    p. cm.
  ISBN 0-321-16077-0 (alk. paper)
  1. Computer graphics. 2. User interfaces
  (Computer systems) I. Title

T385.C4515 2003
006.6—dc22
                                    2003057705

Pearson Education, Inc.
Rights and Contracts Department
75 Arlington Street, Suite 300
Boston, MA 02116
Fax: (617) 848-7047

Text printed on recycled and acid-free paper.

ISBN 0321160770

2 3 4 5 6 7   CRS   07 06 05 04

2nd Printing   October 2004

To Mel and Neel

Contents

Figures

*A color version of this figure is available on the Addison-Wesley Web site at
www.awprofessional.com/titles/0321160770.

Tables

Acknowledgments

FIRST OF ALL, I would like to thank a great team at Addison-Wesley, including Stephane Thomas, John D. Ruley, Michael Mullen, Stephanie Hiebert, and Tyrrell Albaugh, all of whom were very helpful from time to time.

Technical reviewers played a vital role in improving the technical aspects of this book. Their comments and suggestions made me think from various different programming perspectives. I would like to thank technical reviewers Charles Parker, Min Liu, Gilles Khouzam, Jason Hattingh, Chris Garrett, Jeffery Galinovsky, Darrin Bishop, and Deborah Bechtold.

I would also like to thank John O'Donnell for his contribution to the printing chapter of the book (Chapter 11).

Introduction

BY INTRODUCING THE .NET Framework to the programming world, Microsoft has changed the perspective and vision of programming and programmers. Unlike previous programming environments, the .NET Framework is designed with the future of software development in mind. Besides introducing the new C# language and significant additions to Visual Basic .NET and other languages, the .NET Framework provides many new tools and utilities that make a programmer's life easier.

Languages, tools, and utilities aside, the **.NET Framework library** is the real power of the .NET Framework. It's an object-oriented class library that defines an interface to interact with various programming technologies. Any programming language that is designed to work with the .NET Framework can access the library, which makes a programmer's life easier because the methods and properties defined in the library are the same, regardless of the language.

Each class defined in the .NET Framework library belongs to a particular **namespace**—a logical unit that is used to separate a particular programming interface from others. For example, the `System.Windows.Forms` namespace defines classes that are used for Windows Forms development. `System.Data` and its subnamespaces define classes that are used for database development (ADO.NET).

GDI+ is the next-generation graphics device interface, defined in `System.Drawing` and its subnamespaces. This book focuses on how to write graphical Windows and Web applications using GDI+ and C# for the Microsoft .NET Framework.

Who Is This Book For?

This book is designed for intermediate developers who want to write graphics applications for the .NET Framework using GDI+ and C#. Here are the topics we will cover:

- What GDI+ is all about, and how it differs from GDI
- How GDI+ works, and where it is defined in the .NET Framework library
- How to draw text, lines, curves, rectangles, ellipses, and other graphics shapes in GDI+
- How to fill rectangles, ellipses, and other closed curves with different colors, styles, and textures
- Painting and drawing in .NET
- Viewing and manipulating images
- How Windows Forms and Web Forms are related to drawing
- How to write Web-based graphics applications
- Printing in .NET
- Transforming graphics objects, colors, and images
- Interactive color blending and transparent colors
- Using GDI in .NET applications
- Precautions to take when writing GDI+ applications
- Optimizing the performance of GDI+ applications

Prerequisites

There are some things you should know before beginning this book:

- **Language:** This book is written in C#, but developers who want to use GDI+ with other .NET Framework languages—including Visual Basic .NET—can also use this book. Because C# and VB.NET share the same .NET Framework library, there isn't much difference aside from the language syntaxes. Knowledge of C# or VB.NET is not a requirement, however. If you are a C++ developer, you should have no difficulty using this book.

- **Framework:** I used Visual Studio .NET to develop and test the samples in this book. Knowledge of Visual Studio .NET and basics of the .NET Framework is a requirement.
- **Basics of graphics programming:** A basic understanding of graphics programming is a plus but is not mandatory.
- **GDI programming experience:** Experience with GDI programming is a plus but is not mandatory.

What's in This Book That I Won't See in Other Books?

- This book is written by an experienced author who has been watching every .NET move closely since the birth of .NET.
- The author works very closely with the .NET community and has extensive experience developing real-world .NET applications.
- Besides covering GDI+-related namespaces and classes, this book takes a practical approach, discussing all concepts.
- Almost every chapter of the book ends with a real-world application, including FirstWebApp, GDI+Painter, ImageViewer, and many more.
- One chapter (Chapter 13) is dedicated to GDI+ performance techniques, discussing what to do and what *not* to do, when we're writing graphics applications in .NET using GDI+.

Chapter Organization

Before we start, let's take a quick tour of this book. It has 15 chapters and one appendix. Here's a brief introduction:

Chapter 1: GDI+: The Next-Generation Graphics Interface
GDI+ is a new and improved version of GDI. This chapter introduces the GDI+ library, its advantages over previous versions, new features and additions to the library, and how it is related to the .NET Framework.

Chapter 2: Your First GDI+ Application

In the .NET Framework Library, GDI+ functionality is defined in the `System.Drawing` namespace and its subnamespaces. This chapter discusses the contents of these namespaces. After finishing this chapter, you will understand which functionality is defined where and when to which namespace.

Chapter 3: The `Graphics` Class

The `Graphics` class plays a major role in GDI+. Whenever you need to draw a graphics object, you must use the `Graphics` class. This chapter discusses `Graphics` class methods and properties, and how to use them. After completing this chapter, you'll have a pretty good idea how to draw and fill various graphics objects.

Chapter 4: Working with Brushes and Pens

Brushes and pens are used to fill and draw graphics objects. GDI+ provides many classes for working with brushes and pens. This chapter describes how to work with them.

Chapter 5: Colors, Fonts, and Text

This chapter discusses the color-, font-, and text-related classes provided by the .NET Framework class library in more detail.

Chapter 6: Rectangles and Regions

Rectangles and regions can be very useful—and very tricky. This chapter covers them in detail.

Chapter 7: Working with Images

The .NET Framework divides GDI+ functionality between two namespaces: `System.Drawing` and `System.Drawing.Imaging`. This chapter covers the basic imaging-related functionality defined in the `System.Drawing` namespace.

Chapter 8: Advanced Imaging

This chapter discusses more imaging functionality, including the `System.Drawing.Imaging` namespace and how to work with metafiles in the

.NET Framework. We will also see how to maintain the quality and rendering speed of images in GDI+.

Chapter 9: Advanced 2D Graphics

This chapter discusses advanced two-dimensional graphics programming using GDI+. Advanced 2D techniques and tools include blending, matrices, graphics paths, and gradient brushes.

Chapter 10: Transformation

This chapter examines GDI+ transformation. Transformation can be applied not only to graphics shapes, curves, and images, but also to image colors.

Chapter 11: Printing

Printing functionality in the .NET Framework library is defined in the `System.Drawing.Printing` namespace. This chapter explores this namespace and how to write printing applications.

Chapter 12: Developing GDI+ Web Applications

GDI+ can also be used in Web applications. This chapter discusses how to use GDI+ in Web applications with ASP.NET.

Chapter 13: GDI+ Best Practices and Performance Techniques

This chapter concentrates on GDI+ best practices and GDI+-related tips and tricks to improve the quality and performance of drawing.

Chapter 14: GDI Interoperability

This chapter demonstrates how GDI can be used with GDI+ in managed applications.

Chapter 15: Miscellaneous GDI+ Examples

In this chapter we have some fun with GDI+. Among the topics in this chapter are designing interactive GUI applications, creating shaped forms, and adding custom text in images.

Appendix A: Exception Handling in .NET

This appendix introduces exception and error handling in .NET.

Example Source Code

Complete source code for the examples in this book (in both C# and Visual Basic .NET) is available for download at www.awprofessional.com/titles/0321160770.

Exception and Error Handling in the Samples

The .NET Framework supports structured exception handling that's similar to C++ exception handling. The examples in this book do not include exception handling code. Adding exception handling code to every code snippet would have been confusing and redundant. Instead, we discuss exception and error handling concepts in Appendix A. It is highly recommended that you read Appendix A and apply exception and error handling techniques in your applications.

SUMMARY

This introduction explained the book's organization and answered basic questions about the book. In Chapter 1, you will learn the basics of GDI+. Topics we will cover include

- What is GDI+, and why it is a better programming interface than its predecessors?
- How is GDI+ designed and used in the .NET Framework?
- What are the major advantages of GDI+ over GDI?
- How do you write your first graphics application in .NET using GDI+?
- What are some of the basic graphics concepts?

Contact the Author

Mahesh Chand is the founder and administrator of the C# Corner Web site, www.c-sharpcorner.com. You can contact him through his Web site or send him an e-mail at mahesh@c-sharpcorner.com.

▪ 1 ▪
GDI+: The Next-Generation Graphics Interface

W ELCOME TO THE graphics world of GDI+, the next-generation graphics device interface. GDI+ is the gateway to interact with graphics device interfaces in the .NET Framework. If you're going to write .NET applications that interact with graphics devices such as monitors, printers, or files, you will have to use GDI+.

This chapter will introduce GDI+. First we will discuss the theoretical aspects of GDI+, which you should know before starting to write a graphics application.

After reading this chapter, you should understand the following topics:

- What GDI+ is
- How GDI+ is defined
- How to use GDI+ in your applications
- What's new in GDI+
- What the major programming differences between GDI and GDI+ are
- Which major namespaces and classes in the .NET Framework library expose the functionality of GDI+

1.1 Understanding GDI+

If you want to write efficient and optimized graphics applications, it's important to understand the GDI+ class library. In this section we will discuss how GDI+ is defined, and how it can be used in managed and unmanaged applications.

1.1.1 Definition

GDI+ is a library that provides an interface that allows programmers to write Windows and Web graphics applications that interact with graphical devices such as printers, monitors, or files.

All graphical user interface (GUI) applications interact with a hardware device (a monitor, printer, or scanner), that can represent the data in a human-readable form. However, there is no direct communication between a program and a device; otherwise, you would have to write user interface code for each and every device with which your program interacts!

To avoid this monumental task, a third component sits between the program and device. It converts and passes data sent by the program to the device and vice versa. This component is the GDI+ library. Typing a simple "Hello World" on the console, drawing a line or a rectangle, and printing a form are examples in which a program sends data to GDI+, which converts it for use by a hardware device. Figure 1.1 illustrates this process.

Now let's see how GDI+ works. Suppose your program draws a line. A line is displayed as a set of pixels drawn in sequence from the starting location to the ending location. To draw a line on a monitor, the monitor needs to know where to draw the pixels. Instead of telling the monitor to draw pixels, your program calls the DrawLine method of GDI+, and GDI+ draws

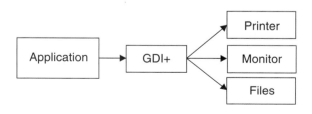

FIGURE 1.1: The role of GDI+

the line from point A to point B. GDI+ reads the point A and point B locations, converts them to a sequence of pixels, and tells the monitor to display the sequence of pixels.

GDI+ allows you to write device-independent managed applications and is designed to provide high performance, ease of use, and multilingual support.

1.1.2 What Is GDI+?

The previous section defined GDI+. But how is it implemented? GDI+ is a set of C++ classes that are located in a class library called `Gdiplus.dll`. `Gdiplus.dll` is a built-in component of the Microsoft Windows XP and Windows Server 2003 operating systems.

▪ TIP

You can use GDI+ on Windows operating systems other than XP. You just need to install GDI+ on the computer, which means that `Gdiplus.dll` must be copied to the system directory. Installing the .NET SDK, Visual Studio .NET, or .NET redistributable copies `Gdiplus.dll` automatically.

Comparing GDI+ to GDI, as we do later in this chapter, is a natural way to introduce GDI+. Note, however, that prior knowledge of GDI is not a prerequisite for learning GDI+ or using this book. This book is about GDI+ development in the .NET Framework, which provides new classes and a new way to write graphics applications. Prior experience with GDI will aid your understanding of the basic concepts, but it is not necessary.

GDI Interoperability

You can use GDI in managed applications with GDI+. GDI interoperability allows you to use GDI functionality in managed applications with GDI+, but you need to take some precautions. We will discuss GDI interoperability in Chapter 14.

1.1.3 The GDI+ Library in the .NET Framework

The previous section said that the GDI+ library is a set of C++ classes that can be used from both managed and unmanaged code. Before we discuss how GDI+ is represented in the .NET Framework library, let's review the concepts of managed and unmanaged code.

1.1.3.1 *Managed and Unmanaged Code*

Code written in the Microsoft .NET development environment is divided into two categories: managed and unmanaged. In brief, code written in the .NET framework that is being managed by the common language runtime (CLR) is called **managed code**. Code that is not being managed by the CLR is called **unmanaged code**.

Managed code enjoys many rich features provided by the CLR, including automatic memory management and garbage collection, cross-language integration, language independence, rich exception handling, improved security, debugging and profiling, versioning, and deployment. With the help of a garbage collector (GC), the CLR automatically manages the life cycle of objects. When the GC finds that an object has not been used after a certain amount of time, the CLR frees resources associated with that object automatically and removes the object from the memory. You can also control the life cycle of objects programmatically.

You can write both managed and unmanaged applications using Microsoft Visual Studio .NET. You can use Visual C++ 7.0 to write unmanaged code in Visual Studio .NET. Managed Extensions to C++ (MC++) is the way to write C++ managed code. Code written using C# and Visual Basic .NET is managed code.

1.1.3.2 *GDI+ in Managed Code*

GDI+ exposes its functionality for both managed and unmanaged code. As noted earlier, GDI+ is a set of unmanaged C++ classes. Programmers tar-

> **■■ NOTE**
> This book targets only managed code development. Unmanaged GDI+ development will not be discussed.

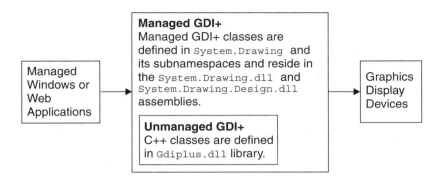

FIGURE 1.2: The managed GDI+ class wrapper

geting unmanaged code can use these C++ classes to write their graphics applications.

The .NET Framework library provides managed classes that are a nice wrapper around GDI+ C++ classes. The GDI+ managed classes provided by the .NET Framework library are defined in the `System.Drawing.dll` and `System.Drawing.Design.dll` assemblies. Figure 1.2 shows a conceptual diagram of the communication between managed Windows and Web applications and display devices through managed GDI+. As the diagram shows, the managed GDI+ classes defined in the `System.Drawing` namespace and its subnamespace are a wrapper around the GDI+ C++ classes defined in the `Gdiplus.dll` unmanaged library.

The managed GDI+ classes provided in the .NET Framework library are defined in the `System.Drawing` namespace and its five subnamespaces: `System.Drawing.Design`, `System.Drawing.Drawing2D`, `System.Drawing.Imaging`, `System.Drawing.Printing`, and `System.Drawing.Text`. We will discuss these namespaces and their classes in more detail in Section 1.4.

1.1.3.3 *GDI+ Revisited*
In brief,

- GDI+ is a component that sits between an application and graphical devices. It converts data into a form compatible with a graphical device, which presents the data in human-readable form.

- GDI+ is implemented as a set of C++ classes that can be used from unmanaged code.
- In the .NET Framework library, GDI+ classes are exposed through `System.Drawing` (and its subnamespaces), which provides a managed class wrapper around the GDI+ C++ classes.

In this book we will be using GDI+ through the namespaces provided by the .NET Framework library. If you want to learn more about GDI+ C++ classes, search for GDI+ references on MSDN. On the GDI+ references page (go to http://msdn.microsoft.com/library, expand **Graphics and Multimedia**, and then click on **GDI+**), you can find all GDI+ classes, functions, constants, enumerations, and structures.

1.1.4 What's New in GDI+ for GDI Programmers?

GDI+ provides significant improvements over its predecessor, GDI. In this section we will take a quick look at these improvements.

GDI+ provides some nice features for 2D vector graphics. One of the many nice features is support for floating point coordinates. For example, the `PointF`, `SizeF`, and `RectangleF` classes represent a floating point, size, and rectangle, respectively. Other objects that use `Point`, `Size`, and `Rectangle` objects also have overloaded methods that can use the `PointF`, `SizeF`, and `RectangleF` objects.

The alpha component, which represents the opacity of a color, is a new addition to the `Color` structure. Alpha blending, anti-aliasing, and color blending are other new additions to the library. We will discuss these topics in more detail in Chapters 5 and 9.

Texture and gradient brushes are another new addition. Some other additions to the basic primitives are compound lines, cardinal splines, scalable regions, inset pens, high-quality filtering and scaling, and many new line styles and line cap options.

Imaging is another area where GDI developers will find many new additions in GDI+. Some of the additions are native support for image file formats such as `.jpeg`, `.png`, `.gif`, `.bmp`, `.tiff`, `.exif`, and `.icon`; support for encoding and decoding raster formats; native image processing support; brightness, contrast, and color balance; and support for transformations, including rotation and cropping.

In color management, support for sRGB, ICM2, and sRGB64 is a new addition. Typography support includes the ClearType, texture, and gradient-filled texts, as well as support for Unicode and Windows 2000 scripts.

1.2 **Exploring GDI+ Functionality**

Microsoft's managed GDI+ documentation divides its functionality into three categories: 2D vector graphics, imaging, and typography. This book divides the GDI+ functionality into five categories:

1. 2D vector graphics
2. Imaging
3. Typography
4. Printing
5. Design

1.2.1 **2D Vector Graphics Programming**

Vector graphics concerns the drawing of shapes that can be specified by sets of points on a coordinate system. Such shapes are called **primitives**; examples include lines, curves, rectangles, and paths. In managed GDI+, a class object or structure represents a graphics primitive. Each class or structure provides members that can be used to get and set a primitive's properties. For example, the `Point` structure provides X and Y properties that represent the x- and y-coordinate values of a point. The `Point` structure also provides methods, including `Ceiling`, `Round`, and `Truncate`. We will discuss these methods in more detail in Chapter 2.

In the .NET Framework library, 2D vector programming is divided into two categories: general and advanced. General 2D vector graphics programming functionality is defined in the `System.Drawing` namespace; advanced functionality is defined in the `System.Drawing.Drawing2D` namespace.

The major 2D vector programming classes defined in the `System.Drawing` namespace are `Pen`, `Pens`, `Brush` (and `Brush`-derived classes), `Brushes`, `Font` (and `Font`-related classes), `Point`, `Rectangle`, and `Size`. We will discuss these classes and their members in more detail in other chapters according to how they are categorized.

The `System.Drawing.Drawing2D` namespace provides blending, color blending, graphics paths, custom line caps, hatch and linear gradient brushes, and matrices. We will discuss these classes and their members in more detail in Chapter 9.

1.2.2 Imaging

Imaging involves viewing and manipulating images. In managed GDI+, imaging functionality is divided into two categories: basic and advanced. The basic functionality is defined in the `Image` class, which also serves as the base class of the `Bitmap` and `Metafile` classes. The `Image` class provides members to load, create, and save images.

The `Bitmap` and `Metafile` classes define functionality for displaying, manipulating, and saving bitmaps and metafiles. Chapters 7 and 8 cover imaging functionality in more detail.

1.2.3 Typography

Typography refers to the design and appearance of text. GDI+ provides classes to create and use fonts. Some of the font-related classes are `Font`, `FontFamily`, and `FontConverter`. GDI+ also provides classes to read all installed fonts on a system. You can also add custom fonts to the font collection. We will cover the capabilities of GDI+ with respect to fonts and typography in Chapter 5.

1.2.4 Printing

GDI+ provides easy-to-use classes that encapsulate Windows printing functionality. The printing classes defined in the .NET Framework class library provide access to and control over available printers, printer sources, paper and paper sources, pages, printer resolution, and so on. GDI+ printing functionality is defined in the `System.Drawing.Printing` namespace. Chapter 11 is dedicated to printing functionality.

1.2.5 **Design**

The GDI+ class library also provides classes that extend design-time user interface (UI) logic and drawing functionality. These classes are defined in the `System.Drawing.Design` namespace. Examples of extended UI functionality include creating custom toolbox items, type-specific value editors, and type converters.

1.3 **GDI+ from a GDI Perspective**

This section is for GDI programmers. To build on your existing knowledge, we will compare and contrast GDI and GDI+. If you've never worked with GDI, we recommend that you skip this section.

We have already mentioned the first and major difference between the two versions: Whereas GDI+ exposes its functionality as both unmanaged and managed classes (through the `System.Drawing` namespace), GDI is unmanaged only. Besides this major difference, some of the important changes in GDI+ are as follows:

- No handles or device contexts
- Object-oriented approach
- Graphics object independence
- Method overloading
- Separate methods for draw and fill
- Regions and their styles

1.3.1 **Elimination of Handles and Device Contexts**

As a GDI programmer, you must be familiar with the **device context**. A device context is a structure that stores information about a particular display device, such as a printer or monitor. This structure specifies how the graphics objects will be drawn on the output device. The device context also stores information about the properties of graphics objects, such as the quality of rendering and so on. To draw an object on a device, first an application needs to get a handle to the device context (HDC), which is used by GDI to send information to the device.

In GDI+, the concept of device context and handle to the device context is replaced by the Graphics object. The Graphics class provides methods and properties to draw various graphics objects; these methods and properties are very easy to use compared to the earlier device context–based programming model.

Suppose that you need to draw a line from point (20, 20) to point (200, 200). In GDI, first an application creates an HDC using the BeginPaint function, which takes a window handle and a PAINTSTRUCT structure. Alternatively, you can call the GetDC function. To draw a line, the application must create a pen object and draw a line using this pen. An application can obtain a pen object by making a call to the CreatePen function, which returns a handle to the pen.

Before starting to draw, the application needs to call the SelectObject function, which takes the device context and pen handle as arguments. Now the application can draw any graphics object. The application calls the EndPaint function to end the drawing process. For example, the code snippet in Listing 1.1 draws a line using the MoveToEx and LineTo functions.

LISTING 1.1: C++ code to draw a line

```cpp
LRESULT APIENTRY MainWndProc(
    HWND hwnd, UINT message, WPARAM wParam,
    LPARAM lParam)
{
    PAINTSTRUCT ps;
    switch (message)
    {
        case WM_PAINT:
            HDC         handle;
            PAINTSTRUCT pstruct;
            HPEN        hPen;
            ...
            ....
            handle = BeginPaint(hWnd, &pstruct);
            hPen = CreatePen(PS_SOLID, 5,
                    RGB(255, 255, 0));
            SelectObject(handle, hPen);
            MoveToEx(handle, 20, 20, NULL);
            LineTo(handle, 200, 200);
            EndPaint(hWnd, &pstruct);
            ...................
            ...................
    }
}
```

Now let's see the same example in GDI+: First you need a `Graphics` object associated with a form, which is usually available on the form's `Form_Paint` event or `OnPaint` method. Once you've got the `Graphics` object associated with a form, you can call its draw and fill methods to draw and fill various graphics objects, such as lines, rectangles, and curves. For example, the code written in Listing 1.2 is the form's paint method. As this code shows, first we get a `Graphics` object associated with the form by using `PaintEventArgs.Graphics`. After that we create a `Pen` object and pass it as an argument to the `DrawLine` method. The `DrawLine` method takes a `Pen` object and the starting and ending points of a line, and draws a line on the form. Notice also in Listing 1.2 that there is no `MoveTo` call.

LISTING 1.2: GDI+ code in C# to draw a line

```
private void Form1_Paint(object sender,
System.Windows.Forms.PaintEventArgs e)
{
Graphics g = e.Graphics;
Pen pn = new Pen(Color.Red, 3);
g.DrawLine(pn, 20, 20, 200, 200);
}
```

> **■ NOTE**
> There are other ways to get a `Graphics` object in your application. We will look at these options in more detail in Chapter 3.

1.3.2 Object-Oriented Approach

If you compare Listings 1.1 and 1.2, it's easy to see that the GDI+ model is more flexible, easier to use, and more object-oriented. GDI provides functions to draw graphics objects; GDI+ provides objects. Each graphics primitive is an object. For example, in GDI+, a pen is represented by a `Pen` object, as opposed to the `HPEN` structure in GDI.

1.3.3 Graphics Object Independence

In GDI, first you select a brush, path, image, or font and pass this object a device context. Then you use the device context handle to draw a graphics object, which means all the objects drawn using that device context will have the same effects.

Unlike GDI, GDI+ provides an object-independent model, which means that pens, brushes, images, or fonts can be created and used independently and can be changed at any time. In addition, an application can even use different pens to draw different graphics objects on the same form, which is not true in the case of a device context.

1.3.4 Method Overloading

GDI+ methods provide many overloaded forms to provide more flexibility to developers. For example, the `DrawRectangle` method has three overloaded forms:

1. `public void DrawRectangle(Pen, Rectangle);`
2. `public void DrawRectangle(Pen, int, int, int, int);`
3. `public void DrawRectangle(Pen, float, float, float, float);`

These forms allow developers to draw a rectangle from a rectangle object, four integer values, or floating point values. The `DrawRectangle` method draws a rectangle specified by a coordinate pair, a width, and a height. The `DrawImage` method, used to draw images, has no fewer than 30 overloaded forms. We will discuss these methods in more detail and see them in action in Chapter 3.

1.3.5 Draw and Fill Methods

Drawing and filling are analogous to writing and painting. When you write, you use a pen to "draw" symbols made up of lines and curves. Painting means you take a brush, dip it into a color, and fill in areas with the color.

In GDI, both actions (fill and draw) are done in one step. For example, consider drawing and filling a rectangle. First an application creates a pen and a brush and calls `SelectObject` to select that pen and brush. Then the application calls the `Rectangle` method, which draws and fills the rectangle. Listing 1.3 shows a code snippet that draws and fills a rectangle.

LISTING 1.3: GDI code to draw and fill a rectangle

```
hBrush = CreateHatchBrush(HS_CROSS, RGB(255, 0, 0));
hPen = CreatePen(PS_SOLID, 3, RGB(255, 0, 0));
SelectObject(hdc, hBrush);
SelectObject(hdc, hPen);
Rectangle(hdc, 20, 20, 200, 200);
```

In GDI+, the `Graphics` class provides separate draw and fill methods. For example, the `DrawRectangle` method takes a `Pen` object and draws an outline of a rectangle, and the `FillRectangle` method takes a `Brush` object and fills the rectangle with the specified brush, as Listing 1.4 shows.

LISTING 1.4: GDI+ code to draw and fill a rectangle

```
Graphics g = e.Graphics;
Pen pn = new Pen(Color.Red, 3);
HatchBrush htchBrush = new HatchBrush(HatchStyle.Cross,
Color.Red, Color.Blue);
g.DrawRectangle(pn, 50, 50, 100, 100);
g.FillRectangle(htchBrush, 20, 20, 200, 200);
```

We will discuss the draw and fill methods in more detail in Chapter 4.

1.3.6 **Regions and Their Styles**

Regions are another area where a GDI developer may find minor changes in GDI+. GDI provides several functions for creating elliptical, round, and polygonal regions. As a GDI programmer, you are probably familiar with the `CreateRectRgn`, `CreateEllipticRgn`, `CreateRoundRectRgn`, `CreatePolygonRgn`, and `CreatePolyPolygonRgn` functions.

In GDI+, the `Region` class represents a region. The `Region` class constructor takes an argument of type `GraphicsPath`, which can have a polygon, a circle, or an ellipse to create a polygonal, round, or elliptical region, respectively. We will discuss regions in more depth in Chapter 6.

1.4 **GDI+ Namespaces and Classes in .NET**

In the .NET Framework library, six namespaces define managed GDI+: `System.Drawing`, `System.Drawing.Design`, `System.Drawing.Drawing2D`,

System.Drawing.Imaging, System.Drawing.Printing, and System.Drawing.Text. Figure 1.3 shows these namespaces. To use any of the classes defined in these namespaces, you must include them in your application.

> **■■ NOTE**
> The .NET Framework class library is also referred as the .NET runtime class library or base class library (BCL).

This section will provide an overview of GDI+ namespaces, their contents, and why and when to use them. These classes and their members will be discussed in more detail in subsequent chapters, according to how they're categorized.

> **■■ NOTE**
> If you are already aware of the .NET Framework library's GDI+ objects and class hierarchy, you may want to skip the rest of this chapter.

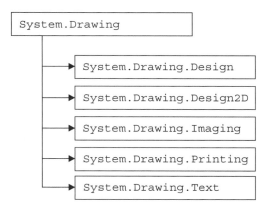

FIGURE 1.3: The GDI+ namespaces in the .NET Framework library

1.4.1 The `System.Drawing` **Namespace**

The `System.Drawing` namespace defines basic GDI+ functionality. This namespace contains the `Graphics` class, which provides methods for filling and drawing graphics objects. It also provides classes that encapsulate GDI+ primitives such as rectangles, points, brushes, and pens. `Brush` and its derived classes are used to fill interiors of graphics objects such as ellipses, rectangles, and polygons with the specified color and pattern. The `Pen` class is used to draw lines and curves with a specified color.

Table 1.1 briefly describes the classes of the `System.Drawing` namespace. We will not discuss these classes in depth here; they are discussed in more detail in later chapters.

The `System.Drawing` namespace also contains some structures that we will be using throughout this book. These structures are `CharacterRange`, `Color`, `Point`, `PointF`, `Rectangle`, `RectangleF`, `Size`, and `SizeF`.

In addition, this namespace defines some delegates and enumerations, which we will discuss in later chapters.

TABLE 1.1: `System.Drawing` classes

Class	Description
Bitmap	Encapsulates a bitmap, which is an image (with its properties) stored in pixel format.
Brush	An abstract base class that cannot be instantiated directly. The `Brush` class provides functionality used by its derived brush classes and represents a brush graphics object. A **brush** is used to fill the interior of a graphical shape with a specified color.
Brushes	Represents brushes with all the standard colors. This class has a static member for each standard color. For example, `Brushes.Blue` represents a blue brush.
ColorConverter	Provides methods and properties to convert colors from one type to another.
ColorTranslator	Provides various methods to translate colors from one type to another.

continues

TABLE 1.1: System.Drawing classes (continued)

Class	Description
Font	Provides members to define the format of font text, name, face, size, and styles. The Font class also provides methods to create a Font object from a window handle to a device context or window handle.
FontConverter	Provides members that convert fonts from one type to another.
FontFamily	Defines a group of typefaces having a similar basic design and certain variations in styles.
Graphics	A key class that encapsulates drawing surfaces. Among many other things, the Graphics class provides members to draw and fill graphical objects.
Icon	Represents a Windows icon. The Icon class provides members to define the size, width, and height of an icon.
IconConverter	Provides members to convert an Icon object from one type to another.
Image	Provides members to define the size, height, width, and format of an image. The Image class also provides methods to create Image objects from a file, a window handle, or a stream; and to save, rotate, and flip images. It is an abstract base class, and its functionality is used through its derived classes: Bitmap, Icon, and Metafile.
ImageAnimator	Provides methods to start and stop animation, and to update frames for an image that has time-based frames.
ImageConverter	Provides members to convert Image objects from one type to another.
ImageFormatConverter	Defines members that can be used to convert images from one format to another.
Pen	Defines a pen with a specified color and width. A **pen** is used to draw graphical objects such as a line, a rectangle, a curve, or an ellipse.

TABLE 1.1: `System.Drawing` classes (continued)

Class	Description
`Pens`	Provides static members for all the standard colors. For example, `Pens.Red` represents a red pen.
`PointConverter`	Defines members that can be used to convert `Point` objects from one type to another.
`RectangleConverter`	Defines members that can be used to convert `Rectangle` objects from one type to another.
`Region`	Represents a region in GDI+, which describes the interior of a graphics shape.
`SizeConverter`	Defines members that can be used to convert size from one type to another.
`SolidBrush`	Inherited from the `Brush` class. This class defines a solid brush of a single color.
`StringFormat`	Provides members to define text format, including alignment, trimming and line spacing, display manipulations, and OpenType features.
`SystemBrushes`	Defines static properties. Each property is a `SolidBrush` object with a Windows display element such as `Highlight`, `HighlightText`, or `ActiveBorder`.
`SystemColors`	Defines static properties of a `Color` structure.
`SystemIcons`	Defines static properties for Windows systemwide icons.
`SystemPens`	Defines static properties. Each property is a `Pen` object with the color of a Windows display element and a width of 1.
`TextureBrush`	Inherited from the `Brush` class. This class defines a brush that has an image as its texture.
`ToolboxBitmapAttribute`	Defines the images associated with a specified component.

1.4.2 **The** `System.Drawing.Design` **Namespace**

As its name suggests, the `System.Drawing.Design` namespace provides additional functionality to develop design-time controls such as custom toolbox items, graphics editors, and type converters. The classes of the `System.Drawing.Design` namespace are described briefly in Table 1.2.

Besides the classes discussed in Table 1.2, the `System.Drawing.Design` namespace also defines a few interfaces, delegates, and enumerations. Table 1.3 lists the interfaces defined in this namespace.

1.4.3 **The** `System.Drawing.Drawing2D` **Namespace**

The `System.Drawing.Drawing2D` namespace defines functionality to develop advanced two-dimensional and vector graphics applications. This namespace provides classes for graphics containers, blending, advanced brushes, matrices, and transformation. Table 1.4 briefly describes these classes.

Besides the classes discussed in Table 1.4, the `System.Drawing.Drawing2D` namespace provides dozens of enumerations. We will discuss these enumerations when we use them in examples in later chapters.

1.4.4 **The** `System.Drawing.Imaging` **Namespace**

Basic imaging functionality is defined in the `System.Drawing` namespace. The `System.Drawing.Imaging` namespace provides functionality for advanced imaging. Before an application uses classes from this namespace, it must reference the `System.Drawing.Imaging` namespace.

Table 1.5 briefly describes the classes of the `System.Drawing.Imaging` namespace. These classes and their use are discussed in more detail in Chapter 8.

1.4.5 **The** `System.Drawing.Printing` **Namespace**

The `System.Drawing.Printing` namespace defines printing-related classes and types in GDI+. Before an application uses classes from this namespace, it must include the namespace.

Table 1.6 briefly discusses the classes provided by the System.Drawing.Printing namespace. These classes and their use are discussed in more detail in Chapter 11.

1.4.6 **The** System.Drawing.Text **Namespace**

The System.Drawing.Text namespace contains only a few classes related to advanced GDI+ typography functionality. Before an application uses classes from this namespace, it must include the namespace. Table 1.7 describes these classes; they will be discussed in more detail in Chapter 5.

TABLE 1.2: System.Drawing.Design classes

Class	Description
BitmapEditor	User interface (UI) for selecting bitmaps using a **Properties** window.
CategoryNameCollection	Collection of categories.
FontEditor	UI for selecting and configuring fonts.
ImageEditor	UI for selecting images in a **Properties** window.
PaintValueEventArgs	Provides data for the PaintValue event.
PropertyValueUIItem	Provides information about the property value UI for a property.
ToolboxComponents-CreatedEventArgs	Provides data for the ComponentsCreated event, which occurs when components are added to the toolbox.
ToolboxComponents-CreatingEventArgs	Provides data for the ComponentsCreating event, which occurs when components are added to the toolbox.
ToolboxItem	Provides a base implementation of a toolbox item.
ToolboxItemCollection	Collection of toolbox items.
UITypeEditor	Provides a base class that can be used to design value editors.

TABLE 1.3: `System.Drawing.Design` interfaces

Interface	Description
`IPropertyValueUIService`	Manages the property list of the **Properties** window.
`IToolboxService`	Provides access to the toolbox.
`IToolboxUser`	Tests the toolbox for toolbox item support capabilities and selects the current tool.

TABLE 1.4: `System.Drawing.Drawing2D` classes

Class	Description
`AdjustableArrowCap`	Represents an adjustable arrow-shaped line cap. Provides members to define the properties to fill, and to set the height and width of an arrow cap.
`Blend`	Gradient blends are used to provide smoothness and shading to the interiors of shapes. A blend pattern contains factor and pattern arrays, which define the position and percentage of color of the starting and ending colors. The `Blend` class defines a blend pattern, which uses `LinearGradientBrush` to fill the shapes. The `Factors` and `Positions` properties represent the array of blend factors and array of positions for the gradient, respectively.
`ColorBlend`	Defines color blending in multicolor gradients. The `Color` and `Position` properties represent the color array and position array, respectively.
`CustomLineCap`	Encapsulates a custom, user-defined line cap.
`GraphicsContainer`	Represents the data of a graphics container. A graphics container is created by `Graphics.BeginContainer` followed by a call to `Graphics.EndContainer`.
`GraphicsPath`	In GDI+, a path is a series of connected lines and curves. This class provides properties to define the path's fill mode and other properties. This class also defines methods to add graphics shapes to a path.

TABLE 1.4: `System.Drawing.Drawing2D` classes (continued)

Class	Description
	For instance, the `AddArc` and `AddCurve` methods add an arc and a curve, respectively, to the path. `Wrap`, `Transform`, `Reverse`, and `Reset` are some of the associated methods.
`GraphicsPathIterator`	A path can contain subpaths. This class provides the ability to find the number of subpaths and iterate through them. `Count` and `SubpathCount` return the number of points and the number of subpaths in a path, respectively.
`GraphicsState`	Represents the state of a `Graphics` object.
`HatchBrush`	Hatch brushes are brushes with a hatch style, a foreground color, and a background color. This class represents a hatch brush in GDI+.
`LinearGradientBrush`	Represents a brush with a linear gradient.
`Matrix`	Encapsulates a 3×3 matrix that represents a geometric **transformation**. This class defines methods for inverting, multiplying, resetting, rotating, scaling, shearing, and translating matrices.
`PathData`	Contains the data in the form of points and types that makes up a path. The `Points` property of the class represents an array of points, and the `Types` property represents the types of the points in a path.
`PathGradientBrush`	Represents a brush with a graphics path. `PathGradientBrush` contains methods and properties for blending, wrapping, scaling, and transformation. This class encapsulates a `Brush` object that fills the interior of a `GraphicsPath` object with a gradient.
`RegionData`	Represents the data stored by a `Region` object. The `Data` property of this class represents the data in the form of an array of bytes.

TABLE 1.5: `System.Drawing.Imaging` classes

Class	Description
BitmapData	Often we don't want to load and refresh all data of a bitmap because rendering each pixel is not only a slow process, but also consumes system resources. With the help of the `BitmapData` class and its `LockBits` and `UnlockBits` methods, we can lock the required data of a bitmap in memory and work with that instead of working with all the data.
ColorMap	Defines a map for converting colors. `ColorMap` is used by the `ImageAttributes` class.
ColorMatrix	Defines a 5×5 matrix that contains coordinates for the ARGB space. `ColorMatrix` is used by the `ImageAttributes` class.
ColorPalette	Defines an array of colors that make up a color palette. `ColorPalette` is used by the `ImageAttributes` class.
Encoder	Represents an encoder, which represents a globally unique identifier (GUID) that identifies the category of an image encoder parameter. `Encoder` is used by the `EncoderParameter` class.
EncoderParameter	An encoder parameter, which sets values for a particular category of an image. This class is used in the Save method with the help of `EncoderParameters`.
EncoderParameters	An array of `EncoderParameter` objects.
FrameDimension	Provides properties to get the frame dimensions of an image.
ImageAttributes	Contains information about how image colors are manipulated during rendering (for more information, see Chapter 7).
ImageCodecInfo	Retrieves information about the installed image codecs.
ImageFormat	Specifies the format of an image.

TABLE 1.5: **System.Drawing.Imaging** classes (continued)

Class	Description
Metafile	Defines a graphic metafile, which contains graphics operations in the form of records that can be recorded (constructed) and played back (displayed).
MetafileHeader	Stores information about a metafile.
MetaHeader	Contains information about a Windows-format (WMF) metafile.
PropertyItem	Encapsulates a metadata property to be included in an image file.
WmfPlaceableFileHeader	Defines a placeable metafile.

TABLE 1.6: **System.Drawing.Printing** classes

Class	Description
Margins	Specifies the margins of a printed page. The Bottom, Left, Right, and Top properties are used to get and set the bottom, left, right, and top margins, respectively, of a page in hundredths of an inch.
MarginsConverter	Provides methods to convert margins, including CanConvertFrom, CanConvertTo, ConvertFrom, and ConvertTo.
PageSettings	Specifies settings of a page, including properties such as Bounds, Color, Landscape, Margins, PaperSize, PaperSource, PrinterResolution, and PrinterSettings.
PaperSize	Specifies the paper size. Its properties include Height, Width, PaperName, and Kind. The Kind property is the type of paper, represented by the PaperKind enumeration, which has members that represent A3, envelopes, sheets, ledgers, and so on.

continues

TABLE 1.6: `System.Drawing.Printing` classes (continued)

Class	Description
`PaperSource`	Specifies the paper tray from which the printer gets paper, with properties `Kind` and `Source-Name`. `SourceName` is a type of `PaperSource` enumeration, which defines members based on the `Kind` property.
`PreviewPageInfo`	Provides print preview information for a single page. The `Image` property returns the image of the printed page, and the `PhysicalSize` property returns the size of the printed page in 1/1000 inch.
`PreviewPrintController`	Displays a document on a screen as a series of images for each page. The `UseAntiAlias` property gets and sets the anti-aliasing when displaying the print preview.
`PrintController`	Controls how a document is printed. The class provides four methods: `OnStartPage`, `OnStartPrint`, `OnEndPage`, and `OnEndPrint`.
`PrintDocument`	Starts the printing process. Creates an instance of this class, sets the printing properties that describe how to print, and calls the `Print` method to start the process.
`PrinterResolution`	Provides properties to return a printer resolution. The `Kind`, `X`, and `Y` properties return the printer resolution, horizontal resolution in dots per inch (dpi), and vertical printer resolution in dpi, respectively.
`PrinterSettings`	Provides methods and properties for setting how a document is printed, including the printer that prints it. Some of the common properties are `MinimumPage`, `MaximumPage`, `Copies`, `MaximumCopies`, `PrinterName`, and so on.
`PrinterSettings .PaperSizeCollection`	Collection of `PaperSize` objects.
`PrinterSettings .PaperSourceCollection`	Collection of `PaperSource` objects.

TABLE 1.6: `System.Drawing.Printing` classes (continued)

Class	Description
`PrinterSettings.Printer-ResolutionCollection`	Collection of `PrinterResolution` objects.
`PrinterUnitConvert`	Specifies a series of conversion methods that are useful when interoperating with the Win32 printing application program interface (API).
`PrintEventArgs`	Provides data for the `BeginPrint` and `EndPrint` events.
`PrintingPermission`	Controls access to printers.
`PrintingPermission-Attribute`	Allows declarative printing permission checks.
`PrintPageEventArgs`	Provides data for the `PrintPage` event.
`QueryPageSettings-EventArgs`	Provides data for the `QueryPageSettings` event.
`StandardPrintController`	Specifies a print controller that sends information to a printer.

TABLE 1.7: `System.Drawing.Text` classes

Class	Description
`FontCollection`	Abstract base class for installed and private font collections. It provides a method to get a list of the font families contained in the collection. Two derived classes from the `FontCollection` class are `InstalledFontCollection` and `PrivateFontCollection`.
`InstalledFontCollection`	Represents the fonts installed on the system.
`PrivateFontCollection`	Represents a collection of font families built from font files that are provided by the client application.

SUMMARY

GDI+ is an improved version of Microsoft's graphics device interface (GDI) API. In this chapter we learned how GDI+ is designed for use in both managed and unmanaged code. `System.Drawing` and its helper namespaces defined in the .NET Framework library provide a managed class wrapper to write managed GDI+ applications. We also learned the basics and definition of GDI+ and what major improvements are offered by GDI+ in comparison to GDI. At the end of this chapter, we took a quick look at the `System.Drawing` namespace and its subnamespaces, and classes defined in these namespaces.

Now that you've learned the basics of GDI+, the next step is to write a fully functional graphics application. In Chapter 2 you will learn how to write your first graphics application using GDI+ in a step-by-step tutorial format.

2

Your First GDI+ Application

I N THIS CHAPTER we move to the more practical aspects of writing graphics applications using GDI+ in the .NET Framework. This chapter is the foundation chapter and discusses vital concepts, including the life cycle of a graphics application. After reading this chapter, you should understand the basics of the GDI+ coordinate system, basic graphics structures used by GDI+, drawing surfaces, and how to write a graphics application using GDI+.

To write a graphics application, a good understanding of drawing surfaces and coordinate systems is necessary. We will begin by discussing these concepts and how they are represented in GDI+. Then you'll learn step-by-step how to write a graphics application in the .NET Framework using GDI+. We will cover the following topics:

- How to add a reference to the GDI+ library
- How to get a drawing surface in the program
- How to create pens and brushes
- How to use pens and brushes to draw graphics objects

At the end of this chapter we will discuss some basic graphics structures and their members. These structures are used in examples throughout this book and include the following:

- Color
- Point and PointF

- `Rectangle` and `RectangleF`
- `Size` and `SizeF`

2.1 Drawing Surfaces

Every drawing application (regardless of the operating system), consists of three common components: a canvas, a brush or pen, and a process.

1. The **canvas** is the space on which objects will be drawn. For example, in a Windows application, a Windows Form is a canvas.
2. A **brush** or a **pen** represents the texture, color, and width of the objects to be drawn on the canvas.
3. The **process** describes how objects are drawn on the canvas.

To draw graphics objects you need to have a pen or a brush, which defines the texture, color, and width of the drawing. For example, if you draw a line or a rectangle, you need to create a pen with a color and width.

The process component of the drawing application includes making a call to draw the line or rectangle on the form.

Each drawing surface has four common properties: width, height, resolution, and color depth.

- The **width** and **height** properties of a surface determine the size of the surface, and they are specified by the number of pixels horizontally and vertically, respectively.
- The **resolution** property of a surface is a measurement of the output quality of graphics objects or images in dots per inch (dpi). For example, a resolution of 72 dpi means that 1 inch of the surface holds 72 horizontal and 72 vertical pixels. For monitors and LCDs, the resolution is frequently specified in terms of the total number of pixels horizontally and vertically rather than a pixel density. Thus a monitor resolution of 1280×1024 means that the screen of the monitor can hold 1,280 horizontal pixels and 1,024 vertical pixels.
- The **color depth** of a surface is the number of colors used to represent each pixel.

> ■ **DEFINITION: PIXEL**
> A **pixel** is the smallest element that participates in the drawing process to display graphics objects or images on the screen. The pixel density is often represented by a value in dots per inch (dpi).

The quality of a pixel is directly proportional to the color depth. The `Color` structure represents a color in GDI+. It has four components: alpha, red, green, and blue. The **RGB (red-green-blue) components** of a color represent the number of possible colors (see Figure 2.1). Each component in RGB has 256 (2^8) color combinations. Hence all three components of GDI+ color represent 256×256×256 possible colors. The **alpha component** determines the transparency of the color, which affects how the color mixes with other colors.

To see the proper colors defined in the GDI+ color structure, a drawing surface must support at least a 24-bit color system (for the RGB components of a color structure), which means that each pixel of the surface must be able to hold 24 bits (8 bits each for the R, G, and B components, as noted already). Surfaces with less than 24 bits per pixel may not display graphics objects and images exactly as defined in a drawing application. We will discuss colors in more detail in Chapter 5.

> ■ **NOTE**
> The color depth of a surface is different from the color depth of a particular display device, such as a monitor or a printer. Most monitors can support over a million colors, and some printers may support only black and white.

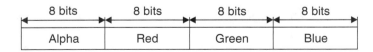

FIGURE 2.1: Color components in GDI+

GDI+ provides three types of drawing surfaces: forms, printers, and bitmaps.

2.1.1 Forms as a Surface

When you write a Windows application that draws something on a form, the form acts as a drawing surface and supports all the properties required by a drawing surface.

2.1.2 Printers as a Surface

When you print from an application, the printer acts as a drawing surface. You can set a printer's resolution and color depth, as well as the height and width of the paper. We will discuss printer-related functionality in Chapter 11.

2.1.3 Bitmaps as a Surface

When you create images in memory and save them as a bitmap, the bitmap functions as a drawing surface. You can set the image width, height, resolution, and color depth properties. Bitmap surfaces are commonly used for writing graphics Web applications. Drawing works a little differently in Web applications. For example, if you want to draw a line and a rectangle in a Web page using GDI+, you need to create an image, use this image as a surface for the line and rectangle objects, set its surface-related properties, and then send the image to the browser. We will discuss Web graphics applications in more detail in Chapter 12.

2.2 The Coordinate System

Understanding the coordinate system is another important part of graphics programming. The coordinate system represents the positions of graphic objects on a display device such as a monitor or a printer.

2.2.1 The Cartesian Coordinate System

The **Cartesian coordinate system** (shown in Figure 2.2) divides a two-dimensional plane into four regions, also called quadrants, and two axes: x and y. The x-axis is represented by a horizontal line and the y-axis by a

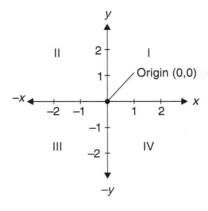

FIGURE 2.2: The Cartesian coordinate system

vertical line. An ordered pair of x and y positions defines a point in a plane. The origin of the plane is a point with $x = 0$ and $y = 0$ values, and the quadrants divide the plane relative to the origin.

To find out which point falls in which quadrant, we compare the point's x- and y-positions relative to the origin:

Quadrant I: $x > 0$ and $y > 0$

Quadrant II: $x < 0$ and $y > 0$

Quadrant III: $x < 0$ and $y < 0$

Quadrant IV: $x > 0$ and $y < 0$

A point with positive x and y values will fall in quadrant I. A point with $+y$ and $-x$ values will fall in quadrant II. A point with $-x$ and $-y$ values will fall in quadrant III, and a point with $+x$ and $-y$ values will fall in quadrant IV. For example, a point at coordinates $(2, -3)$ will fall in quadrant IV, and a point at coordinates $(-3, 2)$ will fall in quadrant II.

2.2.2 The Default GDI+ Coordinate System

Unlike the Cartesian coordinate system, the default **GDI+ coordinate system** starts with the origin in the upper left corner. The default x-axis points to the right, and the y-axis points down. As Figure 2.3 shows, the upper left corner starts with points $x = 0$ and $y = 0$. Points to the left of $x = 0$ are

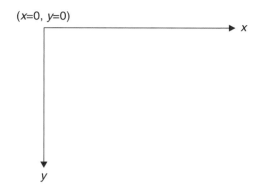

FIGURE 2.3: The GDI+ coordinate system

negative values in the x-direction, and points above $y = 0$ are negative values in the y-direction.

Because the default GDI+ coordinate system starts with ($x = 0$, $y = 0$) in the upper left corner of the screen, by default you can see only the points that have positive x and y values. Objects with either $-x$ or $-y$ values will not be visible on the screen. However, you can apply transformations to move objects with negative values into the visible area.

GDI+ provides three types of coordinate systems: world coordinates, page coordinates, and device coordinates.

1. The coordinate system used in an application is called **world coordinates**. Suppose that your application draws a line from point A (0, 0) to point B (120, 80), as shown in Figure 2.4. If you don't apply any transformation, the line will be displayed at the right location. Now suppose you want to draw a line from point A (–40, –50) to point B (–10, –20). The line drawn using these two points will not be displayed on the screen because the GDI+ coordinate system starts at point (0, 0). However, you can transform the coordinates such that (–40, –50) is the starting point at the top left corner of the surface.

2. The new coordinate system is called **page coordinates**. The process of converting world coordinates to page coordinates is called the *world transformation*.

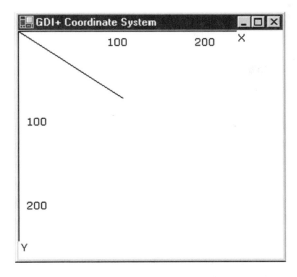

FIGURE 2.4: Drawing a line from point (0, 0) to point (120, 80)

3. You can also control the actual size of graphics objects. For example, if you want to draw a line in inches instead of pixels, you can simply draw a line from point A (1, 1) to point B (1, 2), thereby creating a line that is 1 inch long. The new coordinates are called **device coordinates**. The process of converting page coordinates to device coordinates is called the *page transformation*.

We will discuss coordinate systems and transformation in more detail in Chapter 10.

2.3 Tutorial: Your First GDI+ Application

In this section you'll learn how to write your first GDI+ application, step-by-step. You will create a Windows application and draw a few simple objects, such as lines, rectangles, and ellipses, on a Windows Form.

Here are the steps we will cover:

1. Creating a Windows application
2. Adding references to the GDI+ library
3. Obtaining the graphics surface

4. Setting the graphics surface properties (optional)

5. Drawing or filling graphics shapes

6. Releasing objects

7. Building and running the application

2.3.1 Creating a Windows Application

The first step of this tutorial is to create a Windows application using Visual Studio .NET.

1. Open Visual Studio .NET, select **File | New | Project**, and then choose **Visual C# Projects** under **Project Types** and **Windows Application** under **Templates**, as shown in Figure 2.5.

2. Enter the application name, "FirstGDI+App", and click **OK**.

> **NOTE**
> Clicking the **OK** button creates a Windows application with a form and opens the Form Designer, in which you can build Windows applications.

2.3.2 Adding a Reference to GDI+

As mentioned in Chapter 1, GDI+ functionality resides in the `System.Drawing.dll` namespace and is defined in the `System.Drawing` namespace. Hence the `System.Drawing` namespace must be included in the application. Visual Studio .NET automatically adds a reference to this namespace, which you can see in the beginning of the class. If the namespace is not defined there, you must add a reference manually. To add a reference to the GDI+ library, you use the **Add Reference** dialog.

1. Open the **Add Reference** dialog by selecting **Project | Add Reference**.

2. Select the **System.Drawing.dll** assembly from the libraries listed under the **.NET** tab.

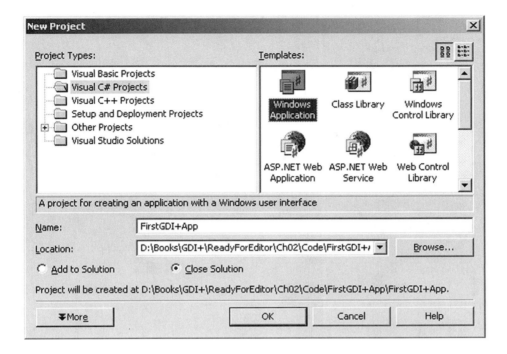

FIGURE 2.5: Creating a Windows application

3. Click the **Select** button to add the library to the **Selected Components** list, as shown in Figure 2.6.

4. Click the **OK** button to add the System.Drawing namespace reference to your project.

5. Go to the **Solution Explorer** window and expand the **References** node. The System.Drawing namespace is listed there Figure 2.7).

▪ NOTE

Visual Studio .NET version 1.0 (or later) automatically adds a reference to the System.Drawing.dll library. In that case, you may not need to add a reference to the library.

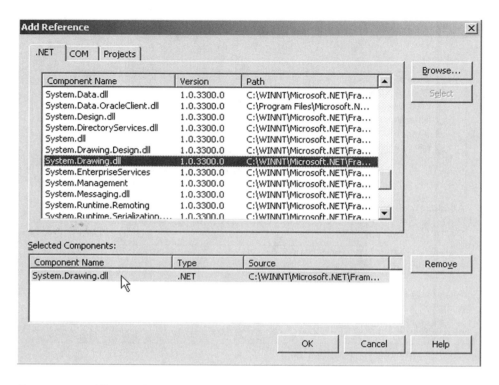

FIGURE 2.6: Adding a reference to `System.Drawing.dll`

FIGURE 2.7: The `System.Drawing` namespace in a project

6. After adding a reference to `System.Drawing.dll`, you must import `System.Drawing` and other related namespaces, depending on the classes your application will use. For now, we will import the `System.Drawing` and `System.Drawing.Drawing2D` namespaces. We add the following two lines to the top of our class:

```
using System.Drawing;
using System.Drawing.Drawing2D;
```

You can also qualify a namespace reference by directly adding it as a prefix of the class. For example, if you don't want to use the `using` statements defined here, you can define a class as follows:

```
System.Drawing.Graphics g = e.Graphics;
```

> **NOTE**
>
> If you create a Windows application using VS.NET, only the line `using System.Drawing.Drawing2D` needs to be written because `using System.Drawing` will already be there.

2.3.3 Getting a `Graphics` Object in an Application

After adding a GDI+ library reference to the project, the next step is to decide on a drawing surface. In a Windows application, a form is a drawing surface. Every form has a `Graphics` object associated with it, which provides the drawing functionality.

In the .NET Framework, the `Graphics` class represents a GDI+ `Graphics` object, which defines methods and properties to draw and fill graphics objects. Whenever an application needs to draw anything, it must go through the `Graphics` object.

> **CAUTION**
>
> There is no way to create a `Graphics` object using the `new` operator. For example, if you write the following code, you will get a compiler error:
>
> ```
> Graphics g = new Graphics ()
> ```

There are several ways to obtain a `Graphics` object associated with a form. Three of them are described in the following sections.

2.3.3.1 *Using the Paint Event of a Form*

You can get a `Graphics` object corresponding to a form using the `PaintEventArgs` property of the form's paint event. For example, the following code gets a `Graphics` object from `PaintEventArgs`:

```
private void form1_Paint(object sender, PaintEventArgs e)
{
        Graphics g = e.Graphics;
}
```

You can add the form's paint event handler using the **Properties** window. As Figure 2.8 shows, we add `Form1_Paint` (the default name) as the paint event handler.

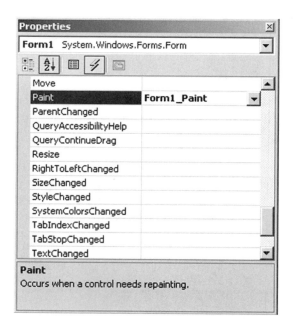

FIGURE 2.8: Adding the `Form_Paint` event handler

> **▪▪ TIP**
> Double-clicking in the paint event drop-down menu in the **Properties** window also adds the event handler.

2.3.3.2 *Overriding the OnPaint Method*

Another way to get a `Graphics` object associated with a form is to override the `OnPaint` method of the form, which uses `PaintEventArgs` in a manner similar to the `Form1_Paint` event. The following code snippet overrides the `OnPaint` method of a form:

```
protected override void OnPaint(PaintEventArgs e)
{
  Graphics g = e.Graphics;
}
```

2.3.3.3 *Using Other Methods*

Sometimes you don't want to use the `OnPaint` method. For example, you might want to draw something on a button or a menu click event handler. The `Form` class provides the `CreateGraphics` method, which returns a `Graphics` object. The following code snippet creates a `Graphics` object using the `CreateGraphics` method and calls a method of the `Graphics` class:

```
Graphics g = this.CreateGraphics();
g.Clear(this.BackColor);
g.Dispose();
```

As this snippet shows, we call the `Clear` method of the `Graphics` class, which sets the background color of the surface as the background color of the form.

> **▪▪ CAUTION**
> When you create a `Graphics` object using the `CreateGraphics` method, you must dispose of that object explicitly by calling the `Dispose` method to release the resources associated with it.

You can also use the `FromImage`, `FromHwnd`, and `FromHdc` static methods of the `Graphics` class to create `Graphics` objects from images, window handles, and window handles to device contexts, respectively. We will discuss these methods in more detail in Chapter 3 (Section 3.2.3.3).

The following code creates a `Bitmap` object and calls the static `FromImage` method, using a `Bitmap` object as an input parameter, which returns a `Graphics` object.

```
Bitmap bmp =
    new Bitmap(600,400,PixelFormat.Format32bppArgb);
Graphics g = Graphics.FromImage(bmp);
```

The following code creates a `Graphics` object from a window handle. In this example, `this` refers to a Windows Form. You can even pass `Form1.Handle` if your form is `Form1`.

```
Graphics g = Graphics.FromHwnd(this.Handle);
```

2.3.4 Creating Pens and Brushes

Once you have a `Graphics` object, the next step is to decide what you're going to draw on the surface. You may need one or more of the three objects: pen, brush, or image. In this chapter we will concentrate on pens and brushes only. Images are discussed in Chapters 7 and 8.

In GDI+ the `Pen` and `Brush` classes represent a pen and a brush, respectively. The abstract `Brush` class functionality is accessed through its derived classes: `SolidBrush` and `HatchBrush`, among others. Pens are used when you need to draw lines, rectangles, and curve boundaries. Brushes are used when you need to fill graphics objects. Chapter 4 discusses pens and brushes in detail.

The `Pen` class constructor takes as arguments the color and width of the pen. The following code creates a red pen with a width of 3 pixels and a black pen with a width of 1 pixel. The `Pens` class provides static members, each of which represents a pen with a particular color.

```
Pen redPen = new Pen(Color.Red, 3);
Pen blackPen = Pens.Black;
```

The SolidBrush class represents a solid brush in GDI+. This class's constructor takes a color as an argument. The following code creates a green solid brush.

```
SolidBrush greenBrush = new SolidBrush(Color.Green);
```

2.3.5 Drawing Graphics Shapes

Once you have the surface, pens, and/or brushes, you can draw lines, shapes, curves, or images. The Graphics class provides draw and fill methods to draw and fill graphics shapes, curves, or images. For example, the FillRectangle method draws a rectangle with a filled color, and DrawRectangle draws the boundary of a rectangle with the specified pen. Draw methods take a pen as an argument, and fill methods take a brush.

We override the OnPaint method and write the code in Listing 2.1 on this method. As Listing 2.1 shows, we first set the smoothing mode of the Graphics object by setting its SmoothingMode property. The Smoothing-Mode enumeration is defined in the System.Drawing.Advanced2D namespace and is used to set the quality of a graphics object. In our code, we set the smoothing mode to anti-aliasing. We will discuss this in more detail in Chapters 8 and 9.

After that we create a rectangle, two pens, and a solid brush. In the next code snippet, we call the DrawRectangle, FillEllipse, and DrawLine methods. The DrawRectangle method draws the boundaries of a rectangle, the FillEllipse method fills an ellipse with the specified brush, and the DrawLine method draws a line using the specified pen. Chapter 3 will discuss the fill and draw methods in more detail.

LISTING 2.1: Drawing lines, rectangles, and ellipses

```
protected override void OnPaint(PaintEventArgs e)
{
  // Obtain the Graphics object
  Graphics g = e.Graphics;
  // Set the smoothing mode of the surface
  g.SmoothingMode = SmoothingMode.AntiAlias;
  // Create a rectangle with height 100 and width 100
  Rectangle rect = new Rectangle(20, 20, 100, 100);
```

continues

```
// Create two Pen objects, one red and one black
Pen redPen = new Pen(Color.Red, 3);
Pen blackPen = Pens.Black;
// Create a SolidBrush object
SolidBrush greenBrush = new SolidBrush(Color.Green);
// Draw shapes and lines
g.DrawRectangle(redPen, rect);
g.FillEllipse(greenBrush, rect);
g.DrawLine(blackPen, 0, 250, this.Width, 250);
g.FillEllipse(Brushes.Blue, 70, 220, 30, 30);
g.FillEllipse(Brushes.SkyBlue, 100, 210, 40, 40);
g.FillEllipse(Brushes.Green, 140, 200, 50, 50);
g.FillEllipse(Brushes.Yellow, 190, 190, 60, 60);
g.FillEllipse(Brushes.Violet, 250, 180, 70, 70);
g.FillEllipse(Brushes.Red, 320, 170, 80, 80);
}
```

2.3.6 Releasing Objects

When you are done using objects, you must release them. In the .NET Framework library, most objects provide a Dispose method, which can be used to dispose of an object. The Dispose method makes sure that all resources allocated for an object are released.

The following code snippet creates Pen and SolidBrush objects as redPen and greenBrush, respectively:

```
Pen redPen = new Pen(Color.Red, 3);
SolidBrush greenBrush = new SolidBrush(Color.Green);
```

When you are done with these objects, call the Dispose method to release the resources allocated with them. For example, the following code snippet disposes of the redPen and greenBrush objects:

```
redPen.Dispose();
greenBrush.Dispose();
```

Now we will Dispose of the previously created objects using the Dispose method to the objects we created in Listing 2.1, as shown in Listing 2.2. (Boldface lines are the new lines added to the listing.)

LISTING 2.2: Using Dispose calls

```
protected override void OnPaint(PaintEventArgs e)
{
  // Obtain the Graphics object
  Graphics g = e.Graphics;
  // Set the composite quality and smoothing mode
  // of the surface
  g.SmoothingMode = SmoothingMode.AntiAlias;
  // Create a rectangle from point (20, 20) to (100, 100)
  Rectangle rect = new Rectangle(20, 20, 100, 100);
  // Create two Pen objects, one red and one black
  Pen redPen = new Pen(Color.Red, 3);
  Pen blackPen = Pens.Black;
  // Create a SolidBrush object
  SolidBrush greenBrush = new SolidBrush(Color.Green);
  // Draw shapes and lines
  g.DrawRectangle(redPen, rect);
  g.FillEllipse(greenBrush, rect);
  g.DrawLine(blackPen, 0, 250, this.Width, 250);
  g.FillEllipse(Brushes.Blue, 70, 220, 30, 30);
  g.FillEllipse(Brushes.SkyBlue, 100, 210, 40, 40);
  g.FillEllipse(Brushes.Green, 140, 200, 50, 50);
  g.FillEllipse(Brushes.Yellow, 190, 190, 60, 60);
  g.FillEllipse(Brushes.Violet, 250, 180, 70, 70);
  g.FillEllipse(Brushes.Red, 320, 170, 80, 80);
  // Dispose of objects
  greenBrush.Dispose();
  // blackPen.Dispose();
  redPen.Dispose();
  g.Dispose();
}
```

Disposing of Objects

In the .NET Framework, the **garbage collector** is responsible for managing resources associated with an object. When you dispose of an object, the garbage collector collects the object right away and frees all the resources associated with that object. If you don't dispose of an object, the garbage collector will keep track of the objects, and if an object is not used for a certain amount of time, it will dispose of it automatically.

It is always best programming practice to dispose of any objects that you create explicitly (using the new operator).

2.3.7 **Building and Running the Application**

The final step in creating an application is to build and run it. To do this, in Visual Studio .NET you can simply select **Debug | Start (F5)** or **Debug | Start Without Debugging (Ctrl+F5)**.

The output of the application looks like Figure 2.9. The application draws a line, a rectangle, and some ellipses with different colors.

Congratulations! You have finished the first step toward becoming a GDI+ expert. Now you can write simple graphics applications in Visual Studio .NET.

2.4 **Some Basic GDI+ Objects**

In previous sections we discussed the steps required to write a simple graphics application using Visual Studio .NET. Before we move on to the next chapter, let's discuss some basic GDI+ objects, such as the color-, point-, and rectangle-related structures provided by the .NET Framework

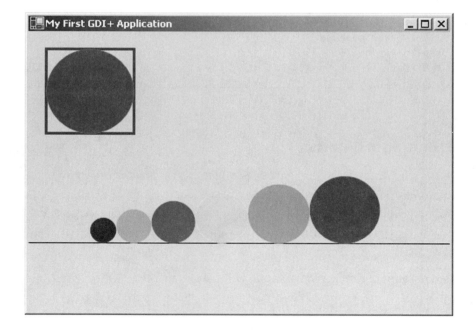

FIGURE 2.9: Your first GDI+ application

library. Understanding these structures is very important because they are used throughout the book.

2.4.1 The `Color` Structure

You may have noticed that we used the `Color` structure in our previous example. The `Color` structure represents a GDI+ ARGB (alpha-red-green-blue) color. This class contains a static property for almost every possible color. For example, `Color.Black` and `Color.Red` represent black and red, respectively. Besides these static properties, this structure has the additional properties defined in Table 2.1.

`IsKnownColor`, `IsNamedColor` and `IsSystemColor` represent members of the `KnownColor` enumeration, which again defines almost every color as a member.

Table 2.2 describes the methods of the `Color` structure.

TABLE 2.1: `Color` properties

Property	Description
`Red, Blue, Green, Aqua, Azure,` and so on	A specified color static property for almost every color.
`A`	Returns the alpha component value in a `Color` structure. We discuss alpha in color-related sections in later chapters.
`R`	Returns the red component value in a `Color` structure.
`G`	Returns the green component value in a `Color` structure.
`B`	Returns the blue component value in a `Color` structure.
`IsEmpty`	Indicates whether a `Color` structure is uninitialized.
`IsKnownColor`	Indicates whether a color is predefined.
`IsNamedColor`	Indicates whether a color is predefined.
`IsSystemColor`	Indicates whether a color is a system color.
`Name`	Returns the name of the color.

TABLE 2.2: Color methods

Method	Description
FromArgb	Creates a Color structure from the four 8-bit ARGB component (alpha-red-green-blue) values.
FromKnownColor	Creates a Color structure from the specified predefined color.
FromName	Creates a Color structure from the specified name of a predefined color.
GetBrightness	Returns the hue-saturation-brightness (HSB) brightness value of this Color structure.
GetHue	Returns the HSB hue value, in degrees, of this Color structure.
GetSaturation	Returns the HSB saturation value of this Color structure.
ToArgb	Returns the 32-bit ARGB value of this Color structure.
ToKnownColor	Returns the KnownColor value of this Color structure.

2.4.2 The Point and PointF Structures

In GDI+, the Point structure represents an ordered pair of integer x- and y-coordinates that define a point in a two-dimensional plane. The Point structure's constructor initializes a new instance of the Point structure. The Point constructor has three overloaded forms that allow you to create a Point object from an integer, a Size object, or two integers as follows:

1. public Point(int);
2. public Point(Size);
3. public Point(int, int);

The following code snippet creates Point objects using all three forms of the constructor:

```
Point pt1 = new Point(10);
Point pt2 = new Point( new Size(20, 20) );
Point pt3 = new Point(30, 30);
```

The `PointF` structure is similar to the `Point` structure, but it uses floating point values instead of integers. Unlike the `Point` structure, `PointF` has only one constructor, which takes two floating point values as *x*- and *y*-coordinates.

```
PointF pt3 = new PointF(30.0f, 30.0f);
```

Both the `Point` and the `PointF` structures define three properties: `IsEmpty`, `X`, and `Y`. The `IsEmpty` property returns `true` if a point is empty, which means that both `X` and `Y` values are zero; otherwise it returns `false`. The `X` and `Y` properties return the *x*- and *y*-coordinates of a point, respectively. The `Empty` static field of the `Point` structure creates a new point with `X` and `Y` values set to zero.

Listing 2.3 creates a point with zero `X` and `Y` values using `Point.Empty` and assigns new coordinate values using the `X` and `Y` properties. This example creates a `Graphics` object using the `Graphics.FromHwnd` method and returns the graphics surface for a form. The `Graphics.FromHwnd` method creates a `Graphics` object from a window handle, which we pass as `this.Handle`. The `DrawLine` method draws a line starting from the first point to the second point using the defined pen. You can test this code on a button or a menu click event handler.

LISTING 2.3: Creating `Point` objects

```
// Create a new Point object
Point pt = new Point(50, 50);
// Create a new point using Point.Empty
Point newPoint = Point.Empty;
// Set X and Y properties of Point
newPoint.X = 100;
newPoint.Y = 200;
// Create a Graphics object from the
// current form's handle
Graphics g = Graphics.FromHwnd(this.Handle);
// Create a new pen with color blue
// and width = 4
Pen pn = new Pen(Color.Blue, 4);
// Draw a line from point pt to
// new point
g.DrawLine(pn, pt, newPoint);
// Dispose of Pen and Graphics objects
pn.Dispose();
g.Dispose();
```

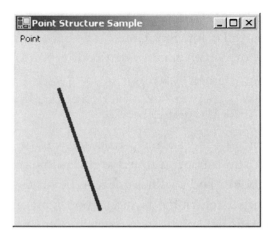

FIGURE 2.10: Using **Point** to draw a line

Figure 2.10 shows the output of Listing 2.3. The program draws a line from point 1 to point 2. The "Point" text in this figure is a menu item.

Like the `Point` structure, `PointF` can also use `Empty`, `X`, and `Y` properties, as shown in Listing 2.4. You can test this code on a button or a menu click event handler.

LISTING 2.4: Creating **PointF** objects

```
// Create a new PointF object
PointF pt = new PointF(50.0F, 50.0F);
// Create a new point using PointF.Empty
PointF newPoint = PointF.Empty;
// Set X and Y properties of PointF
newPoint.X = 100.0F;
newPoint.Y = 200.0F;
// Create a Graphics object from the
// current form's handle
Graphics g = Graphics.FromHwnd(this.Handle);
// Create a new pen with color blue
// and width = 4
Pen pn = new Pen(Color.Blue, 4);
// Draw a line from point pt to
// new point
g.DrawLine(pn, pt, newPoint);
// Dispose of Pen and Graphics objects
pn.Dispose();
g.Dispose();
```

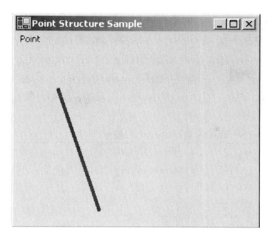

FIGURE 2.11: Using PointF to draw a line

Figure 2.11 shows the output of Listing 2.4. It is identical to Figure 2.10.

The Point structure also defines methods to convert from PointF to Point. The Ceiling method of the Point structure converts a PointF object to a Point object by rounding off the values of the PointF object to the next higher integer values. The Round method converts a PointF object to Point by rounding floating values to the nearest integer values. The Truncate method converts a PointF object to Point by truncating the floating values to integers. Listing 2.5 shows how to use the Ceiling, Round, and Truncate methods. You can test this code on a button or a menu click event handler.

LISTING 2.5: Using the Ceiling, Round, and Truncate methods of Point

```
// Create three points
PointF pt1 = new PointF(30.6f, 30.8f);
PointF pt2 = new PointF(50.3f, 60.7f);
PointF pt3 = new PointF(110.3f, 80.5f);
// Call Ceiling, Round, and Truncate methods
// and return new points
Point pt4 = Point.Ceiling(pt1);
Point pt5 = Point.Round(pt2);
Point pt6 = Point.Truncate(pt3);
// Display results
MessageBox.Show("Value of pt4: " +pt4.ToString());
MessageBox.Show("Value of pt5: " +pt5.ToString());
MessageBox.Show("Value of pt6: " +pt6.ToString());
```

The `Point` structure also defines addition, equality, inequality, subtraction, `Point-to-Size`, and `Point-to-PointF` conversion operators. Listing 2.6 shows how to add and subtract a `Size` object from a `Point` object, convert from `Point` to `PointF`, and convert from a `Point` object to a `Size` object. You can test this code on a button or a menu click event handler.

LISTING 2.6: Some `Point` and `PointF` conversions

```
/ Create a Size object
Size sz = new Size(12, 12);
// Create a Point object
Point pt = new Point(20, 20);
// Add point and size and copy to point
pt = pt+sz;
MessageBox.Show("Addition :"+ pt.ToString());
// Subtract point and size
pt = pt-sz;
MessageBox.Show("Subtraction :"+ pt.ToString());
// Create a PointF object from Point
PointF ptf = pt;
MessageBox.Show("PointF :"+ pt.ToString());
// Convert Point to Size
sz = (Size)pt;
MessageBox.Show("Size :"+ sz.Width.ToString()
+","+ sz.Height.ToString() );
```

2.4.3 The `Rectangle` and `RectangleF` Structures

The `Rectangle` and `RectangleF` structures represent a rectangle in GDI+. A `Rectangle` structure stores the top left corner and height and width of a rectangular region. You can create a `Rectangle` object from `Point` and `Size` objects or by using four integer values as starting and ending coordinates of the rectangle.

The `Rectangle` and `RectangleF` structures provide properties that can be used to get the height, width, and position of the rectangle. Table 2.3 describes the properties of the `Rectangle` and `RectangleF` structures.

LISTING 2.7: Using `Rectangle` properties

```
// Create Point, Size, and Rectangle objects
Point pt = new Point(10, 10);
Size sz = new Size(60, 40);
Rectangle rect1 = Rectangle.Empty;
Rectangle rect2 = new Rectangle(20, 30, 30, 10);
```

TABLE 2.3: `Rectangle` and `RectangleF` properties

Property	Description
Bottom	Returns the *y*-coordinate of the bottom edge.
Height	Represents the rectangle's height.
IsEmpty	Returns `true` if all of the rectangle's values (starting point, height, and width) are zero; otherwise returns `false`.
Left	Returns the *x*-coordinate of the left edge.
Location	Represents the coordinates of the upper left corner.
Right	Returns the *x*-coordinate of the right edge.
Size	Represents the size of a rectangle.
Top	Returns the *y*-coordinate of the top edge.
Width	Represents the width of a rectangle.
X	Represents the *x*-coordinate of the upper left corner.
Y	Represents the *y*-coordinate of the upper left corner.

```
// Set Rectangle properties
if (rect1.IsEmpty)
{
   rect1.Location = pt;
   rect1.Width = sz.Width;
   rect1.Height = sz.Height;
}
// Get Rectangle properties
string str = "Location:"+ rect1.Location.ToString();
str += ", X:" +rect1.X.ToString();
str += ", Y:"+ rect1.Y.ToString();
str += ", Left:"+ rect1.Left.ToString();
str += ", Right:"+ rect1.Right.ToString();
str += ", Top:"+ rect1.Top.ToString();
str += ", Bottom:"+ rect1.Bottom.ToString();
MessageBox.Show(str);
```

Listing 2.8 uses three different methods to create three `Rectangle` objects. The first method creates a `Rectangle` object by using a `Point` and a `Size`. The second and third methods create a `Rectangle` by using four integer values as the starting *x*- and *y*-coordinates and the width and height of the rectangle. After creating the rectangles, the program creates pen and brush objects using the `Pen` and `SolidBrush` classes and calls the fill and draw methods of `Graphics` to draw and fill the rectangles. Finally, we dispose of the objects. You can test this code on a button or a menu click event handler.

LISTING 2.8: Creating `Rectangle` objects

```
// Create a Graphics object
Graphics g = this.CreateGraphics();
int x = 40;
int y = 40;
int height = 120;
int width = 120;
// Create a Point object
Point pt = new Point(80, 80);
// Create a Size object
Size sz = new Size(100, 100);
// Create a rectangle from Point and Size
Rectangle rect1 = new Rectangle(pt, sz);
// Create a rectangle from integers
Rectangle rect2 =
    new Rectangle(x, y, width, height);
// Create a rectangle from direct integers
Rectangle rect3 =
    new Rectangle(10, 10, 180, 180);
// Create pens and brushes
Pen redPen = new Pen(Color.Red, 2);
SolidBrush greenBrush =
    new SolidBrush(Color.Blue);
SolidBrush blueBrush =
    new SolidBrush(Color.Green);
// Draw and fill rectangles
g.DrawRectangle(redPen, rect3);
g.FillRectangle(blueBrush, rect2);
g.FillRectangle(greenBrush, rect1);
// Dispose of the objects
redPen.Dispose();
blueBrush.Dispose();
greenBrush.Dispose();
g.Dispose();
```

Figure 2.12 shows the output from Listing 2.8: three different rectangles.

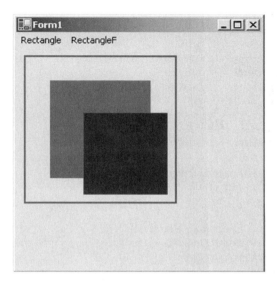

FIGURE 2.12: Using `Rectangle` to create rectangles

You can create a `RectangleF` object in a similar way. The only difference is that `RectangleF` takes floating point arguments instead of integers, `SizeF` instead of `Size`, and `PointF` instead of `Point`. Listing 2.9 creates `RectangleF` objects from `SizeF`, `PointF`, `Size`, and `Point` objects. You can test this code on a button or a menu click event handler.

LISTING 2.9: Creating `RectangleF` objects

```
// Create a Graphics object
Graphics g = this.CreateGraphics();
float x = 40.0f;
float y = 40.0f;
float height = 120.0f;
float width = 120.0f;
// Create a PointF object
PointF pt = new PointF(80.0f, 80.0f);
// Create a SizeF object
SizeF sz = new SizeF(100.0f, 100.0f);
// Create a rectangle from PointF and SizeF
RectangleF rect1 = new RectangleF(pt, sz);
```

continues

```
// Create a rectangle from integers
RectangleF rect2 =
    new RectangleF(x, y, width, height);
// Create a rectangle from direct integers
RectangleF rect3 =
    new RectangleF(10.0f, 10.0f, 180.0f, 180.0f);
// Create pens and brushes
Pen redPen = new Pen(Color.Red, 2);
SolidBrush greenBrush =
    new SolidBrush(Color.Blue);
SolidBrush blueBrush =
    new SolidBrush(Color.Green);
// Draw and fill rectangles
g.DrawRectangle(redPen, rect3.X, rect3.Y,
    rect3.Width, rect3.Height);
g.FillRectangle(blueBrush, rect2);
g.FillRectangle(greenBrush, rect1);
// Dispose of objects
redPen.Dispose();
blueBrush.Dispose();
greenBrush.Dispose();
g.Dispose();
```

Figure 2.13 shows the output from Listing 2.9: three different rectangles, as in Figure 2.12.

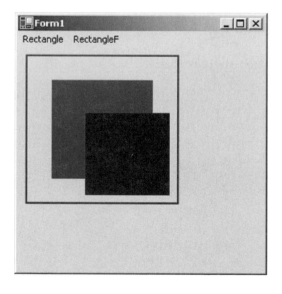

FIGURE 2.13: Using RectangleF to create rectangles

TABLE 2.4: `Rectangle` and `RectangleF` methods

Method	Description
Ceiling	Converts a `RectangleF` object to a `Rectangle` object by rounding the `RectangleF` values to the next higher integer values.
Contains	Determines if the specified point is contained within the rectangular region of a rectangle.
FromLTRB	Creates a rectangle with the specified edge locations.
Inflate	Creates and returns an inflated copy of a rectangle.
Intersect	Replaces a rectangle with the intersection of itself and another rectangle.
IntersectsWith	Determines if a specified rectangle intersects with `rect`.
Offset	Adjusts the location of a specified rectangle by the specified amount.
Round	Converts a `RectangleF` object to a `Rectangle` object by rounding the `RectangleF` values to the nearest integer values.
Truncate	Converts a `RectangleF` object to a `Rectangle` object by truncating the `RectangleF` values.
Union	Returns a rectangle that contains the union of two `Rectangle` structures.

Like the `Point` and `PointF` structures, `Rectangle` and `RectangleF` define `Ceiling`, `Round`, and `Truncate` methods. These methods are described in Table 2.4. Listing 2.10 shows how to use these methods.

LISTING 2.10: Using the **Round, Truncate, Union, Inflate, Ceiling,** and **Intersect** methods of `Rectangle`

```
// Create a Graphics object
Graphics g = this.CreateGraphics();
// Create PointF, SizeF, and RectangleF objects
PointF pt = new PointF(30.8f, 20.7f);
SizeF sz = new SizeF(60.0f, 40.0f);
```

continues

```
RectangleF rect2 =
   new RectangleF(40.2f, 40.6f, 100.5f, 100.0f);
RectangleF rect1 = new RectangleF(pt, sz);
Rectangle rect3 = Rectangle.Ceiling(rect1);
Rectangle rect4 = Rectangle.Truncate(rect1);
Rectangle rect5 = Rectangle.Round(rect2);
// Draw rectangles
g.DrawRectangle(Pens.Black, rect3);
g.DrawRectangle(Pens.Red, rect5);
// Intersect rectangles
Rectangle isectRect =
   Rectangle.Intersect(rect3, rect5);
// Fill new rectangle
g.FillRectangle(
   new SolidBrush(Color.Blue), isectRect);
// Create a Size object
Size inflateSize = new Size(0, 40);
// Inflate rectangle
isectRect.Inflate(inflateSize);
// Draw new rectangle
g.DrawRectangle(Pens.Blue, isectRect);
// Set Rectangle properties
rect4 = Rectangle.Empty;
rect4.Location = new Point(50, 50);
rect4.X = 30;
rect4.Y = 40;
// Union two rectangles
Rectangle unionRect =
   Rectangle.Union(rect4, rect5);
// Draw new rectangle
g.DrawRectangle(Pens.Green, unionRect);
// Dispose of the Graphics object
g.Dispose();
```

Figure 2.14 shows the output from Listing 2.10.

2.4.4 The Size and SizeF Structures

The Size and SizeF structures represent the size of a rectangular area. Like Point/PointF and Rectangle/RectangleF, Size and SizeF also each have an Empty static field, which creates a Size object with zero height and zero width. The only difference between Size and SizeF is that Size uses integer values and SizeF uses floating point values.

You can create Size and SizeF objects by passing the width and height of the Point and PointF objects as constructor arguments, respectively. Listing 2.11 shows different ways to create Size and SizeF objects.

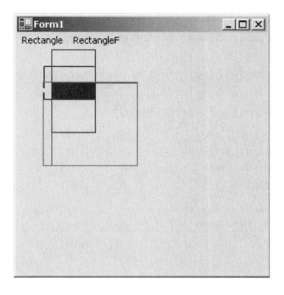

FIGURE 2.14: Using the Round, Truncate, Union, Inflate, Ceiling, and Intersect methods of Rectangle

LISTING 2.11: Creating `Size` and `SizeF` objects

```
Point pt1 = new Point(20, 40);
PointF pt2 = new PointF(50.0f, 80.0f);
Size sz1 = new Size(pt1);
SizeF sz2 = new SizeF(pt2);
Size sz3 = new Size(100, 150);
SizeF sz4 = new SizeF(12.5f, 87.6f);
```

The `Height` and `Width` properties represent the height and width, respectively, of the area represented by the `Size` and `SizeF` structures. The `IsEmpty` property returns `true` if `Size` has zero height and zero width; otherwise it returns `false`.

Like the `Point`/`PointF` and `Rectangle`/`RectangleF` structures, `Size` and `SizeF` have `Ceiling`, `Truncate`, and `Round` static methods. Each method can convert a `SizeF` object to a `Size` object: the `Ceiling` method, by rounding the values of the `Size` structure to the next higher integer values; the `Round` method, by rounding the values of the `Size` structure to the nearest integer values; and the `Truncate` method, by truncating the values to the next lower integer values.

Listing 2.12 shows the use of the `Ceiling`, `Round` and `Truncate` methods. You can test this code on a button or a menu click event handler.

LISTING 2.12: Using the `Ceiling`, `Round`, and `Truncate` methods of `Size` and SizeF

```
PointF pt1 = new PointF(30.6f, 30.8f);
PointF pt2 = new PointF(50.3f, 60.7f);
PointF pt3 = new PointF(110.3f, 80.5f);
SizeF sz1 = new SizeF(pt1);
SizeF sz2 = new SizeF(pt2);
SizeF sz3 = new SizeF(pt3);
Size sz4 = Size.Ceiling(sz1);
Size sz5 = Size.Round(sz2);
Size sz6 = Size.Truncate(sz3);
```

SUMMARY

Before you write a graphics application, a basic understanding of drawing surfaces and coordinate systems is a must. This chapter began with the basics of the drawing surfaces and the coordinate system, describing how drawing surfaces and coordinate systems are represented in GDI+ and how the GDI+ coordinate system differs from other coordinate systems.

Before using any GDI+-related classes defined in the .NET Framework library, you must reference `System.Drawing` and its subnamespaces. In this chapter you learned how to add references to the GDI+ library and how to import the GDI+-related namespaces into your application. After adding a reference to the GDI+ library and namespaces to the application, the next step is to get the `Graphics` object. There are several ways to get a `Graphics` object in an application. This chapter discussed three different ways, and then showed how to use the `Graphics` class methods to draw and fill lines, rectangles, and ellipses. You also learned to dispose of objects when you're finished with them.

Finally, we covered some basic GDI+ structures—including `Color`, `Rectangle`, `RectangleF`, `Point`, `PointF`, `Size`, and `SizeF`—describing their members and how to use them in your applications.

You should now be able to write simple graphics applications using GDI+.

Chapter 3 is all about the `Graphics` class and will demonstrate how quickly you can write real-world applications. By the end of Chapter 3, you will be able to write your own 2D paint application similar to Microsoft's PaintBrush, using your newly acquired GDI+ skills.

3

The Graphics Class

G RAPHICS OBJECTS ARE the heart of GDI+. They are represented by the Graphics class, which defines methods and properties to draw and fill graphics objects. Whenever an application needs to draw or paint something, it has to use the Graphics object. Hence, understanding the Graphics class, its methods, and its properties is very important. We will use Graphics methods and properties in all the chapters that follow.

Specifically, in this chapter we will discuss the methods and properties of the Graphics class, and how to use them in real-world applications, including line charts, pie charts, and our GDI+Painter application. GDI+Painter is similar to the PaintBrush application, which allows you to draw simple graphics objects such as lines, rectangles, and circles and save the images as bitmaps.

3.1 Graphics Class Properties

The Graphics class provides a long list of properties (see Table 3.1) and methods. We will discuss and use these properties and methods in this and following chapters.

TABLE 3.1: Graphics properties

Property	Description
Clip	Gets and sets a Region type that limits the drawing region of the Graphics object.
ClipBounds	Returns a RectangleF structure that bounds the clipping region of this Graphics object. Supports read-only access.
CompositingMode	Returns a value of type CompositingMode enumeration representing how composite images are drawn to the Graphics object.
CompositingQuality	Gets and sets the rendering quality (directly proportional to the visual quality of the output and inversely proportional to the rendering time) of composite images, represented by the CompositingQuality enumeration.
DpiX	Returns the horizontal resolution (dots per inch) of a Graphics object.
DpiY	Returns the vertical resolution (dots per inch) of a Graphics object.
InterpolationMode	Gets and sets the interpolation mode (which determines intermediate values between two endpoints), represented by the InterpolationMode enumerator.
IsClipEmpty	Returns a value indicating whether the clipping region of a Graphics object is empty. When there is no clipping, this property returns false.
IsVisibleClipEmpty	Returns a value indicating whether the visible clipping region of a Graphics object is empty.
PageScale	Gets and sets a value for scaling between world units and page units for this Graphics object.
PageUnit	Gets and sets a value that represents the unit of measure for page coordinates.
PixelOffsetMode	Gets and sets a value for the pixel offset mode (PixelOffsetMode enumeration).
RenderingOrigin	Represents the rendering origin of a Graphics object for dithering and hatch brushes.

TABLE 3.1: `Graphics` properties (continued)

Property	Description
SmoothingMode	Gets and sets the smoothing mode of a `Graphics` object (SmoothingMode enumeration). Does not affect text. `Smoothing` modes include high quality, high speed, and anti-aliasing.
TextContrast	Gets and sets the gamma correction value for rendering anti-aliased and ClearType text values, ranging from 0 to 12. The default is 4.
TextRenderingHint	Gets and sets the text rendering quality (`TextRenderingHint` enumeration). Affects only text drawn on the `Graphics` object.
Transform	Gets and sets the world transformation matrix (transformation is the process of converting graphics objects from one state to another). The transformation state is represented by a transformation matrix.
VisibleClipBounds	Gets and sets the visible clipping region of the `Graphics` object (the intersection of the clipping region of the `Graphics` object and the clipping region of the window).

3.2 `Graphics` **Class Methods**

We can divide `Graphics` class methods into three categories: *draw, fill*, and *miscellaneous*. **Draw methods** are used to draw lines, curves, and outer boundaries of closed curves and images. **Fill methods** fill the interior area of graphics objects. There are also a few miscellaneous methods that fall in neither category—for example, `MeasureString` and `Clear`.

3.2.1 **Draw Methods**

The draw methods of the `Graphics` class are used to draw lines, curves, and outer boundaries of closed curves and images. Table 3.2 lists the draw methods of the `Graphics` class.

3.2.1.1 *Drawing Lines*

The `DrawLine` method draws a line beween two points specified by a pair of coordinates. `DrawLines` draws a series of lines using an array of points.

TABLE 3.2: Graphics draw methods

Method	Description
DrawArc	Draws an arc (a portion of an ellipse specified by a pair of coordinates, a width, a height, and start and end angles).
DrawBezier	Draws a Bézier curve defined by four `Point` structures.
DrawBeziers	Draws a series of Bézier splines from an array of `Point` structures.
DrawClosedCurve	Draws a closed cardinal spline defined by an array of `Point` structures.
DrawCurve	Draws a cardinal spline through a specified array of `Point` structures.
DrawEllipse	Draws an ellipse defined by a bounding rectangle specified by a pair of coordinates, a height, and a width.
DrawIcon	Draws an image represented by the specified `Icon` object at the specified coordinates.
DrawIconUnstretched	Draws an image represented by the specified `Icon` object without scaling the image.
DrawImage	Draws the specified `Image` object at the specified location and with the original size.
DrawImageUnscaled	Draws the specified `Image` object with its original size at the location specified by a coordinate pair.
DrawLine	Draws a line connecting two points specified by coordinate pairs.
DrawLines	Draws a series of line segments that connect an array of `Point` structures.
DrawPath	Draws a `GraphicsPath` object.
DrawPie	Draws a pie shape specified by a coordinate pair, a width, a height, and two radial lines.
DrawPolygon	Draws a polygon defined by an array of `Point` structures.

TABLE 3.2: Graphics draw methods (continued)

Method	Description
DrawRectangle	Draws a rectangle specified by a coordinate pair, a width, and a height.
DrawRectangles	Draws a series of rectangles specified by an array of Rectangle structures.
DrawString	Draws the specified text string at the specified location using the specified Brush and Font objects.

DrawLine has four overloaded methods. The first argument of all Draw-Line methods is a Pen object, with texture, color, and width attributes. The rest of the arguments vary. You can use two points with integer or floating point values, or you can pass four integer or floating point values directly:

1. `public void DrawLine(Pen, Point, Point);`
2. `public void DrawLine(Pen, PointF, PointF);`
3. `public void DrawLine(Pen, int, int, int, int);`
4. `public void DrawLine(Pen, float, float, float, float);`

To draw a line, an application first creates a Pen object, which defines the color and width. The following line of code creates a red pen with a width of 1:

```
Pen redPen = new Pen(Color.Red, 1);
```

After that we define the endpoints of the line:

```
float x1 = 20.0F, y1 = 25.0F;
float x2 = 200.0F, y2 = 100.0F;
```

Finally, we use the pen and points as input to DrawLine:

```
Graphics.DrawLine(redPen, x1, y1, x2, y2);
```

Listing 3.1 shows how to use the different overloaded methods. We create four pens with different colors and widths. After that we call DrawLine with different values—including integer, floating point, and Point structures—to draw four different lines. Three of them start at point (20, 20).

LISTING 3.1: Drawing lines

```
private void Form1_Paint(object sender,
    System.Windows.Forms.PaintEventArgs e)
{
    // Create four Pen objects with red,
    // blue, green, and black colors and
    // different widths
    Pen redPen = new Pen(Color.Red, 1);
    Pen bluePen = new Pen(Color.Blue, 2);
    Pen greenPen = new Pen(Color.Green, 3);
    Pen blackPen = new Pen(Color.Black, 4);
    // Draw line using float coordinates
    float x1 = 20.0F, y1 = 20.0F;
    float x2 = 200.0F, y2 = 20.0F;
    e.Graphics.DrawLine(redPen, x1, y1, x2, y2);
    // Draw line using Point structure
    Point pt1 = new Point(20, 20);
    Point pt2 = new Point(20, 200);
    e.Graphics.DrawLine(greenPen, pt1, pt2);
    // Draw line using PointF structure
    PointF ptf1 = new PointF(20.0F, 20.0F);
    PointF ptf2 = new PointF(200.0F, 200.0F);
    e.Graphics.DrawLine(bluePen, ptf1, ptf2);
    // Draw line using integer coordinates
    int X1 = 60, Y1 = 40, X2 = 250, Y2 = 100;
    e.Graphics.DrawLine(blackPen, X1, Y1, X2, Y2);
    // Dispose of objects
    redPen.Dispose();
    bluePen.Dispose();
    greenPen.Dispose();
    blackPen.Dispose();
}
```

The output from Listing 3.1 is shown in Figure 3.1. We've drawn four lines starting at point (20, 20).

3.2.1.2 *Drawing Connected Lines*

Sometimes we need to draw multiple connected straight line segments. One way to do this is to call the DrawLine method multiple times.

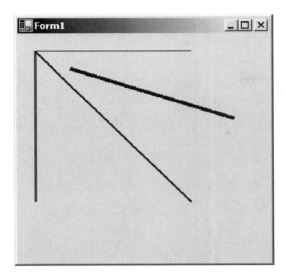

FIGURE 3.1: Using **DrawLine** to draw lines

The Graphics class also provides the DrawLines method, which can be used to draw multiple connected lines. This method has two overloaded forms. One takes an array of Point structure objects, and the other takes an array of PointF structure objects:

1. public void DrawLines(Pen, Point[]);
2. public void DrawLines(Pen, PointF[]);

To draw lines using DrawLines, an application first creates a Pen object, then creates an array of points, and then calls DrawLines. The code in Listing 3.2 draws three line segments.

LISTING 3.2: Using **DrawLines** to draw connected lines

```
PointF[] ptsArray =
{
        new PointF( 20.0F,  20.0F),
        new PointF( 20.0F, 200.0F),
        new PointF(200.0F, 200.0F),
        new PointF(20.0F, 20.0F)

};
e.Graphics.DrawLines(redPen, ptsArray);
```

The code in Listing 3.2 draws what is shown in Figure 3.2.

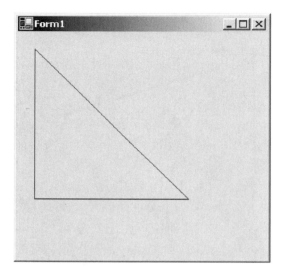

FIGURE 3.2: Using **DrawLines** to draw connected lines

3.2.1.3 *Drawing Rectangles*

The next basic drawing object is a rectangle. When you draw a rectangle through your applications, you need to specify only the starting point, height, and width of the rectangle. GDI+ takes care of the rest.

The Graphics class provides the DrawRectangle method, which draws a rectangle specified by a starting point, a width, and a height. The Graphics class also provides the DrawRectangles method, which draws a series of rectangles specified by an array of Rectangle structures.

DrawRectangle has three overloaded methods. An application can use a Rectangle structure or coordinates of integer or float types to draw a rectangle:

1. `public void DrawRectangle(Pen, Rectangle);`
2. `public void DrawRectangle(Pen, int, int, int, int);`
3. `public void DrawRectangle(Pen, float, float, float, float);`

To draw a rectangle, an application first creates a pen and a rectangle (location, width, and height), and then it calls DrawRectangle. Listing 3.3 draws rectangles using the different overloaded forms of DrawRectangle.

LISTING 3.3: Using `DrawRectangle` to draw rectangles

```
private void Form1_Paint(object sender,
      System.Windows.Forms.PaintEventArgs e)
{
      // Create pens and points
      Pen redPen = new Pen(Color.Red, 1);
      Pen bluePen = new Pen(Color.Blue, 2);
      Pen greenPen = new Pen(Color.Green, 3);
      float x = 5.0F, y = 5.0F;
      float width = 100.0F;
      float height = 200.0F;
      // Create a rectangle
      Rectangle rect = new Rectangle(20, 20, 80, 40);
      // Draw rectangles
      e.Graphics.DrawRectangle(bluePen,
        x, y, width, height);
      e.Graphics.DrawRectangle(redPen,
        60, 80, 140, 50);
      e.Graphics.DrawRectangle(greenPen, rect);
      // Dispose of objects
      redPen.Dispose();
      bluePen.Dispose();
      greenPen.Dispose();
}
```

Figure 3.3 shows the output from Listing 3.3.

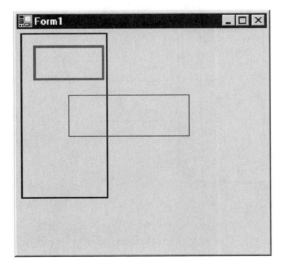

FIGURE 3.3: Drawing individual rectangles

The DrawRectangles method draws a series of rectangles using a single pen. It is useful when you need to draw multiple rectangles using the same pen (if you need to draw multiple rectangles using different pens, you must use multiple calls to DrawRectangle). A single call to DrawRectangles is faster than multiple DrawRectangle calls. DrawRectangles takes two parameters—a pen and an array of Rectangle or RectangleF structures—as shown in Listing 3.4.

LISTING 3.4: Using **DrawRectangles** to draw a series of rectangles

```
Pen greenPen = new Pen(Color.Green, 4);
RectangleF[] rectArray
{
 new RectangleF( 5.0F, 5.0F, 100.0F, 200.0F),
    new RectangleF(20.0F, 20.0F, 80.0F, 40.0F),
    new RectangleF(60.0F, 80.0F, 140.0F, 50.0F)
};
e.Graphics.DrawRectangles(greenPen, rectArray);
greenPen.Dispose()
```

Figure 3.4 shows the output from Listing 3.4. As you can see, it's easy to draw multiple rectangles using the DrawRectangles method.

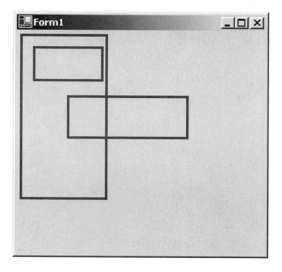

FIGURE 3.4: Drawing a series of rectangles

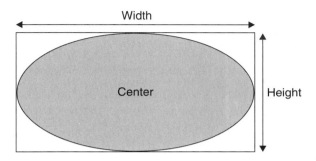

FIGURE 3.5: An ellipse

3.2.1.4 *Drawing Ellipses and Circles*

An **ellipse** is a circular boundary within a rectangle, where each opposite point has the same distance from a fixed point, called the center of the ellipse. An ellipse within a square is called a **circle**. Figure 3.5 shows an ellipse with its height, width, and center indicated.

To draw an ellipse, you need to specify the outer rectangle. GDI+ takes care of the rest. `DrawEllipse` draws an ellipse defined by a rectangle specified by a pair of coordinates, a height, and a width (an ellipse with equal height and width is a circle). `DrawEllipse` has four overloaded methods:

1. `public void DrawEllipse(Pen, Rectangle);`
2. `public void DrawEllipse(Pen, RectangleF);`
3. `public void DrawEllipse(Pen, int, int, int, int);`
4. `public void DrawEllipse(Pen, float, float, float, float);`

To draw an ellipse, an application creates a pen and four coordinates (or a rectangle), and then calls `DrawEllipse`. Listing 3.5 draws ellipses with different options.

LISTING 3.5: Drawing ellipses

```
private void Form1_Paint(object sender,
      System.Windows.Forms.PaintEventArgs e)
{
    // Create pens
    Pen redPen = new Pen(Color.Red, 6 );
```

```
        Pen bluePen = new Pen(Color.Blue, 4 );
        Pen greenPen = new Pen(Color.Green, 2);
        // Create a rectangle
        Rectangle rect =
          new Rectangle(80, 80, 50, 50);
        // Draw ellipses
        e.Graphics.DrawEllipse(greenPen,
          100.0F, 100.0F, 10.0F, 10.0F );
        e.Graphics.DrawEllipse(redPen, rect );
        e.Graphics.DrawEllipse(bluePen, 60, 60, 90, 90);
        e.Graphics.DrawEllipse(greenPen,
          40.0F, 40.0F, 130.0F, 130.0F );
        // Dispose of objects
        redPen.Dispose();
        greenPen.Dispose();
        bluePen.Dispose();
    }
```

Figure 3.6 shows the output from Listing 3.5.

3.2.1.5 *Drawing Text*

This section briefly discusses the drawing of text. Chapter 5 covers this topic in more detail.

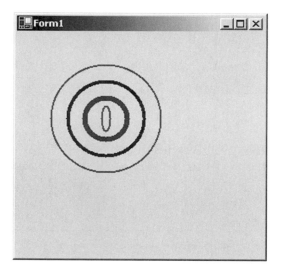

FIGURE 3.6: Drawing ellipses

The `DrawString` method draws a text string on a graphics surface. It has many overloaded forms. `DrawString` takes arguments that identify the text, font, brush, starting location, and string format.

The simplest form of `DrawString` looks like this:

```
public void DrawString(string, Font, Brush, PointF);
```

where `string` is the text that you want to draw, `Font` and `Brush` are the font and brushes used to draw the text, and `PointF` is the starting point of the text.

Listing 3.6 uses the `DrawString` method to draw "Hello GDI+ World!" on a form.

LISTING 3.6: Drawing text

```
private void Form1_Paint(object sender,
System.Windows.Forms.PaintEventArgs e)
{
    e.Graphics.DrawString("Hello GDI+ World!",
        new Font("Verdana", 16),
        new SolidBrush(Color.Red),
        new Point(20, 20));
}
```

■ NOTE

You might notice in Listing 3.6 that we create `Font`, `SolidBrush`, and `Point` objects directly as parameters of the `DrawString` method. This method of creating objects means that we can't dispose of these objects, so some cleanup is left for the garbage collector.

Figure 3.7 shows the output from Listing 3.6.

The `DrawString` method has several overloaded forms, as shown here:

- `public void DrawString(string, Font, Brush, RectangleF);`
- `public void DrawString(string, Font, Brush, PointF, StringFormat);`

FIGURE 3.7: Drawing text

- public void DrawString(string, Font, Brush,
  RectangleF, StringFormat);
- public void DrawString(string, Font, Brush, float,
  float);
- public void DrawString(string, Font, Brush, float,
  float, StringFormat);

Now let's see another example of drawing text—this time using the StringFormat class, which defines the text format. Using StringFormat, you can set flags, alignment, trimming, and other options for the text. (Chapter 5 discusses this functionality in more detail.) Listing 3.7 shows different ways to draw text on a graphics surface. In this example the FormatFlags property is set to StringFormatFlags.DirectionVertical, which draws vertical text.

LISTING 3.7: Using DrawString to draw text on a graphics surface

```
private void Form1_Paint(object sender,
        System.Windows.Forms.PaintEventArgs e)
{
        // Create brushes
```

```
        SolidBrush blueBrush = new SolidBrush(Color.Blue);
        SolidBrush redBrush = new SolidBrush(Color.Red);
        SolidBrush greenBrush = new SolidBrush(Color.Green);
        // Create a rectangle
        Rectangle rect = new Rectangle(20, 20, 200, 100);
        // The text to be drawn
        String drawString = "Hello GDI+ World!";
        // Create a Font object
        Font drawFont = new Font("Verdana", 14);
        float x = 100.0F;
        float y = 100.0F;
        // String format
        StringFormat drawFormat = new StringFormat();
        // Set string format flag to direction vertical,
        // which draws text vertically
        drawFormat.FormatFlags =
          StringFormatFlags.DirectionVertical;
        // Draw string
        e.Graphics.DrawString("Drawing text",
          new Font("Tahoma", 14), greenBrush, rect);
        e.Graphics.DrawString(drawString,
          new Font("Arial", 12), redBrush, 120, 140);
        e.Graphics.DrawString(drawString, drawFont,
          blueBrush, x, y, drawFormat);
        // Dispose of objects
        blueBrush.Dispose();
        redBrush.Dispose();
        greenBrush.Dispose();
        drawFont.Dispose();
}
```

Figure 3.8 shows the output from Listing 3.7.

3.2.1.6 *Creating a Line Chart Application*

As promised, the examples in this book not only show the use of GDI+, but also encourage you to use GDI+ practices in real-world applications, We will create one more real-world application, a line chart application. In this example we will use all the functionality we have discussed so far. Our line chart application will draw lines when a user clicks on a form.

We create a Windows application and add a check box and a button. Then we change the Text properties of the button and the check box to call them **Clear All** and **Rectangle**, respectively. Then we add code to draw two lines and some numbers (using the DrawString method). The initial screen of the line chart application looks like Figure 3.9.

FIGURE 3.8: Drawing text with different directions

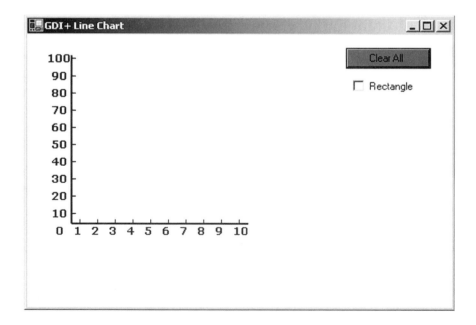

FIGURE 3.9: The line chart application

When you click on the form, the application draws a line. The first line starts from the bottom left corner, where the values of our x- and y-axes are both 0. After a few clicks, the chart looks like Figure 3.10. Every time you click on the form, the application draws a line from the previous point to the current point and draws a small ellipse representing the current point.

The **Clear All** button removes the lines and initializes the first point to (0, 0). Now if you check the **Rectangle** box and click on the form, the chart looks like Figure 3.11. When you click the left mouse button for the first time, the application draws a line from point (0, 0) to the point where you clicked the button.

Now let's see the code. First we declare starting and ending points. These points will be used to draw a line when you click the left mouse button. The default values of both points are shown in the following code fragment, which represents position (0, 0) on the screen:

```
private Point startPoint = new Point(50, 217);
private Point endPoint = new Point(50, 217);
```

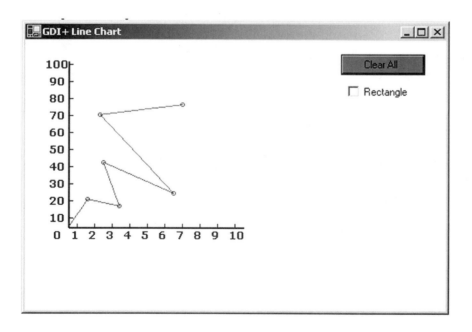

FIGURE 3.10: The line chart application with a chart

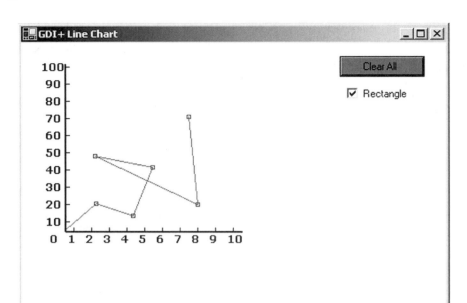

FIGURE 3.11: The line chart with rectangles to mark points

The next step is to draw vertical and horizontal axis lines with index numbers. We do this on the form's paint event handler with the help of the `DrawString` method. Listing 3.8 provides code for the form-paint event handler. As the listing shows, we simply draw a vertical line, a horizontal line, and the marks on these lines.

LISTING 3.8: Drawing lines and marks

```
private void Form1_Paint(object sender,
    System.Windows.Forms.PaintEventArgs e)
{
    Graphics g = e.Graphics;
    Font vertFont =
      new Font("Verdana", 10, FontStyle.Bold);
    Font horzFont =
      new Font("Verdana", 10, FontStyle.Bold);
    SolidBrush vertBrush = new SolidBrush(Color.Black);
    SolidBrush horzBrush = new SolidBrush(Color.Blue);
    Pen blackPen = new Pen(Color.Black, 2);
    Pen bluePen = new Pen(Color.Blue, 2);
    // Drawing a vertical and a horizontal line
    g.DrawLine(blackPen,50,220,50, 25);
    g.DrawLine(bluePen,50,220,250,220);
```

```
// x-axis drawing
g.DrawString("0",horzFont,horzBrush,30, 220);
g.DrawString("1",horzFont,horzBrush,50,220);
g.DrawString("2",horzFont,horzBrush,70,220);
g.DrawString("3",horzFont,horzBrush,90,220);
g.DrawString("4",horzFont,horzBrush,110,220);
g.DrawString("5",horzFont,horzBrush,130,220);
g.DrawString("6",horzFont,horzBrush,150,220);
g.DrawString("7",horzFont,horzBrush,170,220);
g.DrawString("8",horzFont,horzBrush,190,220);
g.DrawString("9",horzFont,horzBrush,210,220);
g.DrawString("10",horzFont,horzBrush,230,220);
// Drawing vertical strings
StringFormat vertStrFormat = new StringFormat();
vertStrFormat.FormatFlags =
  StringFormatFlags.DirectionVertical;

g.DrawString("-",horzFont,horzBrush,
  50, 212, vertStrFormat);
g.DrawString("-",horzFont,horzBrush,
  70, 212, vertStrFormat);
g.DrawString("-",horzFont,horzBrush,
  90, 212, vertStrFormat);
g.DrawString("-",horzFont,horzBrush,
  110, 212, vertStrFormat);
g.DrawString("-",horzFont,horzBrush,
  130, 212, vertStrFormat);
g.DrawString("-",horzFont,horzBrush,
  150, 212, vertStrFormat);
g.DrawString("-",horzFont,horzBrush,
  170, 212, vertStrFormat);
g.DrawString("-",horzFont,horzBrush,
  190, 212, vertStrFormat);
g.DrawString("-",horzFont,horzBrush,
  210, 212, vertStrFormat);
g.DrawString("-",horzFont,horzBrush,
  230, 212, vertStrFormat);
// y-axis drawing
g.DrawString("100-",vertFont,vertBrush, 20,20);
g.DrawString("90 -",vertFont,vertBrush, 25,40);
g.DrawString("80 -",vertFont,vertBrush, 25,60);
g.DrawString("70 -",vertFont,vertBrush, 25,80);
g.DrawString("60 -",vertFont,vertBrush, 25,100);
g.DrawString("50 -",vertFont,vertBrush, 25,120);
g.DrawString("40 -",vertFont,vertBrush, 25,140);
g.DrawString("30 -",vertFont,vertBrush, 25,160);
g.DrawString("20 -",vertFont,vertBrush, 25,180);
g.DrawString("10 -",vertFont,vertBrush, 25,200);
// Dispose of objects
```

continues

```
    vertFont.Dispose();
    horzFont.Dispose();
    vertBrush.Dispose();
    horzBrush.Dispose();
    blackPen.Dispose();
    bluePen.Dispose();
}
```

> **■ NOTE**
>
> The idea in Listing 3.8 is to show an extensive use of the `DrawString`
> method. Alternatively and preferably, you could replace `DrawString`
> with the `DrawLine` and/or `DrawLines` method.

Now on the mouse-down event handler, we draw a line from the starting point (0, 0) to the first mouse click. We store the mouse click position as the starting point for the next line. When we click again, the new line will be drawn from the current starting position to the point where the mouse was clicked. Listing 3.9 shows the mouse-down click event handler. We create a new `Graphics` object using the `CreateGraphics` method. After that we create two `Pen` objects. We store the previous point as the starting point and the current point as the ending point. The X and Y properties of `MouseEventArgs` return the *x*- and *y*-values of the point where the mouse was clicked.

Now we check to see if the **Rectangle** check box is checked. If so, we draw a rectangle to mark the connecting point of the two lines. If not, we draw an ellipse as the connecting point.

LISTING 3.9: The mouse-down event handler

```
private void Form1_MouseDown(object sender,
    System.Windows.Forms.MouseEventArgs e)
{
    if (e.Button == MouseButtons.Left)
    {
        // Create a Graphics object
        Graphics g1 = this.CreateGraphics();
        // Create two pens
        Pen linePen = new Pen(Color.Green, 1);
        Pen ellipsePen = new Pen(Color.Red, 1);
        startPoint = endPoint;
        endPoint = new Point(e.X, e.Y);
```

```
  // Draw the line from the current point
  // to the new point
  g1.DrawLine(linePen, startPoint, endPoint);
  // If Rectangle check box is checked,
  // draw a rectangle to represent the point
  if(checkBox1.Checked)
  {
    g1.DrawRectangle(ellipsePen,
      e.X-2, e.Y-2, 4, 4);
  }
  // Draw a circle to represent the point
  else
  {
    g1.DrawEllipse(ellipsePen,
      e.X-2, e.Y-2, 4, 4);
  }
  // Dispose of objects
  linePen.Dispose();
  ellipsePen.Dispose();
  g1.Dispose();
  }
}
```

The **Clear All** button removes all the lines by invalidating the form's client area and sets the starting and ending points back to their initial values. Code for the **Clear All** button click event handler is given in Listing 3.10.

LISTING 3.10: The Clear All button click event handler

```
private void button1_Click(object sender,
    System.EventArgs e)
{
    startPoint.X = 50;
    startPoint.Y = 217;
    endPoint.X = 50;
    endPoint.Y = 217;
    this.Invalidate(this.ClientRectangle);
}
```

3.2.1.7 *Drawing Arcs*

An **arc** is a portion of an ellipse. For example, Figure 3.12 shows an ellipse that has six arcs. An arc is defined by a bounding rectangle (just as an ellipse), a start angle, and a sweep angle. The **start angle** is an angle in degrees measured clockwise from the *x*-axis to the starting point of the arc.

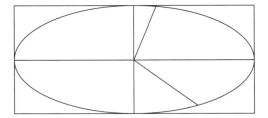

FIGURE 3.12: Arcs in an ellipse

The **sweep angle** is an angle in degrees measured clockwise from the startAngle parameter to the ending point of the arc. So an arc is the portion of the perimeter of the ellipse between the start angle and the start angle plus the sweep angle.

The DrawArc method draws an arc on a graphics surface. DrawArc takes a pen, a pair of coordinates, a width, and a height. There are many DrawArc overloaded methods. An application can use a Rectangle or RectangleF object and integer or float coordinates:

- public void DrawArc(Pen, Rectangle, float, float);
- public void DrawArc(Pen, RectangleF, float, float);
- public void DrawArc(Pen, int, int, int, int, int);
- public void DrawArc(Pen, float, float, float, float, float, float);

The Pen object determines the color, width, and style of the arc; Rectangle or RectangleF represents the bounding rectangle; and the last two parameters are the start angle and sweep angle.

To draw an arc, the application creates Pen and Rectangle objects and defines start and sweep angles. Then it calls the DrawArc method.

Let's create an application that will draw an arc to match the values of the start and sweep angles. We create a Windows application, adding add two text boxes and a button control. The final form looks like Figure 3.13.

We define two floating variables on the class level to store the start and sweep angles:

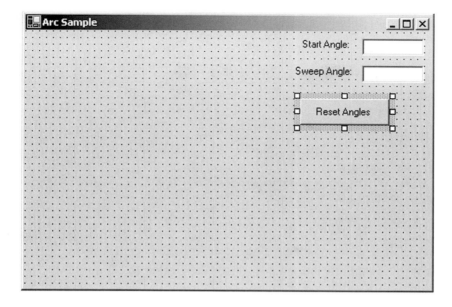

FIGURE 3.13: A sample arc application

```
private float startAngle = 45.0f;
private float sweepAngle = 90.0f;
```

Now let's draw an arc on the form's paint event handler. Listing 3.11 draws an arc. We first create a pen and a rectangle, and we use them in the DrawArc method with start and sweep angles.

LISTING 3.11: The paint event handler

```
private void Form1_Paint(object sender,
      System.Windows.Forms.PaintEventArgs e)
{
    Pen redPen = new Pen(Color.Red, 3);
    Rectangle rect =
        new Rectangle(20, 20, 200, 200);
    e.Graphics.DrawArc(redPen,
      rect, startAngle, sweepAngle);
    redPen.Dispose();
}
```

Now we add code for the **Reset Angles** button. Listing 3.12 simply sets the start and sweep angles by reading values from the text boxes and calls the Invalidate method, which forces GDI+ to call the form's paint event handler.

LISTING 3.12: The Reset Angles button click event handler

```
private void ResetAnglesBtn_Click(object sender,
    System.EventArgs e)
{
    startAngle =
      (float)Convert.ToDouble(textBox1.Text);
    sweepAngle =
      (float)Convert.ToDouble(textBox2.Text);
    Invalidate();
}
```

Figure 3.14 shows the default output from the application.

Now let's change the start and sweep angles to 90 and 180 degrees, respectively, and click the **Reset Angles** button. The new output looks like Figure 3.15.

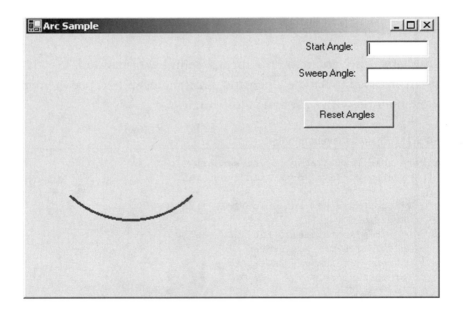

FIGURE 3.14: The default arc, with start angle of 45 degrees and sweep angle of 90 degrees

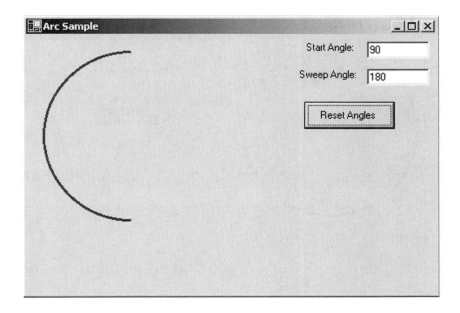

FIGURE 3.15: An arc with start angle of 90 degrees and sweep angle of 180 degrees

Let's change angles one more time. This time our start angle will be 180 degrees, and the sweep angle will be 360 degrees. The new output looks like Figure 3.16.

3.2.1.8 *Drawing Splines and Curves*

A **curve** is a sequence of adjoining points with a tension. The tension of a curve provides its smoothness and removes corners. A **cardinal spline** is a sequence of multiple joined curves. Basically, in a curve there is no straight line between two points. To illustrate, Figure 3.17 shows two curves.

There are two types of curves: open and closed. A **closed curve** is a curve whose starting point is the ending point. A curve that is not a closed curve is called an **open curve**. In Figure 3.18 the first curve is an open curve, and the second curve is a closed curve.

3.2.1.9 *Drawing Open Curves*

Programmatically, a curve is an array of connected points with a tension. A curve has a starting point and an ending point. Between these two points

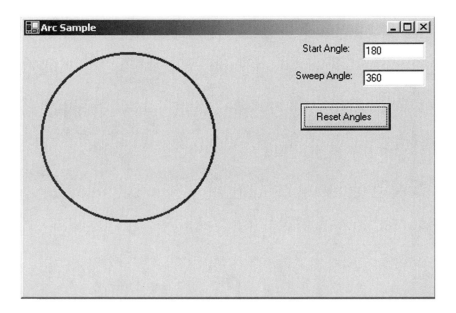

FIGURE 3.16: An arc with start angle of 180 degrees and sweep angle of 360 degree

can be many intermediate points. The Graphics class provides two methods for drawing curves: DrawCurve and DrawClosedCurve. The Draw-Curve method draws a curve specified by an array of Point structures. The DrawClosedCurve draws a closed curve specified by an array of Point structures. Both DrawCurve and DrawClosedCurve have overloaded methods.

DrawCurve has the following overloaded forms:

- public void DrawCurve(Pen, Point[]);
- public void DrawCurve(Pen, PointF[]);
- public void DrawCurve(Pen, Point[], float);
- public void DrawCurve(Pen, PointF[], float);
- public void DrawCurve(Pen, PointF[], int, int);
- public void DrawCurve(Pen, Point[], int, int, float);
- public void DrawCurve(Pen, PointF[], int, int, float);

The simplest form of DrawCurve is

FIGURE 3.17: Two curves

FIGURE 3.18: Open and closed curves

```
public void DrawCurve(Pen pen, Point[] points);
```

where `points` is an array of points.

To test the `DrawCurve` methods, we create a Windows application and add Listing 3.13 to the form's paint event handler. It creates an array of points and draws a curve using the `DrawCurve` method.

LISTING 3.13: Drawing a curve

```
private void Form1_Paint(object sender,
    System.Windows.Forms.PaintEventArgs e)
{
    // Create a pen
    Pen bluePen = new Pen(Color.Blue, 1);
    // Create an array of points
    PointF pt1 = new PointF( 40.0F,  50.0F);
    PointF pt2 = new PointF(50.0F,   75.0F);
    PointF pt3 = new PointF(100.0F,  115.0F);
    PointF pt4 = new PointF(200.0F,  180.0F);
    PointF pt5 = new PointF(200.0F, 90.0F);
    PointF[] ptsArray =
    {
      pt1, pt2, pt3, pt4, pt5
```

continues

```
    };
    // Draw curve
    e.Graphics.DrawCurve(bluePen, ptsArray);
    // Dispose of object
    bluePen.Dispose();
}
```

Figure 3.19 shows the output from our Listing 3.13.

> ■ **NOTE**
> The default tension is 0.5 for this overloaded version of DrawCurve.

The second form of DrawCurve is

```
public void DrawCurve(Pen pen,
    Point[] points,
    float tension
);
```

Here the tension parameter determines the shape of the curve. If the value of tension is 0.0F, the method draws a straight line between the points. The value of tension should vary between 0.0F and 1.0F.

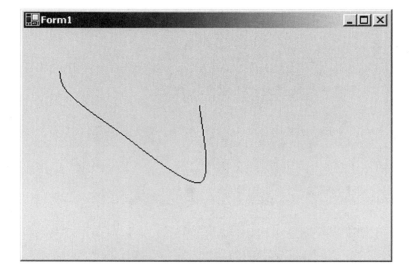

FIGURE 3.19: Drawing a curve

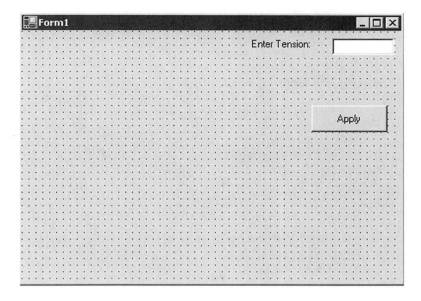

FIGURE 3.20: A curve-drawing application

Now let's update the example in Listing 3.13. We add a text box, a label, and a button to the form. We change the properties of these controls, and the form looks like Figure 3.20.

Now we will update our sample code to draw a curve using the `tension` value entered in the text box. We add a `float` type variable, `tension`, at the class level:

```
private float tension = 0.5F;
```

Then we update the form's paint event handler as shown in Listing 3.14. We provide `tension` as the third argument to the `DrawCurve` method.

LISTING 3.14: Drawing a curve with tension

```
private void Form1_Paint(object sender,
    System.Windows.Forms.PaintEventArgs e)
{
    // Create a pen
    Pen bluePen = new Pen(Color.Blue, 1);
    // Create an array of points
```

continues

```
        PointF pt1 = new PointF( 40.0F,   50.0F);
        PointF pt2 = new PointF(50.0F,   75.0F);
        PointF pt3 = new PointF(100.0F,   115.0F);
        PointF pt4 = new PointF(200.0F,   180.0F);
        PointF pt5 = new PointF(200.0F, 90.0F);
        PointF[] ptsArray =
        {
          pt1, pt2, pt3, pt4, pt5
        };
        // Draw curve
        e.Graphics.DrawCurve(bluePen, ptsArray, tension);
        // Dispose of object
        bluePen.Dispose();
    }
```

Now we add code for the **Apply** button, which simply reads the text box's value and sets it as the tension, as in Listing 3.15.

LISTING 3.15: The Apply button click event handler

```
    private void ApplyBtn_Click(object sender,
    System.EventArgs e)
    {
        tension = (float)Convert.ToDouble(textBox1.Text);
        Invalidate();
    }
```

If you enter "0.0" in the text box and hit **Apply**, the output looks like Figure 3.21, and if you enter the value "1.0" in the text box and hit **Apply**, the output looks like Figure 3.22.

You can also add an offset and specify a number of segments for the curve:

```
    public void DrawCurve(
        Pen pen,
        PointF[] points,
        int offset,
        int numberOfSegments
    );
```

The offset specifies the number of elements to skip in the array of points. The first element after the skipped elements in the array of points becomes the starting point of the curve.

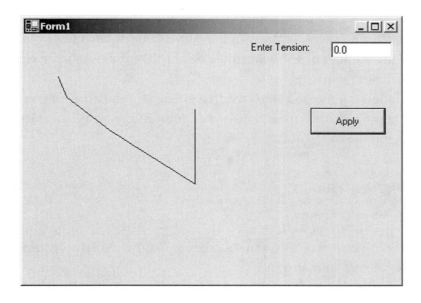

FIGURE 3.21: Drawing a curve with a tension of 0.0F

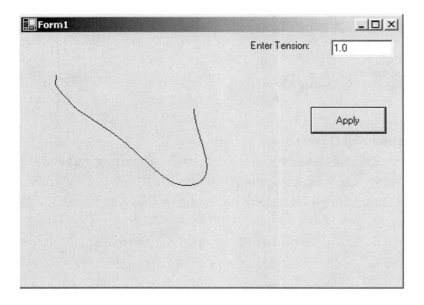

FIGURE 3.22: Drawing a curve with a tension of 1.0F

The `numberOfSegments` property specifies the number of segments, after the starting point, to draw in the curve. It must be at least 1. The offset plus the number of segments must be less than the number of elements in the array of the points.

The following method skips the first element of the array of points and starts drawing a curve from the second point in the array, stopping after three segments:

```
int offset = 1;
int segments = 3;
e.Graphics.DrawCurve(bluePen, ptsArray,
    offset, segments);
```

The final version of `DrawCurve` takes a pen, points array, offset, number of segments, and tension:

```
public void DrawCurve(
    Pen pen,
    Point[] points,
    int offset,
    int numberOfSegments,
    float tension
);
```

Here's an example:

```
int offset = 1;
int segments = 3;
e.Graphics.DrawCurve(bluePen, ptsArray,
    offset, segments, tension);
```

3.2.1.10 *Drawing Closed Curves*

As stated earlier, a closed curve is a curve whose starting and ending points are the same. The `Graphics` class provides the `DrawClosedCurve` method to draw closed curves. It has the following overloaded forms:

- `public void DrawClosedCurve(Pen, Point[]);`
- `public void DrawClosedCurve(Pen, PointF[]);`
- `public void DrawClosedCurve(Pen, Point[], float, FillMode);`

- ```
  public void DrawClosedCurve(Pen, PointF[], float,
  FillMode);
  ```

The simplest form of `DrawClosedCurve` takes two parameters: a pen and an array of points. Listing 3.16 creates an array of points and a pen and calls the `DrawClosedCurve` method.

LISTING 3.16: Drawing closed curves

```
private void Form1_Paint(object sender,
      System.Windows.Forms.PaintEventArgs e)
{

      // Create a pen
      Pen bluePen = new Pen(Color.Blue, 1);
      // Create an array of points
      PointF pt1 = new PointF( 40.0F,   50.0F);
      PointF pt2 = new PointF(50.0F,   75.0F);
      PointF pt3 = new PointF(100.0F,   115.0F);
      PointF pt4 = new PointF(200.0F,   180.0F);
      PointF pt5 = new PointF(200.0F, 90.0F);
      PointF[] ptsArray =
      {
        pt1, pt2, pt3, pt4, pt5
      };
      // Draw curve
      e.Graphics.DrawClosedCurve(bluePen, ptsArray);
      // Dispose of object
      bluePen.Dispose();
}
```

Figure 3.23 shows the output from Listing 3.16. The result is a closed curve.

The second form of `DrawClosedCurve` takes as arguments the tension of the curve and `FillMode`. We have already discussed tension. `FillMode` specifies how the interior of a closed path is filled and clipped. The `FillMode` enumeration represents the fill mode of graphics objects. It has two modes: `Alternate` (the default mode) and `Winding`.

As the documentation says,

To determine the interiors of a closed curve in the Alternate mode, draw a line from any arbitrary start point in the path to some point obviously
```

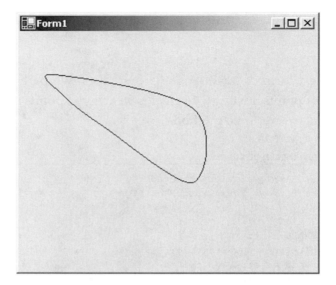

FIGURE 3.23: Drawing a closed curve

outside the path. If the line crosses an odd number of path segments, the starting point is inside the closed region and is therefore part of the fill or clipping area. An even number of crossings means that the point is not in an area to be filled or clipped. An open figure is filled or clipped by using a line to connect the last point to the first point of the figure.

The Winding mode considers the direction of the path segments at each intersection. It adds one for every clockwise intersection, and subtracts one for every counterclockwise intersection. If the result is nonzero, the point is considered inside the fill or clip area. A zero count means that the point lies outside the fill or clip area.

We will clarify these definitions with examples in the discussion of paths in Chapter 9.

Listing 3.17 uses DrawClosedCurve to draw a closed curve with a tension and fill mode.

LISTING 3.17: Drawing a closed curve with a tension and fill mode

```
// Draw curve
float tension = 0.5F;
e.Graphics.DrawClosedCurve(bluePen, ptsArray,
tension, FillMode.Alternate);
```

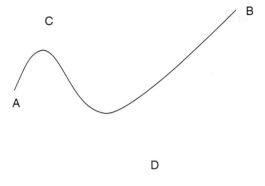

FIGURE 3.24: A Bézier curve

3.2.1.11 *Drawing Bézier Curves*

The Bézier curve, developed by Pierre Bézier in the 1960s for CAD/CAM operations, has become one of the most used curves in drawing. A **Bézier curve** is defined by four points: two endpoints and two control points. Figure 3.24 shows an example of a Bézier curve in which A and B are the starting and ending points and C and D are two control points.

The `Graphics` class provides the `DrawBezier` and `DrawBeziers` methods for drawing Bézier curves. `DrawBezier` draws a Bézier curve defined by four points: the starting point, two control points, and the ending point of the curve. The following example draws a Bézier curve with starting point (30, 20), ending point (140, 50), and control points (80, 60) and (120, 18).

```
e.Graphics.DrawBezier(bluePen, 30, 20,
    80, 60, 120, 180, 140, 50);
```

`DrawBeziers` draws a series of Bézier curves from an array of `Point` structures. To draw multiple beziers, you need $3x + 1$ points, where x is the number of Bézier segments.

Listing 3.18 draws Bézier curves using both `DrawBezier` and `Draw-Beziers`.

LISTING 3.18: Drawing Bézier curves

```
private void Form1_Paint(object sender,
System.Windows.Forms.PaintEventArgs e)
```

continues

```
{
  Graphics g = e.Graphics ;
  // Create pens
  Pen bluePen = new Pen(Color.Blue, 1);
  Pen redPen = new Pen(Color.Red, 1);
  // Create points for curve
  PointF p1 = new PointF(40.0F, 50.0F);
  PointF p2 = new PointF(60.0F, 70.0F);
  PointF p3 = new PointF(80.0F, 34.0F);
  PointF p4 = new PointF(120.0F, 180.0F);
  PointF p5 = new PointF(200.0F, 150.0F);
  PointF p6 = new PointF(350.0F, 250.0F);
  PointF p7 = new PointF(200.0F, 200.0F);
  PointF[] ptsArray =
  {
    p1, p2, p3, p4, p5, p6, p7
  };
  // Draw a Bézier
  e.Graphics.DrawBezier(bluePen, 30, 20,
    80, 60, 120, 180, 140, 50);
  // Draw Béziers
  e.Graphics.DrawBeziers(redPen, ptsArray);
  // Dispose of objects
  redPen.Dispose();
  bluePen.Dispose();
}
```

Figure 3.25 shows the output from Listing 3.18.

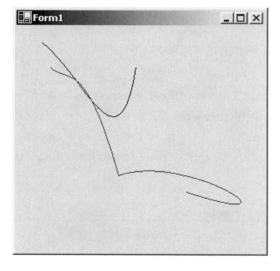

FIGURE 3.25: Drawing Bézier curves

3.2.1.12 *Drawing a Polygon*

A **polygon** is a closed shape with three or more straight sides. Examples of polygons include triangles and rectangles.

The `Graphics` class provides a `DrawPolygon` method to draw polygons. `DrawPolygon` draws a polygon defined by an array of points. It takes two arguments: a pen and an array of `Point` or `PointF` strucures.

To draw a polygon, an application first creates a pen and an array of points and then calls the `DrawPolygon` method with these parameters. Listing 3.19 draws a polygon with five points.

LISTING 3.19: Drawing a polygon

```
private void Form1_Paint(object sender,
    System.Windows.Forms.PaintEventArgs e)
{
  Graphics g = e.Graphics ;
  // Create pens
  Pen greenPen = new Pen(Color.Green, 2);
  Pen redPen = new Pen(Color.Red, 2);
  // Create points for polygon
  PointF p1 = new PointF(40.0F, 50.0F);
  PointF p2 = new PointF(60.0F, 70.0F);
  PointF p3 = new PointF(80.0F, 34.0F);
  PointF p4 = new PointF(120.0F, 180.0F);
  PointF p5 = new PointF(200.0F, 150.0F);
  PointF[] ptsArray =
  {
    p1, p2, p3, p4, p5
  };
  // Draw polygon
  e.Graphics.DrawPolygon(greenPen,ptsArray);
  // Dispose of objects
  greenPen.Dispose();
  redPen.Dispose();
}
```

Figure 3.26 shows the output from Listing 3.19.

3.2.1.13 *Drawing Icons*

The `DrawIcon` and `DrawIconUnstretched` methods are used to draw icons. `DrawIcon` draws an image represented by a specified object at the specified coordinates—stretching the image to fit, if necessary. `DrawIconUnstretched` draws an image represented by an `Icon` object without scaling the image.

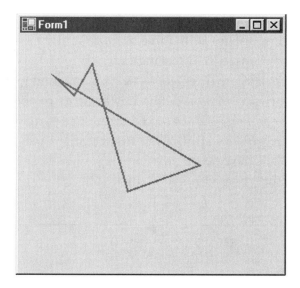

FIGURE 3.26: Drawing a polygon

DrawIcon and DrawIconUnstretched take two arguments: an Icon object and upper left corner coordinates of a rectangle. To draw an icon using these methods, an application first creates an icon and either a Rectangle object or coordinates to the upper left corner at which to draw the icon.

An Icon object represents a Windows icon. An application creates an Icon object using its constructor, which takes arguments of string, Icon, Stream, and Type. Table 3.3 describes the properties of the Icon class.

Table 3.4 describes some of the methods of the Icon class.

TABLE 3.3: Icon properties

Property	Description
Handle	Represents the window handle of an icon.
Height	Represents the height of an icon.
Size	Represents the size of an icon.
Width	Represents the width of an icon.

TABLE 3.4: Icon methods

Method	Description
Clone	Clones an Icon object, creating a duplicate image.
Save	Saves an Icon object to the output stream.
ToBitmap	Converts an Icon object to a Bitmap object.

Listing 3.20 draws icons. The application first creates two Icon objects, then creates a Rectangle object and calls DrawIcon and DrawIcon-Unstretched.

LISTING 3.20: Drawing icons

```
Icon icon1 = new Icon("mouse.ico");
Icon icon2 = new Icon("logo.ico");
int x = 20;
int y = 50;
e.Graphics.DrawIcon(icon1, x, y);
Rectangle rect = new Rectangle(100, 200, 400, 400);
e.Graphics.DrawIconUnstretched(icon2, rect);
```

Figure 3.27 shows the output from Listing 3.20.

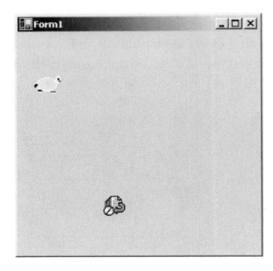

FIGURE 3.27: Drawing icons

3.2.1.14 *Drawing Graphics Paths*

A **graphics path** is a combination of multiple graphics shapes. For example, the graphics path in Figure 3.28 is a combination of lines, an ellipse, and a rectangle.

The GraphicsPath class represents graphics paths. It provides methods to add graphics objects. For example, the AddLine, AddRectangle, Add-Ellipse, AddArc, AddPolygon, AddCurve, and AddBezier methods add a line, a rectangle, an ellipse, an arc, a polygon, a curve, and a Bézier curve, respectively.

GraphicsPath is defined in the System.Drawing.Drawing2D namespace. You must import this namespace using the following line:

```
using System.Drawing.Drawing2D;
```

The Graphics class provides a DrawPath method, which draws a graphics path. It takes two arguments: Pen and GraphicsPath.

To draw a graphics path, first we create a GraphicsPath object, then we add graphics shapes to the path by calling its Add methods, and finally we call DrawPath. For example, the following code creates a graphics path, adds an ellipse to the path, and draws it.

```
GraphicsPath graphPath = new GraphicsPath();
graphPath.AddEllipse(50, 50, 100, 150);
g.DrawPath(greenPen, graphPath);
```

Let's add more shapes to the graph. Listing 3.21 creates a graphics path; adds some lines, an ellipse, and a rectangle; and draws the path.

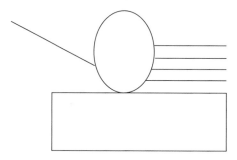

FIGURE 3.28: A path

LISTING 3.21: Drawing a graphics path

```
private void Form1_Paint(object sender,
    System.Windows.Forms.PaintEventArgs e)
{
  // Create a pen
  Pen greenPen = new Pen(Color.Green, 1);
  // Create a graphics path
  GraphicsPath path = new GraphicsPath();
  // Add a line to the path
  path.AddLine(20, 20, 103, 80);
  // Add an ellipse to the path
  path.AddEllipse(100, 50, 100, 100);
  // Add three more lines
  path.AddLine(195, 80, 300, 80);
  path.AddLine(200, 100, 300, 100);
  path.AddLine(195, 120, 300, 120);
  // Create a rectangle and call
  // AddRectangle
  Rectangle rect =
    new Rectangle(50, 150, 300, 50);
  path.AddRectangle(rect);
  // Draw path
  e.Graphics.DrawPath(greenPen, path);
  // Dispose of object
  greenPen.Dispose();
}
```

Figure 3.29 shows the output from Listing 3.21.

3.2.1.15 *Drawing Pie Shapes*

A **pie** is a slice of an ellipse. A pie shape also consists of two radial lines that intersect with the endpoints of the arc. Figure 3.30 shows an ellipse with four pie shapes.

The Graphics class provides the DrawPie method, which draws a pie shape defined by an arc of an ellipse. The DrawPie method takes a Pen object, a Rectangle or RectangleF object, and two radial angles.

Let's create an application that draws pie shapes. We create a Windows application and add two text boxes and a button control to the form. The final form looks like Figure 3.31.

The **Draw Pie** button will draw a pie shape based on the values entered in the **Start Angle** and **Sweep Angle** text boxes. Listing 3.22 shows the code for the **Draw Pie** button click event handler.

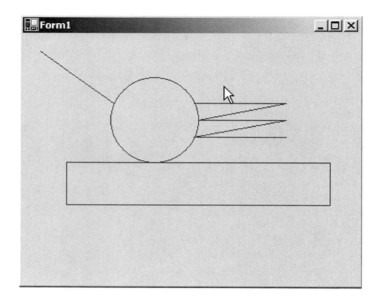

FIGURE 3.29: Drawing a path

LISTING 3.22: Drawing a pie shape

```
private void DrawPieBtn_Click(object sender,
    System.EventArgs e)
{
    // Create a Graphics object
    Graphics g = this.CreateGraphics();
    g.Clear(this.BackColor);
    // Get the current value of start and sweep
    // angles
    float startAngle =
      (float)Convert.ToDouble(textBox1.Text);
    float sweepAngle =
      (float)Convert.ToDouble(textBox2.Text);
    // Create a pen
    Pen bluePen = new Pen(Color.Blue, 1);
    // Draw pie
    g.DrawPie( bluePen, 20, 20, 100, 100,
      startAngle, sweepAngle);
    // Dispose of objects
    bluePen.Dispose();
    g.Dispose();
}
```

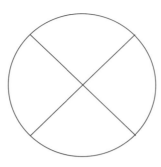

FIGURE 3.30: Four pie shapes of an ellipse

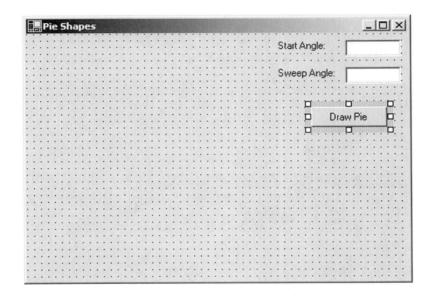

FIGURE 3.31: A pie shape–drawing application

Now let's run the pie shape–drawing application and enter values for the start and sweep angles. Figure 3.32 shows a pie for start and sweep angles of 0.0 and 90 degrees, respectively.

Figure 3.33 shows a pie for start and sweep angles of 45.0 and 180.0 degrees, respectively.

Figure 3.34 shows a pie for start and sweep angles of 90.0 and 45.0 degrees, respectively.

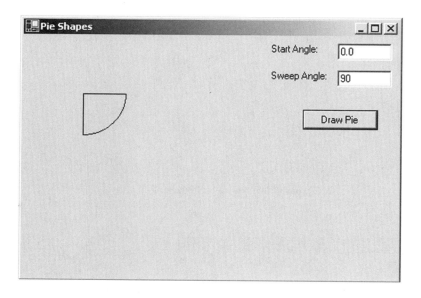

FIGURE 3.32: A pie shape with start angle of 0 degrees and sweep angle of 90 degrees

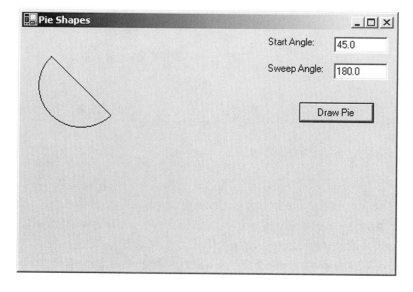

FIGURE 3.33: A pie shape with start angle of 45 degrees and sweep angle of 180 degrees

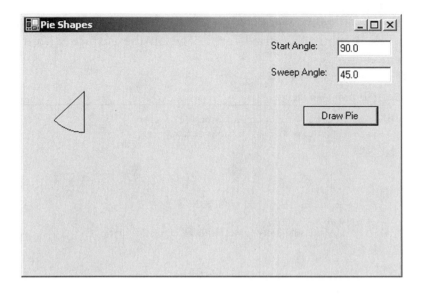

FIGURE 3.34: A pie shape with start angle of 90 degrees and sweep angle of 45 degrees

> **■ NOTE**
> We will see a real-world pie chart application in Section 3.4.

3.2.1.16 *Drawing Images*

The `Graphics` class also provides functionality for drawing images, using `DrawImage` and `DrawImageUnscaled`. `DrawImage` draws an `Image` object with a specified size, and `DrawImageUnscaled` draws an `Image` object without scaling it. The `DrawImage` method has many overloaded forms.

> **■ NOTE**
> Here we discuss simple images. Chapters 7 and 8 discuss the `Image` class, its members, and imaging-related functionality in detail.

An application creates an `Image` object by calling the `Image` class's static `FromFile` method, which takes a file name as an argument. After that you

create the coordinates of a rectangle in which to draw the image and call
DrawImage. Listing 3.23 draws an image on the surface with a size of
ClientRectangle.

LISTING 3.23: Drawing an image

```
private void Form1_Paint(object sender,
    System.Windows.Forms.PaintEventArgs e)
{

    try
    {
     // Create an image from a file
       Image newImage =
         Image.FromFile("dnWatcher.gif");

        // Draw image
        e.Graphics.DrawImage(newImage,
        this.ClientRectangle);
            newImage.Dispose();
    }
    catch (Exception ex)
    {
      MessageBox.Show(ex.Message.ToString());
    }
}
```

Figure 3.35 shows the output from Listing 3.23.

3.2.2 Fill Methods

So far we have seen only the draw methods of the Graphics class. As we
discussed earlier, pens are used to draw the outer boundary of graphics
shapes, and brushes are used to fill the interior of graphics shapes. In this
section we will cover the Fill methods of the Graphics class. You can fill
only certain graphics shapes; hence there are only a few Fill methods
available in the Graphics class. Table 3.5 lists them.

3.2.2.1 *The FillClosedCurve Method*

FillClosedCurve fills the interior of a closed curve. The first parameter of
FillClosedCurve is a brush. It can be a solid brush, a hatch brush, or a
gradient brush. Brushes are discussed in more detail in Chapter 4. The second parameter is an array of points. The third and fourth parameters are

FIGURE 3.35: Drawing an image

optional. The third parameter is a fill mode, which is represented by the `FillMode` enumeration. The fourth and last optional parameter is the tension of the curve, which we discussed in Section 3.2.1.10.

The `FillMode` enumeration specifies the way the interior of a closed path is filled. It has two modes: alternate or winding. The values for alternate and winding are `Alternate` and `Winding`, respectively. The default mode is `Alternate`. The fill mode matters only if the curve intersects itself (see Section 3.2.1.10).

To fill a closed curve using `FillClosedCurve`, an application first creates a `Brush` object and an array of points for the curve. The application can then set the fill mode and tension (which is optional) and call `Fill-ClosedCurve`.

Listing 3.24 creates an array of `PointF` structures and a `SolidBrush` object, and calls `FillClosedCurve`.

LISTING 3.24: Using `FillClosedCurve` to fill a closed curve

```
private void Form1_Paint(object sender,
   System.Windows.Forms.PaintEventArgs e)
```

continues

```
{
  // Create an array of points
    PointF pt1 = new PointF( 40.0F,   50.0F);
    PointF pt2 = new PointF(50.0F,    75.0F);
    PointF pt3 = new PointF(100.0F,   115.0F);
    PointF pt4 = new PointF(200.0F,   180.0F);
    PointF pt5 = new PointF(200.0F, 90.0F);
    PointF[] ptsArray =
    {
      pt1, pt2, pt3, pt4, pt5
    };
    // Fill a closed curve
    float tension = 1.0F;
    FillMode flMode = FillMode.Alternate;
    SolidBrush blueBrush = new SolidBrush(Color.Blue);
    e.Graphics.FillClosedCurve(blueBrush, ptsArray,
      flMode, tension);
    // Dispose of object
    blueBrush.Dispose();
}
```

TABLE 3.5: Graphics fill methods

Method	Description
FillClosedCurve	Fills the interior of a closed cardinal spline curve defined by an array of `Point` structures.
FillEllipse	Fills the interior of an ellipse defined by a bounding rectangle specified by a pair of coordinates, a width, and a height.
FillPath	Fills the interior of a `GraphicsPath` object.
FillPie	Fills the interior of a pie section defined by an ellipse specified by a pair of coordinates, a width, a height, and two radial lines.
FillPolygon	Fills the interior of a polygon defined by an array of points specified by `Point` structures.
FillRectangle	Fills the interior of a rectangle specified by a pair of coordinates, a width, and a height.
FillRectangles	Fills the interiors of a series of rectangles specified by `Rectangle` structures.
FillRegion	Fills the interior of a `Region` object.

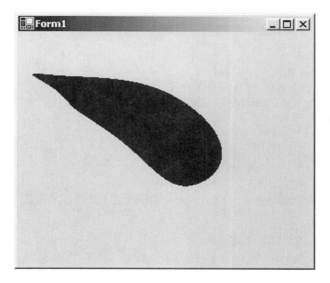

FIGURE 3.36: Filling a closed curve

Figure 3.36 shows the output from Listing 3.24.

3.2.2.2 *The FillEllipse Method*

FillEllipse fills the interior of an ellipse. It takes a Brush object and rectangle coordinates.

To fill an ellipse using FillEllipse, an application creates a Brush and a rectangle and calls FillEllipse. Listing 3.25 creates three brushes and calls FillEllipse to fill an ellipse with a brush.

LISTING 3.25: Filling ellipses

```
private void Form1_Paint(object sender,
  System.Windows.Forms.PaintEventArgs e)
{
  Graphics g = e.Graphics ;
  // Create brushes
  SolidBrush redBrush = new SolidBrush(Color.Red);
  SolidBrush blueBrush = new SolidBrush(Color.Blue);
  SolidBrush greenBrush = new SolidBrush(Color.Green);
  // Create a rectangle
  Rectangle rect =
    new Rectangle(80, 80, 50, 50);
  // Fill ellipses
```

continues

```
g.FillEllipse(greenBrush,
  40.0F, 40.0F, 130.0F, 130.0F );
g.FillEllipse(blueBrush, 60, 60, 90, 90);
g.FillEllipse(redBrush, rect );
g.FillEllipse(greenBrush,
  100.0F, 90.0F, 10.0F, 30.0F );
// Dispose of objects
blueBrush.Dispose();
redBrush.Dispose();
greenBrush.Dispose();
}
```

Figure 3.37 shows the output from Listing 3.25.

3.2.2.3 *The FillPath Method*

FillPath fills the interior of a graphics path. To do this, an application creates Brush and GraphicsPath objects and then calls FillPath, which takes a brush and a graphics path as arguments. Listing 3.26 creates GraphicsPath and SolidBrush objects and calls FillPath.

LISTING 3.26: Filling a graphics path

```
private void Form1_Paint(object sender,
      System.Windows.Forms.PaintEventArgs e)
```

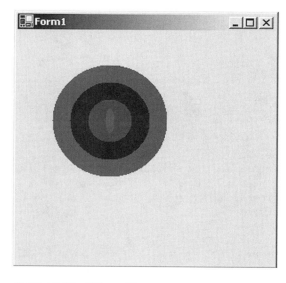

FIGURE 3.37: Filling ellipses

```
    {
        // Create a solid brush
        SolidBrush greenBrush =
          new SolidBrush(Color.Green);
        // Create a graphics path
        GraphicsPath path = new GraphicsPath();
        // Add a line to the path
        path.AddLine(20, 20, 103, 80);
        // Add an ellipse to the path
        path.AddEllipse(100, 50, 100, 100);
        // Add three more lines
        path.AddLine(195, 80, 300, 80);
        path.AddLine(200, 100, 300, 100);
        path.AddLine(195, 120, 300, 120);

        // Create a rectangle and call
        // AddRectangle
        Rectangle rect =
          new Rectangle(50, 150, 300, 50);
        path.AddRectangle(rect);
        // Fill path
        e.Graphics.FillPath(greenBrush, path);
        // Dispose of object
        greenBrush.Dispose();
    }
```

Figure 3.38 shows the output from Listing 3.26. As the figure shows, the fill method fills all the covered areas of a graphics path.

3.2.2.4 *The FillPie Method*

FillPie fills a pie section with a specified brush. It takes four parameters: a brush, the rectangle of the ellipse, and the start and sweep angles. The following code calls FillPie.

```
    g.FillPie(new SolidBrush(Color.Red),
    0.0F, 0.0F, 100, 60, 0.0F, 90.0F);
```

We will discuss the FillPie method in the pie chart application in Section 3.4.

3.2.2.5 *The FillPolygon Method*

FillPolygon fills a polygon with the specified brush. It takes three parameters: a brush, an array of points, and a fill mode. The FillMode enumera-

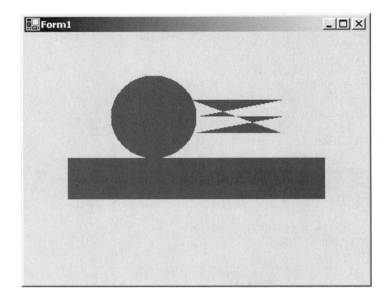

FIGURE 3.38: Filling a graphics path

tion defines the fill mode of the interior of the path. It provides two fill modes: Alternate and Winding. The default mode is Alternate.

In our application we will use a hatch brush. So far we have seen only a solid brush. A **solid brush** is a brush with one color only. A **hatch brush** is a brush with a hatch style and two colors. These colors work together to support the hatch style. The HatchBrush class represents a hatch brush. We will discuss hatch brushes in more detail in Chapter 4.

The code in Listing 3.27 uses FillPolygon to fill a polygon using the Winding mode.

LISTING 3.27: Filling a polygon

```
Graphics g = e.Graphics ;
// Create a solid brush
SolidBrush greenBrush =
    new SolidBrush(Color.Green) ;
// Create points for polygon
PointF p1 = new PointF(40.0F, 50.0F) ;
PointF p2 = new PointF(60.0F, 70.0F) ;
PointF p3 = new PointF(80.0F, 34.0F) ;
PointF p4 = new PointF(120.0F, 180.0F) ;
PointF p5 = new PointF(200.0F, 150.0F) ;
```

```
PointF[] ptsArray =
{
    p1, p2, p3, p4, p5
};
// Draw polygon
e.Graphics.FillPolygon(greenBrush, ptsArray);
// Dispose of object
greenBrush.Dispose();
```

Figure 3.39 shows the output from Listing 3.27. As you can see, the fill method fills all the areas of a polygon.

3.2.2.6 *Filling Rectangles and Regions*

FillRectangle fills a rectangle with a brush. This method takes a brush and a rectangle as arguments. FillRectangles fills a specified *series* of rectangles with a brush, and it takes a brush and an array of rectangles. These methods also have overloaded forms with additional options. For instance, if you're using a HatchStyle brush, you can specify background and foreground colors. Chapter 4 discusses FillRectangle and its options in more detail.

> **▪ NOTE**
>
> The HatchBrush class is defined in the System.Drawing.Drawing2D namespace.

The source code in Listing 3.28 uses FillRectangle to fill two rectangles. One rectangle is filled with a hatch brush, the other with a solid brush.

LISTING 3.28: Filling rectangles

```
private void Form1_Paint(object sender,
    System.Windows.Forms.PaintEventArgs e)
{
    // Create brushes
    SolidBrush blueBrush = new SolidBrush(Color.Blue);
    // Create a rectangle
    Rectangle rect = new Rectangle(10, 20, 100, 50);
    // Fill rectangle
```

continues

```
e.Graphics.FillRectangle(new HatchBrush
  (HatchStyle.BackwardDiagonal,
  Color.Yellow, Color.Black),
  rect);
e.Graphics.FillRectangle(blueBrush,
  new Rectangle(150, 20, 50, 100));

// Dispose of object
blueBrush.Dispose();
}
```

Figure 3.40 shows the output from Listing 3.28.

FillRegion fills a specified region with a brush. This method takes a brush and a region as input parameters. Listing 3.29 creates a Region object from a rectangle and calls FillRegion to fill the region.

LISTING 3.29: Filling regions

```
Rectangle rect = new Rectangle(20, 20, 150, 100);
Region rgn = new Region(rect);
e.Graphics.FillRegion(new SolidBrush(Color.Green)
, rgn);
```

> **■ NOTE**
> Chapter 6 discusses rectangles and regions in more detail.

3.2.3 **Miscellaneous** Graphics **Class Methods**

The Graphics class provides more than just draw and fill methods. Miscellaneous methods are defined in Table 3.6. Some of these methods are discussed in more detail later.

3.2.3.1 *The* Clear *Method*

The Clear method clears the entire drawing surface and fills it with the specified background color. It takes one argument, of type Color. To clear a form, an application passes the form's background color. The following code snippet uses the Clear method to clear a form.

```
form.Graphics g = this.CreateGraphics();
g.Clear(this.BackColor);
g.Dispose();
```

FIGURE 3.39: Filling a polygon

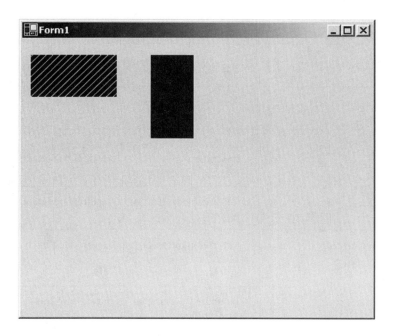

FIGURE 3.40: Filling rectangles

TABLE 3.6: Some miscellaneous `Graphics` methods

Method	Description
AddMetafileComment	Adds a comment to a `Metafile` object.
Clear	Clears the entire drawing surface and fills it with the specified background color.
ExcludeClip	Updates the clip region to exclude the area specified by a `Rectangle` structure.
Flush	Forces execution of all pending graphics operations and returns immediately without waiting for the operations to finish.
FromHdc	Creates a new `Graphics` object from a device context handle.
FromHwnd	Creates a new `Graphics` object from a window handle.
FromImage	Creates a new `Graphics` object from an `Image` object.
GetHalftonePalette	Returns a handle to the current Windows halftone palette.
GetHdc	Returns the device context handle associated with a `Graphics` object.
GetNearestColor	Returns the nearest color to the specified `Color` structure.
IntersectClip	Updates the clip region of a `Graphics` object to the intersection of the current clip region and a `Rectangle` structure.
IsVisible	Returns `true` if a point is within the visible clip region.
MeasureCharacterRanges	Returns an array of `Region` objects, each of which bounds a range of character positions within a string.
MeasureString	Measures a string when drawn with the specified `Font` object.

TABLE 3.6: Some miscellaneous `Graphics` methods (continued)

Method	Description
MultiplyTransform	Multiplies the world transformation and the `Matrix` object.
ReleaseHdc	Releases a device context handle obtained by a previous call to the `GetHdc` method.
ResetClip	Resets the clip region to an infinite region.
ResetTransform	Resets the world transformation matrix to the identity matrix.
Restore	Restores the state of a `Graphics` object to the state represented by a `GraphicsState` object. Takes `GraphicsState` as input, removes the information block from the stack, and restores the `Graphics` object to the state it was in when it was saved.
RotateTransform	Applies rotation to the transformation matrix.
Save	Saves the information block of a `Graphics` object. The information block stores the state of the `Graphics` object. The `Save` method returns a `GraphicsState` object that identifies the information block.
ScaleTransform	Applies the specified scaling operation to the transformation matrix.
SetClip	Sets the clipping region to the `Clip` property.
TransformPoints	Transforms an array of points from one coordinate space to another using the current world and page transformations.
TranslateClip	Translates the clipping region by specified amounts in the horizontal and vertical directions.
TranslateTransform	Prepends the specified translation to the transformation matrix.

3.2.3.2 *The MeasureString Method*

MeasureString measures a string when it is drawn with a Font object and returns the size of the string as a SizeF object. You can use SizeF to find out the height and width of string.

MeasureString can also be used to find the total number of characters and lines in a string. It has seven overloaded methods. It takes two required parameters: the string and font to measure. Optional parameters you can pass include the width of the string in pixels, maximum layout area of the text, string format, and combinations of these parameters.

> **■ NOTE**
> Chapter 5 discusses string operations in detail.

Listing 3.30 uses the MeasureString method to measure a string's height and width and draws a rectangle and a circle around the string. This example also shows how to find the total number of lines and characters of a string.

LISTING 3.30: Using the MeasureString method

```
Graphics g = Graphics.FromHwnd(this.Handle);
g.Clear(this.BackColor);

string testString = "This is a test string";
Font verdana14 = new Font("Verdana", 14);
Font tahoma18 = new Font("Tahoma", 18);
int nChars;
int nLines;

// Call MeasureString to measure a string
SizeF sz = g.MeasureString(testString, verdana14);
string stringDetails = "Height: "+sz.Height.ToString()
+ ", Width: "+sz.Width.ToString();
MessageBox.Show("First string details: "+ stringDetails);
g.DrawString(testString, verdana14, Brushes.Green,
new PointF(0, 100));
g.DrawRectangle(new Pen(Color.Red, 2), 0.0F, 100.0F,
sz.Width, sz.Height);
sz = g.MeasureString("Ellipse", tahoma18,
new SizeF(0.0F, 100.0F), new StringFormat(),
out nChars, out nLines);
```

```
stringDetails = "Height: "+sz.Height.ToString()
+ ", Width: "+sz.Width.ToString()
+ ", Lines: "+nLines.ToString()
+ ", Chars: "+nChars.ToString();
MessageBox.Show("Second string details: "+ stringDetails);

g.DrawString("Ellipse", tahoma18, Brushes.Blue,
new PointF(10, 10));
g.DrawEllipse( new Pen(Color.Red, 3), 10, 10,
sz.Width, sz.Height);g.Dispose()
```

Figure 3.41 shows the output from Listing 3.30.

3.2.3.3 *The FromImage, FromHdc, and FromHwnd Methods*

As we discussed earlier, an application can use Graphics class members to get a Graphics object. The Graphics class provides three methods to create a Graphics object: FromHwnd, FromHdc, and FromImage.

FromImage takes an Image object as input parameter and returns a Graphics object. We will discuss FromImage in more detail in Chapters 7

FIGURE 3.41: Using MeasureString when drawing text

and 8. The following code snippet creates a `Graphics` object from an `Image` object. Once a `Graphics` object has been created, you can call its members.

```
Image img = Image.FromFile("Rose.jpg");
Graphics g = Graphics.FromImage(img);
// Do something
g.Dispose();
```

> **NOTE**
> Make sure you call the `Dispose` method of the `Graphics` object when you're finished with it.

`FromHdc` creates a `Graphics` object from a window handle to a device context. The following code snippet shows an example in which `FromHdc` takes one parameter, of type `IntPtr`.

```
IntPtr hdc = e.Graphics.GetHdc();
Graphics g= Graphics.FromHdc(hdc);
// Do something
e.Graphics.ReleaseHdc(hdc);
g.Dispose();
```

> **NOTE**
> You need to call the `ReleaseHdc` method to release resources allocated by a window handle to a device context, and also make sure you call the `Dispose` method of the `Graphics` object when you're finished with it.

`FromHwnd` returns a `Graphics` object for a form. The following method takes a window handle.

```
Graphics g = Graphics.FromHwnd(this.Handle);
```

To draw on a form, an application can pass this handle. Once an application has a `Graphics` object, it can call any `Graphics` class method to draw graphics objects.

3.3 **The GDI+Painter Application**

Almost every chapter of this book will show a real-world example to illustrate the concepts discussed in it. In this chapter we create an application, GDI+Painter, that you can use to draw and fill simple graphics objects. If you wish, you can add more functionality to the application. Once you are done drawing graphics shapes, the program allows you to save your drawing in bitmap format. You can modify the program to save a drawing in .jpeg or .gif format.

The program is a Windows Forms application and looks like Figure 3.42. It has three draw buttons (line, ellipse, and rectangle) and two fill buttons (rectangle and ellipse). The **Save Image** button allows you to save the image.

Click on a button and the program draws the selected item on the form. Here's how it works:

First we define some private class-level variables:

```
// Variables
private Bitmap bitmap = null;
private Bitmap curBitmap = null;
private bool dragMode = false;
private int drawIndex = 1;
private int curX, curY, x, y;
private int diffX, diffY;
private Graphics curGraphics;
private Pen curPen;
private SolidBrush curBrush;
private Size fullSize;
```

> ■ **NOTE**
> Please download GDI+Painter application source code from online (www.awprofessional.com/titles/0321160770).

The next step is to initialize objects. On the form-load event handler, we create a bitmap and a Graphics object from the bitmap, which represents the entire form. We set its background color to the form's background color by calling the Graphics.Clear method. We also create a Pen object and a Brush object when the form loads. Listing 3.31 gives the form-load event handler code.

LISTING 3.31: The form-load event handler

```
private void Form1_Load(object sender,
  System.EventArgs e)
{
    // Get the full size of the form
    fullSize = SystemInformation
      .PrimaryMonitorMaximizedWindowSize;
    // Create a bitmap using full size
    bitmap = new Bitmap(fullSize.Width,
      fullSize.Height);
    // Create a Graphics object from Bitmap
    curGraphics = Graphics.FromImage(bitmap);
    // Set background color as form's color
    curGraphics.Clear(this.BackColor);
    // Create a new pen and brush as
    // default pen and brush
    curPen = new Pen(Color.Black);
    curBrush = new SolidBrush(Color.Black);
}
```

When we click on a button, we find out which button was selected and save it in the `drawIndex` variable. Listing 3.32 gives code for the button click event handler for all buttons.

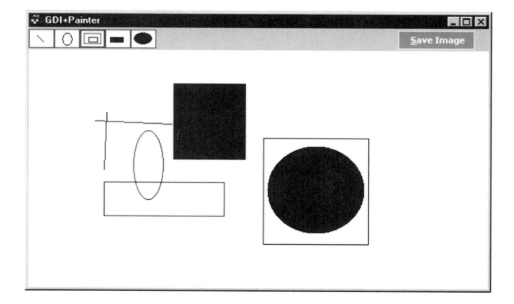

FIGURE 3.42: The GDI+Painter application

LISTING 3.32: Saving a selected button

```
private void LineDraw_Click(object sender,
    System.EventArgs e)
  {
    drawIndex = 1;
  }

  private void RectDraw_Click(object sender,
    System.EventArgs e)
  {
     drawIndex = 2;
  }

  private void EllipseDraw_Click(object sender,
    System.EventArgs e)
  {
    drawIndex = 3;
  }
  private void FilledEllipse_Click(object sender,
    System.EventArgs e)
  {
    drawIndex = 5;
  }
}
```

When we start drawing on the form, we save the starting point on the mouse-down events and the ending point on the mouse-up events (see Listing 3.33). From these two points we can determine the area of the rectangle we're trying to draw. We use this rectangle in draw and fill methods.

On a mouse-move event, we calculate the difference between the ending and starting points that are used to draw the rectangle. Notice also that on mouse down we set dragMode to true, and on mouse up we set dragMode to false. On the basis of the area covered by user selection, we draw or fill objects on mouse up, which gives the user a visible drawing effect. You will also see the RefreshFormBackground method, which we will discuss shortly.

LISTING 3.33: The mouse-down event handler

```
private void Form1_MouseDown(object sender,
  System.Windows.Forms.MouseEventArgs e)
{
    // Store the starting point of
```

continues

```
      // the rectangle and set the drag mode
      // to true
      curX = e.X;
      curY = e.Y;
      dragMode = true;
   }

   private void Form1_MouseMove(object sender,
      System.Windows.Forms.MouseEventArgs e)
   {
      // Find out the ending point of
      // the rectangle and calculate the
      // difference between starting and ending
      // points to find out the height and width
      // of the rectangle
      x = e.X;
      y = e.Y;
      diffX = e.X - curX;
      diffY = e.Y - curY;
      // If dragMode is true, call refresh
      // to force the window to repaint
      if (dragMode)
      {
         this.Refresh();
      }
   }

   private void Form1_MouseUp(object sender,
      System.Windows.Forms.MouseEventArgs e)
   {
      diffX = x - curX;
      diffY = y - curY;
      switch (drawIndex)
      {
         case 1:
         {
            // Draw a line
            curGraphics.DrawLine(curPen,
               curX, curY, x, y);
            break;
         }
         case 2:
         {
            // Draw an ellipse
            curGraphics.DrawEllipse(curPen,
               curX, curY, diffX, diffY);
            break;
         }
         case 3:
         {
```

```
      // Draw a rectangle
      curGraphics.DrawRectangle(curPen,
        curX, curY, diffX, diffY);
      break;
    }
    case 4:
    {
      // Fill the rectangle
      curGraphics.FillRectangle(curBrush,
       curX, curY, diffX, diffY);
      break;
    }
    case 5:
    {
      // Fill the ellipse
      curGraphics.FillEllipse(curBrush,
        curX, curY, diffX, diffY);
      break;
    }
  }
  // Refresh
  RefreshFormBackground();
  // Set drag mode to false
  dragMode = false;
}
```

Now we add code to the form's paint event handler, which draws and fills the object. Listing 3.34 gives the code for the `OnPaint` method.

LISTING 3.34: The **OnPaint** method

```
private void Form1_Paint(object sender,
    System.Windows.Forms.PaintEventArgs e)
  {

  Graphics g = e.Graphics;
  // If dragMode is true, draw the selected
  // graphics shape
  if (dragMode)
  {
    switch (drawIndex)
    {
      case 1:
      {
        g.DrawLine(curPen, curX, curY, x, y);
        break;
      }
```

continues

```
    case 2:
    {
      g.DrawEllipse(curPen,
        curX, curY, diffX, diffY);
      break;
    }
    case 3:
    {
      g.DrawRectangle(curPen,
        curX, curY, diffX, diffY);
      break;
    }
    case 4:
    {
      g.FillRectangle(curBrush,
        curX, curY, diffX, diffY);
      break;
    }
    case 5:
    {
      g.FillEllipse(curBrush,
        curX, curY, diffX, diffY);
      break;
    }
  }
}
}
```

Here's a little trick. You may have noticed that we used the Refresh-FormBackground method. This method sets the current drawing as the background of the form. Listing 3.35 gives code for the method.

LISTING 3.35: The RefreshFormBackground method

```
private void RefreshFormBackground()
{
    curBitmap = bitmap.Clone(
      new Rectangle(0, 0, this.Width, this.Height),
      bitmap.PixelFormat);
    this.BackgroundImage = curBitmap;
}
```

The **Save Image** button allows us to save the image by simply calling the Save method of Bitmap. The Save method takes a file name and format. We use SaveFileDialog to select the file name. Listing 3.36 gives code for the **Save Image** button.

LISTING 3.36: The Save Image button click handler

```csharp
private void SaveBtn_Click(object sender,
  System.EventArgs e)
{
    // Save file dialog
    SaveFileDialog saveFileDlg = new SaveFileDialog();
    saveFileDlg.Filter =
    "Image files (*.bmp)|*.bmp|All files (*.*)|*.*" ;
    if(saveFileDlg.ShowDialog() == DialogResult.OK)
    {
      // Create bitmap and call Save method
      // to save it
      Bitmap tmpBitmap = bitmap.Clone
        (new Rectangle(0, 0,
        this.Width, this.Height),
        bitmap.PixelFormat);
      tmpBitmap.Save(saveFileDlg.FileName,
        ImageFormat.Bmp);
    }
}
```

In the end we release all objects, which we can do on the form-closed event (see Listing 3.37).

LISTING 3.37: The form-closed event handler

```csharp
private void Form1_Closed(object sender, System.EventArgs e)
{
// Dispose of all public objects
curPen.Dispose();
curBrush.Dispose();
curGraphics.Dispose();
}
```

In Chapter 4 we will add functionality to select different pens and brushes to draw and fill graphics shapes.

3.4 Drawing a Pie Chart

Let's look at one more real-world application. In this example we will develop an application that draws pie charts based on a data feed. Pie charts are useful when you need to represent statistical data in a graphical way—for example, the percentage of users visiting a Web site from different

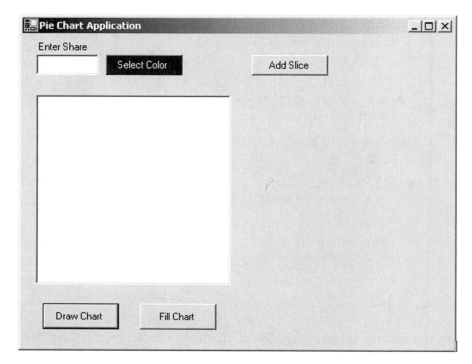

FIGURE 3.43: A pie chart–drawing application

countries, or the percentage grades in different subjects. In our example we will use the `DrawPie` and `FillPie` methods.

First we create a Windows application and add four buttons, a text box, and a list box control. We change the text and names of the text box, and our final form looks like Figure 3.43. In the **Enter Share** text box we will enter a number to represent the share of total items. For example, add five values in the share box: 10, 20, 30, 40, 50. The total is 150. The percentage of the share with value 10 is 10/150.

Listing 3.38 adds variables. You may notice the structure `sliceData`, which has two public variables: `share` and `clr`. The `share` variable represents the share of a slice, and `clr` is its color.

LISTING 3.38: The `sliceData` structure

```
// User-defined variables
private Rectangle rect =
  new Rectangle(250, 150, 200, 200);
```

```
public ArrayList sliceList = new ArrayList();
struct sliceData
{
 public int share;
 public Color clr;
};
private Color curClr = Color.Black;
int shareTotal = 0;
```

The **Select Color** button allows us to select the color for a share. As Listing 3.39 shows, we use `ColorDialog` to select a color.

LISTING 3.39: Selecting a color

```
private void ColorBtn_Click(object sender, System.EventArgs e)
{
 ColorDialog clrDlg = new ColorDialog();
 if (clrDlg.ShowDialog() == DialogResult.OK)
 {
   curClr = clrDlg.Color;
 }
}
```

The **Add Slice** button adds the data to an array to be added to the list for calculation. As Listing 3.40 shows, all data is added to an array. This code also adds the entered data to the `ListBox` control.

LISTING 3.40: Adding pie chart data

```
private void button1_Click(object sender, System.EventArgs e)
{
 int slice = Convert.ToInt32(textBox1.Text);
 shareTotal += slice;
 sliceData dt;
 dt.clr = curClr;
 dt.share = slice;
 sliceList.Add(dt);
 listBox1.Items.Add(
 "Share:"+slice.ToString()+" ," + curClr.ToString() );
}
```

The **Draw Chart** and **Fill Chart** button clicks are used to draw the outer boundary and fill the chart, respectively. These buttons call the `Draw-PieChart` method with a Boolean variable, as shown in Listing 3.41.

LISTING 3.41: The Draw Pie and Fill Pie button click handlers

```
private void DrawPie_Click(object sender, System.EventArgs e)
{
 DrawPieChart(false);
}
private void FillChart_Click(object sender, System.EventArgs e)
{
 DrawPieChart(true);
}
```

The `DrawPieChart` method actually draws the pie chart, as shown in Listing 3.42. Depending on which button—**Fill Chart** or **Draw Chart**—was clicked, we call `FillPie` or `DrawPie`, respectively. We also read each `sliceData` variable of the array and calculate the percentage of a share in the entire chart, represented by an angle.

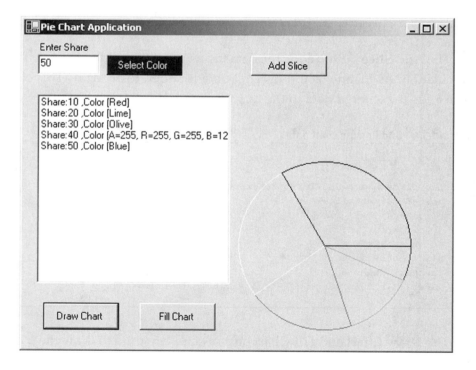

FIGURE 3.44: The Draw Chart button click in action

LISTING 3.42: The `DrawPieChart` method

```
private void DrawPieChart(bool flMode)
{
Graphics g = this.CreateGraphics();
g.Clear(this.BackColor);
Rectangle rect = new Rectangle(250, 150, 200, 200);
float angle = 0;
float sweep = 0;
foreach(sliceData dt in sliceList)
{
sweep = 360f * dt.share / shareTotal;
if(flMode)
g.FillPie(new SolidBrush(dt.clr), rect, angle, sweep);
else
g.DrawPie(new Pen(dt.clr), rect, angle, sweep);
angle += sweep;
}
g.Dispose();
}
```

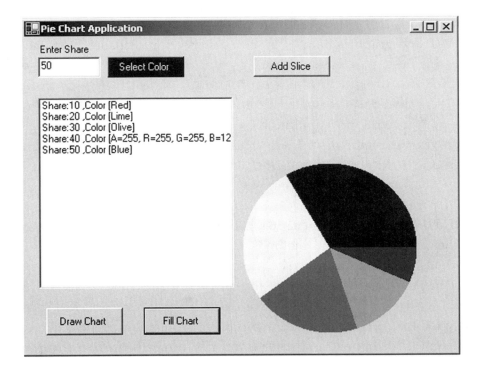

FIGURE 3.45: The Fill Chart button click in action

Let's see this application in action. We add shares 10, 20, 30, 40, and 50 with different colors. The **Draw Chart** button click draws a pie chart, with the output shown in Figure 3.44.

The **Fill Chart** button fills the chart, with the output shown in Figure 3.45.

SUMMARY

In this chapter we have seen that the Graphics object plays a major role in drawing and represents a canvas to draw graphics curves, shapes, and images.

We started this chapter by discussing the Graphics class properties. Then we discussed various Graphics class methods, which are divided into three categories: draw, fill, and miscellaneous. We saw how to use the draw methods to draw lines, rectangles, ellipses, curves, images, paths, and other graphics objects. We also discussed differences between the draw and fill methods and how to use the fill methods to fill rectangles, ellipses, curves, and graphics paths. We then discussed miscellaneous methods, covering the Clear, MeasureString, FromImage, FromHdc, and FromHwnd methods.

This chapter also presented a couple of real-world applications, showing how to write an application to draw line and pie charts. We also used various methods and properties of the Graphics class to write a PaintBrush-like application, GDI+Painter. Using this application, you can draw lines, rectangles, and ellipses and save the resulting image as a bitmap file.

Having completed this chapter, you should have a good understanding of the Graphics class, its methods and properties, and how to use those methods and properties to write real-world applications.

Pens and brushes are two of the most frequently used objects in the graphics world. In this chapter we discussed pens and brushes briefly. Chapter 4 is dedicated to pens and brushes. You will learn how to create different kinds of pens and brushes to write interactive graphics applications. At the end of Chapter 4 we will add different pen and brush options to GDI+Painter, making it more interactive.

4

Working with Brushes and Pens

B RUSHES AND PENS are the two most frequently used objects in graphics applications. **Pens** are used to draw the outlines of graphics objects such as lines and curves; **brushes** are used to fill the graphic objects' interior areas (e.g., filling a rectangle or an ellipse). In this chapter we will discuss how to create and use various types of brushes and pens.

We begin by discussing brushes, brush types, their methods and properties, and how to create and use them in GDI+.

GDI+ provides the `Pen` and `Pens` classes to represent pens. In this chapter we will discuss how to create different kinds of pens using the `Pen` class and its properties, and how to use the `Pen` class methods. We will also discuss how to add line caps, dash caps, line dash styles, and line cap styles. In Sections 4.3 and 4.4 we will discuss the transformation of pens and brushes.

The `SystemPens` and `SystemBrushes` classes represent the system pens and brushes, respectively. In Section 4.5 we will discuss how to use these classes to work with system pens and brushes.

At the end of this chapter we will add color, pen, and brush options to the GDI+Painter application that we created in Chapter 3.

4.1 Understanding and Using Brushes

In the .NET Framework library, brush-related functionality is defined in two namespaces: `System.Drawing` and `System.Drawing.Drawing2D`.

The `System.Drawing` namespace defines general brush-related classes and functionality, and the `System.Drawing.Drawing2D` namespace defines advanced 2D brush-related functionality. For example, the `Brush`, `SolidBrush`, `TextureBrush`, and `Brushes` classes are defined in the `System.Drawing` namespace; and the `HatchBrush` and `GradientBrush` classes are defined in the `System.Drawing.Drawing2D` namespace.

Before using brushes, obviously you must include the corresponding namespace to your application. Alternatively, you can use the namespace as a prefix to the class; for example, `System.Drawing.Brush` represents the `Brush` class if you do not wish to include the `System.Drawing` namespace in your application.

The code snippet in Listing 4.1 creates a red `SolidBrush` object and uses it to draw a rectangle. This code is written on a form's paint event handler. The first line gets the `Graphics` object of the form, and the second line creates a brush using the `SolidBrush` class, which later is used to fill a rectangle. The last line disposes of the `SolidBrush` object.

LISTING 4.1: Creating a solid brush

```
Graphics g = e.Graphics;
SolidBrush redBrush = new SolidBrush(Color.Red);
Rectangle rect = new Rectangle(150, 80, 200, 140);
g.FillRectangle(redBrush, rect);
redBrush.Dispose();
```

4.1.1 The `Brush` Class

In the .NET Framework library, the `Brush` class is an abstract base class, which means you cannot create an instance of it without using its derived classes. All usable classes are inherited from the abstract `Brush` class. Figure 4.1 shows all the `Brush`-derived classes that can be used in your GDI+ applications.

Applications generally call fill methods of the appropriate `Graphics` class, which in turn use brushes to fill GDI+ objects (such as an ellipse, an arc, or a polygon) with a certain kind of brush. GDI+ provides four different kinds of brushes: solid, hatch, texture, and gradient. Figure 4.2 shows the brush types and their classes.

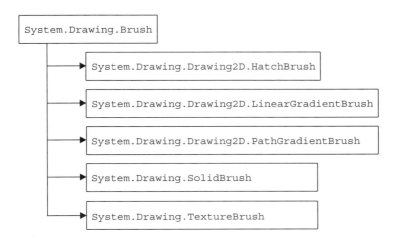

FIGURE 4.1: Classes inherited from the Brush class

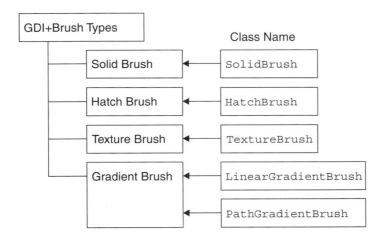

FIGURE 4.2: Brush types and their classes

4.1.2 The Brushes **Class**

The Brushes class is a sealed class (it cannot be inherited). Brushes provides more than 140 static members (properties), and each of these members represents a brush with a particular color (including all the standard colors). For instance, the Brushes.Pink, Brushes.Red, and

Brushes.Green members represent Brush objects with the colors pink, red, and green, respectively.

4.1.3 **Solid Brushes**

A **solid brush** is a brush that fills an area with a single solid color. We create a SolidBrush object by calling its constructor and passing a Color structure as the only parameter. The Color structure represents a color. It has a static property for every possible color. For example, Color.Red represents the color red. The code snippet in Listing 4.2 creates three SolidBrush objects with three different colors: red, green, and blue.

LISTING 4.2: Creating a SolidBrush object

```
SolidBrush redBrush = new SolidBrush(Color.Red);
SolidBrush greenBrush = new SolidBrush(Color.Green);
SolidBrush blueBrush = new SolidBrush(Color.Blue);
```

SolidBrush has only one property of interest: Color, which represents the color of the brush.

Listing 4.3 uses red, green, and blue solid brushes and fills an ellipse, a pie, and a rectangle using the FillEllipse, FillPie, and FillRectangle methods of the Graphics class, respectively.

LISTING 4.3: Using the SolidBrush class

```
private void Form1_Paint(object sender,
System.Windows.Forms.PaintEventArgs e)
{
    Graphics g = e.Graphics;
    // Create three SolidBrush objects
    // using the colors red, green, and blue
    SolidBrush redBrush = new SolidBrush(Color.Red);
    SolidBrush greenBrush = new SolidBrush(Color.Green);
    SolidBrush blueBrush = new SolidBrush(Color.Blue);
    // Fill ellipse using red brush
    g.FillEllipse(redBrush, 20, 40, 100, 120);
    // Fill rectangle using blue brush
    Rectangle rect = new Rectangle(150, 80, 200, 140);
    g.FillRectangle(blueBrush, rect);
    // Fill pie using green brush
    g.FillPie(greenBrush,
      40, 20, 200, 40, 0.0f, 60.0f );
```

```
    // Dispose of objects
    redBrush.Dispose();
    greenBrush.Dispose();
    blueBrush.Dispose();
}
```

The output of Listing 4.3 draws an ellipse, a rectangle, and a pie, as Figure 4.3 shows.

4.1.4 Hatch Brushes

Hatch brushes are brushes with a hatch style, a foreground color, and a background color. **Hatches** are a combination of rectangle lines and the area between the lines. The foreground color defines the color of lines; the background color defines the color between lines.

The `HatchBrush` class constructor takes `HatchStyle` as its first parameter and `Color` as the second parameter. Second and third `Color`

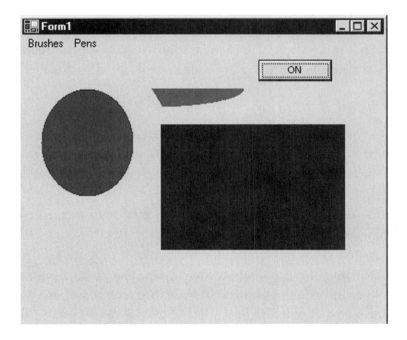

FIGURE 4.3: Graphics objects filled by `SolidBrush`

> **■ NOTE**
>
> The `HatchBrush` class is defined in the `System.Drawing.Drawing2D` namespace. An application needs to provide a reference to `System.Drawing.Drawing2D` before using this class. Alternatively, an application can refer to the `HatchBrush` class as `System.Drawing.Drawing2D.HatchBrush`.

parameters represent the foreground and background colors. The following code snippet shows the constructor signatures:

```
public HatchBrush(HatchStyle, Color);
public HatchBrush(HatchStyle, Color, Color);
```

The following code creates a hatch brush with a dashed-vertical hatch style, blue background, and red foreground:

```
HatchBrush hBrush1 = new HatchBrush
(HatchStyle.DashedVertical, Color.Blue, Color.Red);
```

We can use this hatch brush to fill graphics objects such as rectangles or ellipses. For example, the following code line fills an ellipse using `hBrush1`:

```
g.FillEllipse(hBrush1, 20, 40, 100, 120);
```

`HatchBrush` has three properties: `BackgroundColor`, `ForegroundColor`, and `HatchStyle`. `BackgroundColor` returns the color of spaces between the hatch lines, and `ForegroundColor` represents the color of the hatch lines.

`HatchStyle` returns the hatch brush style of type `HatchStyle` enumeration, whose members are described in Table 4.1.

Let's create a Windows application that looks like Figure 4.4. The combo box will list some of the available hatch styles. The **Pick...** buttons let you select background and foreground colors of the hatch brush, and the **Apply Style** button creates a hatch brush based on the selection and uses it to draw a rectangle.

First we add one `HatchStyle`-type and two `Color`-type class-level variables that represent the current selected hatch style, foreground, and

TABLE 4.1: `HatchStyle` members

Member	Description
BackwardDiagonal	A pattern of lines on a diagonal from upper right to lower left.
Cross	Horizontal and vertical lines that cross.
DarkDownwardDiagonal	Diagonal lines that slant to the right from top points to bottom points, are spaced 50 percent closer together than in `ForwardDiagonal`, and are twice the width of `ForwardDiagonal` lines.
DarkHorizontal	Horizontal lines that are spaced 50 percent closer together than in `Horizontal` and are twice the width of `Horizontal` lines.
DarkUpwardDiagonal	Diagonal lines that slant to the left from top points to bottom points, are spaced 50 percent closer together than `BackwardDiagonal`, and are twice the width of `BackwardDiagonal` lines.
DarkVertical	Vertical lines that are spaced 50 percent closer together than `Vertical` and are twice the width of `Vertical` lines.
DashedDownwardDiagonal	Dashed diagonal lines that slant to the right from top points to bottom points.
DashedHorizontal	Dashed horizontal lines.
DashedUpwardDiagonal	Dashed diagonal lines that slant to the left from top points to bottom points.
DashedVertical	Dashed vertical lines.
DiagonalBrick	A hatch with the appearance of layered bricks that slant to the left from top points to bottom points.
DiagonalCross	Forward diagonal and backward diagonal lines that cross.
Divot	A hatch with the appearance of divots.
DottedDiamond	Forward diagonal and backward diagonal lines, each of which is composed of dots that cross.
DottedGrid	Horizontal and vertical lines, each of which is composed of dots that cross.

continues

TABLE 4.1: HatchStyle members (continued)

Member	Description
ForwardDiagonal	A pattern of lines on a diagonal from upper left to lower right.
Horizontal	A pattern of horizontal lines.
HorizontalBrick	A hatch with the appearance of horizontally layered bricks.
LargeCheckerBoard	A hatch with the appearance of a checkerboard with squares that are twice the size of SmallCheckerBoard.
LargeConfetti	A hatch with the appearance of confetti that is composed of larger pieces than SmallConfetti.
LargeGrid	Horizontal and vertical lines that cross and are spaced 50 percent farther apart than in Cross.
LightDownwardDiagonal	Diagonal lines that slant to the right from top points to bottom points.
LightHorizontal	Horizontal lines that are spaced 50 percent closer together than Horizontal lines.
LightUpwardDiagonal	Diagonal lines that slant to the left from top points to bottom points and are spaced 50 percent closer together than BackwardDiagonal lines.
LightVertical	Vertical lines that are spaced 50 percent closer together than Vertical lines.
Max	Hatch style SolidDiamond.
Min	Hatch style Horizontal.
NarrowHorizontal	Horizontal lines that are spaced 75 percent closer together than Horizontal lines (or 25 percent closer together than LightHorizontal lines).
NarrowVertical	Vertical lines that are spaced 75 percent closer together than Vertical lines (or 25 percent closer together than LightVertical lines).
OutlinedDiamond	Forward diagonal and backward diagonal lines that cross.

TABLE 4.1: `HatchStyle` members (continued)

Member	Description
PercentXX	Percent hatch. The "XX" number after "Percent" represents the ratio of foreground color to background color as XX:100. The values of XX are 05, 10, 20, 25, 30, 40, 50, 60, 70, 75, 80, and 90.
Plaid	A hatch with the appearance of a plaid material.
Shingle	A hatch with the appearance of diagonally layered shingles that slant to the right from top points to bottom points.
SmallCheckerBoard	A hatch with the appearance of a checkerboard.
SmallConfetti	A hatch with the appearance of confetti.
SmallGrid	Horizontal and vertical lines that cross and are spaced 50 percent closer together than Cross lines.
SolidDiamond	A hatch with the appearance of a checkerboard placed diagonally.
Sphere	A hatch with the appearance of spheres laid adjacent to one another.
Trellis	A hatch with the appearance of a trellis.
Vertical	A pattern of vertical lines.
Wave	Horizontal lines that are composed of tildes.
Weave	A hatch with the appearance of a woven material.
WideDownwardDiagonal	Diagonal lines that slant to the right from top points to bottom points, have the same spacing as in ForwardDiagonal, and are triple the width of ForwardDiagonal lines.
WideUpwardDiagonal	Diagonal lines that slant to the left from top points to bottom points, have the same spacing as in BackwardDiagonal, and are triple the width of BackwardDiagonal lines.
ZigZag	Horizontal lines that are composed of zigzags.

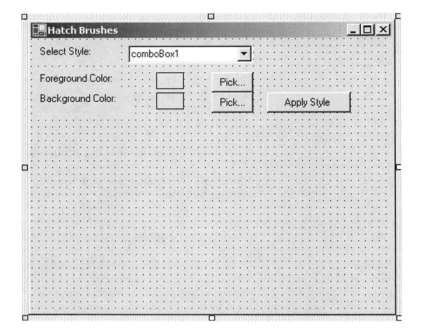

FIGURE 4.4: A sample hatch brush application

background color of a hatch brush, respectively. These variables are defined as follows:

```
private HatchStyle style = new HatchStyle();
private Color forClr = Color.Blue;
private Color backClr = Color.Red;
```

On the form's load event handler (see Listing 4.4), we fill the combo box with different hatch styles and set the background color properties of our two text boxes to the current colors.

LISTING 4.4: The form's load event handler

```
private void Form1_Load(object sender,
    System.EventArgs e)
  {
    // Fill combo box with hatch styles
    FillHatchStyles();
    // Set foreground and background colors
    // of text boxes
    textBox1.BackColor = forClr;
    textBox2.BackColor = backClr;
  }
```

The `FillHatchStyles` method adds different styles to the combo box (see Listing 4.5). We have added only a few styles; many more are available (see Table 4.1).

LISTING 4.5: The `FillHatchStyles` method

```
private void FillHatchStyles()
{
    // Add hatch styles
    comboBox1.Items.Add(
      HatchStyle.BackwardDiagonal.ToString());
    comboBox1.Items.Add(
      HatchStyle.Cross.ToString());
    comboBox1.Items.Add(
      HatchStyle.DashedVertical.ToString());
    comboBox1.Items.Add(
      HatchStyle.DiagonalCross.ToString());
    comboBox1.Items.Add(
      HatchStyle.HorizontalBrick.ToString());
    comboBox1.Items.Add(
      HatchStyle.LightDownwardDiagonal.ToString());
    comboBox1.Items.Add(
      HatchStyle.LightUpwardDiagonal.ToString());
    comboBox1.Text =
      HatchStyle.BackwardDiagonal.ToString();
}
```

The **Pick...** buttons in our combo box (see Figure 4.4) call the `Color-Dialog` method and save the selected foreground and background colors, respectively. These methods also set the background color of the respective text boxes, as Listing 4.6 shows.

LISTING 4.6: The Pick... button click event handler

```
private void ForeColorBtn_Click(object sender,
    System.EventArgs e)
{
    // Use ColorDialog to select a color
    ColorDialog clrDlg = new ColorDialog();
    if (clrDlg.ShowDialog() == DialogResult.OK)
    {
      // Save color as foreground color,
      // and fill text box with this color
```

continues

```
            forClr = clrDlg.Color;
            textBox1.BackColor = forClr;
        }
    }

    private void BackColorBtn_Click(object sender,
        System.EventArgs e)
    {
        // Use ColorDialog to select a color
        ColorDialog clrDlg = new ColorDialog();
        if (clrDlg.ShowDialog() == DialogResult.OK)
        {
            // Save color as background color,
            // and fill text box with this color
            backClr = clrDlg.Color;
            textBox2.BackColor = backClr;
        }
    }
```

The last step is to apply the selected styles and colors, create a hatch brush, and use this brush to draw a rectangle. This is all done on the **Apply Style** button click event handler, which is shown in Listing 4.7. As you can see from this listing, first we create a HatchStyle object based on the user selection in the combo box. Then we create a HatchBrush object using the hatch style, background, and foreground colors. After that we simply fill a rectangle with the hatch brush.

LISTING 4.7: The Apply Style button click event handler

```
private void ApplyBtn_Click(object sender,
    System.EventArgs e)
{
    // Create a Graphics object
    Graphics g = this.CreateGraphics();
    g.Clear(this.BackColor);
    // Read current style from combo box
    string str = comboBox1.Text;
    // Find out the style and set it as the
    // current style
    switch(str)
    {
        case "BackwardDiagonal":
            style = HatchStyle.BackwardDiagonal;
            break;
        case "DashedVertical":
            style = HatchStyle.DashedVertical;
            break;
```

```
case "Cross":
  style = HatchStyle.Cross;
  break;
case "DiagonalCross":
  style = HatchStyle.DiagonalCross;
  break;
case "HorizontalBrick":
  style = HatchStyle.HorizontalBrick;
  break;
case "LightDownwardDiagonal":
  style = HatchStyle.LightDownwardDiagonal;
  break;
case "LightUpwardDiagonal":
  style = HatchStyle.LightUpwardDiagonal;
  break;
default:
  break;
}
// Create a hatch brush with selected
// hatch style and colors
HatchBrush brush =
    new HatchBrush(style, forClr, backClr);
// Fill rectangle
g.FillRectangle(brush, 50, 100, 200, 200);
// Dispose of objects
brush.Dispose();
g.Dispose();
}
```

If you compile and run the application and then click the **Apply Style** button, the default rectangle looks like Figure 4.5.

Let's select `LightDownwardDiagonal` for the hatch style, change the foreground and background colors, and click the **Apply Style** button. Now the output looks like Figure 4.6.

Let's change the hatch style and colors one more time. This time we pick `DiagonalCross` as our hatch style. Now the output looks like Figure 4.7.

4.1.5 Texture Brushes

Texture brushes allow us to use an image as a brush and fill GDI+ objects with the brush. Texture brushes are useful when you need to fill a graphics object with images in a pattern such as tile. In this section we will discuss how to create and use texture brushes in GDI+.

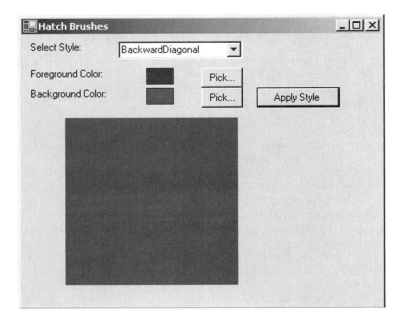

FIGURE 4.5: The default hatch style rectangle

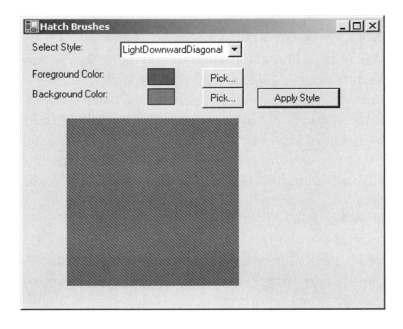

FIGURE 4.6: The LightDownwardDiagonal style with different colors

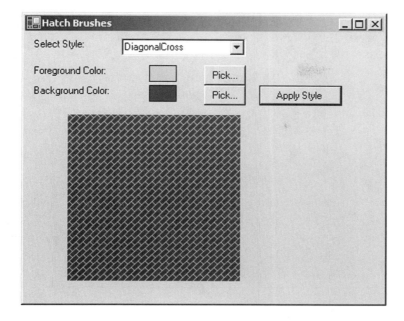

FIGURE 4.7: The DiagonalCross style

In the .NET Framework library, the TextureBrush class represents a texture brush. Table 4.2 describes the properties of the TextureBrush class.

Let's create an application using texture brushes. We create a Windows application. We also add a context menu to the form, along with five context menu items. The final form looks like Figure 4.8.

TABLE 4.2: TextureBrush properties

Property	Description
Image	Returns the Image object associated with a TextureBrush object.
Transform	Represents a Matrix object that defines a local geometric transformation for the image.
WrapMode	Represents a WrapMode enumeration that indicates the wrap mode for a texture brush.

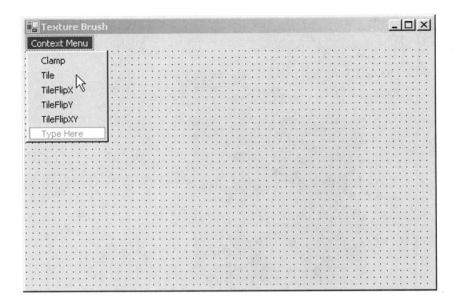

FIGURE 4.8: The texture brush application

> ### ■ NOTE
> The WrapMode enumeration represents the wrap mode for a texture brush. It has five members: Clamp, Tile, TileFlipX, TileFlipY, and TileFlipXY. These members are described later, in Table 4.7.

Now we add a class-level variable of TextureBrush type to the application:

```
private TextureBrush txtrBrush = null;
```

The next step is to create a texture brush from an image and fill a rectangle with that brush. We create an Image object on the form's load event handler from the file smallRoses.gif, which is used to create a TextureBrush object. On the form's paint event handler, we call the Fill-Rectangle method to fill the rectangle with the texture. Listing 4.8 shows the form's load and paint event handler. Note that our rectangle is the ClientRectangle of the form.

LISTING 4.8: Creating a texture brush and filling a rectangle

```
private void Form1_Load(object sender,
      System.EventArgs e)
{
      // Create an image from a file
      Image img = new Bitmap("smallRoses.gif");
      // Create a texture brush from an image
      txtrBrush = new TextureBrush(img);
      img.Dispose();
}

private void Form1_Paint(object sender,
     System.Windows.Forms.PaintEventArgs e)
{
        Graphics g = e.Graphics;
        // Fill a rectangle with a texture brush
        g.FillRectangle(txtrBrush, ClientRectangle);
}
```

■■ **NOTE**

See Chapter 7 for details on the `Image` class.

Now we can add event handlers for the context menu items as shown in Listing 4.9. As you can see from this code, we simply set the `WrapMode` property of the texture brush.

LISTING 4.9: `TextureBrush`'s context menu event handlers

```
private void Clamp_Click(object sender,
      System.EventArgs e)
{
      txtrBrush.WrapMode = WrapMode.Clamp;
      this.Invalidate();
   }

   private void Tile_Click(object sender,
     System.EventArgs e)
   {
     txtrBrush.WrapMode = WrapMode.Tile;
     this.Invalidate();
   }
```

continues

```
private void TileFlipX_Click(object sender,
  System.EventArgs e)
{
  txtrBrush.WrapMode = WrapMode.TileFlipX;
  this.Invalidate();
}

private void TileFlipY_Click(object sender,
  System.EventArgs e)
{
  txtrBrush.WrapMode = WrapMode.TileFlipY;
  this.Invalidate();
}

private void TileFlipXY_Click(object sender,
  System.EventArgs e)
{
  txtrBrush.WrapMode = WrapMode.TileFlipXY;
  this.Invalidate();
}
```

Finally, we need to load the context menu on the right mouse click event handler. As Listing 4.10 shows, we simply set the ContextMenu property of the form.

LISTING 4.10: The right mouse button click event handler

```
private void Form1_MouseDown(object sender,
  System.Windows.Forms.MouseEventArgs e)
{
  if(e.Button == MouseButtons.Right)
  {
    this.ContextMenu = contextMenu1;
  }
}
```

Now let's run the application. Figure 4.9 shows default (tiled) output from the program. The entire client rectangle is filled with the texture.

If we right-click on the form and select the **Clamp** menu item, we get Figure 4.10.

Now let's select the **TileFlipY** option, which generates Figure 4.11.

You can try other options on your own!

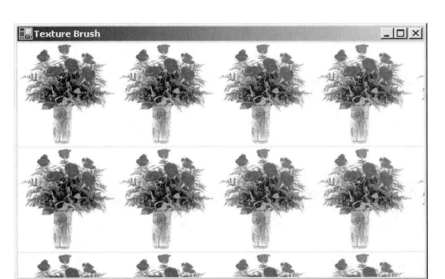

FIGURE 4.9: Using texture brushes

FIGURE 4.10: Clamping a texture

FIGURE 4.11: The TileFlipY texture option

4.1.6 Gradient Brushes

Linear **gradient brushes** allow you to blend two colors together, generating an indefinite range of shades. The Blend class defines a custom falloff for the gradient.

> ■ **NOTE**
> Chapter 9 discusses the Blend class and alpha blending in more detail.

In a gradient, we begin with a starting color and shift to an ending color, with gradual blending in the space between them. In addition to the starting and ending colors, we can specify the direction of the gradient. For example, Figure 4.12 starts with green in the left bottom corner and ends with red in the top right corner. (You may not notice these colors exactly in a black-and-white image.)

You can also specify a range for pattern repetition. For example, you can specify that the gradient will occur from point (0, 0) to point (20, 20) and after that will repeat the same pattern, as in Figure 4.13.

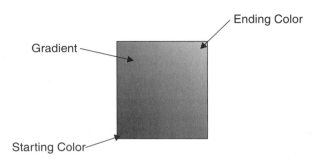

FIGURE 4.12: A color gradient

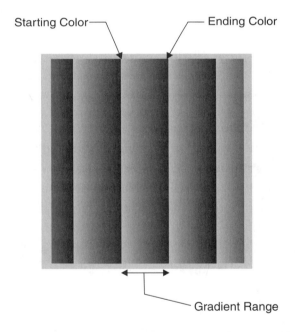

FIGURE 4.13: A gradient pattern with pattern repetition

4.1.6.1 *Linear Gradient Brushes*

The LinearGradientBrush class has eight forms of overloaded constructors. Each constructor takes a starting point, an ending point, and two gradient colors. The orientation and linear gradient mode are optional.

The following code snippet creates a linear gradient brush using the colors red and green:

```
Rectangle rect1 = new Rectangle(20, 20, 50, 50);
LinearGradientBrush lgBrush = new LinearGradientBrush
    (rect1, Color.Red, Color.Green, LinearGradientMode.Horizontal);
```

Here the mode parameter is represented by the `LinearGradientMode` enumeration, which specifies the direction of a linear gradient. The members of the `LinearGradientMode` enumeration are described in Table 4.3.

Now let's look at the properties and methods of the `LinearGradient-Brush` class, which are defined in Tables 4.4 and 4.5, respectively.

> ■ **NOTE**
> Chapters 9 and 10 discuss blending and transformation, respectively, in more detail.

4.1.6.2 *Linear Gradient Brushes Example*

Now let's create an application that uses linear gradient brushes. We create a Windows application, add three label controls, a combo box, two text boxes, four buttons, and two check boxes. We also change the `Text` property and other properties of these controls. The final form looks like Figure 4.14.

The combo box will list the linear gradient modes. The **Pick...** buttons allow the user to pick starting and ending colors for the gradient process. The **Other Rectangle** check box uses a rectangle to specify the range of the

TABLE 4.3: `LinearGradientMode` members

Member	Description
`BackwardDiagonal`	Specifies a gradient from upper right to lower left.
`ForwardDiagonal`	Specifies a gradient from upper left to lower right.
`Horizontal`	Specifies a gradient from left to right.
`Vertical`	Specifies a gradient from top to bottom.

TABLE 4.4: `LinearGradientBrush` properties

Property	Description
Blend	Represents the `Blend` object that specifies gradient position and factors.
GammaCorrection	Represents gamma correction. If it is enabled, the value is `true`; if not, it is `false`.
InterpolationColors	Represents a `ColorBlend` object that defines a multi-color gradient.
LinearColors	Represents the starting and ending colors of a gradient.
Rectangle	Returns a rectangle that defines the starting and ending points of a gradient.
Transform	Represents a `Matrix` object that defines the transformation.
WrapMode	Represents a `WrapMode` enumeration that indicates the wrap mode.

TABLE 4.5: `LinearGradientBrush` methods

Method	Description
MultiplyTransform	Multiplies a `Matrix` object that represents the transformation.
ResetTransform	Resets the `Transform` property to identity.
RotateTransform	Rotates the transformation.
ScaleTransform	Scales the transformation.
SetSigmaBellShape	Creates a gradient falloff based on a bell-shaped curve.
TranslateTransform	Translates the transformation by the specified dimensions.

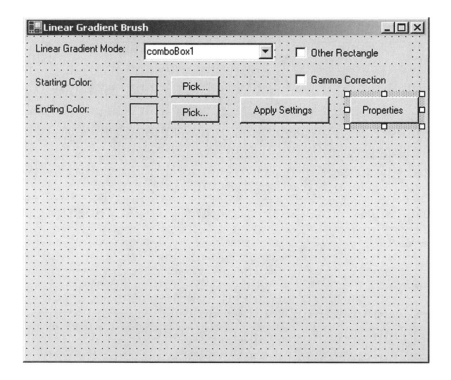

FIGURE 4.14: Our linear gradient brush application

gradient. We will discuss the **Gamma Correction** and **Properties** options later in this section.

Next we add some class-level variables as follows:

```
private LinearGradientBrush lgBrush = null;
private LinearGradientMode mode =
  new LinearGradientMode();
private Color startColor = Color.Red;
private Color endColor = Color.Green;
```

After defining the variables, we add the code from Listing 4.11 on the form's load event handler. As the code shows, we add all gradient modes on the AddGradientMode method. We also set the default background color of text boxes.

LISTING 4.11: Adding available linear gradient modes

```
private void Form1_Load(object sender,
System.EventArgs e)
{
  AddGradientMode();
  textBox1.BackColor = startColor;
  textBox2.BackColor = endColor;
}
private void AddGradientMode()
{
  // Adds linear gradient mode styles to the
  // combo box
  comboBox1.Items.Add(
  LinearGradientMode.BackwardDiagonal);
  comboBox1.Items.Add(
     LinearGradientMode.ForwardDiagonal);
  comboBox1.Items.Add(LinearGradientMode.Horizontal);
  comboBox1.Items.Add(LinearGradientMode.Vertical);
  comboBox1.Text =
     LinearGradientMode.BackwardDiagonal.ToString();
}
```

Next we add code for the **Pick...** buttons, which allow the user to provide color selections for the starting and ending colors. We also set the color of relative text boxes, as shown in Listing 4.12.

LISTING 4.12: The Pick... button click event handler

```
private void StartClrBtn_Click(object sender,
     System.EventArgs e)
{
     // Use ColorDialog to select a color
     ColorDialog clrDlg = new ColorDialog();
     if (clrDlg.ShowDialog() == DialogResult.OK)
     {
       // Save color as foreground color,
       // and fill text box with this color
       startColor = clrDlg.Color;
       textBox1.BackColor = startColor;
     }
  }

  private void EndClrBtn_Click(object sender,
     System.EventArgs e)
  {
```

continues

```
// Use ColorDialog to select a color
ColorDialog clrDlg = new ColorDialog();
if (clrDlg.ShowDialog() == DialogResult.OK)
{
  // Save color as background color,
  // and fill text box with this color
  endColor = clrDlg.Color;
  textBox2.BackColor = endColor;
}
}
```

The last step is to write code for the **Apply Settings** button. This button reads various settings, including the selected gradient mode in the combo box, the starting and ending colors, another rectangle, and gamma correction. As Listing 4.13 shows, the code creates a linear gradient brush using a rectangle, two colors, and the gradient mode selection. After creating the brush, it calls the `FillRectangle` method.

LISTING 4.13: The Apply Settings button click event handler

```
private void ApplyBtn_Click(object sender,
    System.EventArgs e)
{
    Graphics g = this.CreateGraphics();
    g.Clear(this.BackColor);
    // Read current style from combo box
    string str = comboBox1.Text;
    // Find out the mode and set it as the
    // current mode
    switch(str)
    {
      case "BackwardDiagonal":
        mode = LinearGradientMode.BackwardDiagonal;
        break;
      case "ForwardDiagonal":
        mode = LinearGradientMode.ForwardDiagonal;
        break;
      case "Horizontal":
        mode = LinearGradientMode.Horizontal;
        break;
      case "Vertical":
        mode = LinearGradientMode.Vertical;
        break;
    default:
        break;
    }
    // Create rectangle
    Rectangle rect = new Rectangle(50, 140, 200, 220);
```

```
// Create linear gradient brush and set mode
if(checkBox1.Checked)
{
  Rectangle rect1 = new Rectangle(20, 20, 50, 50);
  lgBrush = new LinearGradientBrush
    (rect1, startColor, endColor, mode);
}
else
{
  lgBrush = new LinearGradientBrush
    (rect, startColor, endColor, mode);
}
// Gamma correction check box is checked
if(checkBox1.Checked)
{
  lgBrush.GammaCorrection = true;
}

// Fill rectangle
g.FillRectangle(lgBrush, rect);
// Dispose of objects
if(lgBrush != null)
    lgBrush.Dispose();
g.Dispose();
}
```

When you run the application, the result looks like Figure 4.15.

To generate a different output, let's change the linear gradient mode to Vertical. We'll also change the colors, with the results shown in Figure 4.16.

Let's change the colors and gradient mode again, this time selecting the **Other Rectangle** check box. This option sets a range of the gradient. If the

Gamma Correction

Gamma correction is a process that controls the brightness of images and graphics objects. Some graphics objects that are not properly corrected after color processing can look too dark or bleached out. Gamma correction helps correct this problem by managing the ratio of red, green, and blue components.

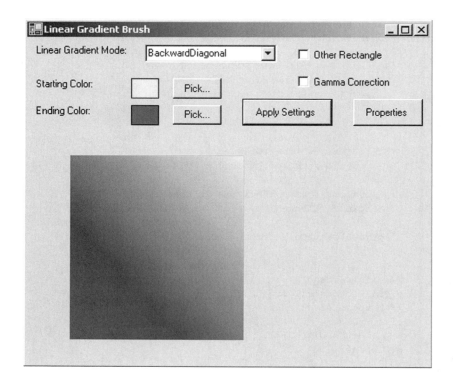

FIGURE 4.15: The default linear gradient brush output

output is out of range, the gradient repeats itself. The new output looks like Figure 4.17.

You can also use the `LinearGradientBrush` class properties and methods to change brush properties programmatically. Listing 4.14 creates a linear gradient brush from two points (starting point and ending point), and sets the `LinearColors` and `GammaCorrection` properties. The correction provides more uniform intensity in the gradient. We write this code on the **Properties** button click event handler.

LISTING 4.14: Using the `LinearColors` and `GammaCorrection` properties of `LinearGradientBrush`

```
private void button1_Click(object sender,
  System.EventArgs e)
{
  Graphics g = this.CreateGraphics();
```

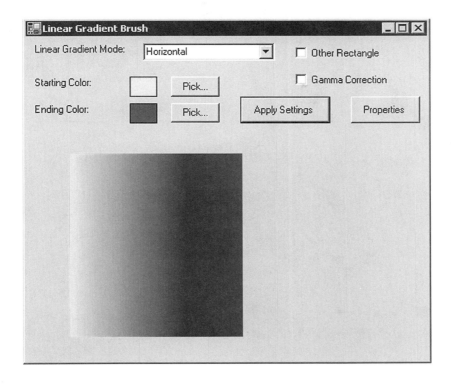

FIGURE 4.16: The `Vertical` linear gradient mode

```
// Create points
Point pt1 = new Point(40, 30);
Point pt2 = new Point(80, 100);
Color [] lnColors = {Color.Black, Color.Red};
// Create a linear gradient brush
LinearGradientBrush lgBrush = new LinearGradientBrush
   (pt1, pt2, Color.Red, Color.Green);
// Set linear colors and gamma correction
lgBrush.LinearColors = lnColors;
lgBrush.GammaCorrection = true;
// Draw rectangle
g.FillRectangle(lgBrush, 50, 140, 200, 200);
// Dispose of objects
lgBrush.Dispose();
g.Dispose();
}
```

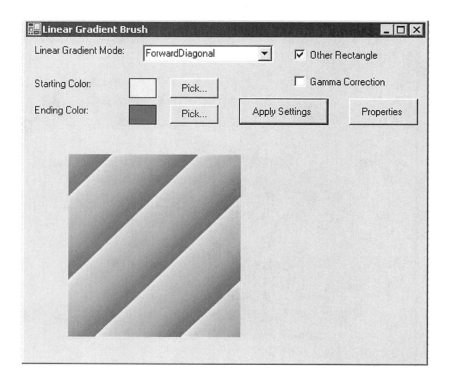

FIGURE 4.17: Using a rectangle in a linear gradient brush

Figure 4.18 shows the output from the **Properties** button click.

4.1.6.3 *Path Gradient Brushes*

A graphics path is a collection of lines and curves. In GDI+, the PathGradientBrush object fills a graphics paths with a gradient. Like LinearGradientBrush, PathGradientBrush is a combination of two colors, but instead of starting with one color and ending with another, PathGradientBrush starts from the center of a graphics path and ends at the outside boundary of the path. In between, you can apply blend factors, positions, and style effects using the PathGradientBrush class members.

Table 4.6 describes the properties of the PathGradientBrush class.

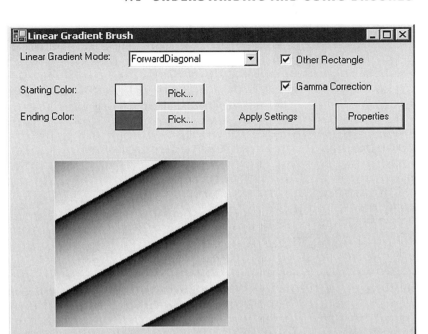

FIGURE 4.18: Using `LinearGradientBrush` properties

Table 4.7 describes the members of the `WrapMode` enumeration.

Like `LinearGradientBrush`, `PathGradientBrush` has five transformation methods: `MultiplyTransform`, `ResetTransform`, `RotateTransform`, `ScaleTransform`, and `TranslateTransform`.

This class also has the methods `SetBlendTriangularShape` and `SetSigmaBellShape`. `SetBlendTriangularShape` creates a gradient with a center color and a linear falloff to one surrounding color. `SetSigmaBellShape` creates a gradient falloff between the center color and the first surrounding color according to a bell-shaped curve.

We will discuss `PathGradientBrush`, its properties, and its methods in more detail in Chapter 9 (Section 9.5).

TABLE 4.6: `PathGradientBrush` properties

Property	Description
Blend	A `Blend` object specifies the positions and factors that define a custom falloff point for a gradient. The `Blend` property takes a `Blend` object.
CenterColor	The center color of the path gradient.
CenterPoint	The center point of the path gradient.
FocusScales	The focus point for the gradient falloff.
InterpolationColors	A `ColorBlend` object defines a multicolor linear gradient, and this property can be used to set a `ColorBlend` object for the brush.
Rectangle	Represents a bounding rectangle for the brush. Outside of this boundary, the brush pattern repeats itself.
SurroundColors	Defines an array of colors for an array of points in the path.
Transform	Specifies a transformation matrix.
WrapMode	Defines how a texture or gradient is tiled when it is larger than the area being filled, using a `WrapMode` enumeration.

TABLE 4.7: `WrapMode` members

Member	Description
Clamp	Clamps the texture or gradient to the object boundary.
Tile	Tiles the gradient or texture.
TileFlipX	Reverses the texture or gradient horizontally and then tiles it.
TileFlipXY	Reverses the texture or gradient horizontally and vertically and then tiles it.
TileFlipY	Reverses the texture or gradient vertically and then tiles it.

4.2 Using Pens in GDI+

Pens are another key object in GDI+. As mentioned earlier, pens are used to draw lines and curves and the outlines of graphics shapes. A pen draws lines and curves with a specified width and style. The Pen object provides members to set the width and style of a pen. Pens can have various kinds of dashed lines and line fill styles. Actually, the process of drawing a line creates a region in the shape of a widened line, and that region is filled with a brush. The dashed lines of pens are represented by **dash styles**. The **fill styles** of lines can be solids or textures depending on the brush used to create a Pen object.

In this section we will discuss how to create and use pens in GDI+; the Pen and Pens classes; and how to create dash styles, cap styles, and line styles for pens.

4.2.1 Creating Pens

The Pen class represents a pen in GDI+. Using the Pen class constructor, an application can create a Pen object from a Brush or Color object with a specified width for the pen.

Listing 4.15 creates pens using Brush and Color objects with and without a specified width.

LISTING 4.15: Using the Pen class constructor to create Pen objects

```
private void menuItem2_Click(object sender,
        System.EventArgs e)
{
    // Create a Graphics object and set it clear
    Graphics g = this.CreateGraphics();
    g.Clear(this.BackColor);
    // Create a solid brush and a hatch brush
    SolidBrush blueBrush =
      new SolidBrush(Color.Blue);
    HatchBrush hatchBrush =
      new HatchBrush(HatchStyle.DashedVertical,
      Color.Black, Color.Green);
    // Create a pen from a solid brush with
    // width 3
    Pen pn1 = new Pen( blueBrush, 3);
```

continues

```
    // Create a pen from a hatch brush
    Pen pn2 = new Pen(hatchBrush, 8);
    // Create a pen from a Color structure
    Pen pn3 = new Pen(Color.Red);
    // Draw a line, ellipse, and rectangle
    g.DrawLine(pn1,
        new Point(10, 40), new Point(10, 90));
    g.DrawEllipse(pn2, 20, 50, 100, 100);
    g.DrawRectangle(pn3, 40, 90, 100, 100);
    // Dispose of objects
    pn1.Dispose();
    pn2.Dispose();
    pn3.Dispose();
    blueBrush.Dispose();
      hatchBrush.Dispose();
    g.Dispose();
}
```

Figure 4.19 shows the output from Listing 4.15.

The Pens class has static properties for all standard colors, which return appropriately colored Pen objects. The following code snippet creates three Pen objects using the Pens class.

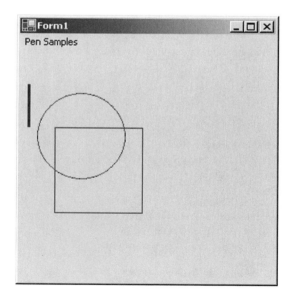

FIGURE 4.19: Creating and using pens

```
Pen pn1 = Pens.Red;
Pen pn2 = Pens.Blue;
Pen pn3 = Pens.Green;
```

4.2.2 Pen **Class Properties and Methods**

The Pen class provides properties to set brush, color, and width programmatically after a Pen object is created. Table 4.8 describes the properties of
the Pen class.

Table 4.9 describes the methods of the Pen class.

4.2.3 **Pen Types**

A pen can draw solid lines, filled lines, texture, and even gradient lines—all
depending on the brush you use to create the pen. For example, if you use
a texture brush to create a pen and then use this pen to create lines, the lines
will be texture lines.

The only way to set a pen's type is to create a brush and use that
brush to create the pen. The PenType property of the Pen class represents
the type of the pen's lines. This property is represented by the PenType
enumeration.

■ **NOTE**

The PenType property is a read-only property.

Table 4.10 describes the members of the PenType enumeration.

4.2.4 **Pens Example**

Now let's create a sample application. In Listing 4.16 we create three
pens from three different brushes: a solid brush, a texture brush, and a
linear gradient brush. After that we create three pens from these brushes,
and then we read the type of each pen and display the types in a message
box.

TABLE 4.8: Pen class properties

Property	Description
Alignment	Alignment for a pen—a type of PenAlignment enumeration, which is defined in Table 4.11.
Brush	Brush object attached with a pen. Setting the Color property after Brush will replace the color of the current brush with the specified color.
Color	Color of a pen. Setting the Brush property after Color will update the color of a pen to the color of the brush.
CompoundArray	Specifies values of a compound pen, which draws compound lines made up of parallel lines and spaces.
CustomEndCap, CustomStartCap, DashCap	A line drawn by a pen can have custom starting and ending caps. The CustomEndCap and CustomStartCap properties represent the ending and starting caps, respectively, of lines drawn by a pen. DashCap is used for dashed lines.
DashOffset	The distance from the start of a line to the beginning of a dash pattern.
DashPattern	An array of custom dashes and spaces.
DashStyle	The style used for dashed lines.
EndCap, StartCap	Ending and starting cap of a line.
LineJoin	The join style for the ends of two consecutive lines.
MiterLimit	Limit of the thickness of the join on a mitered corner.
PenType	The style of lines of a pen. This property is represented by the PenType enumeration.
Transform	The geometric transformation of a pen.
Width	The width of a pen.

TABLE 4.9: **Pen class methods**

Property	Description
Clone	Creates an exact copy of a pen.
MultiplyTransform	Multiplies the transformation matrix of a pen by Matrix.
ResetTransform	Resets the geometric transformation matrix of a pen to identity.
RotateTransform	Rotates the local geometric transformation by the specified angle.
ScaleTransform	Scales the local geometric transformation by the specified factors.
SetLineCap	Sets the values that determine the style of cap used to end lines drawn by a pen.
TranslateTransform	Translates the local geometric transformation by the specified dimensions.

TABLE 4.10: **PenType members**

Member	Description
HatchFill	A hatch fill
LinearGradient	A linear gradient fill
PathGradient	A path gradient fill
SolidColor	A solid fill
TextureFill	A bitmap texture fill

LISTING 4.16: Getting pen types

```
private void GetPenTypes_Click(object sender,
     System.EventArgs e)
{
     // Create a Graphics object
     Graphics g = this.CreateGraphics();
     g.Clear(this.BackColor);
     // Create three different types of brushes
     Image img = new Bitmap("roses.jpg");
     SolidBrush redBrush = new SolidBrush(Color.Red);
     TextureBrush txtrBrush =
       new TextureBrush(img);
     LinearGradientBrush lgBrush =
       new LinearGradientBrush(
       new Rectangle(10, 10, 10, 10),
       Color.Red, Color.Black, 45.0f);
     // Create pens from brushes
     Pen pn1 = new Pen(redBrush, 4);
     Pen pn2 = new Pen(txtrBrush, 20);
     Pen pn3 = new Pen(lgBrush, 20);
     // Drawing objects
     g.DrawEllipse(pn1, 100, 100, 50, 50);
     g.DrawRectangle(pn2, 80, 80, 100, 100);
     g.DrawEllipse(pn3, 30, 30, 200, 200 );

     // Get pen types
     string str = "Pen1 Type: "+
       pn1.PenType.ToString() + "\n";
     str += "Pen2 Type: "+
       pn2.PenType.ToString() + "\n";
     str += "Pen3 Type: "+
       pn3.PenType.ToString();
     MessageBox.Show(str);

     // Dispose of objects
     pn1.Dispose();
     pn2.Dispose();
     pn3.Dispose();
     redBrush.Dispose();
     txtrBrush.Dispose();
     lgBrush.Dispose();
     img.Dispose();
     g.Dispose();
}
```

Figure 4.20 shows the output from Listing 4.16.

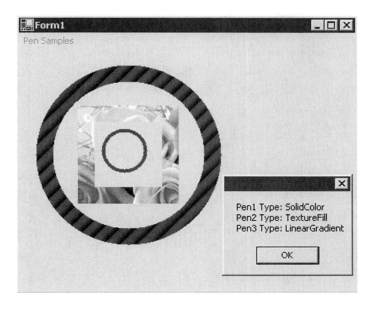

FIGURE 4.20: Displaying pen types

4.2.5 Pen Alignment

The alignment of a pen represents its position respective to a line. The PenAlignment enumeration specifies the alignment of a pen—meaning the center point of the pen width relative to the line. Table 4.11 describes the members of the PenAlignment enumeration.

To see alignment in action, let's create a sample application. We create a Windows application, and add a combo box, three labels, two buttons,

TABLE 4.11: PenAlignment members

Member	Description
Center	The pen is centered.
Inset	The pen is inside the line.
Left	The pen is left of the line.
Outset	The pen is outside of the line.
Right	The pen is right of the line.

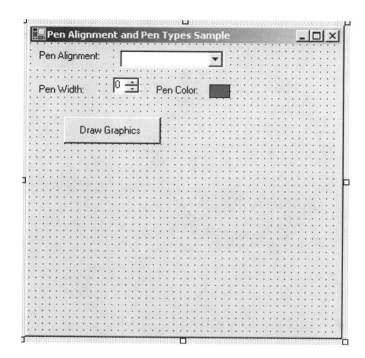

FIGURE 4.21: Our pen alignment application

and a numeric up-down control. We change the control properties, and the final form looks like Figure 4.21.

The **Pen Alignment** combo box lists the alignments of a pen. **Pen Width** represents the width of the pen, and **Pen Color** lets you pick the color of the pen. The **Pen Color** button click event handler simply sets the color of the pen and stores the selected color in a `Color` type variable at the class level, as shown in Listing 4.17.

LISTING 4.17: The Pen Color button click event handler

```
private Color penColor = Color.Red;

private void ColorBtn_Click(object sender,
        System.EventArgs e)
{
    // Use ColorDialog to select a color
    ColorDialog clrDlg = new ColorDialog();
    if (clrDlg.ShowDialog() == DialogResult.OK)
    {
```

```
        // Save color as background color,
        // and fill text box with this color
        penColor = clrDlg.Color;
        ColorBtn.BackColor = penColor;
    }
}
```

Listing 4.18 (on the form's load event handler) loads all alignments to the combo box.

LISTING 4.18: Adding pen alignments to the combo box

```
private void Form1_Load(object sender,
     System.EventArgs e)
{
    AddPenAlignments();

}
private void AddPenAlignments()
{
            // Add pen alignment
    comboBox1.Items.Add(PenAlignment.Center);
    comboBox1.Text =
      PenAlignment.Center.ToString();
    comboBox1.Items.Add(PenAlignment.Inset);
    comboBox1.Items.Add(PenAlignment.Left);
    comboBox1.Items.Add(PenAlignment.Outset);
    comboBox1.Items.Add(PenAlignment.Right);
}
```

Finally, in Listing 4.19 we write code for the **Draw Graphics** button click event handler. We set the Width and Color properties of the pen after reading values from the form's controls. Then we look for the current alignment set by the user in the combo box and set the Alignment property of the pen. In the end, we use this pen to draw a rectangle. We also fill one more rectangle with a linear gradient brush.

LISTING 4.19: Creating a pen with alignment

```
private void DrawBtn_Click(object sender,
     System.EventArgs e)
{
    // Create a Graphics object and set it clear
    Graphics g = this.CreateGraphics();
    g.Clear(this.BackColor);
```

continues

```
// Create a solid brush and a hatch brush
Pen pn1 = new Pen(Color.Blue, 3);
pn1.Width = (float)numericUpDown1.Value;
pn1.Color = ColorBtn.BackColor;
// Find out current pen alignment
string str = comboBox1.Text;
switch(str)
{
  case "Center":
    pn1.Alignment = PenAlignment.Center;
    break;
  case "Inset":
    pn1.Alignment = PenAlignment.Inset;
    break;
  case "Left":
    pn1.Alignment = PenAlignment.Left;
    break;
  case "Outset":
    pn1.Alignment = PenAlignment.Outset;
    break;
  case "Right":
    pn1.Alignment = PenAlignment.Right;
    break;
  default:
    break;
}
// Create a pen from a hatch brush
// Draw a rectangle
g.DrawRectangle(pn1, 80, 150, 150, 150);
// Create a brush
LinearGradientBrush brush =
  new LinearGradientBrush(
  new Rectangle(10, 10, 20, 20), Color.Blue,
  Color.Green, 45.0f);
g.FillRectangle(brush, 90, 160, 130, 130);
// Dispose of objects
pn1.Dispose();
g.Dispose();
}
```

Figure 4.22 shows the output from Listing 4.19. The pen width is 10 and alignment is center.

If we set the alignment as inset, we get Figure 4.23.

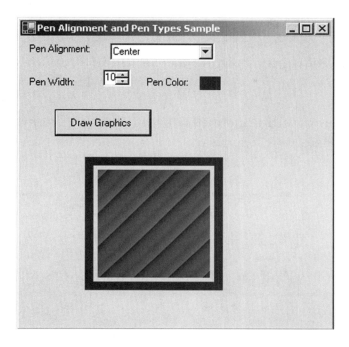

FIGURE 4.22: Drawing with center pen alignment

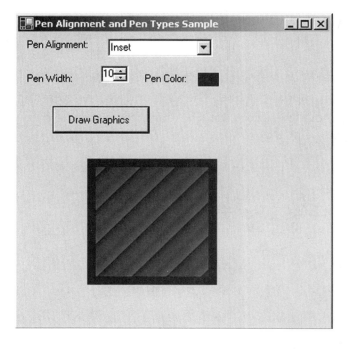

FIGURE 4.23: Drawing with inset pen alignment

4.2.6 LineCap, DashCap, and DashStyle

Pens offer more options than what we have seen so far. A line's caps are the starting and ending points of the line. For example, you may have seen lines with arrows and circles. Figure 4.24 shows some lines with their cap and dash styles.

Using Pen properties and methods, you can draw lines with cap and dash styles. Here we will discuss line cap and line dash styles only briefly (for more details, see Chapter 9).

> ■■ NOTE
>
> We can divide line caps into two types: anchor and nonanchor. The width of an **anchor cap** is bigger than the width of the line; the width of a **nonanchor cap** is the same as the width of the line.

The LineCap property of the Pen class represents the cap style used at the beginning and ending of lines drawn by the pen. You can determine the current cap style of a line by calling the GetLineCap method, which returns a LineCap enumeration. You can also apply a line cap style using the SetLineCap method. This method takes an argument of LineCap enumeration type. Table 4.12 describes the members of the LineCap enumeration.

The SetLineCap method takes the line cap style for the beginning, ending, and dash cap of the line. The first and second parameters of Set-LineCap are of type LineCap. The third parameter is of type DashCap enumeration.

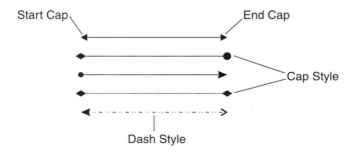

FIGURE 4.24: Line cap and dash styles

TABLE 4.12: `LineCap` members

Member	Description
AnchorMask	A mask used to check whether a line cap is an anchor cap
ArrowAnchor	An arrow-shaped anchor cap
Custom	A custom line cap
DiamondAnchor	A diamond anchor cap
Flat	A flat line cap
NoAnchor	No anchor
Round	A round line cap
RoundAnchor	A round anchor cap
Square	A square line cap
SquareAnchor	A square anchor cap
Triangle	A triangular line cap

TABLE 4.13: `DashCap` members

Member	Description
Flat	A square cap that squares off both ends of each dash
Round	A circular cap
Triangle	A triangular cap

The `DashCap` enumeration specifies the type of graphics shape used on both ends of each dash in a dashed line. Table 4.13 describes the members of the `DashCap` enumeration.

The `DashStyle` enumeration specifies the style of a dashed line drawn by the pen. Table 4.14 describes the members of the `DashStyle` enumeration.

TABLE 4.14: `DashStyle` members

Member	Description
Custom	A user-defined custom dash style
Dash	A line consisting of dashes
DashDot	A line consisting of a repeating dash-dot pattern
DashDotDot	A line consisting of a repeating dash-dot-dot pattern of
Dot	A line consisting of dots
Solid	A solid line

Listing 4.20 shows how to use various styles and properties of the `Pen` class to draw different kinds of dashed lines with different kinds of starting and ending caps. We use the `DashStyle`, `SetLineCap`, `StartCap`, and `EndCap` members of the `Pen` class to set the line dash style, line cap style, start cap style, and end cap style, respectively.

LISTING 4.20: Using the `Pen` class to draw dashed lines

```
private void menuItem4_Click(object sender,
      System.EventArgs e)
{
      Graphics g = this.CreateGraphics();
      g.Clear(this.BackColor);
      // Create three pens
      Pen redPen = new Pen(Color.Red, 6);
      Pen bluePen = new Pen(Color.Blue, 7);
      Pen greenPen = new Pen(Color.Green, 7);
      redPen.Width = 8;
      // Set line styles
      redPen.DashStyle = DashStyle.Dash;
      redPen.SetLineCap(LineCap.DiamondAnchor,
      LineCap.ArrowAnchor, DashCap.Flat);
      greenPen.DashStyle = DashStyle.DashDotDot;
      greenPen.StartCap = LineCap.Triangle;
      greenPen.EndCap = LineCap.Triangle;
      greenPen.DashCap = DashCap.Triangle;
      greenPen.DashStyle = DashStyle.Dot;
      greenPen.DashOffset = 3.4f;
```

```
bluePen.StartCap = LineCap.DiamondAnchor;
bluePen.EndCap = LineCap.DiamondAnchor;
greenPen.SetLineCap(LineCap.RoundAnchor,
  LineCap.Square, DashCap.Round);
// Draw lines
g.DrawLine(redPen, new Point(20, 50),
  new Point(150, 50));
g.DrawLine(greenPen, new Point(30, 80),
  new Point(200, 80));
g.DrawLine(bluePen, new Point(30, 120),
  new Point(250, 120));
// Release resources. If you don't release
// using Dispose, the GC (garbage collector)
// takes care of it for you.
redPen.Dispose();
greenPen.Dispose();
g.Dispose();
}
```

Figure 4.25 shows the output from Listing 4.20.

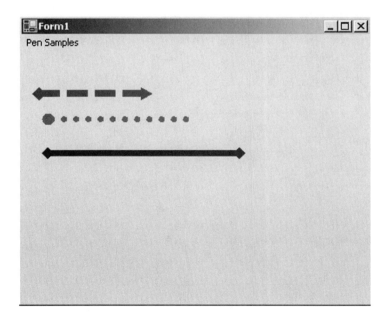

FIGURE 4.25: Drawing dashed lines with different cap styles

4.2.7 Drawing Other Graphics Shapes by Applying Cap and Dashed Line Styles

In the previous section we saw how to draw lines using cap and dash styles. But these styles are not limited to lines only. You can draw other graphics shapes, such as rectangles, ellipses, and curves, using the line cap and dash styles.

As in the previous section, here we will create a pen, set its line cap and line dash styles, and use it—but this time, drawing graphics shapes, rather than simple lines.

Listing 4.21 creates several pens and uses them to draw an arc, Bézier curve, rectangle, and ellipse with the help of the DrawArc, DrawBezier, DrawRectangle, and DrawEllipse methods of the Graphics class (see Chapter 3 for details).

LISTING 4.21: Using different pens to draw various graphics objects

```
private void menuItem6_Click(object sender,
    System.EventArgs e)
{
    Graphics g = this.CreateGraphics();
    g.Clear(this.BackColor);
    Pen redPen = new Pen(
      new SolidBrush(Color.Red), 4);
    Pen bluePen = new Pen(
      new SolidBrush(Color.Blue), 5);
    Pen blackPen = new Pen(
      new SolidBrush(Color.Black), 3);
    // Set line styles
    redPen.DashStyle = DashStyle.Dash;
    redPen.SetLineCap(LineCap.DiamondAnchor,
      LineCap.ArrowAnchor, DashCap.Flat);
    bluePen.DashStyle = DashStyle.DashDotDot;
    bluePen.StartCap = LineCap.Triangle;
    bluePen.EndCap = LineCap.Triangle;
    bluePen.DashCap = DashCap.Triangle;
    blackPen.DashStyle = DashStyle.Dot;
    blackPen.DashOffset = 3.4f;
    blackPen.SetLineCap(LineCap.RoundAnchor,
      LineCap.Square, DashCap.Round);
    // Draw objects
    g.DrawArc(redPen, 10.0F, 10.0F, 50,
      100, 45.0F, 90.0F);
    g.DrawRectangle(bluePen, 60, 80, 140, 50);
```

```
    g.DrawBezier(blackPen, 20.0F, 30.0F,
       100.0F, 200.0F, 40.0F, 400.0F,
       100.0F, 200.0F);
    g.DrawEllipse(redPen, 50, 50, 200, 100 );
    // Dispose of objects
    redPen.Dispose();
    bluePen.Dispose();
    blackPen.Dispose();
    g.Dispose();
}
```

Figure 4.26 shows the output of Listing 4.21. All of the elements drawn have line cap and dash styles.

4.3 **Transformation with Pens**

Transformation is the process of changing graphics objects from one state to another. Rotation, scaling, reflection, translation, and shearing are examples of transformation.

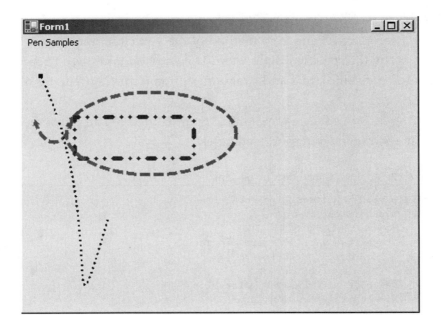

FIGURE 4.26: Graphics shapes with cap and dash styles

The Pen class provides methods for transformation and rotation. The RotateTransform method rotates a transformation by an angle. This method takes a rotation angle of type float. The second argument, MatrixOrder, is an optional parameter that provides an order for matrix transformation operations. The MatrixOrder enumeration defines the matrix order, which has two members: Append and Prepend. The matrix order is the order in which a matrix is multiplied with other matrices.

The difference between Append and Prepend is the order of the operation. For example, if two operations are participating in a process, the second operation will be performed after the first when the matrix order is Append; when the order is Prepend, the second operation will be performed before the first.

The MultiplyTransform method multiplies a transformation matrix by a pen. Its first argument is a Matrix object, and the optional second argument is the matrix order of type MatrixOrder enumeration.

> **■ NOTE**
> The Matrix class is discussed in more detail in Chapter 10.

The TranslateTransform method of the Pen class translates a transformation by the specified dimension. This method takes two float type values for translation in *x* and *y*, and an optional third parameter of type MatrixOrder.

Listing 4.22 uses the ScaleTransform and RotateTransform methods to apply rotation on pens and rectangles.

LISTING 4.22: Applying transformation on pens

```
private void menuItem5_Click(object sender,
    System.EventArgs e)
{
    Graphics g = this.CreateGraphics();
    g.Clear(this.BackColor);
    // Create a Pen object
    Pen bluePen = new Pen(Color.Blue, 10);
    Pen redPen = new Pen(Color.Red, 5);
    // Apply rotate and scale transformations
```

```
    bluePen.ScaleTransform(3, 1);
    g.DrawEllipse(bluePen, 20, 20, 100, 50);
    g.DrawRectangle(redPen, 20, 120, 100, 50);
    bluePen.RotateTransform(90, MatrixOrder.Append);
    redPen.ScaleTransform(4, 2, MatrixOrder.Append);
    g.DrawEllipse(bluePen, 220, 20, 100, 50);
    g.DrawRectangle(redPen, 220, 120, 100, 50);
    // Dispose of objects
    redPen.Dispose();
    bluePen.Dispose();
    g.Dispose();
}
```

Figure 4.27 shows the output from Listing 4.22. The first ellipse and rectangle are drawn normally. The second ellipse and rectangle are drawn after rotation and scaling have been applied to their pens.

Chapter 10 discusses rotation, scaling, and other transformation methods in more detail.

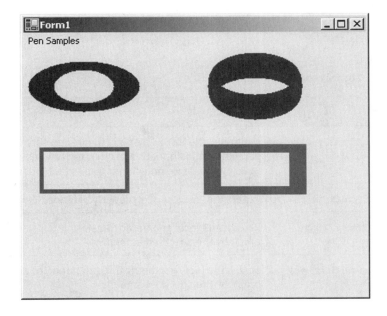

FIGURE 4.27: Rotation and scaling

> **NOTE**
> You need to reference the `System.Drawing.Drawing2D` namespace in order to run the code in the listings of this section because the `Matrix` class and the `MatrixOrder` enumeration are defined in this name-space.

4.4 Transformation with Brushes

The `TextureBrush`, `LinearGradientBrush`, and `PathGradientBrush` classes also provide transformation methods. Brush transformation is not used very often, but it may be useful in some cases, as the following example will show.

A transformation on a `TextureBrush` object is a transformation of the image used as the texture. `TextureBrush` provides the methods `MultiplyTransform`, `ResetTransform`, `RotateTransform`, `Scale-Transform`, and `TranslateTransform` (see Table 4.15).

The `TextureBrush` class also provides a `Transform` property, which can be used to apply a transformation on a texture brush.

TABLE 4.15: **TextureBrush** methods

Method	Description
MultiplyTransform	Multiplies the Matrix object that represents the local geometric transformation of a texture brush by the specified Matrix object in the specified order.
ResetTransform	Resets the Transform property of a texture to identity.
RotateTransform	Rotates the local geometric transformation of a texture brush by the specified amount.
ScaleTransform	Scales the local geometric transformation of a texture brush by the specified amount.
TranslateTransform	Translates the local geometric transformation of a tex-ture brush by the specified dimensions in the specified order.

Listing 4.23 uses the `Translate`, `MultiplyTransform`, `ScaleTrans-`
`form`, and `RotateTransform` methods of the `Pen` class to apply rotation on
pens, and draws a line and rectangles.

LISTING 4.23: **Transformation in texture brushes**

```
private void TextureBrush_Click(object sender,
    System.EventArgs e)
{
    Graphics g = this.CreateGraphics();
    g.Clear(this.BackColor);
    // Create a TextureBrush object
    TextureBrush txtrBrush = new TextureBrush(
      new Bitmap("smallRoses.gif"));
    // Create a transformation matrix
    Matrix M = new Matrix();
    // Rotate the texture image by 90 degrees
    txtrBrush.RotateTransform(90,
      MatrixOrder.Prepend);
    // Translate
    M.Translate(50, 0);
    // Multiply the transformation matrix
    // of txtrBrush by translateMatrix
    txtrBrush.MultiplyTransform(M);
    // Scale operation
    txtrBrush.ScaleTransform(2, 1,
      MatrixOrder.Prepend);
    // Fill a rectangle with texture brush
    g.FillRectangle(txtrBrush, 240, 0, 200, 200);
    // Reset transformation
    txtrBrush.ResetTransform();
    // Fill rectangle after resetting transformation
    g.FillRectangle(txtrBrush, 0, 0, 200, 200);
    // Dispose of objects
    txtrBrush.Dispose();
    g.Dispose();
}
```

Figure 4.28 shows the output from Listing 4.23, with the original image
on the left and the transformed image on the right.

A transformation on a linear gradient brush is a transformation of the
colors of the brush. The `LinearGradientBrush` class provides all common
transformation methods and `Transform` properties. Listing 4.24 shows
how to use transformation in linear gradient brushes.

FIGURE 4.28: Transformation in `TextureBrush`

LISTING 4.24: Transformation in linear gradient brushes

```
private void LinearGradientBrush_Click(object sender,
     System.EventArgs e)
{
     Graphics g = this.CreateGraphics();
     g.Clear(this.BackColor);
     // Create a LinearGradientBrush object
     Rectangle rect = new Rectangle(20, 20, 200, 100);
     LinearGradientBrush lgBrush =
          new LinearGradientBrush(
          rect, Color.Red, Color.Green, 0.0f, true);
     Point[] ptsArray = {new Point(20, 50),
          new Point(200,50), new Point(20, 100)};
     Matrix M = new Matrix(rect, ptsArray);
     // Multiply transformation
     lgBrush.MultiplyTransform(M, MatrixOrder.Prepend);
     // Rotate transformation
     lgBrush.RotateTransform(45.0f, MatrixOrder.Prepend);
     // Scale transformation
     lgBrush.ScaleTransform(2, 1, MatrixOrder.Prepend);
```

```
    // Draw a rectangle after transformation
    g.FillRectangle(lgBrush, 0, 0, 200, 100);
    // Reset transformation
    lgBrush.ResetTransform();
    // Draw a rectangle after reset transformation
    g.FillRectangle(lgBrush, 220, 0, 200, 100);
    // Dispose of objects
    lgBrush.Dispose();
    g.Dispose();
}
```

Figure 4.29 shows the output from Listing 4.24. The second rectangle results from various transformation operations, and the first rectangle is a result of a call to ResetTransform.

PathGradientBrush provides similar mechanisms to transform path gradient brushes. As Listing 4.25 shows, we create a PathGradientBrush object and set its CenterColor and SurroundColors properties. Then we create a Matrix object and call its methods to apply various transformation operations, such as translation, rotation, scaling, and shearing, and we apply the Matrix object to the PathGradientBrush object by calling its MultiplyTransform method.

FIGURE 4.29: Transformation in linear gradient brushes

LISTING 4.25: Transformation in path gradient brushes

```csharp
private void PathGradientBrush_Click(object sender,
    System.EventArgs e)
{
    Graphics g = this.CreateGraphics();
    g.Clear(this.BackColor);
    // Create a GraphicsPath object
    GraphicsPath path = new GraphicsPath();
    // Create a rectangle and add it to path
    Rectangle rect = new Rectangle(20, 20, 200, 200);
    path.AddRectangle(rect);
    // Create a path gradient brush
    PathGradientBrush pgBrush =
        new PathGradientBrush(path.PathPoints);
    // Set its center and surrounding colors
    pgBrush.CenterColor = Color.Green;
    pgBrush.SurroundColors = new Color[] {Color.Blue};
    // Create matrix
    Matrix M = new Matrix();
    // Translate
    M.Translate(20.0f, 10.0f, MatrixOrder.Prepend);
    // Rotate
    M.Rotate(10.0f, MatrixOrder.Prepend);
    // Scale
    M.Scale(2, 1, MatrixOrder.Prepend);
    // Shear
    M.Shear(.05f, 0.03f, MatrixOrder.Prepend);
    // Apply matrix to the brush
    pgBrush.MultiplyTransform(M);
    // Use brush after transformation
    // to fill a rectangle
    g.FillRectangle(pgBrush, 20, 100, 400, 400);
    // Dispose of objects
    pgBrush.Dispose();
    g.Dispose();
}
```

Figure 4.30 shows the output from Listing 4.25. The original rectangle started at point (10, 10) with height and width 200 each, but after various transformation methods have been applied, the output rectangle is totally different.

FIGURE 4.30: Transformation in path gradient brushes

4.5 **System Pens and System Brushes**

System pens and **system brushes** are pens and brushes that are used to create system colors. In this section we will discuss how to create and use system pens and brushes.

There are two ways to create system pens and brushes. First, you can create pens and brushes using the `SystemColors` class. `SystemColors` represents the system colors in GDI+, providing static properties for system colors, such as `ActiveBorder` and `ControlText`. The second way to create system pens and brushes uses the `SystemPens` and `SystemBrushes` classes.

For performance reasons, it is a good idea to use the `SystemPens` and `SystemBrushes` classes rather than creating pens and brushes by using the `SystemColors` class.

4.5.1 **System Pens**

The SystemPens class represents a pen created with the system colors. This class has a static property for each system color that represents the system pen with that particular color. Table 4.16 lists the properties of the System-Pens class.

The SystemPens class also provides a method—FromSystemColor—that creates a Pen object from a Color structure. To create a system pen, we

TABLE 4.16: **SystemPens** properties

Property	Description
ActiveCaptionText	Pen with active window's title bar color
Control	Pen with control color
ControlDark	Pen with the shadow color of a 3D element.
ControlDarkDark	Pen with the dark shadow color of a 3D element.
ControlLight	Pen with the light color of a 3D element.
ControlLightLight	Pen with the highlight color of a 3D element.
ControlText	Pen with the control text color
GrayText	Pen with disabled color
Highlight	Pen with highlighting
HighlightText	Pen with highlighted text color
InactiveCaptionText	Pen with inactive title bar color
InfoText	Pen with the color of the text of a ToolTip
MenuText	Pen with the color of a menu's text
WindowFrame	Pen with the color of a window frame
WindowText	Pen with the color of the text in the client area of a window

pass a SystemColors object. The following code shows how to use the FromSystemColor method:

```
Pen pn = SystemPens.FromSystemColor(
        SystemColors.HotTrack);
```

4.5.2 System Brushes

The SystemBrushes class represents a Brush object using the system colors. All properties of SystemBrushes are static read-only properties. Table 4.17 describes these properties.

TABLE 4.17: SystemBrushes properties

Property	Description
ActiveBorder	Brush object with the color of the active window's border
ActiveCaption	Brush object with the background color of the active window's title bar
ActiveCaptionText	Brush object with the color of the text in the active window's title bar
AppWorkspace	Brush object with the color of the application workspace
Control	Brush object with the face color of a 3D element
ControlDark	Brush object with the shadow color of a 3D element
ControlDarkDark	Brush object with the dark shadow color of a 3D element
ControlLight	Brush object with the light color of a 3D element
ControlLightLight	Brush object with the highlight color of a 3D element
ControlText	Brush object with the color of text in a 3D element
Desktop	Brush object with the color of the desktop

continues

TABLE 4.17: `SystemBrushes` properties (continued)

Property	Description
Highlight	Brush object with the color of the background of selected items
HighlightText	Brush object with the color of the text of selected items
HotTrack	Brush object with the color used to designate a hot-tracked item
InactiveBorder	Brush object with the color of an inactive window's border
InactiveCaption	Brush object with the color of the background of an inactive window's title bar
Info	Brush object with the color of the background of a ToolTip
Menu	Brush object with the color of a menu's background
ScrollBar	Brush object with the color of the background of a scroll bar
Window	Brush object with the color of the background in the client area of a window
WindowText	Brush object with the color of the text in the client area of a window

■ NOTE

The MSDN documentation states that the `SystemBrushes` properties return a `SolidBrush` object, but that statement is not quite accurate. These properties return a `Brush` object that must be cast to a `SolidBrush` object. If you run the code without casting them, the compiler throws an error.

The `SystemBrushes` class also provides a `FromSystemColor` method, which creates a `Brush` object from a specified system color. The following code shows how to use the `FromSystemColor` method:

```
SolidBrush brush =
    (SolidBrush)SystemBrushes.FromSystemColor
    (SystemColors.ActiveCaption);
```

Disposing of System Pens and Brushes

You cannot dispose of system pens and brushes. If you try to dispose of them, GDI+ generates an error because these objects belong to the system.

Listing 4.26 uses `SystemBrushes` and `SystemPens` objects to draw two lines and a rectangle.

LISTING 4.26: Using the **SystemBrushes** and **SystemPens** classes

```
private void Form1_Paint(object sender,
    System.Windows.Forms.PaintEventArgs e)
{
    Graphics g = e.Graphics;
    // Create a pen using SystemPens
    Pen pn = SystemPens.FromSystemColor(
      SystemColors.HotTrack);
    // Create a brush using SystemBrushes
    SolidBrush brush =
       (SolidBrush)SystemBrushes.FromSystemColor
       (SystemColors.ActiveCaption);
    // Draw lines and rectangles
    g.DrawLine(pn, 20, 20, 20, 100);
    g.DrawLine(pn, 20, 20, 100, 20);
    g.FillRectangle(brush, 30, 30, 50, 50);
    // YOU CAN'T DISPOSE OF SYSTEM PENS AND
    // BRUSHES. IF YOU TRY, GDI+ WILL GENERATE
    // AN ERROR.
    //pn.Dispose();
    //brush.Dispose();
}
```

Figure 4.31 shows the output from Listing 4.26.

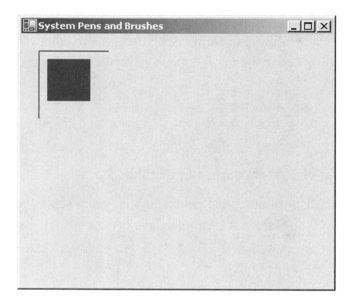

FIGURE 4.31: Using system pens and system brushes

4.6 A Real-World Example: Adding Colors, Pens, and Brushes to the GDI+Painter Application

In Chapter 3 we created the GDI+Painter application, which allows us to draw simple objects, such as a line, a rectangle, and an ellipse. In this section we will extend the functionality of GDI+Painter by adding support for brushes and pens. After completing this section, you will be able to select a pen color and its width, color transparency, and brush color.

Figure 4.32 shows the modified version of GDI+Painter without any objects..

Transparency is a component of the color in GDI+. In the .NET Framework library, the `Color` structure represents a color. It has four components: alpha (A), red (R), green (G), and blue (B). The **alpha component** of the `Color` structure represents the transparency of a color. The alpha component values vary from 0 to 255, where 0 is fully transparent and 255 is fully opaque. To create a transparent brush or pen, we create a color using the alpha value and use the color to create a pen or a brush. We will discuss

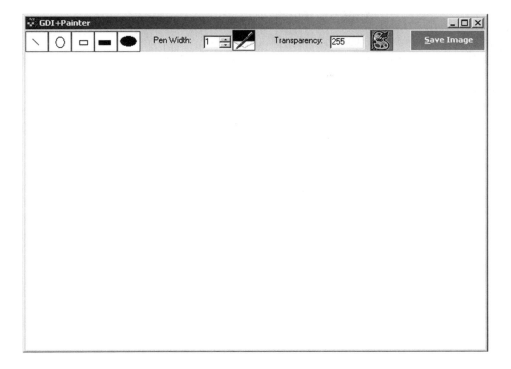

FIGURE 4.32: GDI+Painter with pen and brush support

colors and alpha transparency in more detail in Chapter 5 (ARGB is the focus of Section 5.2).

The following code snippet shows how to create a color with transparency. We use the same method to add transparency to our application.

```
Color clr = Color.FromArgb(Convert.ToInt16
    (TransCounter.Value.ToString()),
    PenBtn.BackColor.R,
    PenBtn.BackColor.G, PenBtn.BackColor.B);
```

In our modified version of GDI+Painter, the width selector numeric up-down control allows you to select the width of the pen. A pen is used when we draw the outlines of graphics shapes. A brush is used when we draw filled graphics shapes.

The `Pen` color and `Brush` color buttons launch `ColorDialog`, which lets us select a color and set the color of the button itself, which later is used by the program when creating a `Pen` or `Brush` object. Listing 4.27 shows the code for these two button click event handlers. This code also sets the background color of the respective buttons to set the current selected color of our brush and pen.

LISTING 4.27: Selecting pen and brush colors

```
private void PenSettings_Click(object sender,
System.EventArgs e)
{
    ColorDialog colorDlg = new ColorDialog();
    colorDlg.ShowDialog();
    PenBtn.BackColor = colorDlg.Color;
}
private void BrushSettings_Click(object sender,
System.EventArgs e)
{
    ColorDialog colorDlg = new ColorDialog();
    colorDlg.ShowDialog();
    BrushBtn.BackColor = colorDlg.Color;
}
```

When we draw a graphics shape, we set the color, width, and transparency of the pen and brush according to the selection. The last two changes in our revised version of GDI+Painter are on the mouse-up event handler and the form's paint event handler, respectively.

The modified mouse-up event handler is shown in Listing 4.28. In it, we use the color buttons to create our current pen and brush from the selected colors.

LISTING 4.28: The mouse-up event handler

```
private void Form1_MouseUp(object sender,
    System.Windows.Forms.MouseEventArgs e)
{
    // Set the pen's color
    curPen.Color = Color.FromArgb(Convert.ToInt16(
      TransCounter.Value.ToString()),
      PenBtn.BackColor.R, PenBtn.BackColor.G,
      PenBtn.BackColor.B);
    // Set the pen's width
    curPen.Width = (float)PenWidthCounter.Value;
    // Set the brush's color
    curBrush.Color = Color.FromArgb(Convert.ToInt16(
      TransCounter.Value.ToString()),
```

```csharp
    BrushBtn.BackColor.R, BrushBtn.BackColor.G,
    BrushBtn.BackColor.B);

diffX = x - curX;
diffY = y - curY;
switch (drawIndex)
{
  case 1:
  {
    // Draw a line
    curGraphics.DrawLine(curPen,
      curX, curY, x, y);
    break;
  }
  case 2:
  {
    // Draw an ellipse
    curGraphics.DrawEllipse(curPen,
      curX, curY, diffX, diffY);
    break;
  }
  case 3:
  {
    // Draw a rectangle
    curGraphics.DrawRectangle(curPen,
      curX, curY, diffX, diffY);
    break;
  }
  case 4:
  {
    // Fill rectangle
    curGraphics.FillRectangle(curBrush,
     curX, curY, diffX, diffY);
    break;
  }
  case 5:
  {
    // Fill ellipse
    curGraphics.FillEllipse(curBrush,
      curX, curY, diffX, diffY);
    break;
  }
}
// Refresh
RefreshFormBackground();
// Set dragMode to false
dragMode = false;
}
```

The same procedure is applied to the form's paint event handler, shown in Listing 4.29. This code sets the `Color` and `Width` properties of our pen and the `Color` property of our brush according to the current values.

LISTING 4.29: The form's paint event handler

```
private void Form1_Paint(object sender,
      System.Windows.Forms.PaintEventArgs e)
{
      // Set current pen's color
      curPen.Color = Color.FromArgb(
        Convert.ToInt16(
        TransCounter.Value.ToString()),
        PenBtn.BackColor.R,
        PenBtn.BackColor.G,
        PenBtn.BackColor.B);
      // Set pen's width
      curPen.Width = (float)PenWidthCounter.Value;
      // Set current brush's color
      curBrush.Color = Color.FromArgb(
        Convert.ToInt16(
        TransCounter.Value.ToString()),
        BrushBtn.BackColor.R,
        BrushBtn.BackColor.G,
        BrushBtn.BackColor.B);

      Graphics g = e.Graphics;
      // If dragMode is true, draw selected
      // graphics shape
      if (dragMode)
      {
        switch (drawIndex)
        {
          case 1:
          {
            g.DrawLine(curPen, curX, curY, x, y);
            break;
          }
          case 2:
          {
            g.DrawEllipse(curPen,
              curX, curY, diffX, diffY);
            break;
          }
          case 3:
          {
            g.DrawRectangle(curPen,
              curX, curY, diffX, diffY);
            break;
```

```
        }
        case 4:
        {
          g.FillRectangle(curBrush,
            curX, curY, diffX, diffY);
          break;
        }
        case 5:
        {
          g.FillEllipse(curBrush,
            curX, curY, diffX, diffY);
          break;
        }
      }
    }
  }
}
```

If you run the revised GDI+Painter application, you can set the colors of the brush and the pen, the pen's width, and the transparency of both the pen and the brush. Figure 4.33 shows lines, rectangles, and ellipses drawn with different sizes and transparency.

4.6.1 Improvements in GDI+Painter

You can improve the functionality of the GDI+Painter application (or your own applications) even more: As we have discussed in our examples, you can add a brush selection feature. You can allow users to select a brush type, style, and other properties. If users pick a gradient brush, they can select colors. You can also allow users to select cap and line styles. For solid brushes, users should be able to pick a color; for texture brushes, they should be able to pick an image; and for hatch and gradient brushes, they should be able to pick styles, background, foreground, and other color properties. You can even add transformation and other options—all of which we've discussed in this chapter.

On the basis of this example, you can write your own graphics tool library with support for many more options than the standard Windows PaintBrush application!

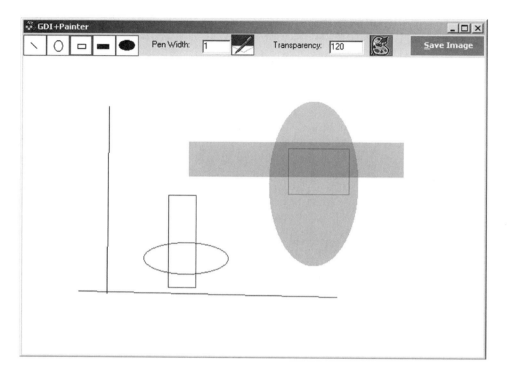

FIGURE 4.33: GDI+Painter in action

SUMMARY

In this chapter we learned how to work with pens and brushes by using classes from the GDI+ .NET Framework class library. The chapter began by showing how to represent various kinds of brushes in GDI+. We learned the classes for the different brushes and how to use their properties and methods.

After covering brushes, the discussion moved on to pens and how to represent them using GDI+ classes. We learned pen-related classes and their properties and methods, and how to add various styles to pens, such as cap, line, and dash styles. We also discussed system pens and brushes, and how to use GDI+ classes to represent and use system pens and brushes.

At the end of the chapter we added options for pens and brushes to the GDI+Painter application. You should now have a pretty good idea of how to use pens and brushes in your own applications.

After pens and brushes, the next most frequently used graphics objects are text, fonts, and colors. We will discuss these in Chapter 5.

5
Colors, Fonts, and Text

THREE TYPES OF objects that are used to build graphics-intensive applications are colors, fonts, and text. In this chapter you will learn about the representation of colors, fonts, and text in the .NET Framework class library. We will cover the following topics:

- Basics of colors, fonts, and text and how they are represented in Windows
- Namespaces, classes, and other objects provided by the .NET Framework library to work with colors, fonts, and text
- System fonts, colors, brushes, and pens
- Color conversions and translations
- System and private font collections
- Formatting text using hinting, tab stops, and other methods
- Setting the quality and performance of text rendering
- Writing a simple text editor application
- Text transformation operations such as scaling, rotation, and translation
- Advanced typography

5.1 **Accessing the** `Graphics` **Object**

There are several ways an application can use the code from this chapter. It can execute code using the `OnPaint` method or `Form_Paint` event, or it can use code with a button or menu click event handler. If an application executes code with `Form_Paint` or `OnPaint`, you will need to include the following line at the beginning of the method.

```
Graphics g = e.Graphics;
```

If an application executes code from a button or menu click event handler or elsewhere, you will need to create a `Graphics` object using `CreateGraphics` or another method (see Chapter 3 for details) and call the `Dispose` method to dispose of objects when you're finished with them. The following code snippet gives an example:

```
Graphics g = this.CreateGraphics();

// YOUR CODE HERE

// Dispose of GDI+ objects
g.Dispose();
```

> ▪▫ **NOTE**
>
> To test code from this chapter, we will create a Windows application with code written on the menu item click event handlers.

5.2 **Working with Colors**

In this section we will examine color representation in GDI+ and how to use color-related functionality in real-world applications.

In GDI+, a color is represented by a 32-bit structure made up of four components: alpha (A), red (R), green (G), and blue (B), referred to as **ARGB mode**. Components' values range from 0 to 255. The **alpha component** (the first 8 bits) of the color represents transparency, which determines how a color is blended with the background. An alpha value of 0 represents a fully transparent color, and a value of 255 represents a fully opaque color; intermediate values produce results between these extremes. Real-world examples of alpha use include drawing translucent graphics shapes and images. Chapter 9 discusses the alpha component in more detail (see Section 9.6).

5.2.1 Color Spaces

It's hard for human beings—as perceptual entities—to describe and represent colors. **Color spaces** provide a common frame of reference that helps represent colors. A color space contains components called **color channels**. For example, RGB space is a three-dimensional space with red, green, and blue color channels. To limit our discussion, we will cover the RGB (red-green-blue), HSV (hue-saturation-value), and HLS (hue-lightness-saturation) color spaces.

The **RGB** color space is the most commonly used namespace in computer programming because it closely matches the structure of most display hardware—which commonly includes separate red, green, and blue subpixel structures. It can be thought of as a cube in which length indicates the intensity of red, width indicates the intensity of green, and height indicates the intensity of blue. The corner indicated by (0, 0, 0) is black, and the opposite corner (255, 255, 255) is white. Every other color available is represented somewhere between those corners.

The **HSV**, sometimes called HSB (hue-saturation-brightness), and **HLS** color spaces can be thought of as single and double cones. The **hue component** represents the position on the cone as an angular measurement. The 0-, 120-, and 240-degree values of hue represent the colors red, green, and blue, respectively.

The **saturation component** describes the color intensity. A saturation value of 0 means gray (colorless), and the maximum value of saturation indicates pure color and brightness for the values specified by the hue and value components.

The **value**, or **brightness**, **component** represents the brightness of the color. A value of 0 indicates the color black (no brightness), and a maximum value indicates that the color is brightest (closest to white).

The `Color` structure provided by the .NET Framework library is based on the RGB color space. In Section 5.2.2 we will discuss how to use it in our applications.

5.2.2 The `Color` Structure

The `Color` structure represents ARGB colors in GDI+. This class has a static member property for almost every possible color. For example, `Color.Black` and `Color.Red` represent the colors black and red, respectively. Besides these static properties, this structure includes read-only properties—A, R, G, and B—that represent the alpha, red, green, and blue components, respectively.

The `IsEmpty` property checks whether a `Color` structure has been initialized (if not, there is no color). The `KnownColor` enumeration contains more than 300 colors, and each color is represented by its name. For example, `Blue` and `Black` members represent the colors blue and black, respectively. `KnownColor` also defines color combinations, such as `LimeGreen` and `LightBlue`. You can also find system colors such as `ActiveBorder`, `ActiveCaption`, `Control`, `ControlText`, `Highlight`, and `Inactive-Border`, using the `IsSystemColor` enumeration. The `Name` property represents the name of the color, which is a read-only property. The `Transparent` property is a static property that represents a transparent color.

The `Color` structure also provides some methods. The `FromArgb` method creates a color from the four ARGB components. This method has different overloaded forms with which an application can create a `Color` object from an alpha value only; from an alpha value with a `Color` object only; from three values (red, green, and blue); and from all four values (alpha, red, green, and blue).

The `FromKnownColor` and `FromName` methods create a `Color` object from a predefined color or from the name of a predefined color, respectively. The `FromKnownColor` method takes only one argument, of `Known-Color` enumeration. The `FromName` method takes one argument of string type as the color name. All members defined in the `KnownColor` enumeration are valid names for this method.

> ▪▪ **NOTE**
>
> All three "from" methods (FromArgb, FromKnownColor, and From-
> Name) are static.

The ToArgb and ToKnownColor methods convert an ARGB or Known-
Color value, respectively, to a Color structure.

Listing 5.1 illustrates different ways to create Color objects and use
them in an application to draw various graphics objects, including a filled
ellipse with a red brush, a filled rectangle with a blue brush, and a line with
a green pen. The application first creates four Color objects via the From-
Argb, FromName, FromKnownColor, and Empty methods. The FromArgb
method creates a translucent pure red Color object, using parameters 120,
255, 0, and 0. The FromName method creates a Color object from the string
"Blue". The FromKnownColor method creates a color object from the
known color Green.

LISTING 5.1: Using the methods and properties of the Color structure

```
private void ColorStructMenu_Click(object sender,
    System.EventArgs e)
{
    // Create Graphics object
    Graphics g = this.CreateGraphics();
    // Create Color object from ARGB
    Color redColor = Color.FromArgb(120, 255, 0, 0);
    // Create Color object form color name
    Color blueColor = Color.FromName("Blue");
    // Create Color object from known color
    Color greenColor =
      Color.FromKnownColor(KnownColor.Green);
    // Create empty color
    Color tstColor = Color.Empty;
    // See if a color is empty
    if(tstColor.IsEmpty)
    {
      tstColor = Color.DarkGoldenrod;
    }
    // Create brushes and pens from colors
```

continues

```
        SolidBrush redBrush = new SolidBrush(redColor);
        SolidBrush blueBrush = new SolidBrush(blueColor);
        SolidBrush greenBrush = new SolidBrush(greenColor);
        Pen greenPen = new Pen(greenBrush, 4);
        // Draw GDI+ objects
        g.FillEllipse(redBrush, 10, 10, 50, 50);
        g.FillRectangle(blueBrush, 60, 10, 50, 50);
        g.DrawLine(greenPen, 20, 60, 200, 60);
        // Check property values
        MessageBox.Show("Color Name :"+ blueColor.Name +
          ", A:"+blueColor.A.ToString() +
          ", R:"+blueColor.R.ToString() +
          ", B:"+blueColor.B.ToString() +
          ", G:"+blueColor.G.ToString() );
        // Dispose of GDI+ objects
        redBrush.Dispose();
        blueBrush.Dispose();
        greenBrush.Dispose();
        greenPen.Dispose();
        g.Dispose();
}
```

Figure 5.1 shows the output from Listing 5.1.

The GetBrightness, GetHue, and GetSaturation methods return a color's brightness, hue, and saturation component values, respectively. Listing 5.2 reads the hue, saturation, and brightness components of a color and displays their values on the form by using the DrawString method.

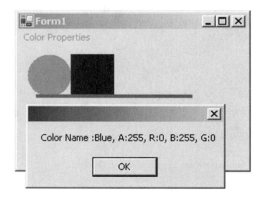

FIGURE 5.1: Creating colors using different methods

LISTING 5.2: Getting brightness, hue, and saturation of a color

```
private void HSBMenu_Click(object sender,
    System.EventArgs e)
{
    // Create a Graphics object
    Graphics     g = this.CreateGraphics();
    // Create a color
    Color clr = Color.FromArgb(255, 200, 0, 100);
    // Get hue, saturation, and brightness components
    float h = clr.GetHue();
    float s = clr.GetSaturation();
    float v = clr.GetBrightness();
    string str = "Hue: "+ h.ToString() + "\n" +
            "Saturation: "+ s.ToString() + "\n" +
            "Brightness: "+ v.ToString();
    // Display data
    g.DrawString(str, new Font("verdana", 12),
      Brushes.Blue, 50, 50);
    // Dispose of object
    g.Dispose();
}
```

Figure 5.2 shows the output from Listing 5.2. The values of hue, saturation, and brightness in this particular color are 330, 1, and 0.3921569, respectively.

5.2.3 System Colors

The SystemColors class represents the Windows system colors; it provides 26 read-only properties, each of which returns a Color object. Table 5.1 lists the properties of the SystemColors class.

The following code snippet uses the SystemColors class to set colors of a few Windows controls. In this code we set the background colors of a text box, a radio button, and a button to inactive border, active caption, and control dark system colors, respectively.

```
textBox1.BackColor = SystemColors.InactiveBorder;
radioButton1.BackColor = SystemColors.ActiveCaption;
button1.BackColor = SystemColors.ControlDarkDark;
```

If you're wondering whether you can create a brush or a pen from the SystemColors class to fill and draw shapes, curves, and text, the answer is, absolutely. The following code snippet uses SystemColors to create

FIGURE 5.2: Getting brightness, hue, and saturation components of a color

TABLE 5.1: SystemColors properties

Property	Description
ActiveBorder	Active window border color
ActiveCaption	Active window title bar background color
ActiveCaptionText	Active window title bar text color
AppWorkspace	Multiple-document interface (MDI) workspace background color
Control	Control background color
ControlDark	3D control shadow color
ControlDarkDark	3D control dark shadow color
ControlLight	3D control highlight color
ControlLightLight	3D control light highlight color
ControlText	Text color of controls

TABLE 5.1: `SystemColors` properties (continued)

Property	Description
Desktop	Windows desktop color
GrayText	Disabled text color
Highlight	Highlighted text background color
HighlightText	Highlighted text color
HotTrack	Hot track color
InactiveBorder	Inactive window border color
InactiveCaption	Inactive window caption bar color
InactiveCaptionText	Inactive window caption bar text color
Info	ToolTip background color
InfoText	ToolTip text color
Menu	Menu background color
MenuText	Menu text color
ScrollBar	Background color of scroll bars
Window	Background color of window
WindowFrame	Thin window frame color
WindowText	Window text color

`SolidBrush` and `Pen` objects. This code creates a solid brush and a pen from active caption system and highlight text system colors, respectively.

```
SolidBrush brush =
new SolidBrush(SystemColors.ActiveCaption);
Pen pn = new Pen(SystemColors.HighlightText);
```

For performance reasons, GDI+ provides `SystemPens` and `System-Brushes` classes, which should be used instead of creating a brush or pen from the `SystemColors` class. For example, the following method is advisable for creating system brushes and pens. This code snippet creates a solid brush and a pen from active caption and highlight text system colors, respectively.

```
SolidBrush brush1 =
(SolidBrush)SystemBrushes.FromSystemColor
(SystemColors.ActiveCaption);
Pen pn1 = SystemPens.FromSystemColor
(SystemColors.HighlightText);
```

Listing 5.3 uses the SystemBrushes and SystemPens classes to create a SolidBrush object and three Pen objects, which are used later to draw and fill graphics objects. The solid brush is created from the active caption system color, and the three pens are created from highlight text, control light light, and control dark system colors, respectively. Later the brush and pens are used to draw two lines, a rectangle, and an ellipse.

LISTING 5.3: Using SystemPens and SystemBrushes

```
private void SystemColorsMenu_Click(object sender,
    System.EventArgs e)
{
    // Create a Graphics object
    Graphics g = this.CreateGraphics();
    // Create brushes and pens
    SolidBrush brush1 =
        (SolidBrush)SystemBrushes.FromSystemColor
        (SystemColors.ActiveCaption);
    Pen pn1 = SystemPens.FromSystemColor
        (SystemColors.HighlightText);
    Pen pn2 = SystemPens.FromSystemColor
        (SystemColors.ControlLightLight);
    Pen pn3 = SystemPens.FromSystemColor
        (SystemColors.ControlDarkDark);
    // Draw and fill graphics objects
    g.DrawLine(pn1, 10, 10, 10, 200);
    g.FillRectangle(brush1, 60, 60, 100, 100);
    g.DrawEllipse(pn3, 20, 20, 170, 170);
    g.DrawLine(pn2, 10, 10, 200, 10);
    // Dispose of object
    g.Dispose();
}
```

Figure 5.3 shows the output from Listing 5.3. System colors were used to draw two lines, an ellipse, and a rectangle.

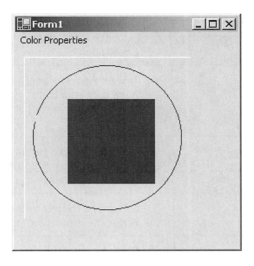

FIGURE 5.3: Using system colors to draw graphics objects

> **▪ NOTE**
>
> When you create pens using `SystemPens`, you cannot modify the width or other properties of the pen. The code will compile but will throw an unhandled exception when executed. If you create a pen using `SystemColors`, however, you can modify its width like this:
>
> ```
> Pen pn = new Pen(SystemColors.HighlightText);
> Pn.Width = 4;
> ```

5.2.4 **The** `ColorConverter` **and** `ColorTranslator` **Classes**

The `ColorConverter` class is used to convert colors from one data type to another. This class is inherited from the `TypeConverter` class, which defines the functionality for conversion of types and accessing values and properties of types. The `TypeConverter` class serves as a base class for many conversion classes, and `ColorConverter` and `FontConverter` are two of them. We will discuss `FontConverter` in more detail later in this chapter. Some of the common methods of the `TypeConverter` class (which are available in the `ColorConverter` class) are described in Table 5.2.

TABLE 5.2: Common **TypeConverter** methods

Method	Description
CanConvertFrom	Takes a type as a parameter and returns true if the converter can convert an object to the type of the converter; otherwise returns false.
CanConvertTo	Takes a type as a parameter and returns true if the converter can convert an object to a given type; otherwise returns false.
ConvertFrom	Converts an object to the type of the converter and returns the converted object.
ConvertTo	Converts a specified object to a new type and returns the object.
GetStandardValues	Returns a collection of standard values (collection type) for the data type for which this type converter is designed.
GetStandardValuesSupported	Identifies whether this object supports a standard set of values.

Listing 5.4 uses the ColorConverter class methods to convert colors. We store a color in a string and call the ConvertFromString method, which returns the Color object. Later we will use the Color objects to create two brushes that we will use to fill a rectangle and an ellipse.

LISTING 5.4: Using the **ColorConverter** class to convert colors

```
private void ColorConvert_Click(object sender,
    System.EventArgs e)
{
    Graphics g = this.CreateGraphics();
    g.Clear(this.BackColor);
    string str = "#FF00FF";
    ColorConverter clrConverter = new ColorConverter();
    Color clr1 =
        (Color)clrConverter.ConvertFromString(str);
    // Use colors
    SolidBrush clr2 = new SolidBrush(clr1);
    SolidBrush clr3 = new SolidBrush(clr1);
    // Draw GDI+ objects
    g.FillEllipse(clr2, 10, 10, 50, 50);
```

FIGURE 5.4: Converting colors

```
g.FillRectangle(clr3, 60, 10, 50, 50);
// Dispose of objects
clr2.Dispose();
clr3.Dispose();
g.Dispose();
}
```

Figure 5.4 shows the output from Listing 5.4.

The `ColorTranslator` class provides methods to translate colors to and from HTML, OLE, and Win32 color values. These methods are useful when you're using legacy color structures that pre-date the .NET Framework. For example, you may have legacy code that gives the HTML color representation of a color. Table 5.3 describes the methods of the `Color-Translator` class. All of the methods are static.

Listing 5.5 uses the `ColorTranslator` class to translate colors from Win32 and HTML colors. Later these colors will be used to create brushes.

LISTING 5.5: Translating colors

```
private void ColorTranslator_Click(object sender,
    System.EventArgs e)
{
    Graphics g = this.CreateGraphics();
    // Translate colors
    Color win32Color =
        ColorTranslator.FromWin32(0xFF0033);
    Color htmlColor =
        ColorTranslator.FromHtml("#00AAFF");
```

continues

TABLE 5.3: ColorTranslator methods

Method	Description
FromHtml	Translates from an HTML color representation to a Color structure.
FromOle	Translates from an OLE color value to a Color structure.
FromWin32	Translates from a Windows color value to a Color structure.
ToHtml	Translates from a Color structure to an HTML color representation.
ToOle	Translates from a Color structure to an OLE color.
ToWin32	Translates from a Color structure to a Windows color.

```
        // Use colors
        SolidBrush clr1 = new SolidBrush(win32Color);
        SolidBrush clr2 = new SolidBrush(htmlColor);
        // Draw GDI+ objects
        g.FillEllipse(clr1, 10, 10, 50, 50);
        g.FillRectangle(clr2, 60, 10, 50, 50);
        // Dispose of objects
        clr1.Dispose();
        clr2.Dispose();
        g.Dispose();
    }
```

In a manner similar to the "from" methods just discussed, you can translate a Color structure into Win32, HTML, and OLE values using the ToWin32, ToHtml, and ToOle methods, respectively.

> ■■ NOTE
>
> You can also transform colors using transformation methods. Some of the transformation methods are for scaling, translating, rotating, and shearing. We cover this functionality in Chapter 10.

5.3 Working with Fonts

In this section we will concentrate on fonts. The discussion starts with a description of the types of fonts in the Windows operating system, followed by a little background material on fonts. After these basic concepts are covered, the discussion turns to how fonts are handled in GDI+ and .NET.

5.3.1 Font Types in Windows

Windows supports two types of fonts: GDI fonts and device fonts. **Device fonts** are native to output devices such as a monitor or a printer. **GDI fonts** are stored in files on your system—normally in the `Windows\Fonts` directory. Each font has its own file. For example, Arial, Arial Black, Arial Bold, Arial Italic, Arial Black Italic, Arial Bold Italic, Arial Narrow, Arial Narrow Bold Italic, and Arial Narrow Italic are different fonts in the Arial font family, and each one has its own file (see Figure 5.5).

GDI fonts can be further divided into four major categories: raster, stroke, TrueType, and OpenType. The raster and stroke fonts are the oldest

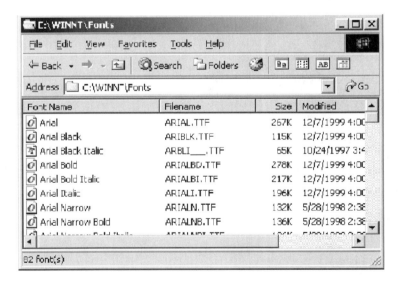

FIGURE 5.5: Fonts available in Windows

way to display text (they pre-date Windows 3.1!). **Raster fonts** (also known as bitmap fonts) store each character in pixel format. Each raster font is designed for a specific aspect ratio and character size, which are generally not scalable to other sizes. The main advantage of raster fonts is high performance because rendering a raster font usually just requires copying it to video memory. Raster fonts support boldface, italics, underlining, and strikethrough formatting.

Stroke fonts (also known as vector fonts) are defined as a series of lines and dots—in much the same way that characters are drawn with a pen plotter. Stroke fonts are thus quite scalable (they can be increased or decreased to any size), and they can be used with output devices of any resolution. Examples of stroke fonts include Modern, Roman, and Script. Like raster fonts, stroke fonts support boldface, italics, underlining, and strikethrough formatting.

Next we come to **TrueType fonts**, which were developed by Apple and Microsoft and are supported by many manufacturers. TrueType fonts are also called outline fonts because the individual characters are defined by filled outlines of straight lines and curves. Altering the coordinates that define the outlines provides great scalability. The original 13 TrueType fonts were

1. Courier New
2. Courier New Bold
3. Courier New Italic
4. Courier New Bold Italic
5. Times New Roman
6. Times New Roman Bold
7. Times New Roman Italic
8. Times New Roman Bold Italic
9. Arial
10. Arial Bold
11. Arial Italic
12. Arial Bold Italic
13. Symbol

Adobe and Microsoft announced yet another format in 1997, called **OpenType**. It is a combination of TrueType and the Type 1 outline format of Adobe's page-description language. Windows 2000 installs 82 fonts, including TrueType fonts, OpenType fonts, and other types. The TrueType fonts are represented by a "T" icon, and OpenType fonts are represented by an "O" icon in Windows Explorer, as shown in Figure 5.6.

The file extension of both TrueType and OpenType fonts is .ttf. If you double-click on the Verdana OpenType font file, it displays the information shown in Figure 5.7.

The Arial Black Italic TrueType font file, on the other hand, looks like Figure 5.8.

In 1998, Microsoft announced a new display technology called **ClearType**. ClearType increases the readability and smoothness of text on existing LCDs (liquid crystal displays), such as laptop screens, flat-screen monitors, and Pocket PC screens. In normal displays, a pixel has only two states: on and off. ClearType technology adds additional information to a pixel besides the on and off states. With ClearType, the words on the display device look almost as sharp and clear as those on the printed page.

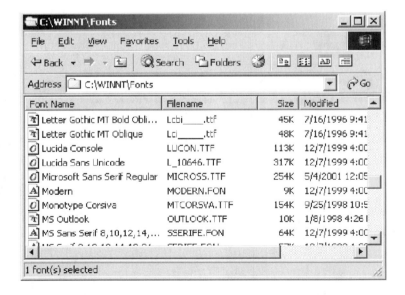

FIGURE 5.6: Font icons represent font types

FIGURE 5.7: An OpenType font

FIGURE 5.8: A TrueType font

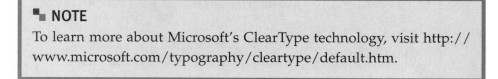

NOTE

To learn more about Microsoft's ClearType technology, visit http://www.microsoft.com/typography/cleartype/default.htm.

5.3.1.1 *Attributes or Styles*

In typography, the combination of a **typeface name** (sometimes referred to as a face name) and a **point size** (sometimes referred to as the em size) represents a font. A typeface name is a combination of a font family and the font style (also referred to as font attributes). Each typeface belongs to a font family such as Times New Roman, Arial, or Courier. The Courier family, for example, includes the typefaces Courier New, Courier New Bold, and Courier New Italic.

Generally, when we talk about a font, we are referring to more than just one component. A typical font is a combination of three components: font family, font style, and font size. Figure 5.9 shows the components of a typical font.

A complete example of a font is "Times New Roman, size 10, Bold | Italic". Here the font family is Times New Roman, the size is 10-point, and the style is both bold and italic.

5.3.1.2 *Font Height and Line Spacing*

The size of a font is expressed in points, where a **point** is usually 1/72 (0.013888) inch. The measurement of the size of a font is a little confusing because characters have different heights. If all alphabetic characters had

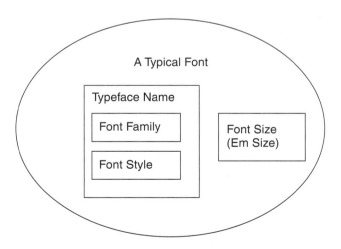

FIGURE 5.9: Font components

the same height, it would be easier to calculate the size of a font. For example, consider the characters *b* and *q*. Technically they have the same height (or size), but they are situated in different locations along a straight line. In other words, the character's size may not be the same as the point size, also called **em size**. The font size is related to the line spacing. We will discuss line spacing in more detail in Section 5.3.4.

5.3.2 Fonts in .NET

Before we use fonts and draw text, let's see what classes GDI+ provides related to text and fonts, and how to use them.

Typography Namespaces

In the .NET framework library, two namespaces define the font-related functionality: `System.Drawing` and `System.Drawing.Text`. The `System.Drawing` namespace contains general typography functionality, and `System.Drawing.Text` contains advanced typography functionality. Before using any of the typography-related classes in your application, you must include the appropriate namespace. We will discuss advanced typography in Section 5.6.

The `Font` class provides functionality for fonts, including methods and properties to define functionalities such as font style, size, name, and conversions. Before we discuss the `Font` class, we will introduce the `FontStyle` enumeration and the `FontFamily` class, which we will use to create `Font` objects.

5.3.3 The `FontStyle` Enumeration

The `FontStyle` enumeration defines the common styles of a font. The members of `FontStyle` are described in Table 5.4.

5.3.4 The `FontFamily` Class

The `FontFamily` class provides methods and properties to work with font families. Table 5.5 describes the properties of the `FontFamily` class.

TABLE 5.4: `FontStyle` members

Member	Description
Bold	Bold text
Italic	Italic text
Regular	Normal text
Strikeout	Text with a line through the middle
Underline	Underlined text

TABLE 5.5: `FontFamily` properties

Property	Description
Families	Returns an array of all the font families associated with the current graphics context.
GenericMonospace	Returns a monospace font family.
GenericSansSerif	Returns a sans serif font family.
GenericSerif	Returns a serif font family.
Name	Returns the name of a font family.

> **◼ NOTE**
>
> The `GetFamilies` method of the `FontCollection` class returns all families, as we will discuss in Section 5.6.

Table 5.6 describes the methods of the `FontFamily` class.

Table 5.6 introduces some new terms, including *base line*, *ascent*, and *descent*. Let's see what they mean. Figure 5.10 shows a typical font in Windows. As you can see, although the letters *b* and *q* are the same size, their starting points and ending points (top and bottom locations) are different. The total height of a font—including ascent, descent, and extra space—is

TABLE 5.6: FontFamily methods

Method	Description
GetCellAscent	Returns the cell ascent, in font design units, of a font family.
GetCellDescent	Returns the cell descent, in font design units, of a font family.
GetEmHeight	Returns the height, in font design units, of the em square for the specified style.
GetFamilies	Returns an array that contains all font families available for a graphics object. This method takes an argument of Graphics type.
GetLineSpacing	Returns the amount of space between two consecutive lines of text for a font family.
GetName	Returns the name, in the specified language, of a font family.

IsStyleAvailable	Before applying a style to a font, you may want to know whether the font family in question supports that style. This method returns true if a font style is available. For example, the following code snippet checks whether or not the Arial font family supports italics:
	
	`FontFamily ff = new FontFamily("Arial");`
	`if(ff.IsStyleAvailable(FontStyle.Italic))`
	`// do something`

called the **line spacing**. **Ascent** is the height above the base line, and **descent** is the height below the base line. As Figure 5.10 shows, two characters may have different positions along the base line. For some fonts, the extra value is 0, but for others it is not.

For some fonts, line spacing is the sum of ascent and descent. Listing 5.6 creates a new font; uses get methods to get the values of line spacing, ascent, and descent; and calculates the extra space by subtracting ascent and descent from the line space. The following list identifies the get methods of a FontFamily object:

- GetCellAscent returns the cell ascent, in font design units.
- GetCellDescent returns the cell descent, in font design units.

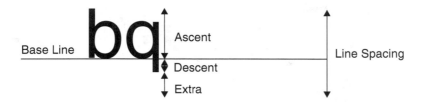

FIGURE 5.10: Font metrics

- GetEmHeight returns the em height, in font design units.
- GetLineSpacing returns the line spacing for a font family.

In addition to these get methods, the Font class provides GetHeight, which returns the height of a Font object.

As Listing 5.6 shows, we use GetLineSpacing, GetLineAscent, Get-LineDescent, and GetEmHeight to get line spacing, ascent, descent, and font height, respectively, and then we display the output in a message box.

LISTING 5.6: Getting line spacing, ascent, descent, and font height

```
private void Properties_Click(object sender,
      System.EventArgs e)
{
    // Create a Graphics object
    Graphics g = this.CreateGraphics();
    // Create a Font object
    Font fnt = new Font("Verdana", 10);
    // Get height
    float lnSpace = fnt.GetHeight(g);
    // Get line spacing
    int cellSpace =
      fnt.FontFamily.GetLineSpacing(fnt.Style);
    // Get cell ascent
    int cellAscent =
      fnt.FontFamily.GetCellAscent(fnt.Style);
    // Get cell descent
    int cellDescent =
      fnt.FontFamily.GetCellDescent(fnt.Style);
    // Get font height
    int emHeight =
      fnt.FontFamily.GetEmHeight(fnt.Style);
    // Get free space
    float free = cellSpace - (cellAscent + cellDescent);
```

continues

```
       // Display values
       string str = "Cell Height:" + lnSpace.ToString() +
         ", Line Spacing: "+cellSpace.ToString() +
         ", Ascent:"+ cellAscent.ToString() +
         ", Descent:"+ cellDescent.ToString() +
         ", Free:"+free.ToString() +
         ", EM Height:"+ emHeight.ToString() ;
       MessageBox.Show(str.ToString());
       // Dispose of objects
       fnt.Dispose();
       g.Dispose();
     }
```

Figure 5.11 shows the output from Listing 5.6. We get cell height, line spacing, ascent, descent, free (extra) space, and em height.

5.3.5 The `GraphicsUnit` Enumeration

You can define the unit of measure of a font when you construct a `Font` object. The `Font` class constructor takes an argument of type `Graphics-Unit` enumeration, which specifies the unit of measure of a font. The default unit of measure for fonts is the point (1/72 inch). You can get the current unit of a font by using the `Unit` property of the `Font` class. The following code snippet returns the current unit of the font:

```
Font fnt = new Font("Verdana", 10);
MessageBox.Show(fnt.Unit.ToString());
```

The members of the `GraphicsUnit` enumeration are described in Table 5.7.

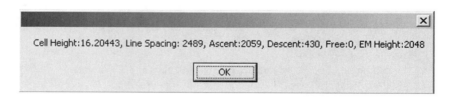

FIGURE 5.11: Getting line spacing, ascent, descent, free (extra) space, and height of a font

TABLE 5.7: `GraphicsUnit` members

Member	Unit of Measure
`Display`	1/75 inch
`Document`	1/300 inch
`Inch`	1 inch
`Millimeter`	1 millimeter
`Pixel`	1 pixel
`Point`	1/72 inch
`World`	The world unit (we'll discuss world coordinates in Chapter 10)

5.3.6 **The `Font` Class**

The `Font` class combines a font and methods and properties to define functionalities such as font style, size, name, and conversions. Table 5.8 describes the properties of the `Font` class.

The following code creates a `Font` object of font family Arial with size 16 and uses the `Font` class properties to find out the details of the `Font` object.

```
Font arialFont = new Font( "Arial", 16,
FontStyle.Bold|FontStyle.Underline|FontStyle.Italic);
MessageBox.Show("Font Properties = Name:"+arialFont.Name
+" Size:"+arialFont.Size.ToString()
+" Style:"+ arialFont.Style.ToString()
+" Default Unit:"+ arialFont.Unit.ToString()
+" Size in Points:"+ arialFont.SizeInPoints.ToString());
```

The `Font` class provides three static methods: `FromHdc`, `FromHfont`, and `FromLogFont`. These methods create a `Font` object from a window handle to a device context, a window handle, and a GDI `LOGFONT` structure, respectively. The `GetHeight` method returns the height of a `Font` object. The `ToHfont` and `ToLogFont` methods convert a `Font` object to a window handler and a GDI `LOGFONT` structure, respectively.

TABLE 5.8: Font properties

Property	Description
Bold	Returns `true` if the font is bold.
FontFamily	Every font belongs to a font family. This property returns the `FontFamily` object associated with a `Font` object.
GdiCharSet	Returns a string containing all characters.
GdiVerticalFont	Returns `true` if a font is derived from a GDI vertical font; otherwise returns `false`.
Height	Returns the height of a font.
Italic	Returns `true` if a font is italic.
Name	Returns the face name of a font.
Size	Returns the em size of a font in font design units.
SizeInPoints	Returns the size, in points, of a font.
Strikeout	Returns `true` if a font specifies a horizontal line through the font.
Style	Returns style information for a font, which is a type of `FontStyle` enumeration.
Underline	Returns `true` if a font is underlined.
Unit	Returns the unit of measure for a font.

In the following example, you must import the GDI library by adding the following code at the beginning of your class before using any GDI fonts, because we will be using `GetStockObject`:

```
[System.Runtime.InteropServices.DllImportAttribute("gdi32.dll")]
private static extern IntPtr GetStockObject(int fnObj);
```

Listing 5.7 creates a font from a GDI handle and draws a string on the form. The `FromHfont` method creates a `Font` object from a GDI handle.

LISTING 5.7: Using the `FromHfont` method

```
private void FromHfontMenu_Click(object sender,
      System.EventArgs e)
{

      // Create the Graphics object
      Graphics g = this.CreateGraphics();
      // Create a brush
      SolidBrush brush = new SolidBrush(Color.Red);
      // Get a handle
      IntPtr hFont = GetStockObject(0);
      // Create a font from the handle
      Font hfontFont = Font.FromHfont(hFont);
      // Draw text
      g.DrawString("GDI HFONT", hfontFont,
        brush, 20, 20);
      // Dispose of objects
      brush.Dispose();
      hfontFont.Dispose();
      g.Dispose();
}
```

Figure 5.12 shows the output from Listing 5.7.

5.3.7 **Constructing a** `Font` **Object**

A `Font` object belongs to the `FontFamily` class, so before we construct a `Font` object, we need to construct a `FontFamily` object. The following code snippet creates two `FontFamily` objects, belonging to the Verdana and Arial font families, respectively.

```
// Create font families
FontFamily verdanaFamily = new FontFamily("Verdana");
FontFamily arialFamily = new FontFamily("Arial");
```

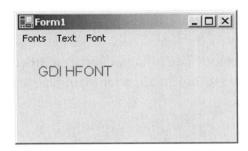

FIGURE 5.12: Using the `FromHFont` method

The Font class provides more than a dozen overloaded constructors, which allow an application to construct a Font object in different ways, either from string names of a font family and size or from a FontFamily object with font style and optional GraphicsUnit values.

The simplest way to create a Font object is to pass the font family name as the first argument and the point size as the second argument of the Font constructor. The following code snippet creates a Times New Roman 12-point font:

```
Font tnwFont = new Font("Times New Roman", 12);
```

The following code snippet creates three fonts in different styles belonging to the Verdana, Tahoma, and Arial font families, respectively:

```
// Create font families
FontFamily verdanaFamily = new FontFamily("Verdana");
FontFamily arialFamily = new FontFamily("Arial");
// Construct Font objects
Font verdanaFont = new Font( verdanaFamily, 14,
    FontStyle.Regular, GraphicsUnit.Pixel);
Font tahomaFont = new Font( new FontFamily("Tahoma"), 10,
    FontStyle.Bold|FontStyle.Italic, GraphicsUnit.Pixel);
Font arialFont = new Font(arialFamily, 16, FontStyle.Bold,
    GraphicsUnit.Point);
Font tnwFont = new Font("Times New Roman", 12);
```

> **■ NOTE**
>
> As the code example here shows, you can use the FontStyle and GraphicsUnit enumerations to define the style and units of a font, respectively.

If you don't want to create and use a FontFamily object in constructing a font, you can pass the font family name and size directly when you create a new Font object. The following code snippet creates three fonts from the Verdana, Arial, and Tahoma font families, respectively, with different sizes and styles:

```
// Construct Font objects
Font verdanaFont = new Font( "Verdana", 12);
```

```
Font arialFont = new Font( arialFamily, 10);
Font tahomaFont = new Font( "Arial", 14,
   FontStyle.Underline|FontStyle.Italic);
```

5.4 Working with Text and Strings

As we discussed in Chapter 3, the DrawString method of the Graphics class can be used to draw text on a graphics surface. The DrawString method takes a string, font, brush, and starting point.

Listing 5.8 creates three different fonts and draws text on a form using the DrawString method. Each DrawString method uses a different color and font to draw the string.

LISTING 5.8: Drawing text on a graphics surface

```
private void DrawText_Click(object sender,
      System.EventArgs e)
{
     // Create a Graphics object
     Graphics g = this.CreateGraphics();
     // Create font families
     FontFamily verdanaFamily = new FontFamily("Verdana");
     FontFamily arialFamily = new FontFamily("Arial");
     // Construct Font objects
     Font verdanaFont = new Font( "Verdana", 10);
     Font arialFont =
       new Font( arialFamily, 16, FontStyle.Bold);
     Font tahomaFont = new Font( "Tahoma", 24,
       FontStyle.Underline|FontStyle.Italic);
     // Create Brush and other objects
     PointF pointF = new PointF(30, 10);
     SolidBrush solidBrush =
       new SolidBrush(Color.FromArgb(255, 0, 0, 255));
     // Draw text using DrawString
     g.DrawString("Drawing Text", verdanaFont,
       new SolidBrush(Color.Red), new PointF(20,20) );
     g.DrawString("Drawing Text", arialFont,
       new SolidBrush(Color.Blue), new PointF(20, 50) );
     g.DrawString("Drawing Text", tahomaFont,
       new SolidBrush(Color.Green), new PointF(20, 80) );
     // Dispose of objects
     solidBrush.Dispose();
     g.Dispose();
}
```

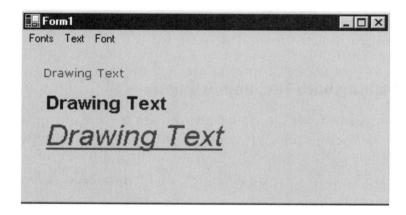

FIGURE 5.13: Fonts with different styles and sizes

Figure 5.13 shows the output from Listing 5.8. The first text is 10-point Verdana; the second, 14-point Arial Bold; and the third, 24-point Tahoma Italic.

> **■ NOTE**
> See Chapter 3 (Section 3.2.1.5) for more overloaded forms of the Draw-String method.

5.4.1 Drawing Formatted Text

The DrawString method can also be used to draw formatted text. To format text, the .NET Framework library provides the StringFormat class, which can be passed as a parameter of the DrawString methods. The StringFormat class provides members to set alignment, line spacing, digit substitution, trimming, and tab stops. These classes are defined in the System.Drawing namespace.

5.4.1.1 Alignment and Trimming

The Alignment and Trimming properties of the StringFormat class are used to set and get alignment and trimming of text. The Alignment property takes a value of type StringAlignment enumeration, and the Trimming property takes a value of type StringTrimming enumeration.

The `LineAlignment` property represents the line alignment of text, which also takes a value of type `StringAlignment` enumeration.

The `StringAlignment` enumeration specifies the alignment of a text string. Table 5.9 describes the members of the `StringAlignment` enumeration.

The `StringTrimming` enumeration specifies how to trim characters from a string that does not completely fit into a layout shape. Table 5.10 describes the members of the `StringTrimming` enumeration.

Listing 5.9 uses `Alignment` and `Trimming` properties to align and trim text strings and draws the text to a form. We use two `String-Format` objects: `strFormat1` and `strFormat2`. For `strFormat1`, we set the alignment to `Center`, line alignment to `Center`, and trimming to `EllipsisCharacter`. For `strFormat2`, we set the alignment to `Far`, string

TABLE 5.9: `StringAlignment` members

Member	Description
Center	Text is aligned in the center of a rectangle.
Far	Text is aligned as far as possible from the origin position of a rectangle.
Near	Text is aligned as close as possible to the origin position of a rectangle.

TABLE 5.10: `StringTrimming` members

Member	Description
Character	Text is trimmed to the nearest character.
EllipsisCharacter	Text is trimmed to the nearest character, and an ellipsis is inserted at the end of a trimmed line.
EllipsisPath	The center is removed from trimmed lines and replaced by an ellipsis.
EllipsisWord	Text is trimmed to the nearest word, and an ellipsis is inserted at the end of a trimmed line.
None	No trimming.
Word	Text is trimmed to the nearest word.

alignment to Near, and trimming to Character. Then we use strFormat1 and strFormat2 as parameters of the DrawString method to apply a string format to the text.

LISTING 5.9: Using the **Trimming** and **Alignment** properties of **StringFormat**

```
private void menuItem11_Click(object sender,
    System.EventArgs e)
{
    // Create a Graphics object
    Graphics g = this.CreateGraphics();
    g.Clear(this.BackColor);

    string text = "Testing GDI+ Text and Font" +
      " functionality for alignment and trimming.";
    // Create font families
        FontFamily arialFamily = new FontFamily("Arial");
    // Construct Font objects
    Font verdanaFont =
      new Font( "Verdana", 10, FontStyle.Bold);
    Font arialFont = new Font( arialFamily, 16);
    // Create rectangles
    Rectangle rect1 = new Rectangle(10, 10, 100, 150);
    Rectangle rect2 = new Rectangle(10, 165, 150, 100);
    // Construct string format and alignment
    StringFormat strFormat1 = new StringFormat();
    StringFormat strFormat2 = new StringFormat();
    // Set alignment, line alignment, and trimming
    // properties of string format
    strFormat1.Alignment = StringAlignment.Center;
    strFormat1.LineAlignment = StringAlignment.Center;
    strFormat1.Trimming =
      StringTrimming.EllipsisCharacter;
    strFormat2.Alignment = StringAlignment.Far;
    strFormat2.LineAlignment = StringAlignment.Near;
    strFormat2.Trimming = StringTrimming.Character;
    // Draw GDI+ objects
    g.FillEllipse(new SolidBrush(Color.Blue), rect1);
    g.DrawRectangle( new Pen(Color.Black), rect2);
    g.DrawString(text, verdanaFont,
      new SolidBrush(Color.White) , rect1,  strFormat1);
    g.DrawString(text, arialFont,
      new SolidBrush(Color.Red), rect2, strFormat2);
    // Dispose of objects
    arialFont.Dispose();
    arialFont.Dispose();
    verdanaFont.Dispose();
    arialFamily.Dispose();
    g.Dispose();
}
```

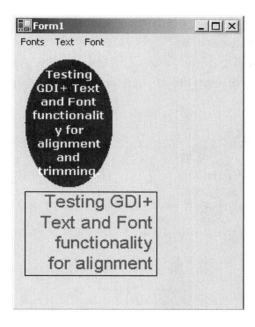

FIGURE 5.14: Alignment and trimming options

Figure 5.14 shows the output from Listing 5.9. Text inside the rectangle is trimmed to fit.

5.4.2 Using Tab Stops

Along with the properties discussed in the preceding section, the String-Format class provides some methods. The GetTabStops and SetTab-Stops methods can be used to get and set tab stops, respectively. Each of these methods takes two arguments: firstTabOffset and tabStops. The first parameter, firstTabOffset, is a float value that represents the number of spaces between the beginning of a line of text and the first tab stop. The second parameter, tabStops, is an array of float values that represents the number of spaces between tabs.

An application can use the SetTabStops method to generate tabular output on a graphics surface. For example, Listing 5.10 uses SetTabStops to generate a tabular data report. In this example we create a String-Format object and set its tab stops using the SetTabStops method, and then we call the DrawString method.

In Listing 5.10 we create a table that lists the grades of a student in tabular format. The table has four columns: ID, Math, Physics, and Chemistry. These columns list the grades obtained by a student. As the listing shows, we create a `StringFormat` object and set the tab stops using the `SetTabStops` method.

LISTING 5.10: Using tab stops to draw tabular data on a graphics surface

```
private void menuItem12_Click(object sender,
    System.EventArgs e)
{
  // Create a Graphics object
  Graphics g = this.CreateGraphics();
  g.Clear(this.BackColor);
  // Some text data
  string text = "ID\tMath\tPhysics\tChemistry \n";
  text = text +
    "————-\t————-\t————-\t————-\n";
  text = text + "1002\t76\t89\t92\n";
  text = text + "1003\t53\t98\t90\n";
  text = text + "1008\t99\t78\t65\n";
  // Create a font
  Font verdanaFont =
    new Font( "Verdana", 10, FontStyle.Bold);
  Font tahomaFont =
    new Font( "Tahoma", 16);
  // Create brushes
  SolidBrush blackBrush = new SolidBrush(Color.Black);
  SolidBrush redBrush = new SolidBrush(Color.Red);
  // Create a rectangle
  Rectangle rect = new Rectangle(10, 50, 350, 250);
  // Create a StringFormat object
  StringFormat strFormat = new StringFormat();
  // Set tab stops of string format
  strFormat.SetTabStops(5, new float[]
    {80, 100, 80, 80});
  // Draw string
  g.DrawString("Student Grades Table",
    tahomaFont,
    blackBrush, new Rectangle
    (10, 10, 300, 100));
  g.DrawString("=============",
    tahomaFont, blackBrush,
    new Rectangle(10, 23, 300, 100));
  // Draw string with tab stops
  g.DrawString(text, verdanaFont,
    redBrush, rect, strFormat);
```

```
    // Dispose of GDI+ objects
    tahomaFont.Dispose();
    redBrush.Dispose();
    blackBrush.Dispose();
    g.Dispose();
}
```

Figure 5.15 shows the output from Listing 5.10. It's easy to present text data in a tabular form by simply using the `StringFormat` class and its properties.

5.4.3 The `FormatFlags` Property

The `FormatFlags` property is useful when an application needs to draw text strings in different layouts—such as drawing vertical text. `Format-Flags` takes a value of the `StringFormatFlags` enumeration. Table 5.11 describes the members of the `StringFormatFlags` enumeration.

> ### ▪ NOTE
>
> An application can apply more than one `StringFormatFlags` member by using bitwise combinations.

As Listing 5.11 shows, our sample code draws two strings. One string is drawn from right to left, and the other is vertical. Using `FormatFlags` is pretty simple. An application creates a `StringFormat` object, sets its `FormatFlags` property, and then uses the `StringFormat` object in the `DrawString` method. Note that an application can use more than one instance of `FormatFlags` for the same `StringFormat` object.

Student Grades Table

ID	Math	Physics	Chemistry
1002	76	89	92
1003	53	98	90
1008	99	78	65

FIGURE 5.15: Drawing tabbed text on a form

TABLE 5.11: `StringFormatFlags` members

Member	Description
DirectionRightToLeft	Draws text right to left in a given rectangle using the `DrawString` method.
DirectionVertical	Draws vertical text in a given rectangle using the `DrawString` method. The default alignment is left (use the `Alignment` property to change the text alignment).
DisplayFormatControl	Causes control characters such as the paragraph mark to be shown in the output with a representative glyph (e.g., ¶).
FitBlackBox	Specifies that no part of any glyph will overhang the bounding rectangle.
LineLimit	Specifies that only complete lines will be laid out in the formatting rectangle.
MeasureTrailingSpaces	By default, the boundary rectangle returned by the `MeasureString` method excludes any space at the end of each line. Set this flag to include that space in the measurement.
NoClip	By default, clipping is on, which means that any text outside of the formatting rectangle is not displayed. `NoClip` disables clipping.
NoFontFallback	By default, if the specified font is not found, an alternative font will be used. `NoFontFallback` disables that option and displays an open square for the missing character(s).
NoWrap	By default, wrapping is on. `NoWrap` disables wrapping.

LISTING 5.11: Using `FormatFlags` to format string text

```
private void menuItem16_Click(object sender,
    System.EventArgs e)
{
    // Create a Graphics object
    Graphics g = this.CreateGraphics();
    // Create a rectangle
    Rectangle rect = new Rectangle(50, 50, 350, 250);
    // Create two StringFormat objects
```

```
StringFormat strFormat1 = new StringFormat();
StringFormat strFormat2 = new StringFormat();
// Set format flags of StringFormat objects
// with direction right to left
strFormat1.FormatFlags =
  StringFormatFlags.DirectionRightToLeft;
// Set direction vertical
strFormat2.FormatFlags =
  StringFormatFlags.DirectionVertical;
// Set alignment
strFormat2.Alignment = StringAlignment.Far;
// Draw rectangle
g.DrawRectangle(new Pen(Color.Blue), rect);
string str =
      "Horizontal Text: This is horizontal "
    + "text inside a rectangle";
// Draw strings
g.DrawString(str,
  new Font("Verdana", 10, FontStyle.Bold),
  new SolidBrush(Color.Green),
  rect, strFormat1);
g.DrawString("Vertical: Text String",
  new Font("Arial", 14),
  new SolidBrush(Color.Red),
  rect, strFormat2);
  // Dispose of GDI+ objects
g.Dispose();
}
```

Figure 5.16 shows the output from Listing 5.11. One text string is drawn from right to left (aligned right) in the drawing rectangle, and the other text string is drawn vertically on the left-hand side. An application can even use `Alignment`, `Trimming`, and other properties to align and trim text.

> **▪ NOTE**
>
> Using the `Alignment` property will remove the effect of `String-FormatFlags.DirectionRightToLeft;`.

5.4.4 Setting Digital Substitution

The `SetDigitSubstitution` method can be used to substitute digits in a string on the basis of a user's local area. `SetDigitSubstitution` takes a parameter of the `StringDigitSubstitute` enumeration, the members of which are described in Table 5.12.

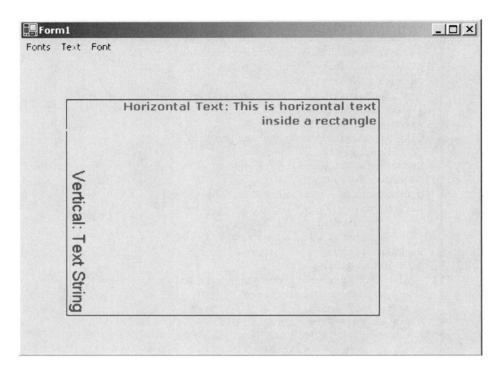

FIGURE 5.16: Using **FormatFlags** to draw vertical and right-to-left text

TABLE 5.12: **StringDigitSubstitute** members

Member	Description
National	Provides substitution digits based on the national language of the user's locale.
None	Disables substitutions.
Traditional	Provides substitution digits based on user's native script or language.
User	Provides a user-defined substitution.

5.5 **Rendering Text with Quality and Performance**

In Chapter 3 (Section 3.1) I said that we would discuss some of the Graphics class members in later chapters. Here we will discuss the TextRenderingHint property of the Graphics class.

> **NOTE**
> The TextRenderingHint enumeration is defined in the System. Drawing.Text namespace.

The TextRenderingHint property of the Graphics class defines the quality of text rendered on graphics surfaces. The quality also affects drawing performance. For best performance, select low-quality rendering. Better quality will produce slower rendering. For LCD displays, ClearType text provides the best quality.

The TextRenderingHint property takes a value of type TextRenderingHint enumeration. The members of the TextRenderingHint enumeration are described in Table 5.13.

Listing 5.12 uses the TextRenderingHint property to draw text with different options. This code draws four different text strings using different text rendering hint options.

LISTING 5.12: Using **TextRenderingHint** to set the quality of text

```
private void menuItem17_Click(object sender,
    System.EventArgs e)
{
    Graphics g = this.CreateGraphics();
    g.Clear(this.BackColor);

    SolidBrush redBrush = new SolidBrush(Color.Red);
    Font verdana16 = new Font("Verdana", 16);
    string text1 = "Text with SingleBitPerPixel";
    string text2 = "Text with ClearTypeGridFit";
    string text3 = "Text with AntiAliasing";
    string text4 = "Text with SystemDefault";
    // Set TextRenderingHint property of surface
    // to single bit per pixel
    g.TextRenderingHint =
      TextRenderingHint.SingleBitPerPixel;
```

continues

TABLE 5.13: `TextRenderingHint` members

Member	Description
`AntiAlias`	Characters are rendered by anti-aliasing without hinting. `AntiAlias` offers good quality, but slow performance.
`AntiAliasGridFit`	Characters are anti-aliased with hinting. `AntiAliasGridFit` offers good quality and high performance.
`ClearTypeGridFit`	Characters are drawn by a ClearType bitmap with hinting. This is the highest-quality setting, with slow performance. It takes advantage of ClearType font features, if available.
`SingleBitPerPixel`	Characters are drawn with each glyph's bitmap. Hinting is not used.
`SingleBitPerPixelGridFit`	Characters are drawn with each glyph's bitmap. Hinting is used to improve character appearance on stems and curvature.
`SystemDefault`	Characters are drawn with each glyph's bitmap, with the system's default rendering hint.

```
// Draw string
g.DrawString(text1, verdana16, redBrush,
  new PointF(10, 10));
// Set TextRenderingHint property of surface
// to ClearType grid fit
g.TextRenderingHint =
  TextRenderingHint.ClearTypeGridFit;
// Draw string
g.DrawString(text2, verdana16, redBrush,
  new PointF(10, 60));
// Set TextRenderingHint property of surface
// to AntiAlias
g.TextRenderingHint = TextRenderingHint.AntiAlias;
// Draw string
g.DrawString(text3, verdana16, redBrush,
  new PointF(10, 100));
// Set TextRenderingHint property of surface
// to SystemDefault
g.TextRenderingHint =
  TextRenderingHint.SystemDefault;
```

```
  // Draw string
  g.DrawString(text4, verdana16, redBrush,
    new PointF(10, 150));
  // Dispose of objects
  redBrush.Dispose();
  g.Dispose();
}
```

Figure 5.17 shows the output from Listing 5.12. Different `TextRender-ingHint` options result in text with higher or lower quality. (How clearly this shows up will vary on different displays—and it may be hard to see in print.)

5.6 Advanced Typography

Besides the text functionality defined in the `System.Drawing` namespace, the .NET Framework class library defines more advanced typography functionality in the `System.Drawing.Text` namespace. As usual, before using any of the `System.Drawing.Text` classes or other objects, you need to add a namespace reference to the project.

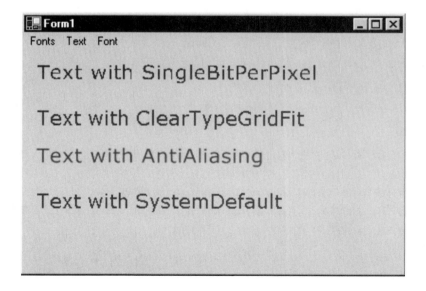

FIGURE 5.17: Using different `TextRenderingHint` settings to draw text

The `System.Drawing.Text` namespace provides three font collection classes: `FontCollection`, `InstalledFontCollection`, and `Private-FontCollection`. The `FontCollection` class works as a base class for the other two classes and provides a property (`Families`) that returns an array containing a list of all font families in the collection.

The `InstalledFontCollection` class represents all the fonts installed on the system. The `Families` property returns a collection of all font families available on the system.

> **■ NOTE**
>
> Before using any of the `System.Drawing.Text` namespace classes, an application must add a reference to the namespace with the "using" directive:
>
> `using System.Drawing.Text;`
>
> Alternatively, you can qualify a class using the namespace as a prefix.

5.6.1 Getting All Installed Fonts on a System

As stated in the previous section, the `InstalledFontCollection` class represents all available font families on a system. The `Families` property returns an array of `FontFamily` type.

Listing 5.13 returns all available fonts on a system. To test this application, add a combo box to a form and write this code on the form-load event handler or a button or menu click event handler.using `System.Drawing.Text` Before executing this code, an application must add the following line:

```
using System.Drawing.Text
```

LISTING 5.13: Using `InstalledFontCollection` to get all installed fonts on a system

```
// Create InstalledFontCollection object
InstalledFontCollection
  sysFontCollection = new InstalledFontCollection();
// Get the array of FontFamily objects
FontFamily[] fontFamilies = sysFontCollection.Families;
```

```
// Read all font familes and add to the combo box
for(int i = 0; i < fontFamilies.Length; ++i)
{
    comboBox1.Items.Add(fontFamilies[i].Name);
}
```

5.6.2 Private Font Collection

The PrivateFontCollection class is used to create a private collection of fonts, for use only by your application. A private collection may include the fonts available on a system, as well as fonts that are not installed on the system. Such a collection is useful when you want to use third-party fonts. The AddFontFile method is used to add a font file to the collection. The AddMemoryFont method reads fonts from system memory and adds them to the collection. The IsStyleAvailable method, which takes a FontStyle enumeration value, indicates whether a style is available.

Normally all system fonts are installed in your Windows\Fonts directory. On our test machine, all fonts are installed in the directory C:\WinNT\Fonts. You can also browse and add fonts from other locations to a private font collection by passing the full path of the font file in the AddFontFile method. For example, the following code snippet adds four fonts to a private font collection.

```
// Create a private font collection
PrivateFontCollection pfc =
    new PrivateFontCollection();
// Add font files to the private font collection
pfc.AddFontFile("tekhead.ttf");
pfc.AddFontFile("DELUSION.TTF");
pfc.AddFontFile("HEMIHEAD.TTF");
pfc.AddFontFile("C:\\WINNT\\Fonts\\Verdana.ttf");
```

In this code we add four fonts to the private font collection. Verdana is available on all machines. The other three fonts can be downloaded from http://www.fontfreak.com (click Enter on site's home page to access naviagation area).

You can even add styles to an existing font. In Listing 5.14 we add four fonts to the private font collection with the AddFontFile method. Then we see if these font families have different styles. If not, we add new styles to the font families and draw text using the new fonts. In the end, we print out the font name on the form.

LISTING 5.14: Using the `PrivateFontCollection` class

```
private void menuItem2_Click(object sender,
    System.EventArgs e)
{
    Graphics g = this.CreateGraphics();
    PointF pointF = new PointF(10, 20);
    string fontName;
    // Create a private font collection
    PrivateFontCollection pfc =
      new PrivateFontCollection();
    // Add font files to the private font collection
    pfc.AddFontFile("tekhead.ttf");
    pfc.AddFontFile("DELUSION.TTF");
    pfc.AddFontFile("HEMIHEAD.TTF");
    // MAKE SURE YOU HAVE THE Verdana.ttf FILE IN THE SPECIFIED
    // FOLDER, OR CHANGE THE FOLDER LOCATION
pfc.AddFontFile("C:\\WINNT\\Fonts\\Verdana.ttf");
    // Return all font families from the collection
    FontFamily[] fontFamilies = pfc.Families;
    // Get font families one by one,
    // add new styles, and draw
    // text using DrawString
    for(int j = 0; j < fontFamilies.Length; ++j)
    {
      // Get the font family name
      fontName = fontFamilies[j].Name;

      if(fontFamilies[j].IsStyleAvailable(
        FontStyle.Italic) &&
        fontFamilies[j].IsStyleAvailable(
        FontStyle.Bold) &&
        fontFamilies[j].IsStyleAvailable(
        FontStyle.Underline) &&
        fontFamilies[j].IsStyleAvailable(
        FontStyle.Strikeout) )
      {
        // Create a font from the font name
        Font newFont = new Font(fontName,
          20, FontStyle.Italic | FontStyle.Bold
          |FontStyle.Underline, GraphicsUnit.Pixel);
        // Draw string using the current font
        g.DrawString(fontName, newFont,
          new SolidBrush(Color.Red), pointF);
        // Set location
        pointF.Y += newFont.Height;
      }
    }
    // Dispose of object
    g.Dispose();
}
```

> **NOTE**
> You may need to change the directory path in Listing 5.14 to match your machine.

To test Listing 5.14, create a Windows application and insert the sample code on the form-paint, a button click, or a menu click event handler, and run the application. Figure 5.18 shows the ouput of the application. All the available fonts in the private font collection are listed.

FIGURE 5.18: Using a private font collection

5.7 A Simple Text Editor

Now let's see how to write a simple text editor in just a few minutes, using the functionality we have discussed in this chapter so far.

First we create a Windows application and add some controls to the form. As Figure 5.19 shows, we add two label controls and set their `Text` properties to **Available Fonts** and **Size**, respectively. Then we add a combo box, a `NumericUpDown` control, and two button controls with the `Text`

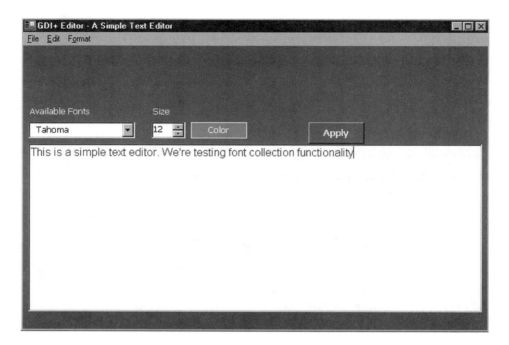

FIGURE 5.19: A simple text editor application

properties set to **Color** and **Apply**, respectively. We will use the combo box control to display all installed fonts, the `NumericUpDown` control to set the size of text, and the **Color** button to set the text color. We also add a `RichTextBox` control to the form and size it appropriately.

Now we add the following line to our application:

```
using System.Drawing.Text;
```

We also add two private variables of types `Color` and `int`, respectively, as follows:

```
private Color textColor;
private int textSize;
```

Finally, we double-click on the form and insert the code from Listing 5.15 on the form-load event handler, thereby setting the `NumericUp-Down` control's `Value` property to 10 and adding all installed fonts to the combo box control.

LISTING 5.15: The form-load event handler

```
private void Form1_Load(object sender,
     System.EventArgs e)
{
     numericUpDown1.Value = 10;
     // Create InstalledFontCollection object
     InstalledFontCollection
       sysFontCollection =
       new InstalledFontCollection();
     // Get the array of FontFamily objects
     FontFamily[] fontFamilies =
       sysFontCollection.Families;
     // Read all font familes and
     // add to the combo box
     foreach (FontFamily ff in fontFamilies)
     {
       comboBox1.Items.Add(ff.Name);
     }
     comboBox1.Text = fontFamilies[0].Name;
}
```

The **Color** button click event handler simply calls `ColorDialog`, which allows the user to pick the text color (see Listing 5.16).

LISTING 5.16: Getting color from `ColorDialog`

```
private void button1_Click(object sender,
     System.EventArgs e)
{
     // Create a color dialog and let
     // the user select a color.
     // Save the selected color.
     ColorDialog colorDlg = new ColorDialog();
     if(colorDlg.ShowDialog() == DialogResult.OK)
     {
       textColor = colorDlg.Color;
     }
}
```

The **Apply** button reads the selected font name from the combo box and the size from the `NumericUpDown` control. Then it creates a `Font` object using the font family name and size. Finally, we set the `ForeColor` and `Font` properties of the `RichTextBox` control (see Listing 5.17).

LISTING 5.17: Setting the font and foreground color of `RichTextBox`

```
private void button2_Click(object sender,
    System.EventArgs e)
{
    // Get size of text from
    // the numeric up-down control
    textSize = (int)numericUpDown1.Value;
    // Get current font name from the list
    string selFont = comboBox1.Text;
    // Create new font from the current selection
    Font textFont = new Font(selFont, textSize);
    // Set color and font of rich-text box
    richTextBox1.ForeColor = textColor;
    richTextBox1.Font = textFont;
}
```

By extending this simple application and the `RichTextBox` features, you can develop a complete text editor with features that include open and save, find, change font styles, and so on. We'll leave this to you as an exercise!

5.8 Transforming Text

Transformation is a process of moving objects from one place to another by applying a series of operations such as scaling, rotation, and translation. In this section we will see how to transform text using the `Graphics` object.

Transformation using `Graphics` class methods and properties is pretty simple. The `Graphics` class provides the methods `ScaleTransform`, `RotateTransform`, `TranslateTransform` and others.

> ■ NOTE
> See Chapter 10 for detailed information about transformations and how to use various transformation techniques.

Let's look at a simple yet useful example of text transformation. First we draw some text on a form using the code in Listing 5.18.

LISTING 5.18: Drawing text on a form

```
Graphics g = e.Graphics;
string str = "Colors, fonts, and text are common elements "+
"of graphics programming. In this chapter, you learned " +
" about the colors, fonts, and text representations in the "+
".NET Framework class library. You learned how to create "+
"these elements and use them in GDI+.";
g.DrawString(str, new Font("Verdana", 10),
new SolidBrush(Color.Blue), new Rectangle(50,20,200,300) );
```

Figure 5.20 shows the output of Listing 5.18. The text is drawn normally.

Now let's scale the text using the `ScaleTransform` method by writing the following line before the `DrawString` method call. Scaling changes the text size by application of a scaling factor. For example, the following code line doubles the size of text. This code must be added before the `DrawString` method call:

```
g.ScaleTransform(2, 1);
```

Now our text on the form looks like Figure 5.21. It is scaled to twice the regular size.

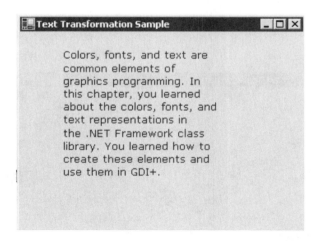

FIGURE 5.20: Drawing text on a form

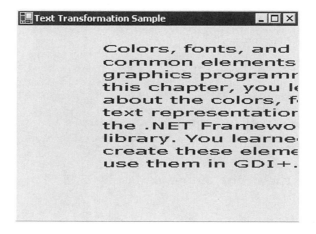

FIGURE 5.21: Using `ScaleTransform` to scale text

Now let's rotate the text, which we can do by calling the `RotateTrans-form` method, which takes a rotation angle. We rotate the text 45 degrees by adding the following line before the `DrawString` method call:

```
g.RotateTransform(45.0f,
System.Drawing.Drawing2D.MatrixOrder.Prepend);
```

Now the text on the form looks like Figure 5.22. It is rotated from its previous position.

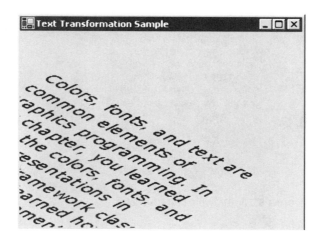

FIGURE 5.22: Using `RotateTransform` to rotate text

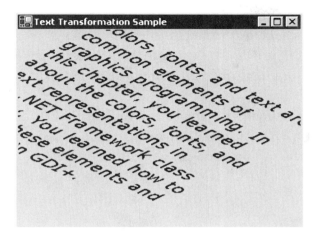

FIGURE 5.23: Using **TranslateTransform** to translate text

Finally, let's call `TranslateTransform`, which takes two values related to the *x*- and *y*-axes. We add the following line after `RotateTransform`:

```
g.TranslateTransform(-20, -70);
```

and our final form looks like Figure 5.23. The text has been moved (or "translated") from its previous position.

SUMMARY

We started this chapter by discussing the basics of colors, fonts, and text-related functionality and classes defined in the .NET Framework. In the colors section, we covered how to use the `Color` class and its members, including system colors. We also discussed color spaces, and how to translate colors from one to another.

In the fonts section, we discussed how to use the `Font` class and related classes to create various types of fonts with different sizes and colors. We also discussed how to control the font families, including system and private font collections, and use them in our application.

The text section covered some uses of fonts and strings. We discussed how to format text, including aligning, tab stops, trimming, and hinting. We also discussed how to improve the quality and speed of text rendering by using various settings. Then we created a text editor illustrating how to use color-, font-, and text-related functionality in a real-world application.

At the end of the chapter we discussed some text transformation techniques, including scaling, rotation, and translation of text from one position to another.

Chapter 3 mentioned rectangles and regions only briefly, but regions and rectangles play a major role in application development and rendering performance. In Chapter 6 we will discuss rectangles and regions in detail.

▪ 6▪
Rectangles and Regions

I N PREVIOUS CHAPTERS we discussed rectangles and how to draw and fill them using the draw and fill methods of the `Graphics` class. In this chapter we will discuss additional functionality of rectangles and regions.

We will cover the following key topics:

- .NET Framework objects that work with rectangles and regions and their members
- `Graphics` class members that work with rectangles and regions
- Writing applications using objects
- The `Rectangle` structure and its members
- The `Region` class and its members
- Invalidating and clipping regions
- Examples of real-world applications using regions and rectangles

A rectangle has three properties: starting point, height, and width. Figure 6.1 shows these properties where the starting point is the top left.

Suppose you wanted to draw a rectangle from point (1, 2) with height 7 and width 6. The final rectangle would look like Figure 6.2.

The filled rectangle occupies the entire area within the range of its height and width.

Starting Point (x, y)

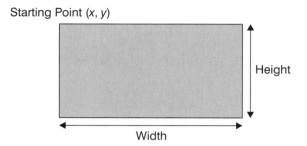

Height

Width

FIGURE 6.1: A rectangle

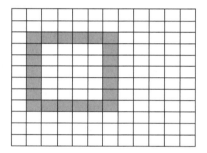

FIGURE 6.2: A rectangle with starting point (1, 2), height 7, and width 6

6.1 The `Rectangle` Structure

In Chapter 2 we discussed the `Rectangle` and `RectangleF` structures, and how to use their properties and methods. In this chapter we will discuss the functionality that we missed in Chapter 2. To refresh your memory, let's take a quick look at the `Rectangle` structure.

A `Rectangle` object stores the top left corner and height and width of a rectangular region. In this section we will see how to create and use the `Rectangle` structure.

6.1.1 Constructing a `Rectangle` Object

There are several ways to create a `Rectangle` object. For example, you can create a `Rectangle` object from four integer values representing the starting point and size of the rectangle, or from `Point` and `Size` structures. Listing 6.1 creates `Rectangle` objects from `Size`, `Point`, and direct values. As this code shows, a `Rectangle` constructor can take a `Point` and a `Size` object or, alternatively, the starting point (as separate variables `x` and `y`), width, and height.

LISTING 6.1: Constructing `Rectangle` objects

```
int x = 20;
int y = 30;
int height = 30;
int width = 30;
// Create a starting point
Point pt = new Point(10, 10);
// Create a size
Size sz = new Size(60, 40);
// Create a rectangle from a point
// and a size
Rectangle rect1 = new Rectangle(pt, sz);
Rectangle rect2 =
new Rectangle(x, y, width, height);
```

6.1.2 **Constructing a** `RectangleF` **Object**

You can also create a `RectangleF` object in several ways: from four floating point numbers with the starting and ending points and height and width of the rectangle, or from a point and a size. `RectangleF` is a mirror of `Rectangle`, including properties and methods. The only difference is that `RectangleF` takes floating point values. For example, instead of `Size` and `Point`, `RectangleF` uses `SizeF` and `PointF`. Listing 6.2 creates `RectangleF` objects in two different ways.

LISTING 6.2: Constructing `RectangleF` objects

```
// Create a starting point
PointF pt = new PointF(30.8f, 20.7f);
// Create a size
SizeF sz = new SizeF(60.0f, 40.0f);
// Create a rectangle from a point and
// a size
RectangleF rect1 = new RectangleF(pt, sz);
// Create a rectangle from floating points
RectangleF rect2 =
new RectangleF(40.2f, 40.6f, 100.5f, 100.0f);
```

6.1.3 Rectangle **Properties and Methods**

The Rectangle structure provides properties that include Bottom, Top, Left, Right, Height, Width, IsEmpty, Location, Size, X, and Y. Listing 6.3 creates two rectangles (rect1 and rect2), reads these properties, and displays their values in a message box.

LISTING 6.3: Using the the Rectangle structure properties

```csharp
private void PropertiesMenu_Click(object sender,
    System.EventArgs e)
{
    // Create a point
    PointF pt = new PointF(30.8f, 20.7f);
    // Create a size
    SizeF sz = new SizeF(60.0f, 40.0f);
    // Create a rectangle from a point and
    // a size
    RectangleF rect1 = new RectangleF(pt, sz);
    // Create a rectangle from floating points
    RectangleF rect2 =
      new RectangleF(40.2f, 40.6f, 100.5f, 100.0f);
    // If rectangle is empty,
    // set its Location, Width, and Height
    // properties
    if (rect1.IsEmpty)
    {
      rect1.Location = pt;
      rect1.Width = sz.Width;
      rect1.Height = sz.Height;
    }
    // Read properties and display
    string str =
      "Location:"+ rect1.Location.ToString();
    str += "X:"+rect1.X.ToString() + "\n";
    str += "Y:"+ rect1.Y.ToString() + "\n";
    str += "Left:"+ rect1.Left.ToString() + "\n";
    str += "Right:"+ rect1.Right.ToString() + "\n";
    str += "Top:"+ rect1.Top.ToString() + "\n";
    str += "Bottom:"+ rect1.Bottom.ToString();
    MessageBox.Show(str);
}
```

As we discussed in Chapter 2, the Rectangle structure provides methods that include Round, Truncate, Inflate, Ceiling, Intersect, and Union.

- The `Round` method converts a `RectangleF` object to a `Rectangle` object by rounding off the values of `RectangleF` to the nearest integer.

- The `Truncate` method converts a `RectangleF` object to a `Rectangle` object by truncating the values of `RectangleF`.

- The `Inflate` method creates a rectangle inflated by the specified amount.

- The `Ceiling` method converts a `RectangleF` object to a `Rectangle` object by rounding to the next higher integer values.

- The `Intersect` method replaces a rectangle by its intersection with a supplied rectangle.

- The `Union` method gets a rectangle that contains the union of two rectangles.

Listing 6.4 shows how to use the `Round`, `Truncate`, `Inflate`, `Ceiling`, `Intersect`, and `Union` methods.

LISTING 6.4: Using the `Rectangle` structure methods

```
private void MethodsMenu_Click(object sender,
    System.EventArgs e)
{
    // Create a Graphics object
    Graphics g = this.CreateGraphics();
    // Create a point and a size
    PointF pt = new PointF(30.8f, 20.7f);
    SizeF sz = new SizeF(60.0f, 40.0f);
    // Create two rectangles
    RectangleF rect1 = new RectangleF(pt, sz);
    RectangleF rect2 =
      new RectangleF(40.2f, 40.6f, 100.5f, 100.0f);
    // Ceiling a rectangle
    Rectangle rect3 = Rectangle.Ceiling(rect1);
    // Truncate a rectangle
    Rectangle rect4 = Rectangle.Truncate(rect1);
    // Round a rectangle
    Rectangle rect5 = Rectangle.Round(rect2);
    // Draw rectangles
    g.DrawRectangle(Pens.Black, rect3);
    g.FillRectangle(Brushes.Red, rect5);
```

continues

```
    // Intersect a rectangle
    Rectangle isectRect =
      Rectangle.Intersect(rect3, rect5);
    // Fill rectangle
    g.FillRectangle(
      new SolidBrush(Color.Blue), isectRect);
    // Inflate a rectangle
    Size inflateSize = new Size(0, 40);
    isectRect.Inflate(inflateSize);
    // Draw rectangle
    g.DrawRectangle(Pens.Blue, isectRect);
    // Empty rectangle and set its properties
    rect4 = Rectangle.Empty;
    rect4.Location = new Point(50, 50);
    rect4.X = 30;
    rect4.Y = 40;
    // Union rectangles
    Rectangle unionRect =
      Rectangle.Union(rect4, rect5);
    // Draw rectangle
    g.DrawRectangle(Pens.Green, unionRect);
    // Displose of objects
    g.Dispose();
}
```

Figure 6.3 shows the output of Listing 6.3.

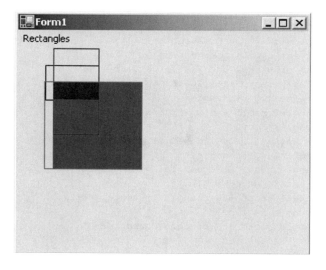

FIGURE 6.3: Using `Rectangle` methods

6.1.3.1 *The Contains Method and Hit Test*

The Contains method is used to determine whether a rectangle or point is inside the current rectangle. If a point is inside the current rectangle, the Contains method returns true; otherwise it returns false. One of the common uses of Contains is to find out if a mouse button was clicked inside a rectangle.

6.1.3.2 *Hit Test Example*

To see proper use of the Contains method, let's create a Windows application and draw a rectangle on the form. Whether the user clicks inside or outside of the rectangle, we will have the application generate an appropriate message.

First we define a class-level Rectangle variable as follows:

```
Rectangle bigRect = new Rectangle(50, 50, 100, 100);
```

Then we use the form's paint event handler because we want to render graphics whenever the form needs to refresh. The form's paint event handler code looks like this:

```
private void Form1_Paint(object sender,
System.Windows.Forms.PaintEventArgs e)
{
    SolidBrush brush = new SolidBrush(Color.Green);
    e.Graphics.FillRectangle(brush, bigRect);
    brush.Dispose();
}
```

Our last step is to determine whether the user clicked inside the rectangle. We track the user's mouse-down event and write code for the left mouse button click event handler. The MouseEventArgs enumeration provides members to find out which mouse button is clicked. The MouseButtons enumeration has members that include Left, Middle, None, Right, Xbutton1, and Xbutton2, which represent the mouse buttons.

We check to see if the mouse button clicked was the left button, then create a rectangle, and (if the mouse button was clicked) generate a message. Listing 6.5 shows the code for this process.

LISTING 6.5: Determining whether a mouse was clicked inside a rectangle

```
private void Form1_MouseDown(object sender,
System.Windows.Forms.MouseEventArgs e)
{
  if(e.Button == MouseButtons.Left)
  {
    if (bigRect.Contains( new Point(e.X, e.Y)) )
      MessageBox.Show("Clicked inside rectangle");
    else
      MessageBox.Show("Clicked outside rectangle");
  }
}
```

When you run the application and click on the rectangle, the output looks like Figure 6.4.

The `Contains` method also allows us to find out whether a rectangle fits inside another rectangle. Listing 6.6 checks whether `smallRect` is within `bigRect`.

LISTING 6.6: Checking if one rectangle is within another

```
Point pt = new Point(0, 0);
Size sz = new Size(200, 200);
```

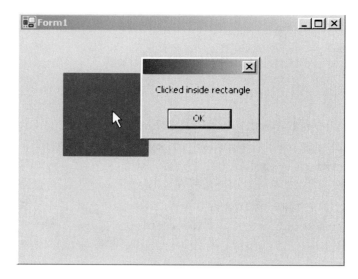

FIGURE 6.4: Hit test using the `Contains` method

```
Rectangle bigRect = new Rectangle(pt, sz);
Rectangle smallRect = new Rectangle(30, 20, 100, 100);
if (bigRect.Contains(smallRect) )
  MessageBox.Show("Rectangle "+smallRect.ToString()
  +" is inside Rectangle "+ bigRect.ToString() );
```

6.2 **The** `Region` **Class**

A **region** describes the interior of a closed graphics shape, or form. A form has two areas: a nonclient area and a client area. The **nonclient area** (which does not allow for user-drawn graphics objects) includes the title bar—and, depending on the application, horizontal and vertical scroll bars. This area cannot be used to draw graphics objects. The **client area** is used to draw controls and graphics objects.

In the .NET Framework library, the `Region` class object represents a region. If you have ever developed a complex .NET graphics application that requires a lot of rendering, you may have used this object a lot.

6.2.1 **Constructing a** `Region` **Object**

The `Region` class provides five overloaded forms. Using these forms, you can construct a `Region` object from a `Rectangle`, `RectangleF`, `Graphics-Path`, or `RegionData` object, or with no parameters. The following code snippet creates `Region` objects in different ways using different arguments.

```
// Create two rectangles
Rectangle rect1 =
   new Rectangle(20, 20, 60, 80);
RectangleF rect2 =
   new RectangleF(100, 20, 60, 100);
// Create a graphics path
GraphicsPath path = new GraphicsPath();
// Add a rectangle to the graphics path
path.AddRectangle(rect1);
// Create a region from rect1
Region rectRgn1 = new Region(rect1);
// Create a region from rect2
Region rectRgn2 = new Region(rect2);
// Create a region from GraphicsPath
Region pathRgn = new Region(path);
```

The `Region` class has no properties. After constructing a region, an application can use the `Graphics` class's `FillRegion` method to fill the region.

Table 6.1 describes the methods of the `Region` class briefly. They are discussed in detail in Sections 6.2.2 through 6.2.4.

6.2.2 **The** `Complement, Exclude,` **and** `Union` **Methods**

We saw the `Region` class methods in Table 6.1. Now let's use these methods in our applications.

The `Complement` method updates the portion of a `Region` object (specified by a rectangle or a region) that does not intersect the specified region. It takes an argument of type `Rectangle`, `RectangleF`, `GraphicsPath`, or `Region` and updates the region. Listing 6.7 creates two `Region` objects and draws rectangles with different pens. The `Complement` method updates only the portion of the first region that falls within the second region.

LISTING 6.7: Using the `Complement` method of the `Region` class

```
// Create Graphics object
Graphics g = this.CreateGraphics();
// Create two rectangles
Rectangle rect1 = new Rectangle(20, 20, 60, 80);
Rectangle rect2 = new Rectangle(50, 30, 60, 80);
// Create two regions
Region rgn1 = new Region(rect1);
Region rgn2 = new Region(rect2);
// Draw rectangles
g.DrawRectangle(Pens.Green, rect1);
g.DrawRectangle(Pens.Black, rect2);
// Complement can take Rectangle, RectangleF,
// Region, or GraphicsPath as an argument
rgn1.Complement(rgn2);
// rgn1.Complement(rect2);
g.FillRegion(Brushes.Blue, rgn1);
// Dispose of object
g.Dispose();
```

Figure 6.5 shows the output from Listing 6.7. Our code updates a portion of `rgn1` that doesn't intersect with `rgn2`. It is useful when you need to update only a specific part of a region. For example, suppose you're writing a shooting game application and your program updates the targets only after gunfire. In this scenario you need to update only the target region, not the entire form.

TABLE 6.1: `Region` methods

Method	Description
`Clone`	Creates an exact copy of a region.
`Complement`	Updates a region to the portion of a rectangle that does not intersect with the region.
`Exclude`	Updates a region to the portion of its interior that does not intersect with a rectangle.
`FromHrgn`	Creates a new `Region` object from a handle to the specified existing GDI region.
`GetBounds`	Returns a `RectangleF` structure that represents a rectangle that bounds a region.
`GetHrgn`	Returns a window handle for a region.
`GetRegionData`	Returns a `RegionData` object for a region. `RegionData` contains information describing a region.
`GetRegionScans`	Returns an array of `RectangleF` structures that approximate a region.
`Intersect`	Updates a region to the intersection of itself with another region.
`IsEmpty`	Returns `true` if a region is empty; otherwise returns `false`.
`IsInfinite`	Returns `true` if a region has an infinite interior; otherwise returns `false`.
`IsVisible`	Returns `true` if the specified rectangle is contained within a region.
`MakeEmpty`	Marks a region as empty.
`MakeInfinite`	Marks a region as infinite.
`Transform`	Applies the transformation matrix to the region.
`Translate`	Offsets the coordinates of a region by the specified amount.
`Union`	Updates a region to the union of itself and the given graphics path.
`Xor`	Updates a region to the union minus the intersection of itself with the given graphics path.

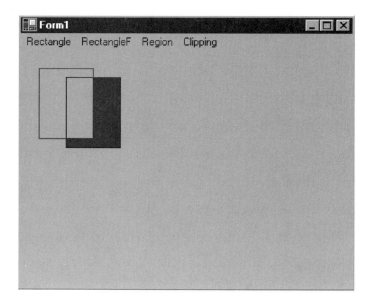

FIGURE 6.5: Complementing regions

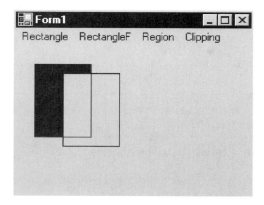

FIGURE 6.6: Excluding regions

The `Exclude` method updates the part of a region that does not interact with the specified region or rectangle. Like `Complement`, `Exclude` takes an argument of type `Rectangle`, `RectangleF`, `GraphicsPath`, or `Region` and updates the region. Listing 6.8 creates two `Region` objects and draws rectangles with different pens, then calls `Exclude`.

LISTING 6.8: Using the `Exclude` method of the `Region` class

```
Rectangle rect1 = new Rectangle(20, 20, 60, 80);
Rectangle rect2 = new Rectangle(50, 30, 60, 80);
Region rgn1 = new Region(rect1);
Region rgn2 = new Region(rect2);
g.DrawRectangle(Pens.Green, rect1);
g.DrawRectangle(Pens.Black, rect2);
rgn1.Exclude(rgn2);
g.FillRegion(Brushes.Blue, rgn1);
```

Figure 6.6 shows the output from Listing 6.8. Only the excluded part of the region is updated.

From the code of Listing 6.8, replacing the line

```
rgn1.Exclude(rgn2);
```

with

```
rgn1.Union(rgn2);
```

produces Figure 6.7, which updates the union of both regions (or rectangles). Like `Exclude` and `Complement`, the `Union` method can take `Rectangle`, `RectangleF`, `GraphicsPath`, or `Region` as an argument.

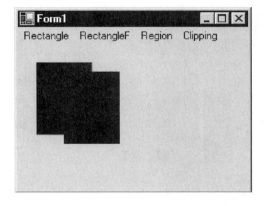

FIGURE 6.7: Applying `Union` on regions

6.2.3 **The** Xor **and** Intersect **Methods**

The Xor method updates the union of both regions (or rectangles) except the intersection area of the rectangle itself. Replacing Exclude with Xor, as shown in Listing 6.9, generates Figure 6.8.

LISTING 6.9: Using the Xor method of the Region class

```
// Create Graphics object
Graphics g = this.CreateGraphics();
g.Clear(this.BackColor);
// Create rectangles
Rectangle rect1 = new Rectangle(20, 20, 60, 80);
Rectangle rect2 = new Rectangle(50, 30, 60, 80);
// Create regions
Region rgn1 = new Region(rect1);
Region rgn2 = new Region(rect2);
// Draw rectangles
g.DrawRectangle(Pens.Green, rect1);
g.DrawRectangle(Pens.Black, rect2);
// Xor two regions
rgn1.Xor(rgn2);
// Fill the region after Xoring
g.FillRegion(Brushes.Blue, rgn1);
// Dispose of object
g.Dispose();
```

The Intersect method is the reverse of Xor. It updates only the intersection region of two regions or rectangles. For example, if you replace line

```
rgn1.Xor(rgn2);
```

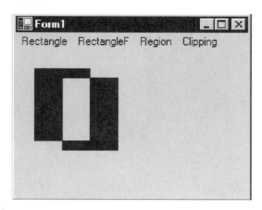

FIGURE 6.8: Using the Xor method of the Region class

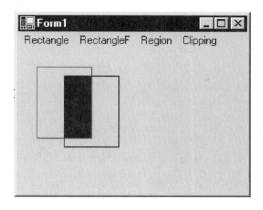

FIGURE 6.9: Using the `Intersect` method of the `Region` class

with the following code:

```
rgn1.Intersect(rgn2);
```

the new output will look like Figure 6.9.

6.2.4 `GetBounds` **and Other Methods**

The `IsEmpty` method takes a `Graphics` object as an argument and returns `true` if a region is empty. Otherwise it returns `false`. `IsInfinite` returns `true` if a region is infinite (otherwise it returns `false`), and it takes a `Graphics` object as the only argument.

The `MakeEmpty` and `MakeInfinite` methods make a region empty or infinite, respectively. An infinite region completely covers the area of a control.

The `GetBounds` method returns the bounds of a region. This method also takes a `Graphics` object as an argument.

The code in Listing 6.10 uses these methods. It makes `rgn2` infinite and fills it with a red pen, which fills the entire form with red.

LISTING 6.10: Using `GetBounds` and other methods of the `Region` class

```
// Create a Graphics object
Graphics g = this.CreateGraphics();
g.Clear(this.BackColor);
```

continues

```
// Create rectangles and regions
Rectangle rect1 =
   new Rectangle(20, 20, 60, 80);
Rectangle rect2 =
   new Rectangle(50, 30, 60, 80);
Region rgn1 = new Region(rect1);
Region rgn2 = new Region(rect2);
// If region is not empty, empty it
if (! rgn1.IsEmpty(g))
   rgn1.MakeEmpty();
// If region is not infinite, make it infinite

if (! rgn2.IsInfinite(g))
   rgn2.MakeInfinite();
// Get bounds of the infinite region
RectangleF rect = rgn2.GetBounds(g);
// Display
   MessageBox.Show(rect.ToString());
// Fill the region
g.FillRegion(Brushes.Red, rgn2);
// Dispose of object
g.Dispose();
```

An infinite region's starting coordinates are negative numbers, and its height and width are large positive numbers, as Figure 6.10 shows. Using `FillRegion` on an infinite region fills the entire form.

6.3 **Regions and Clipping**

As we discussed in Chapter 3, the `Graphics` class provides methods to clip regions. Using these methods, an application can restrict where graphics objects are drawn. One major use of clipping regions is to repaint only part of a control. In some cases painting an entire form is costly in terms of time

FIGURE 6.10: Bounds of an infinite region

and memory resources. Clipping plays a vital role by painting only the desired area. The Graphics class provides the SetClip, ResetClip, IntersectClip, ExcludeClip, and TranslateClip methods to use in clipping operations.

ExcludeClip excludes the area specified by an argument of type Rectangle or a Region and updates the clipping region. Listing 6.11 fills a rectangle, excluding one small rectangle and a region.

LISTING 6.11: Using ExcludeClip to clip regions

```
// Create a Graphics object
Graphics g = this.CreateGraphics();
g.Clear(this.BackColor);
// Create rectangles
Rectangle rect1 = new Rectangle(20, 20, 60, 80);
Rectangle rect2 = new Rectangle(100, 100, 30, 40);
// Create a region
Region rgn1 = new Region(rect2);
// Exclude clip
g.ExcludeClip(rect1);
g.ExcludeClip(rgn1);
// Fill rectangle
g.FillRectangle(Brushes.Red, 0, 0, 200, 200);
// Dispose of object
g.Dispose();
```

Figure 6.11 shows output from Listing 6.11. The small rectangle and small region are not updated.

SetClip sets the clipping region of a Graphics object. This method has many overloaded forms and takes parameters of type Rectangle, RectangleF, Region, GraphicsPath, and Graphics with or without the CombineMode enumeration. The CombineMode enumeration defines how different clipping regions can be combined (see Table 6.2).

The ResetClip method resets the clipping region to infinity. Listing 6.12 uses the SetClip, ResetClip, and IntersectClip methods.

LISTING 6.12: Using the SetClip, ResetClip, and IntersectClip methods

```
// Create a Graphics object
Graphics g = this.CreateGraphics();
g.Clear(this.BackColor);
```

continues

```
// Create rectangles and regions
Rectangle rect1 = new Rectangle(20, 20, 200, 200);
Rectangle rect2 = new Rectangle(100, 100, 200, 200);
Region rgn1 = new Region(rect1);
Region rgn2 = new Region(rect2);
// Call SetClip
g.SetClip(rgn1, CombineMode.Exclude);
// Call IntersectClip
g.IntersectClip(rgn2);
// Fill rectangle
g.FillRectangle(Brushes.Red, 0, 0, 300, 300);
// Call ResetClip
g.ResetClip();
// Draw rectangles
g.DrawRectangle(Pens.Green, rect1);
g.DrawRectangle(Pens.Yellow, rect2);
// Dispose of object
g.Dispose();
```

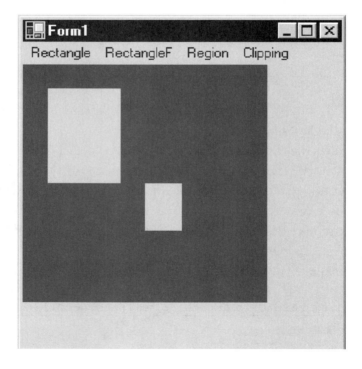

FIGURE 6.11: ExcludeClip output

TABLE 6.2: **CombineMode** members

Member	Description
Complement	The existing region is replaced by the result of the existing region being removed from the new region.
Exclude	The existing region is replaced by the result of the new region being removed from the existing region.
Intersect	Two clipping regions are combined, and the result is their intersection.
Replace	One clipping region replaces the other.
Union	Two clipping regions are combined, and the result is their union.
Xor	Two clipping regions are combined, and the result is their union minus their intersection.

> **NOTE**
> The CombineMode enumeration is defined in the System.Drawing.Drawing2D namespace.

Figure 6.12 shows the output from Listing 6.12.

TranslateClip translates the clipping region as specified. Listing 6.13 uses the TranslateClip method to translate a region by 20 and 30 points.

LISTING 6.13: Using **TranslateClip** to translate a region

```
// Create a Graphics object
Graphics g = this.CreateGraphics();
g.Clear(this.BackColor);
// Create a RectangleF rectangle
RectangleF rect1 =
new RectangleF(20.0f, 20.0f, 200.0f, 200.0f);
// Create a region
Region rgn1 = new Region(rect1);
// Call SetClip
g.SetClip(rgn1, CombineMode.Exclude);
```

continues

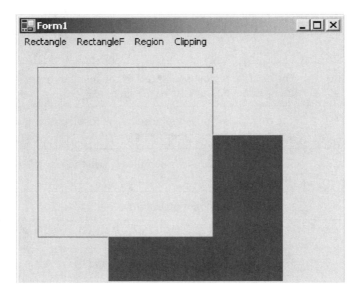

FIGURE 6.12: Using Clip methods

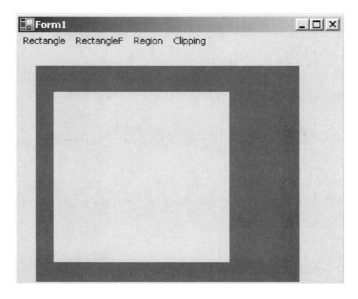

FIGURE 6.13: Using TranslateClip

```
float h = 20.0f;
float w = 30.0f;
// Call TranslateClip with h and w
g.TranslateClip(h, w);
// Fill rectangle
g.FillRectangle(Brushes.Green, 20, 20, 300, 300);
```

Figure 6.13 shows the output from Listing 6.13.

6.4 **Clipping Regions Example**

Listing 6.14 uses Xor to clip regions.

LISTING 6.14: Using the **Xor** method

```
Pen pen = new Pen(Color.Red, 5);
SolidBrush brush = new SolidBrush(Color.Red);
Rectangle rect1 = new Rectangle(50, 0, 50, 150);
Rectangle rect2 = new Rectangle(0, 50, 150, 50);
Region region = new Region(rect1);
region.Xor(rect2);
g.FillRegion(brush, region);
```

Figure 6.14 shows the output from Listing 6.14.

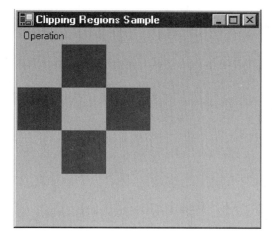

FIGURE 6.14: Result of the **Xor** method

Now if we replace Xor with Union:

```
region.Union(rect2);
```

the new output looks like Figure 6.15.

Now let's replace Union with Exclude:

```
region.Exclude(rect2);
```

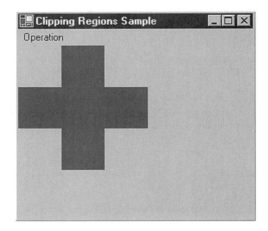

FIGURE 6.15: Result of the Union method

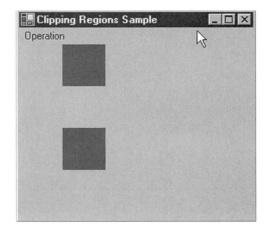

FIGURE 6.16: Result of the Exclude method

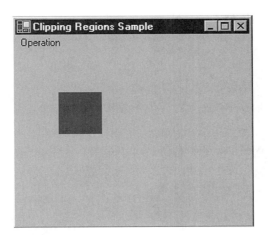

FIGURE 6.17: Result of the `Intersect` method

The output looks like Figure 6.16.

If we use the `Intersect` method:

```
region.Intersect(rect2);
```

the output looks like Figure 6.17.

6.5 Regions, Nonrectangular Forms, and Controls

When we're writing Windows applications with drawing functionality, it becomes important to understand the roles of regions, client areas, and nonclient areas. This section will describe an exciting and wonderful use of regions.

Figure 6.18 shows a typical rectangular form. As you can see, the title bar area usually contains the title of the form, as well as minimize, maximize, and close buttons. This is the nonclient area; the rest of the form is the client area. Graphics objects can be drawn only in the client area. The combination of both client and nonclient areas is the default region of a form.

What exactly is a region? A **region** is a collection of pixels that represents part of a control. GDI+ is responsible only for drawing the region associated with a window (a form or control). The default region of a window includes both client and nonclient areas, so GDI+ draws the entire window.

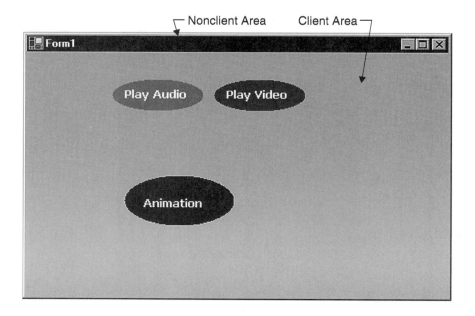

FIGURE 6.18: Client and nonclient areas of a form

However, you can force the operating system to display only part of a window. This is where regions are useful.

6.5.1 The Application

This section will show you the importance of regions and how you can use them in real-world applications.

Have you ever thought about writing nonrectangular forms or controls? How about writing circular, triangular, or polygonal forms, buttons, labels, or text boxes? Our example is a Windows application in which the user can select the shape of the form. The user will have options to change the default rectangular form to a circular, triangular, or polygonal form. You will also learn how to create nonrectangular controls such as buttons.

How can we write nonrectangular forms and controls? GDI+ draws only the regions associated with a form or a control. But setting a nonrectangular region should do the trick. This is what we will do in our application. One of the nonrectangular forms of the final application might look like Figure 6.19. As you can see, this technique can be used to build cool-looking Windows applications.

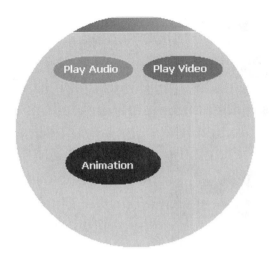

FIGURE 6.19: A nonrectangular form and controls

6.5.2 **Coding**

In Windows Forms, every control, including a form, is derived from the `Control` class. The `Region` property of the control class represents the region of control. If you set the `Region` property of a control, only the area covered by that region will be visible to the user. Sections 6.5.2.1 through 6.5.2.6 describe the steps involved in writing code for nonrectangular shapes.

6.5.2.1 *Step 1: Create the Application*

We create a Windows application, put three controls on the form, and change the `Text` properties of the buttons. We also add a context menu and four menu items, as Figure 6.20 shows. In addition, we add menu and button click event handlers.

6.5.2.2 *Step 2: Add the* `Shape` *Class*

Now we add a class to the project. Our class name is `Shape`, as Listing 6.15 shows. We add two methods to this class: `GetPolyRegion` and `Get-RectRegion`. Both of these methods return a `Region` object. The `GetPoly-Region` method takes an array of `Point` objects as its only argument. We create a graphics path from the points by calling `AddPolygon`. After that we

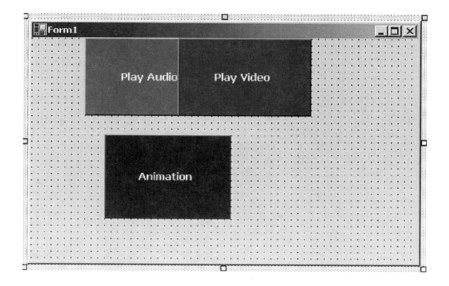

FIGURE 6.20: The nonrectangular forms application

create a region from the path and return it. See Chapters 3 and 9 for more about the GraphicsPath class. Similarly, we create a region from a rectangle in the GetRectRegion method.

LISTING 6.15: The Shape class

```
// The Shape class contains the functionality
// of shaped controls
public class Shape
{
    public Shape()
    {
    }
    public Region GetPolyRegion(Point[] pts)
    {
        // Create a graphics path
        GraphicsPath path =
            new GraphicsPath(FillMode.Alternate);
        path.AddPolygon(pts);
        // Create a Region object from the path
        // and set it as the form's region
        Region rgn = new Region(path);
        return rgn;
    }
```

```
public Region GetRectRegion(Rectangle rct)
{
    // Create a graphics path
    GraphicsPath path =
        new GraphicsPath(FillMode.Alternate);
    path.AddEllipse(rct);
    // Create a Region object from the path
    // and set it as the form's region
    Region rgn = new Region(path);
    return rgn;
}
}
```

6.5.2.3 *Step 3: Load the Context Menu*

Now we load the context menu on the right mouse click of the form. In Listing 6.16, we set the `ContextMenu` property of the form as the context menu control.

LISTING 6.16: The mouse-down click event handler

```
private void Form1_MouseDown(object sender,
System.Windows.Forms.MouseEventArgs e)
{
  if(e.Button == MouseButtons.Right)
  {
    this.ContextMenu = this.contextMenu1;
  }
}
```

6.5.2.4 *Step 4: Call the `Shape` Class Methods*

Now we call `GetRectRegion` and `GetPolyRegion` from the context menu click event handlers to get the region for a rectangle or a polygon. After getting a `Region` object corresponding to a rectangle or a polygon, we just need to set the `Region` property of the form. Listing 6.17 shows the code for the context menu click event handlers.

LISTING 6.17: Menu item click event handlers

```
private void CircleMenu_Click(object sender,
    System.EventArgs e)
{
    // Create a rectangle
    Rectangle rect =
```

continues

```
        new Rectangle(50, 0, 300, 300);
    // Create a Shape object and call
    // the GetRectRegion method
    Shape shp = new Shape();
    this.Region = shp.GetRectRegion(rect);
    this.BackColor = Color.BurlyWood;
}

private void RectMenu_Click(object sender,
    System.EventArgs e)
{
    // A Points array for a rectangle
    // Same points as the original form
    Point[] pts =
    {
        new Point(0, 0),
        new Point(0, originalSize.Height),
        new Point(originalSize.Width, originalSize.Height),
        new Point(originalSize.Width, 0)
    };
    // Create a Shape object and call
    // the GetPolyRegion method
    Shape shp = new Shape();
    this.Region = shp.GetPolyRegion(pts);
    // Set background color
    this.BackColor = Color.DarkGoldenrod;
}

private void TriangleMenu_Click(object sender,
    System.EventArgs e)
{
    // Add three lines to the path representing
    // three sides of a triangle
    Point[] pts =
    {
        new Point(50, 0),
        new Point(0,300),
        new Point(300, 300),
        new Point(50, 0)
    };
    this.BackColor = Color.CornflowerBlue;
    // Create a Shape object and call
    // the GetPolyRegion method
    Shape shp = new Shape();
    this.Region = shp.GetPolyRegion(pts);
}
```

The code in Listing 6.18 for the **Close** menu item simply closes the form.

LISTING 6.18: The Close menu click event handler

```
private void CloseMenu_Click(object sender,
System.EventArgs e)
{
   this.Close();
}
```

6.5.2.5 *Step 5: Display Nonrectangular Shapes*

Using similar methods, you can set the Region property of controls such as Button or TextBox to display nonrectangular shapes. If you don't want to use the Shape class, you can directly set the Region property of a control. Listing 6.19 sets the Region properties of three buttons. We write this code on the form's load event handler.

LISTING 6.19: Setting the **Region** properties of buttons

```
originalSize = this.Size;
// Create a Region object from the path
GraphicsPath path1 =
    new GraphicsPath(FillMode.Alternate);
path1.AddEllipse(new Rectangle(30, 30,
AudioBtn.Width -60, AudioBtn.Height-60));
AudioBtn.Region = new Region(path1);

GraphicsPath path2 =
    new GraphicsPath(FillMode.Alternate);
path2.AddEllipse(new Rectangle(30, 30,
VideoBtn.Width -60, VideoBtn.Height-60));
VideoBtn.Region = new Region(path2);

GraphicsPath path3 =
    new GraphicsPath(FillMode.Alternate);
path3.AddEllipse(new Rectangle(20, 20,
VideoBtn.Width -40, VideoBtn.Height-40));
AnimationBtn.Region = new Region(path3);
```

6.5.2.6 *Step 6: Build and Run*

The last step is to run the application and right-click on the form. Figure 6.21 shows the result of selecting the **Circle** menu option.

Figure 6.22 shows the result of selecting the **Triangle** menu option.

Using this technique, you can build Windows forms and controls of virtually any shape.

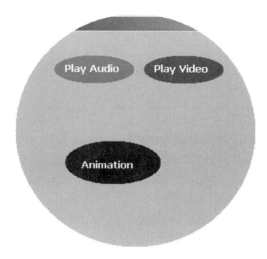

FIGURE 6.21: A circular form

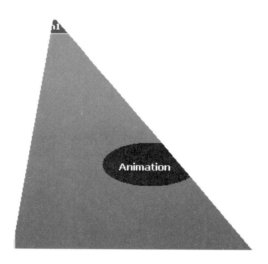

FIGURE 6.22: A triangular form

SUMMARY

In this chapter we discussed some common uses of rectangles and regions. You learned several ways to create `Rectangle` and `RectangleF` objects, and how to use the `Round`, `Truncate`, `Union`, `Inflate`, `Ceiling`, and

`Intersect` methods in your applications. After that you saw an example of a hit test. Then we discussed the `Region` class and its members, and how to use `Complement`, `Union`, `Exclude`, `Xor`, and other methods of the `Region` class. We also saw a sample of clipping regions. At the end of this chapter we saw an interesting sample application that uses regions to create nonrectangular forms and controls.

Imaging is a vital part of graphics. GDI+ provides rich imaging functionality. We will cover this functionality in Chapter 7.

7

Working with Images

I N VIEWING AND manipulating images, GDI+ provides significant improvements over its predecessor, GDI. In this chapter we will discuss the following topics:

- Basic imaging-related classes defined in the .NET Framework library
- The difference between raster and vector images
- The `Image` class, its properties, and its methods
- Writing an image viewer application
- Opening and viewing images
- Retrieving image properties
- Creating thumbnails
- Rotating and flipping images
- Zooming in and out on images
- Saving and skewing images
- Changing the resolution and scaling of images
- Playing animated images
- The `Bitmap` class, its properties, and its methods
- Using the `Icon` class to work with icons
- Drawing transparent images
- Using the `PictureBox` control to draw images

As we said earlier, the graphics-related functionality in the .NET Framework class library is defined in the `System.Drawing` namespace and its helper namespaces. The imaging functionality is divided into two categories by separation into two namespaces. Basic imaging functionality is defined in the `System.Drawing` namespace; advanced imaging functionality is defined in the `System.Drawing.Imaging` namespace. This chapter covers the former; Chapter 8 will focus on the latter.

7.1 Raster and Vector Images

The graphics world divides images into two types: raster and vector.

A **raster image** (also called **bitmap**) is a collection of one or more pixels. Each pixel of the image can be controlled individually, which means that each pixel of the image can have a different color or shade. In a raster image that contains a line and a rectangle, the line and rectangle are each a sequence of pixels. Raster images require higher resolutions and anti-aliasing for a smooth appearance and are best suited for photographs and images with shading.

A **vector image** is a collection of one or more vectors. Mathematically, a **vector** is a combination of a magnitude and a direction, which can be used to represent the relationships between points, lines, curves, and filled areas. In vector images, a vector is the entity to be controlled. Each vector can have a separate color or shade. So a vector image with a line and a rectangle is a set of vectors in which each vector has different properties, such as color or shade. Vector graphics are mathematically described and appear smooth at any size or resolution, and they are often used by mechanical and architectural engineers.

Vector images can be transformed from one state to another without any loss of data. Transforming raster images, however, may cause data loss or reduce the quality of images. For example, in the zoomed raster image shown in Figure 7.1, the outer boundary of the image is blurry.

In the zoomed vector image of Figure 7.2, however, the outer boundary of the image is sharper.

FIGURE 7.1: A zoomed raster image

FIGURE 7.2: A zoomed vector image

7.1.1 **Raster Image Formats**

A bitmap is usually stored in an array of bits that specify the color of each pixel in a rectangular array of pixels. The bitmap's height and width are measured in pixels. The number of bits per pixel specifies the number of colors that can be assigned to that pixel, according to the equation

$$N_c = 2^{Bp}$$

where

N_c = the number of colors that each pixel can display

Bp = the number of bits per pixel

For example, if $Bp = 8$, then $N_c = 2^8 = 256$ colors. If $Bp = 24$, then $N_c = 2^{24}$ = 16,777,216 colors. Table 7.1 shows the number of bits and number of possible colors that can be assigned to a pixel.

Bitmaps with 1 bit per pixel are called **monochrome images**. Monochrome images generally store two colors: black and white.

7.1.2 Graphics File Formats

There are many bitmap image formats, including the following:

- BMP
- GIF
- JPEG
- EXIF
- PNG
- TIFF

7.1.2.1 *BMP*

BMP is a standard Windows format to store device-independent and application-independent bitmap images. The number of bits per pixel (1, 4, 8, 16, 24, 32, or 64) for a given BMP file is specified in a file header. BMP files with 24 bits per pixel are common.

TABLE 7.1: Number of bits and possible number of colors per pixel

Bits	Colors
1	$2^1 = 2$
2	$2^2 = 4$
4	$2^4 = 16$
8	$2^8 = 256$
16	$2^{16} = 65,536$
24	$2^{24} = 16,777,216$

7.1.2.2 *GIF*

Graphics Interchange Format (GIF) is a common format for images that appear on Web pages. GIF uses Lempel-Ziv-Welch (LZW) compression to minimize file size. No information is lost in the compression process; a decompressed image is exactly the same as the original. GIF files can use a maximum of 8 bits per pixel, so they are limited to 256 colors.

7.1.2.3 *JPEG*

Joint Photographic Experts Group (JPEG) is another popular format used on Web pages. JPEG can store 24 bits per pixel, so it is capable of displaying more than 16 million colors. Some information is lost during JPEG conversion, but it usually doesn't affect the perceived quality of the image. JPEG is not a file format; it is a compression scheme. **JPEG File Interchange Format (JFIF)** is a file format commonly used for storing and transferring images that have been compressed according to the JPEG scheme.

7.1.2.4 *EXIF*

Exchangeable Image File (EXIF) is a file format used by digital cameras. It was originally developed by the Japan Electronic Industry Development Association. The EXIF file contains an image compressed according to the JPEG specification.

7.1.2.5 *PNG*

Portable Network Graphics (PNG) format provides the advantages of the GIF format but supports greater color depth. PNG files can store colors with 8, 24, 32, or 48 bits per pixel, and grayscales with 1, 2, 4, 8, or 16 bits per pixel. PNG also supports alpha channel, so it's a suitable format for storing images that support a high number of colors with transparency.

7.1.2.6 *TIFF*

Tag Image File Format (TIFF or **TIF)** can store images with arbitrary color depth, using a variety of compression algorithms. The TIFF format can be extended as needed by the approval and addition of new tags. This format is used by engineers when they need to add information in the image itself.

Almost all image file formats can also store metadata related to the image, such as scanner manufacturer, host computer, type of compression, orientation, samples per pixel, and so on.

7.2 Working with Images

Before we write any imaging code, let's explore the .NET Framework library and see what kind of imaging support it offers. The `Bitmap` class provides functionality to work with raster images, and the `Metafile` class provides functionality to work with vector images. Both classes are inherited from the `Image` class. In this chapter we will discuss the `Image` and `Bitmap` classes and their members. The `Metafile` class will be discussed in Chapter 8.

We'll start this discussion with the `Image` class, which is defined in the `System.Drawing` namespace. Understanding this class is important because we will be using its members in our samples throughout this chapter and the next.

The `Image` class is an abstract base class for the `Bitmap`, `Metafile`, and `Icon` classes. Some common `Image` class properties (all read-only) are described in Table 7.2.

The Pixel Format

The **pixel format** (also known as color depth) defines the number of bits within each pixel. The format also defines the order of color components within a single pixel of data. In the .NET Framework library, the `Pixel-Format` enumeration represents the pixel format.

Besides the properties discussed in Table 7.2, the `Image` class provides methods, which are described in Table 7.3.

7.2.1 An Image Viewer Application

Now we will write an application that will use some of the properties and methods of the `Image` class. You will learn how to open, view, manipulate, and save images. The application is a simple image viewer.

TABLE 7.2: `Image` class properties

Property	Description
`Flags`	Gets or sets attribute flags for an image.
`FrameDimensionsList`	Returns an array of GUIDs that represent the dimensions of frames within an image.
`Height, Width`	Returns the height and width of an image.
`HorizontalResolution`	Returns the horizontal resolution, in pixels per inch, of an image.
`Palette`	Gets or sets the color palette used for an image.
`PhysicalDimension`	Returns the width and height of an image.
`PixelFormat`	Returns the pixel format for an image.
`PropertyIdList`	Returns an array of the property IDs stored in an image.
`PropertyItems`	Returns an array of `PropertyItem` objects for an image.
`RawFormat`	Returns the format of an image.
`Size`	Returns the width and height of an image.
`VerticalResolution`	Returns the vertical resolution, in pixels per inch, of an image.

To begin:

1. Use Visual Studio .NET to create a Windows application project called ImageViewer.
2. Add a `MainMenu` control and some menu items to the form.
3. Change the text of the menu items to **File**, **Open File**, **Save File**, and **Exit**, and the name of these menu items to `FileMenu`, `OpenFileMenu`, `SaveFileMenu`, and `ExitMenu`, respectively. The final form looks like Figure 7.3.
4. Write menu click event handlers for the `OpenFileMenu`, `SaveFileMenu`, and `ExitMenu` items by simply double-clicking on them.

The OpenFileMenu click event handler will allow us to browse and select one image and display it, the SaveFileMenu click event handler will save the image as a new file name, and the ExitMenu click event handler will simply close the application.

Before we write code for these menu event handlers, let's see how to create an Image object from a file and how to display it using the Draw-Image method of the Graphics class.

TABLE 7.3: Image class methods

Method	Description
FromFile, FromHbitmap, FromStream	Creates an Image object from a file, a window handle, and a stream, respectively.
GetBounds	Returns the bounding rectangle for an image.
GetEncoderParameterList	Returns parameters supported by an image encoder.
GetFrameCount	Returns the total number of frames available in an image. Some images include multiple frames. Each frame is a separate layer with different properties. For example, an animated GIF can have multiple frames with different text and other properties.
GetPixelFormatSize	Returns the color depth.
GetPropertyItem	Returns the property item.
GetThumbnailImage	Returns the thumbnail for an image.
IsAlphaPixelFormat	Returns true if the pixel format for an Image object contains alpha information.
IsCanonicalPixelFormat	Returns true if the pixel format is canonical. This is a reserved format.
IsExtendedPixelFormat	Returns true if the pixel format is extended. This is a reserved format.
RemovePropertyItem	Removes the property item.
RotateFlip	Rotates and/or flips an image.

TABLE 7.3: `Image` class methods (continued)

Method	Description
`Save`	Saves an image in a specified format.
`SaveAdd`	Takes one parameter of type `Encoder-Parameters` that defines parameters required by the image encoder that is used by the save-add operation.
`SelectActiveFrame`	Selects a frame specified by the dimension and index. The first parameter of this method is the frame dimension, which can be used to identify an image by its time, resolution, or page number. The second parameter is the frame index of the active frame. Calling this method causes all changes made to the previous frame to be discarded.
`SetPropertyItem`	Sets the value of a property item.

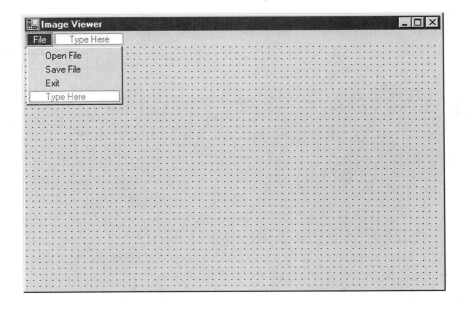

FIGURE 7.3: A simple image viewer application

7.2.2 **Creating an** `Image` **Object**

The `Image` class provides three static methods to create an `Image` object: `FromFile`, `FromHbitmap`, and `FromStream`.

1. `FromFile` creates an `Image` object from a file.
2. `FromHbitmap` creates an `Image` object from a window handle to a bitmap.
3. `FromStream` creates an `Image` object from a stream of bytes (in a file or a database).

For example, in the following line, `FromFile` constructs an `Image` object. Here `curFileName` is a string variable that holds the file name:

```
Image curImage = Image.FromFile(curFileName);
```

We will see how to create `Image` objects from streams and bitmaps in later chapters.

7.2.3 **Drawing an Image**

After creating an `Image` object, you'll want to view the image. GDI+ and Windows Forms offer many ways to view images. You can use a `Form`, `PictureBox`, or `Button` control as a container to view images. In most of our samples, we will draw an image on a graphics surface (a form).

> ■ **TIP**
>
> You can also use a picture box to view images. The `PictureBox` control is easy to use, but using a form as a viewer provides more control and flexibility. For instance, use a `PictureBox` control when you do not need to manipulate or resize images. If you need to manipulate images using operations such as zooming in and zooming out, scaling, and skewing, use a `Form` object as the container because it is easy to change the size of `Form`. Later in this chapter you will see how to use a picture box to draw images.

As we saw in Chapter 3, the `DrawImage` method of the `Graphics` class is used to draw an image. It has 30 overloaded forms. The simplest form of `DrawImage` takes an `Image` object and the starting point where it will be drawn. You can also specify the area of a rectangle in which the image will be drawn. `GraphicsUnit` and `ImageAttributes` are optional parameters, which we will discuss later in this chapter.

The following code snippet creates an `Image` object from a file, and draws the image using the `DrawImage` method. The starting point of the image is (10, 10). You can put this code on the form's paint event handler.

```
Graphics g = e.Graphics;
Image curImage = Image.FromFile(curFileName);
g.DrawImage(curImage, 10, 10);
```

The following code will fit an image into a rectangle that starts at point (10, 10) and has a width of 100 and a height of 100.

```
Graphics g = e.Graphics;
Image curImage = Image.FromFile(curFileName);
Rectangle rect = new Rectangle(20, 20, 100, 100);
g.DrawImage(curImage, rect);
```

If you want to fill the entire form with an image, you can use the `ClientRectangle` property of the form as the default rectangle.

```
Graphics g = e.Graphics;
Image curImage = Image.FromFile(curFileName);
g.DrawImage(curImage, this.ClientRectangle);
```

Before we write code for the menu items event handler, we define `string` and `Image` type variables in the application scope. Add the following at the beginning of the class:

```
// User-defined variables
private string curFileName = null;
private Image curImage = null;
```

Listing 7.1 shows the code for the `OpenFileMenu` click event handler. We use `OpenFileDialog` to browse images and save the file name in the string variable after the user selects a file. Thus we create an `Image` object from the selected file by using `Image.FromFile`. We also call `Invalidate`, which forces the form to repaint and call the paint event handler, where we will be viewing the image.

LISTING 7.1: The `OpenFileMenu` click event handler

```csharp
private void OpenFileMenu_Click(object sender,
    System.EventArgs e)
{
    // Create OpenFileDialog
    OpenFileDialog opnDlg = new OpenFileDialog();
    // Set a filter for images
    opnDlg.Filter =
        "All Image files|*.bmp;*.gif;*.jpg;*.ico;"+
        "*.emf;,*.wmf|Bitmap Files(*.bmp;*.gif;*.jpg;"+
        "*.ico)|*.bmp;*.gif;*.jpg;*.ico|"+
        "Meta Files(*.emf;*.wmf;*.png)|*.emf;*.wmf;*.png";
    opnDlg.Title = "ImageViewer: Open Image File";
    opnDlg.ShowHelp = true;
    // If OK, selected
    if(opnDlg.ShowDialog() == DialogResult.OK)
    {
        // Read current selected file name
        curFileName = opnDlg.FileName;
        // Create the Image object using
        // Image.FromFile
        try
        {
            curImage = Image.FromFile(curFileName);
        }
        catch(Exception exp)
        {
            MessageBox.Show(exp.Message);
        }
    }
    // Repaint the form, which forces the paint
    // event handler
    Invalidate();
}
```

Now we write the `Graphics.DrawImage` method on the form's paint event handler. You can write a paint event handler from the **Properties** window of the form by double-clicking on the paint event available in the events list. Listing 7.2 shows our code, which simply calls `DrawImage`, using the default rectangle coordinates as `AutoScrollPosition`, and the image's width and height.

LISTING 7.2: The paint event handler of the form

```
private void Form1_Paint(object sender,
    System.Windows.Forms.PaintEventArgs e)
{
        Graphics g = e.Graphics;
        if(curImage != null)
        {
            // Draw image using the DrawImage method
            g.DrawImage(curImage,
                AutoScrollPosition.X,
                AutoScrollPosition.Y,
                curImage.Width,
                curImage.Height );
        }
}
```

Now we're ready to view images. Compile and run the application, use the **Open File** menu item to select an image file, and the program will view it. In Figure 7.4, we open a file called `031.jpg`.

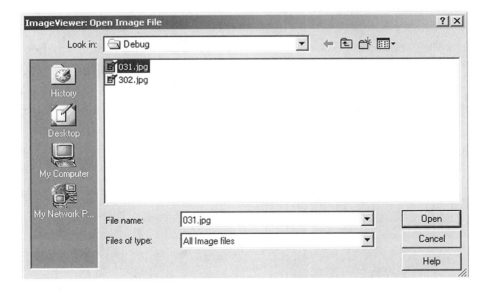

FIGURE 7.4: Browsing a file

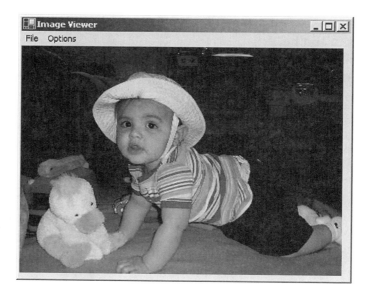

FIGURE 7.5: Viewing an image

Clicking the **Open** button brings up the file for viewing, as shown in Figure 7.5.

7.2.4 Saving Images

Now we move to the **Save File** menu item. It allows you to save images in different file formats.

The Image class provides the Save method, which is used to save images to a specified format. The Save method takes a file name (as string type) or a stream (a Stream object), and a specified format of type Image-Format class. Table 7.4 describes the properties of the ImageFormat class.

> **NOTE**
>
> The Emf and Wmf properties in the ImageFormat enumeration do not save a real metafile, but save the bitmap as one metafile record. It will still be a bitmap.

TABLE 7.4: `ImageFormat` properties

Property	Description
Bmp	Specifies BMP format.
Emf	Specifies EMF (Enhanced Metafile Format). We will discuss this format in Chapter 8.
Exif	Specifies EXIF format.
Gif	Specifies GIF format.
Guid	Specifies a GUID structure that represents the `ImageFormat` object.
Icon	Specifies Windows icon format.
Jpeg	Specifies JPEG format.
MemoryBmp	Specifies memory bitmap format.
Png	Specifies PNG format.
Tiff	Specifies TIFF format.
Wmf	Specifies WMF (Windows Metafile Format). We will discuss this format in Chapter 8.

Now we add code for the `SaveFileMenu` click event handler, as shown in Listing 7.3. We use `SaveFileDialog`, which lets us specify the file name and saves an image using the format specified in the dialog. We read the extension of the file name entered by the user, and on that basis we pass the `ImageFormat` property in the `Save` method.

> **■ NOTE**
>
> The `ImageFormat` enumeration is defined in the `System.Drawing.Imaging` namespace. Don't forget to add a reference to this namespace in your application.

LISTING 7.3: Using the Save method to save images

```csharp
private void SaveFileMenu_Click(object sender,
    System.EventArgs e)
{
    // If image is created
    if(curImage == null)
        return;
    // Call SaveFileDialog
    SaveFileDialog saveDlg = new SaveFileDialog();
    saveDlg.Title = "Save Image As";
    saveDlg.OverwritePrompt = true;
    saveDlg.CheckPathExists = true;
    saveDlg.Filter =
        "Bitmap File(*.bmp)|*.bmp|" +
        "Gif File(*.gif)|*.gif|" +
        "JPEG File(*.jpg)|*.jpg|" +
        "PNG File(*.png)|*.png" ;
    saveDlg.ShowHelp = true;
    // If selected, save
    if(saveDlg.ShowDialog() == DialogResult.OK)
    {
        // Get the user-selected file name
        string fileName = saveDlg.FileName;
        // Get the extension
        string strFilExtn =
            fileName.Remove(0, fileName.Length - 3);
        // Save file
        switch(strFilExtn)
        {
            case "bmp":
                curImage.Save(fileName, ImageFormat.Bmp);
                break;
            case "jpg":
                curImage.Save(fileName, ImageFormat.Jpeg);
                break;
            case "gif":
                curImage.Save(fileName, ImageFormat.Gif);
                break;
            case "tif":
                curImage.Save(fileName, ImageFormat.Tiff);
                break;
            case "png":
                curImage.Save(fileName, ImageFormat.Png);
                break;
            default:
                break;
        }
    }
}
```

Now we write code for the ExitMenu click event handler. This menu simply closes the application. Hence we call the Form.Close method on this event handler, as shown in Listing 7.4.

LISTING 7.4: The **ExitMenu** click event handler

```
private void ExitMenu_Click(object sender,
    System.EventArgs e)
{
    this.Close();
}
```

7.2.5 Retrieving Image Properties

Table 7.2 listed the Image class properties. Now we will read and display the properties of an image. We add a **Properties** menu item to the main menu and write the code in Listing 7.5 as this menu click event handler. We read the size, format, resolution, and pixel format of an image.

LISTING 7.5: Getting image properties

```
private void PropertiesMenu_Click(object sender,
    System.EventArgs e)
{
    if(curImage != null)
    {
        // Viewing image properties
        string imageProperties = "Size:"+ curImage.Size;
        imageProperties += ",\n RawFormat:"+
            curImage.RawFormat.ToString();
        imageProperties += ",\n Vertical Resolution:"
            + curImage.VerticalResolution.ToString();
        imageProperties += ",\n Horizontal Resolution:"
            + curImage.HorizontalResolution.ToString();
        imageProperties += ",\n PixelFormat:"+
            curImage.PixelFormat.ToString();
        MessageBox.Show(imageProperties);
    }
}
```

Figure 7.6 shows the properties of an image.

Size:{Width=415, Height=303},
RawFormat:[ImageFormat: b96b3cae-0728-11d3-9d7b-0000f81ef32e],
Vertical Resolution:150,
Horizontal Resolution:150,
PixelFormat:Format24bppRgb

OK

FIGURE 7.6: Reading the properties of an image

7.3 **Manipulating Images**

In the previous section we covered how to read, view, and save images. In this section we will manipulate images and cover the following topics:

- Creating image thumbnails
- Rotating
- Flipping and zooming in and out (magnifying and demagnifying) images

7.3.1 **Creating a Thumbnail of an Image**

A **thumbnail** is a small representation of an image. The Image class provides a method called GetThumbnailImage, which is used to create a thumbnail. This method's first two parameters are the width and height of the thumbnail image. The third parameter is Image.GetThumbnail-ImageAbort, which is not used in GDI+ version 1.0 but must be passed in for compatibility. The fourth parameter must be of type IntPtr.Zero. This parameter is not used in the current version. If both the width and height parameters are 0, GDI+ will return the embedded thumbnail if there is one in the image; otherwise a system-defined size is used. For most JPEG images from digital cameras, it is better to pass both zeros in for both parameters to get the embedded thumbnail.

To test the thumbnail code, we add a menu named **Options** to the Main-Menu control, as well as a **Create Thumbnail** menu item. We add **Create Thumbnail** as a submenu item or on a button click event handler, as Listing 7.6 shows. We create an `Image.GetThumbnailImageAbort` parameter, and then we call `GetThumbnailImage` with one-fourth the width and height of the original size, followed by the `DrawImage` method.

LISTING 7.6: Creating and drawing a thumbnail image

```
private void ThumbnailMenu_Click(object sender,
    System.EventArgs e)
{
    if(curImage != null)
    {
        // Callback
        Image.GetThumbnailImageAbort tnCallBack =
            new Image.GetThumbnailImageAbort(tnCallbackMethod);
        // Get the thumbnail image
        Image thumbNailImage = curImage.GetThumbnailImage
            (100, 100, tnCallBack, IntPtr.Zero);
        // Create a Graphics object
        Graphics tmpg = this.CreateGraphics();
        tmpg.Clear(this.BackColor);
        // Draw thumbnail image
        tmpg.DrawImage(thumbNailImage, 40, 20);
        // Dispose of Graphics object
        tmpg.Dispose();
    }
}
// Must be called, but not used
public bool tnCallbackMethod()
{
    return false;
}
```

Now we run the application and open `Nee101.jpg`. If we click the **Create Thumbnail** menu item, the new thumbnail image looks like Figure 7.7.

7.3.2 Rotating and Flipping Images

Rotating and flipping are common operations in many imaging programs. **Rotation** rotates an image at an angle that is a multiple of 90. **Flipping** reflects an image on an axis.

The `RotateFlip` method allows us to rotate and flip images. The value of `RotateFlip` is of type `RotateFlipType` enumeration, which defines the direction of rotation and flipping. The members of the `RotateFlipType` enumeration (listed in Table 7.5) are easy to understand.

FIGURE 7.7: A thumbnail image

To rotate and/or flip an image, call `RotateFlip` and pass in any of the values in Table 7.5. The following code snippets show different rotation and flip options.

- Rotating 90 degrees:
  ```
  curImage.RotateFlip(RotateFlipType.Rotate90FlipNone);
  ```
- Rotating 180 degrees:
  ```
  curImage.RotateFlip(RotateFlipType.Rotate180FlipNone);
  ```
- Rotating 270 degrees:
  ```
  curImage.RotateFlip(RotateFlipType.Rotate270FlipNone);
  ```
- Flipping on the *x*-axis only, with no rotation:
  ```
  curImage.RotateFlip(RotateFlipType.RotateNoneFlipX);
  ```
- Flipping on the *y*-axis only, with no rotation:
  ```
  curImage.RotateFlip(RotateFlipType.RotateNoneFlipY);
  ```
- Flipping on the *x*- and *y*-axes, with no rotation:
  ```
  curImage.RotateFlip(RotateFlipType.RotateNoneFlipXY);
  ```
- Rotating 180 degrees and flipping on the *x*-axis:
  ```
  curImage.RotateFlip(RotateFlipType.Rotate180FlipX);
  ```

7.3.3 Adding Rotate and Flip Options to the Image Viewer

Now let's add rotate and flip options to the ImageViewer application.

We add four submenus to the **Options** menu—**Rotate**, **Flip**, **Fit**, and **Zoom**. We will cover the **Rotate** and **Flip** options in this section, and **Fit** and **Zoom** in Sections 7.3.4 and 7.3.5, respectively.

TABLE 7.5: `RotateFlipType` members

Member	Description
`Rotate180FlipNone`	180-degree rotation without flipping
`Rotate180FlipX`	180-degree rotation with a horizontal flip
`Rotate180FlipXY`	180-degree rotation with horizontal and vertical flips
`Rotate180FlipY`	180-degree rotation with a vertical flip
`Rotate270FlipNone`	270-degree rotation without flipping
`Rotate270FlipX`	270-degree rotation with a horizontal flip
`Rotate270FlipXY`	270-degree rotation with horizontal and vertical flips
`Rotate270FlipY`	270-degree rotation with a vertical flip
`Rotate90FlipNone`	90-degree rotation without flipping
`Rotate90FlipX`	90-degree rotation with a horizontal flip
`Rotate90FlipXY`	90-degree rotation with horizontal and vertical flips
`Rotate90FlipY`	90-degree rotation with a vertical flip
`RotateNoneFlipNone`	No rotation and no flipping
`RotateNoneFlipX`	No rotation, with a horizontal flip
`RotateNoneFlipXY`	No rotation, with horizontal and vertical flips
`RotateNoneFlipY`	No rotation, with a vertical flip

We add three items to the **Rotate** submenu: **90**, **180**, and **270** (see Figure 7.8). These items rotate an image 90, 180, and 270 degrees, respectively. You can add as many items as you want. You can even allow users to enter an arbitrary angle.

Now we add three items to the **Flip** submenu: **FlipX**, **FlipY**, and **FlipXY** (see Figure 7.9). These items flip an image about the *x*-, *y*-, and *xy*-axes, respectively. You can add more items if you wish.

Within our program we give the menu items meaningful names. For example, the **90**, **180**, and **270** menu items are represented by `Rotate90Menu`,

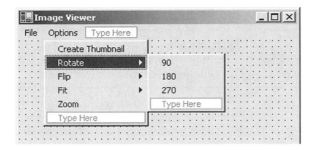

FIGURE 7.8: Rotate menu items

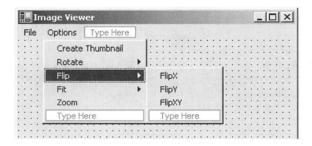

FIGURE 7.9: Flip menu items

`Rotate180Menu`, and `Rotate270Menu`, respectively. And we use `FlipX-Menu`, `FlipYMenu`, and `FlipXYMenu` to represent the **FlipX**, **FlipY**, and **FlipXY** menu items, respectively.

The next step is to write code for the menu item event handlers. To add them, we simply double-click on the menu items. The code for the **Rotate** menu items is given in Listing 7.7. We check whether the `Image` object has been created and then call `RotateFlip` with the appropriate value. We also call `Invalidate` to redraw the image with the new settings.

LISTING 7.7: Rotate menu item event handlers

```
// Rotate 90 degrees
private void Rotate90Menu_Click(object sender,
    System.EventArgs e)
{
    if(curImage != null)
    {
        curImage.RotateFlip(
```

```
                RotateFlipType.Rotate90FlipNone);
            Invalidate();
        }
    }
    // Rotate 180 degrees
    private void Rotate180Menu_Click(object sender,
        System.EventArgs e)
    {
        if(curImage != null)
        {
            curImage.RotateFlip(
                RotateFlipType.Rotate180FlipNone);
            Invalidate();
        }
    }
    // Rotate 270 degrees
    private void Rotate270Menu_Click(object sender,
        System.EventArgs e)
    {
        if(curImage != null)
        {
            curImage.RotateFlip(
                RotateFlipType.Rotate270FlipNone);
            Invalidate();
        }
    }
```

Now let's run and test the application. We open an image, and it looks like Figure 7.10.

Selecting **Rotate | 90** generates the image shown in Figure 7.11.

Selecting **Rotate | 180** generates the image shown in Figure 7.12.

Selecting **Rotate | 270** generates the image shown in Figure 7.13.

We also add code for the **Flip** menu item click event handlers, as shown in Listing 7.8. We simply call RotateFlip with an appropriate value.

LISTING 7.8: Flip menu item event handlers

```
    // Flip X
    private void FlipXMenu_Click(object sender,
        System.EventArgs e)
    {
        if(curImage != null)
        {
            curImage.RotateFlip(
                RotateFlipType.RotateNoneFlipX);
            Invalidate();
```

continues

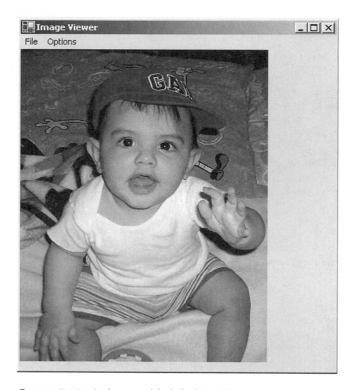

FIGURE 7.10: An image with default settings

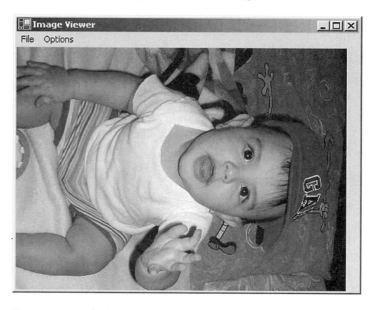

FIGURE 7.11: The image of Figure 7.10, rotated 90 degrees

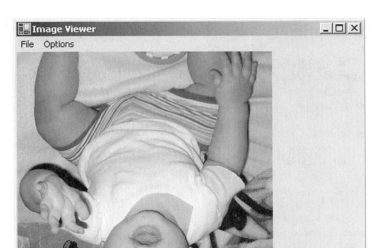

FIGURE 7.12: The image of Figure 7.10, rotated 180 degrees

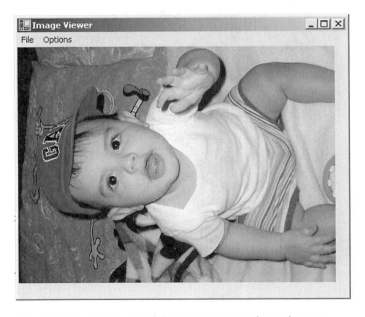

FIGURE 7.13: The image of Figure 7.10, rotated 270 degrees

```
        }
    }
    // Flip Y
    private void FlipYMenu_Click(object sender,
        System.EventArgs e)
    {
        if(curImage != null)
        {
            curImage.RotateFlip(
                RotateFlipType.RotateNoneFlipY);
            Invalidate();
        }
    }
    // Flip X and Y both
    private void FlipXYMenu_Click(object sender,
        System.EventArgs e)
    {
        if(curImage != null)
        {
            curImage.RotateFlip(
                RotateFlipType.RotateNoneFlipXY);
            Invalidate();
        }
    }
}
```

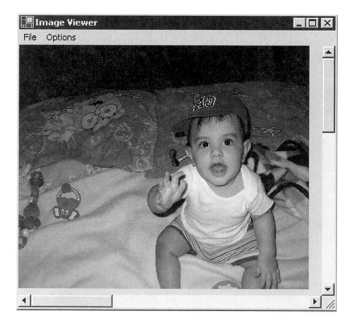

FIGURE 7.14: The image of Figure 7.10, flipped in the *x*-direction

Now if we flip the image shown in Figure 7.10, we can see the difference. The **FlipX** option generates the image shown in Figure 7.14.

The **FlipY** option generates the image shown in Figure 7.15.

The **FlipXY** option generates the image shown in Figure 7.16.

7.3.4 Fitting Images

An application that manipulates images often needs to fit them within the height and/or width of a drawing surface. A fit-width option sets the width of an image to the width of the surface (a form or a control), and a fit-height option sets the height of an image to the height of the surface. The fit-all option sets both the height and the width of an image to the height and width of the surface.

Let's add fit options to our ImageViewer application. We add four menu items to the **Fit** submenu: **Fit Height**, **Fit Width**, **Fit Original**, and **Fit All**,

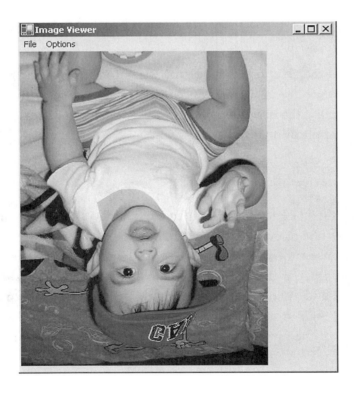

FIGURE 7.15: The image of Figure 7.10, flipped in the *y*-direction

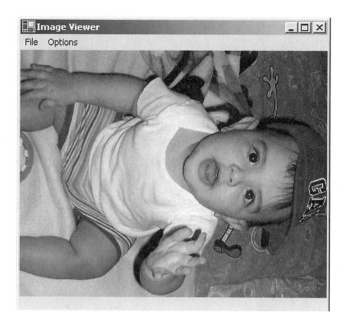

FIGURE 7.16: The image of Figure 7.10, flipped in both the *x*-and the *y*-directions

which will fit the height, width, original size of the image, and both height and width, respectively (see Figure 7.17).

To implement the fit options, we need to add `Rectangle` and `Size` variables at the application level, as follows:

```
private Rectangle curRect;
private Size originalSize = new Size(0,0);
```

We will use `curRect` to store the current rectangle of the image and `originalSize` for the original size of the image.

Now we need to modify the `OpenFileMenu` click event handler. The new code is given in Listing 7.9. We activate autoscrolling by setting the `AutoScroll` and `AutoScrollMinSize` properties of the form to `true`. We create a rectangle from the current size of the image. We also save the current size of the image by setting the `Width` and `Height` properties of `originalSize`.

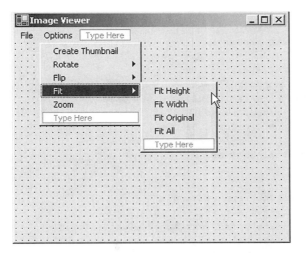

FIGURE 7.17: Fit menu items

LISTING 7.9: Modified Open File menu click event handler

```
private void OpenFileMenu_Click(object sender,
        System.EventArgs e)
{
    // Create OpenFileDialog
    OpenFileDialog opnDlg = new OpenFileDialog();
    // Set a filter for images
    opnDlg.Filter =
        "All Image files|*.bmp;*.gif;*.jpg;*.ico;"+
        "*.emf;,*.wmf|Bitmap Files(*.bmp;*.gif;*.jpg;"+
        "*.ico)|*.bmp;*.gif;*.jpg;*.ico|"+
        "Meta Files(*.emf;*.wmf;*.png)|*.emf;*.wmf;*.png";
    opnDlg.Title = "ImageViewer: Open Image File";
    opnDlg.ShowHelp = true;
    // If OK, selected
    if(opnDlg.ShowDialog() == DialogResult.OK)
    {
        // Read current selected file name
        curFileName = opnDlg.FileName;
        // Create the Image object using
        // Image.FromFile
        try
        {
            curImage = Image.FromFile(curFileName);
        }
```

continues

```
        catch(Exception exp)
        {
            MessageBox.Show(exp.Message);
        }
        // Activate scrolling
        this.AutoScroll = true;
        this.AutoScrollMinSize = new Size
            ((int)(curImage.Width),
            (int)(curImage.Height));
        // Repaint the form, which forces the paint
        // event handler
        this.Invalidate();
    }
    // Create current rectangle
    curRect = new Rectangle(0, 0,
        curImage.Width, curImage.Height);
    // Save original size of the image
    originalSize.Width = curImage.Width;
    originalSize.Height = curImage.Height;
}
```

The paint event handler must also be modified. The new code is given in Listing 7.10. We use the curRect rectangle to view the image.

LISTING 7.10: Modified paint event handler

```
private void Form1_Paint(object sender,
    System.Windows.Forms.PaintEventArgs e)
{
    Graphics g = e.Graphics;
    if(curImage != null)
    {
        // Draw image using the DrawImage method
        g.DrawImage(curImage, new Rectangle
            (this.AutoScrollPosition.X,
            this.AutoScrollPosition.Y,
            (int)(curRect.Width),
            (int)(curRect.Height)));
    }
}
```

The last step is to add event handler code for the **Fit Height**, **Fit Width**, **Fit Original**, and **Fit All** menu options, as shown in Listing 7.11. For the **Fit Width** option, we set the width of the current rectangle to the width of the form; for the **Fit Height** option, we set the height of the current rectangle to the height of the form; for the **Fit All** option, we set both the height and width of the current rectangle to the height and width of the form; and for **Fit Original**, we set the current rectangle's height and width to the height and width of the original file saved as `originalSize`.

LISTING 7.11: **Fit menu item event handlers**

```
private void FitWidthMenu_Click(object sender,
    System.EventArgs e)
{
    if(curImage != null)
    {
        curRect.Width = this.Width;
        Invalidate();
    }
}

private void FitHeightMenu_Click(object sender,
    System.EventArgs e)
{
    if(curImage != null)
    {
        curRect.Height = this.Height;
        Invalidate();
    }
}

private void FitOriginalMenu_Click(object sender,
    System.EventArgs e)
{
    if(curImage != null)
    {
        curRect.Height = originalSize.Height;
        curRect.Width = originalSize.Width;
        Invalidate();
    }
}

private void FitAllMenu_Click(object sender,
    System.EventArgs e)
{
    if(curImage != null)
    {
        curRect.Height = this.Height;
        curRect.Width = this.Width;
        Invalidate();
    }
}
```

Now we compile and run the application, and we view an image. The original image looks like Figure 7.18.

The **Fit Width** option generates the image shown in Figure 7.19.

The **Fit Height** option generates the image shown in Figure 7.20.

Aspect Ratio

To see an image correctly, you may want to maintain its **aspect ratio** (the ratio of height to width). To do so, you need to modify the code so that when you select **Fit Width** or **Fit Height,** the width and the height are changed according to the original ratio.

The **Fit Original** option generates the image shown in Figure 7.21.

The **Fit All** option generates the image shown in Figure 7.22.

7.3.5 Zooming In and Out

Before we finish our ImageViewer application, let's add one more option: zooming.

Adding zoom-in and zoom-out features requires only one operation: multiplying the height and width of the image by a zoom factor. The **zoom factor** is the ratio of the current size of the image to the desired new size of the image. For example, suppose that we want to zoom in an image by 200 percent. We must multiply the current size of the image by 200 percent,

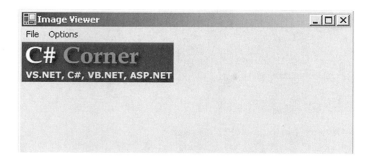

FIGURE 7.18: An image in ImageViewer

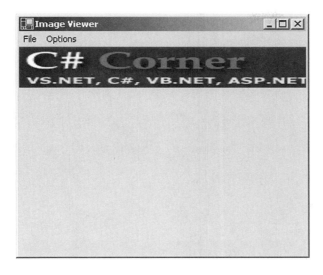

FIGURE 7.19: The image of Figure 7.18 after Fit Width

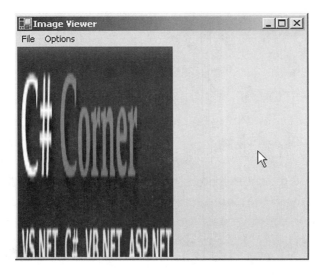

FIGURE 7.20: The image of Figure 7.18 after Fit Height

FIGURE 7.21: The image of Figure 7.18 after Fit Original

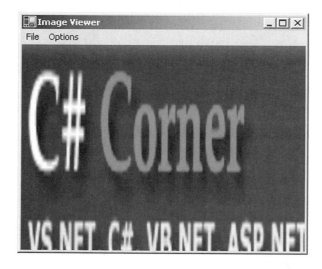

FIGURE 7.22: The image of Figure 7.18 after Fit All

or 2 (200/100 = 2 times). If we want to zoom out an image by 25 percent, we need to multiply the size of the image by 25 percent, or 0.25 (25/100 = 0.25 times).

Now let's add the zoom features to our application. As is typically done, we add five items to the **Zoom** submenu: **25**, **50**, **100**, **200**, and **500** (see Figure 7.23). In our code we use Zoom25, Zoom50, Zoom100, Zoom200, and Zoom500, respectively, to represent these menu items, and we add the appropriate menu item click event handlers by double-clicking on the menu items.

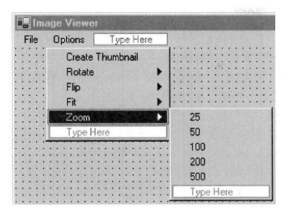

FIGURE 7.23: Zoom menu items

Now we add a double variable that represents the zoom factor. The default zoom factor is 1.0. We add the following line to the class at the application level:

```
private double curZoom = 1.0;
```

Next we modify the `OpenFileMenu` click event handler slightly. We change the `AutoScrollMinSize` property as follows:

```
this.AutoScrollMinSize = new Size
    ((int)(curImage.Width * curZoom),
    (int)(curImage.Height * curZoom));
```

We multiply the image height and width by the zoom factor to represent an image with an appropriate zoom setting.

The next step is to modify the paint event handler. Here we need to multiply the height and width of the image by the zoom factor. The new `Draw-Image` method, shown here, calls the paint event handler of Listing 7.10:

```
// Draw image using the DrawImage method
g.DrawImage(curImage, new Rectangle
    (this.AutoScrollPosition.X,
    this.AutoScrollPosition.Y,
    (int)(curRect.Width * curZoom),
    (int)(curRect.Height * curZoom)));
```

The last step is to add **Zoom** menu item click event handlers and calculate the zoom factor. Listing 7.12 shows the code for the **Zoom** menu item click event handlers. We calculate the zoom factor by dividing the zoom value by 100. We also call the `Invalidate` method to repaint the image with the new zoom setting.

LISTING 7.12: Zoom menu item event handlers

```
private void Zoom25_Click(object sender,
    System.EventArgs e)
{
    if(curImage != null)
    {
        curZoom = (double)25/100;
        Invalidate();
    }
}
private void Zoom50_Click(object sender,
    System.EventArgs e)
{
    if(curImage != null)
    {
        curZoom = (double)50/100;
        Invalidate();
    }
}
private void Zoom100_Click(object sender,
    System.EventArgs e)
{
    if(curImage != null)
    {
        curZoom = (double)100/100;
        Invalidate();
    }
}
private void Zoom200_Click(object sender,
    System.EventArgs e)
{
    if(curImage != null)
    {
        curZoom = (double)200/100;
        Invalidate();
    }
}
private void Zoom500_Click(object sender,
    System.EventArgs e)
{
    if(curImage != null)
```

```
    {
        curZoom = (double)500/100;
        Invalidate();
    }
}
```

Using the method just described, we can zoom an image in and out to any percentage. Let's run the application and open an image. Our original image looks like Figure 7.24.

The **Zoom | 25** option generates the image shown in Figure 7.25.

FIGURE 7.24: An image in ImageViewer

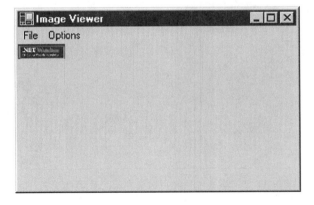

FIGURE 7.25: The image of Figure 7.24 with 25 percent zoom

The **Zoom | 50** option generates the image shown in Figure 7.26.

The **Zoom | 200** option generates the image shown in Figure 7.27.

The **Zoom | 500** option generates the image shown in Figure 7.28.

Congratulations! You have successfully written an image viewer application that can be used for various purposes. Now we will discuss some additional imaging options.

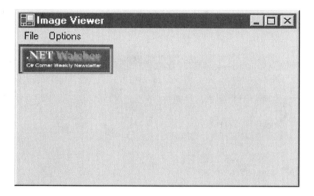

FIGURE 7.26: The image of Figure 7.24 with 50 percent zoom

FIGURE 7.27: The image of Figure 7.24 with 200 percent zoom

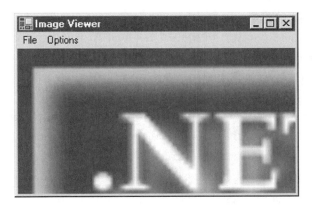

FIGURE 7.28: The image of Figure 7.24 with 500 percent zoom

7.4 **Playing Animations in GDI+**

So far we have been dealing with static image formats, such as BMP. Each of these formats holds image data for a single picture. Other formats—such as GIF, AVI (Audio Video Interleaved), and MPEG (Moving Picture Experts Group)—contain image data that, when played back in quick succession, gives the illusion of movement. These images are called **animated images**. GIF is one of the common formats used for animated images. An animated image is a series of images, also called **frames** (e.g., see Figure 7.29).

You can create animated images by using graphics tools such as Macromedia Fireworks or CorelDRAW, but GDI+ doesn't support the creation of animated images. When you create animated images, you must specify the order of frames and the time interval between them.

FIGURE 7.29: An animated image with three frames

The GDI+ library provides the `ImageAnimator` class to deal with animated file formats using time-based frames. At this time, GDI+ supports only multiframe GIFs and TIFFs. `ImageAnimator` has four static methods: `Animate`, `CanAnimate`, `StopAnimate`, and `UpdateFrames`.

1. The `Animate` method displays a framed image as an animation. This method takes parameters of type `Image` and `EventHandler`. `Image` is the image you want to animate. The event is triggered when the currently displayed frame is changed.

2. The `CanAnimate` method returns `true` when an image has time-based frames.

3. The `StopAnimate` method terminates an animation. It takes parameters of type `Image` and `EventHandler`.

4. The `UpdateFrames` method will move to the next frame and render it the next time the image is drawn.

Now let's write an application that will play animated images. We create a Windows application and add a `MainMenu` control and two button controls to the form. We also add two menu items: **Open File** and **Exit**. We change the text and names of the menu items and button controls as shown in Figure 7.30.

We add two variables of type `Image` and `string` as follows:

```
private Image curImage = null;
private string curFileName = null;
```

The **Open File** menu item allows us to browse images, and the **Exit** menu item closes the form. Listing 7.13 gives the code for the click event handlers for these two menu items.

LISTING 7.13: The Open File and Exit menu item click event handlers

```
private Image curImage;

private void OpenFileMenu_Click(object sender,
    System.EventArgs e)
{
    // Create OpenFileDialog
    OpenFileDialog opnDlg = new OpenFileDialog();
```

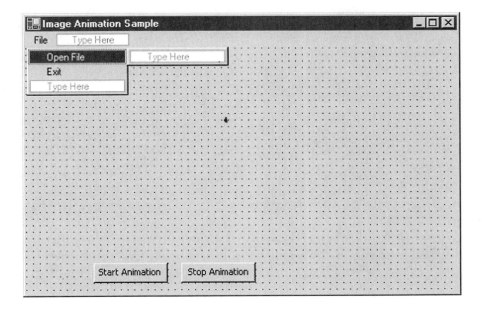

FIGURE 7.30: An image animation example

```
    opnDlg.Filter = "Animated Gifs|*.gif;";
    // If OK, selected
    if(opnDlg.ShowDialog() == DialogResult.OK)
    {
        // Read current selected file name
        curFileName = opnDlg.FileName;
    }
}
private void ExitMenu_Click(object sender,
    System.EventArgs e)
{
    this.Close();
}
```

Now we rename the two buttons **Start Animation** and **Stop Animation**, respectively, and write click event handlers by double-clicking on them. The code for the `StartAnimationBtn` event handler is given in Listing 7.14. We create an `Image` object by calling `FromImage`, which takes an image file as its only argument. Then we use the `CanAnimate` method to check if the image can be animated. If it can, we call `Animate`, which plays the animation.

LISTING 7.14: The **StartAnimationBtn** click event handler

```
private void StartAnimationBtn_Click(object sender,
System.EventArgs e)
{
    curImage = Image.FromFile(curFileName);
    if( ImageAnimator.CanAnimate(curImage) )
    {
        ImageAnimator.Animate(curImage,
        new EventHandler(this.OnFrameChanged));
    }
    else
    MessageBox.Show("Image doesn't have frames");
}
```

On the StopAnimationBtn click event handler, we check whether there is an Image object, and we call StopAnimate to stop the animation as shown in Listing 7.15.

LISTING 7.15: The **StopAnimationBtn** click event handler

```
private void StopAnimationBtn_Click(object sender,
System.EventArgs e)
{
    if(curImage != null)
    {
        ImageAnimator.StopAnimate(curImage,
        new EventHandler(this.OnFrameChanged));
    }
}
```

Now we add OnPaint and OnFrameChanged methods to the application. The code for these methods is given in Listing 7.16. In the OnPaint method, we call the UpdateFrames method of ImageAnimator and then call DrawImage to draw the image. In the OnFrameChanged method, we repaint the form by calling Invalidate.

LISTING 7.16: The **OnPaint** and **OnFrameChanged** methods

```
protected override void OnPaint(PaintEventArgs e)
{
    if(curImage != null)
    {
        ImageAnimator.UpdateFrames();
```

```
            e.Graphics.DrawImage(curImage, new Point(0, 0));
        }
    }
}
private void OnFrameChanged(object o, EventArgs e)
{
    this.Invalidate();
}
```

Now compile and run the application. You can browse animated images on your system or download the files from online and select a file. The **Start Animation** button will start playing the animation. The **Stop Animation** button will stop the animation.

Figure 7.31 shows the first frame of the animation sample provided with this book (download code from online).

Figure 7.32 shows the second frame of the sample.

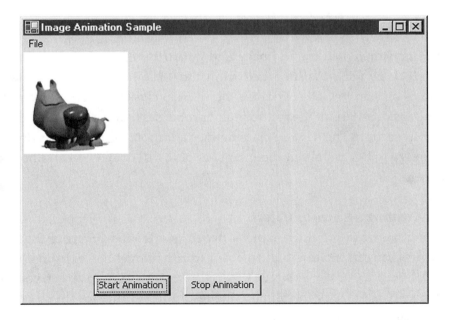

FIGURE 7.31: The first frame of an animated image

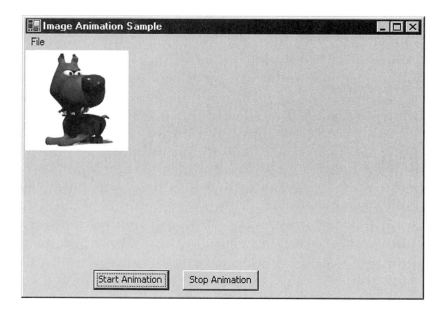

FIGURE 7.32: The second frame of an animated image

7.5 **Working with Bitmaps**

A **bitmap** stores data for an image and its attributes in pixel format. The Bitmap class, which is inherited from the Image class, encapsulates a graphics bitmap in GDI+. Because the Bitmap class is inherited from the Image class, it offers all the methods and properties that we discussed in the previous section. The Bitmap class defines additional functionality. In this section we will learn about the members of the Bitmap class and how to use them.

7.5.1 **Creating a** Bitmap **Object**

The Bitmap class provides about a dozen overloaded forms of the constructors. You can create a Bitmap object from a bitmap file, or from Image, Stream, string, or Type objects. When you create a Bitmap object, you can also specify the size of the bitmap, the resolution of the Graphics object, and the pixel format of the bitmap.

The code snippet in Listing 7.17 creates Bitmap objects from an Image and file name with or without the size of the Bitmap included.

LISTING 7.17: Creating `Bitmap` objects from different sources

```
// Creating an Image object
Image curImage = Image.FromFile("myfile.gif");
// Creating a Bitmap object from a file name
Bitmap curBitmap1 = new Bitmap("myfile.gif");
// Creating a Bitmap object from an Image object
Bitmap curBitmap2 = new Bitmap(curImage);
// Creating a Bitmap object with size and image
Bitmap curBitmap3 =
new Bitmap(curImage, new Size(200, 100) );
// Creating a Bitmap object with no images
Bitmap curBitmap4 = new Bitmap(200, 100);
```

Besides the constructor, the `Bitmap` class provides two static methods—`FromHicon` and `FromResource`—which can be used to create a `Bitmap` object from a window handle to an icon and from a Windows resource (`.res` file), respectively.

7.5.2 Viewing a Bitmap

Viewing a bitmap using the `Bitmap` class is similar to viewing an image. After constructing a `Bitmap` object, you just pass it as a parameter to `Draw-Image`. The following code snippet creates a `Bitmap` object from a file and views the bitmap by calling the `DrawImage` method of a `Graphics` object associated with a form. You can write this code on a menu or a button click event handler.

```
Graphics g = this.CreateGraphics();
Bitmap bitmap = new Bitmap("myfile.jpg");
g.DrawImage(bitmap, 20, 20);
g.Dispose();
```

7.5.3 The `Bitmap` Class Methods and Properties

The `Bitmap` class doesn't define any properties beyond those defined in the `Image` class. However, `Bitmap` does provide additional methods. Among them are `FromHicon`, `FromResource`, `GetHbitmap`, `GetHicon`, `GetPixel`, `LockBits`, `MakeTransparent`, `SetPixel`, `SetResolution`, and `UnlockBits`.

The `FromHicon` and `FromResource` methods create a `Bitmap` object from a window handle to an icon and from a Windows resource, respectively.

The GetHbitmap and GetHicon methods create a Windows HBITMAP structure and a window handle to an icon.

The GetPixel and SetPixel methods get and set the color of the specified pixel of an image. These methods are useful when an application
needs to blur images, change the color of specific pixels, change the contrast
of pixels, and so on. You can blur an image by reducing the color depth of
pixels. We will use GetPixel and SetPixel in examples in this chapter
and the next.

The following line of code returns the color of a pixel at positions $x = 10$
and $y = 10$:

```
Color curColor = curBitmap.GetPixel(10, 10);
```

The following code snippet uses SetPixel to change all pixels between
point (50, 50) and point (60, 60) to red:

```
for (int i = 50; i < 60; i++)
{
    for (int j = 50; j < 60; j++)
    {
        curBitmap.SetPixel(i, j, Color.Red);
    }
}
```

SetResolution sets the resolution of a bitmap. This method takes two
parameters of type float, which represent the horizontal resolution and
vertical resolution in dots per inch.

MakeTransparent makes the default color transparent to a bitmap. This
method takes either no arguments or a single argument of type Color:

```
Color curColor = curBitmap.GetPixel(10, 10);
curBitmap.MakeTransparent();
```

or

```
curBitmap.MakeTransparent(curColor);
```

To test the methods and properties of Bitmap, we create a Windows
application and add **Open File** and **Exit** menu items as in the previous

examples. Then we add controls for a group box, text boxes, a button, a check box, and some labels. The final form looks like Figure 7.33. We can set the resolution and transparency of the bitmap from here.

We add the following application-level variables to the application:

```
// Variables
private Bitmap curBitmap;
private float imgHeight;
private float imgWidth;
private string curFileName;
```

As usual, we browse images on the **Open File** menu item click event handler and close the form on the **Exit** menu item click event handler. We also create a `Bitmap` object from the selected file and store the height and width of the image, as Listing 7.18 shows.

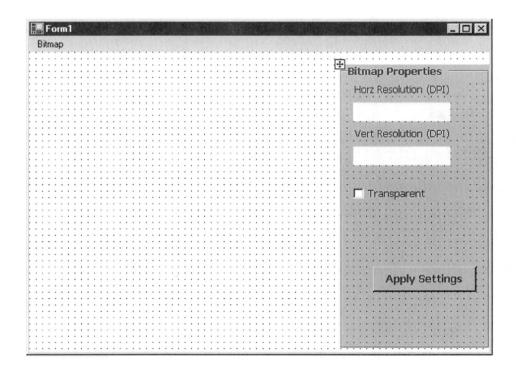

FIGURE 7.33: A bitmap example

LISTING 7.18: The Open File and Exit menu item event handlers

```
private void OpenBmpMenu_Click(object sender,
    System.EventArgs e)
{
    OpenFileDialog openDlg = new OpenFileDialog();
    openDlg.Filter =
        "All Bitmap files|*.bmp;*.gif;*.jpg;";
    string filter = openDlg.Filter;
    openDlg.Title = "Open Bitmap File";
    openDlg.ShowHelp = true;
    if(openDlg.ShowDialog() == DialogResult.OK)
    {
        curFileName = openDlg.FileName;
        curBitmap = new Bitmap(curFileName);
        imgHeight = curBitmap.Height;
        imgWidth = curBitmap.Width;
    }
    Invalidate();
}
private void ExitMenu_Click(object sender,
    System.EventArgs e)
{
    this.Close();
}
```

Now we write code on the paint event handler to view the bitmap (see Listing 7.19).

LISTING 7.19: The paint event handler

```
private void Form1_Paint(object sender,
    System.Windows.Forms.PaintEventArgs e)
{
    Graphics g = e.Graphics;
    if(curBitmap != null)
    {
        g.DrawImage(curBitmap,
            AutoScrollPosition.X, AutoScrollPosition.Y,
            imgWidth, imgHeight);
    }
}
```

The code for the **Apply Settings** button click event handler is given in Listing 7.20. It reads values for horizontal and vertical resolution from two text boxes and sets values for a bitmap using the SetResolution method. It also uses the MakeTransparent and SetPixel methods.

LISTING 7.20: The Apply Settings button click event handler

```
private void ApplyBtn_Click(object sender,
    System.EventArgs e)
{
    if(curBitmap == null)
        return;
    float hDpi = 90;
    float vDpi = 90;
    // Create dpi settings
    if(textBox1.Text.ToString() != "")
            hDpi = Convert.ToInt32(textBox1.Text);
    if(textBox1.Text.ToString() != "")
        vDpi = Convert.ToInt32(textBox2.Text);
    curBitmap.SetResolution(hDpi, vDpi);
    // If Transparent check box is checked
    if(checkBox1.Checked)
    {
        Color curColor =
            curBitmap.GetPixel(10, 10);
        curBitmap.MakeTransparent();
    }
    // Set pixel colors to red
    for (int i = 50; i < 60; i++)
    {
        for (int j = 50; j < 60; j++)
        {
            curBitmap.SetPixel(i, j, Color.Red);
        }
    }
    // Redraw
    Invalidate();
}
```

If we run the application and click the **Apply Settings** button (see Figure 7.34), a small red rectangle appears, showing that the color of that part of the image has been changed to red.

The LockBits and UnlockBits methods are used to lock and unlock a bitmap into system memory. LockBits takes three parameters—of type Rectangle, ImageLockMode enumeration, and PixelFormat enumeration—and returns an object of type BitmapData. The rectangle is the portion of the bitmap that will be locked in system memory.

ImageLockMode provides the access level on the data. Its members include ReadOnly, ReadWrite, UserInputBuffer, and WriteOnly. The PixelFormat enumeration defines the format of color data for each pixel.

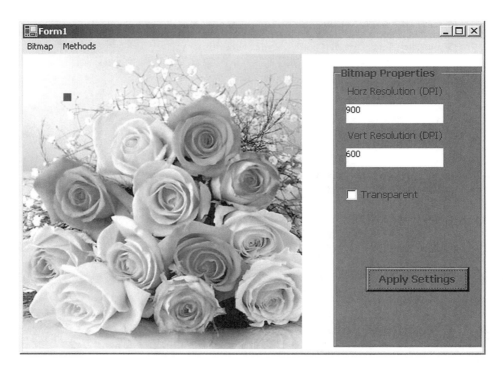

FIGURE 7.34: Changing the pixel colors of a bitmap

NOTE

We will discuss these methods and enumerations in more detail in Chapter 8.

7.6 Working with Icons

The Icon class represents a Windows **icon**, which is a small transparent bitmap. Just like the Bitmap class, this class is inherited from the Image class.

An application can create an Icon object from a stream, string, icon, icon file, or type by using the Icon class constructors with the size of the icon as an optional parameter. The Icon class provides four read-only properties—Handle, Height, Size, and Width—which return a window handle to the icon, height, size, and width of an icon, respectively.

Listing 7.21 creates an Icon object from an icon file and sets the icon of a form using the Form class's Icon property.

LISTING 7.21: **Creating an icon and setting a form's Icon property**

```
private void Form1_Load(object sender,
    System.EventArgs e)
{
    // Create an icon
    Icon curIcon = new Icon("mouse.ico");
    // Set form's icon
    this.Icon = curIcon;
    // Get icon properties
    float h = curIcon.Height;
    float w = curIcon.Height;
    Size sz = curIcon.Size;
}
```

The FromHandle method of the Icon class creates an Icon object from a window handle to an icon (HICON). The Save method saves an Icon object to a stream, and the ToBitmap method converts an Icon object to a Bitmap object. Listing 7.22 creates a Bitmap object from an Icon object using ToBitmap and draws the bitmap using DrawImage.

LISTING 7.22: **Creating a bitmap from an icon and displaying it**

```
private void Form1_Paint(object sender,
    System.Windows.Forms.PaintEventArgs e)
{
    // Create an icon
    Icon curIcon = new Icon("mouse.ico");
    // Create a bitmap from an icon
    Bitmap bmp = curIcon.ToBitmap();
    // Draw bitmap
    Graphics g = e.Graphics;
    g.Clear(this.BackColor);
    g.DrawImage(bmp, 10, 10);
    g.Dispose();
}
```

Figure 7.35 shows the output from Listings 7.21 and 7.22.

FIGURE 7.35: Viewing icons

Sometimes you will need to convert a `Bitmap` object into an `Icon` object. The following code snippet shows how to do this:

```
Icon curIcon;
curIcon = Icon.FromHandle(bmp.GetHicon());
```

7.7 Skewing Images

So far, we have seen that we can draw various images on graphics surfaces by using `DrawImage`. We have also seen how to implement rotate, flip, fit-height, fit-width, and zoom features. An imaging application may need to provide even more features, including scaling, skewing, and high-performance rendering. Using GDI+, we can do all of this very easily. We will discuss some of these issues in this chapter and some of them in Chapter 8.

The `DrawImage` method has about two dozen overloaded forms—one of which lets us provide the destination points for an image. The original image will be drawn after its coordinates are mapped to the destination points—a process called **skewing**. We will see an example in a moment. First let's examine the necessary form of DrawImage.

To translate an image from its original coordinates to the mapped coordinates, an application needs to create an array of new coordinates and call DrawImage, passing this array as the second parameter. For example, the following code snippet creates an array of points and passes it to the Draw-Image method.

```
Point[] pts =
{
    new Point(X0, Y0),
    new Point(X1, Y1),
    new Point(X2, Y2)
};
g.DrawImage(curImage, pts);
```

Now let's create a Windows application and add a MainMenu control with an **Open File** menu item. Let's also add a button to the form. Our final form will look like Figure 7.36.

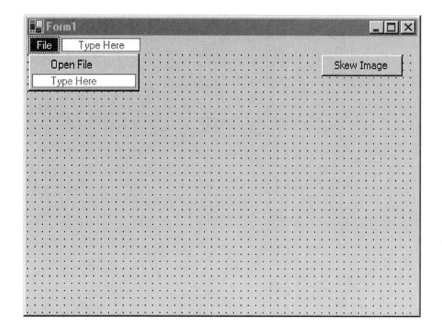

FIGURE 7.36: A skewing application

Now we add the following variables to the application:

```
private Bitmap curBitmap = null;
private bool skewImage = false;
Point[] pts =
{
    new Point(150, 20),
    new Point(20, 50),
    new Point(150, 300)
};
```

The complete code is given in Listing 7.23. The **Open File** menu item click event handler opens an image and creates a `Bitmap` object from the selected file. The paint event handler views the image. If `skewImage` is `true`, the paint event handler calls the `DrawImage` method with an array of points. The **Skew Image** button click event handler simply sets `skew-Image` to `true`.

LISTING 7.23: Skew Image button click event handler

```
private void OpenFileMenu_Click(object sender,
    System.EventArgs e)
{
    OpenFileDialog openDlg = new OpenFileDialog();
    openDlg.Filter =
        "All Bitmap files|*.bmp;*.gif;*.jpg;";
    string filter = openDlg.Filter;
    openDlg.Title = "Open Bitmap File";
    openDlg.ShowHelp = true;
    if(openDlg.ShowDialog() == DialogResult.OK)
    {
        curBitmap = new Bitmap(openDlg.FileName);
    }
    Invalidate();
}
private void Form1_Paint(object sender,
    System.Windows.Forms.PaintEventArgs e)
{
    // Create a Graphics object
    Graphics g = e.Graphics;
    g.Clear(this.BackColor);
    if(curBitmap != null)
    {
        if(skewImage)
        {
```

```
                g.DrawImage(curBitmap, pts);
            }
            else
            {
                g.DrawImage(curBitmap, 0, 0);
            }
        }
        // Dispose of object
        g.Dispose();
    }

    private void SkewImageBtn_Click(object sender,
        System.EventArgs e)
    {
        skewImage = true;
        Invalidate();
    }
```

If you run the application and open an image, the normal view looks like Figure 7.37.

If you click **Skew Image**, the new output looks like Figure 7.38.

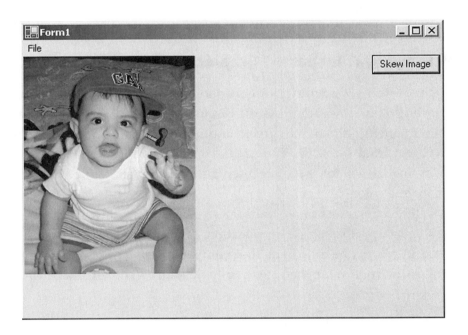

FIGURE 7.37: Normal view of an image

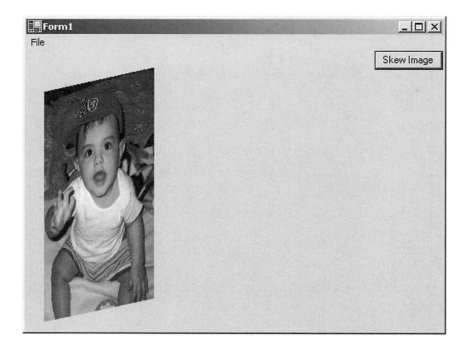

FIGURE 7.38: Skewed image

7.8 Drawing Transparent Graphics Objects

Sometimes we need to draw objects on top of images—and these objects may need to be transparent. As we discussed earlier, color in GDI+ has four components: alpha, red, green, and blue. The value of each component varies from 0 to 255. The alpha component represents the transparency in GDI+ color. Zero represents a fully transparent color; 255, a fully opaque color.

An application must create transparent pens and brushes to draw transparent graphics objects. An application can use the Color.FromArgb method to specify the ratio of all four components in a color. For example, the following code snippet creates a fully opaque green pen and brush.

```
Pen solidPen =
  new Pen(Color.FromArgb(255, 0, 255, 0), 10);
SolidBrush solidColorBrush =
  new SolidBrush(Color.FromArgb(255, 0, 255, 0));
```

The following code snippet creates semitransparent colors and brushes.

```
Pen transPen =
  new Pen(Color.FromArgb(128, 0, 255, 0), 10);
SolidBrush semiTransBrush =
  new SolidBrush(Color.FromArgb(60, 0, 255, 0));
```

Listing 7.24 views an image and draws lines and a rectangle with different transparencies.

LISTING 7.24: Drawing transparent graphics objects

```
private void Form1_Paint(object sender,
    System.Windows.Forms.PaintEventArgs e)
{
    Graphics g = e.Graphics;
    // Create an image from a file
    Image curImage = Image.FromFile("myphoto.jpg");
    // Draw image
    g.DrawImage(curImage, 0, 0,
        curImage.Width, curImage.Height);
    // Create pens with different opacity
    Pen opqPen =
        new Pen(Color.FromArgb(255, 0, 255, 0), 10);
    Pen transPen =
        new Pen(Color.FromArgb(128, 0, 255, 0), 10);
    Pen totTransPen =
        new Pen(Color.FromArgb(40, 0, 255, 0), 10);
    // Draw Graphics object using transparent pens
    g.DrawLine(opqPen, 10, 10, 200, 10);
    g.DrawLine(transPen, 10, 30, 200, 30);
    g.DrawLine(totTransPen, 10, 50, 200, 50);
    SolidBrush semiTransBrush =
        new SolidBrush(Color.FromArgb(60, 0, 255, 0));
    g.FillRectangle(semiTransBrush, 20, 100, 200, 100);
}
```

Figure 7.39 shows the output from Listing 7.24.

7.9 Viewing Multiple Images

Sometimes we need to draw multiple images on the same spot, one on top of the other. In the previous section we discussed how to draw transparent

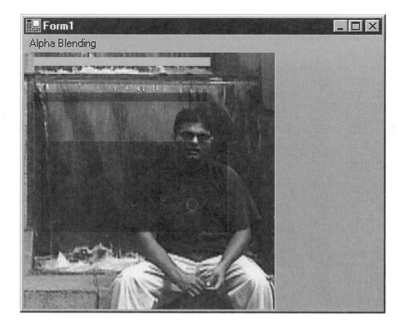

FIGURE 7.39: Drawing transparent graphics objects

graphics objects on top of images. In this section we will discuss how to draw images (transparent or opaque) on top of other images.

Drawing transparent images is different from drawing transparent graphics objects such as lines, rectangles, or ellipses. To draw transparent graphics objects, we simply create a transparent color and use this color when we create a pen or a brush.

Drawing transparent images is controlled by the color matrix (represented by the `ColorMatrix` class), which defines the transparency of the image. A color matrix is applied to an image when we call `DrawImage`. The `DrawImage` method takes an argument of type `ImageAttributes`. The `SetColorMatrix` method of `ImageAttributes` sets a color matrix to the `ImageAttributes` type. Passing `ImageAttributes` to `DrawImage` applies the color matrix to the image. Chapter 8 discusses this process in more detail.

As usual, we create a Windows application. In this application we will draw a large image, and a small image on top of the large image. To make this application more interesting, we add a transparency control to the application so that we can adjust the transparency of the top image. The final form looks like Figure 7.40.

Now let's add a `TrackBar` control to the form. We set the `Maximum` and `Minimum` properties of `TrackBar` to 10 and 0, respectively. Then we write a `TrackBar` control scroll event so that when we scroll the track bar, it can manage the transparency of the image.

> ### ■ NOTE
>
> We have defined a `float` type variable in the class as follows:
> ```
> float tpVal = 1.0f;
> ```

Now we convert the `TrackBar` value to a floating value so that we can use it in the `ColorMatrix` class to set the color of the image, as Listing 7.25

FIGURE 7.40: Drawing multiple images

shows. The `ColorMatrix` class constructor takes an array, which contains the values of matrix items. The `Item` property of this class represents a cell of the matrix and can be used to get and set cell values. Besides the `Item` property, the `ColorMatrix` class provides 25 `MatrixXY` properties, which represent items of the matrix at row (x + 1) and column (y + 1). `MatrixXY` properties can be used to get and set an item's value. See Chapter 10 (Section 10.7.1) for more details.

LISTING 7.25: The `TrackBar` scroll event handler

```
private void trackBar1_Scroll(object sender,
System.EventArgs e)
{
    tpVal = (float)trackBar1.Value/10;
    this.Invalidate();
}
```

We will now view both images on the form's paint event, as Listing 7.26 shows. We create an `Image` object and view the first image. Then we create a `ColorMatrix` object with transparency and set it with the `Image-Attribute` property. Later we attach the `ImageAttribute` property to the second image when we draw it using the `DrawImage` method.

LISTING 7.26: Viewing multiple images on the form-load event

```
private void Form1_Paint(object sender,
    System.Windows.Forms.PaintEventArgs e)
{
    // Create an Image object (first image) from a file
    curImage = Image.FromFile("roses.jpg");
    // Draw first image
    e.Graphics.DrawImage(curImage,
        AutoScrollPosition.X, AutoScrollPosition.Y,
        curImage.Width, curImage.Height );
    // Create an array of ColorMatrix points
    float[][] ptsArray =
    {
        new float[] {1, 0, 0, 0, 0},
        new float[] {0, 1, 0, 0, 0},
        new float[] {0, 0, 1, 0, 0},
        new float[] {0, 0, 0, tpVal, 0},
        new float[] {0, 0, 0, 0, 1}
    };
```

```
        // Create a ColorMatrix object
        ColorMatrix clrMatrix = new ColorMatrix(ptsArray);
        // Create image attributes
        ImageAttributes imgAttributes = new ImageAttributes();
        // Set color matrix
        imgAttributes.SetColorMatrix(clrMatrix,
            ColorMatrixFlag.Default,
            ColorAdjustType.Bitmap);
        // Create second Image object from a file
        Image smallImage = Image.FromFile("smallRoses.gif");
        // Draw second image with image attributes
        e.Graphics.DrawImage(smallImage,
            new Rectangle(100, 100, 100, 100),
            0, 0, smallImage.Width, smallImage.Height,
            GraphicsUnit.Pixel, imgAttributes );
    }
```

7.10 **Using a Picture Box to View Images**

So far in our sample applications, we have used a form as the drawing surface for images. You can also use a `PictureBox` control to view images. Picture boxes are easy to use, and this control optimizes the rendering process with a built-in double buffering feature. A **picture box** is recommended for viewing (but not manipulating) images when you know the exact size of the image.

The `PictureBox` class is defined in the `System.Windows.Forms` namespace. The `Image` property, which takes an `Image` object, sets the image to the picture box that you want to display. You can also set the position and clipping, using the `SizeMode` property. `SizeMode`, which is of type `PictureBoxSizeMode` enumeration, specifies how an image is positioned within a picture box. The members of the `PictureBoxSizeMode` enumeration are defined in Table 7.6.

To view an image in a `PictureBox` control, we simply create an `Image` object using any of the `Image` class methods and set the `PictureBox.Image` property to that image.

Listing 7.27 views an image in a picture box. To test this code, create a Windows application, add a `PictureBox` control to the form by dragging it from the toolbox, and add code to the form-load event handler.

LISTING 7.27: Viewing an image in a picture box

```
Image curImage = Image.FromFile("roses.jpg");
pictureBox1.Image = curImage;
pictureBox1.SizeMode = PictureBoxSizeMode.StretchImage;
```

Figure 7.41 shows the output from Listing 7.27.

TABLE 7.6: `PictureBoxSizeMode` members

Member	Description
AutoSize	The picture box is automatically set to the same size as the image.
CenterImage	The image is displayed in the center of the picture box.
Normal	The image is placed in the upper left corner of the picture box and clipped if it is larger than the control.
StretchImage	The image is stretched or shrunk to fit the size of the picture box.

FIGURE 7.41: Viewing an image in a picture box

7.11 **Saving Images with Different Sizes**

Sometimes we need to save an image with a different size than it originally had. As we discussed earlier, the Save method of the Image class is used to save images. This method also allows us to specify the size of a saved image.

To make our program even more interesting, we will determine the size of the saved image at runtime. Create a Windows application and add two text boxes, two tables, and a button control to the form. The text boxes are used to specify the height and width of the saved image, and the button is used to save the image with the new size, as shown in Figure 7.42.

First we specify an Image private variable:

```
private Image curImage;
```

Then we create and view the image at the form's paint event handler, as shown in Listing 7.28.

FIGURE 7.42: Saving images with different sizes

LISTING 7.28: **Viewing an image**

```
private void Form1_Paint(object sender,
System.Windows.Forms.PaintEventArgs e)
{
    curImage = Image.FromFile("roses.jpg");
    e.Graphics.DrawImage(curImage,
        AutoScrollPosition.X, AutoScrollPosition.Y,
        curImage.Width, curImage.Height );
}
```

On the **Save Image** button click, we ask the user to specify a file name and we call the `Save` method of the `Image` class, which saves an image in the given format. As Listing 7.29 shows, we also read the size of the new image from `textBox1` and `textBox2` and specify the size when we create a new `Bitmap` object from the existing image.

LISTING 7.29: **Saving an image with the given size**

```
private void SaveImageBtn_Click(object sender,
System.EventArgs e)
{
    if(curImage == null)
    return;
    int height = Convert.ToInt16(textBox1.Text);
    int width = Convert.ToInt16(textBox2.Text);
    SaveFileDialog saveDlg = new SaveFileDialog();
    saveDlg.Title = "Save Image As";
    saveDlg.OverwritePrompt = true;
    saveDlg.CheckPathExists = true;
    saveDlg.Filter =
        "Bitmap File(*.bmp)|*.bmp|Gif File(*.gif)|*.gif| " +
        "JPEG File(*.jpg)|*.jpg";
    saveDlg.ShowHelp = true;
    if(saveDlg.ShowDialog() == DialogResult.OK)
    {
        string fileName = saveDlg.FileName;
        string extn =
            fileName.Substring(fileName.Length - 3, 3);
        Bitmap newImage = new Bitmap(curImage,
            new Size(width, height));
        if(extn.Equals("bmp"))
            newImage.Save(fileName,ImageFormat.Bmp);
        else if(extn.Equals("gif"))
            newImage.Save(fileName,ImageFormat.Gif);
        else if(extn.Equals("jpg"))
            newImage.Save(fileName,ImageFormat.Jpeg);
    }
}
```

FIGURE 7.43: New image, with width of 200 and height of 200

Now we save an image with a width of 200 and a height of 200. The results are shown in Figure 7.43.

SUMMARY

GDI+ provides a significant improvement in imaging over GDI. In this chapter we discussed the basic imaging capabilities of GDI+, as defined in the System.Drawing namespace. We focused mainly on the Image and Bitmap classes, and by now you should understand how to use the .NET Framework to work with images. We saw how to open, view, save, and manipulate images. We also saw some interesting functionality, including creating thumbnail images, rotating and flipping, zooming in and out, skewing and stretching, and animation.

In addition, we covered some advanced imaging features, including drawing transparent images and setting bitmap resolution and color.

Throughout this chapter, we developed a real-world application that you can use in your programming career.

Imaging functionality doesn't end here. Advanced imaging functionality, which is defined in the `System.Drawing.Imaging` namespace, will be the focus of Chapter 8. Some of the topics yet to be discussed are bitmaps, metafiles, color maps, encoding and decoding images, and details of the color matrix.

8
Advanced Imaging

IN CHAPTER 7 WE discussed the imaging functionality defined in the `System.Drawing` namespace. This chapter will cover the advanced imaging functionality defined in the `System.Drawing.Imaging` namespace. We will explore how to implement this functionality in our applications. The topics will include

- Understanding `LockBits` and `UnlockBits`
- Working with metafiles and metafile enhancements
- Working with the color matrix, color map, and color palette
- Using the `Encoder` and `EncoderCollection` classes
- An overview of tagged data in TIFF files
- Converting metafiles

8.1 Rendering Partial Bitmaps

In Chapter 7 we saw that the `Bitmap` class provides the `LockBits` and `UnlockBits` methods, but we didn't get to use them. `LockBits` and `UnlockBits` lock and unlock bitmap pixels in system memory. Each call to `LockBits` should be followed by a call to `UnlockBits`.

Why might you want to lock bitmap pixels? Rendering (painting) bitmaps and images is a resource-consuming operation, and it is one of the

> **■ NOTE**
>
> The code used in this chapter uses classes defined in the System. Drawing.Imaging namespace, so be sure to add a reference to this namespace in your applications.

most frequently performed graphics operations. Suppose you want to change the color or intensity level of a bitmap. You could always loop though the bitmap pixel by pixel and use SetPixel to modify its properties, but that is a huge time- and resource-consuming operation.

A better option would be to use LockBits and UnlockBits. These methods allow you to control any part of the bitmap by specifying a range of pixels, eliminating the need to loop through each pixel of the bitmap.

To use this option, first call LockBits, which returns the BitmapData object. BitmapData specifies the attributes of a bitmap. Before we examine the members of the BitmapData class, let's take a look at the LockBits and UnlockBits methods. The LockBits method is defined as follows:

```
public BitmapData LockBits( Rectangle rect,
ImageLockMode flags, PixelFormat format);
```

LockBits takes three parameters of type Rectangle, ImageLockMode enumeration, and PixelFormat enumeration, and it returns an object of type BitmapData. The rectangle defines the portion of the bitmap to be locked in system memory.

UnlockBits takes a single parameter of type BitmapData, which was returned by LockBits. This method is defined as follows:

```
public void UnlockBits(BitmapData bitmapdata);
```

The ImageLockMode enumeration used in LockBits provides the access level to the data. Table 8.1 describes the members of ImageLockMode.

The pixel format defines the number of bits of memory associated with one pixel of data, as well as the order of the color components within a single pixel. Generally the number of bits per pixel is directly proportional to the quality of the image because the pixel can store more colors.

TABLE 8.1: `ImageLockMode` members

Member	Description
ReadOnly	The locked portion of the bitmap is for reading only.
ReadWrite	The locked portion of the bitmap is for reading or writing.
UserInputBuffer	The buffer used for reading or writing pixel data is allocated by the user.
WriteOnly	The locked portion of the bitmap is for writing only.

The `PixelFormat` enumeration represents the pixel, which is useful when you need to change the format of a bitmap or a portion of it. The members of the `PixelFormat` enumeration are described in Table 8.2.

8.1.1 Drawing Grayscale or Other Color Images

To demonstrate the use of `LockBits` and `UnlockBits`, we will change the pixels of a bitmap using the `GetPixel` and `SetPixel` methods. As we discussed in Chapter 7, an application can use `GetPixel` and `SetPixel` to get and set the colors of each pixel of a bitmap. To set a bitmap color to grayscale or other colors, an application reads the current color using `GetPixel`, calculates the grayscale value, and calls `SetPixel` to apply the new color.

In the following code snippet we read the color of a pixel; calculate the grayscale value by applying a formula to the red, green, and blue components; and call `SetPixel` to set the pixel's new grayscale color.

```
Color curColor = curBitmap.GetPixel(i, j);
int ret = (curColor.R + curColor.G + curColor.B) / 3;
curBitmap.SetPixel(i, j, Color.FromArgb(ret, ret, ret));
```

Listing 8.1 draws an image with its original color settings and later redraws it in grayscale. The `Width` and `Height` properties of the `Bitmap` class are used to loop through each pixel of the bitmap, and `SetPixel` is used to set the pixel's color to grayscale.

TABLE 8.2: `PixelFormat` members

Member	Description
Alpha	The pixel data contains alpha values that are not pre-multiplied.
DontCare	No pixel format is specified.
Format1bppIndexed	1 bit per pixel, using indexed color. The color table therefore has two colors in it.
Format4bppIndexed	4 bits per pixel, using indexed color.
Format8bppIndexed	8 bits per pixel, using indexed color.
Format16bppArgb1555	16 bits per pixel, giving 32,768 colors; 5 bits each are used for red, green, and blue, and 1 bit is used for alpha.
Format16bppGrayScale	16 bits per pixel, giving 65,536 shades of gray.
Format16bppRgb555	16 bits per pixel; 5 bits each are used for red, green, and blue. The last bit is not used.
Format16bppRgb565	16 bits per pixel; 5 bits are used for red, 6 bits for green, and 5 bits for blue.
Format24bppRgb	24 bits per pixel; 8 bits each are used for red, green, and blue.
Format32bppArgb	32 bits per pixel; 8 bits each are used for alpha, red, green, and blue. This is the default GDI+ color combination.
Format32bppPArgb	32 bits per pixel; 8 bits each are used for alpha, red, green, and blue. The red, green, and blue components are premultiplied according to the alpha component.
Format32bppRgb	32 bits per pixel; 8 bits each are used for red, green, and blue. The last 8 bits are not used.
Format48bppRgb	48 bits per pixel; 16 bits each are used for red, green, and blue.
Format64bppArgb	64 bits per pixel; 16 bits each are used for alpha, red, green, and blue.

TABLE 8.2: `PixelFormat` members (continued)

Member	Description
`Format64bppPArgb`	64 bits per pixel; 16 bits each are used for alpha, red, green, and blue. The red, green, and blue components are premultiplied according to the alpha component.
`Gdi`	GDI colors.
`Indexed`	Color-indexed values, which are an index to colors in the system color table, as opposed to individual color values.
`Max`	The maximum value for this enumeration.
`PAlpha`	The format contains premultiplied alpha values.
`Undefined`	The format is undefined.

LISTING 8.1: Using `SetPixel` to change the color scale of a bitmap

```
// Create a Graphics object from a button
// or menu click event handler
Graphics g = this.CreateGraphics();
g.Clear(this.BackColor);
// Create a Bitmap object
Bitmap curBitmap = new Bitmap("roses.jpg");
// Draw bitmap in its original color
g.DrawImage(curBitmap, 0, 0, curBitmap.Width,
curBitmap.Height);
// Set each pixel to grayscale using GetPixel
// and SetPixel
for (int i = 0; i < curBitmap.Width; i++)
{
    for (int j = 0; j < curBitmap.Height; j++)
    {
        Color curColor = curBitmap.GetPixel(i, j);
        int ret = (curColor.R + curColor.G + curColor.B) / 3;
            curBitmap.SetPixel(i, j,
            Color.FromArgb(ret, ret, ret));
    }
}
// Draw bitmap again with gray settings
g.DrawImage(curBitmap, 0, 0, curBitmap.Width,
    curBitmap.Height);
// Dispose of object
g.Dispose();
```

8.1.2 Using `BitmapData` to Change Pixel Format

In the previous section we discussed how to set the pixel format of a bitmap by reading pixels one by one. You can also set the pixel format by using the `BitmapData` class and its members.

The `BitmapData` object specifies the attributes of a bitmap, including size, pixel format, starting address of the pixel data in memory, and length of each scan line (**stride**). These properties are described in Table 8.3. All of the properties have both get and set types.

Now let's set the color of pixels in a bitmap by using `LockBits` and `UnlockBits`. This approach is faster than using the `SetPixel` method. Listing 8.2 uses `LockBits` and `UnlockBits` to set a bitmap pixel format. First we create an `Image` object from a file, followed by a `Bitmap` object from the `Image` object. Then we call `LockBits`, which returns a `Bitmap-Data` object. Next we call `PixelFormat` to set the pixel format. You can use any of the `PixelFormat` enumeration values. Finally, we call `UnlockBits` to unlock the locked bits. Notice that the `lockedRect` rectangle in the `LockBits` method is the size of the bitmap.

LISTING 8.2: Using `LockBits` and `UnlockBits` to set the grayscale of a bitmap

```
private void Form1_Paint(object sender,
    System.Windows.Forms.PaintEventArgs e)
{
    Image img = Image.FromFile("roses.jpg");
    Bitmap curImage =
        new Rectangle(0,0,curImage.Width,curImage.Height);
```

TABLE 8.3: `BitmapData` properties

Property	Description
Height	Represents the pixel height.
PixelFormat	Represents the format of the pixels using the `PixelFormat` enumeration.
Scan0	Represents the address of the first pixel data in the bitmap.
Stride	Represents stride (also called scan width).
Width	Represents the pixel width.

```
    Rectangle lockedRect =
        new Rectangle(0, 0, curImage.Width, curImage.Height);
    BitmapData bmpData = curImage.LockBits(lockedRect,
        ImageLockMode.ReadWrite,
        PixelFormat.Format24bppRgb);
    // Set the format of BitmapData pixels
    bmpData.PixelFormat = PixelFormat.Max;
    // Unlock the locked bits
    curImage.UnlockBits(bmpData);
    // Draw image with new pixel format
    e.Graphics.DrawImage(curImage, 0, 0,
        curImage.Width, curImage.Height);
}
```

Figure 8.1 shows the output from Listing 8.2. The entire bitmap is grayscale.

If a bitmap is huge and we want to change the format of only a few pixels, `LockBits` and `UnlockBits` really help. Using these methods, we can lock and render only the part of a bitmap we want to work on instead of rendering the entire bitmap. Suppose we want to change the pixel format

FIGURE 8.1: Using `BitmapData` to set grayscale

of only the section of the bitmap starting at point (50, 50) and ending at point (200, 200). We simply change the rectangle passed to LockBits.

Listing 8.3 locks only that portion of the image specified by a rectangle.

LISTING 8.3: Changing the pixel format of a partial bitmap

```
private void Form1_Paint(object sender,
    System.Windows.Forms.PaintEventArgs e)
{
    Image img = Image.FromFile("roses.jpg");
    Bitmap curImage =
        new Bitmap(img, new Size(img.Width, img.Height));
    // Call LockBits, which returns a BitmapData object
    Rectangle lockedRect = new Rectangle(50,50,200,200);
    /* Rectangle lockedRect =
        new Rectangle(0,0,curImage.Width,curImage.Height);
        */
    BitmapData bmpData = curImage.LockBits(lockedRect,
        ImageLockMode.ReadWrite,
        PixelFormat.Format24bppRgb);
    // Set the format of BitmapData pixels
    bmpData.PixelFormat = PixelFormat.Max;
    // Unlock the locked bits
    curImage.UnlockBits(bmpData);
    // Draw image with new pixel format
    e.Graphics.DrawImage(curImage, 0, 0,
        curImage.Width, curImage.Height);
}
```

Figure 8.2 shows the output from Listing 8.3. You may not see any difference between this illustration and Figure 8.1, but if you run the sample code yourself, you will notice that the color of only a small rectangle in the image is changed.

GetPixel/SetPixel versus LockBits/UnlockBits

Comparing the two samples used in Listings 8.1 and 8.2 shows that the LockBits/UnlockBits method is significantly faster than the GetPixel/SetPixel method. To draw the same image, the Get-Pixel/SetPixel method takes about 150 milliseconds, and the Lock-Bits/UnlockBits method takes about 50 milliseconds.

FIGURE 8.2: Changing the pixel format of a partial bitmap

8.2 **Working with Metafiles**

Metafiles contain information about how an image was created—including lists of graphics operations—rather than storing the image in pixel format. Graphics operations in a metafile are stored as records, which can be controlled (recorded and played back) individually.

The `Metafile` class provides functionality to work with different metafile formats including Windows Metafile Format (WMF), Enhanced Metafile Format (EMF), and an extension to Enhanced Metafile Format (EMF+). The `Metafile` class provides about 40 overloaded forms of its constructor.

Loading and viewing a metafile is similar to viewing a bitmap. An application can load a metafile from a stream, string, or `IntPtr` instance with different formats and locations. The simplest way to load and view a metafile is to pass the file name in the `Metafile` constructor and call `DrawImage`.

GDI+ and Metafiles

Even though GDI+ is capable of reading both WMF and EMF files, it creates only EMF files. EMF files that contain GDI+ records are called EMF+ files.

The `Metafile` class is derived from the `Image` class and has no methods and properties besides those inherited from the `Image` class.

Let's create an application to test metafile functionality. We will create a Windows application and add a `MainMenu` control to the form. Then we'll add a menu item to `MainMenu` to test the code in this and subsequent sections.

As Listing 8.4 shows, first we create a `Graphics` object using `this.CreateGraphics`. Then we create a `Metafile` object from a file and use `DrawImage` to view it.

LISTING 8.4: Viewing a metafile

```
private void ViewFile_Click(object sender,
    System.EventArgs e)
{
    // Create a Graphics object
    Graphics g = this.CreateGraphics();
    g.Clear(this.BackColor);
    // Create a Metafile object from a file name
    Metafile curMetafile = new Metafile("mtfile.wmf");
    // Draw metafile using DrawImage
    g.DrawImage(curMetafile, 0, 0) ;
    // Dispose of object
    g.Dispose();
}
```

Figure 8.3 shows the output from Listing 8.4.

8.2.1 `Metafile` Class Method

As mentioned already, the `Metafile` class provides a long list of over-loaded constructors. It also provides three methods: `GetHenhmetafile`, `GetMetafileHeader`, and `PlayRecord`.

`GetHenhmetafile` returns a window handle to a metafile. `Get-Metafileheader`, which has five overloaded forms, returns a metafile

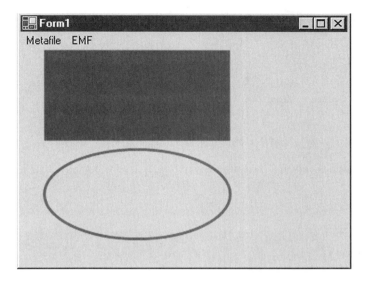

FIGURE 8.3: Viewing a metafile

header in the form of a `MetafileHeader` object. `PlayRecord` plays (reads and displays) an extended metafile.

8.2.2 Creating Metafiles Programmatically

The `Metafile` object can create a metafile programmatically. Three simple steps are required to create a metafile:

1. Creating a `Metafile` object with a file name
2. Using `FromImage` to create a `Graphics` object from the `Metafile` object
3. Adding graphics lines and shapes

Now let's create a metafile programmatically. In Listing 8.5 we use `GetHdc` to get the handle to a device context (HDC), and we use this handle to create a metafile called `newFile.wmf`. After creating the metafile, we use the `FillRectangle`, `FillEllipse`, and `DrawString` methods to add a rectangle, an ellipse, and a string, respectively. Calling these methods adds records describing the respective objects to the metafile. Finally, we release the objects.

LISTING 8.5: Creating a metafile

```
private void CreateMetaFile_Click(object sender,
    System.EventArgs e)
{
    Metafile curMetafile = null;
    // Create a Graphics object
    Graphics g = this.CreateGraphics();
    // Get HDC
    IntPtr hdc = g.GetHdc();
    // Create a rectangle
    Rectangle rect = new Rectangle(0, 0, 200, 200);
    // Use HDC to create a metafile with a name
    try
    {
        curMetafile =
            new Metafile("newFile.wmf", hdc);
    }
    catch(Exception exp)
    {
        MessageBox.Show(exp.Message);
        g.ReleaseHdc(hdc);
        g.Dispose();
        return;
    }
    // Create a Graphics object from the Metafile object
    Graphics g1 = Graphics.FromImage(curMetafile);
    // Set smoothing mode
    g1.SmoothingMode = SmoothingMode.HighQuality;
    // Fill a rectangle on the Metafile object
    g1.FillRectangle(Brushes.Green, rect);
    rect.Y += 110;
    //  Draw an ellipse on the Metafile object
    LinearGradientBrush lgBrush =
        new LinearGradientBrush(
        rect, Color.Red, Color.Blue, 45.0f);
    g1.FillEllipse(lgBrush, rect);
    // Draw text on the Metafile object
    rect.Y += 110;
    g1.DrawString("MetaFile Sample",
        new Font("Verdana", 20),
        lgBrush, 200, 200,
        StringFormat.GenericTypographic);
    // Release objects
    g.ReleaseHdc(hdc);
    g1.Dispose();
    g.Dispose();
}
```

Running the code in Listing 8.5 will create a new metafile in your application's folder. Figure 8.4 shows the image described by the metafile.

As mentioned earlier, after creating a metafile, you can view it as you would any other image, using the `DrawImage` method of the `Graphics` class.

TIP

Using the same approach, you can easily create a metafile editor similar to GDI+Painter, in which you can draw graphics objects and save them as metafiles. You can even change the GDI+Painter application code to do so.

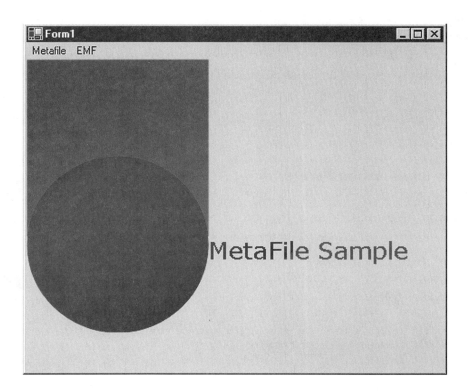

FIGURE 8.4: A metafile created programmatically

8.2.3 **Enhanced Metafiles**

Using enhanced metafiles, you can add personalized data to a metafile as defined in the MSDN documentation:

> The enhanced Windows metafile (EMF) format contains a comment mechanism for embedding data within the metafile. This comment mechanism is used to embed GDI+ records within an EMF file. Applications that cannot read or recognize the comment data skip the comment records and render the records they do understand. If the EMF+ file is played back by GDI+, then the GDI+ records are used to render the metafile; otherwise, the GDI records (if present) are used.

There are three types of EMFs: EMF only, EMF+ dual, and EMF+ only. The `EmfType` enumeration is used to find out the type of EMF programmatically. This enumeration provides three members: `EmfOnly`, `EmfPlusDual`, and `EmfPlusOnly`. The `EmfOnly` and `EmfPlusDual` types of records can be played by both GDI and GDI+; `EmfPlusOnly` types of records can be played only by GDI+.

You can use the `Metafile` object constructors to specify the type of EMF you want to create. The following code creates an EMF+ dual metafile:

```
Metafile curMetafile =
new Metafile(hdc, EmfType.EmfPlusDual,
"emfPlusDual.emf");
```

8.2.4 **How Metafiles Work**

The `EnumerateMetafile` method can be used to read and play back records of a metafile one by one. Each record is sent to `Graphics.EnumerateMetafileProc`, which is used to read the data for a record. This method has many overloaded forms.

`Graphics.EnumerateMetafileProc` takes five parameters and is defined as follows:

```
public delegate bool Graphics.EnumerateMetafileProc(
   EmfPlusRecordType recordType,
   int flags,
   int dataSize,
   IntPtr data,
   PlayRecordCallback callbackData
);
```

GDI/GDI+ Record

Each metafile record describes a command that is capable of drawing, filling, or changing the graphics state of a surface. For example, clearing a graphics object, drawing a rectangle, filling an ellipse, creating a graphics container, and ending a graphics container are all examples of records. After creating a metafile programmatically, if you call `DrawRectangle`, one record will be added to the metafile. When you play back the metafile, GDI+ reads the record (`DrawRectangle`) and draws a rectangle.

The `EmfPlusRecordType` enumeration defines the available metafile record types.

Whereas `recordType` is of type `EmfPlusRecordType` enumeration and specifies the type of metafile, the `flags` parameter is a set of flags that specify attributes of the record. The `dataSize` parameter represents the number of bytes in the record data, and `data` is an array of bytes that contains the record data. The `callbackData` parameter is a `PlayRecordCallback` delegate supplied by the .NET Framework to play a record of metafile data.

Listing 8.6 reads records from a metafile and displays data for these records individually. In the `EnumMetaCB` callback, we check whether the record type is `FillEllipse`, `FillRects`, `DrawEllipse`, or `DrawRects` and display the corresponding data.

LISTING 8.6: Reading metafile records

```
private void EnumerateMetaFile_Click(object sender,
    System.EventArgs e)
{
    // Create a Graphics object
    Graphics g = this.CreateGraphics();
    g.Clear(this.BackColor);
    // Create a Metafile object from a file
    Metafile curMetafile = new Metafile("mtfile.wmf");
    // Set EnumerateMetafileProc property
    Graphics.EnumerateMetafileProc enumMetaCB =
        new Graphics.EnumerateMetafileProc(EnumMetaCB);
```

continues

```
    // Enumerate metafile
    g.EnumerateMetafile(curMetafile,
        new Point(0, 0), enumMetaCB);
    // Dispose of objects
    curMetafile.Dispose();
    g.Dispose();
}
private bool EnumMetaCB(EmfPlusRecordType recordType,
    int flags, int dataSize,
    IntPtr data, PlayRecordCallback callbackData)
{
    string str = "";
    // Play only EmfPlusRecordType.FillEllipse records
    if (recordType == EmfPlusRecordType.FillEllipse
        || recordType == EmfPlusRecordType.FillRects
        || recordType == EmfPlusRecordType.DrawEllipse
        || recordType == EmfPlusRecordType.DrawRects )
    {
        str = "Record type:"+ recordType.ToString()+
            ", Flags:"+ flags.ToString()+
            ", DataSize:"+ dataSize.ToString()+
            ", Data:"+data.ToString() ;
        MessageBox.Show(str);
    }
    return true;
}
```

Figure 8.5 shows the output from Listing 8.6. Our program displays the record type, flag, data size, and data. The record in this example contains only `FillRectangle` methods. If more records are used to create a metafile, you will see messages for the various record types.

8.2.5 Reading a Metafile Header

A metafile header contains attributes such as type, size, and version of a metafile. It is represented by the `MetafileHeader` class. `GetMetafileHeader` returns a metafile header and has many overloaded methods.

The `MetafileHeader` class has the eight methods listed in Table 8.4.

FIGURE 8.5: Reading metafile records

TABLE 8.4: `MetafileHeader` methods

Method	Description
`IsDisplay`	Returns `true` if a metafile is device-dependent.
`IsEmf`	Returns `true` if a metafile is in the Windows EMF format.
`IsEmfOrEmfPlus`	Returns `true` if a metafile is in the Windows EMF or EMF+ format.
`IsEmfPlus`	Returns `true` if a metafile is in the Windows EMF+ format.
`IsEmfPlusDual`	Returns `true` if a metafile is in the dual EMF format, which supports both the enhanced and the enhanced plus format.
`IsEmfPlusOnly`	Returns `true` if a metafile supports only the Windows EMF+ format.
`IsWmf`	Returns `true` if a metafile is in the Windows WMF format.
`IsWmfPlaceable`	Returns `true` if a metafile is in the Windows placeable WMF format.

Properties of the `MetafileHeader` class represent various attributes of metafiles, including size, version, and type, as Table 8.5 shows. All of these properties are read-only.

Reading metafile attributes is simple: Create a `Metafile` object, get its header attributes using `GetMetafileHeader`, and display the value of these attributes in a message box. Listing 8.7 reads metafile header attributes, including type, bounds, size, and version.

LISTING 8.7: Reading metafile header attributes

```
private void MetafileHeaderInfo_Click(object sender,
    System.EventArgs e)
{
    // Create a Metafile object
    Metafile curMetafile = new Metafile("mtfile.wmf");
    // Get metafile header
    MetafileHeader header = curMetafile.GetMetafileHeader();
```

continues

TABLE 8.5: MetafileHeader properties

Property	Description
Bounds	Gets the bounds of a metafile in the form of a rectangle.
DpiX	Gets the horizontal resolution, in dots per inch, of a metafile in the form of a rectangle.
DpiY	Gets the vertical resolution, in dots per inch, of a metafile in the form of a rectangle.
EmfPlusHeaderSize	Gets the size, in bytes, of an enhanced metafile plus header file.
LogicalDpiX	Gets the logical horizontal resolution, in dots per inch, of a metafile.
LogicalDpiY	Gets the logical vertical resolution, in dots per inch, of a metafile.
MetafileSize	Gets the size, in bytes, of a metafile.
Type	Gets the type of a metafile.
Version	Gets the version number of a metafile.
WmfHeader	Gets the WMF header of a metafile.

```
// Read metafile header attributes
string mfAttributes = "";
mfAttributes += "Type :"+ header.Type.ToString();
mfAttributes += ", Bounds:"+ header.Bounds.ToString();
mfAttributes += ", Size:"+ header.MetafileSize.ToString();
mfAttributes += ", Version:"+ header.Version.ToString();
// Display message box
MessageBox.Show(mfAttributes);
// Dispose of object
curMetafile.Dispose();
}
```

Figure 8.6 shows the output from Listing 8.7.

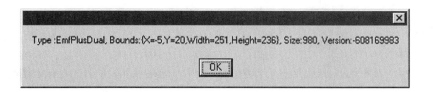

Type :EmfPlusDual, Bounds:(X=-5,Y=20,Width=251,Height=236), Size:980, Version:-608169983

OK

FIGURE 8.6: Reading metafile header attributes

8.3 **Color Mapping Using Color Objects**

The `System.Drawing.Imaging` namespace provides three color objects that can be used to apply color mappings to images. These three objects are `ColorMap`, `ColorMatrix`, and `ColorPalette`. In this section we will discuss the use and importance of these objects.

8.3.1 **The Color Remap Table**

A **color remap table** is used to convert the existing colors of an image to new colors by applying a color mapping to them. The `ColorMap` class represents a color remap table. It defines the mapping between existing colors and the new colors to which they will be converted. When the map is applied to an image, any pixel of the old color is converted to the new color.

The `ColorMap` class has only two properties—`NewColor` and `Old-Color`—both of type `Color`. `OldColor` represents an existing color, and `NewColor` represents the new color to which the existing color will be converted.

A color map is applied to an image through the `ImageAttributes` parameter of `DrawImage`. The `ImageAttributes` class provides the `Set-RemapTable` method, which is used to apply a `ColorMap` object array to the image attributes.

> ■■ **NOTE**
> Each `ColorMap` object maps a single color. To map multiple colors, you must create multiple `ColorMap` objects.

To see `ColorMap` in action, we create a Windows application and add a `MainMenu` control to the form. We also add three menu items to the main menu and use their menu item click event handlers to test our code.

Listing 8.8 gives code for the `ColorMap` menu click event handler. As usual, we create `Graphics` and `Image` objects. We will map the red, yellow, and blue colors to green, navy, and aqua, respectively. We create three `ColorMap` objects and a `ColorMap` array from these objects, and we set their `OldColor` and `NewColor` properties to the desired colors. Then we create an `ImageAttributes` object and apply the `ColorMap` array to it by calling the `SetRemapTable` method. After that the `ImageAttributes` object is used as a parameter of `DrawImage`.

LISTING 8.8: Applying the color remap table

```csharp
private void ColorMap_Click(object sender,
    System.EventArgs e)
{
    // Create a Graphics object
    Graphics g = this.CreateGraphics();
    g.Clear(this.BackColor);
    // Create an Image object
    Image image = new Bitmap("Sample.bmp");
    // Create ImageAttributes
    ImageAttributes  imageAttributes =
        new ImageAttributes();
    // Create three ColorMap objects
    ColorMap colorMap1 = new ColorMap();
    ColorMap colorMap2 = new ColorMap();
    ColorMap colorMap3 = new ColorMap();
    // Set the ColorMap objects' properties
    colorMap1.OldColor = Color.Red;
    colorMap1.NewColor = Color.Green;
    colorMap2.OldColor = Color.Yellow;
    colorMap2.NewColor = Color.Navy;
    colorMap3.OldColor = Color.Blue;
    colorMap3.NewColor = Color.Aqua;
    // Create an array of ColorMap objects
    // because SetRemapTable takes an array
    ColorMap[] remapTable =
    {
        colorMap1,
        colorMap2,
        colorMap3
    };
```

```
    imageAttributes.SetRemapTable(remapTable,
        ColorAdjustType.Bitmap);
    // Draw image
    g.DrawImage(image, 10, 10, image.Width, image.Height);
    // Draw image with color map
    g.DrawImage(
        image,
        new Rectangle(150, 10, image.Width, image.Height),
        0, 0, image.Width, image.Height,
        GraphicsUnit.Pixel,
        imageAttributes);
    // Dispose of objects
    image.Dispose();
    g.Dispose();
}
```

Figure 8.7 shows the output from Listing 8.8. The original image is on the left; the image on the right shows remapped colors. On your system you will notice that the red, yellow, and blue colors are converted to green, navy, and aqua.

8.3.2 **The Color Matrix**

The `ColorMatrix` class defines a 5×5 matrix that contains coordinates for the ARGB (alpha, red, green, and blue) space (from 0,0 to 4,4). The `Item` property of this class represents a cell of the matrix and can be used to get and set cell values. Besides the `Item` property, the `ColorMatrix` class provides 25 `MatrixXY` properties, which represent items of the matrix at the

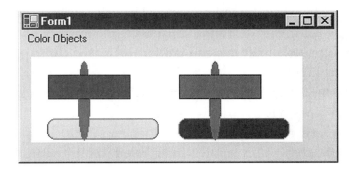

FIGURE 8.7: Applying a color remap table

*x*th row and *y*th column. The `MatrixXY` properties can be used to get and set item values.

You can use an array of points to initialize a `ColorMatrix` object, or you can assign values directly to the `ColorMatrix` properties. The following code snippet creates an array of points that is used as an argument to the `ColorMatrix` constructor, and then sets the values of `Matrix34` and `Matrix11`.

```
float[][] ptsArray ={
   new float[] {1, 0, 0, 0, 0},
   new float[] {0, 1, 0, 0, 0},
   new float[] {0, 0, 1, 0, 0},
   new float[] {0, 0, 0, 0.5f, 0},
   new float[] {0, 0, 0, 0, 1}};
ColorMatrix clrMatrix = new ColorMatrix(ptsArray);
if( clrMatrix.Matrix34 <= 0.5) //3rd row, 4th col
{
   clrMatrix.Matrix34 = 0.8f;
   clrMatrix.Matrix11 = 0.3f;    //1st row, 1st col
}
```

The `SetColorMatrix` method of the `ImageAttributes` class uses a color matrix. We will see how to use a color matrix in your applications in the sample applications that follow. Chapter 10 discusses `ColorMatrix` in more detail.

8.3.3 The Color Palette

A **color palette** defines an array of colors that make up a color palette. The colors in the palette are limited to 32-bit ARGB colors (8 bits each for the alpha, red, green, and blue components). The color palette can be used to increase the color intensity without increasing the number of colors used. This process creates a halftone, and it offers increased contrast at a cost of decreased resolution.

The `ColorPalette` class defines an array of colors that make up a color palette. This class has only two properties: `Entries` and `Flags`. The `Entries` property returns an array of colors, and the `Flags` property represents how the color information is interpreted. Table 8.6 lists valid values for the `Flags` property.

TABLE 8.6: ColorPalette.Flags values

Value	Description
0x00000001	The color values in the array contain alpha information.
0x00000002	The colors in the array are grayscale values.
0x00000004	The colors in the array are halftone values.

8.4 Image Attributes and the ImageAttributes Class

Images represented by the Image class and its inherited classes can also store attributes. The ImageAttributes class represents the attributes of an image. DrawImage can take a parameter of type ImageAttributes, which represents how the colors are applied to an image when it is rendered. The ImageAttributes class has no properties, but it provides many useful methods. Let's take a look at the methods provided by the Image-Attributes class.

8.4.1 The SetWrapMode Method

Sometimes we need to fill a graphics shape with a texture that's smaller or larger than the graphics shape. The **wrap mode**—represented by the Wrap-Mode enumeration—specifies how a texture is tiled when it is larger or smaller than the area being filled. The members of the WrapMode enumeration are described in Table 8.7.

SetWrapMode is used to set the wrap mode of a texture or gradient. This method takes three parameters: a wrap mode (WrapMode), a color (Color), and a clamp (Boolean). The last two parameters are optional. If the clamp value is true, the texture will be clamped to the image boundary; otherwise there is no clamping.

Listing 8.9 uses this method. First we create an ImageAttributes object and set the wrap mode using SetWrapMode. Then we create an Image object using FromFile, followed by a call to DrawImage with an argument of the ImageAttributes object. DrawImage draws an image on the form, rendered using the colors defined by ImageAttributes.

TABLE 8.7: WrapMode members

Member	Description
Clamp	Clamps the texture or gradient to the object boundary.
Tile	Tiles the gradient or texture.
TileFlipX	Reverses the texture or gradient horizontally and then tiles it.
TileFlipXY	Reverses the texture or gradient horizontally and vertically and then tiles it.
TileFlipY	Reverses the texture or gradient vertically and then tiles it.

LISTING 8.9: Using the SetWrapMode method of ImageAttributes

```
private void SetWrapMode_Click(object sender,
    System.EventArgs e)
{
    Graphics g = this.CreateGraphics();
    g.Clear(this.BackColor);
    // Create ImageAttributes object
    ImageAttributes ImgAttr = new ImageAttributes();
    // Set wrap mode to tile
    ImgAttr.SetWrapMode(WrapMode.Tile);
    // Create an image
    Image curImage = Image.FromFile("dnWatcher.gif");
    // Draw image
    Rectangle rect = new Rectangle(0, 0, 400, 400);
    g.DrawImage(curImage, rect, 0, 0, 400, 400,
        GraphicsUnit.Pixel, ImgAttr);
    // Dispose of object
    g.Dispose();
}
```

Figure 8.8 shows the output from Listing 8.9. If the image is smaller than the surface, images are wrapped.

> ■ NOTE
> The WrapMode enumeration is defined in the System.Drawing.Drawing2D namespace. Don't forget to add the namespace reference to the project.

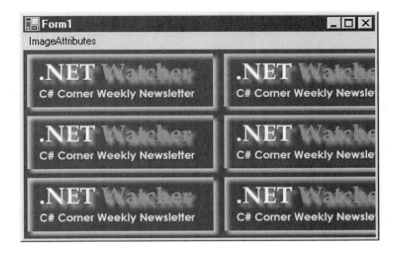

FIGURE 8.8: Wrapping images

8.4.2 **The** SetGamma **Method**

The SetGamma method sets the **gamma value**, which represents the brightness of a graphics shape, for all graphics objects, including images, brushes, and pens. Gamma values range from 0.1 to 5.0 (normally 0.1 to 2.2), with 0.1 being the brightest and 5.0 the darkest.

This method takes a floating type parameter as gamma value and a second optional parameter of the ColorAdjustType enumeration type. Using the ColorAdjustType enumeration from the Imaging namespace, you can even specify which GDI+ objects use this color adjustment. For example, if you want to apply gamma values on text only, you can do so using ColorAdjustType.Text, which is described in Table 8.8. The following code snippet sets the gamma value of ImageAttributes.

```
ImageAttributes ImgAttr = new ImageAttributes();
imageAttr.SetGamma(2.0f, ColorAdjustType.Default);
```

Now you can use this ImageAttributes object as a parameter of the DrawImage method.

8.4.3 **The** SetColorMatrix **Method**

A **color matrix** represents how colors are represented in an Image object. As we saw in Section 8.3.2, the ColorMatrix object represents a color matrix.

TABLE 8.8: `ColorAdjustType` members

Member	Description
Any	Reserved
Bitmap	For `Bitmap` objects only
Brush	For `Brush` objects only
Count	The number of types specified (used internally by GDI+)
Default	For all objects that do no have their own color adjustment information
Pen	For `Pen` objects only
Text	For text only

`SetColorMatrix` applies a color matrix to an image. This method takes a parameter of the `ColorMatrix` class, with two optional parameters of `ColorMatrixFlag` and `ColorAdjustType` enumerations.

Often we don't want all graphics objects to be affected by a color adjustment. Suppose we have some graphics shapes, an image, and some text, and we want only the image to be affected by the color adjustment specified by the `SetColorMatrix` method. The `ColorAdjustType` enumeration allows us to specify which graphics objects use the color adjustment information. Table 8.8 describes the members of the `ColorAdjustType` enumeration.

`ColorMatrixFlag` specifies the types of images and colors that will be affected by the color adjustment settings. The `ColorMatrixFlag` enumeration has three members: `AltGrays`, `Default`, and `SkipGrays`. `AltGrays` is not available for use except by the .NET Framework internally, so basically `ColorMatrixFlag` provides the option of affecting gray colors or not. The `Default` value means that all colors will be affected; `SkipGrays` means that gray shades will not be affected. (You may want to skip some of the gray shades that are used when you're smoothing images.)

In Listing 8.10 we create `ColorMatrix` and `ImageAttributes` objects. Then we call `SetColorMatrix` to add a color matrix to `ImageAttributes`. `ImageAttributes.SetColorMatrix` takes `ColorMatrix` as its first argument.

LISTING 8.10: Drawing semitransparent images

```
private void SetColorMatrix_Click(object sender,
    System.EventArgs e)
{
    Graphics g = this.CreateGraphics();
    g.Clear(this.BackColor);
    Rectangle rect = new Rectangle(20, 20, 200, 100);
    Bitmap bitmap = new Bitmap("MyPhoto.jpg");
    // Create an array of matrix points
    float[][] ptsArray =
    {
        new float[] {1, 0, 0, 0, 0},
        new float[] {0, 1, 0, 0, 0},
        new float[] {0, 0, 1, 0, 0},
        new float[] {0, 0, 0, 0.5f, 0},
        new float[] {0, 0, 0, 0, 1}
    };
    // Create a color matrix
    ColorMatrix clrMatrix = new ColorMatrix(ptsArray);
    // Set ColorMatrix properties
    if( clrMatrix.Matrix34 <= 0.5)
    {
        clrMatrix.Matrix34 = 0.8f;
        clrMatrix.Matrix11 = 0.3f;
    }
    // Create image attributes
    ImageAttributes imgAttributes = new ImageAttributes();
    // Set color matrix
    imgAttributes.SetColorMatrix(clrMatrix,
        ColorMatrixFlag.Default,
        ColorAdjustType.Bitmap);
    g.FillRectangle(Brushes.Red, rect);
    rect.Y += 120;
    g.FillEllipse(Brushes.Black, rect);
    // Draw image
    g.DrawImage(bitmap,
        new Rectangle(0, 0, bitmap.Width, bitmap.Height),
        0, 0, bitmap.Width, bitmap.Height,
        GraphicsUnit.Pixel, imgAttributes);
    // Dispose of object
    g.Dispose();
}
```

Figure 8.9 shows the output from Listing 8.10. A rectangle and a circle
are drawn, and then an image with lower color resolution, as specified by
ImageAttributes.

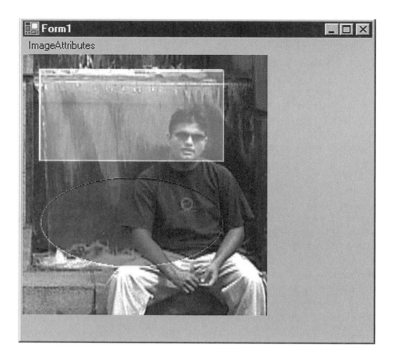

FIGURE 8.9: Drawing semitransparent images

8.4.4 The SetNoOp and SetColorKey Methods

The SetNoOp method sets the NoOp correction value for Graphics objects. When NoOp is set, no adjustments to the color will be made during the rendering process.

SetColorKey sets the low and high color values for graphics objects and shapes. The SetColorKey method takes a parameter of type Color-AdjustType enumeration (see Table 8.8) that specifies the type of the graphics objects and shapes to be affected by SetColorKey.

Listing 8.11 applies gamma effect and sets color key values using the SetColorKey method.

LISTING 8.11: Applying SetGamma and SetColorKey

```
private void SetNoOp_Click(object sender,
    System.EventArgs e)
{
    // Create a Graphics object
    Graphics g = this.CreateGraphics();
    g.Clear(this.BackColor);
```

```
    // Create two colors
    Color lClr = Color.FromArgb(245,0,0);
    Color uClr = Color.FromArgb(255,0,0);
    // Create ImageAttributes object
    ImageAttributes ImgAttr = new ImageAttributes();
    // Set color key
    ImgAttr.SetColorKey(lClr, uClr,
        ColorAdjustType.Default);
    // Set gamma
    ImgAttr.SetGamma(2.0f, ColorAdjustType.Default);
    // Set NoOp
    // ImgAttr.SetNoOp(ColorAdjustType.Default);
    // Create an Image object
    Image curImage = Image.FromFile("dnWatcher.gif");
    // Draw image
    Rectangle rect = new Rectangle(0, 0, 400, 400);
    g.DrawImage(curImage, rect, 0, 0, 400, 400,
        GraphicsUnit.Pixel, ImgAttr);
    // Dispose of object
    g.Dispose();
}
```

Figure 8.10 shows the output from Listing 8.11.

Now if we uncomment the following line in Listing 8.11:

```
//ImgAttr.SetNoOp(ColorAdjustType.Default);
```

the output will look like Figure 8.11. Using SetNoOp cancels all image attribute effects.

8.4.5 **The** SetThreshold **Method**

The SetThreshold method sets the transparency range (threshold) for a specified category. This method takes one parameter representing a

FIGURE 8.10: Applying SetGamma and SetColorKey

FIGURE 8.11: Using the `SetNoOp` method

threshold value ranging between 0.0 and 1.0, and an optional second parameter of type `ColorAdjustType`. The value of the threshold specifies a cutoff point for each component of color. For example, suppose that the threshold is set to 0.8 and the value of the red component is 240. Because the value of the red component (240) is greater than 0.8, the red component will be changed to 255 (full intensity).

```
imageAttr.SetThreshold(0.8f, ColorAdjustType.Default);
```

8.4.6 The `SetBrushRemapTable` Method

We have already discussed how the `SetRemapTable` method sets a remap table to the specified `ColorMap` object. The `OldColor` and `NewColor` properties of `ColorMap` represent old and new colors, respectively. `SetBrushRemapTable` converts only the colors of brushes. The `ColorMap` class also provides both `OldColor` and `NewColor` properties.

Listing 8.12 creates a `ColorMap` object, sets its `OldColor` and `New-Color` properties, and then calls `SetBrushRemapTable` with the `ColorMap` object.

LISTING 8.12: Using `SetBrushRemapTable`

```
private void SetBrushRemapTable_Click(object sender,
    System.EventArgs e)
{
    Graphics g = this.CreateGraphics();
    g.Clear(this.BackColor);
    ColorMap[] clrMapTable = new ColorMap[1];
    clrMapTable[0] = new ColorMap();
    clrMapTable[0].OldColor = Color.Red;;
    clrMapTable[0].NewColor = Color.Green;
```

```
    ImageAttributes ImgAttr = new ImageAttributes();
    ImgAttr.SetBrushRemapTable(clrMapTable);
    Image curImage = Image.FromFile("Sample.bmp");
    g.DrawImage(curImage, 0, 0);
    Rectangle rect = new Rectangle(0, 0, 400, 400);
    g.DrawImage(curImage, rect, 0, 0, 400, 400,
        GraphicsUnit.Pixel, ImgAttr);
    // Dispose of object
    g.Dispose();
}
```

8.4.7 **The Clear Methods**

The ImageAttributes class provides a "clear" method for almost every set method we have discussed in this section. The clear methods take either no parameter or an optional parameter of ColorAdjustType enumeration. These clear methods are listed in Table 8.9.

TABLE 8.9: The clear methods of **ImageAttributes**

Method	Description
ClearBrushRemapTable	Clears color remap table for brush.
ClearColorKey	Clears color key values for the graphics objects specified by the ColorAdjustType enumeration.
ClearColorMatrix	Clears color adjust matrix to all zeros.
ClearGamma	Clears gamma effect for the graphics objects specified by the ColorAdjustType enumeration.
ClearNoOp	Clears NoOp setting for all graphics objects.
ClearOutputChannel	Clears output channel selection for graphics objects specified by the ColorAdjustType enumeration.
ClearOutputChannel-ColorProfile	Clears output channel selection and color profile file for graphics objects specified by the ColorAdjustType enumeration.
ClearRemapTable	Clears color remap table for graphics objects specified by the ColorAdjustType enumeration.
ClearThreshold	Clears threshold value for graphics objects specified by theColorAdjustType enumeration.

Suppose that we wanted to clear the color key values for all graphics objects. We would use the `ClearColorKey` method as follows:

```
imageAttr.ClearColorKey(ColorAdjustType.Default);
```

8.5 Encoder Parameters and Image Formats

In Chapter 7 we discussed how the `Save` method of the `Image` class can be used to save images in different formats. This is what our code in Chapter 7 looked like to save an image as a TIFF file:

```
curImage.Save(fileName, ImageFormat.Tiff);
```

In fact, the `Save` method does much more than just save an image in different formats. An overloaded `Save` method can take an argument of type `EncoderParameters`, which represents an encoder. An **encoder** is responsible for converting a file from one format to another, and a **decoder** reverses it. The encoder is responsible for saving an image to a format defined by codec parameters.

Two forms of the `Save` method with `EncoderParameters` are

```
public void Save(Stream, ImageCodecInfo, EncoderParameters);
public void Save(string, ImageCodecInfo, EncoderParameters);
```

Another method is `SaveAdd`. This method adds information to an `Image` object. `EncoderParameters` determines how the new information is incorporated into the existing image.

The `SaveAdd` method has two overloaded forms. The first form adds a frame to the file or stream specified in a previous call to the `Save` method. This method can be used to save selected frames from a multiple-frame image to another multiple-frame image.

```
public void SaveAdd(EncoderParameters);
```

The second form, which takes two parameters (`Image` and `Encoder-Parameters`) adds a frame to the file or stream specified in a previous call to the `Save` method.

```
public void SaveAdd(Image, EncoderParameters);
```

8.5.1 **The** `Encoder`, `EncoderCollection`, **and** `Image` **Relationship**

Unfortunately, mostly because of inadequate documentation and samples in MSDN, it is a little difficult to understand how encoder and decoder parameters relate to images. To help clear this up, look at Figure 8.12, which shows how the different elements relate to each other.

As you can see, the `Save` method of the `Image` class consumes `EncoderParameters`, which is a collection of type `EncoderParameter`. An `EncoderParameter` object represents an encoder. We use the `Encoder` property to attach an `Encoder` object to the `EncoderParameter` object.

8.5.2 **The** `Encoder` **and** `EncoderParameter` **Classes**

An `Encoder` object encapsulates a globally unique identifier (GUID) that identifies the category of an image encoder parameter represented by `EncoderParameter`. This `Encoder` object is attached to an `Encoder-Parameter` object through its `Encoder` property.

An `Encoder` object is created by use of the `Encoder` class constructor, which takes one parameter of type `Guid`.

The `Encoder` class provides one property, `Guid`, and a set of static fields, which represent the encoder properties. The `Guid` property of the

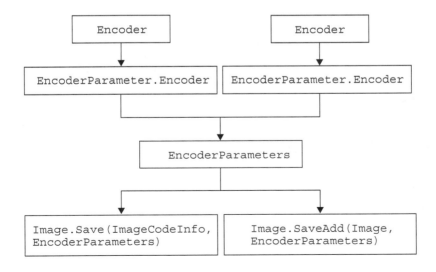

FIGURE 8.12: The relationship among `Encoder`, `EncoderCollection`, and `Image`

Encoder class returns a GUID attached to an encoder. Table 8.10 describes the fields.

EncoderParameter represents an array of values that is used to pass values to an image encoder. The EncoderParameter constructor takes an argument of Encoder object type. Table 8.11 describes the properties of the EncoderParameter class.

The EncoderParameters class represents an array of Encoder-Parameter objects. You will have to create an EncoderParameters object because the Save and SaveAdd methods take a parameter of type EncoderParameters.

Suppose that you want to save a JPEG file to a TIFF file with 24-bit compression. In Listing 8.13 we first create an EncoderParameters object. Then we create an array of ImageCodecInfo objects, which provide members to retrieve information about installed image codecs, including the codec name, MIME type, format, version, and signature. The properties of

TABLE 8.10: Encoder fields

Field	Description
ChrominanceTable	Specifies chrominance table as the parameter category.
ColorDepth	Specifies color depth as the parameter category.
Compression	Specifies compression as the parameter category.
LuminanceTable	Specifies luminance table as the parameter category.
Quality	Specifies quality as the parameter category.
RenderMethod	Specifies rendering method as the parameter category.
SaveFlag	Specifies save flag as the parameter category.
ScanMethod	Specifies scan method as the parameter category.
Transformation	Specifies transformation as the parameter category.
Version	Specifies version as the parameter category.

TABLE 8.11: `EncoderParameter` properties

Property	Description
`Encoder`	Represents an encoder associated with this encoder parameter. Both get and set types.
`NumberOfValues`	Returns the number of elements in the array of values stored in an encoder parameter.
`Type`	Returns the type of an encoder parameter.
`ValueType`	Returns the data type of the values stored in an encoder parameter.

the `ImageCodecInfo` class are listed in Table 8.12. All of these properties have both get and set types.

GDI+ provides several built-in image encoders and decoders. The `ImageCodecInfo` class provides two static methods: `GetImageEncoders` and `GetImageDecoders`, which return the built-in GDI+ image encoders and decoders in an array of `ImageCodecInfo` objects.

MIME Types

MIME stands for "Multipurpose Internet Mail Extensions." It is a standard way of classifying file types on the Internet. By specifying a MIME type, applications can easily identify the type of file and can extract more information and attributes about a file. Here are some useful links to Web resources that provide information about MIME types:

http://www.mhonarc.org/~ehood/MIME/MIME.html

http://msdn.microsoft.com/library/default.asp?url=/workshop/networking/moniker/overview/appendix_a.asp

ftp://ftp.isi.edu/in-notes/iana/assignments/media-types/media-types/

TABLE 8.12: `ImageCodecInfo` properties

Property	Description
`Clsid`	Returns the `Guid` structure that contains a GUID identifying a specific codec.
`CodecName`	Returns a string containing the name of the codec.
`DllName`	Returns a string containing the path name of the codec's DLL. If there is no DLL, returns `null`.
`FilenameExtension`	Returns a string containing the file name extension(s) used by the codec. The extensions are separated by semicolons.
`Flags`	Returns a 32-bit combination of flags from the `ImageCodecFlags` enumeration.
`FormatDescription`	Returns a string describing the codec's file format.
`FormatID`	Returns a `Guid` structure containing a GUID that identifies the codec's format.
`MimeType`	Returns a string containing the codec's Multipurpose Internet Mail Extensions (MIME) type.
`SignatureMasks`	Returns a two-dimensional array of bytes that can be used as a filter.
`SignaturePatterns`	Returns a two-dimensional array of bytes representing the signature of the codec.
`Version`	Returns the version number of the codec.

In Listing 8.13, after creating an `EncoderParameters` object, we use the `Encoder` and `EncoderParameter` objects to create three encoder parameters. These encoder parameters are responsible for changing image color depth, compression, and transformation. We use the `Encoder` class and set its `ColorDepth` property. Later the `Encoder` object is used as an argument to `EncoderParameter`, which subsequently is added to `EncoderParameters`. Then we also set the `Transformation` and `Compression` properties to `CompressionLZW` and `TransformRotation180`, respectively.

When we are done adding `EncoderParameter` objects to `Encoder-Parameters`, we call the `Save` method of `Bitmap` with the `EncoderParameters` object. Our sample saves the bitmap to a TIFF file with 24 color depth, and LZW compression.

LISTING 8.13: Saving an image with encoder properties

```
private void button1_Click(object sender,
    System.EventArgs e)
{

    ImageCodecInfo imgCodecInfo = null;
    Encoder encoder = null;
    EncoderParameter encoderParam = null;
    EncoderParameters encoderParams =
        new EncoderParameters(3);
    // Create a Bitmap object from a file
    Bitmap curBitmap = new Bitmap("roses.jpg");
    // Define mimeType
    string mimeType = "image/tiff";
    ImageCodecInfo[] encoders;
    encoders = ImageCodecInfo.GetImageEncoders();
    for(int i = 0; i < encoders.Length; ++i)
    {
        if(encoders[i].MimeType == mimeType)
            imgCodecInfo = encoders[i];
    }
    // Set color depth to 24 pixels
    encoder = Encoder.ColorDepth;
    encoderParam = new EncoderParameter(encoder, 24L);
    encoderParams.Param[0] = encoderParam;
    // Set compression mode to LZW
    encoder = Encoder.Compression;
    encoderParam = new EncoderParameter(encoder,
        (long)EncoderValue.CompressionLZW);
    encoderParams.Param[1] = encoderParam;
    // Set transformation to 180 degrees
    encoder = Encoder.Transformation;
    encoderParam = new EncoderParameter(encoder,
        (long)EncoderValue.TransformRotate180);
    encoderParams.Param[2] = encoderParam;
    // Save file as a TIFF file
    curBitmap.Save("newFile.tif", imgCodecInfo,
        encoderParams);
    // Dispose of object
    curBitmap.Dispose();
}
```

8.5.3 Retrieving Information from Digital Images or Tagged Data of TIFF Files

The `PropertyItems` property of the `Image` class returns an array of `PropertyItem` objects, which describe the attributes of an image. Each instance of `PropertyItem` has four properties—Id, Len, Type, and Value—which represent the identifier, length, type, and value of the property, respectively.

One common use of `PropertyItem` is to read the tagged data of TIFF files or the information from the JPEG images taken from a digital camera. Listing 8.14 opens a JPEG file and uses the `Image.PropertyItems` property to get an array of `PropertyItem` objects. After that we make a loop and read all property item IDs and values.

You can add this code to a button or a menu click event handler. Don't forget to add a reference to the `System.Drawing.Imaging` namespace.

LISTING 8.14: Retrieving information from digital images

```
Graphics g = this.CreateGraphics();
g.Clear(this.BackColor);
Image curImage = Image.FromFile("DSCF0105.JPG");
// Return an array of property items using
// Image's PropertyItems property
PropertyItem [] imgProperties = curImage.PropertyItems;
// Total items
string str = imgProperties.Length.ToString();
MessageBox.Show("Properties "+str);
// Read items and display in a message box
for (int i=0; i< imgProperties.Length; i++)
{
    str = string.Empty;
      str = "Id :"+imgProperties[i].Id.ToString();
    str += " ,Value:"
    +BitConverter.ToString(imgProperties[i].Value);
    MessageBox.Show(str);
}
// Dispose of object
g.Dispose();
```

8.5.4 Converting a Bitmap to Other Formats

Saving a bitmap as a PNG file or any another format is simple if we use `ImageCodecInfo` settings. We create an `ImageCodecInfo` object with

MIME type `image/png` and use it as the second argument to the `Save` method of the `Bitmap` class. Listing 8.15 converts `Shapes.bmp` to `Shape0.png`.

LISTING 8.15: Converting from JPEG to PNG

```
private void ConvertToPNG_Click(object sender,
    System.EventArgs e)
{

    ImageCodecInfo imgCodecInfo = null;
    // Create a bitmap from a file
    Bitmap curBitmap = new Bitmap("Shapes.bmp");
    int j;
    // Set MIME type. This defines the format of
    // the new file.
    string mimeType = "image/png";
    ImageCodecInfo[] encoders;
    // Get GDI+ built-in image encoders
    encoders = ImageCodecInfo.GetImageEncoders();
    // Compare with our MIME type and copy it to
    // ImageCodecInfo
    for(j = 0; j < encoders.Length; ++j)
    {
        if(encoders[j].MimeType == mimeType)
            imgCodecInfo = encoders[j];
    }
    // Save as PNG file
    curBitmap.Save("Shape0.png",
        imgCodecInfo, null);
    // Dispose of object
    curBitmap.Dispose();
}
```

Listing 8.15 will save `Shapes.bmp` to `Shape0.png`. You can save a file to other formats by changing the MIME type.

SUMMARY

This chapter covered more advanced imaging concepts. We discussed the `System.Drawing.Imaging` namespace classes, their members, and how to use them. At the beginning of the chapter you learned how to set grayscale images using `SetPixel`, `LockBits`, and `UnlockBits`. In the same section we discussed how to set the color of a bitmap.

In the section covering the `Metafile` class and related functionality, you learned the metafile types supported by GDI+, how to create new metafiles, and how to read and enumerate existing metafiles. We also saw how to read metafile header information.

The `Graphics` class provides methods to set the attributes of images. We covered how to set the colors and other attributes of images using the color map table, color matrix, and color palette. In this section we saw some real-world applications, such as drawing transparent images, wrapping images, and setting gamma values of images.

This chapter also discussed how to use the `Encoder`, `EncoderParameter`, `EncoderParameters`, and `ImageCodecInfo` classes and their members to encode images. We discussed some real-world scenarios in which you may want to change the color depth and compression of images. We also learned how to read tagged data from TIFF files and how to convert among different image formats.

Chapter 9 will concentrate on the `System.Drawing.Drawing2D` namespace.

9

Advanced 2D Graphics

I N CHAPTERS 7 AND 8 we learned how to use advanced imaging functions of the `Image`, `Bitmap`, and other classes defined in the `System.Drawing` and `System.Drawing.Imaging` namespaces. In this chapter we will discuss advanced two-dimensional GDI+ programming. The .NET Framework library defines this functionality in a separate namespace: `System.Drawing.Drawing2D`. Among the advanced 2D techniques we will discuss are blending, matrices, graphics paths, and gradient brushes.

> **■ NOTE**
>
> Before using any class discussed in this chapter, an application should reference the `System.Drawing.Drawing2D` namespace by adding the following line:
>
> `using System.Drawing.Drawing2D`

Apart from blending, gradient brushes, graphics containers, graphics paths, and matrix-related classes, the `System.Drawing.Drawing2D` namespace provides many enumerations. Some of the enumerations we have discussed in previous chapters; the rest will be covered in this chapter.

Table 9.1 lists the classes provided by `System.Drawing.Drawing2D`. Several of these classes were mentioned in previous chapters. We will discuss them here in more detail.

TABLE 9.1: `System.Drawing.Drawing2D` classes

Class	Description
AdjustableArrowCap	An adjustable, arrow-shaped line cap.
Blend	A blend pattern used by linear gradient brushes.
ColorBlend	An array of colors and positions in a multicolor gradient.
CustomLineCap	A custom user-defined line cap.
GraphicsContainer	The internal data of a graphics container. The `BeginContainer` and `EndContainer` methods are used to save the state of a `Graphics` object.
GraphicsPath	A graphics path, which contains a series of connected lines and curves.
GraphicsPathIterator	A graphics path can have many subpaths. This class provides a way to iterate through them.
GraphicsState	Graphics object state, which is returned by the `BeginContainer` method.
HatchBrush	A hatch brush. Discussed in Chapter 4.
LinearGradientBrush	Linear gradient brush. Discussed in Chapter 4.
Matrix	A 3×3 affine matrix that represents a geometric transformation.
PathData	Contains the graphical data of a graphics path.
PathGradientBrush	A brush that fills a graphics path with a gradient.
RegionData	Data of a region.

9.1 Line Caps and Line Styles

In previous chapters we saw how to draw lines and curves using Draw-Line, DrawCurve, and related methods of the Graphics class. In these cases we drew only solid lines and curves. Lines and curves can also have styles. For example, you can draw a dotted line with circular caps.

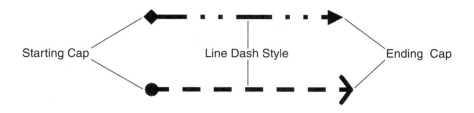

FIGURE 9.1: Lines with different starting cap, ending cap, and dash styles

A line has three parts: the line body, starting cap, and ending cap. The line starts with a **starting cap** and ends with an **ending cap**. The part that connects these two caps is the **line body**. The caps and body of a line can have different styles. Figure 9.1 shows two lines with different starting and ending cap and body styles.

The ends of a line can have different caps. Table 9.2 shows some of the available line cap styles.

A line body can have its own style, called the **dash style**. Figure 9.2 shows four different dash styles.

Each line dash style can also have its own cap style, which is called a **line dash cap**. Figure 9.3 shows three different line dash caps.

TABLE 9.2: Line cap styles

Style	Description
	Triangle
	AnchorMask (or flat or square)
	ArrowAnchor
	DiamondAnchor
	Round
	RoundAnchor
	SquareAnchor

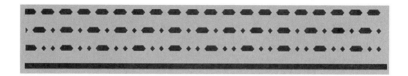

FIGURE 9.2: Line dash style

FIGURE 9.3: Line dash caps

9.1.1 Line Caps and Styles Specified by the Pen Class

The Pen object specifies the line caps and line styles being used to draw lines. To create a line with caps and styles, we create a Pen object, set its line cap and line style properties (or methods) and use the Pen object to draw the lines.

Table 9.3 lists the members of the Pen class that can be used to set line caps and line styles.

9.1.2 Adding Line Caps and Styles

There is no direct way to apply line caps and line styles to a line. We must go through the Pen object. As we covered in previous chapters, to draw a line we must have a Pen object specifying the color and width of the pen used when we call the DrawLine method of the Graphics class. The Pen object also provides members for attaching line caps and line styles to a pen. After we attach line caps and styles to a pen, we use this pen to draw lines.

In Listing 9.1 we create a Pen object with a specified color and width. Then we set the line caps using the StartCap and EndCap properties of the Pen class, followed by the DashStyle and DashOffset properties. After that we call DrawLine and dispose of the objects.

TABLE 9.3: `Pen` Class members for setting line caps and styles

Member	Description
StartCap	Property that gets or sets the cap style used at the beginning of the line. Takes a `LineCap` enumeration member.
EndCap	Property that gets or sets the cap style used at the end of the line. Takes a `LineCap` enumeration member.
CustomStartCap	Property that gets or sets a custom cap to use at the beginning of the line. Takes a `CustomLineCap` object.
CustomEndCap	Property that gets or sets a custom cap to use at the ending of the line. Takes a `CustomLineCap` object.
DashCap	Property that gets or sets the cap style used at the end of the dashes that make up a dashed line. Takes a `DashCap` enumeration, which has only three members: `Flat`, `Round`, and `Triangle`.
DashOffset	Property that gets and sets the dash offset—that is, the distance from the start of a line to the beginning of a dash pattern.
DashPattern	Property that specifies the length of each dash and space in a dash pattern. Takes an array of floating values. The first element of this array sets the length of a dash, the second element sets the length of a space, the third element sets the length of a dash, and so on.
DashStyle	Dash lines can have their own styles. This property gets and sets dash line styles, which are represented by the `DashStyle` enumeration. The `DashStyle` enumeration has six members—`Custom`, `Dash`, `DashDot`, `DashDotDot`, `Dot`, and `Solid`—that represent lines consisting of a custom pattern, dashes, a dash-dot repeating pattern, a dash-dot-dot repeating pattern, dots, and a solid line, respectively.
SetLineCap	Method that sets the values of all three parts (the starting line cap, ending line cap, and dash style) of a line.

LISTING 9.1: Setting line caps and line styles

```
Graphics g = this.CreateGraphics();
g.Clear(this.BackColor);
// Create a pen
Pen blackPen = new Pen(Color.Black, 10);
// Set the line caps and line styles
blackPen.StartCap = LineCap.Triangle;
blackPen.EndCap = LineCap.Triangle;
blackPen.DashStyle = DashStyle.Dash;
blackPen.DashOffset = 40;
g.DrawLine(blackPen, 20, 10, 200, 10);
// Dispose of objects
blackPen.Dispose();
g.Dispose();
```

We will cover line caps and styles in more detail in Sections 9.1.3 through 9.1.5.

9.1.3 Getting and Setting Line Caps and Styles

In the previous sections we discussed the LineCap, DashStyle, and DashCap enumerations, which represent the line cap, line dash style, and dash cap, respectively. Now we will write an application and use these enumerations.

We create a Windows application and a MainMenu control with three menu items on the form. We call these menu items GetCapStyle, LineDashStyle, and LineDashCap, respectively, and write menu click event handlers by double-clicking on them. On the GetCapStyle menu item click event handler, we will read different line caps and generate output using these line caps; on the LineDashStyle menu item click event handler, we will generate lines with different dash styles; and on the LineDashCap menu item click event handler, we will generate output with different line dash caps.

The GetCapStyle menu item click event handler is shown in Listing 9.2. We create a pen and set the starting and ending caps using the StartCap and EndCap properties of the Pen object, and then we draw a line.

LISTING 9.2: Getting line caps

```
private void GetCapStyles_Click(object sender,
    System.EventArgs e)
{
```

```
Graphics g = this.CreateGraphics();
g.Clear(this.BackColor);
// Create a pen
Pen blackPen = new Pen(Color.Black, 10);
// Set line styles
blackPen.StartCap = LineCap.Triangle;
blackPen.EndCap = LineCap.Triangle;
g.DrawLine(blackPen, 20, 10, 200, 10);
blackPen.StartCap = LineCap.Square;
blackPen.EndCap = LineCap.AnchorMask;
g.DrawLine(blackPen, 20, 30, 200, 30);
blackPen.StartCap = LineCap.ArrowAnchor;
blackPen.EndCap = LineCap.ArrowAnchor;
g.DrawLine(blackPen, 20, 50, 200, 50);
blackPen.StartCap = LineCap.DiamondAnchor;
blackPen.EndCap = LineCap.DiamondAnchor;
g.DrawLine(blackPen, 20, 70, 200, 70);
blackPen.StartCap = LineCap.Flat;
blackPen.EndCap = LineCap.Flat;
g.DrawLine(blackPen, 20, 90, 200, 90);
blackPen.StartCap = LineCap.Round;
blackPen.EndCap = LineCap.Round;
g.DrawLine(blackPen, 20, 110, 200, 110);
blackPen.StartCap = LineCap.RoundAnchor;
blackPen.EndCap = LineCap.RoundAnchor;
g.DrawLine(blackPen, 20, 130, 200, 130);
blackPen.StartCap = LineCap.Square;
blackPen.EndCap = LineCap.Square;
g.DrawLine(blackPen, 20, 150, 200, 150);
blackPen.StartCap = LineCap.SquareAnchor;
blackPen.EndCap = LineCap.SquareAnchor;
g.DrawLine(blackPen, 20, 170, 200, 170);
blackPen.StartCap = LineCap.Flat;
blackPen.EndCap = LineCap.Flat;
g.DrawLine(blackPen, 20, 190, 200, 190);
// Dispose of objects
blackPen.Dispose();
g.Dispose();
}
```

The output of Listing 9.2 looks like Figure 9.4, in which the lines have different caps.

The LineDashStyle menu item click event handler code is given in Listing 9.3. We create a pen and set the dash style and dash offset values using the DashStyle and DashOffset properties of the Pen object, and then we draw lines.

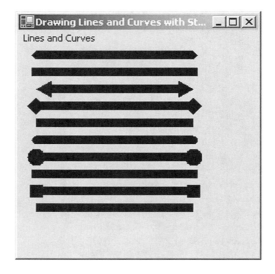

FIGURE 9.4: Reading line caps

LISTING 9.3: Getting line dash styles

```
private void LineDashStyle_Click(object sender,
    System.EventArgs e)
{
    Graphics g = this.CreateGraphics();
    g.Clear(this.BackColor);
    // Create a pen
    Pen blackPen = new Pen(Color.Black, 6);
    // Set line styles
    blackPen.DashStyle = DashStyle.Dash;
    blackPen.DashOffset = 40;
    blackPen.DashCap = DashCap.Triangle;
    g.DrawLine(blackPen, 20, 10, 500, 10);
    blackPen.DashStyle = DashStyle.DashDot;
    g.DrawLine(blackPen, 20, 30, 500, 30);
    blackPen.DashStyle = DashStyle.DashDotDot;
    g.DrawLine(blackPen, 20, 50, 500, 50);
    blackPen.DashStyle = DashStyle.Dot;
    g.DrawLine(blackPen, 20, 70, 500, 70);
    blackPen.DashStyle = DashStyle.Solid;
    g.DrawLine(blackPen, 20, 70, 500, 70);
    // Dispose of objects
    blackPen.Dispose();
    g.Dispose();
}
```

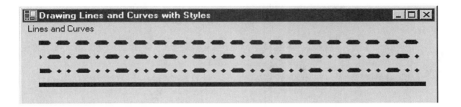

FIGURE 9.5: Reading line dash styles

Figure 9.5 shows the output from Listing 9.3. The lines have different dash styles.

The GetCapStyle menu item click event handler code is given in Listing 9.4. We create a pen and set the dash cap styles using the DashCap property of the Pen object.

LISTING 9.4: Getting dash caps

```
private void LineDashCap_Click(object sender,
    System.EventArgs e)
{
    Graphics g = this.CreateGraphics();
    g.Clear(this.BackColor);
    // Create a pen
    Pen blackPen = new Pen(Color.Black, 10);
    // Set DashCap styles
    blackPen.DashStyle = DashStyle.DashDotDot;
    blackPen.DashPattern = new float[]{10};
    blackPen.DashCap = DashCap.Triangle;
    g.DrawLine(blackPen, 20, 10, 500, 10);
    blackPen.DashCap = DashCap.Flat;
    g.DrawLine(blackPen, 20, 30, 500, 30);
    blackPen.DashCap = DashCap.Round;
    g.DrawLine(blackPen, 20, 50, 500, 50);
    // Dispose of objects
    blackPen.Dispose();
    g.Dispose();
}
```

Figure 9.6 shows the output from Listing 9.4. The lines have different dash caps: triangular, flat, and round, respectively.

FIGURE 9.6: Getting line dash caps

9.1.4 Drawing Other Objects with Line Caps and Styles

So far we have applied line caps and line styles only to lines, but these effects can also be applied to other objects, including curves, rectangles, and ellipses. However, some of these objects impose limitations. For example, rectangles, ellipses, and closed curves do not have starting and ending caps, so the StartCap and EndCap properties of a pen will not affect them.

Let's add one more menu item to MainMenu, called OtherObjects. The code for its menu item click event handler is given in Listing 9.5. We create three pens with different colors and widths; set their line cap, dash style, and dash cap properties; and draw a rectangle, an ellipse, and a curve.

LISTING 9.5: Drawing other objects using line caps, dash styles, and dash caps

```
private void OtherObjects_Click(object sender,
    System.EventArgs e)
{
    Graphics g = this.CreateGraphics();
    g.Clear(this.BackColor);
    g.SmoothingMode = SmoothingMode.AntiAlias;
    // Create pen objects
    Pen blackPen = new Pen(Color.Black, 5);
    Pen bluePen = new Pen(Color.Blue, 8);
    Pen redPen = new Pen(Color.Red, 4);
    // Set DashCap styles
    blackPen.StartCap = LineCap.DiamondAnchor;
    blackPen.EndCap = LineCap.SquareAnchor;
    blackPen.DashStyle = DashStyle.DashDotDot;
    blackPen.DashPattern = new float[]{10};
    blackPen.DashCap = DashCap.Triangle;
```

```
    // Set blue pen dash style and dash cap
    bluePen.DashStyle = DashStyle.DashDotDot;
    bluePen.DashCap = DashCap.Round;
    // Set red pen line cap and line dash styles
    redPen.StartCap = LineCap.Round;
    redPen.EndCap = LineCap.DiamondAnchor;
    redPen.DashCap = DashCap.Triangle;
    redPen.DashStyle = DashStyle.DashDot;
    redPen.DashOffset = 3.4f;
    // Draw a rectangle
    g.DrawRectangle(blackPen, 20, 20, 200, 100);
    // Draw an ellipse
    g.DrawEllipse(bluePen, 20, 150, 200, 100);
    // Draw a curve
    PointF pt1 = new PointF( 90.0F,  40.0F);
    PointF pt2 = new PointF(130.0F,  80.0F);
    PointF pt3 = new PointF(200.0F, 100.0F);
    PointF pt4 = new PointF(220.0F, 120.0F);
    PointF pt5 = new PointF(250.0F, 250.0F);
    PointF[] ptsArray =
    {
        pt1, pt2, pt3, pt4, pt5
    };
    g.DrawCurve(redPen, ptsArray);
    // Dispose of objects
    blackPen.Dispose();
    g.Dispose();
}
```

Figure 9.7 shows the output from Listing 9.5. Each graphics object—rectangle, ellipse, and curve—has a different style.

9.1.5 Customizing Line Caps

Sometimes we need to use custom caps. Figure 9.8 shows a line with customized caps of different sizes.

The CustomLineCap and AdjustableArrowCap classes provide functionality to draw custom line caps. CustomLineCap allows us to define custom caps, which can be attached to a pen—then an application can use the pen to draw graphics objects.

The CustomLineCap class constructor takes two parameters of type GraphicsPath. The first parameter defines the **fill path**, which identifies the fill for the custom cap. The second parameter defines the **stroke path**, which defines the outline of the custom cap. The fill path and stroke path parameters cannot be used at the same time.

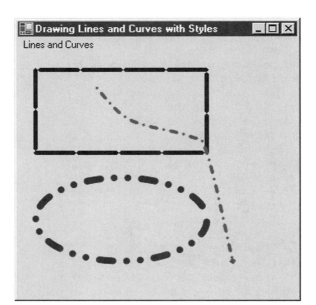

FIGURE 9.7: A rectangle, an ellipse, and a curve with different line styles

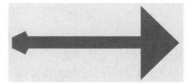

FIGURE 9.8: A line with custom caps

To create a `CustomLineCap` object, first we create a `GraphicsPath` object and add items to the path such as a line, ellipse, or rectangle using any of the add methods. Then we pass the `GraphicsPath` object as an argument to `CustomLineCap`. The following code snippet shows how to create a `CustomLineCap` object:

```
GraphicsPath path1 = new GraphicsPath();
// Add items to GraphicsPath
CustomLineCap cap1 = new CustomLineCap(null, path1);
```

Once we have a `CustomLineCap` object, we can set the `CustomStart-Cap` and `CustomEndCap` properties of the pen to apply custom line caps. We will see a full working example of custom line caps in a moment.

Table 9.4 describes the properties of the `CustomLineCap` class.

9.1.5.1 *Line Joins*

A **line join** defines how lines and curves are joined in a graphics path. The `LineJoin` enumeration represents a line join. Its members are described in Table 9.5.

We can set the line join of a pen using its `LineJoin` property. To see the line joins, we create a Windows application and add a group box, four radio buttons, and a button to the form. The final form looks like Figure 9.9.

TABLE 9.4: `CustomLineCap` properties

Property	Description
BaseCap	The base line cap. LineCap enumeration type.
BaseInset	The distance between the cap and the line.
StrokeJoin	How lines and curves in the path that will be stroked are joined. LineJoin enumeration type.
WidthScale	Width scale of custom line cap. A WidthScale value of 2 means that the cap will be double the pen size that is drawing the line cap.

TABLE 9.5: `LineJoin` members

Member	Description
Bevel	Beveled join with a diagonal corner.
Miter	Mitered join with a sharp corner or a clipped corner.
MiterClipped	Mitered join with a sharp corner or a beveled corner.
Round	Circular join with a smooth, circular arc between the lines.

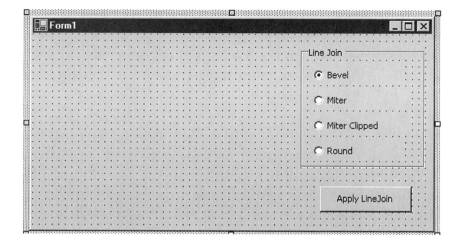

FIGURE 9.9: The line join test application

When we select different line join types and hit the **Apply LineJoin** button, the application draws lines with different joins.

The code for the **Apply LineJoin** button click event handler and DrawJoinedLines method is given in Listing 9.6. As the listing shows, the **Apply LineJoin** button click event handler calls the DrawJoinedLines method with a LineJoin value determined by the current selection.

LISTING 9.6: The Apply LineJoin button click event handler

```
private void ApplyJoin_Click(object sender,
    System.EventArgs e)
{
    // Create a Graphics object
    Graphics g = this.CreateGraphics();
    g.Clear(this.BackColor);
    // Line join type
    if(BevelRadBtn.Checked)
    {
        DrawJoinedLines(g, LineJoin.Bevel);
    }
    if(MiterRadBtn.Checked)
    {
        DrawJoinedLines(g, LineJoin.Miter);
    }
```

```
        if(MiterClippedRadBtn.Checked)
        {
            DrawJoinedLines(g, LineJoin.MiterClipped);
        }
        if(RoundRadBtn.Checked)
        {
            DrawJoinedLines(g, LineJoin.Round);
        }
        // Dispose of object
        g.Dispose();
    }

private void DrawJoinedLines(Graphics g,
    LineJoin joinType)
{
    // Set smoothing mode
    g.SmoothingMode = SmoothingMode.AntiAlias;
    // Create a pen with width 20
    Pen redPen = new Pen(Color.Red, 20);
    // Set line join
    redPen.LineJoin = joinType;
    // Create an array of points
    Point[] pts =
        {
            new Point(150, 20),
            new Point(50, 20),
            new Point(80, 60),
            new Point(50, 150),
            new Point(150, 150)
        };
    // Create a rectangle using lines
    Point[] pts1 =
        {
            new Point(200, 20),
            new Point(300, 20),
            new Point(300, 120),
            new Point(200, 120),
            new Point(200, 20)
        };
    // Draw lines
    g.DrawLines(redPen, pts);
    g.DrawLines(redPen, pts1);
    // Dispose of object
    redPen.Dispose();
}
```

Now if we run the code, the Bevel line join output looks like Figure 9.10. The Miter line join output looks like Figure 9.11. The Round line join output looks like Figure 9.12.

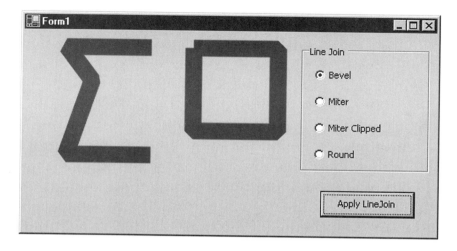

FIGURE 9.10: The **Bevel** line join effect

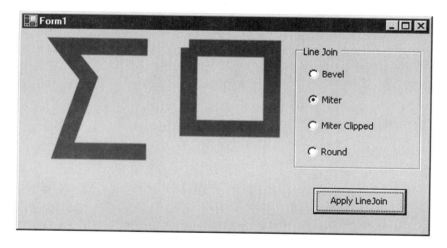

FIGURE 9.11: The **Miter** line join effect

9.1.5.2 *Stroke Caps*

We have already seen how to use the StartCap and EndCap properties of a Pen object to set the starting and ending caps of lines. We have also seen how to use the StartCustomCap and EndCustomCap properties to set customized starting and ending caps.

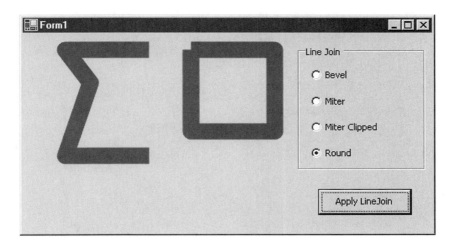

FIGURE 9.12: The Round line join effect

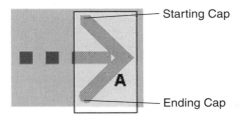

FIGURE 9.13: Customized starting and ending caps

To understand caps better, take a look at Figure 9.13. The rectangle A is a line cap. The starting cap is triangular, and the ending cap is round.

The `GetStrokeCaps` and `SetStrokeCaps` methods of the `Custom-LineCap` class can also be used to get and set the starting and ending caps of a custom cap. The `SetStrokeCaps` method takes two arguments of type `LineCap` enumeration and sets the caps for the starting and ending points of lines. Listing 9.7 creates custom line caps and sets them using the `Set-StrokeCaps` method. After creating custom line caps, we create a pen and set its `CustomStartCap` and `CustomEndCap` properties, which use the pen to draw a line.

LISTING 9.7: Using `SetStrokeCaps`

```csharp
private void SetStrokeCapsMenu_Click(object sender,
    System.EventArgs e)
{
    // Create a Graphics object
    Graphics g = this.CreateGraphics();
    g.Clear(this.BackColor);
    // Create a path for custom line cap. This
    // path will have two lines from points
    // (-3, -3) to (0, 0) and (0, 0) to (3, -3).
    Point[] points =
    {
        new Point(-3, -3),
        new Point(0, 0),
        new Point(3, -3)
    };
    GraphicsPath path = new GraphicsPath();
    path.AddLines(points);
    // Create a custom line cap from the path
    CustomLineCap cap =
        new CustomLineCap(null, path);
    // Set the starting and ending caps of the custom cap
    cap.SetStrokeCaps(LineCap.Round, LineCap.Triangle);
    // Create a Pen object and set its starting and ending
    // caps
    Pen redPen = new Pen(Color.Red, 15);
    redPen.CustomStartCap = cap;
    redPen.CustomEndCap = cap;
    redPen.DashStyle = DashStyle.DashDotDot;
    // Draw the line
    g.DrawLine(redPen,
        new Point(100, 100),
        new Point(400, 100));
    // Dispose of object
    g.Dispose();
}
```

Figure 9.14 shows the output from Listing 9.7.

9.1.5.3 *Adjustable Arrow Caps*

Adjustable arrow caps allow you to set the size of the cap's base cap, height, width, and joins. The `AdjustableArrowCap` class, which is inherited from the `CustomLineCap` class, represents an adjustable arrow-shaped line cap.

The `AdjustableArrowCap` class constructor takes three parameters: the width of the arrow as a floating value, the height of the arrow as a floating

FIGURE 9.14: Setting customized starting and ending caps

value, and a Boolean value (optional) that, if `true`, indicates that the arrow cap is filled.

The following code snippet creates an `AdjustableArrowCap` object:

```
float w = 2;
float h = 5;
bool fill = false;
AdjustableArrowCap myArrow =
   new AdjustableArrowCap(w, h, fill);
```

Besides having `CustomLineCap` methods and properties, `Adjustable-ArrowCap` provides four properties: `Filled`, `Height`, `Width`, and `Middle-Inset`. The `Height` and `Width` properties represent the height and the width, respectively, of an arrow cap. The `Filled` property indicates whether an arrow cap is filled. The `MiddleInset` property represents the distance between the outline of the arrow cap and the fill.

Now let's add an `AdjustableArrowCap` option to our application. We add one menu item to the form, along with a menu item click event handler, as shown in Listing 9.8. We create two `AdjustableArrowCap` objects and set their `BaseCap`, `BaseInset`, `StrokeJoin`, and `WidthScale` properties. Then we create a black `Pen` object with a width of 15 and set the `Custom-StartCap` and `CustomEndCap` properties of the pen as `AdjustableArrow-Cap` objects. Finally, we use this pen to draw a line with `DrawLine`.

LISTING 9.8: Using adjustable arrow caps

```
private void AdjustableRowCapMenu_Click(object sender,
    System.EventArgs e)
{
    // Create a Graphics object
    Graphics g = this.CreateGraphics();
    g.Clear(this.BackColor);
    // Create two AdjustableArrowCap objects
    AdjustableArrowCap cap1 =
        new AdjustableArrowCap(1, 1, false);
    AdjustableArrowCap cap2 =
        new AdjustableArrowCap(2, 1);
    // Set cap properties
    cap1.BaseCap = LineCap.Round;
    cap1.BaseInset = 5;
    cap1.StrokeJoin = LineJoin.Bevel;
    cap2.WidthScale = 3;
    cap2.BaseCap = LineCap.Square;
    cap2.Height = 1;
    // Create a pen
    Pen blackPen = new Pen(Color.Black, 15);
    // Set CustomStartCap and CustomEndCap properties
    blackPen.CustomStartCap = cap1;
    blackPen.CustomEndCap = cap2;
    // Draw line
    g.DrawLine(blackPen, 20, 50, 200, 50);
    // Dispose of objects
    blackPen.Dispose();
    g.Dispose();
}
```

Figure 9.15 shows the output from Listing 9.8. The end caps have different sizes.

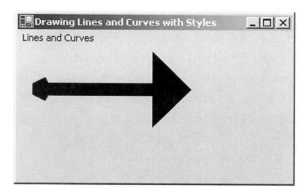

FIGURE 9.15: Adjustable arrow caps

9.2 **Understanding and Using Graphics Paths**

In Chapter 3 we briefly discussed how to create a graphics path, add graphics items to the path, and draw and fill graphics paths using `FillPath` and `DrawPath`.

A **graphics path** is a set of connected lines, curves, and other simple graphics objects, including rectangles, ellipses, and text. A path works as a single graphics object, so an effect applied to the graphics path will be applied to all the components of the path. For example, if a graphics path contains a line, a rectangle, and an ellipse and we draw the path using a red pen, all three components (line, rectangle, and ellipse) of the graphics path will be drawn with the red pen.

To create and use a graphics path, we create a `GraphicsPath` object and add its components by using add methods. For example, you can use the `AddLine`, `AddRectangle`, and `AddEllipse` methods to add a line, a rectangle, and an ellipse, respectively, to the graphics path. After adding components to a path, you can use `DrawPath` or `FillPath` to draw and fill it.

By default, all graphics shapes of a path are connected to one another and treated as a single entity with a collection of points and point types. But by using `StartFigure` and `CloseFigure`, an application can draw more than one image.

9.2.1 **Creating a** `GraphicsPath` **Object**

The `GraphicsPath` class represents a graphics path in the .NET Framework library. It provides six overloaded constructors, which take as arguments a fill mode, array of points, and array of bytes (an array of `PathPointTypes` enumerations that defines the type of each corresponding point in the point array) to construct a `GraphicsPath` object. The following code snippet uses different overloaded constructors to create `GraphicsPath` objects.

```
GraphicsPath path1 = new GraphicsPath();
GraphicsPath path2 = new GraphicsPath(FillMode.Winding);
GraphicsPath path3 =
    new GraphicsPath(pts, PathPointTypes, FillMode.Alternate);
```

In this function, `pts` represents an array of `Point` structures, and `types` represents an array of bytes, which takes the `PathPointType` enumeration types, defined as follows:

```
byte[] types = {
    (byte)PathPointType.Start,
    (byte)PathPointType.Line,
    (byte)PathPointType.DashMode };
```

The `GraphicsPath` object includes an array of points and an array of types. Point types that make up shapes include starting points, ending points, and Bézier curve points. The `PathPointType` enumeration defines the type of a point in a graphics path. The members of the `PathPointType` enumeration are described in Table 9.6.

Using `GraphicsPath`'s **Add Methods**

You can create a `GraphicsPath` object from an array of points with `PathPointType` values, but I recommend that you use the methods of `GraphicsPath` to add various objects, instead of using `PathPoint-Type`.

Now let's create a simple graphics path. Listing 9.9 gives the code for a simple graphics path with a line, a rectangle, and an ellipse. To test this code, create a Windows application, add a reference to the `System.Draw-ing.Advanced2D` namespace, and add the code on the form's load, or a button, or a menu item click event handler. The code creates a graphics path using `GraphicsPath`; adds two lines, a rectangle, and an ellipse using `AddLine`, `AddRectangle`, and `AddEllipse`, respectively; and draws the path using a red pen.

LISTING 9.9: Creating a simple graphics path

```
private void Sample_Click(object sender,
    System.EventArgs e)
{
    Graphics g = this.CreateGraphics();
    g.Clear(this.BackColor);
    // Create a graphics path
```

TABLE 9.6: `PathPointType` members

Member	Description
Bezier	Default Bézier curve.
Bezier3	Cubic Bézier curve. There is no practical difference between `Bezier` and `Bezier3`.
CloseSubpath	Ending point of a subpath.
DashMode	Dashed segment.
Line	Line segment.
PathMarker	Path marker, which allows easy traversal of a path by marking the points.
PathTypeMask	Mask point, which allows us to show or hide points.
Start	Starting point of a graphics path.

```
GraphicsPath path = new GraphicsPath();
// Add two lines, a rectangle, and
// an ellipse
path.AddLine(20, 20, 200, 20);
path.AddLine(20, 20, 20, 200);
path.AddRectangle(new Rectangle(30, 30, 100, 100));
path.AddEllipse(new Rectangle(50, 50, 60, 60));
// Draw path
Pen redPen = new Pen(Color.Red, 2);
g.DrawPath(redPen, path);
// Dispose of objects
redPen.Dispose();
g.Dispose();
}
```

Figure 9.16 shows the output from Listing 9.9: two lines, a rectangle, and an ellipse.

You can also fill a path with `FillPath`. Iif you replace the `DrawPath` line in Listing 9.9 with:

```
g.FillPath(new SolidBrush(Color.Black), path);
```

the code will generate a new figure that looks like Figure 9.17.

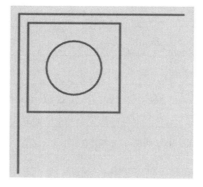

FIGURE 9.16: A simple graphics path

FIGURE 9.17: A filled graphics path

> **■ NOTE**
> In a graphics path, all lines and curves are connected, even though you don't connect them explicitly. Objects like rectangles and circles may not be connected (unless you connect them explicitly) but they are still part of the path.

9.2.2 Shaped Forms and Graphics Paths

Graphics paths are very useful when you need to create shaped (non-rectangular) forms and controls. Using a graphics path, you can also write a form with a text-based shape. For example, you can write a form application that looks like Figure 9.18, which includes a text string, two ellipses, and two rectangles.

Writing applications with shaped forms is easy if we use graphics paths. First we create a `GraphicsPath` object and add components (such as rectangles, ellipses, or text) to the path. Then we create a `Region` object from the graphics path and set it as the form's `Region` property. For example, Listing 9.10 adds text, two rectangles, and two ellipses to a graphics path, creates a `Region` object from this graphics path, and sets it as the `Region` property of the form. The output of this code will generate a form that looks like Figure 9.18.

LISTING 9.10: Using graphics paths to create shaped forms

```
GraphicsPath path = new GraphicsPath(FillMode.Alternate);
path.AddString("Close? Right Click!",
    new FontFamily("Verdana"),
    (int)FontStyle.Bold, 50, new Point(0, 0),
    StringFormat.GenericDefault );
path.AddRectangle(new Rectangle(20, 70, 100, 100));
path.AddEllipse(new Rectangle(140, 70, 100, 100));
path.AddEllipse(new Rectangle(260, 70, 100, 100));
path.AddRectangle(new Rectangle(380, 70, 100, 100));
Region rgn = new Region(path);
this.Region = rgn;
```

To test this code, create a Windows application and add this code to the form's load event handler.

FIGURE 9.18: A shaped form

9.2.3 GraphicsPath Properties and Methods

Let's examine the properties and methods of the GraphicsPath class before we start using them. Table 9.7 describes the properties.

The following code snippet reads some of the GraphicsPath properties:

```
// Getting GraphicsPath properties
FillMode fMode = path.FillMode;
PathData data = path.PathData;
PointF [] pts = path.PathPoints;
byte [] ptsTypes = path.PathTypes;
int count = path.PointCount;
```

The GraphicsPath class provides more than a dozen add methods to add graphics objects to a path. Among these methods are AddArc, AddBezier, AddBeziers, AddCloseCurve, AddCurve, AddEllipse, Add-Line, AddLines, AddPath, AddPie, AddPolygon, AddRectangle, Add-Rectangles, and AddString. These methods are used to add an arc, a Bézier, a set of Béziers, a closed curve, a curve, an ellipse, a line, a set of

TABLE 9.7: GraphicsPath properties

Property	Description
FillMode	Represents the fill mode of a graphics path, which determines how the interior of a graphics path is filled. This property is a FillMode enumeration type and has two values: Alternate and Winding.
PathData	Returns a PathData object containing path data for a graphics path. The path data of a graphics path is composed of arrays of points and types. The Points property of PathData returns an array of points, and the Types property returns an array of types of points.
PathPoints	Represents all points in a path.
PathTypes	Represents types of the corresponding points in the PathPoints array.
PointCount	Represents the total number of items in PathPoints.

Alternate and Winding Modes

As defined in the MSDN documentation, the **alternate mode** specifies that areas are filled according to the even-odd parity rule. According to this rule, you can determine whether a test point is inside or outside a closed curve as follows: Draw a line from the test point to a point that is distant from the curve. If that line crosses the curve an odd number of times, the test point is inside the curve; otherwise the test point is outside the curve.

The **winding mode** specifies that areas are filled according to the nonzero winding rule, which says that you can determine whether a test point is inside or outside a closed curve as follows: Draw a line from a test point to a point that is distant from the curve. Count the number of times the curve crosses the test line from left to right, and the number of times the curve crosses the test line from right to left. If those two numbers are the same, the test point is outside the curve; otherwise the test point is inside the curve.

lines, a path, a pie, a polygon, a rectangle, a set of rectangles, and a string, respectively. Other methods, which don't belong to the add category, are described in Table 9.8.

9.2.4 Subpaths

A graphics path can contain many subpaths. Having subpaths provides better control over individual paths. An application can break a graphics path into subpaths by using the `StartFigure` method. It can close open subpaths by using the `CloseFigure` or `CloseAllFigures` methods. `StartFigure` starts a new subpath of a path, and `CloseFigure` closes the opened subpath. `CloseAllFigures` closes all subpaths of a graphics path.

Listing 9.11 uses the `StartFigure` method to create three subpaths, and the `CloseFigure` and `CloseAllFigures` methods to close open figures. The first path contains an arc and a line, the second path contains two lines and a curve, and the third path contains two lines.

TABLE 9.8: Some `GraphicsPath` methods

Method	Description
ClearMarkers	Clears all markers from a path if any were set with `PathPointType.PathMarker`.
CloseAllFigures	Closes all open figures in a path.
CloseFigure	Closes the current figure.
Flatten	Approximates each curve in a path with a sequence of connected line segments.
GetLastPoint	Returns the last point in the `PathPoints` array.
Reset	Removes all points and types from a path and sets the fill mode to `Alternative`.
Reverse	Reverses the order of points in the `PathPoints` array of a path.
SetMarkers	Sets a marker on a path.
StartFigure	Starts a new figure.
Transform	Transforms a path by applying a matirix on the path.
Warp	Applies a warp transformation.
Widen	Replaces a path with curves that enclose the area that is filled when the path is drawn by the specified pen.

LISTING 9.11: Creating graphics subpaths

```
private void SubPathMenu_Click(object sender,
    System.EventArgs e)
{
    // Create a Graphics object
    Graphics g = this.CreateGraphics();
    g.Clear(this.BackColor);
    // Create a GraphicsPath object
    GraphicsPath path = new GraphicsPath();
    // Create an array of points
    Point[] pts =
    {
        new Point(40, 80),
        new Point(50, 70),
```

```
        new Point(70, 90),
        new Point(100, 120),
        new Point(80, 120)
    };
    // Start first figure and add an
    // arc and a line
    path.StartFigure();
    path.AddArc(250, 80, 100, 50, 30, -180);
    path.AddLine(180, 220, 320, 80);
    // Close first figure
    path.CloseFigure();
    // Start second figure, add two lines
    // and a curve, and close all figures
    path.StartFigure();
    path.AddLine(50, 20, 5, 90);
    path.AddLine(50, 150, 150, 180);
    path.AddCurve(pts, 5);
    path.CloseAllFigures();
    // Create third figure and don't close
    // it
    path.StartFigure();
    path.AddLine(200, 230, 250, 200);
    path.AddLine(200, 230, 250, 270);
    // Draw path
    g.DrawPath(new Pen(Color.FromArgb(255, 255, 0, 0), 2)
        , path);
    // path.Reverse();
    // path.Reset();
    // Dispose of object
    g.Dispose();
}
```

Figure 9.19 shows the output from Listing 9.11. There are three uncon-nected subpaths.

The `Reverse` method can be used to reverse the order of points in a path, and the `Reset` method to remove (empty) all points from a path. The following code snippet shows how to use these two methods:

```
path.Reverse();
path.Reset();
```

9.2.5 **The Graphics Path Iterator**

As mentioned earlier, a graphics path is a set of graphics subpaths. We can determine the number of subpaths and the related data of a subpath by using the `GraphicsPathIterator` class. This class allows us to iterate through all the subpaths of a graphics path.

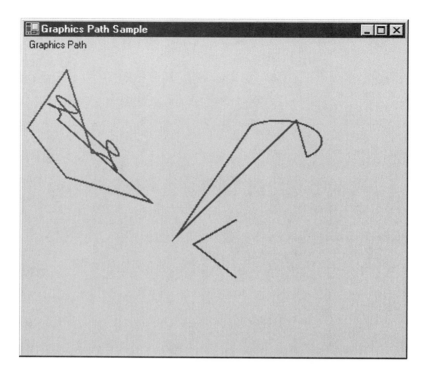

FIGURE 9.19: Three subpaths

The Count and SubpathCount properties of GraphicsPathIterator return the total number of points and the number of subpaths in a graphics path, respectively. The CopyData method can be used to copy the points of a path and their types. It returns the number of points, which is also the number of types copied.

The HasCurves method returns true if a path has curves in it; otherwise it returns false. The NextMarker method moves the iterator to the next marker in the path. The NextPathType method returns the starting and ending indices of the next group of data points that all have the same type.

The NextSubpath method returns the starting index, ending index, and a Boolean value of true if the subpath is closed (false if the subpath is open), and moves to the next subpath. The Rewind method resets the iterator to the beginning of the path.

Listing 9.12 creates and draws a graphics path and uses Graphics-PathIterator to find and show the data for all subpaths.

LISTING 9.12: Iterating through subpaths

```
private void GraphicsPathIterator_Paint(object sender,
    System.Windows.Forms.PaintEventArgs e)
{
    // Get the Graphics object
    Graphics g = e.Graphics;
    // Create a rectangle
    Rectangle rect = new Rectangle(50, 50, 100, 50);
    // Create a graphics path
    GraphicsPath path = new  GraphicsPath();
    PointF[] ptsArray =
    {
        new PointF(20, 20),
        new PointF(60, 12),
        new PointF(100, 20)
    };
    // Add a curve, a rectangle, an ellipse, and a line
    path.AddCurve(ptsArray);
    path.AddRectangle(rect);
    rect.Y += 60;
    path.AddEllipse(rect);
    path.AddLine(120, 50, 220, 100);
    // Draw path
    g.DrawPath(Pens.Blue, path);
    // Create a graphics path iterator
    GraphicsPathIterator pathIterator =
        new GraphicsPathIterator(path);
    // Display total points and subpaths
    string str = "Total points = "
        + pathIterator.Count.ToString();
    str += ", Sub paths = "
        + pathIterator.SubpathCount.ToString();
    MessageBox.Show(str);
    // Rewind
    pathIterator.Rewind();
    // Read all subpaths and their properties
    for(int i=0; i<pathIterator.SubpathCount; i++)
    {
        int strtIdx, endIdx;
        bool bClosedCurve;
        pathIterator.NextSubpath(out strtIdx,
            out endIdx, out bClosedCurve);
        str = "Start Index = " + strtIdx.ToString()
            + ", End Index = " + endIdx.ToString()
            + ", IsClosed = " + bClosedCurve.ToString();
        MessageBox.Show(str);
    }
}
```

9.3 **Graphics Containers**

Suppose that you have a surface with 100 different graphics objects (text, shapes, and images), and you want to anti-alias just one object, perhaps for performance reasons. Without graphics containers, you would have to create a `Graphics` object and set the `SmoothingMode` property to `AntiAlias`—which would set anti-aliasing for everything drawn on the object. How do you set the smoothing mode of only one particular object on a surface? That's where containers come in.

The `Graphics` class provides methods and properties to define the attributes of graphics objects. For example, you can set the rendering quality of text using the `TextRenderingHint` property. The smoothing mode represents the quality of the graphics objects, the compositing quality represents the quality of composite images, the compositing mode represents whether pixels from a source image overwrite or are combined with background pixels, and the interpolation mode represents how intermediate values between two endpoints are calculated. These attributes are set with the `SmoothingMode`, `CompositingMode`, `CompositingQuality`, and `InterpolationMode` properties—which are applicable for an entire `Graphics` object. For example, if you set the `SmoothingMode` property of a `Graphics` object to `AntiAlias`, all graphics objects attached to that `Graphics` object will be anti-aliased.

A **graphics container** is a temporary graphics object that acts as a canvas for graphics shapes, allowing an application to set a container property separately from the main `Graphics` object. An application can apply properties to a `Graphics` object within a container, and these properties won't be available outside of that container. Thus we can selectively apply properties to `Graphics` objects.

In Figure 9.20, for example, a `Graphics` object includes three graphics containers, each with different properties. These properties are not available outside of their containers. All graphics objects inside a container may be affected by the container property. It's also possible to have nested containers.

`Graphics` containers do not inherit their parent's settings. In Figure 9.20, for example, the `Graphics` object is a container whose composit-

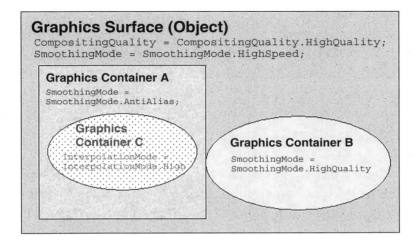

FIGURE 9.20: Nested containers

ing quality is set to high, and whose smoothing mode is set to high-speed. The graphics containers won't have high-speed and high-quality rendering unless we set them within the container itself. The smoothing mode of graphics container A is set to anti-aliasing; that of graphics container B is set to high quality. Graphics container C is a nested container within graphics container A, with interpolation mode set to high.

Before we discuss graphics containers in more detail, let's take a look at graphics states.

9.3.1 Understanding Graphics States

During the life cycle of a `Graphics` object, the object maintains a list of graphics states. These graphics states fall into various categories depending on the operations being applied to the `Graphics` object. For example, setting the compositing quality of a `Graphics` object changes the object's state.

Graphics states can be divided into three categories:

1. Quality settings
2. Transformations
3. Clipping region

The first state of the `Graphics` object involves the quality of shapes and images. This state changes when you set the quality of a `Graphics` object using the `SmoothingMode`, `TextRenderingHint`, `Compositing-Mode`, `CompositingQuality`, and `InterpolationMode` properties of the `Graphics` class.

Transformation is another state that a `Graphics` object maintains. Transformation is the process of changing graphics objects from one state to another by rotation, scaling, reflection, translation, and shearing.

The `Graphics` object maintains two transformation states: world and page. The **world transformation** defines the conversion of world coordinates to page coordinates. **World coordinates** are coordinates that you define in your program, and **page coordinates** are coordinates that GDI+ uses to expose the object coordinates. The **page transformation** defines the conversion of page coordinates to device coordinates. **Device coordinates** determine how a graphics object will be displayed on a particular display device.

The `Graphics` class provides the `ScaleTransform`, `RotateTransform`, and `TranslateTransform` methods, as well as the `Transform` property, to support transformations.

> **■ NOTE**
> Chapter 10 discusses transformations and transformation-related classes, methods, and properties in greater detail.

The world unit (by default) is always defined as a pixel. For example, in the following code snippet a rectangle will be drawn starting at 0 pixels from the left edge and 0 pixels from the top edge, with width and height of 100 and 50 pixels, respectively.

```
Graphics g = this.CreateGraphics();
g.DrawRectangle(Pens.Green, 0, 0, 100, 50);
```

Page coordinates may be different from world coordinates, depending on the page unit and page scaling of the `Graphics` object. For example, if the page unit is an inch, the page coordinates will start at point (0, 0), but

TABLE 9.9: `GraphicsUnit` members

Member	Description
Display	1/75 inch as the unit of measure.
Document	The document unit (1/300 inch) as the unit of measure.
Inch	An inch as the unit of measure.
Millimeter	A millimeter as the unit of measure.
Pixel	A pixel as the unit of measure.
Point	A printer's point (1/72 inch) as the unit of measure.
World	The world unit as the unit of measure.

the width and height of the rectangle will be 100 inches and 50 inches, respectively.

The `PageScale` and `PageUnit` properties define a page transformation. The `PageUnit` property defines the unit of measure used for page coordinates, and the `PageScale` property defines the scaling between world and page units for a `Graphics` object. The `PageUnit` property takes a value of type `GraphicsUnit` enumeration, which is defined in Table 9.9.

Listing 9.13 draws three ellipses with the same size but different `PageUnit` values: `Pixel`, `Millimeter`, and `Point`.

LISTING 9.13: Setting page transformation

```
private void TransformUnits_Click(object sender,
    System.EventArgs e)
{
    // Create a Graphics object and set its
    // background as form's background
    Graphics g = this.CreateGraphics();
    g.Clear(this.BackColor);
    // Draw an ellipse with default units
    g.DrawEllipse(Pens.Red, 0, 0, 100, 50);
    // Draw an ellipse with page unit as pixel
    g.PageUnit = GraphicsUnit.Pixel;
    g.DrawEllipse(Pens.Red, 0, 0, 100, 50);
```

continues

```
// Draw an ellipse with page unit as millimeter
g.PageUnit = GraphicsUnit.Millimeter;
g.DrawEllipse(Pens.Blue, 0, 0, 100, 50);
// Draw an ellipse with page unit as point
g.PageUnit = GraphicsUnit.Point;
g.DrawEllipse(Pens.Green, 0, 0, 100, 50);
// Dispose of object
g.Dispose();
}
```

Figure 9.21 shows the output from Listing 9.13. Although the parameters to DrawEllipse are the same, we get results of different sizes because of the different PageUnit settings.

The third state of the Graphics object is the clipping region. A Graphics object maintains a clipping region that applies to all items drawn by that object. You can set the clipping region by calling the SetClip method. It has six overloaded forms, which vary in using a Graphics object, graphics path, region, rectangle, or handle to a GDI region as the first parameter. The second parameter in all six forms is CombineMode, which has six values: Complement, Exclude, Intersect, Replace, Union, and Xor. The Clip property of the Graphics object specifies a Region

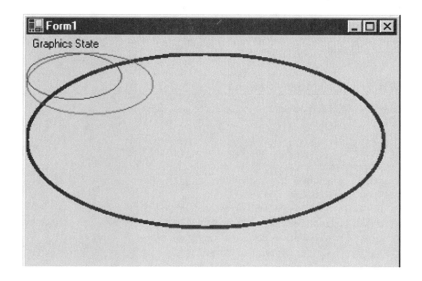

FIGURE 9.21: Drawing with different PageUnit values

object that limits the portion of a `Graphics` object that is currently available for drawing. The `ClipBounds` property returns a `RectangleF` structure that represents a bounding rectangle for the clipping region of a `Graphics` object.

> ■ **NOTE**
> Chapter 6 discussed clipping regions and the `CombineMode` enumeration in detail.

9.3.2 Saving and Restoring Graphics States

The `GraphicsState` class represents the state of a `Graphics` object. This class does not have any useful properties or methods, but it is used by the `Save` and `Restore` methods of the `Graphics` object. A call to the `Save` method saves a `GraphicsState` object as an information block on the stack and returns it. When this object is passed to the `Restore` method, the information block is removed from the stack and the graphics state is restored to the saved state.

You can make multiple calls to `Save` (even nested), and each time a new state will be saved and a new `GraphicState` object will be returned. When you call `Restore`, the block will be freed on the basis of the `GraphicsState` object you pass as a parameter.

Now let's see how this works in our next example. We create a Windows application, add a `MainMenu` control and its items, and write click event handlers for these items. Listing 9.14 creates and saves graphics states using the `Save` method, then restores them one by one. The first saved state stores page units and a rotation transformation; the second state stores a translation transformation. We save the first graphics state as `gs1`. Then we call the `TranslateTransform` method, which translates and transforms the graphics object. We save the new graphics state as `gs2`. Now we call `ResetTransform`, which removes all the transformation effects. Then we draw an ellipse. We restore the graphics states by calling `Graphics-State.Restore` methods for both `gs1` and `gs2`, and we fill a rectangle and draw an ellipse, respectively.

LISTING 9.14: Saving and restoring graphics states

```csharp
private void SaveRestoreMenu_Click(object sender,
    System.EventArgs e)
{
    // Create a Graphics object and set its
    // background as the form's background
    Graphics g = this.CreateGraphics();
    g.Clear(this.BackColor);
    // Page transformation
    g.PageUnit = GraphicsUnit.Pixel;
    // World transformation
    g.RotateTransform(45, MatrixOrder.Append);
    // Save first graphics state
    GraphicsState gs1 = g.Save();
    // One more transformation
    g.TranslateTransform(0, 110);
    // Save graphics state again
    GraphicsState gs2 = g.Save();
    // Undo all transformation effects by resetting
    // the transformation
    g.ResetTransform();
    // Draw a simple ellipse with no transformation
    g.DrawEllipse(Pens.Red, 100, 0, 100, 50);
    // Restore first graphics state, which means
    // that the new item should rotate 45 degrees
    g.Restore(gs1);
    g.FillRectangle(Brushes.Blue, 100, 0, 100, 50);
    // Restore second graphics state
    g.Restore(gs2);
    g.DrawEllipse(Pens.Green, 100, 50, 100, 50);
    // Dispose of Graphics object
    g.Dispose();
}
```

Figure 9.22 shows the output from Listing 9.14. The first ellipse has no transformation effects, but the rectangle and ellipse below do have transformation effects.

9.3.3 **Working with Graphics Containers**

Graphics containers were introduced earlier in this chapter. Now let's see how to create and use them in our applications.

9.3.3.1 *Creating a Graphics Container*

The BeginContainer method of the Graphics class creates a container. Each BeginContainer method is paired with an EndContainer method.

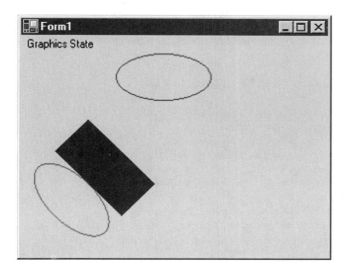

FIGURE 9.22: Saving and restoring graphics states

You can also create nested containers. The following code snippet creates two containers:

```
GraphicsContainer gContrainer1 = g.BeginContainer();
// Do something here
GraphicsContainer gContrainer2 = g.BeginContainer();
// Do something here
g.EndContainer(gContrainer2);
g.EndContainer(gContrainer1);
```

9.3.3.2 *Using Graphics Containers to Draw Text*

As mentioned earlier, graphics containers are temporary canvases. Let's see how to set the quality of different text for different containers. Listing 9.15 creates two containers, and each has different properties. The first container sets the `TextRenderingHint` property to `AntiAlias` and the `TextContrast` property to 4. The second container sets `TextRendering-Hint` to `AntiAliasGridFit` and `TextContrast` to 12. After creating `Font` and `SolidBrush` objects, we set the `TextRenderingHint` property of the `Graphics` object, and then we call `DrawString`. Finally, we call `End-Container` to terminate the container scope.

LISTING 9.15: Using different graphics containers to draw text

```
private void DrawTextMenu_Click(object sender,
    System.EventArgs e)
{
    // Create a Graphics object and set its
    // background as the form's background
    Graphics g = this.CreateGraphics();
    g.Clear(this.BackColor);
    // Create font and brushes
    Font tnrFont = new Font("Times New Roman", 40,
        FontStyle.Bold, GraphicsUnit.Pixel);
    SolidBrush blueBrush = new SolidBrush(Color.Blue);
    g.TextRenderingHint = TextRenderingHint.SystemDefault;
    // First container boundary starts here
    GraphicsContainer gContrainer1 = g.BeginContainer();
    // Gamma correction value 0 - 12. Default is 4.
    g.TextContrast = 4;
    g.TextRenderingHint = TextRenderingHint.AntiAlias;
    g.DrawString("Text String", tnrFont, blueBrush,
        new PointF(10, 20));
    // Second container boundary starts here
    GraphicsContainer gContrainer2 = g.BeginContainer();
    g.TextContrast = 12;
    g.TextRenderingHint =
        TextRenderingHint.AntiAliasGridFit;
    g.DrawString("Text String", tnrFont, blueBrush,
        new PointF(10, 50));
    // Second container boundary finishes here
    g.EndContainer(gContrainer2);
    // First container boundary finishes here
    g.EndContainer(gContrainer1);
    // Draw string outside of the container
    g.DrawString("Text String", tnrFont, blueBrush,
        new PointF(10, 80));
    // Dispose of Graphics object
    blueBrush.Dispose();
    g.Dispose();
}
```

> **NOTE**
>
> The TextRenderingHint enumeration is defined in the System.Drawing.Text namespace. Don't forget to add this namespace reference.

Figure 9.23 shows the output from Listing 9.15. Notice the quality difference in the text.

9.3.3.3 *Using Graphics Containers to Draw Shapes*

In the previous section we saw how we can use containers to draw text with different rendering quality and performance. We can draw other shapes using `SmoothingMode`, `CompositingQuality`, and other properties.

Listing 9.16 uses the `AntiAlias`, `GammaCorrected`, and `HighSpeed` options to draw rectangles and ellipses. We create a container by calling `BeginContainer`, set the smoothing mode to anti-aliasing, and set the compositing quality and gamma correction of the `Graphics` object. Then we draw an ellipse and a rectangle. After that we create a second graphics container by making another call to `BeginContainer` and set the smoothing mode and compositing quality to high speed, and then we draw a new ellipse and rectangle. Finally, we make two calls to the `EndContainer` method to close the containers.

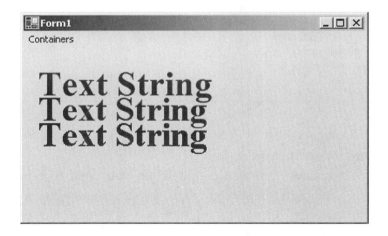

FIGURE 9.23: Using graphics containers to draw text

Listing 9.16: Using graphics containers to draw shapes

```
private void DrawShapesMenu_Click(object sender,
    System.EventArgs e)
{
    // Create a Graphics object and set its
    // background as the form's background
    Graphics g = this.CreateGraphics();
    g.Clear(this.BackColor);
    // Create pens
    Pen redPen = new Pen(Color.Red, 20);
    Pen bluePen = new Pen(Color.Blue, 10);
    // Create first graphics container
    GraphicsContainer gContainer1 = g.BeginContainer();
    // Set its properties
    g.SmoothingMode = SmoothingMode.AntiAlias;
    g.CompositingQuality =
        CompositingQuality.GammaCorrected;
    // Draw graphics objects
    g.DrawEllipse(redPen, 10, 10, 100, 50);
    g.DrawRectangle(bluePen, 210, 0, 100, 100);
    // Create second graphics container
    GraphicsContainer gContainer2 = g.BeginContainer();
    // Set its properties
    g.SmoothingMode = SmoothingMode.HighSpeed;
    g.CompositingQuality = CompositingQuality.HighSpeed;
    // Draw graphics objects
    g.DrawEllipse(redPen, 10, 150, 100, 50);
    g.DrawRectangle(bluePen, 210, 150, 100, 100);
    // Destroy containers
    g.EndContainer(gContainer2);
    g.EndContainer(gContainer1);
    // Dispose of objects
    redPen.Dispose();
    bluePen.Dispose();
    g.Dispose();
}
```

Figure 9.24 shows the output from Listing 9.16 The first ellipse and rectangle are smoother than the second set.

Graphics containers are also useful when you need to render large images either with high quality or at high speed. For example, if you have two large images and only one is quality-sensitive, you can create two graphics containers and set high quality for the first container and high speed for the second.

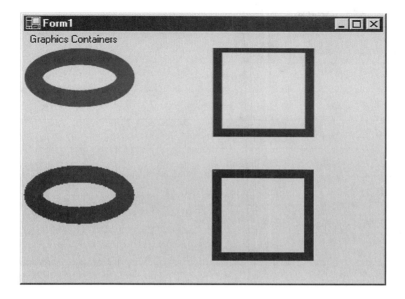

FIGURE 9.24: Using graphics containers to draw shapes

9.4 **Reading Metadata of Images**

If you have ever worked with mechanical and engineering drawings or digital images, you are probably aware of metadata. **Metadata** is information about the image, that's not part of the image itself. When an engineer draws an image, metadata is often added, such as the following information: last updated, updated by, date, place, and names. A photograph might include metadata such as image title, manufacturer, and model.

In the .NET Framework library, the `PropertyItem` object is used as a placeholder for metadata. The `PropertyItem` class provides four properties: `Id`, `Len`, `Type`, and `Value`. All of these properties have both read and write access.

The `Id` property is a tag, which identifies the metadata item. Table 9.10 describes `Id` tag values.

The `Value` property is an array of values whose format is determined by the `Type` property. The `Len` property represents the length of the array of values in bytes. The `Type` property represents the data type of values stored in the array. Table 9.11 describes the format of the `Type` property values.

TABLE 9.10: `Id` values

Hexadecimal Value	Description
0x0320	Image title
0x010F	Equipment manufacturer
0x0110	Equipment model
0x9003	ExifDTOriginal
0x829A	EXIF exposure time
0x5090	Luminance table
0x5091	Chrominance table

TABLE 9.11: Format of `Type` property values

Numeric Value	Description
1	A `Byte` object
2	An array of `Byte` objects encoded as ASCII
3	A 16-bit integer
4	A 32-bit integer
5	An array of two `Byte` objects that represent a rational number
6	Not used
7	Undefined
8	Not used
9	`SLong`
10	`SRational`

An `Image` object may contain more than one `PropertyItem` object. The `PropertyItems` property of the `Image` class represents an array of `PropertyItem` objects corresponding to an image. The `PropertyIdList` property of the `Image` class returns an array of property IDs stored in an image object. Listing 9.17 uses the `PropertyItems` property of the `Image` class and reads all property items of an image.

LISTING 9.17: Reading the metadata of a bitmap

```
private void Form1_Load(object sender,
    System.EventArgs e)
{
    // Create an image from a file
    Graphics g = this.CreateGraphics();
    Image curImage = Image.FromFile("roses.jpg");
    Rectangle rect = new Rectangle(20, 20, 100, 100);
    g.DrawImage(curImage, rect);
    // Create an array of PropertyItem objects and read
    // items using PropertyItems
    PropertyItem[] propItems = curImage.PropertyItems;
    // Create values of PropertyItem members
    foreach (PropertyItem propItem in propItems)
    {
        System.Text.ASCIIEncoding encoder =
            new System.Text.ASCIIEncoding();
        string str = "ID ="+propItem.Id.ToString("x");
        str += ", Type ="+ propItem.Type.ToString();
        str += ", Length = "+ propItem.Len.ToString();
        str += ", Value ="
            + encoder.GetString(propItem.Value);
        MessageBox.Show(str);
    }
    // Dispose of object
    g.Dispose();
}
```

Figure 9.25 shows the output from Listing 9.17.

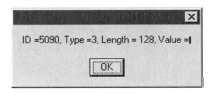

FIGURE 9.25: Reading the metadata of a bitmap

9.5 **Blending Explained**

If you have experience working with graphics, you may have heard some terms related to blending. *Blending*, *alpha blending*, and *color blending* are a few of these. In general, **blending** refers to mixing or combining two colors: a source color and a background color. The resulting blended color is used to draw graphics shapes, lines, and curves.

In this chapter blending is divided into three categories: color blending, alpha blending, and mixed blending. **Color blending**, which produces what are known as color **gradients**, involves drawing and filling graphics shapes, lines, and curves starting with a color at one end and finishing with another color at the other end. Figure 9.26 shows a good example of color blending.

Alpha blending is used to draw and fill transparent shapes, lines, and curves. Pens and brushes are used to create alpha blending. First we create a pen or brush using the alpha component value as the color of a brush or pen, and then we use that brush or pen to fill and draw shapes, lines, and

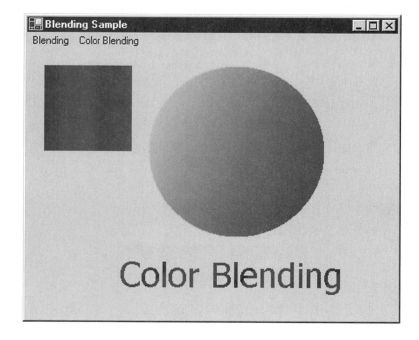

FIGURE 9.26: Color blending examples

> **NOTE**
>
> Images in this book are not colored, so you may not see the exact effects described in the text. To see the exact effects, run the sample code.

curves. Semitransparent or translucent graphics shapes, lines, and curves are examples of alpha blending. For example, Figure 9.27 contains three lines with opaque and semitransparent colors, and a string with semitransparent color on top of an image—a perfect example of alpha blending.

Mixed blending is probably a new concept to most readers. You won't find it mentioned in the MSDN documentation. Mixed blending is a combination of color and alpha blending. Figure 9.28 shows an example. If you run the sample code, you will see that the output consists of not only a transparent image, but also a color blending sample.

FIGURE 9.27: Transparent graphics shapes in an image using alpha blending

FIGURE 9.28: Mixed blending effects

9.5.1 **Color Blending**

Gradient brushes play a major role in color blending. LinearGradient-Brush and PathGradientBrush both represent brush objects with color blending.

As we discussed in Chapter 4, a linear gradient brush is a brush with two colors: a starting color and an ending color. A path gradient brush is used to fill graphics paths. Instead of starting a color from one end, the path gradient brush starts a color from the center of the path and ends with the second color at the outer boundary of the path.

A **blend pattern** is a combination of two colors (a starting color and an ending color) defined by factors and positions. The Blend class represents a blend pattern in the .NET Framework. It provides two properties: Factors and Positions. The Factors property specifies the percentage of the starting color and the ending color to be used at the corresponding position. The Positions property specifies the percentages of distance for each gradation of color along the gradient line. The values of `Factors` and `Positions` must be between 0 and 1, where 0 represents the starting position and 1 represents the ending position. For example, `0.4f` specifies that a point is 40 percent of the total distance from the starting point.

After creating a `Blend` object, you can attach it to a linear gradient brush by setting the `Blend` property of the `LinearGradientBrush` object. In Listing 9.18 we create a `Blend` object and its `Factors` and `Positions` properties, and then we set the `Blend` property of the `LinearGradientBrush` object. We can use this brush to fill graphics shapes.

LISTING 9.18: Creating a `Blend` object and setting its `Factors` and `Positions` properties

```
LinearGradientBrush brBrush = new LinearGradientBrush(
    new Point(0, 0), new Point(50, 20),
    Color.Blue, Color.Red);
Blend blend = new Blend();
float[] factArray = {0.0f, 0.3f, 0.5f, 1.0f};
float[] posArray  = {0.0f, 0.2f, 0.6f, 1.0f};
blend.Factors = factArray;
blend.Positions = posArray;
brBrush.Blend = blend;
```

The `ColorBlend` class defines arrays of colors and positions used for interpolating color blending in a multicolor gradient. The `Positions` property, an array of floating points (values vary between 0.0 and 1.0), represents the positions of the colors along a gradient line; and the `Colors` property, an array of `Color` objects, represents the color to use at corresponding positions. Each position defined in `Positions` has a corresponding color in the `Colors` array. Hence if six positions are defined in the `Positions` array, the `Colors` array will have six `Color` objects.

To use a `ColorBlend` object, create the object and set its `Positions` and `Colors` properties, as shown in Listing 9.19. The `InterpolationColors` property of the `LinearGradientBrush` and `PathGradientBrush` classes uses the `ColorBlend` object.

LISTING 9.19: Creating a `ColorBlend` object and setting its `Colors` and `Positions` properties

```
LinearGradientBrush brBrush = new LinearGradientBrush(
    new Point(0, 0), new Point(50, 20),
   Color.Blue, Color.Red);
// Create color and points arrays
Color[] clrArray =
{
    Color.Red, Color.Blue, Color.Green,
    Color.Pink, Color.Yellow,
    Color.DarkTurquoise
};
float[] posArray =
{
    0.0f, 0.2f, 0.4f,
    0.6f, 0.8f, 1.0f
};
// Create a ColorBlend object and set its Colors and
// Positions properties
ColorBlend colorBlend = new ColorBlend();
colorBlend.Colors = clrArray;
colorBlend.Positions = posArray;
brBrush.InterpolationColors = colorBlend;
```

9.5.2 Blending Using `LinearGradientBrush` Objects

The `LinearGradientBrush` object represents a linear gradient brush, which lets us specify the starting and ending colors, and the starting and ending points, of the gradient pattern.

> ■ **NOTE**
>
> See Chapter 4 for more detail on brushes and pens.

The linear gradient brushes work differently from solid and hatch brushes. For solid and hatch brushes, an application creates a brush and uses the brush to fill graphics shapes; the brush pattern applies to the entire shape. For linear gradient brushes, an application creates a linear gradient brush with a rectangle. The rectangle passed in the constructor of the `LinearGradientBrush` object defines the boundaries of a gradient pattern. For example, Listing 9.20 creates a linear gradient brush with starting point (0, 0), ending point (50, 50), starting color red, and ending color green. Then the code fills a rectangle starting at point (0, 0) and ending at point (200, 50):

LISTING 9.20: Creating a `LinearGradientBrush` object

```
LinearGradientBrush rgBrush =
new LinearGradientBrush
(
    new RectangleF(0, 0, 50, 50),
    Color.Red, Color.Green,
    LinearGradientMode.Horizontal
);
g.FillRectangle(rgBrush, 0, 0, 200, 50);
```

Figure 9.29 shows the output from Listing 9.20. After point (50, 50) the gradient pattern repeats itself.

Now let's create one more linear gradient brush using code from Listing 9.21. The brush's range is greater, and the rectangle starts at point (50, 50), with height and width 200 and 50, respectively.

LISTING 9.21: Setting a brush's rectangle

```
LinearGradientBrush rgBrush =
new LinearGradientBrush
(
    new RectangleF(0, 0, 200, 200),
    Color.Red, Color.Green,
    LinearGradientMode.Horizontal
);
g.FillRectangle(rgBrush, 50, 50, 200, 50);
```

As the output of Listing 9.21 shows (see Figure 9.30), the pattern repeats after it crosses point (200, 200).

The `LinearGradientBrush` class also provides two methods—`Set-BlendTriangularShape` and `SetSigmaBellShape`—which can be used to set gradient properties. `SetBlendTriangularShape` creates a gradient

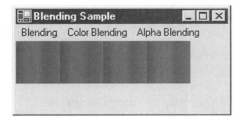

FIGURE 9.29: Using linear gradient brushes

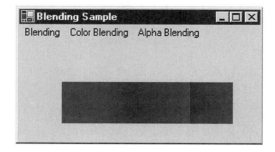

FIGURE 9.30: Using a rectangle in the linear gradient brush

with a center color and a linear falloff color. This method takes two parameters—representing focus and scale—both floating point values that vary from 0 to 1. The focus parameter is optional. Listing 9.22 shows the Set-BlendTriangularShape method being used.

LISTING 9.22: Using the **SetBlendTriangularShape** method

```
private void SetBlendTriangularShapeMenu_Click(object sender,
    System.EventArgs e)
{
    Graphics g = this.CreateGraphics();
    g.Clear(this.BackColor);
    // Create a rectangle
    Rectangle rect = new Rectangle(20, 20, 100, 50);
    // Create a linear gradient brush
    LinearGradientBrush rgBrush =
        new LinearGradientBrush(
        rect, Color.Red, Color.Green,
        0.0f, true);
    // Fill rectangle
    g.FillRectangle(rgBrush, rect);
    rect.Y = 90;
    // Set blend triangular shape
    rgBrush.SetBlendTriangularShape(0.5f, 1.0f);
    // Fill rectangle again
    g.FillRectangle(rgBrush, rect);
    // Dispose of object
    g.Dispose();
}
```

Figure 9.31 shows the output from Listing 9.22. The first image starts with red and ends with green; the second image has green as the center, and red as both the starting and the ending edge color.

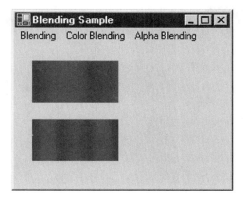

FIGURE 9.31: Using the `SetBlendTriangularShape` method

The `SetSigmaBellShape` method creates a gradient falloff based on a bell-shaped curve. Much like `SetBlendTriangularShape`, this method takes two parameters—representing focus and scale (the focus parameter is optional)—whose values vary from 0 to 1. Listing 9.23 shows the `SetSigmaBellShape` method being used.

LISTING 9.23: Using the `SetSigmaBellShape` method

```
private void SetSigmaBellShapeMenu_Click(object sender,
    System.EventArgs e)
{
    Graphics g = this.CreateGraphics();
    g.Clear(this.BackColor);
    // Create a rectangle
    Rectangle rect = new Rectangle(20, 20, 100, 50);
    // Create a linear gradient brush
    LinearGradientBrush rgBrush =
        new LinearGradientBrush(
        rect, Color.Red, Color.Green,
        0.0f, true);
    // Fill rectangle
    g.FillRectangle(rgBrush, rect);
    rect.Y = 90;
    // Set signma bell shape
    rgBrush.SetSigmaBellShape(0.5f, 1.0f);
    // Fill rectangle again
    g.FillRectangle(rgBrush, rect);
    // Dispose of object
    g.Dispose();
}
```

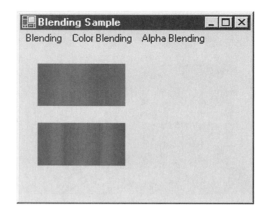

FIGURE 9.32: Using the `SetSigmaBellShape` method

Figure 9.32 shows the output from Listing 9.23. The first image starts with red and ends with green. After the sigma bell shape is set, the image's center is green, and its starting and ending edges are red.

Now let's compare the effects of `SetSigmaBellShape` and `SetBlend-TriangularShape`. Listing 9.24 draws three rectangles: one using the `LinearGradient` brush with no effects, one using `SetSigmaBellShape`, and one using `SetBlendTriangularShape`.

LISTING 9.24: Comparing the effects of `SetBlendTriangularShape` and `SetSigmaBellShape`

```
private void CompBlendTSigmaBell_Click(object sender,
    System.EventArgs e)
{
    Graphics g = this.CreateGraphics();
    g.Clear(this.BackColor);
    // Create a rectangle
    Rectangle rect = new Rectangle(0, 0, 40, 20);
    // Create a linear gradient brush
    LinearGradientBrush rgBrush =
        new LinearGradientBrush(
        rect, Color.Black, Color.Blue,
        0.0f, true);
    // Fill rectangle
    g.FillRectangle(rgBrush,
        new Rectangle(10, 10, 300, 100));
    // Set sigma bell shape
    rgBrush.SetSigmaBellShape(0.5f, 1.0f);
```

```
    // Fill rectangle again
    g.FillRectangle(rgBrush,
        new Rectangle(10, 120, 300, 100));
    // Set blend triangular shape
    rgBrush.SetBlendTriangularShape(0.5f, 1.0f);
    // Fill rectangle again
    g.FillRectangle(rgBrush,
        new Rectangle(10, 240, 300, 100));
    // Dispose of object
    g.Dispose();
}
```

Figure 9.33 shows the output from Listing 9.24. The first image is the original image, the second image is a sigma bell shape, and the third image is a blend triangular shape. `SetBlendTriangularShape` produces a glassy effect in the center of the color, and `SetSigmaBellShape` produces a faded effect.

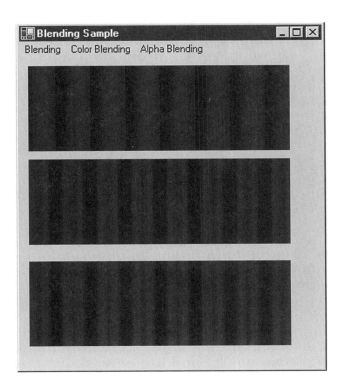

FIGURE 9.33: Comparing the effects of `SetBlendTriangularShape` and `SetSigmaBellShape`

The first parameter of `SetBlendTriangularShape` and `SetSigma-BellShape` represents the center of the gradient (color), which varies between `0.0f` and `1.0f`, where `0.0f` is the starting point and `1.0f` is the ending point of the gradient.

Now let's change the center of the gradient by modifying the two relevant lines of Listing 9.24 as follows:

```
rgBrush.SetSigmaBellShape(0.8f, 1.0f);
rgBrush.SetBlendTriangularShape(0.2f, 1.0f);
```

The new output looks like Figure 9.34. The center of the gradient in the second and third images is visibly different.

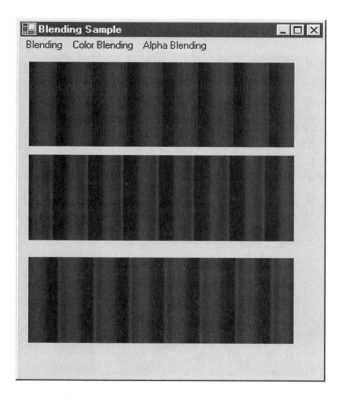

FIGURE 9.34: Setting the center of a gradient

9.5.3 **Adding Multicolor Support to Gradients**

So far in this section, we have been using only two colors (the default supported by `LinearGradientBrush`). What if we want to use more than two colors? No problem!

The `LinearGradientBrush` class provides properties that are useful for blending. Two of these properties are `InterpolationColors` and `Blend`. The `Blend` property is represented by the `Blend` object, and `InterpolationColors` is represented by the `ColorBlend` object. To apply multicolor gradients, simply create `Blend` and `ColorBlend` objects, attach these objects to a `LinearGradientBrush` object, and use the brush to fill shapes.

Listing 9.25 creates a `ColorBlend` object, sets its `Colors` and `Positions` properties, and sets the `InterpolationColors` property of the brush.

LISTING 9.25: Using the **InterpolationColors** property of
LinearGradientBrush

```
private void InterpolationColorsMenu_Click
    (object sender, System.EventArgs e)
{
    Graphics g = this.CreateGraphics();
    g.Clear(this.BackColor);
    // Create a LinearGradientBrush object
    LinearGradientBrush brBrush =
        new LinearGradientBrush(
        new Point(0, 0), new Point(50, 20),
        Color.Blue, Color.Red);
    Rectangle rect =
        new Rectangle(20, 20, 200, 100);
    // Create color and points arrays
    Color[] clrArray =
    {
        Color.Red, Color.Blue, Color.Green,
        Color.Pink, Color.Yellow,
        Color.DarkTurquoise
    };
    float[] posArray =
    {
        0.0f, 0.2f, 0.4f,
        0.6f, 0.8f, 1.0f
    };
```

continues

```
// Create a ColorBlend object and
// set its Colors and Positions properties
ColorBlend colorBlend = new ColorBlend();
colorBlend.Colors = clrArray;
colorBlend.Positions = posArray;
// Set InterpolationColors property
brBrush.InterpolationColors = colorBlend;
// Draw shapes
g.FillRectangle(brBrush, rect);
rect.Y = 150;
rect.Width = 100;
rect.Height = 100;
g.FillEllipse(brBrush, rect);
// Dispose of object
g.Dispose();
}
```

Figure 9.35 shows the output from Listing 9.25. The gradient has multiple colors.

FIGURE 9.35: A multicolor gradient

The `Blend` property of `LinearGradientBrush` allows you to attach a `Blend` object to the brush, which represents the positions and factors of the blend. Listing 9.26 creates a `Blend` object and sets its `Factors` and `Positions` properties, as well as the `Blend` property of the brush.

LISTING 9.26: Using the `Blend` property of `LinearGradientBrush`

```
private void BlendPropMenu_Click(object sender,
    System.EventArgs e)
{
    Graphics g = this.CreateGraphics();
    g.Clear(this.BackColor);
    // Create a linear gradient brush
    LinearGradientBrush brBrush =
        new LinearGradientBrush(
        new Point(0, 0), new Point(50, 20),
        Color.Blue, Color.Red);
    // Create a Blend object
    Blend blend = new Blend();
    float[] factArray = {0.0f, 0.3f, 0.5f, 1.0f};
    float[] posArray  = {0.0f, 0.2f, 0.6f, 1.0f};
    // Set Blend's Factors and Positions properties
    blend.Factors = factArray;
    blend.Positions = posArray;
    // Set Blend property of the brush
    brBrush.Blend = blend;
    // Fill a rectangle and an ellipse
    g.FillRectangle(brBrush, 10, 20, 200, 100);
    g.FillEllipse(brBrush, 10, 150, 120, 120);
    // Dispose of object
    g.Dispose();
}
```

Figure 9.36 shows the output from Listing 9.26. The blend's position and colors are controlled by the `Factors` property.

9.5.4 Using Gamma Correction in Linear Gradient Brushes

We use **gamma correction** when we want to display a drawing accurately on a computer screen. Gamma correction controls the overall brightness of an image. Images that are not properly corrected may look either too dark or bleached out. By setting the gamma correction, we tell GDI+ to change the brightness and set the best ratios of red to green to blue.

FIGURE 9.36: Using blending in a linear gradient brush

The GammaCorrection property, a Boolean type, is used to apply gamma correction on a linear gradient brush. This property can be true (enabled) or false (disabled). Brushes with gamma correction have more uniform intensity than brushes with no gamma correction.

Listing 9.27 draws two rectangles. The first has no gamma correction; the second does have gamma correction. If you run this code, you will notice that the second rectangle has a more uniform gradation.

LISTING 9.27: Applying gamma correction on linear gradient brushes

```
private void GammaCorrectionMenu_Click(
    object sender, System.EventArgs e)
{
    Graphics g = this.CreateGraphics();
    g.Clear(this.BackColor);
    // Create a rectangle
    Rectangle rect =
        new Rectangle(20, 20, 100, 50);
    // Create a linear gradient brush
    LinearGradientBrush rgBrush =
        new LinearGradientBrush(
        rect, Color.Red, Color.Green,
        0.0f, true);
```

```
            // Fill rectangle
            g.FillRectangle(rgBrush, rect);
            rect.Y = 90;
            // Set gamma correction of the brush
            rgBrush.GammaCorrection = true;
            // Fill rectangle
            g.FillRectangle(rgBrush, rect);
            // Dispose of object
            g.Dispose();
        }
```

9.5.5 Blending Using PathGradientBrush Objects

As we discussed in Chapter 4 (Section 4.1.6), the PathGradientBrush object is used to fill a graphics path with a gradient. We can specify the center and boundary colors of a path.

The CenterColor and SurroundColors properties are used to specify the center and boundary colors. Listing 9.28 uses the CenterColor and SurroundColors properties; it sets the center color of the path to red and the surrounding color to green.

LISTING 9.28: Blending using PathGradientBrush

```
    private void PathGBBlend_Click(object sender,
        System.EventArgs e)
    {
        Graphics g = this.CreateGraphics();
        g.Clear(this.BackColor);
        // Create Blend object
        Blend blend = new Blend();
        // Create point and position arrays
        float[] factArray = {0.0f, 0.3f, 0.5f, 1.0f};
        float[] posArray  = {0.0f, 0.2f, 0.6f, 1.0f};
        // Set Factors and Positions properties of Blend
        blend.Factors = factArray;
        blend.Positions = posArray;
        // Set smoothing mode of Graphics object
        g.SmoothingMode = SmoothingMode.AntiAlias;
        // Create path and add a rectangle
        GraphicsPath path = new GraphicsPath();
        Rectangle rect = new Rectangle(10, 20, 200, 200);
        path.AddRectangle(rect);
        // Create path gradient brush
        PathGradientBrush rgBrush =
            new PathGradientBrush(path);
```

continues

```
            // Set Blend and FocusScales properties
            rgBrush.Blend = blend;
            rgBrush.FocusScales = new PointF(0.6f, 0.2f);
            Color[] colors = {Color.Green};
            // Set CenterColor and SurroundColors properties
            rgBrush.CenterColor = Color.Red;
            rgBrush.SurroundColors = colors;
            g.FillEllipse(rgBrush, rect);
            // Dispose of object
            g.Dispose();
    }
```

If you run the code from Listing 9.28, you will see that the focus is the center of the ellipse, and there is scattering in a faded color toward the boundary of the ellipse. The center is red, and the border is green (see Figure 9.37).

The FocusScales property changes the focus point for the gradient falloff. The following code snippet sets the FocusScales property:

```
rgBrush.FocusScales = new PointF(0.6f, 0.2f);
```

After FocusScales is set, the color of the ellipse changes from the center of the ellipse to a rectangle. Figure 9.38 shows the new output.

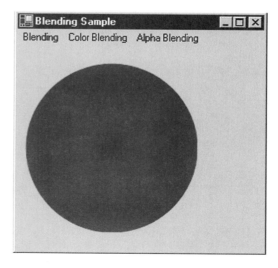

FIGURE 9.37: Blending using PathGradientBrush

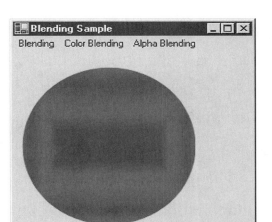

FIGURE 9.38: Setting the focus scale

We can even specify multiple surrounding colors. For example, we can create an array of different colors and use them for the Surround-Colors property of the brush. To do so, we replace the following line of Listing 9.28:

```
Color[] colors = {Color.Green};
```

with the following code snippet:

```
Color[] colors =
{Color.Green, Color.Blue,
Color.Red, Color.Yellow};
rgBrush.SurroundColors = colors;
```

If you add this code to the application, you will see a totally different output. As Figure 9.39 shows, the new ellipse has four different boundary colors.

Like LinearGradientBrush, the PathGradientBrush class provides Blend and InterpolationColors properties. Listing 9.29 shows the InterpolationColors property in use.

FIGURE 9.39: Blending multiple colors

LISTING 9.29: Using the **InterpolationColors** property of
PathGradientBrush

```
private void PathGBInterPol_Click(object sender,
    System.EventArgs e)
{
    Graphics g = this.CreateGraphics();
    g.Clear(this.BackColor);
    // Create color and points arrays
    Color[] clrArray =
        {Color.Red, Color.Blue, Color.Green,
            Color.Pink, Color.Yellow,
            Color.DarkTurquoise};
    float[] posArray =
        {0.0f, 0.2f, 0.4f, 0.6f, 0.8f, 1.0f};
    // Create a ColorBlend object and set its Colors and
    // Positions properties
    ColorBlend colorBlend = new ColorBlend();
    colorBlend.Colors = clrArray;
    colorBlend.Positions = posArray;
    // Set smoothing mode of Graphics object
    g.SmoothingMode = SmoothingMode.AntiAlias;
    // Create a graphics path and add a rectangle
    GraphicsPath path = new GraphicsPath();
    Rectangle rect = new Rectangle(10, 20, 200, 200);
    path.AddRectangle(rect);
```

```
// Create a path gradient brush
PathGradientBrush rgBrush =
        new PathGradientBrush(path);
// Set interpolation colors and focus scales
rgBrush.InterpolationColors =  colorBlend;
rgBrush.FocusScales = new PointF(0.6f, 0.2f);
Color[] colors = {Color.Green};
// Set center and surrounding colors
rgBrush.CenterColor = Color.Red;
rgBrush.SurroundColors = colors;
// Draw ellipse
g.FillEllipse(rgBrush, rect);
// Dispose of object
g.Dispose();
}
```

Figure 9.40 shows the output from Listing 9.29.

You can even apply blending on a path gradient brush using the Blend property. Listing 9.30 creates a Blend object and sets the Blend property of the brush.

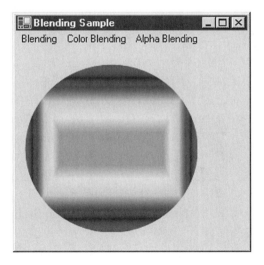

FIGURE 9.40: Using the **InterpolationColors** property of **PathGradientBrush**

LISTING 9.30: Using the `Blend` property of `PathGradientBrush`

```
private void PathGBBlend_Click(object sender,
    System.EventArgs e)
{
    Graphics g = this.CreateGraphics();
    g.Clear(this.BackColor);
    // Create Blend object
    Blend blend = new Blend();
    // Create point and position arrays
    float[] factArray = {0.0f, 0.3f, 0.5f, 1.0f};
    float[] posArray  = {0.0f, 0.2f, 0.6f, 1.0f};
    // Set Factors and Positions properties of Blend
    blend.Factors = factArray;
    blend.Positions = posArray;
    // Set smoothing mode of Graphics object
    g.SmoothingMode = SmoothingMode.AntiAlias;
    // Create path and add a rectangle
    GraphicsPath path = new GraphicsPath();
    Rectangle rect = new Rectangle(10, 20, 200, 200);
    path.AddRectangle(rect);
    // Create path gradient brush
    PathGradientBrush rgBrush =
        new PathGradientBrush(path);
    // Set Blend and FocusScales properties
    rgBrush.Blend = blend;
    rgBrush.FocusScales = new PointF(0.6f, 0.2f);
    Color[] colors =
    {
        Color.Green, Color.Blue,
        Color.Red, Color.Yellow
    };
    // Set CenterColor and SurroundColors
    rgBrush.CenterColor = Color.Red;
    rgBrush.SurroundColors = colors;
    g.FillEllipse(rgBrush, rect);
    // Dispose of object
    g.Dispose();
}
```

Figure 9.41 shows the output from Listing 9.30. Blending is done with four different colors.

Just as with `LinearGradientBrush`, you can use the `SetBlend-TriangularShape` and `SetSigmaBellShape` methods with `Path-GradientBrush`.

FIGURE 9.41: Multicolor blending using `PathGradientBrush`

9.6 Alpha Blending

In GDI+, every color is a combination of ARGB components; each of the alpha, red, green, and blue components is represented by 8 bits. The alpha component in a color structure represents the transparency of the color, which varies from 0 to 255. The value 0 represents full transparency, and 255 represents full opacity.

The final color of an ARGB color structure is calculated by the following formula:

Final Color = (Source Color × alpha / 255) +
[Background Color × (255 – alpha) / 255]

This formula is applied on each component of the source color and background color.

In alpha blending, an application creates a color with an alpha component and uses this color to create a pen or a brush. This pen or brush is used to draw and fill graphics shapes, and it calculates the final color. Alpha blending may sound unfamiliar, but programmatically it is simply a method of setting the alpha component (transparency) of a color, and using it to fill and draw graphics shapes.

9.6.1 **Brushes, Pens, and Alpha Blending**

The process of alpha blending involves three simple steps. First an application creates a color with transparency (the alpha component). The following line creates a `Color` object with alpha component value 40:

```
Color clr = Color.FromArgb(40, 255, 255, 255);
```

The second step is to create a brush or pen using that color. The following lines create a transparent pen and a brush:

```
Pen transPen = new Pen(clr, 10);
SolidBrush semiTransBrush = new SolidBrush(clr);
```

Finally, the application uses the transparent brush or pen to fill and draw graphics shapes, lines, and curves. The following code uses the `Pen` and `Brush` objects we created in the previous steps to draw a line and to draw and fill a rectangle:

```
g.DrawLine(transPen, 10, 30, 200, 30);
g.FillRectangle(semiTransBrush, rect);
```

Listing 9.31 uses this approach to draw lines, a rectangle, an ellipse, and text objects with varying transparency. You can add this code to a menu item or a button click event handler.

LISTING 9.31: Using alpha blending to draw non-opaque or semi-opaque graphics shapes

```
private void AlphaBPensBrushes_Click(object sender,
    System.EventArgs e)
{
    Graphics g = this.CreateGraphics();
    g.Clear(this.BackColor);
    // Create pens with semitransparent colors
    Rectangle rect =
        new Rectangle(220, 30, 100, 50);
    Pen transPen =
        new Pen(Color.FromArgb(128, 255, 255, 255), 10);
    Pen totTransPen =
        new Pen(Color.FromArgb(40, 0, 255, 0), 10);
    // Draw line, rectangle, ellipse, and string using
    // semitransparent colored pens
    g.DrawLine(transPen, 10, 30, 200, 30);
    g.DrawLine(totTransPen, 10, 50, 200, 50);
```

```
    g.FillRectangle(new SolidBrush(
        Color.FromArgb(40, 0, 0, 255)), rect);
    rect.Y += 60;
    g.FillEllipse(new SolidBrush(
        Color.FromArgb(20, 255, 255, 0)), rect);
    SolidBrush semiTransBrush =
        new SolidBrush(Color.FromArgb(90, 0, 50, 255));
    g.DrawString("Some Photo \nDate: 04/09/2001",
        new Font("Verdana", 14), semiTransBrush,
        new RectangleF(20, 100, 300, 100) );
    // Dispose of object
    g.Dispose();
}
```

Figure 9.42 shows the output from Listing 9.31. The lines, rectangle, ellipse, and text on this form are semitransparent.

9.6.2 Alpha Blending and Images

We often see a semitransparent date and place name on a photo. You can draw transparent graphics shapes on images using the same method: Create a graphics shape using semi- or non-opaque colors, and then draw on the image.

Listing 9.32 draws graphics shapes on an image. First we create an Image object and call DrawImage to draw an image. Then we create transparent pens and brushes and call fill and draw methods to draw graphics

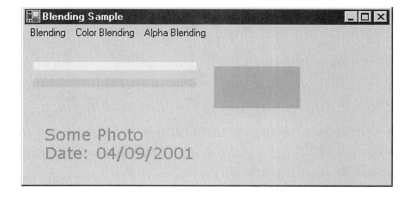

FIGURE 9.42: Drawing semitransparent graphics shapes

shapes. You can add the code in Listing 9.32 to any menu item or button click event handler.

LISTING 9.32: Drawing semitransparent graphics shapes on an image

```
private void AlphaBImages_Click(object sender,
    System.EventArgs e)
{
    Graphics g = this.CreateGraphics();
    g.Clear(this.BackColor);
    // Draw an image
    Image curImage =
        Image.FromFile("Neel3.jpg");
    g.DrawImage(curImage, 0, 0,
        curImage.Width, curImage.Height);
    // Create pens and a rectangle
    Rectangle rect =
        new Rectangle(220, 30, 100, 50);
    Pen opqPen =
        new Pen(Color.FromArgb(255, 0, 255, 0), 10);
    Pen transPen =
        new Pen(Color.FromArgb(128, 255, 255, 255), 10);
    Pen totTransPen =
        new Pen(Color.FromArgb(40, 0, 255, 0), 10);
    // Draw lines, rectangle, ellipse, and string
    g.DrawLine(opqPen, 10, 10, 200, 10);
    g.DrawLine(transPen, 10, 30, 200, 30);
    g.DrawLine(totTransPen, 10, 50, 200, 50);
    g.FillRectangle(new SolidBrush(
        Color.FromArgb(140, 0, 0, 255)), rect);
    rect.Y += 60;
    g.FillEllipse(new SolidBrush(
        Color.FromArgb(150, 255, 255, 255)), rect);
    SolidBrush semiTransBrush =
        new SolidBrush(Color.FromArgb(90, 255, 255, 50));
    g.DrawString("Some Photo \nDate: 04/09/2001",
        new Font("Verdana", 14), semiTransBrush,
        new RectangleF(20, 100, 300, 100) );
    // Dispose of object
    g.Dispose();
}
```

Figure 9.43 shows the output from Listing 9.32. Lines, text, a rectangle, and an ellipse are drawn on top of the image, but you can see through them because these shapes are semitransparent.

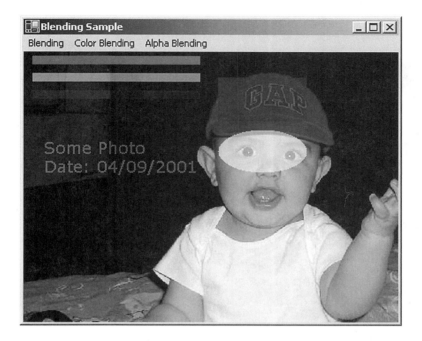

FIGURE 9.43: Drawing semitransparent shapes on an image

9.6.3 Compositing Mode and Blending

As mentioned earlier, blending is a process of combining two colors: a source color and a background color. The compositing mode specifies how source colors are combined with background colors.

The `CompositingMode` property of the `Graphics` class represents the compositing mode of a graphics surface, which applies to all graphics shapes for that surface. The `CompositingMode` enumeration has two members: `SourceCopy` and `SourceOver`. `SourceCopy` specifies that when a color is rendered, it overwrites the background color, and `SourceOver` specifies that when a color is rendered, it is blended with the background color using the alpha component.

The following code snippet shows how to set the `CompositingMode` property of a `Graphics` object.

```
Graphics g = this.CreateGraphics();
g.Clear(this.BackColor);
g.CompositingMode = CompositingMode.SourceCopy;
```

```
g.CompositingMode = CompositingMode.SourceOver;
// Dispose of object
g.Dispose();
```

CompositingMode may be helpful in scenarios where you need to draw overlapped images. Suppose you draw one rectangle and one ellipse, and an area of the ellipse overlaps a small area of the rectangle. You may or may not want to show the overlapped area of the rectangle. The compositing mode provides you the option of doing either.

Instead of applying CompositingMode to all of the graphics, you can apply it to selected shapes. One way to do this is to create a temporary Graphics object (a new surface), draw all the shapes you need and apply the compositing mode on this object. You can also create graphics containers and apply the necessary settings to each graphics container.

The quality of compositing is inversely proportional to the rendering speed: The higher the quality, the slower the rendering. The Compositing-Quality property of the Graphics object represents the quality of a composition process, which takes a value of type CompositingQuality enumeration. The CompositingQuality enumeration is defined in Table 9.12.

Listing 9.33 draws two sets of shapes. Each set has a rectangle and an ellipse. First we create a Bitmap object, and then we create a temporary Graphics object using the FromImage method by passing the Bitmap object. We set the CompositingMode property of this Graphics object to

TABLE 9.12: CompositingQuality members

Member	Description
AssumeLinear	Assume linear values. Better than the default quality.
Default	Default quality.
GammaCorrected	Gamma correction is used.
HighQuality	High quality, low speed.
HighSpeed	High speed, low quality.
Invalid	Invalid quality.

SourceOver, which means that the color rendered overwrites the background color. Then we draw a rectangle and an ellipse.

LISTING 9.33: Using `CompositingMode` to draw graphics shapes

```
private void AlphaBCompGammaCorr_Click(object sender,
    System.EventArgs e)
{
    Graphics g = this.CreateGraphics();
    g.Clear(this.BackColor);
    // Create two rectangles
    Rectangle rect1 =
        new Rectangle(20, 20, 100, 100);
    Rectangle rect2 =
        new Rectangle(200, 20, 100, 100);
    // Create two SolidBrush objects
    SolidBrush redBrush =
        new SolidBrush(Color.FromArgb(150, 255, 0, 0));
    SolidBrush greenBrush =
        new SolidBrush(Color.FromArgb(180, 0, 255, 0));
    // Create a Bitmap object
    Bitmap tempBmp = new Bitmap(200, 150);
    // Create a Graphics object
    Graphics tempGraphics =
        Graphics.FromImage(tempBmp);
    // Set compositing mode and compositing
    // quality of Graphics object
    tempGraphics.CompositingMode =
        CompositingMode.SourceOver;
    tempGraphics.CompositingQuality =
        CompositingQuality.GammaCorrected;
    // Fill rectangle
    tempGraphics.FillRectangle(redBrush, rect1);
    rect1.X += 30;
    rect1.Y += 30;
    // Fill ellipse
    tempGraphics.FillEllipse(greenBrush, rect1);
    g.CompositingQuality =
        CompositingQuality.GammaCorrected;
    // Draw image
    g.DrawImage(tempBmp, 0, 0);
    // Fill rectangle
    g.FillRectangle(Brushes.Red, rect2);
    rect2.X += 30;
    rect2.Y += 30;
    // Fill ellipse
    g.FillEllipse(Brushes.Green, rect2);
```

continues

```
    // Dispose of objects
    greenBrush.Dispose();
    redBrush.Dispose();
    tempBmp.Dispose();
    g.Dispose();
}
```

Figure 9.44 shows the output from Listing 9.33. You can clearly see that an ellipse copies over the color of a rectangle.

Now we change the value of `CompositingMode` to `SourceCopy` by using the following code snippet:

```
tempGraphics.CompositingMode =
        CompositingMode.SourceCopy;
```

Figure 9.45 shows the new output. The color of the rectangle and the color of ellipse do not overlap now, but the color of the rectangle is gone and that area is overridden by the ellipse.

9.6.4 Mixed Blending

Mixed blending is a combination of both alpha blending and color blending. It is useful when you need to draw transparent and blended graphics shapes—for example, drawing a transparent image with transparent shapes using a blended linear gradient brush.

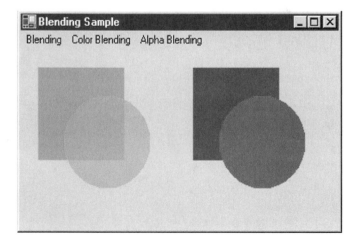

FIGURE 9.44: Using `CompositingMode.SourceOver`

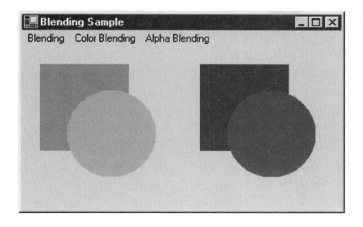

FIGURE 9.45: Blending with `CompositingMode.SourceCopy`

Listing 9.34 shows how to mix these two types of blending. Using the
`InterpolationColors` property, we create a `LinearGradientBrush`
object and set its `Colors` and `Positions` properties to specify the blending
colors and positions. After that we create a `Bitmap` object and apply a color
matrix using `SetColorMatrix`. Then we draw a rectangle and an ellipse,
and we call `DrawImage`.

LISTING 9.34: Mixed blending example

```
private void MixedBlending_Click(object sender,
    System.EventArgs e)
{
    Graphics g = this.CreateGraphics();
    g.Clear(this.BackColor);
    // Create a LinearGradientBrush object
    LinearGradientBrush brBrush =
        new LinearGradientBrush(
        new Point(0, 0), new Point(50, 20),
        Color.Blue, Color.Red);
    Rectangle rect =
        new Rectangle(20, 20, 200, 100);
    // Create color and points arrays
    Color[] clrArray =
    {
        Color.Red, Color.Blue, Color.Green,
        Color.Pink, Color.Yellow,
        Color.DarkTurquoise
    };
```

continues

```
float[] posArray =
{
    0.0f, 0.2f, 0.4f,
    0.6f, 0.8f, 1.0f
};
// Create a ColorBlend object and
// set its Colors and Positions properties
ColorBlend colorBlend = new ColorBlend();
colorBlend.Colors = clrArray;
colorBlend.Positions = posArray;
// Set InterpolationColors property
brBrush.InterpolationColors = colorBlend;
// Create a Bitmap object from a file
Bitmap bitmap = new Bitmap("MyPhoto.jpg");
// Create a points array
float[][] ptsArray =
{
    new float[] {1, 0, 0, 0, 0},
    new float[] {0, 1, 0, 0, 0},
    new float[] {0, 0, 1, 0, 0},
    new float[] {0, 0, 0, 0.5f, 0},
    new float[] {0, 0, 0, 0, 1}
};
// Create a ColorMatrix object using pts array
ColorMatrix clrMatrix =
    new ColorMatrix(ptsArray);
// Create an ImageAttributes object
ImageAttributes imgAttributes =
    new ImageAttributes();
// Set color matrix of ImageAttributes
imgAttributes.SetColorMatrix(clrMatrix,
    ColorMatrixFlag.Default,
    ColorAdjustType.Bitmap);
// Fill rectangle
g.FillRectangle(brBrush, rect);
rect.Y += 120;
// Fill ellipse
g.FillEllipse(brBrush, rect);
// Draw image using ImageAttributes
g.DrawImage(bitmap,
    new Rectangle(0, 0,
    bitmap.Width, bitmap.Height),
    0, 0, bitmap.Width, bitmap.Height,
    GraphicsUnit.Pixel, imgAttributes);
// Dispose of objects
brBrush.Dispose();
bitmap.Dispose();
g.Dispose();
}
```

FIGURE 9.46: A mixed blending example

Figure 9.46 shows the output from Listing 9.34. The rectangle and ellipse are blended (multicolor) and translucent (alpha-blended).

9.7 **Miscellaneous Advanced 2D Topics**

So far in this chapter, we have covered line caps and line styles, graphics paths, graphics containers, graphics container states, color blending and alpha blending, and the use of linear and path gradient brushes. The `System.Drawing.Advanced2D` namespace contains topics that don't fall into any of these categories. In this section we will cover a few of these topics:

- Region data
- The `SmoothingMode` enumeration
- The `PixelOffsetMode` enumeration

9.7.1 **Region Data**

Sometimes we need to get and set a region's data or create a `Region` object from an array of bytes. A region's data is an array of bytes that specify the region. The `RegionData` class can be used to read or write the array. This class has only one property, `Data`, which returns an array of bytes that describe the region.

Listing 9.35 uses `RegionData` to read the data of a region.

LISTING 9.35: Using **`RegionData`** to read the data of a region

```
// Create a rectangle
Rectangle rect = new Rectangle(20, 20, 200, 200);
Region rgn = new Region(rect);
// Create a RegionData object
RegionData rgnData = rgn.GetRegionData();
// Get data
byte[] btArry = rgnData.Data;
MessageBox.Show("Number of bytes :"
    + rgnData.Data.Length.ToString()
);
```

9.7.2 **The `SmoothingMode` and `PixelOffsetMode` Enumerations**

`SmoothingMode` and `PixelOffsetMode` are two enumerations defined in the `Drawing.Drawing2D` namespace. In this section we will take a quick look at these enumerations.

9.7.2.1 *The `SmoothingMode` Enumeration*

The smoothing mode specifies the rendering quality of graphics drawn on a surface. The `SmoothingMode` property is used to get and set the smoothing mode of a graphics surface, and it takes a value of `SmoothingMode` enumeration.

`SmoothingMode` defines anti-aliasing for lines, curves, and images. This property does not affect text; the `TextRenderingHint` property is used for text. `SmoothingMode` has six members, which are defined in Table 9.13.

To see `SmoothingMode` in action, let's draw a few graphics shapes. Listing 9.36 draws a rectangle, an ellipse, and a line. The line that sets the smoothing mode of the `Graphics` object is commented out.

TABLE 9.13: `SmoothingMode` members

Member	Description
AntiAlias	Anti-aliased rendering.
Default	No anti-aliasing (the default mode).
HighQuality	High-quality, low-speed rendering.
HighSpeed	High-speed, low-quality rendering.
Invalid	Invalid mode. Raises exception.
None	Specifies no anti-aliasing.

LISTING 9.36: **Drawing with the default smoothing mode**

```
private void GeneralMenu_Click(object sender,
    System.EventArgs e)
{
    // Create a Graphics object
    Graphics g = this.CreateGraphics();
    g.Clear(this.BackColor);
    // Create three pens
    Pen redPen = new Pen(Color.Red, 6);
    Pen bluePen = new Pen(Color.Blue, 10);
    Pen blackPen = new Pen(Color.Black, 5);
    // Set smoothing mode
    // g.SmoothingMode = SmoothingMode.AntiAlias;
    // Draw a rectangle, an ellipse, and a line
    g.DrawRectangle(bluePen, 10, 20, 100, 50);
    g.DrawEllipse(redPen, 10, 150, 100, 50);
    g.DrawLine(blackPen, 150, 100, 250, 220);
    // Dispose of objects
    redPen.Dispose();
    bluePen.Dispose();
    blackPen.Dispose();
    g.Dispose();
}
```

Figure 9.47 shows the output from Listing 9.36. The outer edges of the shapes are not smooth.

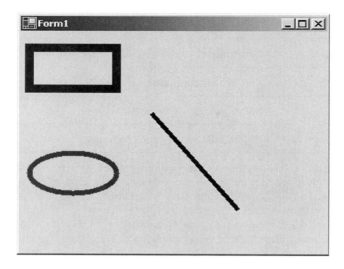

FIGURE 9.47: Drawing with `SmoothingMode` set to `Default`

Now let's uncomment the `SmoothingMode` line in Listing 9.36 and run the program again:

```
g.SmoothingMode = SmoothingMode.AntiAlias;
```

Figure 9.48 shows the new output. The shapes have smooth outer edges and look better overall.

9.7.2.2 *The* `PixelOffsetMode` *Enumeration*

`PixelOffsetMode` determines how pixels are offset during rendering. By offsetting pixels during rendering, we can improve rendering quality, but at the expense of speed. The `PixelOffsetMode` property of the `Graphics` class, with the help of `SmoothingMode`, is used to draw enhanced anti-aliasing images. The `PixelOffsetMode` enumeration is defined in Table 9.14.

The `PixelOffsetMode` property helps when we want to enhance anti-aliased graphics. Here's how to set this property:

```
g.SmoothingMode = SmoothingMode.AntiAlias;
g.PixelOffsetMode = PixelOffsetMode.HighQuality;
```

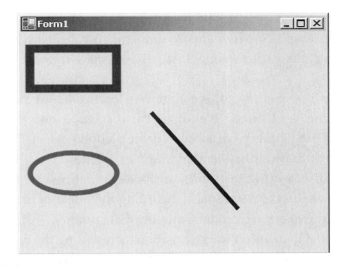

FIGURE 9.48: Drawing with `SmoothingMode` set to `AntiAlias`

TABLE 9.14: `PixelOffsetMode` members

Member	Description
Default	The default mode.
Half	Pixels are offset by -0.5 units, both horizontally and vertically, for high-speed anti-aliasing.
HighQuality	High-quality, low-speed rendering.
HighSpeed	High-speed, low-quality rendering.
Invalid	Invalid mode.
None	No pixel offset.

SUMMARY

The `System.Drawing.Drawing2D` namespace defines advanced functionality to work with 2D graphics objects. In this chapter we discussed the functionality defined in this namespace. We started the chapter by discussing the line caps and line styles. We saw sample code that set the line cap, line dash style, and line dash caps.

Next we covered graphics paths and graphics containers. We saw the usefulness of graphics paths and containers, and their advantages over nongraphics paths and containers. We also discussed graphics container states.

In the blending section of this chapter, we learned about color blending, alpha blending, and mixed blending. We discussed how to use linear gradient and path gradient brushes to draw blended objects. We saw how to use colors to draw alpha-blended graphics objects.

We also discussed other topics and classes defined in the `System.Drawing.Advanced2D` namespace, including metadata of images, how to set gamma correction, region data, and drawing quality.

Chapter 10 will focus on transformations, presenting the basics of transformations, matrices, and matrix operations, and how to apply transformation in practice.

10
Transformation

IN CHAPTER 9 we delved into advanced 2D graphics programming. In this chapter we will explore GDI+ transformations. A **transformation** is a process that changes graphics objects from one state to another. Rotation, scaling, reflection, translation, and shearing are some examples of transformation. Transformations can be applied not only to graphics shapes, curves, and images, but even to image colors.

In this chapter we will cover the following topics:

- The basics of transformation, including coordinate systems and matrices
- Global, local, and composite transformations
- Transformation functionality provided by the `Graphics` class
- Transformation concepts such as shearing, rotation, scaling, and translation
- The `Matrix` and `ColorMatrix` classes, and their role in transformation
- Matrix operations in image processing, including rotation, translation, shearing, and scaling
- Color transformation and recoloring
- Text transformation
- Composite transformations and the matrix order

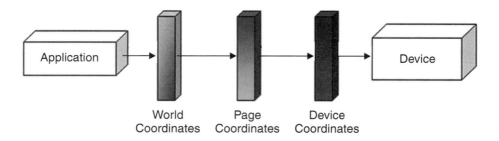

FIGURE 10.1: Steps in the transformation process

Any drawing process involves a source and a destination. The source of a drawing is the application that created it, and the destination is a display or printer device. For example, the process of drawing a simple rectangle starts with a command telling GDI+ to draw on the screen, followed by GDI+ iterating through multiple steps before it finally renders a rectangle on the screen. In the same way, transformation involves some steps before it actually renders the transformed object on a device. These steps are shown in Figure 10.1, which shows that GDI+ is responsible for converting world coordinates to page coordinates and device coordinates before it can render a transformed object.

10.1 Coordinate Systems

Before we discuss transformations, we need to understand coordinate systems. GDI+ defines three types of coordinate spaces: world, page, and device. When we ask GDI+ to draw a line from point A ($x1$, $y1$) to point B ($x2$, $y2$), these points are in the world coordinate system.

Before GDI+ draws a graphics shape on a surface, the shape goes through a few transformation stages (conversions). The first stage converts world coordinates to page coordinates. Page coordinates may or may not be the same as world coordinates, depending on the transformation. The process of converting world coordinates to page coordinates is called **world transformation**.

The second stage converts page coordinates to device coordinates. Device coordinates represent how a graphics shape will be displayed on a

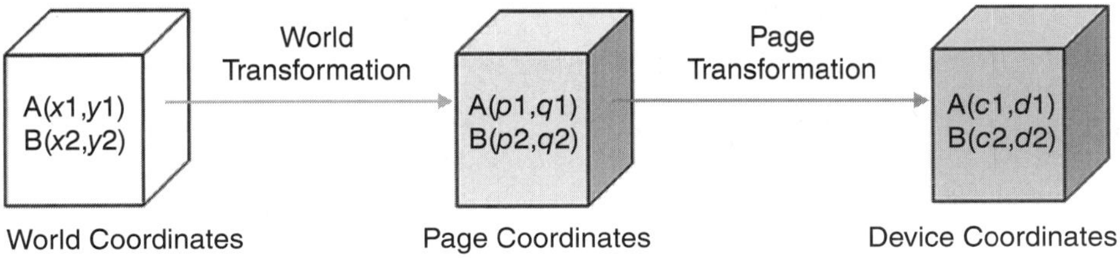

World
Transformation

Page
Transformation

A(x1,y1)
B(x2,y2)

A(p1,q1)
B(p2,q2)

A(c1,d1)
B(c2,d2)

World Coordinates

Page Coordinates

Device Coordinates

FIGURE 10.2: Transformation stages

device such as a monitor or printer. The process of converting page coordinates to device coordinates is called **page transformation**. Figure 10.2 shows the stages of conversion from world coordinates to device coordinates.

In GDI+, the default origin of all three coordinate systems is point $(0, 0)$, which is at the upper left corner of the client area. When we draw a line from point A $(0, 0)$ to point B $(120, 80)$, the line starts 0 pixels from the upper left corner in the x-direction and 0 pixels from the upper left corner in the y-direction, and it will end 120 pixels over in the x-direction and 80 pixels down in the y-direction. The line from point A $(0, 0)$ to point B $(120, 80)$ is shown in Figure 10.3.

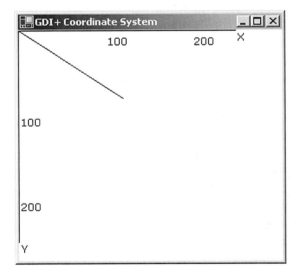

FIGURE 10.3: Drawing a line from point (0, 0) to point (120, 80)

Drawing this line programmatically is very simple. We must have a Graphics object associated with a surface (a form or a control). We can get a Graphics object in several ways. One way is to accept the implicit object provided by a form's paint event handler; another is to use the Create-Graphics method. Once we have a Graphics object, we call its draw and fill methods to draw and fill graphics objects. Listing 10.1 draws a line from starting point A (0, 0) to ending point B (120, 80). You can add this code to a form's paint event handler.

LISTING 10.1: Drawing a line from point (0, 0) to point (120, 80)

```
Graphics g = e.Graphics;
Point A = new Point(0, 0);
Point B = new Point(120, 80);
g.DrawLine(Pens.Black, A, B);
```

Figure 10.3 shows the output from Listing 10.1. All three coordinate systems (world, page, and device) draw a line starting from point (0, 0) in the upper left corner of the client area to point (120, 80).

Now let's change to the page coordinate system. We draw a line from point A (0, 0) to point B (120, 80), but this time our origin is point (50, 40) instead of the upper left corner. We shift the page coordinates from point (0, 0) to point (50, 40). The TranslateTransform method of the Graphics class does this for us. We will discuss this method in more detail in the discussion that follows. For now, let's try the code in Listing 10.2.

LISTING 10.2: Drawing a line from point (0, 0) to point (120, 80) with origin (50, 40)

```
Graphics g = e.Graphics;
g.TranslateTransform(50, 40);
Point A = new Point(0, 0);
Point B = new Point(120, 80);
g.DrawLine(Pens.Black, A, B);
```

Figure 10.4 shows the output from Listing 10.2. The page coordinate system now starts at point (50, 40), so the line starts at point (0, 0) and ends at point (120, 80). The world coordinates in this case are still (0, 0) and (120, 80), but the page and device coordinates are (50, 40) and (170, 120). The

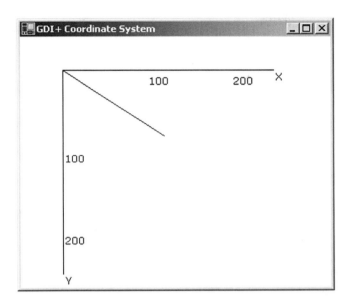

FIGURE 10.4: Drawing a line from point (0, 0) to point (120, 80) with origin (50, 40)

device coordinates in this case are the same as the page coordinates because the page unit is in the pixel (default) format.

What is the difference between page and device coordinates? Device coordinates determine what we actually see on the screen. They can be represented in many formats, including pixels, millimeters, and inches. If the device coordinates are in pixel format, the page coordinates and device coordinates will be the same (this is typically true for monitors, but not for printers).

The `PageUnit` property of the `Graphics` class is of type `GraphicsUnit` enumeration. In Listing 10.3 we set the `PageUnit` property to inches. Now graphics objects will be measured in inches, so we need to pass inches instead of pixels. If we draw a line from point (0, 0) to point (2, 1), the line ends 2 inches from the left side and 1 inch from the top of the client area in the page coordinate system. In this case the starting and ending points are (0, 0) and (2, 1) in both world and page coordinates, but the device coordinate system converts them to inches. Hence the starting and ending points in the device coordinate system are (0, 0) and (192, 96), assuming a resolution of 96 dots per inch.

LISTING 10.3: Setting the device coordinate system to inches

```
g.PageUnit = GraphicsUnit.Inch;
g.DrawLine(Pens.Black, 0, 0, 2, 1);
```

Figure 10.5 shows the output from Listing 10.3. The default width of the pen is 1 page unit, which in this case gives us a pen 1 inch wide.

Now let's create a new pen with a different width. Listing 10.4 creates a pen that's 1 pixel wide (it does so by dividing the number of pixels we want—in this case 1—by the page resolution, which is given by DpiX). We draw the line again, this time specifying a red color.

LISTING 10.4: Using the `GraphicsUnit.Inch` option with a pixel width

```
Pen redPen = new Pen(Color.Red, 1/g.DpiX);
g.PageUnit = GraphicsUnit.Inch;
g.DrawLine(Pens.Black, 0, 0, 2, 1);
```

FIGURE 10.5: Drawing with the `GraphicsUnit.Inch` option

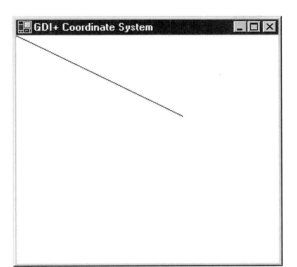

FIGURE 10.6: Drawing with the `GraphicsUnit.Inch` option and a pixel width

Figure 10.6 shows the output from Listing 10.4.

We can also combine the use of page and device coordinates. In Listing 10.5 we transform page coordinates to 1 inch from the left and 0.5 inch from the top of the upper left corner of the client area. Our new page coordinate system has starting and ending points of (1, 0.5) and (3, 1.5), but the device coordinate system converts them to pixels. Hence the starting and ending points in device coordinates are (96, 48) and (288, 144), assuming a resolution of 96 dots per inch.

LISTING 10.5: Combining page and device coordinates

```
Pen redPen = new Pen(Color.Red, 1/g.DpiX);
g.TranslateTransform(1, 0.5f);
g.PageUnit = GraphicsUnit.Inch;
g.DrawLine(redPen, 0, 0, 2, 1);
```

Figure 10.7 shows the output from Listing 10.5.

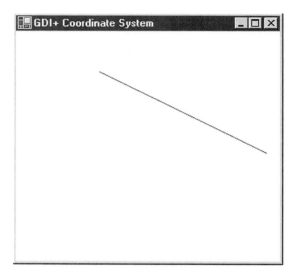

FIGURE 10.7: Combining page and device coordinates

10.2 Transformation Types

There are many types of transformations.

Translation is a transformation of the xy plane that moves a graphics object toward or away from the origin of the surface in the x- or y-direction. For example, moving an object from point A $(x1, y1)$ to point B $(x2, y2)$ is a translation operation in which an object is being moved $(y2 - y1)$ points in the y-direction.

Rotation moves an object around a fixed angle around the center of the plane.

In the **reflection** transformation, an object moves to a position in the opposite direction from an axis, along a line perpendicular to the axis. The resulting object is the same distance from the axis as the original point, but in the opposite direction.

Simple transformations, including rotation, scaling, and reflection are called **linear transformations**. A linear transformation followed by translation is called an **affine transformation**.

The **shearing** transformation skews objects based on a shear factor. In the sample applications discussed throughout this chapter, will see how to use these transformations in GDI+.

So far we've looked at only simple transformations. Now let's discuss some more complex transformation-related functionality defined in the .NET Framework library.

What Can You Transform?

You have just seen the basics of transforming lines. We can also transform graphics objects such as points, curves, shapes, images, text, colors, and textures, as well as colors and images used in pens and brushes.

10.3 **The Matrix Class and Transformation**

Matrices play a vital role in the transformation process. A **matrix** is a multi-dimensional array of values in which each item in the array represents one value of the transformation operation, as we will see in the examples later in this chapter.

In GDI+, the Matrix class represents a 3×2 matrix that contains x, y, and w values in the first, second, and third columns, respectively.

> **NOTE**
> Before using the Matrix class in your applications, you need to add a reference to the System.Drawing.Drawing2D namespace.

We can create a Matrix object by using its overloaded constructors, which take an array of points (hold the matrix items) as arguments. The following code snippet creates three Matrix objects from different overloaded constructors. The first Matrix object has no values for its items. The second and third objects have integer and floating point values, respectively, for the first six items of the matrix.

```
Matrix M1 = new Matrix();
Matrix M2 = new Matrix(2, 1, 3, 1, 0, 4);
Matrix M3 =
  new Matrix(0.0f, 1.0f, -1.0f, 0.0f, 0.0f, 0.0f);
```

TABLE 10.1: **Matrix** properties

Property	Description
Elements	Returns an array containing matrix elements.
IsIdentity	Returns true if the matrix is an identity matrix; otherwise returns false.
IsInvertible	Returns true if a matrix is invertible; otherwise returns false.
OffsetX	Returns the *x* translation value of a matrix.
OffsetY	Returns the *y* translation value of a matrix.

The Matrix class provides properties for accessing and setting its member values. Table 10.1 describes these properties.

The Matrix class provides methods to invert, rotate, scale, and transform matrices. The Invert method is used to reverse a matrix if it is invertible. This method takes no parameters.

> ■ **NOTE**
>
> The Transform property of the Graphics class is used to apply a transformation in the form of a Matrix object. We will discuss this property in more detail in Section 10.4.

Listing 10.6 uses the Invert method to invert a matrix. We create a Matrix object and read its original values. Then we call the Invert method and read the new values.

LISTING 10.6: Inverting a matrix

```
private void InvertMenu_Click(object sender,
    System.EventArgs e)
{
    string str = "Original values: ";
    // Create a Matrix object
    Matrix X = new Matrix(2, 1, 3, 1, 0, 4);
    // Write its values
    for(int i=0; i<X.Elements.Length; i++)
    {
```

```
        str += X.Elements[i].ToString();
        str += ", ";
    }
    str += "\n";
    str += "Inverted values: ";
    // Invert matrix
    X.Invert();
    float[] pts = X.Elements;
    // Read inverted matrix
    for(int i=0; i<pts.Length; i++)
    {
        str += pts[i].ToString();
        str += ", ";
    }
    // Display result
    MessageBox.Show(str);
}
```

The `Multiply` method multiplies a new matrix against an existing matrix and stores the result in the first matrix. `Multiply` takes two arguments. The first is the new matrix by which you want to multiply the existing matrix, and the second is an optional `MatrixOrder` argument that indicates the order of multiplication.

The `MatrixOrder` enumeration has two values: `Append` and `Prepend`. `Append` specifies that the new operation is applied after the preceding operation; `Prepend` specifies that the new operation is applied before the preceding operation during cumulative operations. Listing 10.7 multiplies two matrices. We create two `Matrix` objects and use the `Multiply` method to multiply the second matrix by the first. Then we read and display the resultant matrix.

LISTING 10.7: Multiplying two matrices

```
private void MultiplyMenu_Click(object sender,
    System.EventArgs e)
{
    string str = null;
    // Create two Matrix objects
    Matrix X =
        new Matrix(2.0f, 1.0f, 3.0f, 1.0f, 0.0f, 4.0f);
    Matrix Y =
        new Matrix(0.0f, 1.0f, -1.0f, 0.0f, 0.0f, 0.0f);
    // Multiply two matrices
    X.Multiply(Y, MatrixOrder.Append);
```

continues

```
    // Read the resultant matrix
    for(int i=0; i<X.Elements.Length; i++)
    {
        str += X.Elements[i].ToString();
        str += ", ";
    }
    // Display result
    MessageBox.Show(str);
}
```

The `Reset` method resets a matrix to the identity matrix (see Figure 10.21 for an example of an identity matrix). If we call the `Reset` method and then apply a matrix to transform an object, the result will be the original object.

The `Rotate` and `RotateAt` methods are used to rotate a matrix. The `Rotate` method rotates a matrix at a specified angle. This method takes two arguments: a floating point value specifying the angle, and (optionally) the matrix order. The `RotateAt` method is useful when you need to change the center of the rotation. Its first parameter is the angle; the second parameter (of type `float`) specifies the center of rotation. The third (optional) parameter is the matrix order.

Listing 10.8 simply creates a `Graphics` object using the `Create-Graphics` method and calls `DrawLine` and `FillRectangle` to draw a line and fill a rectangle, respectively.

LISTING 10.8: Drawing a line and filling a rectangle

```
private void Rotate_Click(object sender,
    System.EventArgs e)
{
    // Create a Graphics object
    Graphics g = this.CreateGraphics();
    g.Clear(this.BackColor);
    // Draw a line
    g.DrawLine(new Pen(Color.Green, 3),
        new Point(120, 50),
        new Point(200, 50));
    // Fill a rectangle
    g.FillRectangle(Brushes.Blue,
        200, 100, 100, 60);
    // Dispose of object
    g.Dispose();
}
```

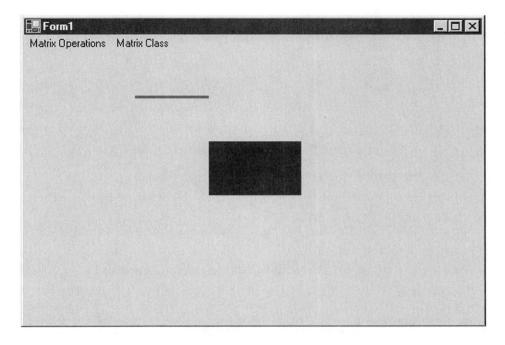

FIGURE 10.8: Drawing a line and filling a rectangle

Figure 10.8 shows the output from Listing 10.8.

Now let's rotate our graphics objects, using the `Matrix` object. In Listing 10.9 we create a `Matrix` object, call its `Rotate` method to rotate the matrix 45 degrees, and apply the `Matrix` object to the `Graphics` object by setting its `Transform` property.

LISTING 10.9: Rotating graphics objects

```
private void Rotate_Click(object sender,
    System.EventArgs e)
{
    // Create a Graphics object
    Graphics g = this.CreateGraphics();
    g.Clear(this.BackColor);
    // Create a Matrix object
    Matrix X = new Matrix();
    // Rotate by 45 degrees
    X.Rotate(45, MatrixOrder.Append);
    // Apply Matrix object to the Graphics object
```

continues

```
        // (i.e., to all the graphics items
        // drawn on the Graphics object)
        g.Transform = X;
        // Draw a line
        g.DrawLine(new Pen(Color.Green, 3),
            new Point(120, 50),
            new Point(200, 50));
        // Fill a rectangle
        g.FillRectangle(Brushes.Blue,
            200, 100, 100, 60);
        // Dispose of object
        g.Dispose();
}
```

Figure 10.9 shows the new output. Both objects (line and rectangle) have been rotated 45 degrees.

Now let's replace `Rotate` with `RotateAt`, as in Listing 10.10.

FIGURE 10.9: Rotating graphics objects

LISTING 10.10: Using the `RotateAt` method

```
private void RotateAtMenu_Click(object sender,
    System.EventArgs e)
{
    // Create a Graphics object
    Graphics g = this.CreateGraphics();
    g.Clear(this.BackColor);
    // Create a Matrix object
    Matrix X = new Matrix();
    // Create a point
    PointF pt = new PointF(180.0f, 50.0f);
    // Rotate by 45 degrees
    X.RotateAt(45, pt, MatrixOrder.Append);
    // Apply the Matrix object to the Graphics object
    // (i.e., to all the graphics items
    // drawn on the Graphics object)
    g.Transform = X;
    // Draw a line
    g.DrawLine(new Pen(Color.Green, 3),
        new Point(120, 50),
        new Point(200, 50));
    // Fill a rectangle
    g.FillRectangle(Brushes.Blue,
        200, 100, 100, 60);
    // Dispose of object
    g.Dispose();
}
```

This new code generates Figure 10.10.

If we call the `Reset` method in Listing 10.10 after `RotateAt` and before `g.Transform`, like this:

```
X.RotateAt(45, pt, MatrixOrder.Append);
// Reset the matrix
X.Reset();
// Apply the Matrix object to the Graphics object
// (i.e., to all the graphics items
// drawn on the Graphics object)
g.Transform = X;
```

the revised code generates Figure 10.11, which is the same as Figure 10.8. There is no rotation because the `Reset` method resets the transformation.

The `Scale` method scales a matrix in the *x*- and *y*-directions. This method takes two floating values (scale factors), for the *x*- and *y*-axes,

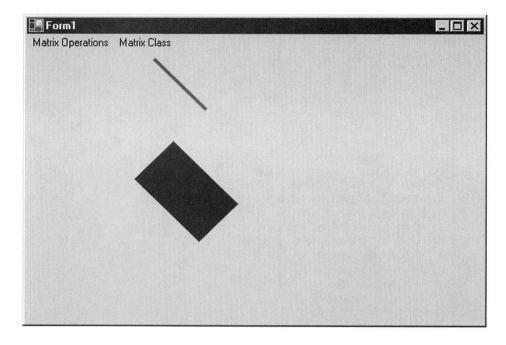

FIGURE 10.10: Using the `RotateAt` method

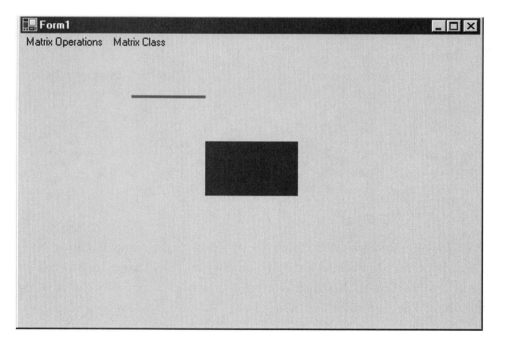

FIGURE 10.11: Resetting a transformation

respectively. In Listing 10.11 we draw a rectangle with a width of 20 and a height of 30. Then we create a `Matrix` object and scale it by calling its `Scale` method with arguments 3 and 4 in the *x*- and *y*-directions, respectively.

LISTING 10.11: Scaling graphics objects

```
private void Scale_Click(object sender,
    System.EventArgs e)
{
    // Create Graphics object
    Graphics g = this.CreateGraphics();
    g.Clear(this.BackColor);
    // Draw a filled rectangle with
    // width 20 and height 30
    g.FillRectangle(Brushes.Blue,
        20, 20, 20, 30);
    // Create Matrix object
    Matrix X = new Matrix();
    // Apply 3X scaling
    X.Scale(3, 4, MatrixOrder.Append);
    // Apply transformation on the form
    g.Transform = X;
    // Draw a filled rectangle with
    // width 20 and height 30
    g.FillRectangle(Brushes.Blue,
        20, 20, 20, 30);
    // Dispose of object
    g.Dispose();
}
```

Figure 10.12 shows the output from Listing 10.11. The first rectangle is the original rectangle; the second rectangle is the scaled rectangle, in which the *x* position (and width) is scaled by 3, and the *y* position (and height) is scaled by 4.

The `Shear` method provides a shearing transformation and takes two floating point arguments, which represent the horizontal and vertical shear factors, respectively. In Listing 10.12 we draw a filled rectangle with a hatch brush. Then we call the `Shear` method to shear the matrix by 2 in the vertical direction, and we use `Transform` to apply the `Matrix` object.

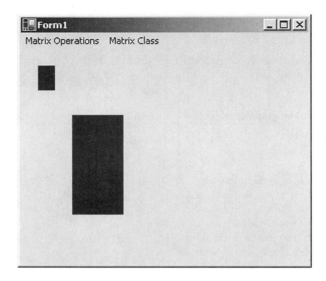

FIGURE 10.12: Scaling a rectangle

LISTING 10.12: Shearing graphics objects

```
private void Shear_Click(object sender,
    System.EventArgs e)
{
    // Create a Graphics object
    Graphics g = this.CreateGraphics();
    g.Clear(this.BackColor);
    // Create a brush
    HatchBrush hBrush = new HatchBrush
        (HatchStyle.DarkVertical,
        Color.Green, Color.Yellow);
    // Fill a rectangle
    g.FillRectangle(hBrush,
        100, 50, 100, 60);
    // Create a Matrix object
    Matrix X = new Matrix();
    // Shear
    X.Shear(2, 1);
    // Apply transformation
    g.Transform = X;
    // Fill rectangle
    g.FillRectangle(hBrush,
        10, 100, 100, 60);
    // Dispose of objects
    hBrush.Dispose();
    g.Dispose();
}
```

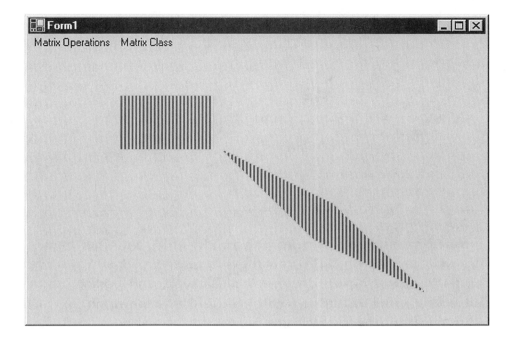

FIGURE 10.13: Shearing a rectangle

Figure 10.13 shows the output from Listing 10.12. The first rectangle in this figure is the original; the second is sheared.

The `Translate` method translates objects by the specified value. This method takes two floating point arguments, which represent the x and y offsets. For example, Listing 10.13 translates the original rectangle by 100 pixels each in the x- and y-directions.

LISTING 10.13: Translating graphics objects

```
private void Translate_Click(object sender,
    System.EventArgs e)
{
    // Create a Graphics obhect
    Graphics g = this.CreateGraphics();
    g.Clear(this.BackColor);
    // Draw a filled rectangle
    g.FillRectangle(Brushes.Blue,
        50, 50, 100, 60);
```

continues

```
    // Create a Matrix object
    Matrix X = new Matrix();
    // Translate by 100 in the x direction
    // and 100 in the y direction
    X.Translate(100, 100);
    // Apply transformation
    g.Transform = X;
    // Draw a filled rectangle after
    // translation
    g.FillRectangle(Brushes.Blue,
        50, 50, 100, 60);
    // Dispose of object
    g.Dispose();
}
```

Here we draw two rectangles with a width of 100 and a height of 60. Both rectangles start at (50, 50), but the code generates Figure 10.14. Even though the rectangles were drawn with the same size and location, the second rectangle after translation is now located 100 points away in the x- and y-directions from the first rectangle.

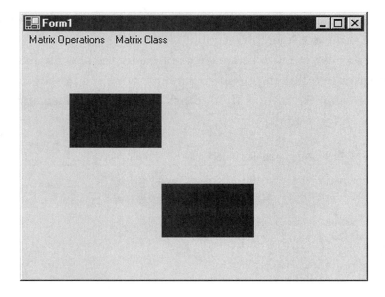

FIGURE 10.14: Translating a rectangle

10.4 **The Graphics Class and Transformation**

In Chapter 3 we saw that the Graphics class provides some transformation-related members. Before we move to other transformation-related classes, let's review the transformation functionality defined in the Graphics class, as described in Table 10.2. We will see how to use these members in the examples throughout this chapter.

The Transform property of the Graphics class represents the world transformation of a Graphics object. It is applied to all items of the object. For example, if you have a rectangle, an ellipse, and a line and set the

TABLE 10.2: Transformation-related members defined in the Graphics class

Member	Description
MultiplyTransform	Method that multiplies the world transformation of a Graphics object and a Matrix object. The Matrix object specifies the transformation action (scaling, rotation, or translation).
ResetTransform	Method that resets the world transformation matrix of a Graphics object to the identity matrix.
RotateTransform	Method that applies a specified rotation to the transformation matrix of a Graphics object.
ScaleTransform	Method that applies a specified scaling operation to the transformation matrix of a Graphics object by prepending it to the object's transformation matrix.
Transform	Property that represents the world transformation for a Graphics object. Both get and set.
TransformPoints	Method that transforms an array of points from one coordinate space to another using the current world and page transformations of a Graphics object.
TranslateClip	Method that translates the clipping region of a Graphics object by specified amounts in the horizontal and vertical directions.
TranslateTransform	Method that prepends the specified translation to the transformation matrix of a Graphics object.

Transform property of the Graphics object, it will be applied to all three items. The Transform property is a Matrix object. The following code snippet creates a Matrix object and sets the Transform property:

```
Matrix X = new Matrix();
X.Scale(2, 2, MatrixOrder.Append);
g.Transform = X;
```

The transformation methods provided by the Graphics class are MultiplyTransform, ResetTransform, RotateTransform, Scale-Transform, TransformPoints, TranslateClip, and TranslateTrans-form. The MultiplyTransform method multiplies a transformation matrix by the world transformation coordinates of a Graphics object. It takes an argument of Matrix type. The second argument, which specifies the order of multiplication operation, is optional. The following code snippet creates a Matrix object with the Translate transformation. The MultiplyTransform method multiplies the Matrix object by the world coordinates of the Graphics object, translating all graphics items drawn by the Graphics object.

```
Matrix X = new Matrix();
X. Translate(200.0F, 100.0F);
g.MultiplyTransform(X, MatrixOrder.Append);
```

RotateTransform rotates the world transform by a specified angle. This method takes a floating point argument, which represents the rotation angle, and an optional second argument of MatrixOrder. The following code snippet rotates the world transformation of the Graphics object by 45 degrees:

```
g.RotateTransform(45.0F, MatrixOrder.Append);
```

The ScaleTransform method scales the world transformation in the specified x- and y-directions. The first and second arguments of this method are x- and y-direction scaling factors, and the third optional argument is MatrixOrder. The following code snippet scales the world transformation by 2 in the x-direction and by 3 in the y-direction:

```
g.ScaleTransform(2.0F, 3.0F, MatrixOrder.Append);
```

The `TranslateClip` method translates the clipping region in the horizontal and vertical directions. The first argument of this method represents the translation in the *x*-direction, and the second argument represents the translation in the *y*-direction:

```
e.Graphics.TranslateClip(20.0f, 10.0f);
```

The `TranslateTransform` method translates the world transformation by the specified *x*- and *y*-values and takes an optional third argument of `MatrixOrder`:

```
g.TranslateTransform(100.0F, 0.0F, MatrixOrder.Append);
```

We will use all of these methods in our examples.

10.5 **Global, Local, and Composite Transformations**

Transformations can be divided into two categories based on their scope: global and local. In addition, there are composite transformations. A **global transformation** is applicable to all items of a `Graphics` object. The `Transform` property of the `Graphics` class is used to set global transformations.

A **composite transformation** is a sequence of transformations. For example, scaling followed by translation and rotation is a composite translation. The `MultiplyTransform`, `RotateTransform`, `ScaleTransform`, and `TranslateTransform` methods are used to generate composite transformations.

Listing 10.14 draws two ellipses and a rectangle, then calls `Scale-Transform`, `TranslateTransform`, and `RotateTransform` (a composite transformation). The items are drawn again after the composite transformation.

LISTING 10.14: Applying a composite transformation

```
private void GlobalTransformation_Click(object sender,
    System.EventArgs e)
{
    // Create a Graphics object
    Graphics g = this.CreateGraphics();
```

continues

```
        g.Clear(this.BackColor);
        // Create a blue pen with width of 2
        Pen bluePen = new Pen(Color.Blue, 2);
        Point pt1 = new Point(10, 10);
        Point pt2 = new Point(20, 20);
        Color [] lnColors = {Color.Black, Color.Red};
        Rectangle rect1 = new Rectangle(10, 10, 15, 15);
        // Create two linear gradient brushes
        LinearGradientBrush lgBrush1 = new LinearGradientBrush
            (rect1, Color.Blue, Color.Green,
            LinearGradientMode.BackwardDiagonal);
        LinearGradientBrush lgBrush = new LinearGradientBrush
            (pt1, pt2, Color.Red, Color.Green);
        // Set linear colors
        lgBrush.LinearColors = lnColors;
        // Set gamma correction
        lgBrush.GammaCorrection = true;
        // Fill and draw rectangle and ellipses
        g.FillRectangle(lgBrush, 150, 0, 50, 100);
        g.DrawEllipse(bluePen, 0, 0, 100, 50);
        g.FillEllipse(lgBrush1, 300, 0, 100, 100);
        // Apply scale transformation
        g.ScaleTransform(1, 0.5f);
        // Apply translate transformation
        g.TranslateTransform(50, 0, MatrixOrder.Append);
        // Apply rotate transformation
        g.RotateTransform(30.0f, MatrixOrder.Append);
        // Fill ellipse
        g.FillEllipse(lgBrush1, 300, 0, 100, 100);
        // Rotate again
        g.RotateTransform(15.0f, MatrixOrder.Append);
        // Fill rectangle
        g.FillRectangle(lgBrush, 150, 0, 50, 100);
        // Rotate again
        g.RotateTransform(15.0f, MatrixOrder.Append);
        // Draw ellipse
        g.DrawEllipse(bluePen, 0, 0, 100, 50);
        // Dispose of objects
        lgBrush1.Dispose();
        lgBrush.Dispose();
        bluePen.Dispose();
        g.Dispose();
    }
```

Figure 10.15 shows the output from Listing 10.14.

A **local transformation** is applicable to only a specific item of a Graph-ics object. The best example of local transformation is transforming a graphics path. The Translate method of the GraphicsPath class trans-

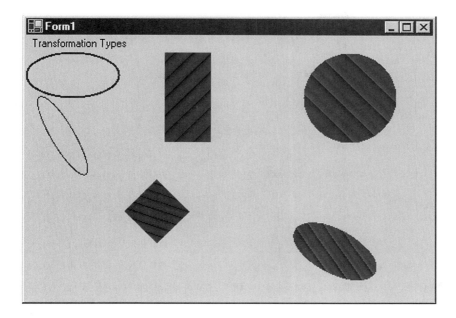

FIGURE 10.15: Composite transformation

lates only the items of a graphics path. Listing 10.15 translates a graphics path. We create a `Matrix` object and apply rotate and translate transformations to it.

LISTING 10.15: Translating graphics path items

```
private void LocalTransformation_Click(object sender,
    System.EventArgs e)
{
    // Create a Graphics object
    Graphics g = this.CreateGraphics();
    g.Clear(this.BackColor);
    // Create a GraphicsPath object
    GraphicsPath path = new GraphicsPath();
    // Add an ellipse and a line to the
    // graphics path
    path.AddEllipse(50, 50, 100, 150);
    path.AddLine(20, 20, 200, 20);
    // Create a blue pen with a width of 2
    Pen bluePen = new Pen(Color.Blue, 2);
```

continues

```
// Create a Matrix object
Matrix X = new Matrix();
// Rotate 30 degrees
X.Rotate(30);
// Translate with 50 offset in x direction
X.Translate(50.0f, 0);
// Apply transformation on the path
path.Transform(X);
// Draw a rectangle, a line, and the path
g.DrawRectangle(Pens.Green, 200, 50, 100, 100);
g.DrawLine(Pens.Green, 30, 20, 200, 20);
g.DrawPath(bluePen, path);
// Dispose of objects
bluePen.Dispose();
path.Dispose();
g.Dispose();
}
```

Figure 10.16 shows the output from Listing 10.15. The transformation affects only graphics path items (the ellipse and the blue [dark] line).

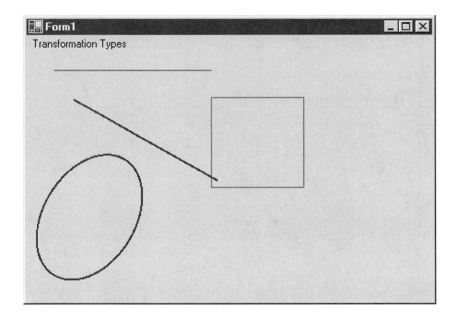

FIGURE 10.16: Local transformation

10.6 **Image Transformation**

Image transformation is exactly the same as any other transformation process. In this section we will see how to rotate, scale, translate, reflect, and shear images. We will create a `Matrix` object, set the transformation process by calling its methods, set the `Matrix` object as the `Transform` property or the transformation methods of the `Graphics` object, and call `DrawImage`.

Rotating images is similar to rotating other graphics. Listing 10.16 rotates an image. We create a `Graphics` object using the `CreateGraphics` method. Then we create a `Bitmap` object from a file and call the `DrawImage` method, which draws the image on the form. After that we create a `Matrix` object, call its `Rotate` method, rotate the image by 30 degrees, and apply the resulting matrix to the surface using the `Transform` property. Finally, we draw the image again using `DrawImage`.

LISTING 10.16: **Rotating images**

```
private void RotationMenu_Click(object sender,
    System.EventArgs e)
{
    Graphics g = this.CreateGraphics();
    g.Clear(this.BackColor);
    Bitmap curBitmap = new Bitmap(@"roses.jpg");
    g.DrawImage(curBitmap, 0, 0, 200, 200);
    // Create a Matrix object, call its Rotate method,
    // and set it as Graphics.Transform
    Matrix X = new Matrix();
    X.Rotate(30);
    g.Transform = X;
    // Draw image
    g.DrawImage(curBitmap,
        new Rectangle(205, 0, 200, 200),
        0, 0, curBitmap.Width,
        curBitmap.Height,
        GraphicsUnit.Pixel) ;
    // Dispose of objects
    curBitmap.Dispose();
    g.Dispose();
}
```

Figure 10.17 shows the output from Listing 10.16. The first image is the original; the second image is rotated.

FIGURE 10.17: Rotating images

Now let's apply other transformations. Replacing the `Rotate` method in Listing 10.16 with the following line scales the image:

```
X.Scale(2, 1, MatrixOrder.Append);
```

The scaled image is shown in Figure 10.18.

Replacing the `Rotate` method in Listing 10.16 with the following line translates the image with 100 offset in the *x*- and *y*-directions:

```
X.Translate(100, 100);
```

The new output is shown in Figure 10.19.

Replacing the `Rotate` method in Listing 10.16 with the following line shears the image:

```
X.Shear(2, 1);
```

FIGURE 10.18: Scaling images

FIGURE 10.19: Translating images

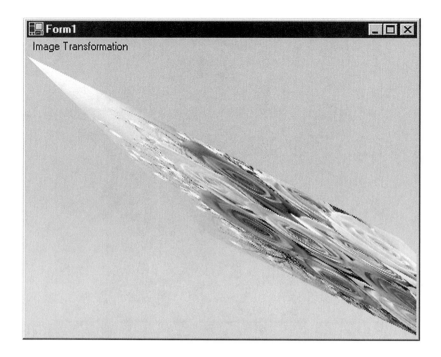

FIGURE 10.20: Shearing images

The new output is shown in Figure 10.20.

You have probably noticed that image transformation is really no different from the transformation of other graphics objects. We recommend that you download the source code samples from online to see the detailed code listings.

10.7 Color Transformation and the Color Matrix

So far we have seen the transformation of graphics shapes from one state to another, but have you ever thought about transforming colors? Why *would* you want to transform an image's colors? Suppose you wanted to provide grayscale effects, or needed to adjust the contrast, brightness, or even "redness" of an image. For example, images retrieved from video and still cameras often need correction. In these cases, a color matrix is very useful.

As we discussed in earlier chapters, the color of each pixel of a GDI+ image or bitmap is represented by a 32-bit number, of which 8 bits each are used for the red, green, blue, and alpha components. Each of the four components is a number from 0 to 255. For red, green, and blue, 0 represents no intensity and 255 represents full intensity. For the alpha component, 0 represents transparent and 255 represents fully opaque. A color vector includes four items: A, R, G, and B. The minimum values for this vector are (0, 0, 0, 0), and the maximum values are (255, 255, 255, 255).

GDI+ allows the use of values between 0 and 1, where 0 represents the minimum intensity and 1 the maximum intensity. These values are used in a color matrix to represent the intensity and opacity of color components. For example, the color vector with minimum values is (0, 0, 0, 0), and the color vector with maximum values is (1, 1, 1, 1).

In a color transformation we can apply a color matrix on a color vector by multiplying a 4×4 matrix. However, a 4×4 matrix supports only linear transformations such as rotation and scaling. To perform nonlinear transformations such as translation, we must use a 5×5 matrix. The element of the fifth row and the fifth column of the matrix must be 1, and all of the other entries in the five columns must be 0.

The elements of the matrix are identified according to a zero-based index. The first element of the matrix is M[0][0], and the last element is M[4][4]. A 5×5 identity matrix is shown in Figure 10.21. In this matrix the elements M[0][0], M[1][1], M[2][2], and M[3][3] represent the red, blue, green, and alpha factors, respectively. The element M[4][4] means nothing, and it must always be 1.

Now if we want to double the intensity of the red component of a color, we simply set M[0][0] equal to 2. For example, the matrix shown in Figure 10.22 doubles the intensity of the red component, decreases the

$$\begin{bmatrix} 1 & 0 & 0 & 0 & 0 \\ 0 & 1 & 0 & 0 & 0 \\ 0 & 0 & 1 & 0 & 0 \\ 0 & 0 & 0 & 1 & 0 \\ 0 & 0 & 0 & 0 & 1 \end{bmatrix}$$

FIGURE 10.21: An identity matrix

$$
\begin{bmatrix}
2 & 0 & 0 & 0 & 0 \\
0 & 0.5 & 0 & 0 & 0 \\
0 & 0 & 3 & 0 & 0 \\
0 & 0 & 0 & 0.5 & 0 \\
0 & 0 & 0 & 0 & 1
\end{bmatrix}
$$

FIGURE 10.22: A matrix whose components have different intensities

intensity of the green component by half, triples the intensity of the blue component, and decreases the opacity of the color by half (making it semi-transparent).

In the matrix shown in Figure 10.22, we multiplied the intensity values. We can also add intensity values by using other matrix elements. For example, the matrix shown in Figure 10.23 will double the intensity of the red component and add 0.2 to each of the red, green, and blue component intensities.

10.7.1 **The ColorMatrix Class**

In this section we will discuss the ColorMatrix class. As you might guess from its name, this class defines a matrix of colors. In the preceding sections we discussed the Matrix class. The ColorMatrix class is not very different from the Matrix class. Whereas the Matrix class is used in general transformation to transform graphics shapes and images, the ColorMatrix class is specifically designed to transform colors. Before we see practical use of the color transformation, we will discuss the ColorMatrix class, its properties, and its methods.

$$
\begin{bmatrix}
2 & 0 & 0 & 0 & 0 \\
0 & 1 & 0 & 0 & 0 \\
0 & 0 & 1 & 0 & 0 \\
0 & 0 & 0 & 1 & 0 \\
0.2 & 0.2 & 0.2 & 0 & 1
\end{bmatrix}
$$

FIGURE 10.23: A color matrix with multiplication and addition

The `ColorMatrix` class constructor takes an array that contains the values of matrix items. The `Item` property of this class represents a cell of the matrix and can be used to get and set cell values. Besides the `Item` property, the `ColorMatrix` class provides 25 `MatrixXY` properties, which represent items of the matrix at row $(x + 1)$ and column $(y + 1)$. `MatrixXY` properties can be used to get and set an item's value.

Listing 10.17 creates a `ColorMatrix` object with item $(4, 4)$ set to 0.5 (half opacity). Then it sets the values of item $(3, 4)$ to 0.8 and item $(1, 1)$ to 0.3.

LISTING 10.17: Creating a `ColorMatrix` object

```
float[][] ptsArray ={
   new float[] {1, 0, 0, 0, 0},
   new float[] {0, 1, 0, 0, 0},
   new float[] {0, 0, 1, 0, 0},
   new float[] {0, 0, 0, 0.5f, 0},
   new float[] {0, 0, 0, 0, 1}};
ColorMatrix clrMatrix = new ColorMatrix(ptsArray);
if( clrMatrix.Matrix34 <= 0.5)
{
    clrMatrix.Matrix34 = 0.8f;
        clrMatrix.Matrix11 = 0.3f;
}
```

Section 10.8 will describe how to apply color matrices to the transformation of colors.

10.8 **Matrix Operations in Image Processing**

Recoloring, the process of changing image colors, is a good example of color transformation. Recoloring includes changing colors, intensity, contrast, and brightness of an image. It can all be done via the `Image-Attributes` class and its methods.

The color matrix can be applied to an image via the `SetColorMatrix` method of the `ImageAttributes` class. The `ImageAttributes` object is used as a parameter when we call `DrawImage`.

10.8.1 **Translating Colors**

Translating colors increases or decreases color intensities by a set amount (not by multiplying them). Each color component (red, green, and blue) has

255 different intensity levels ranging from 0 to 255. For example, assume that the current intensity level for the red component of a color is 100. Changing its intensity level to 150 would imply translating by 50.

In a color matrix representation, the intensity varies from 0 to 1. The last row's first four elements represent the translation of red, green, blue, and alpha components of a color, as shown in Figure 10.22. Hence, adding a value to these elements will transform a color. For example, the t1, t2, t3, and t4 values in the following color matrix represent the red, green, blue, and alpha component translations, respectively:

```
Color Matrix = {
{1,  0,  0,  0, 0},
{0,  1,  0,  0, 0},
{0,  0,  1,  0, 0},
{0,  0,  0,  1, 0},
{t1, t2, t3, t4, 1}};
```

Listing 10.18 uses a ColorMatrix object to translate colors. We change the current intensity of the red component to 0.90. First we create a Graphics object using the CreateGraphics method, and we create a Bitmap object from a file. Next we create an array of ColorMatrix elements and create a ColorMatrix object from this array. Then we create an ImageAttributes object and set the color matrix using SetColorMatrix, which takes the ColorMatrix object as its first parameter. After all that, we draw two images. The first image has no effects; the second image shows the result of our color matrix transformation. Finally, we dispose of the objects.

LISTING 10.18: Using ColorMatrix to translate colors

```
private void TranslationMenu_Click(object sender,
    System.EventArgs e)
{
    // Create a Graphics object
    Graphics g = this.CreateGraphics();
    g.Clear(this.BackColor);
    // Create a Bitmap object
    Bitmap curBitmap = new Bitmap("roses.jpg");
    // Color matrix elements
    float[][] ptsArray =
    {
        new float[] {1,  0,  0,  0, 0},
```

```
        new float[] {0,  1,  0,  0, 0},
        new float[] {0,  0,  1,  0, 0},
        new float[] {0,  0,  0,  1, 0},
        new float[] {.90f, .0f, .0f, .0f, 1}
    };
    // Create a ColorMatrix object
    ColorMatrix clrMatrix = new ColorMatrix(ptsArray);
    // Create image attributes
    ImageAttributes imgAttribs = new ImageAttributes();
    // Set color matrix
    imgAttribs.SetColorMatrix(clrMatrix,
        ColorMatrixFlag.Default,
        ColorAdjustType.Default);
    // Draw image with no effects
    g.DrawImage(curBitmap, 0, 0, 200, 200);
    // Draw image with image attributes
    g.DrawImage(curBitmap,
        new Rectangle(205, 0, 200, 200),
        0, 0, curBitmap.Width, curBitmap.Height,
        GraphicsUnit.Pixel, imgAttribs) ;
    // Dispose of objects
    curBitmap.Dispose();
    g.Dispose();
}
```

Figure 10.24 shows the output from Listing 10.18. The original image is on the left; on the right we have the results of our color translation. If you

FIGURE 10.24: Translating colors

change the values of other components (red, blue, and alpha) in the last row of the color matrix, you'll see different results.

10.8.2 Scaling Colors

Scaling color involves multiplying a color component value by a scaling factor. For example, the t1, t2, t3, and t4 values in the following color matrix represent the red, green, blue, and alpha components, respectively. If we change the value of M[2][2] to 0.5, the transformation operation will multiply the green component by 0.5, cutting its intensity by half.

```
Color Matrix = {
{t1,  0,   0,   0, 0},
{0,   t2,  0,   0, 0},
{0,   0,   t3,  0, 0},
{0,   0,   0,   t4, 0},
{0,   0,   0,   0, 1}};
```

Listing 10.19 uses the `ColorMatrix` object to scale image colors.

LISTING 10.19: Scaling colors

```
private void ScalingMenu_Click(object sender,
    System.EventArgs e)
{
    // Create a Graphics object
    Graphics g = this.CreateGraphics();
    g.Clear(this.BackColor);
    // Create a Bitmap object
    Bitmap curBitmap = new Bitmap("roses.jpg");
    // Color matrix elements
    float[][] ptsArray =
    {
        new float[] {1,   0,   0,   0, 0},
        new float[] {0,   0.8f, 0,   0, 0},
        new float[] {0,   0,   0.5f, 0, 0},
        new float[] {0,   0,   0,   0.5f, 0},
        new float[] {0, 0, 0, 0, 1}
    };
    // Create a ColorMatrix object
    ColorMatrix clrMatrix = new ColorMatrix(ptsArray);
    // Create image attributes
    ImageAttributes imgAttribs = new ImageAttributes();
    // Set color matrix
    imgAttribs.SetColorMatrix(clrMatrix,
        ColorMatrixFlag.Default,
        ColorAdjustType.Default);
```

```
    // Draw image with no effects
    g.DrawImage(curBitmap, 0, 0, 200, 200);
    // Draw image with image attributes
    g.DrawImage(curBitmap,
        new Rectangle(205, 0, 200, 200),
        0, 0, curBitmap.Width, curBitmap.Height,
        GraphicsUnit.Pixel, imgAttribs) ;
    // Dispose of objects
    curBitmap.Dispose();
    g.Dispose();
}
```

Figure 10.25 shows the output from Listing 10.19. The original image is on the left; on the right is the image after color scaling. If you change the values of t1, t2, t3, and t4, you will see different results.

10.8.3 Shearing Colors

Earlier in this chapter we discussed image shearing. It can be thought of as anchoring one corner of a rectangular region and stretching the opposite corner horizontally, vertically, or in both directions. Shearing colors is the same process, but here the object is the color instead of the image.

Color shearing increases or decreases a color component by an amount proportional to another color component. For example, consider the

FIGURE 10.25: Scaling colors

transformation in which the red component is increased by one half the value of the blue component. Under such a transformation, the color (0.2, 0.5, 1) would become (0.7, 0.5, 1). The new red component is 0.2 + (0.5)(1) = 0.7. The following color matrix is used to shear image colors.

```
float[][] ptsArray = {
 new float[] {1,   0,   0,   0, 0},
 new float[] {0,   1,   0,   0, 0},
 new float[] {.50f,   0,   1,   0, 0},
 new float[] {0,   0,   0,   1, 0},
 new float[] {0, 0, 0, 0, 1}};
ColorMatrix clrMatrix = new ColorMatrix(ptsArray);
```

If we substitute this color matrix into Listing 10.19, the output will look like Figure 10.26.

FIGURE 10.26: Shearing colors

10.8.4 Rotating Colors

As explained earlier, color in GDI+ has four components: red, green, blue, and alpha. Rotating all four components in a four-dimensional space is hard to visualize. However, such rotation can be visualized in a three-dimensional space. To do this, we drop the alpha component from the color structure and assume that there are only three colors—red, green, and blue—as shown in Figure 10.27. The three colors—red, green, and blue—are perpendicular to each other, so the angle between any two primary colors is 90 degrees.

Suppose that the red, green, and blue colors are represented by points (1, 0, 0), (0, 1, 0), and (0, 0, 1), respectively. If we rotate a color with a green component of 1, and red and blue components of 0 each, by 90 degrees, the new color will have a red component of 1, and green and blue components of 0 each. If we rotate the color less than 90 degrees, the new color will be located somewhere between green and red.

Figure 10.28 shows how to initialize a color matrix to perform rotations about each of the three components: red, green, and blue.

Listing 10.20 rotates the colors by 45 degrees from the red component.

LISTING 10.20: Rotating colors

```
private void RotationMenu_Click(object sender,
    System.EventArgs e)
{
    float degrees = 45.0f;
    double r = degrees*System.Math.PI/180;
    // Create a Graphics object
    Graphics g = this.CreateGraphics();
    g.Clear(this.BackColor);
    // Create a Bitmap object from a file
    Bitmap curBitmap = new Bitmap("roses.jpg");
```

continues

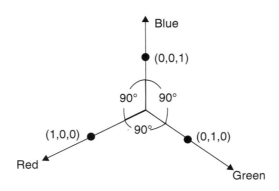

FIGURE 10.27: RGB rotation space

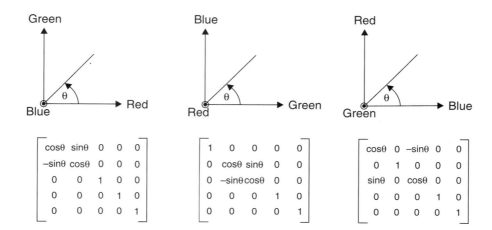

$$
\begin{bmatrix}
\cos\theta & \sin\theta & 0 & 0 & 0 \\
-\sin\theta & \cos\theta & 0 & 0 & 0 \\
0 & 0 & 1 & 0 & 0 \\
0 & 0 & 0 & 1 & 0 \\
0 & 0 & 0 & 0 & 1
\end{bmatrix}
\quad
\begin{bmatrix}
1 & 0 & 0 & 0 & 0 \\
0 & \cos\theta & \sin\theta & 0 & 0 \\
0 & -\sin\theta & \cos\theta & 0 & 0 \\
0 & 0 & 0 & 1 & 0 \\
0 & 0 & 0 & 0 & 1
\end{bmatrix}
\quad
\begin{bmatrix}
\cos\theta & 0 & -\sin\theta & 0 & 0 \\
0 & 1 & 0 & 0 & 0 \\
\sin\theta & 0 & \cos\theta & 0 & 0 \\
0 & 0 & 0 & 1 & 0 \\
0 & 0 & 0 & 0 & 1
\end{bmatrix}
$$

FIGURE 10.28: RGB initialization

```
// Color matrix elements
float[][] ptsArray =
{
    new float[] {(float)System.Math.Cos(r),
                 (float)System.Math.Sin(r),
                 0,  0,  0},
    new float[] {(float)-System.Math.Sin(r),
                  (float)-System.Math.Cos(r),
                   0,  0,  0},
    new float[] {.50f,  0,  1,  0,  0},
    new float[] {0,  0,  0,  1,  0},
    new float[] {0, 0, 0, 0, 1}
};
// Create a ColorMatrix object
ColorMatrix clrMatrix = new ColorMatrix(ptsArray);
// Create image attributes
ImageAttributes imgAttribs = new ImageAttributes();
// Set ColorMatrix to ImageAttributes
imgAttribs.SetColorMatrix(clrMatrix,
    ColorMatrixFlag.Default,
    ColorAdjustType.Default);
// Draw image with no effects
g.DrawImage(curBitmap, 0, 0, 200, 200);
// Draw image with image attributes
g.DrawImage(curBitmap,
    new Rectangle(205, 0, 200, 200),
    0, 0, curBitmap.Width, curBitmap.Height,
    GraphicsUnit.Pixel, imgAttribs) ;
// Dispose of objects
curBitmap.Dispose();
g.Dispose();
}
```

FIGURE 10.29: Rotating colors

Figure 10.29 slows the output from Listing 10.20. On the left is the original image; on the right is the image after color rotation.

10.9 Text Transformation

In Chapter 5 we discussed how to use the `ScaleTransform`, `Rotate-Transform`, and `TranslateTransform` methods to transform text. We can also use a transformation matrix to transform text.

We create a `Matrix` object with the transformation properties and apply it to the surface using the `Transform` property of the `Graphics` object. Listing 10.21 creates a `Matrix` object and sets it as the `Transform` property. We then call `DrawString`, which draws the text on the form. To test this code, add the code to a form's paint event handler.

LISTING 10.21: Text transformation example

```
Graphics g = e.Graphics;
string str =
"Colors, fonts, and text are common" +
" elements of graphics programming." +
"In this chapter, you learned " +
" about the colors, fonts, and text" +
" representations in the "+
".NET Framework class library. "+
"You learned how to create "+
"these elements and use them in GDI+.";
// Create a Matrix object
Matrix M = new Matrix(1, 0, 0.5f, 1, 0, 0);
g.RotateTransform(45.0f,
System.Drawing.Drawing2D.MatrixOrder.Prepend);
g.TranslateTransform(-20, -70);
g.Transform = M;
g.DrawString(str,
new Font("Verdana", 10),
new SolidBrush(Color.Blue),
new Rectangle(50,20,200,300) );
```

Figure 10.30 shows the outcome of Listing 10.21.

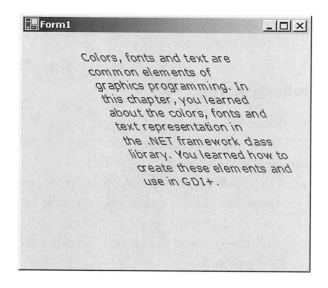

FIGURE 10.30: Using the transformation matrix to transform text

We can apply shearing and other effects by changing the values of `Matrix`. For example, if we change `Matrix` as follows:

```
Matrix M = new Matrix(1, 0.5f, 0, 1, 0, 0);
```

the new code will generate Figure 10.31.

We can reverse the text just by changing the value of the `Matrix` object as follows:

```
Matrix M = new Matrix(1, 1, 1, -1, 0, 0);
```

with the results shown in Figure 10.32.

10.10 **The Significance of Transformation Order**

The `Matrix` object can store a single transformation or a sequence of transformations. As we learned in Section 10.5, a sequence of transformations is called a *composite transformation*, which is a result of multiplying the matrices of the individual transformations.

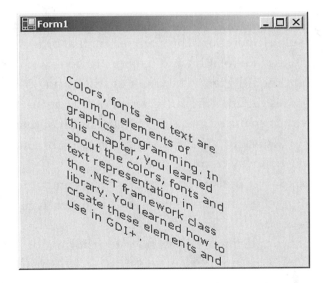

FIGURE 10.31: Using the transformation matrix to shear text

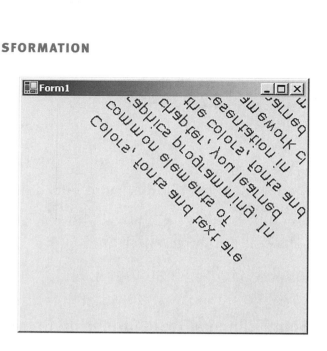

FIGURE 10.32: Using the transformation matrix to reverse text

In a composite transformation, the order of the individual transformations is very important. Matrix operations are not cumulative. For example, the result of a Graphics → Rotate → Translate → Scale → Graphics operation will be different from the result of a Graphics → Scale → Rotate → Translate → Graphics operation. The main reason that order is significant is that transformations like rotation and scaling are done with respect to the origin of the coordinate system. The result of scaling an object that is centered at the origin is different from the result of scaling an object that has been moved away from the origin. Similarly, the result of rotating an object that is centered at the origin is different from the result of rotating an object that has been moved away from the origin.

The MatrixOrder enumeration, which is an argument to the transformation methods, represents the transformation order. It has two values: Append and Prepend.

Let's write an application to see how transformation order works. We create a Windows application and add a MainMenu control and three menu items to the form. The MatrixOrder class is defined in the System.Drawing.Drawing2D namespace, so we also add a reference to this namespace.

Listing 10.22 draws a rectangle before and after applying a Scale → Rotate → Translate transformation sequence.

LISTING 10.22: Scale → Rotate → Translate transformation order

```
private void First_Click(object sender,
    System.EventArgs e)
{
    // Create a Graphics object
    Graphics g = this.CreateGraphics();
    g.Clear(this.BackColor);
    // Create a rectangle
    Rectangle rect =
        new Rectangle(20, 20, 100, 100);
    // Create a solid brush
    SolidBrush brush =
        new SolidBrush(Color.Red);
    // Fill rectangle
    g.FillRectangle(brush, rect);
    // Scale
    g.ScaleTransform(1.75f, 0.5f);
    // Rotate
    g.RotateTransform(45.0f, MatrixOrder.Append);
    // Translate
    g.TranslateTransform(150.0f, 50.0f,
        MatrixOrder.Append);
    // Fill rectangle again
    g.FillRectangle(brush, rect);
    // Dispose of objects
    brush.Dispose();
    g.Dispose();
}
```

Figure 10.33 shows the output from Listing 10.22. The original rectangle is in the upper left; on the lower right is the rectangle after composite transformation.

Now let's change the order of transformation to Translate → Rotate → Scale with Append, as shown in Listing 10.23.

LISTING 10.23: Translate → Rotate → Scale transformation order with Append

```
private void Second_Click(object sender,
    System.EventArgs e)
{
    // Create a Graphics object
    Graphics g = this.CreateGraphics();
```

continues

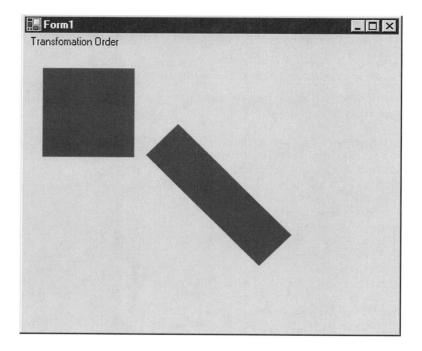

FIGURE 10.33: Scale → Rotate → Translate composite transformation

```
g.Clear(this.BackColor);
// Create a rectangle
Rectangle rect =
    new Rectangle(20, 20, 100, 100);
// Create a solid brush
SolidBrush brush =
    new SolidBrush(Color.Red);
// Fill rectangle
g.FillRectangle(brush, rect);
// Translate
g.TranslateTransform(100.0f, 50.0f,
    MatrixOrder.Append);
// Scale
g.ScaleTransform(1.75f, 0.5f);
// Rotate
g.RotateTransform(45.0f,
    MatrixOrder.Append);
// Fill rectangle again
g.FillRectangle(brush, rect);
// Dispose of objects
brush.Dispose();
g.Dispose();
}
```

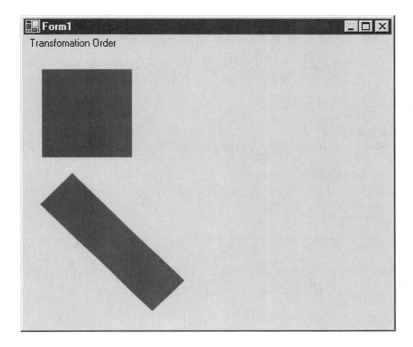

FIGURE 10.34: Translate → Rotate → Scale composite transformation with `Append`

Figure 10.34 shows the output from Listing 10.23. The original rectangle is in the same place, but the transformed rectangle has moved.

Now let's keep the code from Listing 10.23 and change only the matrix transformation order from `Append` to `Prepend`, as shown in Listing 10.24.

LISTING 10.24: Translate → Rotate → Scale transformation order with `Prepend`

```
private void Third_Click(object sender,
    System.EventArgs e)
{
    // Create a Graphics object
    Graphics g = this.CreateGraphics();
    g.Clear(this.BackColor);
    // Create a rectangle
    Rectangle rect =
        new Rectangle(20, 20, 100, 100);
    // Create a solid brush
    SolidBrush brush =
        new SolidBrush(Color.Red);
```

continues

```
    // Fill rectangle
    g.FillRectangle(brush, rect);
    // Translate
    g.TranslateTransform(100.0f, 50.0f,
        MatrixOrder.Prepend);
    // Rotate
    g.RotateTransform(45.0f,
        MatrixOrder.Prepend);
    // Scale
    g.ScaleTransform(1.75f, 0.5f);
    // Fill rectangle again
    g.FillRectangle(brush, rect);
    // Dispose of objects
    brush.Dispose();
    g.Dispose();
}
```

The new output is shown in Figure 10.35. The matrix order affects the result.

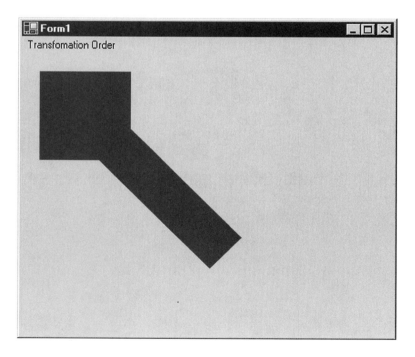

FIGURE 10.35: Translate → Rotate → Scale composite transformation with `Prepend`

SUMMARY

In this chapter we first discussed the basics of transformation, coordinate systems, the role of coordinate systems in the transformation process, and transformation functionality. We learned

- How to distinguish among global, local, and composite transformations
- How to use the `Graphics` class transformations in applications
- How to translate, scale, shear, and rotate graphics objects

Matrices play a vital role in transformation. We can customize the transformation process and its variables by creating and applying a transformation matrix. This chapter showed

- How to use the `Matrix` and `ColorMatrix` classes, and their role in transformation
- How to use the matrix operations for image processing, including translation, scaling, shearing, and rotation
- How to use recoloring and color transformation to manipulate the colors of graphics objects
- How to perform color transformations

Transformations can be applied not only to graphics images and objects, but also to text strings. Drawing vertical or skewed text is one example of text transformation. This chapter explained how to transform text.

Printing also plays an important part in GDI+. In Chapter 11 you will learn various components of the `System.Drawing.Printing` namespace and how to use them.

■ 11 ■
Printing

S OONER OR LATER you will need to print out application data. Perhaps you have created documents or test data and now you want to
see them on paper. You may be drawing something and want to print it out.
Printing data from a database and printing images are other possibilities.
With the .NET Framework you will find it easy to create applications that
talk your printer's language. This chapter covers printing functionality in
the .NET Framework. The aim is to give you the knowledge to handle basic
(and some not so basic) printing needs.

We'll begin with a brief history of printing, followed by an introduction
to the printing classes available in .NET. Toward the end of the chapter we
will delve deep into printing functionality. After reading this chapter, you
should have a good idea of printing functionality defined in the .NET
Framework, and how to implement this functionality in your applications.
Here are some of the topics we will discuss in this chapter:

- A brief history of printing in Microsoft Windows
- The printing process (i.e., how printing works)
- Printing in Microsoft .NET
- The `System.Drawing.Printing` namespace and its classes
- Getting and setting page and printer settings
- The basic framework of printing-enabled applications

- How to print text, images, and graphics objects
- How to use various print dialogs and their classes
- Writing your own custom printing and page setup dialogs
- Printing multipage documents
- Understanding the print controller and its related classes

11.1 A Brief History of Printing with Microsoft Windows

If you are running Microsoft Windows today, you can more or less print to any available printer, from a $100 bargain-basement inkjet to a $1,000 Tektronix color printer. This versatility is possible only because of software standardization.

When Microsoft DOS was the standard PC desktop operating system, every application had to supply its own printing software or printer drivers. If you bought a piece of software from Company X, you had to hope that it supported your printer. Thus, often you had to check which printers your new software supported and buy one of those. Either that, or wait until Company X supported your printer, which, more often than not, never happened.

Companies tended to produce printer drivers for only a select few of the popular printers on the market, such as the HP LaserJet. Even worse, you might have a printer driver for your laser printer when using a drawing package, but if you wanted to use a word processor from a different company, it would not be surprising to find that your printer was not supported!

11.1.1 Hewlett-Packard Chooses Standards

During this time, companies like Hewlett-Packard were driving the printer business and introducing standards that could only make things better. At this point HP had been in the printer business a long time and had introduced many different types of printers and plotters. It had already introduced a standard language (Hewlett-Packard Graphics Language, or HPGL) for drawing graphics on a plotter, which allowed the user to issue draw commands like, "Draw a line from point A to point B."

Hewlett-Packard introduced the LaserJet series of laser printers, which became extremely successful because of their high quality and low cost. These printers were driven by a language called PCL (Printer Control Language). (Even today, printers manufactured by HP and several other companies support PCL.) Even if you don't have the exact printer driver you need, if your printer supports PCL you can at least get some output from it.

Moreover, Hewlett-Packard used PCL with all its printers, so if you wrote an application to communicate with the HP LaserJet Series II, you could be pretty certain that the code would work with later printers in the range. Although HP is not the only printer manufacturer, it can certainly be credited with jump-starting the market.

While companies like Hewlett-Packard were making printing easier, the software problems still existed. If you did not have an appropriate printer driver for your application, you would not get anything out of your printer.

When a Printer Has No Driver

Be aware, though, that even today, if you rush out and buy the latest and greatest printer, you may get home and find that the printer has not come supplied with a printer driver—or the version of Windows you have may not support that particular printer. So what do you do?

In most cases you can just choose a driver from an earlier model in the same line. For instance you could use an HP LaserJet II driver to drive an HP LaserJet 4 printer. This works because Hewlett-Packard uses PCL to control it sprinters, so even though the LaserJet II may use an older version of PCL, the LaserJet 4 still supports it. The message here is that when you're buying your next printer, make sure the operating system you intend to use supports it!

With the release of Microsoft Windows in its various forms, the printing crisis was more or less over. Windows provided a standard graphical user interface, or GUI, and anything that you could draw on-screen could be printed out. Microsoft provided Windows drivers for the most common printers. Over time, as new versions of Windows came out, more and more printers were supported. Now all that the programmers had to do was write code for Windows, and they could use that same code to talk to any printer that Windows supported.

11.2 Overview of the Printing Process

Before we write our first printing application, it's important to understand how printing works in Windows and what role GDI+ plays in the process.

GDI+ is an application-level library that allows applications to interact with display devices such as monitors, printers, and scanners through the device drivers. Figure 11.1 illustrates the role of GDI+ in the drawing process. The application passes data to GDI+. GDI+ is responsible for converting the data into graphics format (pixels) with the help of display drivers and sending it to the display driver, which displays the data on a device such as a monitor.

The printing process, which is very similar to the drawing process, is shown in Figure 11.2. The application sends data to GDI+, which communicates with a printer driver that sends data to the printer.

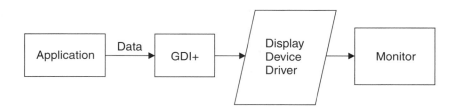

FIGURE 11.1: A simple drawing process

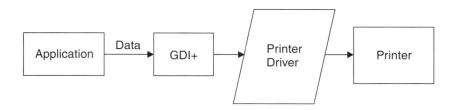

FIGURE 11.2: A simple printing process

11.2.1 **How Is Drawing Different from Printing?**

The drawing process involves a **surface**, which is the container for graphics shapes. In Windows applications, a **form** works as a drawing surface. In previous chapters we used the Graphics object associated with a form to access the surface associated with a form.

There are several ways to get the Graphics object associated with a form. The simplest way is to use the form's paint event handler and PaintEventArgs.Graphics property, which returns the Graphics object for the form to which this paint event handler belongs. Another way is to use the CreateGraphics method. Listing 11.1 uses PaintEvent-Args.Graphics to get the Graphics object associated with a form. Once you have the drawing surface (Graphics object), you can use draw and fill methods.

LISTING 11.1: Drawing graphics shapes

```
private void Form1_Paint(object sender,
  System.Windows.Forms.PaintEventArgs e)
{
  Graphics g = e.Graphics;
  SolidBrush redBrush =
    new SolidBrush(Color.Red);
  Rectangle rect =
    new Rectangle(150, 80, 200, 140);
  g.FillPie(greenBrush, 40, 20, 200,
    40, 0.0f, 60.0f );
  g.FillRectangle(blueBrush, rect);
}
```

The printing process is somewhat different from the drawing process. In a printing process, a printer works as a drawing surface. In a drawing process, we already have a form as a drawing surface. To print something on a printer, however, we need the printer object. The basic steps of a printing process are

1. Specify the printer you want to use.
2. Retrieve the printer's surface, which is a Graphics object.
3. Call the draw and fill methods of the Graphics object.

In Sections 11.2.2 and 11.2.3 we will discuss the printing process in more detail.

11.2.2 Conceptual Flow of the Printing Process

Before we discuss the programmatic flow of a printing process, let's look at the conceptual flow. Every printing process involves five basic steps, as illustrated in Figure 11.3.

Step 1: Specify a printer. In this step we select a printer to be used in the printing process. You may want to select a printer from multiple printers available to your application.

Step 2: Set the printer properties. In this step we can set properties such as color, paper tray, paper size, and print quality. This step is optional; if we do not set printer properties, the process uses default settings.

Step 3: Get the printer surface. Unlike the drawing surface (a form), which is available on the form's paint event handler, the printer surface is available only through the print-page event handler. As such, this step requires creating a print-page event handler. One parameter of the event handler is of type `PrintPageEventArgs`,

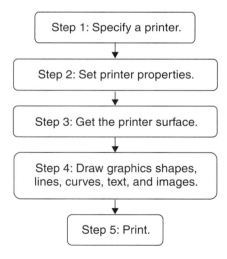

FIGURE 11.3: Conceptual flow of the printing process

whose `Graphics` member represents the printer surface associated with this print-page event handler. In Section 11.2.3 we will see how to implement the print-page event handler programmatically.

Step 4: Draw graphics shapes, lines, curves, text, and images. Once we have the printer surface, everything works in much the same way as the drawing process. We can call draw and fill methods to draw lines, curves, shapes, text, and images.

Step 5: Print. After we call the draw and fill methods of the `Graphics` object associated with a printer, the final step is to print the objects.

11.2.3 Programmatic Flow of the Printing Process

The previous section dealt with the conceptual flow of the printing process. In this section we will examine the *programmatic* flow.

Figure 11.4 is a flowchart displaying the four programmatic steps of the printing process.

Step 1: Create a `PrintDocument` object and specify the printer. This printer will be used as a surface.

Step 2: Set the printer and page properties. We set the `Printer-Settings` and `PageSettings` objects for this optional step. If we don't set these properties, the default settings of the printer will be used. We will cover `PrinterSettings` and `PageSettings` in more detail later.

Step 3: Set the print-page event handler. The print-page event handler is responsible for printing. We create a print-page event handler by setting the `PrintDocument.PrintPage` member. Process A (see Figure 11.5) is called from the print-page event handler, as illustrated in Figure 11.4.

Step 4: Print the document. Finally, we call the `PrintDocument.Print` method, which sends printing objects to the printer.

Process A, which is shown in Figure 11.5, describes how and what to send to the printer. This process is defined as the print-page event handler:

```
public void pd_PrintPage(object sender,
PrintPageEventArgs ev)
```

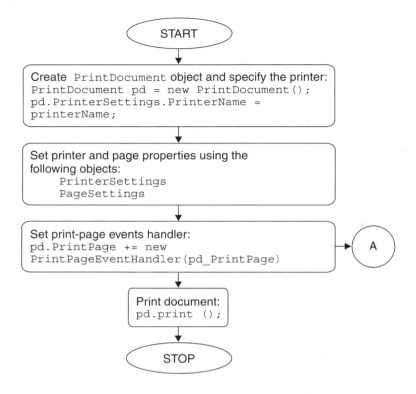

FIGURE 11.4: A flowchart of the printing process

The second parameter, `PrintPageEventArgs`, provides access to the printer surface through its `Graphics` member. As Figure 11.5 shows, first we get the `Graphics` object from `PrintPageEventArgs`.

The next step is to set the page and paper setting using the `Margin-Bounds`, `PageBounds`, and `PageSettings` members of the `Print-PageEventArgs` enumeration. We will discuss these properties in more detail later.

The final step of this process is to call draw and fill methods of the `Graphics` object as we used to do in the drawing process. We will see a working example of this process in Section 11.3.

11.2.4 The `System.Drawing.Printing` Namespace
In the .NET Framework, printing functionality is defined in the `System.Drawing.Printing` namespace, which resides in the `System.`

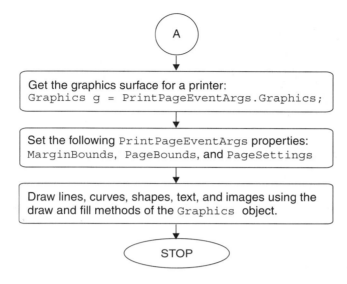

FIGURE 11.5: Process A

`Drawing.dll` assembly. The reference to this assembly is automatically added to an application when we create a new project using Visual Studio .NET. To use the printing-related classes, we can simply add the following line to the application:

```
using System.Drawing.Printing;
```

Alternatively, we can use the `System.Drawing.Printing` namespace by adding it to the classes directly.

> **■ NOTE**
> Before you use any printer-related classes in your application, a printer must be installed on your machine.

11.3 Your First Printing Application

We just saw how the printing process works in the .NET Framework. Now let's talk about how to write your first simple printing application. In this application we will send the text "Hello Printer!" to the printer from a Windows application. To create this application, follow the simple steps described here.

Using Visual Studio .NET, create a Windows application project named HelloPrinterSamp, as shown in Figure 11.6.

After we create the project, we add the following line to it:

```
using System.Drawing.Printing;
```

Then we add controls for a label, a combo box, and a button to the form. We change the `Text` and `Name` properties of the form and these controls. (See the online source code for more details.) The final form should look like Figure 11.7.

When you run this application, the combo box will display the available printers on your machine. You can select any printer from this list, and when you click the **Hello Printer** button, it will print "Hello Printer!" on your printer.

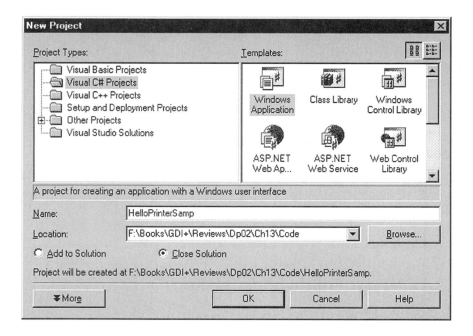

FIGURE 11.6: Creating a Windows application

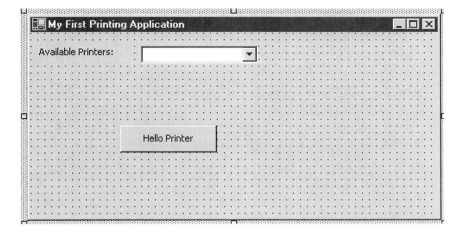

FIGURE 11.7: Your first printing application

We load the available printers on the form's load event handler. The `PrinterSettings.InstalledPrinters` property returns the installed printers on a machine. `PrinterSettings.InstalledPrinters.Count` returns the total number of printers. In Listing 11.2 we check if printers are installed on the machine, read them, and add them to the printer list combo box.

LISTING 11.2: Getting all installed printers

```
private void Form1_Load(object sender,
  System.EventArgs e)
{
  // See if any printers are installed
  if( PrinterSettings.InstalledPrinters.Count <= 0)
  {
    MessageBox.Show("Printer not found!");
    return;
  }
  // Get all available printers and add them to the
  // combo box
  foreach(String printer in
    PrinterSettings.InstalledPrinters)
  {
    printersList.Items.Add(printer.ToString());
  }
}
```

The next step is to add code to the **Hello Printer** button click event handler (see Listing 11.3). This code is responsible for printing. We create a `PrintDocument` object and set the `PrintDocument.PrinterSettings.PrinterName` property to the printer selected from the printer list combo box. Then we add a print-page event handler and call the `Print-Document.Print` method, which prints the document.

LISTING 11.3: The Hello Printer button click event handler

```
private void HelloPrinterBtn_Click(object sender,
  System.EventArgs e)
{
  // Create a PrintDocument object
  PrintDocument pd = new PrintDocument();
  // Set PrinterName as the selected printer
  // in the printers list
  pd.PrinterSettings.PrinterName =
    printersList.SelectedItem.ToString();
  // Add PrintPage event handler
  pd.PrintPage +=
    new PrintPageEventHandler(pd_PrintPage);
  // Print the document
  pd.Print();
}
```

The last step is to add the print-page event handler code (see Listing 11.4). This code is responsible for creating a `Graphics` object for the printer. It calls the `DrawString` method, which is responsible for drawing text. First we create a `Graphics` object from `PrintPageEvent-Args.Graphics`. Then we create `Font` and `SolidBrush` objects and call `DrawString` to draw some text on the printer. The `DrawString` method takes a string that represents the text to be drawn; the font; a brush; and a layout rectangle that represents the starting point, width, and height of a rectangle for the text.

> ▗▖ **NOTE**
> See Chapter 3 for more detail on the `DrawString` method. And for more about solid brushes and fonts, see Chapters 4 and 5, respectively.

LISTING 11.4: The print-page event handler

```
// The PrintPage event handler
public void pd_PrintPage(object sender,
  PrintPageEventArgs ev)
{
  // Get the Graphics object
  Graphics g = ev.Graphics;
  // Create a font Arial with size 16
  Font font = new Font("Arial", 16);
  // Create a solid brush with black color
  SolidBrush brush =
    new SolidBrush(Color.Black);
// Draw "Hello Printer!"
g.DrawString("Hello Printer!",
  font, brush,
  new Rectangle(20, 20, 200, 100));
  }
```

Now you can run the application, select a printer from the list, and click the **Hello Printer** button. You should see "Hello Printer!" on your printed page.

11.4 **Printer Settings**

Before writing our next printing application, let's examine printer settings. **Printer settings** specify the properties of a print process, such as the paper size, print quality, number of copies, number of pages, and so on. In this section we will first discuss how to access and set printer settings using the `PrinterSettings` class properties. Then we will write an application that allows us to read and set printer settings programmatically.

11.4.1 **The `PrinterSettings` Class**

The `PrinterSettings` object is the gateway to reading and setting printer settings. `PrinterSettings` specifies how a document will be printed during a print process.

After creating a `PrinterSettings` object instance, we usually use the `PrintDocument.PrinterSettings` or `PageSettings.Printer-Settings` property to access the `PrinterSettings` objects corresponding to the `PrintDocument` and `PageSettings` objects, respectively. We will discuss these in more detail in a moment.

The following code snippet creates a `PrinterSettings` object:

```
PrinterSettings prs = new PrinterSettings();
```

The `PrinterSettings` class provides the following 22 properties: `CanDuplex`, `Collate`, `Copies`, `DefaultPageSettings`, `Duplex`, `FromPage`, `InstalledPrinters`, `IsDefaultPrinter`, `IsPlotter`, `IsValid`, `LandscapeAngle`, `MaximumCopies`, `MaximumPage`, `MinimumPage`, `PaperSizes`, `PaperSources`, `PrinterName`, `PrinterResolutions`, `PrintRange`, `PrintToFile`, `SupportsColor`, and `ToPage`. In the sections that follow, we will discuss each of these properties in turn.

11.4.1.1 *The `InstalledPrinters` Property*

The `InstalledPrinters` static property returns the names of all available printers on a machine, including printers available on the network. This property returns all the printer names in a `PrinterSettings.StringCollection` object.

Listing 11.5 iterates through all the available printers on a machine.

LISTING 11.5: Getting all installed printers on a machine

```
foreach(String printer in
    PrinterSettings.InstalledPrinters)
{
    string str = printer.ToString();
}
```

11.4.1.2 *The `PaperSizes` Property*

The `PaperSizes` property returns the paper sizes supported by a printer. It returns all the paper sizes in a `PrinterSettings.PaperSizeCollection` object.

Listing 11.6 iterates through all the available paper sizes.

LISTING 11.6: Reading all available paper sizes

```
PrinterSettings prs = new PrinterSettings();
foreach(PaperSize ps in prs.PaperSizes)
{
    string str = ps.ToString();
}
```

11.4.1.3 *The PrinterResolutions Property*

The PrinterResolutions property returns all the resolutions supported by a printer. It returns all the printer resolutions in a PrinterSettings.PrinterResolutionCollection object that contains PrinterResolution objects.

Listing 11.7 reads the printer resolutions and adds them to a ListBox control. Here YourPrinterName is the name of the printer you want to use. If you do not set a printer name, the default printer will be used.

LISTING 11.7: Getting printer resolution

```
PrinterSettings ps = new PrinterSettings();
// Set the printer name
ps.PrinterName = YourPrinterName;
foreach(PrinterResolution pr in ps.PrinterResolutions)
{
   listBox2.Items.Add(pr.ToString());
}
```

The PrinterResolution class, which represents the resolution of a printer, is used by the PrinterResolutions and PrinterResolution properties of PrinterSettings to get and set printer resolutions. Using these two properties, we can get all the printer resolutions available on a printer. We can also use it to set the printing resolution for a page.

The PrinterResolution class has three properties: Kind, X, and Y. The Kind property is used to determine whether the printer resolution is the PrinterResolutionKind enumeration type or Custom. If it's Custom, the X and Y properties are used to determine the printer resolution in the horizontal and vertical directions, respectively, in dots per inch. If the Kind property is not Custom, the value of X and Y each is –1.

11.4.1.4 *The CanDuplex and Duplex Properties*

The CanDuplex property is used to determine whether a printer can print on both sides of a page. If so, we can set the Duplex property to true to print on both sides of a page.

Listing 11.8 determines whether your printer can print on both sides of a page. If your program responds true, you have a very good printer.

LISTING 11.8: Using the `CanDuplex` property

```
PrinterSettings ps = new PrinterSettings();
MessageBox.Show("Supports Duplex?");
MessageBox.Show("Answer = " + ps.CanDuplex.ToString());
```

The `Duplex` enumeration specifies the printer's duplex settings, which are used by `PrinterSettings`. The members of the `Duplex` enumeration are described in Table 11.1.

11.4.1.5 *The `Collate` Property*

The `Collate` property (both get and set) is used only if we choose to print more than one copy of a document. If the value of `Collate` is `true`, an entire copy of the document will be printed before the next copy is printed. If the value is `false`, all copies of page 1 will be printed, then all copies of page 2, and so on.

The code snippet that follows sets the `Collate` property of `PrinterSettings` to `true`:

```
PrinterSettings ps = new PrinterSettings();
ps.Collate=true;
```

11.4.1.6 *The `Copies` Property*

The `Copies` property (both get and set) allows us to enter the number of copies of a document that we want to print. Not all printers support this feature (in which case this setting will be ignored). The `MaximumCopies` property, which is described in Section 11.4.1.9, tells us how many copies the printer can print.

TABLE 11.1: `Duplex` members

Member	Description
Default	Default duplex setting
Horizontal	Double-sided, horizontal printing
Simplex	Single-sided printing
Vertical	Double-sided, vertical printing

Duplex Printing: A Problem

Duplex printing (the ability to print on both sides of a page) is a feature usually found on higher-end laser and inkjet printers. It is generally found only on more expensive printers because either the printer needs to be able to print on both sides of a sheet, or it must have an internal mechanism to turn the page over and print on the other side.

Let's assume you have a low-end printer and need to print on both sides of the page. To do this, you would need to create a custom software solution. Let's also assume that your application is printing a 100-page text document. Because the document consists of text alone, this is not too difficult to achieve. You would simply read from a text stream and keep track of whether you have the space to print the next line. If not, you would tell the printer to go to another page. In this scenario you would end up with 100 single-sided pages.

So how do you get double-sided printing? In the tradition of good programming, you cheat, of course! The solution to this problem is to track the page number, and on the first pass print only odd-numbered pages (1, 3, 5, and so on). Once you have done this, display a dialog box that tells you to take all the sheets of paper just printed and reload them into the printer so they will be fed into the printer upside down. Now you can print the even-numbered pages (2, 4, 6, and so on). Voilà! The user gets duplex printing functionality from a cheap printer.

The following code sets the `Copies` property of `PrinterSettings`:

```
PrinterSettings ps = new PrinterSettings();
// We want 10 copies of our document
ps.Copies=10;
```

11.4.1.7 *The IsPlotter Property*

The `IsPlotter` property tells us if the printer we're using is actually a plotter that can accept plotter commands.

The following code snippet indicates whether the printer is a plotter:

```
PrinterSettings ps = new PrinterSettings();
MessageBox.Show(ps.IsPlotter.ToString());
```

11.4.1.8 *The PrinterName and IsValid Properties*

If we print without setting the PrinterName property, our printout will be sent to the default printer. The PrinterName property allows us to specify a printer to use. The IsValid property tells us whether the PrinterName value we have selected represents a valid printer on our system.

Listing 11.9 checks if the printer is valid.

LISTING 11.9: Using the IsValid property

```
PrinterSettings ps = new PrinterSettings();
ps.PrinterName=("Invalid Printer Name");
MessageBox.Show("Is this a valid printer name?");
MessageBox.Show(ps.IsValid.ToString());
```

11.4.1.9 *The MaximumCopies Property*

The MaximumCopies property determines how many copies the printer can print. Some printers do not allow us to print more than one copy at a time.

Listing 11.10 reads the maximum number of copies that a printer can print.

LISTING 11.10: Reading the maximum number of copies

```
PrinterSettings ps = new PrinterSettings();
MessageBox.Show("Maximum number of copies: ");
MessageBox.Show(ps.MaximumCopies);
```

11.4.1.10 *The SupportsColor Property*

The SupportsColor property tells us whether the current printer supports printing in color. It will return true if the printer supports color printing and false otherwise.

Listing 11.11 reads the value of the SupportsColor property to find out whether a printer supports colors.

LISTING 11.11: Using the SupportsColor property

```
PrinterSettings ps = new PrinterSettings();
MessageBox.Show("Does this printer support color:");
MessageBox.Show(ps.SupportsColor.ToString());
```

11.4.1.11 *Other* `PrinterSettings` *Properties*

Besides the properties discussed already, the `PrinterSettings` class provides the additional properties listed in Table 11.2. We will discuss these properties in detail in our examples.

11.4.2 **The** `PaperSize` **Class**

Most printers can use papers of more than one size (height and width). The `PaperSize` class is used to read and set the paper size used by a printer.

The `PaperSize` class represents the size of paper used in printing. This class is used by `PrinterSettings` through its `PaperSizes` property to get and set the paper sizes for the printer.

TABLE 11.2: Other `PrinterSettings` properties

Property	Description
`DefaultPageSettings`	Returns the default page settings.
`FromPage`	Returns the page number of the first page to print. Both get and set.
`IsDefaultPrinter`	Returns `true` if the current printer is the default printer.
`LandscapeAngle`	Returns the angle, in degrees, by which the portrait orientation is rotated to produce the landscape orientation. Valid rotation values are 90 and 270 degrees. If landscape is not supported, the only valid rotation value is 0 degrees.
`MaximumPage`	Returns the maximum value of `FromPage` or `ToPage` that can be selected in a print dialog. Both get and set.
`MinimumPage`	Returns the minimum value of `FromPage` or `ToPage` that can be selected in a print dialog. Both get and set.
`PrintRange`	Returns the page numbers that the user has specified to be printed. Both get and set.
`PrintToFile`	Returns a value indicating whether the printing output is sent to a file instead of a port. Both get and set.
`ToPage`	Returns the page number of the last page to print. Both get and set.

The PaperSize class has four properties: Height, Kind, PaperName, and Width. Height, Width, and PaperName have both get and set access. The Height and Width properties are used to get and set the paper's height and width, respectively, in hundredths of an inch. The PaperName property is used to get and set the name of the type of paper, but it can be used only when the Kind property is set to Custom. The Kind property returns the type of paper.

We can construct custom paper sizes using the PaperSize class. Listing 11.12 reads the PaperSize properties.

LISTING 11.12:　Reading PaperSize properties

```
PrinterSettings ps = new PrinterSettings();
Console.WriteLine("Paper Sizes");
foreach(PaperSize psize in ps.PaperSizes)
{
 string str1 = psize.Kind.ToString();
 string str2 = psize.PaperName.ToString();
 string str3 = psize.Height.ToString();
 string str4 = psize.Width.ToString();
}
```

11.4.3 The PaperSource Class

The PaperSource class specifies the paper tray from which the printer retrieves the paper for the current printing task. This class is used by PrinterSettings through its PaperSources property to get and set the paper source trays that are available on the printer. The PaperSize class has two properties: Kind and SourceName. The Kind property returns an enumerated value for the paper source, and SourceName returns the name of the paper source as a string.

Listing 11.13 reads all the paper sources and displays them in a message box.

LISTING 11.13:　Reading paper sources

```
PrinterSettings ps = new PrinterSettings();
foreach(PaperSource p in ps.PaperSources)
{
 MessageBox.Show(p.SourceName);
}
```

11.4.4 **The `PrinterResolutionKind` Enumeration**

The `PrinterResolutionKind` enumeration specifies a printer resolution, as described in Table 11.3. This enumeration is used by the `Printer-Resolution`, `PrinterSettings`, and `PageSettings` classes.

11.4.5 `PrinterSettings` **Collection Classes**

Besides the `PrinterSettings` class, the `System.Drawing.Printing` namespace provides three `PrinterSettings` collection classes. These collection classes provide members to count total items in a collection, and to add items to and remove items from a collection. These classes are

1. **`PrinterSettings.PaperSizeCollection`**. A printer may support different kinds of papers, including papers of different sizes. This class returns a collection including all paper sizes supported by the printer. `PaperSizeCollection` contains `PaperSizes` objects.

2. **`PrinterSettings.PaperSourceCollection`**. A printer may support different paper sources (trays). This class represents a collection of paper sources (trays) provided by a printer. `Paper-SourceCollection` is available via the `PaperSources` property and contains `PaperSource` objects.

3. **`PrinterSettings.PrinterResolutionCollection`**. A printer may support different resolutions. This class represents a collection of resolutions supported by a printer. `PrinterResolution-Collection` is accessible via the `PrinterResolutions` property and contains `PrinterResolution` objects.

TABLE 11.3: `PrinterResolutionKind` members

Member	Description
Custom	Custom resolution
Draft	Draft-quality resolution
High	High resolution
Low	Low resolution
Medium	Medium resolution

All of these collection classes provide `Count` and `Item` properties. The `Count` property returns the total number of items in a collection, and the `Item` property returns the item at the specified index. We will use these classes in our samples.

11.4.6 A Printer Settings Example

On the basis of the preceding discussion of printer settings, and of printer-related classes and their members, let's write an application using these classes. In this application we will display available printers, the resolutions they support, available paper sizes, and other printer properties. This application will also allow us to set printer properties.

First we create a Windows application and add a combo box, two list boxes, three buttons, six check boxes, and two text boxes to the form. The final form looks like Figure 11.8. Then we add a reference to the `System.Drawing.Printing` namespace.

Next we write code. The **Available Printers** combo box displays all available installed printers on the machine in the `ListBox` control. We load all installed printers on the form's load event. As Listing 11.14 shows, we use the `InstalledPrinters` static property of `PrinterSettings`, which returns all installed printer names. We check if the installed printers count is more than 0 and add the installed printers to the combo box.

LISTING 11.14:　Reading all available printers

```
private void Form1_Load(object sender,
  System.EventArgs e)
{
  // See if any printers are installed
  if( PrinterSettings.InstalledPrinters.Count <= 0)
  {
    MessageBox.Show("Printer not found!");
    return;
  }
  // Get all the available printers and add them to the
  // combo box
  foreach(String printer in
    PrinterSettings.InstalledPrinters)
  {
    PrintersList.Items.Add(printer.ToString());
  }
}
```

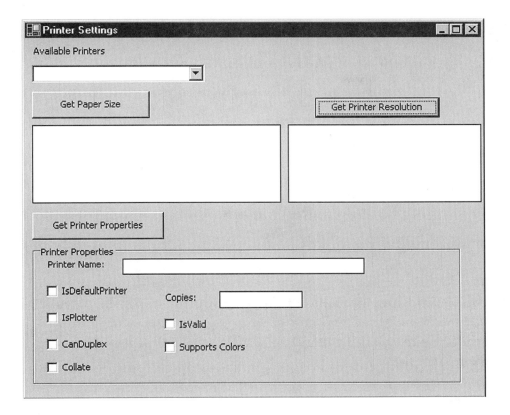

FIGURE 11.8: The printer settings form

The **Get Printer Resolution** button returns resolutions supported by a printer selected in ListBox1. The PrinterResolutions property of PrinterSettings returns the printer resolutions supported by the printer. Listing 11.15 reads all available resolutions for the selected printer in List-Box1 and adds them to ListBox2.

LISTING 11.15: Reading printer resolutions

```
private void button2_Click(object sender,
  System.EventArgs e)
{
  // If no printer is selected
  if(PrintersList.Text == string.Empty)
  {
```

continues

```
      MessageBox.Show("Select a printer from the list");
      return;
    }
    // Get the current selected printer from the
    // list of printers
    string str = PrintersList.SelectedItem.ToString();
    // Create a PrinterSettings object
    PrinterSettings ps = new PrinterSettings();
    // Set the current printer
    ps.PrinterName = str;
    // Read all printer resolutions and add
    // them to the list box
    foreach(PrinterResolution pr
          in ps.PrinterResolutions)
    {
      ResolutionsList.Items.Add(pr.ToString());
    }
  }
```

The **Get Paper Size** button returns the available paper sizes. Again we use the `PaperSizes` property of `PrinterSettings`, which returns all available paper sizes. Listing 11.16 reads all available paper sizes and adds them to the list box.

LISTING 11.16: Reading paper sizes

```
private void button3_Click(object sender,
  System.EventArgs e)
{
  // If no printer is selected
  if(PrintersList.Text == string.Empty)
  {
    MessageBox.Show("Select a printer from the list");
    return;
  }
  // Create printer settings
  PrinterSettings prs = new PrinterSettings();
  // Get the current selected printer from the
  // list of printers
  string str = PrintersList.SelectedItem.ToString();
  prs.PrinterName = str;
  // Read paper sizes and add them to the list box
  foreach(PaperSize ps in prs.PaperSizes)
  {
    PaperSizesList.Items.Add(ps.ToString());
  }
}
```

The **Get Printer Properties** button gets the printer properties and sets the check boxes and text box controls according to the values returned. The **Get Printer Properties** button click event handler code is given in Lising 11.17. We read many printer properties that were discussed earlier in this chapter.

LISTING 11.17: Reading printer properties

```
private void GetProperties_Click(object sender,
  System.EventArgs e)
{
  // If no printer is selected
  if(PrintersList.Text == string.Empty)
  {
    MessageBox.Show("Select a printer from the list");
    return;
  }
  PrinterSettings ps = new PrinterSettings();
  string str = PrintersList.SelectedItem.ToString();
  ps.PrinterName = str;
  // Check if the printer is valid
  if(!ps.IsValid)
  {
    MessageBox.Show("Not a valid printer");
    return;
  }
  // Set printer name and copies
  textBox1.Text = ps.PrinterName.ToString();
  textBox2.Text = ps.Copies.ToString();

  // If printer is the default printer
  if (ps.IsDefaultPrinter == true)
    IsDefPrinterChkBox.Checked = true;
  else
    IsDefPrinterChkBox.Checked = false;
  // If printer is a plotter
  if (ps.IsPlotter)
    IsPlotterChkBox.Checked = true;
  else
    IsPlotterChkBox.Checked = false;
  // Duplex printing possible?
  if (ps.CanDuplex)
    CanDuplexChkBox.Checked = true;
  else
    CanDuplexChkBox.Checked = false;
```

continues

```
    // Collate?
    if (ps.Collate)
      CollateChkBox.Checked = true;
    else
      CollateChkBox.Checked = false;
    // Printer valid?
    if (ps.IsValid)
      IsValidChkBox.Checked = true;
    else
      IsValidChkBox.Checked = false;
    // Color printer?
    if (ps.SupportsColor)
      SuppColorsChkBox.Checked = true;
    else
      SuppColorsChkBox.Checked = false;
  }
```

Now let's run the application. By default, the **Available Printers** combo box displays all available printers. Select a printer from the list, and click the **Get Printer Resolution** button, which displays the printer resolutions supported by the selected printer. Also click on the **Get Paper Size** and **Get Printer Properties** buttons. The final output of the application is shown in Figure 11.9.

We will be using many `PrinterSettings` class members throughout this chapter.

11.5 **The** `PrintDocument` **and** `Print` **Events**

So far we have seen how to print simple text and how to read and set printer settings. In the previous sections we saw that in a printing application, we create a `PrintDocument` object, set its printer name, set the print-page event handler, and then call the `Print` method. `PrintDocument` offers more than this. In this section we will cover `PrintDocument` members and print events.

The `PrintDocument` class is used to tell the printing system how printing will take place. Table 11.4 describes the properties of the `Print-Document` class.

Besides the properties described in Table 11.4, `PrintDocument` also provides printing-related methods that invoke print events. These methods are described in Table 11.5.

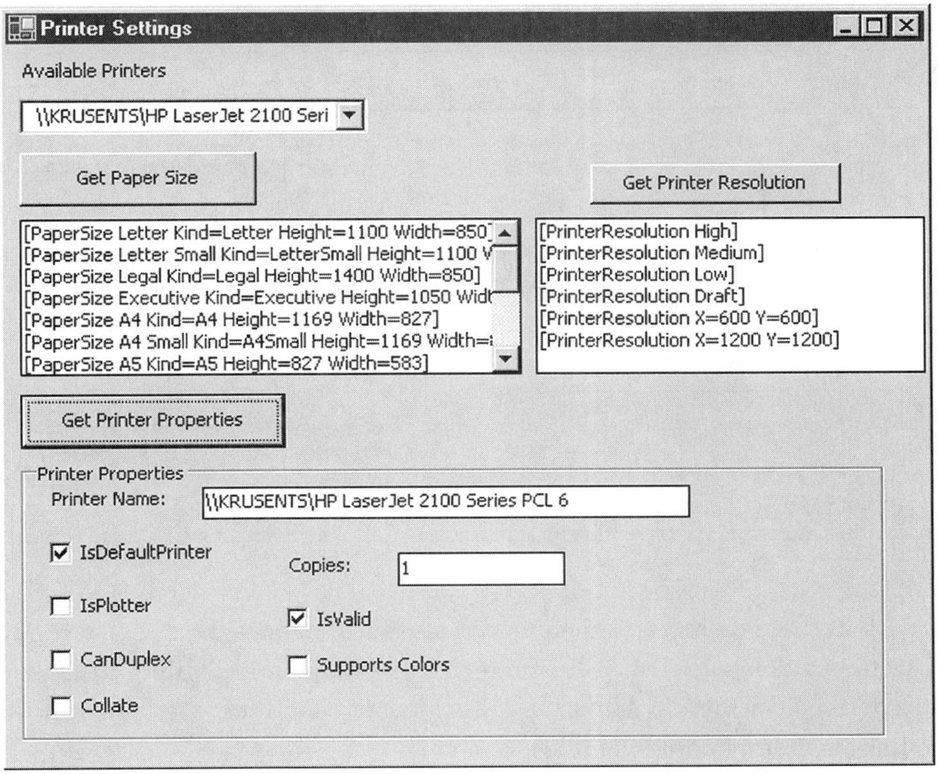

FIGURE 11.9: Reading printer properties

TABLE 11.4: `PrintDocument` properties

Property	Description
`DefaultPageSettings`	Represents the page settings using a `PageSettings` object.
`DocumentName`	Returns the name of the document to be displayed in a print status dialog box or printer queue while printing the document.
`PrintController`	Returns the print controller that guides the printing process.
`PrinterSettings`	Returns the printer settings represented by a `PrinterSettings` object.

TABLE 11.5: `PrintDocument` methods

Method	Description
OnBeginPrint	Raises the `BeginPrint` event, which is called after the `Print` method and before the first page of the document is printed.
OnEndPrint	Raises the `EndPrint` event, which is called when the last page of the document has been printed.
OnPrintPage	Raises the `PrintPage` event, which is called before a page prints.
OnQueryPageSettings	Raises the `QueryPageSettings` event, which is called immediately before each `PrintPage` event.
Print	Starts the document's printing process.

All of these methods allow derived classes to handle the event without attaching a delegate. This is the preferred technique for handling the event in a derived class. We will discuss these methods and their events, and how to handle them, in our examples.

11.5.1 Understanding `Print` Events

During the printing process, the printing system fires events according to the stage of a printing process. The three common events are `BeginPrint`, `PrintPage`, and `EndPrint`. As their names indicate, the `BeginPrint` event occurs when the `Print` method is called, and the `EndPrint` event occurs when the last page of the document has been printed. The `PrintPage` event occurs for each page being printed (as in Figure 11.10) when the `Print` method is called and after the `BeginPrint` event has occurred.

Figure 11.10 shows a flowchart for the print events during a printing process. The `BeginPrint` event is raised after the `Print` method is called. Then the printing process checks if there are any pages. If there are, the `PrintPage` event occurs, which is responsible for the actual printing, and the control goes back to check if there are more pages to print. When all pages are done printing, the `EndPage` event is fired.

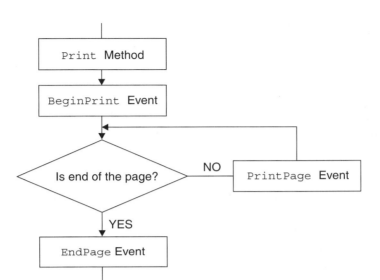

FIGURE 11.10: Print events

The `PrintEventArgs` class provides data for `BeginPrint` and `End-Print` events. This class is inherited from `CancelEventArgs`, which implements a single property called `Cancel`, that indicates if an event should be canceled (in the current .NET Framework release, `PrintEventArgs` is reserved for future use).

The `BeginPrint` event occurs when the `Print` method is called and before the first page prints. `BeginPrint` takes a `PrintEventArgs` object as an argument. This event is the best place to initialize resources. The `PrintEventHandler` method, which is used to handle the event code, is called whenever the `BeginPrint` event occurs.

The `PrintPage` event occurs when the `Print` method is called and before a page prints. When we create a `PrintPageEventHandler` delegate, we identify a method that handles the `PrintPage` event. The event handler is called whenever the `PrintPage` event occurs.

The code snippet that follows creates a `PrintPageEventHandler` delegate, where pd_PrintPage is an event handler:

```
PrintDocument pd = new PrintDocument();
pd.PrintPage +=
  new PrintPageEventHandler(pd_PrintPage);
```

PrintPageEventHandler takes a PrintPageEventArgs object as its second argument, which has the six properties described in Table 11.6.

The following code snippet shows how to get the Graphics object from PrintPageEventArgs:

```
public void pd_PrintPage(object sender,
  PrintPageEventArgs ev)
{
 // Get the Graphics object attached to
 // PrintPageEventArgs
 Graphics g = ev.Graphics;
 // Use g now
}
```

The EndPrint event occurs when the last page of the document has been printed. It takes a PrintEventArgs object as an argument. This is the best place to free your resources. The PrintEventHandler method is called whenever the EndPrint event occurs and is used to handle the event code.

Now let's write an application that shows how to use these events. We create a Windows application and add a a combo box and a button to the form. We set ComboBox.Name to printersList and the text of the button to **PrintEvents Start**. The final form looks like Figure 11.11.

TABLE 11.6: `PrintPageEventArgs` properties

Property	Description
Cancel	Indicates whether the print job should be canceled. Both get and set.
Graphics	Returns the Graphics object.
HasMorePages	Indicates whether an additional page should be printed. Used in multipage documents before the Print method is called. Both get and set.
MarginBounds	Returns the portion of the page inside the margins.
PageBounds	Returns the total area of the page.
PageSettings	Returns page settings for the current page.

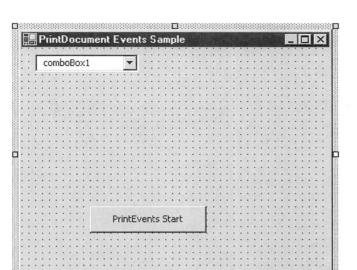

FIGURE 11.11: The print events application

Next we add a reference to the System.Drawing.Printing namespace as follows:

```
using System.Drawing.Printing;
```

Then we add code on the form's load event handler that adds all installed printers to the combo box (see Listing 11.18).

LISTING 11.18: Loading all installed printers

```
private void Form1_Load(object sender,
  System.EventArgs e)
{
  // See if any printers are installed
  if( PrinterSettings.InstalledPrinters.Count <= 0)
  {
    MessageBox.Show("Printer not found!");
    return;
  }
  // Get all available printers and add them to the
  // combo box
  foreach(String printer in
    PrinterSettings.InstalledPrinters)
  {
    printersList.Items.Add(printer.ToString());
  }
}
```

Now we write code for the button click event handler. Listing 11.19 creates all three print event handlers, attaches them to a `PrintDocument` object, and calls `PrintDocument`'s print methods.

LISTING 11.19: Attaching `BeginPrint`, `EndPrint`, and `PagePrint` event handlers

```
private void PrintEvents_Click(object sender,
  System.EventArgs e)
{
  // Get the selected printer
  string printerName =
  printersList.SelectedItem.ToString();
  // Create a PrintDocument object and set the
  // current printer
  PrintDocument pd = new PrintDocument();
  pd.PrinterSettings.PrinterName = printerName;
  // BeginPrint event
  pd.BeginPrint +=
    new PrintEventHandler(BgnPrntEventHandler);
  // PrintPage event
  pd.PrintPage +=
    new PrintPageEventHandler(PrntPgEventHandler);
  // EndPrint event
  pd.EndPrint +=
    new PrintEventHandler(EndPrntEventHandler);
  // Print the document
  pd.Print();
}
```

As stated earlier, the `BeginPrint` event handler can be used to initialize resources before printing starts, and the `EndPrint` event handler can be used to free allocated resources. Listing 11.20 shows all three print event handlers. The `PrintPage` event handler uses the properties for `Print-PageEventArgs` and calls `DrawRectangle` and `FillRectangle` to print the rectangles. This example simply shows how to call these events. You can use the `PrintPage` event handler to draw anything you want to print, as we have seen in previous examples.

LISTING 11.20: The `BeginPrint`, `EndPrint`, and `PagePrint` event handlers

```
public void BgnPrntEventHandler(object sender,
  PrintEventArgs peaArgs)
{
  // Create a brush and a pen
  redBrush = new SolidBrush(Color.Red);
  bluePen = new Pen(Color.Blue, 3);
}
```

```
public void EndPrntEventHandler(object sender,
   PrintEventArgs peaArgs)
{
  // Release brush and pen objects
  redBrush.Dispose();
  bluePen.Dispose();
}

public void PrntPgEventHandler(object sender,
   PrintPageEventArgs ppeArgs)
{
  // Create PrinterSettings object
  PrinterSettings ps = new PrinterSettings();
  // Get Graphics object
  Graphics g = ppeArgs.Graphics;
  // Create PageSettings object
  PageSettings pgSettings = new PageSettings(ps);
  // Set page margins
  ppeArgs.PageSettings.Margins.Left = 50;
  ppeArgs.PageSettings.Margins.Right = 100;
  ppeArgs.PageSettings.Margins.Top = 50;
  ppeArgs.PageSettings.Margins.Bottom = 100;
  // Create two rectangles
  Rectangle rect1 = new Rectangle(20, 20, 50, 50);
  Rectangle rect2 =
    new Rectangle(100, 100, 50, 100);
  // Draw and fill rectangles
  g.DrawRectangle(bluePen, rect1);
  g.FillRectangle(redBrush, rect2);
}
```

As this discussion has shown, the print event can be handy when you need to initialize or free resources.

11.6 Printing Text

So far we have printed simple text and graphics items from the program itself. How about reading a text file and printing it from our program? Do you remember the GDI+ editor from Chapter 5? We can make the editor open a text file and add print functionality to print the text file. In this section we will read a text file and print it.

As usual, we create a Windows application and add a reference to the `System.Drawing.Printing` namespace. We then add a text box and four buttons to the form. We also change the `Name` and `Text` properties of the

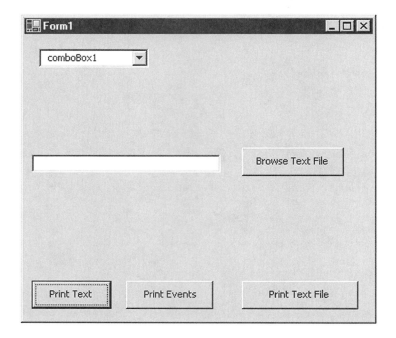

FIGURE 11.12: The form with text file printing options

button controls. The final form looks like Figure 11.12. As you might guess, the **Browse Text File** button allows us to browse for text files.

The code for the **Browse Text File** button is given in Listing 11.21. This button allows you to browse a file and adds the selected file name to the text box. Clicking the **Print Text File** button prints the selected text file. We use an `OpenFileDialog` object to open a text file and set `textBox1.Text` as the selected file name. The functionality of the **Print Text** and **Print Events** buttons is obvious.

> **■■ NOTE**
>
> C# Corner's FAQ (http://www.c-sharpcorner.com/faq.asp) includes a long list of .NET how-tos and frequently asked questions and contains the code for these simple functionalities.

LISTING 11.21: The Browse Text File button click event handler

```
private void BrowseBtn_Click(object sender,
  System.EventArgs e)
{
  // Create an OpenFileDialog object
  OpenFileDialog fdlg = new OpenFileDialog();
  // Set its properties
  fdlg.Title = "C# Corner Open File Dialog" ;
  fdlg.InitialDirectory = @"c:\" ;
  fdlg.Filter =
  "Text files (*.txt)|*.txt|All files (*.*)|*.*" ;
  fdlg.FilterIndex = 2 ;
  fdlg.RestoreDirectory = true ;
  // Show dialog and set the selected file name
  // as the text of the text box
  if(fdlg.ShowDialog() == DialogResult.OK)
  {
    textBox1.Text = fdlg.FileName ;
  }
}
```

Now let's add code for the **Print Text File** button click. First we add two private variables to the application as follows:

```
private Font verdana10Font;
private StreamReader reader;
```

Then we proceed as shown in Listing 11.22. The code is pretty simple. First we make sure that the user has selected a file name. Then we create a StreamReader object and read the file by passing the file name as the only argument. Next we create a font with font family Verdana and size 10 (see Chapter 5 for more on fonts). After that we create a PrintDocument object, add a PrintPage event handler, and call the Print method. The rest is done by the PrintPage event handler.

> **NOTE**
> The StreamReader class is defined in the System.IO namespace.

LISTING 11.22: The Print Text File button click event handler

```
private void PrintTextFile_Click(object sender,
  System.EventArgs e)
{
  // Get the file name
  string filename = textBox1.Text.ToString();
  // Check if it's not empty
  if(filename.Equals(string.Empty))
  {
    MessageBox.Show("Enter a valid file name");
    textBox1.Focus();
    return;
  }
  // Create a StreamReader object
  reader = new StreamReader(filename);
  // Create a Verdana font with size 10
  verdana10Font = new Font("Verdana", 10);
  // Create a PrintDocument object
  PrintDocument pd = new PrintDocument();
  // Add PrintPage event handler
  pd.PrintPage += new PrintPageEventHandler
    (this.PrintTextFileHandler);
  // Call Print method
  pd.Print();
  // Close the reader
  if(reader != null)
    reader.Close();
}
```

The code for the `PrintPage` event handler `PrintTextFileHandler` is given in Listing 11.23. Here we read one line at a time from the text file, using the `StreamReader.ReadLine` method, and call `DrawString`, which prints each line until we reach the end of the file. To give the text a defined size, we use the `verdana10Font.GetHeight` method.

> ■ **NOTE**
> See Chapter 3 and 5 for details about the `DrawString` method and fonts, respectively.

LISTING 11.23: Adding a print-page event handler

```
private void PrintTextFileHandler(object sender,
  PrintPageEventArgs ppeArgs)
{
  // Get the Graphics object
  Graphics g = ppeArgs.Graphics;
  float linesPerPage = 0;
  float yPos = 0;
  int count = 0;
  // Read margins from PrintPageEventArgs
  float leftMargin = ppeArgs.MarginBounds.Left;
  float topMargin = ppeArgs.MarginBounds.Top;
  string line = null;
  // Calculate the lines per page on the basis of
  // the height of the page and the height of
  // the font
  linesPerPage = ppeArgs.MarginBounds.Height /
    verdana10Font.GetHeight(g);
  // Now read lines one by one, using StreamReader
  while(count < linesPerPage &&
    ((line = reader.ReadLine()) != null))
  {
    // Calculate the starting position
    yPos = topMargin + (count *
      verdana10Font.GetHeight(g));
    // Draw text
    g.DrawString(line, verdana10Font, Brushes.Black,
      leftMargin, yPos, new StringFormat());
    // Move to next line
    count++;
  }
  // If PrintPageEventArgs has more pages
  // to print
  if(line != null)
    ppeArgs.HasMorePages = true;
  else
    ppeArgs.HasMorePages = false;
}
```

You should be able to add code for the **Print Text** and **Print Events** buttons yourself. Their functionality should be obvious.

Now run the application, browse a text file, and hit the **Print Text File** button, and you should be all set.

> **■ NOTE**
> Using the same method, you can easily add printing functionality to the GDI+ editor. You can add a menu item called **Print** to the editor that will print an opened text file.

11.7 Printing Graphics

We just saw how to print text files. Now let's talk about how to print images and graphics items such as lines, rectangles, and ellipses. You probably have a pretty good idea how printing works. It's all in the magic of the Graphics object available through PrintPageEventArgs. Once we have a printer's Graphics object, we call draw and fill methods to print graphics items. In this section we will create an application that shows how to print simple graphics objects, including lines, curves, rectangles, and images.

Again, we create a Windows application and add a main menu to the form. We add four menu items to the main menu. The final form looks like Figure 11.13. As you might guess, the **Draw Items** and **View Image** menu items will draw graphics objects and show an image, respectively. The **Print Image** and **Print Graphics Items** menu items will print the image and the graphics items, respectively.

The next step is to add a reference to the System.Drawing.Printing namespace.

11.7.1 Printing Graphics Items

Let's write code for the menu items. We'll do the **Draw Items** first, as in Listing 11.24. This menu item draws two lines, a rectangle, and an ellipse. First we create a Graphics object using the Form.CreateGraphics method and call the DrawLine, DrawRectangle, and FillEllipse methods. See Chapter 3 for more on these methods.

LISTING 11.24: Drawing graphics items

```
private void DrawItems_Click(object sender,
  System.EventArgs e)
{
  // Create a Graphics object
  Graphics g = this.CreateGraphics();
```

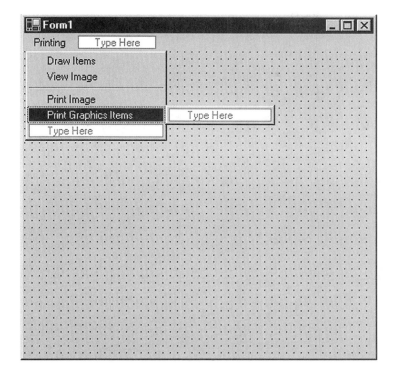

FIGURE 11.13: A graphics-printing application

```
g.Clear(this.BackColor);
// Draw graphics items
g.DrawLine(Pens.Blue, 10, 10, 10, 100);
g.DrawLine(Pens.Blue, 10, 10, 100, 10);
g.DrawRectangle(Pens.Yellow, 20, 20, 200, 200);
g.FillEllipse(Brushes.Gray, 40, 40, 100, 100);
// Dispose of object
g.Dispose();
}
```

Figure 11.14 shows the output from Listing 11.24.

Now let's write code for **Print Graphics Items**. We want to print the output shown in Figure 11.14. We create a `PrintDocument` object, add a `PrintPage` event handler, and call the `Print` method. The `PrintPage` event handler draws the graphics items.

Listing 11.25 contains two methods. The `PrintGraphicsItems_Click` method is a menu click event handler that creates a `PrintDocument` object,

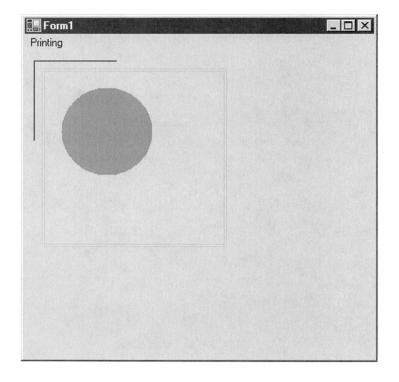

FIGURE 11.14: Drawing simple graphics items

sets its PrintPage event, and calls the Print method. The second method, PrintGraphicsItemsHandler, simply calls the draw and fill methods of PrintPageEventArgs.Graphics.

LISTING 11.25: Printing graphics items

```
private void PrintGraphicsItems_Click(object sender,
  System.EventArgs e)
{
  // Create a PrintDocument object
  PrintDocument pd = new PrintDocument();
  // Add PrintPage event handler
  pd.PrintPage += new PrintPageEventHandler
    (this.PrintGraphicsItemsHandler);
  // Print
  pd.Print();
}
private void PrintGraphicsItemsHandler(object sender,
  PrintPageEventArgs ppeArgs)
{
```

```
    // Create a printer Graphics object
    Graphics g = ppeArgs.Graphics;
    // Draw graphics items
    g.DrawLine(Pens.Blue, 10, 10, 10, 100);
    g.DrawLine(Pens.Blue, 10, 10, 100, 10);
    g.DrawRectangle(Pens.Yellow, 20, 20, 200, 200);
    g.FillEllipse(Brushes.Gray, 40, 40, 100, 100);
}
```

If you run the application and click on **Print Graphics Items**, the printer will generate output that looks like Figure 11.14.

11.7.2 **Printing Images**

If you did not skip Chapters 7 and 8, then you already know how the Draw-Image method of the Graphics object is used to draw images. Similarly, the DrawImage method of PrintPageEventArgs.Graphics prints an image to the printer, which then prints that image onto paper.

Before we add code for the **View Image** menu item, we need to add two application scope variables as follows:

```
private Image curImage = null;
private string curFileName = null;
```

View Image lets us browse for an image and then draws it on the form. As Listing 11.26 shows, we create a Graphics object using Form.Create-Graphics. Then we use OpenFileDialog to browse files on the system. Once a file has been selected, we create the Image object by using Image.FromFile, which takes the file name as its only parameter. Finally, we use DrawImage to draw the image.

LISTING 11.26: Viewing an image

```
private void ViewImage_Click(object sender,
  System.EventArgs e)
{
  // Create a Graphics object
  Graphics g = this.CreateGraphics();
  g.Clear(this.BackColor);
  // Call OpenFileDialog, which allows us to browse
  // images
```

continues

```
OpenFileDialog openDlg = new OpenFileDialog();
openDlg.Filter =
  "All Image files|*.bmp;*.gif;*.jpg;*.ico;"+
  "*.emf,*.wmf|Bitmap Files(*.bmp;*.gif;*.jpg;"+
  "*.ico)|*.bmp;*.gif;*.jpg;*.ico|"+
  "Meta Files(*.emf;*.wmf)|*.emf;*.wmf";
string filter = openDlg.Filter;
// Set InitialDirectory, Title, and ShowHelp
// properties
openDlg.InitialDirectory =
  Environment.CurrentDirectory;
openDlg.Title = "Open Image File";
openDlg.ShowHelp = true;
// If OpenFileDialog is OK
if(openDlg.ShowDialog() == DialogResult.OK)
{
  // Get the file name
  curFileName = openDlg.FileName;
  // Create an Image object from file name
  curImage = Image.FromFile(curFileName);
}
if(curImage != null)
{
  // Draw image using the DrawImage method
  g.DrawImage(curImage, AutoScrollPosition.X,
    AutoScrollPosition.Y,
      curImage.Width, curImage.Height );
}
// Dispose of object
g.Dispose();
}
```

Now we run the application and select an image. Figure 11.15 shows the output.

> **NOTE**
> See Chapters 7 and 8 for more on viewing and manipulating images.

Now let's write a **Print Image** menu item click handler. This option prints an image that we're currently viewing on the form. As in the previous example, we create a PrintDocument object, add a PrintPage event handler, and call the Print method. This time, however, instead of using

FIGURE 11.15: Viewing an image

the `DrawRectangle` and `DrawLine` methods, we use the `DrawImage` method, which draws the image.

As Listing 11.27 shows, our code creates a `PrintDocument` object, sets the `PrintPage` event of `PrintDocument` and the `PrintPage` event handler, and calls `PrintDocument.Print`. The `PrintPage` event handler calls `DrawImage`.

LISTING 11.27: Printing an image

```
private void PrintImage_Click(object sender,
  System.EventArgs e)
{
  // Create a PrintDocument object
  PrintDocument pd = new PrintDocument();
  // Add the PrintPage event handler
  pd.PrintPage += new PrintPageEventHandler
    (this.PrintImageHandler);
```

continues

```
  // Print
  pd.Print();
}

private void PrintImageHandler(object sender,
  PrintPageEventArgs ppeArgs)
{
  // Get the Graphics object from
  // PrintPageEventArgs
  Graphics g = ppeArgs.Graphics;
  // If Graphics object exists
  if(curImage != null)
  {
    // Draw image using the DrawImage method
    g.DrawImage(curImage, 0, 0,
      curImage.Width, curImage.Height );
  }
}
```

If we run the application, open and view a file, and click the **Print Image** menu item, we get a printout that looks like Figure 11.15.

11.8 **Print Dialogs**

In the beginning of this chapter we said that all printing functionality is defined in the `System.Drawing.Printing` namespace. That statement is not entirely true. Actually, a few printing-related classes are defined in the `System.Windows.Forms` namespace. These classes are

- `PrintDialog`
- `PrintPreviewDialog`
- `PrintPreviewControl`
- `PageSetupDialog`

These classes are also available as Windows Forms controls in Visual Studio .NET; we can add them to a form by dragging the control from the toolbox. The toolbox with the three print dialogs is shown in Figure 11.16.

However, adding and using these controls programmatically is even easier than using the toolbox, as we will soon see. Before you learn how to use them, let's explore their functionality.

FIGURE 11.16: Print dialogs in the Visual Studio .NET toolbox

11.8.1 **The** `PrintDialog` **Control**

The `PrintDialog` class represents the `PrintDialog` control in the .NET Framework library. This class represents a standard Windows printer dialog, which allows the user to select a printer and choose which portions of the document to print. Table 11.7 describes the `PrintDialog` class properties. By default, all of these properties are `false` when a `PrintDialog` object is created, and all the properties have both get and set options.

Besides the properties defined in Table 11.7, `PrintDialog` has one method called `Reset`. This method resets all options, the last selected printer, and the page settings to their default values.

Listing 11.28 creates a `PrintDialog` object, sets its properties, calls `ShowDialog`, and prints the document.

LISTING 11.28: Creating and using the `PrintDialog` control

```
PrintDialog printDlg = new PrintDialog();
PrintDocument printDoc = new PrintDocument();
printDoc.DocumentName = "Print Document";
printDlg.Document = printDoc;
```

continues

TABLE 11.7: `PrintDialog` properties

Property	Description
AllowSelection	Indicates whether the **From... To... Page** option button is enabled.
AllowSomePages	Indicates whether the **Pages** option button is enabled.
Document	Identifies the `PrintDocument` object used to obtain printer settings.
PrinterSettings	Identifies the printer settings that the dialog box modifies.
PrintToFile	Indicates whether the **Print** to file check box is checked.
ShowHelp	Indicates whether the **Help** button is displayed.
ShowNetwork	Indicates whether the **Network** button is displayed.

```
printDlg.AllowSelection = true;
printDlg.AllowSomePages = true;

// Call ShowDialog
if (printDlg.ShowDialog() == DialogResult.OK)
  printDoc.Print();
```

11.8.2 The `PageSetupDialog` Control

The `PageSetupDialog` class represents the `PageSetupDialog` control in the .NET Framework library. This class represents a standard Windows page setup dialog that allows users to manipulate page settings, including margins and paper orientation. Users can also set a `PageSettings` object through `PageSetupDialog`'s `PageSettings` property. Table 11.8 describes the properties of the `PageSetupDialog` class. All of these properties have both get and set options.

As with `PrintDialog`, the `PageSetupDialog` class has a `Reset` method that resets all the default values for the dialog.

Listing 11.29 creates a `PageSetupDialog` object, sets its properties, calls `ShowDialog`, and prints the document.

TABLE 11.8: `PageSetupDialog` properties

Property	Description
`AllowMargins`	Indicates whether the margins section of the dialog box is enabled. By default, true when a `PageSetup-Dialog` object is created.
`AllowOrientation`	Indicates whether the orientation section of the dialog box (landscape versus portrait) is enabled. By default, `true` when a `PageSetupDialog` object is created.
`AllowPaper`	Indicates whether the paper section of the dialog box (paper size and paper source) is enabled. By default, `true` when a `PageSetupDialog` object is created.
`AllowPrinter`	Indicates whether the **Printer** button is enabled. By default, `true` when a `PageSetupDialog` object is created.
`Document`	Identifies the `PrintDocument` object from which to get page settings. By default, `null` when a `Page-SetupDialog` object is created.
`MinMargins`	Indicates the minimum margins the user is allowed to select, in hundredths of an inch. By default, `null` when a `PageSetupDialog` object is created.
`PageSettings`	Identifies the page settings to modify. By default, `null` when a `PageSetupDialog` object is created.
`PrinterSettings`	Identifies the printer settings that the dialog box will modify when the user clicks the **Printer** button. By default, `null` when a `PageSetupDialog` object is created.
`ShowHelp`	Indicates whether the **Help** button is visible. By default, `false` when a `PageSetupDialog` object is created.
`ShowNetwork`	Indicates whether the **Network** button is visible. By default, `true` when a `PageSetupDialog` object is created.

LISTING 11.29: Creating and using the `PageSetupDialog` control

```
setupDlg = new PageSetupDialog();
printDlg = new PrintDialog();
printDoc = new PrintDocument();
printDoc.DocumentName = "Print Document";

// PageSetupDialog settings
setupDlg.Document = printDoc;
setupDlg.AllowMargins = false;
setupDlg.AllowOrientation = false;
setupDlg.AllowPaper = false;
setupDlg.AllowPrinter = false;
setupDlg.Reset();

if (setupDlg.ShowDialog() == DialogResult.OK)
{
printDoc.DefaultPageSettings =
  setupDlg.PageSettings;
printDoc.PrinterSettings =
  setupDlg.PrinterSettings;
}
```

11.8.3 The `PrintPreviewDialog` Control

The `PrintPreviewDialog` class represents the `PrintPreviewDialog` control in the .NET Framework library. This class represents a standard Windows print preview dialog, which allows users to preview capabilities before printing. The `PrintPreviewDialog` class is inherited from the `Form` class, which means that this dialog contains all the functionality defined in `Form`, `Control`, and other base classes.

In addition to the properties provided by the base classes, this class has its own properties. Many of these properties are very common and are provided by many controls. Table 11.9 describes a few important `Print-PreviewDialog` class properties. All of these properties have both get and set options.

Listing 11.30 creates a `PrintPreviewDialog` object, sets its properties, calls `ShowDialog`, and prints the document.

LISTING 11.30: Creating and using the `PrintPreviewDialog` control

```
// Create a PrintPreviewDialog object
PrintPreviewDialog previewDlg =
  new PrintPreviewDialog();
```

TABLE 11.9: Some `PrintPreviewDialog` properties

Property	Description
Document	Identifies the document shown in preview.
HelpButton	Indicates whether a help button should be displayed in the caption box of the form. The default value is `false`.
KeyPreview	Indicates whether the form will receive key events before the event is passed to the control that has focus. The default value is `false`.
ShowInTaskbar	Indicates whether the form is displayed in the Windows taskbar. The default value is `true`.
TransparencyKey	Identifies the color that will represent transparent areas of the form.
UseAntiAlias	Indicates whether printing uses the anti-aliasing features of the operating system.
WindowState	Identifies the form's window state.

```
// Create a PrintDocument object
PrintDocument printDoc =
  new PrintDocument();
// Set Document property
previewDlg.Document = printDoc;
previewDlg.WindowState =
  FormWindowState.Normal;
// Show dialog
previewDlg.ShowDialog();
```

11.8.4 Print Dialogs in Action

Now let's create a Windows application. In this application you will see how to use the print dialogs in your Windows applications.

We create a Windows application and add a `MainMenu` control to the form. We also add four menu items and a separator to the `MainMenu` control. The final form looks like Figure 11.17.

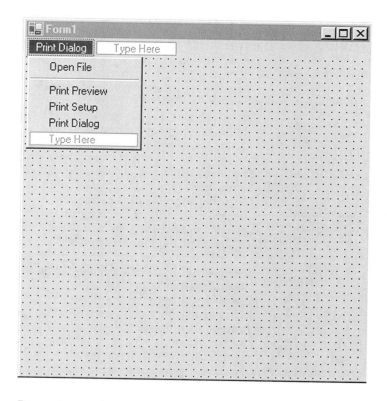

FIGURE 11.17: The print dialog application

As usual, our first step is to add some private variables to the project, as follows:

```
// Variables
private Image curImage = null;
private string curFileName = null;
private PrintPreviewDialog previewDlg = null;
private PageSetupDialog setupDlg = null;
private PrintDocument printDoc = null;
private PrintDialog printDlg = null;
We also add the following namespaces to the project:
using System.Drawing.Printing;
using System.Drawing.Imaging;
using System.Drawing.Drawing2D;
using System.Drawing.Text;
```

On our form's load event, we initialize these dialogs. We also create a `PrintPage` event handler and add it to the `PrintDocument` object, as shown in Listing 11.31.

LISTING 11.31: Initializing print dialogs

```
private void Form1_Load(object sender,
  System.EventArgs e)
{
  // Create print preview dialog
  // and other dialogs
  previewDlg = new PrintPreviewDialog();
  setupDlg = new PageSetupDialog();
  printDlg = new PrintDialog();
  printDoc = new PrintDocument();
  // Set document name
  printDoc.DocumentName = "Print Document";
  // PrintPreviewDialog settings
  previewDlg.Document = printDoc;
  // PageSetupDialog settings
  setupDlg.Document = printDoc;
  // PrintDialog settings
  printDlg.Document = printDoc;
  printDlg.AllowSelection = true;
  printDlg.AllowSomePages = true;
  // Create a PrintPage event handler
  printDoc.PrintPage +=
    new PrintPageEventHandler(this.pd_Print);
}
```

Now we add the `PrintPage` event handler, which calls `DrawGraphics-Items` as shown in Listing 11.32. We pass `PrintPageEventArgs.Graphics` as the only parameter to `DrawGraphicsItems`.

LISTING 11.32: The `PrintPage` event handler

```
private void pd_Print(object sender,
PrintPageEventArgs ppeArgs)
{
  DrawGraphicsItems(ppeArgs.Graphics);
}
```

The `DrawGraphicsItems` method draws an image and text on the printer or the form, depending on the `Graphics` object. If we pass `Form.Graphics`, the `DrawGraphicsItems` method will draw graphics objects on the form, but if we pass `PrintPageEventArgs.Graphics`, this method will send drawings to the printer.

The code for the `DrawGraphicsItems` method is given in Listing 11.33. This method also sets the smoothing mode and text qualities via the `SmoothingMode` and `TextRenderingHint` properties. After that it calls `DrawImage` and `DrawText`.

LISTING 11.33: The **DrawGraphicsItems** method

```
private void DrawGraphicsItems(Graphics gObj)
{
  // Set text and image quality
  gObj.SmoothingMode =
    SmoothingMode.AntiAlias;
  gObj.TextRenderingHint =
    TextRenderingHint.AntiAlias;
  if(curImage != null)
  {
    // Draw image using the DrawImage method
    gObj.DrawImage(curImage,
      AutoScrollPosition.X,
      AutoScrollPosition.Y,
      curImage.Width, curImage.Height );
  }
  // Draw a string
  gObj.DrawString("Printing Dialogs Test",
    new Font("Verdana", 14),
    new SolidBrush(Color.Blue), 0, 0);
}
```

There's just one more thing to do before we write the menu item event handlers. We call `DrawGraphicsItems` from the form's paint event handler, as Listing 11.34 shows. Adding this code will display the drawing on the form.

LISTING 11.34: The form's paint event handler

```
private void Form1_Paint(object sender,
System.Windows.Forms.PaintEventArgs e)
{
 DrawGraphicsItems(e.Graphics);
}
```

Now we can write code for the menu items. The **Open File** menu item just lets us browse images and creates an `Image` object by calling the `Image.FromFile` method, as Listing 11.35 shows.

LISTING 11.35: The Open File menu handler

```
private void OpenFile_Click(object sender,
  System.EventArgs e)
{
  // Create a Graphics object
  Graphics g = this.CreateGraphics();
  g.Clear(this.BackColor);
  // Create open file dialog
  OpenFileDialog openDlg = new OpenFileDialog();
  // Set filter as images
  openDlg.Filter =
    "All Image files|*.bmp;*.gif;*.jpg;*.ico;"+
    "*.emf,*.wmf|Bitmap Files(*.bmp;*.gif;*.jpg;"+
    "*.ico)|*.bmp;*.gif;*.jpg;*.ico|"+
    "Meta Files(*.emf;*.wmf)|*.emf;*.wmf";
  string filter = openDlg.Filter;
  // Set title and initial directory
  openDlg.InitialDirectory =
    Environment.CurrentDirectory;
  openDlg.Title = "Open Image File";
  openDlg.ShowHelp = true;
  // Show dialog
  if(openDlg.ShowDialog() == DialogResult.OK)
  {
    // Get the file name and create
    // Image object from file
    curFileName = openDlg.FileName;
    curImage = Image.FromFile(curFileName);
  }
  // Paint the form, which
  // forces a call to the paint event
  Invalidate();
}
```

The code for `PrintPreviewDialog`, `PageSetupDialog`, and `Print-Dialog` is given in Listing 11.36. We show `PrintDialog` and call its `Print-Document.Print` method if the user selects **OK** on the print dialog. We set `PageSetupDialog` page and printer settings when the user selects **OK** on the page setup dialog. For the print preview dialog, we set the `Use-AntiAlias` property and call `ShowDialog`.

LISTING 11.36: Print dialogs

```csharp
private void PrintDialog_Click(object sender,
  System.EventArgs e)
{
  if (printDlg.ShowDialog() == DialogResult.OK)
   printDoc.Print();
}
private void PageSetupDialog_Click(object sender,
  System.EventArgs e)
{
  if (setupDlg.ShowDialog() == DialogResult.OK)
  {
    printDoc.DefaultPageSettings =
      setupDlg.PageSettings;
    printDoc.PrinterSettings =
      setupDlg.PrinterSettings;
  }
}
private void PrintPreview_Click(object sender,
  System.EventArgs e)
{
  previewDlg.UseAntiAlias = true;
  previewDlg.WindowState =
    FormWindowState.Normal;
  previewDlg.ShowDialog();
}
```

Now when we run the application and browse an image using the **Open File** menu item, the form looks like Figure 11.18.

If we click on **Print Preview**, our program will display the print preview dialog, as shown in Figure 11.19.

As stated earlier, the page setup dialog allows us to set the page properties, including size, sources, orientation, and margins. Clicking on **Print Setup** on the dialog menu brings up the page setup dialog, which is shown in Figure 11.20.

Clicking on **Print Dialog** calls up the standard print dialog, shown in Figure 11.21.

We can use these dialogs as we would in any other Windows applications.

FIGURE 11.18: Viewing an image and text

FIGURE 11.19: The print preview dialog

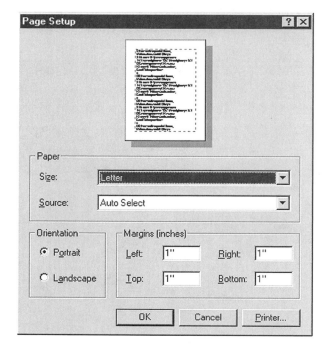

FIGURE 11.20: The page setup dialog

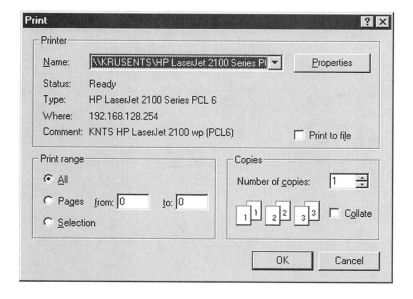

FIGURE 11.21: The print dialog

11.9 **Customizing Page Settings**

We have already discussed `PageSetupDialog`, which allows us to adjust page settings. This is all taken care of by the dialog internally. But what if we need a custom page setup dialog? Sometimes we won't want to use the default dialogs provided by Windows. For example, suppose we want to change the text of the dialog or don't want the user to have page selection or anything else that is not available on the default Windows dialogs.

The `System.Drawing.Printing` namespace also defines functionality to manage page settings programmatically.

11.9.1 **The `PageSettings` Class**

Page settings are the properties of a page that are being used when a page is printed, including color, page margins, paper size, page bounds, and page resolution.

The `PageSettings` class represents page settings in the .NET Framework library. This class provides members to specify page settings. It is used by the `PrintDocument.DefaultPageSettings` property to specify the page settings of a `PrintDocument` object. Table 11.10 describes the properties of the `PageSettings` class.

Besides the properties described in Table 11.10, the `PageSettings` class provides three methods: `Clone`, `CopyToHdevmode`, and `SetHdevmode`. The `Clone` method simply creates a copy of the `PageSettings` object. `Copy-ToHdevmode` copies relevant information from the `PageSettings` object to the specified `DEVMODE` structure, and `SetHdevmode` copies relevant information to the `PageSettings` object from the specified `DEVMODE` structure. The `DEVMODE` structure is used by Win32 programmers.

11.9.2 **Page Margins**

The `Margins` class represents a page margin in the .NET Framework library. It allows you to get the current page margin settings and set new margin settings. This class has four properties—`Left`, `Right`, `Top`, and `Bottom`—which represent the left, right, top, and bottom margins, respectively, in hundredths of an inch. This class is used by the `Margins` property of the `PageSettings` class. We will use this class and its members in our examples.

TABLE 11.10: `PageSettings` properties

Property	Description
Bounds	Returns the size of the page.
Color	Indicates whether the page should be printed in color. Both get and set. The default is determined by the printer.
Landscape	Indicates whether the page is printed in landscape or portrait orientation. Both get and set. The default is determined by the printer.
Margins	Identifies the page margins. Both get and set.
PaperSize	Identifies the paper size. Both get and set.
PaperSource	Identifies the paper source (a printer tray). Both get and set.
PrinterResolution	Identifies the printer resolution for the page. Both get and set.
PrinterSettings	Identifies the printer settings associated with the page. Both get and set.

11.9.3 Creating a Custom Paper Size

As mentioned earlier, the `PaperSize` class specifies the size and type of paper. You can create your own custom paper sizes. For example, Listing 11.37 creates a custom paper size with a height of 200 and a width of 100.

LISTING 11.37: Creating a custom paper size

```
// Create a custom paper size and add it to the list
PaperSize customPaperSize = new PaperSize();
customPaperSize.PaperName = "Custom Size";
customPaperSize.Height = 200;
customPaperSize.Width = 100;
```

11.9.4 The `PaperKind` Enumeration

The `PaperKind` enumeration, as we saw earlier, is used by the `Kind` property to specify standard paper sizes. This enumeration has over 100 members. Among them are `A2`, `A3`, `A3Extra`, `A3ExtraTransverse`, `A3Rotated`, `A3Transverse`, `A4`, `A5`, `A6`, `Custom`, `DCEnvelope`, `Executive`, `Invite-Envelope`, `ItalyEnvelope`, `JapanesePostcard`, `Ledger`, `Legal`, `Legal-Extra`, `Letter`, `LetterExtra`, `LetterSmall`, `Standard10x11` (`10x14`, `10x17`, `12x11`, `15x11`, `9x11`), `Statement`, and `Tabloid`.

11.9.5 **The** `PaperSourceKind` **Enumeration**

The `PaperSourceKind` enumeration represents standard paper sources. Table 11.11 describes the members of the `PaperSourceKind` enumeration.

TABLE 11.11: `PaperSourceKind` members

Member	Description
`AutomaticFeed`	Automatically fed paper
`Cassette`	A paper cassette
`Custom`	A printer-specific paper source
`Envelope`	An envelope
`FormSource`	The printer's default input bin
`LargeCapacity`	The printer's large-capacity bin
`LargeFormat`	Large-format paper
`Lower`	The lower bin of a printer
`Manual`	Manually fed paper
`ManualFeed`	Manually fed envelope
`Middle`	The middle bin of a printer
`SmallFormat`	Small-format paper
`TractorFeed`	A tractor feed
`Upper`	The upper bin of a printer

11.9.6 Page Settings in Action

Now let's create an application that will allow us to get and set page settings. In this application we will create a custom dialog.

We start by creating a new Windows application in VS.NET. We add some controls to the form, with the result shown in Figure 11.22. The **Available Printers** combo box displays all available printers. The **Size** and **Source** combo boxes display paper sizes and sources, respectively. The **Paper Orientation** section indicates whether paper is oriented in landscape mode or portrait mode. The **Paper Margins** text boxes obviously represent left, right, top, and bottom margins. The Bounds property is represented by the **Bounds (Rectangle)** text box. The **Color Printing** check box indicates whether the printer supports color printing. The **Set Properties** button allows us to enter new values in the controls.

The form's load event (see Listing 11.38), loads all the required Page-Settings-related settings using the LoadPrinters, LoadPaperSizes, LoadPaperSources, and ReadOtherSettings methods.

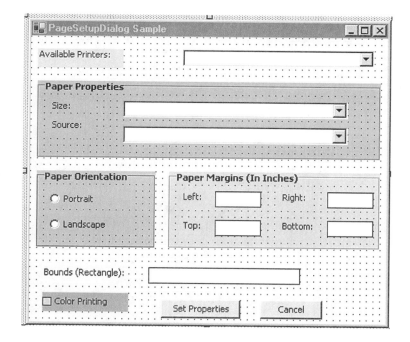

FIGURE 11.22: The custom page settings dialog

LISTING 11.38: The form's load event handler

```
private void Form1_Load(object sender,
  System.EventArgs e)
{
  // Load all available printers
  LoadPrinters();
  // Load paper sizes
  LoadPaperSizes();
  // Load paper sources
  LoadPaperSources();
  // Load other settings
  ReadOtherSettings();
}
```

The `LoadPrinters`, `LoadPaperSizes`, `LoadPaperSources`, and `ReadOtherSettings` methods are used to load printers, paper sizes, paper sources, and other properties, respectively. The `LoadPrinters` method is given in Listing 11.39. We simply read the `InstalledPrinters` property of `PrinterSettings` and add printers to the `printersList` combo box.

LISTING 11.39: Loading printers

```
private void LoadPrinters()
{
  // Load all available printers
  foreach(String printer in
    PrinterSettings.InstalledPrinters)
  {
    printersList.Items.Add(printer.ToString());
  }
  printersList.Select(0, 1);
}
```

The `LoadPaperSizes` method (see Listing 11.40), loads all available paper sizes to the combo box. We read the `PaperSizes` property of `PrinterSettings` and add the paper type to the combo box. Then we create a custom paper size and add this to the combo box as well. This example will give you an idea of how to create your own custom paper sizes.

LISTING 11.40: Loading paper sizes

```
private void LoadPaperSizes()
{
  PaperSizeCombo.DisplayMember = "PaperName";
  PrinterSettings settings = new PrinterSettings();
  // Get all paper sizes and add them to the combo box list
  foreach(PaperSize size in settings.PaperSizes)
  {
    PaperSizeCombo.Items.Add(size.Kind.ToString());
    // You can even read the paper name and all PaperSize
    // properties by uncommenting these two lines:
    // PaperSizeCombo.Items.Add
      // (size.PaperName.ToString());
    // PaperSizeCombo.Items.Add(size.ToString());
  }
  // Create a custom paper size and add it to the list
  PaperSize customPaperSize =
    new PaperSize("Custom Size", 50, 100);
  // You can also change properties
  customPaperSize.PaperName = "New Custom Size";
  customPaperSize.Height = 200;
  customPaperSize.Width = 100;
  // Don't assign the Kind property. It's read-only.
  // customPaperSize.Kind = PaperKind.A4;
  // Add custom size
  PaperSizeCombo.Items.Add(customPaperSize);
}
```

The `LoadPaperSources` method (see Listing 11.41), reads all available paper sources and adds them to the `PaperSourceCombo` combo box. We use the `PaperSources` property of `PrinterSettings` to read the paper sources.

LISTING 11.41: Loading paper sources

```
private void LoadPaperSources()
{
  PrinterSettings settings = new PrinterSettings();
  PaperSourceCombo.DisplayMember="SourceName";
  // Add all paper sources to the combo box
  foreach(PaperSource source in settings.PaperSources)
  {
    PaperSourceCombo.Items.Add(source.ToString());
    // You can even add Kind and SourceName
      // by uncommenting the following two lines:
    // PaperSourceCombo.Items.Add
      // (source.Kind.ToString());
```

```
    // PaperSourceCombo.Items.Add
      // (source.SourceName.ToString());
  }
}
```

The last method, ReadOtherSettings, reads other properties of a printer, such as whether it supports color, margins, and bounds. Listing 11.42 shows the ReadOtherSettings method.

LISTING 11.42: Loading other properties of a printer

```
private void ReadOtherSettings()
{
  // Set other default properties
  PrinterSettings settings = new PrinterSettings();
  PageSettings pgSettings =
    settings.DefaultPageSettings;
  // Color printing
  if(pgSettings.Color)
    ColorPrintingBox.Checked = true;
  else
    ColorPrintingBox.Checked = false;
  // Page margins
  leftMarginBox.Text =
    pgSettings.Bounds.Left.ToString();
  rightMarginBox.Text =
    pgSettings.Bounds.Right.ToString();
  topMarginBox.Text =
    pgSettings.Bounds.Top.ToString();
  bottomMarginBox.Text =
    pgSettings.Bounds.Bottom.ToString();
  // Landscape or portrait
  if(pgSettings.Landscape)
    landscapeButton.Checked = true;
  else
    portraitButton.Checked = true;
  // Bounds
  boundsTextBox.Text =
    pgSettings.Bounds.ToString();
}
```

▪■ **NOTE**

Remember that you need to add a reference to the System. Drawing.Printing namespace to your application whenever you use classes from this namespace.

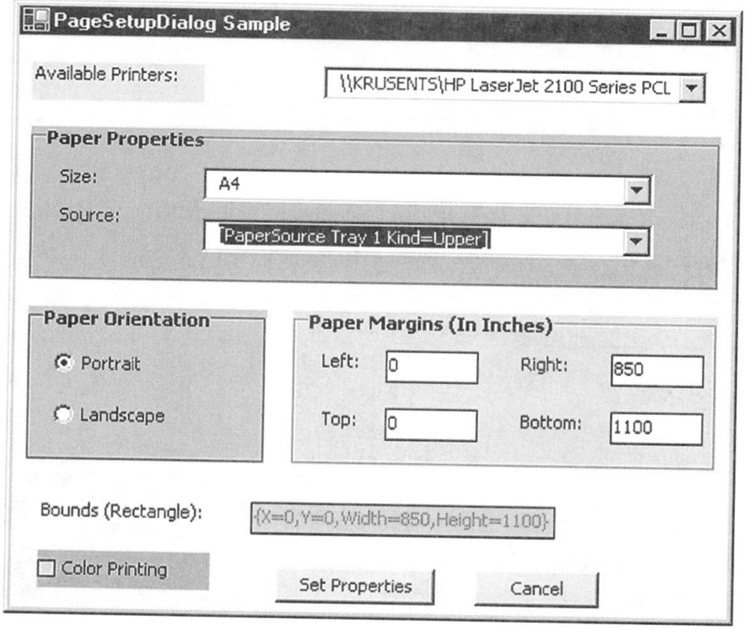

FIGURE 11.23: The `PageSetupDialog` sample in action

Now if we run the application, its form looks like Figure 11.23. Each of the Windows controls displays its intended property.

Finally, we want to save settings through the **Set Properties** button click and write code for a **Cancel** button. On the **Set Properties** button click, we set the properties using `PrinterSettings`. Make sure a printer is available in the **Available Printers** combo box. The **Cancel** button simply closes the dialog.

The code for the **Set Properties** and **Cancel** button click event handlers is given in Listing 11.43, in which we set the page settings, color, and landscape properties of a page.

LISTING 11.43: Saving paper settings

```
private void SetPropertiesBtn_Click(object sender,
    System.EventArgs e)
{
  // Set other default properties
  PrinterSettings settings = new PrinterSettings();
  PageSettings pgSettings =
    settings.DefaultPageSettings;
```

```
  // Color printing?
  if (ColorPrintingBox.Checked )
    pgSettings.Color = true;
  else
    pgSettings.Color = false;

  // Landscape or portrait?
  if(landscapeButton.Checked )
    pgSettings.Landscape = true;
  else
    pgSettings.Landscape = false;
}

private void CancelBtn_Click(object sender,
  System.EventArgs e)
{
  this.Close();
}
```

The preceding discussion should enable you to customize page settings in the way that you want, instead of using the standard page settings dialog provided in the `PageSettingsDialog` class.

> ### NOTE
> Even though the printing functionality defined in the `System.Drawing.Printing` namespace allows developers to customize the standard Windows dialogs, I recommend that you use the standard Windows dialogs unless you can't live without customizing them.

11.9.7 The `PrintRange` Enumeration

The `PrintRange` enumeration is used to specify the part of a document to print. This enumeration is used by the `PrinterSettings` and `PrintDialog` classes. Table 11.12 describes the members of the `PrintRange` enumeration.

You can use the `PrintRange` property of the `PrinterSettings` object to set the print range. Here's an example of code that does this:

```
PrinterSettings.PrintRange = PrintRange.SomePages;
```

TABLE 11.12: `PrintRange` members

Member	Description
AllPages	All pages are printed.
Selection	The selected pages are printed.
SomePages	The pages between `FromPage` and `ToPage` are printed.

11.10 Printing Multiple Pages

So far we have discussed printing only an image or a single-page file. Printing multipage files is another important part of printing functionality that developers may need to implement when writing printer applications. Unfortunately, the .NET Framework does not keep track of page numbers for you, but it provides enough support for you to keep track of the current page, the total number of pages, the last page, and a particular page number. Basically, when printing a multipage document, you need to find out the total number of pages and print them from first to last. You can also specify a particular page number. If you are using the default Windows printing dialog, then you don't have to worry about it because you can specify the pages in the dialog, and the framework takes care of this for you.

To demonstrate how to do this, our next program produces a useful printout showing all the fonts installed on your computer. This program is a useful tool for demonstrating the calculation of how many pages to print when you're using graphical commands to print.

We will use the `PrintPreview` facility to display the output in case you don't have access to a printer. In this example we need to track how many fonts have been printed and how far down the page we are. If we're going to go over the end of the page, we drop out of the `pd_PrintPage` event handler and set `ev.HasMorePages` to `true` to indicate that we have another page to print.

To see this functionality in action, let's create a Windows application and add a menu with three menu items and a `RichTextBox` control to the form. The final form is shown in Figure 11.24.

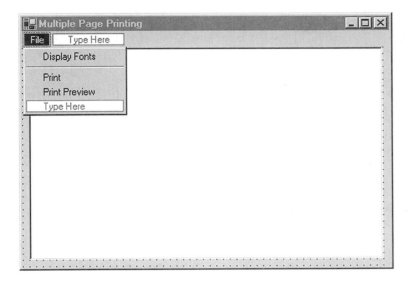

FIGURE 11.24: A form for printing multiple pages

The **Display Fonts** menu displays available fonts on the machine. Before we add code to this menu, we add the following variables:

```
private int fontcount;
private int fontposition = 1;
private float ypos = 1;
private PrintPreviewDialog previewDlg = null;
```

The code for the **Display Fonts** menu click is given in Listing 11.44. Here we read installed fonts on the system and display them in the rich text box. We use `InstalledFontCollection` to read all installed fonts on a machine. Then we use the `InstalledFontCollection.Families` property and make a loop to read all the font families. We also check if these families support different styles, including regular, bold, italic, and underline, and we add some text to the rich text box with the current font.

■■ NOTE
See Chapter 5 for details about fonts and font collections.

LISTING 11.44: Displaying fonts

```
private void DisplayFonts_Click_1(object sender,
System.EventArgs e)
{
  // Create InstalledFontCollection object
  InstalledFontCollection ifc =
    new InstalledFontCollection();
  // Get font families
  FontFamily[] ffs = ifc.Families;
  Font f;
  // Make sure rich text box is empty
  richTextBox1.Clear();
  // Read font families one by one,
  // set font to some text,
  // and add text to the text box
  foreach(FontFamily ff in ffs)
  {
    if (ff.IsStyleAvailable(FontStyle.Regular))
      f = new Font(ff.GetName(1),
        12, FontStyle.Regular);
    else if(ff.IsStyleAvailable(FontStyle.Bold))
      f = new Font(ff.GetName(1),
        12, FontStyle.Bold);
    else if (ff.IsStyleAvailable(FontStyle.Italic))
      f = new Font(ff.GetName(1),
        12, FontStyle.Italic);
    else
      f = new Font(ff.GetName(1),
        12, FontStyle.Underline);
    richTextBox1.SelectionFont=f;
    richTextBox1.AppendText(
    ff.GetName(1)+"\r\n");
    richTextBox1.SelectionFont=f;
    richTextBox1.AppendText(
      "abcdefghijklmnopqrstuvwxyz\r\n");
    richTextBox1.SelectionFont=f;
    richTextBox1.AppendText(
      "ABCDEFGHIJKLMNOPQRSTUVWXYZ\r\n");
    richTextBox1.AppendText(
      "==============================\r\n");
  }
}
```

The code for the **Print Preview** and **Print** menu items is given in Listing 11.45. This code should look familiar to you. We simply create `Print-Document` and `PrintPreviewDialog` objects, set their properties, add a print-page event handler, and call the `Print` and `Show` methods.

LISTING 11.45: The Print Preview and Print menu items

```
private void PrintPreviewMenuClick(object sender,
  System.EventArgs e)
{
  // Create a PrintPreviewDialog object
  previewDlg = new PrintPreviewDialog();
  // Create a PrintDocument object
  PrintDocument pd = new PrintDocument();
  // Add print-page event handler
  pd.PrintPage +=
    new PrintPageEventHandler(pd_PrintPage);
  // Set Document property of PrintPreviewDialog
  previewDlg.Document = pd;
  // Display dialog
  previewDlg.Show();
}

private void PrintMenuClick(object sender,
  System.EventArgs e)
{
  // Create a PrintPreviewDialog object
  previewDlg = new PrintPreviewDialog();
  // Create a PrintDocument object
  PrintDocument pd = new PrintDocument();
  // Add print-page event handler
  pd.PrintPage +=
    new PrintPageEventHandler(pd_PrintPage);
  // Print
  pd.Print();
}
```

The print-page event handler, pd_PrintPage, is given in Listing 11.46.
We print fonts using DrawString, and we set PrintPageEventArgs.Has-
MorePages to true. To make sure the text fits, we increase the *y*-position by
60 units.

LISTING 11.46: The print-page event handler

```
public void pd_PrintPage(object sender,
  PrintPageEventArgs ev)
{
  ypos = 1;
  float pageheight = ev.MarginBounds.Height;
  // Create a Graphics object
  Graphics g = ev.Graphics;
```

continues

```
// Get installed fonts
InstalledFontCollection ifc =
  new InstalledFontCollection();
// Get font families
FontFamily[] ffs = ifc.Families;
// Draw string on the paper
while(ypos+60 < pageheight &&
  fontposition < ffs.GetLength(0))
{
  // Get the font name
  Font f =
    new Font(ffs[fontposition].GetName(0),25);
  // Draw string
  g.DrawString(ffs[fontposition].GetName(0), f,
    new SolidBrush(Color.Black),1,ypos);
  fontposition = fontposition+1;
  ypos = ypos + 60;
}
if (fontposition < ffs.GetLength(0))
{
  // Has more pages??
  ev.HasMorePages = true;
}
}
```

That's it. If we run the program, the **Print** menu prints multiple pages, and the **Print Preview** menu shows the print preview on two pages (see Figure 11.25).

As you can see, it's pretty easy to create multipage report generators. Now you can use the print options to print documents with multiple pages.

11.10.1 **The** DocumentName **Property**

If you want to display the name of the document you're printing, you can use the DocumentName property of the PrintDocument object:

```
pd.DocumentName="A Test Document";
```

The new result is shown in Figure 11.26.

We have seen that using the DocumentPrintPreview class is fairly straightforward. In reality, all that's happening is that this control is passed a graphics class representing each page in a printout.

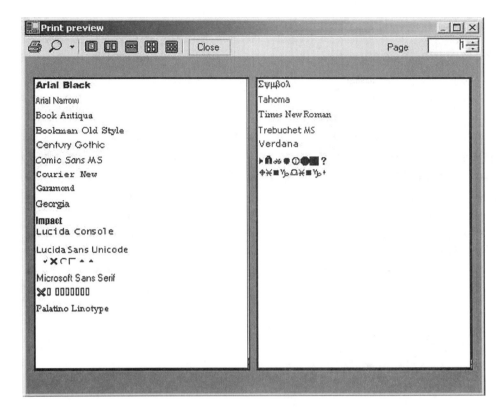

FIGURE 11.25: Print preview of multiple pages

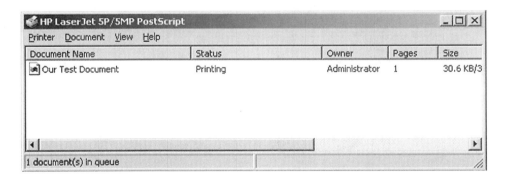

FIGURE 11.26: Setting a document name

11.11 Marginal Printing: A Caution

Although it's exciting to be able to draw graphics on a printout, keep in mind that printers have limits. Never try to print at the extreme edges of the page because you cannot be sure that a printer will print in exactly the same place. You could have two printers of the same model and manufacturer, and yet when you print you may notice they print in different places. Some printers are more accurate than others, but usually a sheet of paper will move slightly as it moves through the printer. Laser printers tend to be able to print closer to the edges of the paper than inkjet printers because of the mechanism that is used to transport the sheet of paper through the printer.

To see a marginal-printing sample, let's create a Windows application. We add two buttons to the form. The final form is shown in Figure 11.27.

Now we add code for the **Normal Printing** and **Marginal Printing** button click event handlers, as in Listing 11.47. Each handler creates a `Print-Document` object, adds a `PrintPage` event handler, and calls the `Print` method. The `PrintPage` event handlers for **Normal Printing** and **Marginal Printing** are `NormalPrinting` and `MarginPrinting`, respectively.

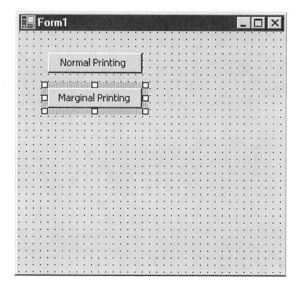

FIGURE 11.27: Marginal-printing test application

LISTING 11.47: The Normal Printing and Marginal Printing button event handlers

```
private void NormalBtn_Click(object sender,
  System.EventArgs e)
{
  // Create a PrintDocument object
  PrintDocument pd = new PrintDocument();
  // Add PrintPage event handler
  pd.PrintPage +=
    new PrintPageEventHandler(NormalPrinting);
  // Print
  pd.Print();
}
private void MarginalBtn_Click(object sender,
  System.EventArgs e)
{
  // Create a PrintDocument object
  PrintDocument pd = new PrintDocument();
  // Add PrintPage event handler
  pd.PrintPage +=
    new PrintPageEventHandler(MarginPrinting);
  // Print
  pd.Print();
}
```

Now let's look at the `NormalPrinting` handler (see Listing 11.48). We start with the top location of the text as unit 1. Then we calculate the next line's position using the height of the font and draw four lines with the values of the top, left, bottom, and right margins. In the end we draw a rectangle with the default bounds of the page.

LISTING 11.48: The **NormalPrinting** event handler

```
public void NormalPrinting(object sender,
  PrintPageEventArgs ev)
{
  // Set the top position as 1
  float ypos = 1;
  // Get the default left margin
  float leftMargin = ev.MarginBounds.Left;
  // Create a font
  Font font = new Font("Arial",16);
  // Get the font's height
  float fontheight = font.GetHeight(ev.Graphics);
```

continues

```
    // Draw four strings
    ev.Graphics.DrawString("Top Margin = "
        + ev.MarginBounds.Top.ToString(),
        font, Brushes.Black,
        leftMargin, ypos);
    ypos = ypos + fontheight;
    ev.Graphics.DrawString("Bottom Margin = "
        + ev.MarginBounds.Bottom.ToString(),
        font, Brushes.Black,
        leftMargin, ypos);
    ypos = ypos + fontheight;
    ev.Graphics.DrawString ("Left Margin = "
        + ev.MarginBounds.Left.ToString(),
        font, Brushes.Black,
        leftMargin, ypos);
    ypos = ypos + fontheight;
    ev.Graphics.DrawString ("Right Margin = "
        + ev.MarginBounds.Right.ToString(),
        font, Brushes.Black,
        leftMargin, ypos);
    ypos = ypos + fontheight;
    // Draw a rectangle with default margins
    ev.Graphics.DrawRectangle(
        new Pen(Color.Black),
        ev.MarginBounds.X,
        ev.MarginBounds.Y,
        ev.MarginBounds.Width,
        ev.MarginBounds.Height);
}
```

If we run the application, we will see text describing the four margin values printed outside the rectangle.

Next comes code for the `MarginPrinting` event handler (see Listing 11.49). We use the default margin of the page as the top location for the first text. Everything else is the same as in Listing 11.48.

LISTING 11.49: The **MarginPrinting** event handler

```
public void MarginPrinting(object sender,
    PrintPageEventArgs ev)
{
    // Set the top position as the default margin
    float ypos = ev.MarginBounds.Top;
    // Get the default left margin
    float leftMargin = ev.MarginBounds.Left;
    // Create a font
    Font font = new Font("Arial",16);
```

```
// Get the font's height
float fontheight = font.GetHeight(ev.Graphics);
// Draw four strings
ev.Graphics.DrawString("Top Margin = " +
  ev.MarginBounds.Top.ToString(),
  font, Brushes.Black,
  leftMargin, ypos);
ypos = ypos + fontheight;
ev.Graphics.DrawString("Bottom Margin = " +
  ev.MarginBounds.Bottom.ToString(),
  font, Brushes.Black,
  leftMargin, ypos);
ypos = ypos + fontheight;
ev.Graphics.DrawString ("Left Margin = " +
  ev.MarginBounds.Left.ToString(),
  font, Brushes.Black,
  leftMargin, ypos);
ypos = ypos + fontheight;
ev.Graphics.DrawString ("Right Margin = "
  + ev.MarginBounds.Right.ToString(),
  font,Brushes.Black,
  leftMargin, ypos);
ypos = ypos + fontheight;
// Draw a rectangle with default margins
ev.Graphics.DrawRectangle(
  new Pen(Color.Black),
  ev.MarginBounds.X,
  ev.MarginBounds.Y,
  ev.MarginBounds.Width,
  ev.MarginBounds.Height);
}
```

When we run this code, we will see text appearing inside the rectangle printed using the page margin values.

11.12 Getting into the Details: Custom Controlling and the Print Controller

At this point you must feel like a printer master and have the confidence you need to write a printing application. We have covered almost every aspect of printing in .NET, but guess what! There are still a few surprises hidden in System.Drawing.Printing. You will probably never use the classes that we're going to discuss in this section, but it's not a bad idea to know about them.

So far in this chapter we've created a `PrintDocument` object, created a `PrintPage` event handler, and called the `Print` method of `PrintDocument`. `PrintDocument` took care of everything internally for us. Now we will see how to control `PrintDocument`. For this, we need a print controller, which controls how a `PrintDocument` object handles printing.

The `PrintController` class represents print controllers in the .NET Framework library. It's an abstract base class, so its functionality comes from its three derived classes: `PreviewPrintController`, `StandardPrintController`, and `PrintControllerWithStatusDialog`. `PrintController` and its derived classes are shown schematically in Figure 11.28.

Normally `PrintController` is used by `PrintDocument`. When `PrintDocument` starts printing by calling the `Print` method, it invokes the print controller's `OnStartPrint`, `OnEndPrint`, `OnStartPage`, and `OnEndPage` methods, which determine how a printer will print the document. Usually the `OnStartPrint` method of `PrintController` is responsible for obtaining the `Graphics` object, which is later used by the `PrintPage` event handler.

The `StandardPrintController` class is used to send pages to the printer. We set the `PrintController` property of `PrintDocument` to `PrintController.StandardPrintController`. `PrintControllerWithStatusDialog` adds a status dialog to the printing functionality. It shows the name of the document currently being printed. To attach `PrintControllerWithStatusDialog`, we set `PrintDocument`'s `PrintCon-`

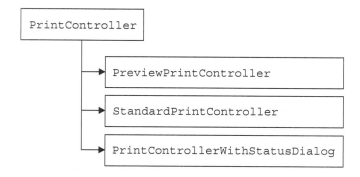

FIGURE 11.28: **PrintController-derived** classes

troller property to `PrintController.PrintControllerWithStatus-Dialog`.

The `PreviewPrintController` class is used for generating previews of pages being printed. Besides the methods defined in the `PrintController` class, `PreviewPrintController` provides one property (`UseAntiAlias`) and one method (`GetPreviewPageInfo`). The `UseAntiAlias` property indicates whether anti-aliasing will be used when the print preview is being displayed.

The `GetPreviewPageInfo` method captures the pages of a document as a series of images and returns them as an array called `PreviewPageInfo`. The `PreviewPageInfo` class provides print preview information for a single page. This class has two properties: `Image` and `PhysicalSize`. The `Image` property returns an `Image` object, which represents an image of the printed page, and `PhysicalSize` represents the size of the printed page in hundredths of an inch.

Let's write a sample application. We create a Windows application, and we add a `MainMenu` control, an item, and a `StatusBar` control to the form. Our final form looks like Figure 11.29.

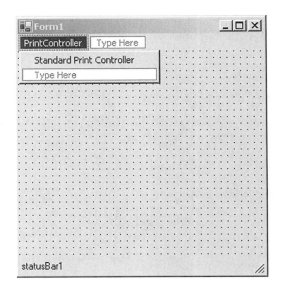

FIGURE 11.29: Print controller test form

Before adding any code to this form, we create a `MyPrintController` class, which is inherited from `StandardPrintController`. You can use the `PreviewPrintController` or `PrintControllerWithStatusDialog` classes in the same way. The code for the `MyPrintController` class is given in Listing 11.50. We override all four methods: `OnStartPrint`, `OnStartPage`, `OnEndPrint`, and `OnEndPage`. On these methods we notify the status bar about the status of the printing process. This information could be useful for displaying page numbers or other print status information when we're printing multipage documents.

LISTING 11.50: The **MyPrintController** class

```csharp
// Print controller class
class MyPrintController: StandardPrintController
{
  private StatusBar statusBar;
  private string str = string.Empty;

  public MyPrintController(StatusBar sBar) : base()
  {
    statusBar = sBar;
  }
  public override void OnStartPrint
    (PrintDocument printDoc,
    PrintEventArgs peArgs)
  {
    statusBar.Text = "OnStartPrint Called";
    base.OnStartPrint(printDoc, peArgs);
  }
  public override Graphics OnStartPage
    (PrintDocument printDoc,
    PrintPageEventArgs ppea)
  {
    statusBar.Text = "OnStartPage Called";
    return base.OnStartPage(printDoc, ppea);
  }
  public override void OnEndPage
    (PrintDocument printDoc,
    PrintPageEventArgs ppeArgs)
  {
    statusBar.Text = "OnEndPage Called";
    base.OnEndPage(printDoc, ppeArgs);
  }
  public override void OnEndPrint
    (PrintDocument printDoc,
    PrintEventArgs peArgs)
  {
```

```
        statusBar.Text = "OnEndPrint Called";
        statusBar.Text = str;
        base.OnEndPrint(printDoc, peArgs);
    }
}
```

To call the `MyPrintController` class, we need to set the `Print-Controller` property of `PrintDocument` to invoke `MyPrintController`'s overridden methods. Let's write a menu click event handler and set the `PrintDocument.PrintController` property there. In Listing 11.51 we create a `PrintDocument` object, set its `DocumentName` and `Print-Controller` properties, enable the `PrintPage` event handler, and call `Print` to print the document.

LISTING 11.51: Setting the `PrintController` property of `PrintDocument`

```
private void StandardPrintControllerMenu_Click(
    object sender, System.EventArgs e)
{
    PrintDocument printDoc = new PrintDocument();
    printDoc.DocumentName =
        "PrintController Document";
    printDoc.PrintController =
        new MyPrintController(statusBar1);
    printDoc.PrintPage +=
        new PrintPageEventHandler(PrintPageHandler);
    printDoc.Print();
}
```

Listing 11.52 gives the code for the `PrintPage` event handler, which just draws some text on the printer.

LISTING 11.52: The `PrintPage` event handler

```
void PrintPageHandler(object obj,
    PrintPageEventArgs ppeArgs)
{
    Graphics g = ppeArgs.Graphics;
    SolidBrush brush =
        new SolidBrush(Color.Red);
    Font verdana20Font =
        new Font("Verdana", 20);
    g.DrawString("Print Controller Test",
        verdana20Font,
        brush, 20, 20);
}
```

FIGURE 11.30: Print controller output

If we run the application and print, we will see that the status bar displays the status of the printing process. The first event message is shown in Figure 11.30.

You can extend this functionality to write your own custom print controllers.

SUMMARY

Printing functionality in the .NET Framework library is defined in the `System.Drawing.Printing` namespace. In this chapter we discussed almost every possible aspect of printing. We began by discussing the history of printing in Microsoft Windows. Then we discussed printing-related functionality in the Microsoft .NET Framework.

After a basic introduction to printing in .NET, you learned the basic steps required to write a printing application and how printing differs from on-screen drawing. You also learned how to print simple text; graphics objects such as lines, rectangles, and circles; images; text files; and other documents.

The `PrinterSettings` class provides members to get and set printer settings. We discussed how to use this class and its members.

The .NET Framework library provides printing-related standard dialogs. You learned to use the `PrintDialog`, `PrintPreviewDialog`, and `PageSetupDialog` classes to provide a familiar Windows look and feel in your applications.

Multipage printing can be a bit tricky. You learned how to write an application with multipage printing functionality.

At the end of this chapter we discussed how to write custom printing and page setup dialogs using `PageSettings` and related classes. We also discussed the advanced custom print controller–related classes and how to use them in applications.

More Printing Samples

For more printing-related samples, C# Corner's section on printing (www.c-sharpcorner.com/printing.asp) is a good resource. There you will find many useful and handy sample code downloads, including printing a form and its contents, printing a data grid, and much more.

Using GDI+ in Web applications is a requirement for Web developers. Chapter 12 will cover the use of GDI+ to draw on the Web.

■ 12 ■
Developing GDI+ Web Applications

I N PREVIOUS CHAPTERS we covered almost every aspect of drawing using Windows Forms. This chapter will introduce you to drawing on the Web and show how GDI+ can be used to write powerful graphics Web applications. From a programmer's perspective, GDI+ treats both Windows and Web applications in the same way.

This chapter covers the following topics:

- A quick introduction to ASP.NET
- Developing your first Web application using ASP.NET in Visual Studio .NET
- Understanding the process of drawing on the Web
- Creating `Bitmap` and `Graphics` objects
- Drawing simple rectangles and other graphics objects on Web Forms
- Drawing images on Web Forms
- Setting the alpha value and quality of graphics objects
- Using linear and path gradient brushes on the Web
- Drawing line charts
- Drawing and filling pie charts

If we want to draw a rectangle on the Web, we create a `Graphics` object and call its `DrawRectangle` method. However, getting a `Graphics` object for a Web page is different from getting one for a Windows Form, as we will discuss in greater detail later.

Another restriction in Web applications is the fact that a browser can display only images. If we wanted to draw a rectangle on a Web page, the rectangle would first have to be drawn and converted into an image and then sent to the browser for display.

To draw graphics shapes in a Windows Forms application, we simply call the draw or fill method, and GDI+ draws the shape on the form, as Figure 12.1 shows.

Drawing in Web Forms involves one extra step. When you call a draw or fill method, GDI+ doesn't communicate directly with the Web Forms. Instead, it allows us to save a graphics shape as an image. Later we send the image to the browser for display. This process is shown in Figure 12.2.

After completing this chapter, you will be amazed by the power and flexibility of GDI+ and ASP.NET.

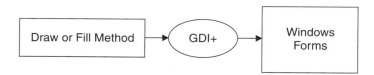

FIGURE 12.1: Drawing in Windows Forms

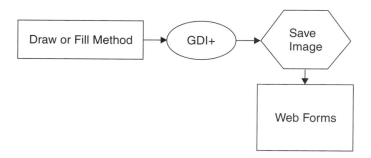

FIGURE 12.2: Drawing in Web Forms

12.1 Creating Your First ASP.NET Web Application

Discussing ASP.NET in depth is beyond the scope of this book. In this chapter we will take an "as needed" approach, discussing only the techniques we will use in our applications. If you are looking for an introductory ASP.NET book, try *Essential ASP.NET* by Fritz Onion (published by Addison-Wesley).

To understand ASP.NET and Visual Studio .NET integration, we will write a simple non-GDI+ Web application. In this application we will add some controls to a Web page: a generic button, a text box, and an **Image** button. After adding these controls, we will write code in the button click event handler that will read the contents of the text box as a file name and display the file in the **Image** button. Let's get started!

12.1.1 Creating a Web Application Project

Creating a new ASP.NET Web application using Visual Studio .NET is simple: First we create a new project by choosing **File | New | Project | Visual C# Projects** and then selecting the **ASP.NET Web Application** template. As Figure 12.3 shows, we give our application the name FirstWebApp. It resides in the `GDIPlusGuide` folder of `localhost`, which is the default Web server on our local machine.

The **Location** box displays the default option of `http://localhost` and the application name. Here `localhost` represents the default IIS server running on our local machine. The default virtual directory for `localhost` is `C:\Inetpub\wwwroot`.

> **■ NOTE**
> If you are using a remote server for your development, you'll need to provide your server name instead of `localhost`. You can either create the project in the root of the server or create a new folder.

Clicking the **OK** button creates a new directory, `FirstWebApp`, in the server's virtual directory. It also creates a new Web application and sends us to the default `WebForm1.aspx` page (see Figure 12.4).

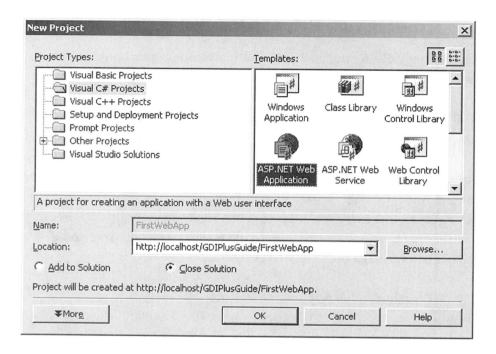

FIGURE 12.3: The FirstWebApp project

From here we can edit our page's HTML. Two modes are available: **Design** and **HTML** (see the bottom left corner of Figure 12.4). We click the **HTML** button to edit the code, as shown in Figure 12.5.

The HTML view shows us the HTML code of a page, its controls, and its control properties. The HTML editor also lets us edit the HTML manually. (Although we can edit the code of a page manually in HTML view, we will not need to do that for the examples in this book.)

If we switch back to the design mode and right-click on the page, we see several options: **View HTML Source**, **Build Style**, **View in Browser**, **View Code**, **Synchronize Document Outline**, and so on.

We can set the properties of a page by selecting **Properties** from the context menu (which we bring up with a right mouse-click). The **Properties** menu opens the **DOCUMENT Property Pages** window (see Figure 12.6). Three tabs are available in this window: **General**, **Color and Margins**, and **Keywords**. Most of the properties are self-explanatory. The **General** tab

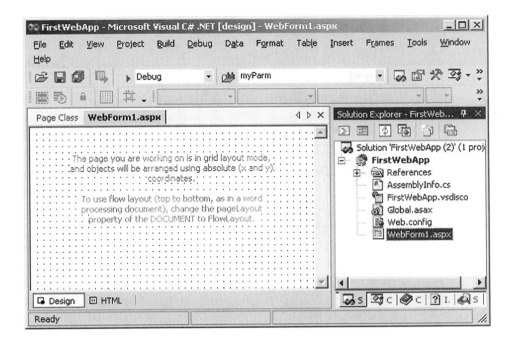

FIGURE 12.4: The default `WebForm1.aspx` page

FIGURE 12.5: The HTML view of `WebForm1.aspx`

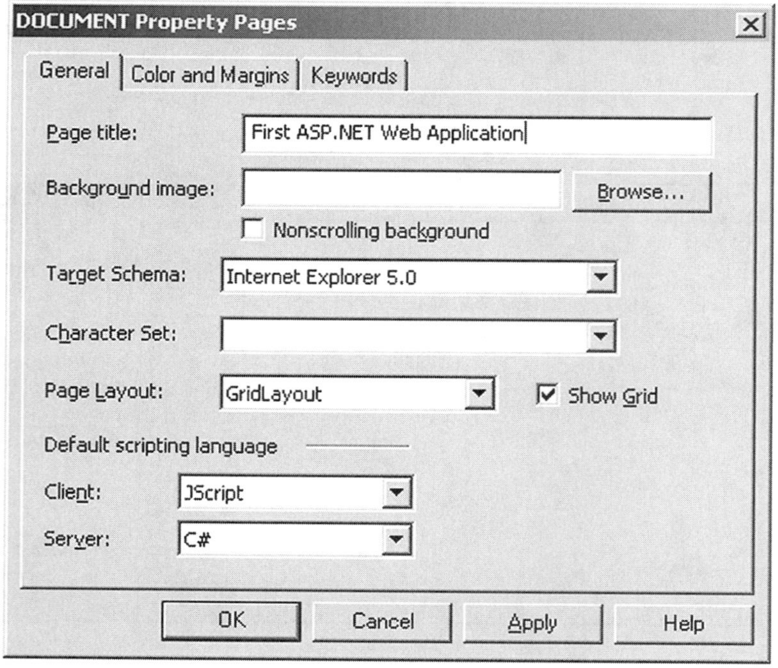

FIGURE 12.6: An ASP.NET document's page properties

contains page title, background image, target schema, character set, page layout, and client and server language properties.

The **Page Layout** property has two options: **GridLayout** and **FlowLayout**. We use **GridLayout** when we want to drop controls to the page and reposition them. If we want to add text to the page, we must set the page layout to **FlowLayout**. After we set the **Page Layout** property to **FlowLayout**, the editor works as a text editor.

12.1.2 Adding Web Controls to a Web Form

Visual Studio .NET provides a Web Forms control toolbox that's similar to the Windows control toolbox. We can open the toolbox by selecting the **View | Toolbox** main menu item. The **Web Forms** category of the toolbox contains the server-side controls (controls available on the server, for which all processing is done on the server). When a browser requests a control, ASP.NET converts the request into HTML and sends it to the browser. The

HTML category contains HTML controls. HTML controls are simple HTML tags with all processing done on the client side. As a result, HTML controls are often faster than server-side controls.

Let's switch the page back to the **Design** and **GridLayout** mode and add a button, a text box, and an `Image` control to the page by dragging these controls from the Web Forms toolbox to `WebForm1.aspx`. We will use the **View Image** button to view an image. The `ImageUrl` property of the **View Image** button represents the image that this control will view.

The page should now look like Figure 12.7 (after you position your controls). As the figure shows, we change the button's text to "View Image" by right-clicking on the **Properties** menu item, which launches the **Properties** window.

12.1.3 **Writing Code on the Button Click Event Handler**

The last step of this tutorial is to add an event handler for the button click event, which will set the `ImageUrl` property of the **Image** button. This is similar to adding a control event in a Windows Forms application. You can double-click on the button to add a button click event handler.

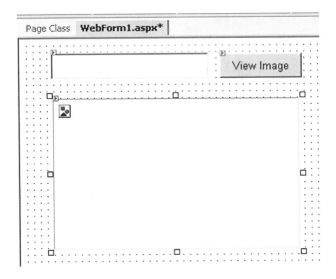

FIGURE 12.7: The `WebForm1.aspx` design mode after the addition of Web Forms controls

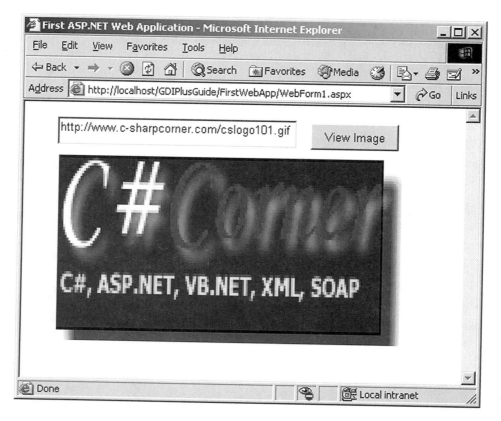

FIGURE 12.8: Viewing an image in an **Image** control

Double-clicking on the button adds a `Button1_Click` method to the `WebForm1.aspx.cs` class, which hosts code for the page controls and events. Now we write a line of code that sets the `ImageUrl` property of the `Image` control as the text of the `TextBox` control. The button click event handler code is given in Listing 12.1.

LISTING 12.1: The button click event handler

```
private void Button1_Click(object sender,
System.EventArgs e)
{
Image1.ImageUrl = TextBox1.Text;
}
```

Now compile and run the project. In the text box we type "http://www.c-sharpcorner.com/cslogo101.gif" (or any valid image URL) as the URL name and click the **View Image** button. The output of the program looks like Figure 12.8.

Now that we have seen how to create a simple Web application using Visual Studio .NET and ASP.NET, in the next section we will move on to GDI+ and show how to use GDI+ to write graphics Web applications.

12.2 Your First Graphics Web Application

Now it's time to use GDI+ in Web applications. First we'll write some code, and then we'll discuss how GDI+ Web applications work.

In this application we will draw a few simple graphics objects, including lines and rectangles. First we create a Web Application using Visual Studio .NET. After creating a Web application, we need to add a GDI+-related namespace to the project. We import namespaces as follows:

```
using System.Drawing;
using System.Drawing.Drawing2D;
using System.Drawing.Imaging;
```

> ■ **NOTE**
>
> See Chapter 1 to learn more about GDI+ namespaces and classes. If you use Visual Studio .NET to create your Web application, the wizard will add `System` and `System.Drawing` namespace references automatically.

Now we add code to draw graphics objects. Listing 12.2 draws two lines and a rectangle. You can write the code on the page-load event handler or on a button click event handler.

LISTING 12.2: Drawing simple graphics objects on the Web

```
private void Page_Load(object sender,
    System.EventArgs e)
  {
```

continues

```
// Create pens and brushes
Pen redPen = new Pen(Color.Red, 3);
HatchBrush brush =
 new HatchBrush(HatchStyle.Cross,
 Color.Red, Color.Yellow);
// Create a Bitmap object
Bitmap curBitmap = new Bitmap(200, 200);
// Create a Graphics object from Bitmap
Graphics g = Graphics.FromImage(curBitmap);
// Draw and fill rectangles
g.FillRectangle(brush, 50, 50, 100, 100);
g.DrawLine(Pens.WhiteSmoke, 10, 10, 180, 10);
g.DrawLine(Pens.White, 10, 10, 10, 180);
// Save the Bitmap object and send response to the
// browser
curBitmap.Save(Response.OutputStream,
 ImageFormat.Jpeg);
// Dispose of Graphics and Bitmap objects
curBitmap.Dispose();
 g.Dispose();
  }
```

We will discuss this code in more detail in the following section. If you are using a text editor to write your applications, you can write the code given in Listing 12.3.

LISTING 12.3: Using a text editor to draw simple graphics

```
<%@ Import Namespace="System" %>
<%@ Import Namespace="System.Drawing" %>
<%@ Import Namespace="System.Drawing.Drawing2D" %>
<%@ Import Namespace="System.Drawing.Imaging" %>

<script language="C#" runat="server">

void Page_Load(Object sender, EventArgs e)
{
Pen redPen = new Pen(Color.Red, 3);
HatchBrush brush = new HatchBrush(HatchStyle.Cross,
Color.Red, Color.Yellow);
Bitmap curBitmap = new Bitmap(200, 200);
Graphics g = Graphics.FromImage(curBitmap);
g.FillRectangle(brush, 50, 50, 100, 100);
g.DrawLine(Pens.WhiteSmoke, 10, 10, 180, 10);
g.DrawLine(Pens.White, 10, 10, 10, 180);
curBitmap.Save(Response.OutputStream,
 ImageFormat.Jpeg);
g.Dispose();
}
</script>
```

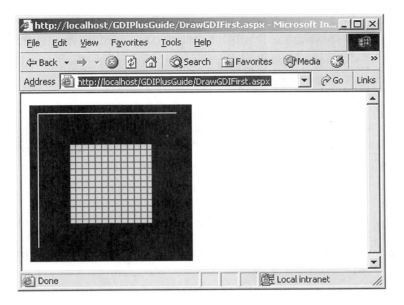

FIGURE 12.9: Drawing simple graphics objects on the Web

Now when we run our application, the output generated by Listing 12.2 or 12.3 should look like Figure 12.9.

12.2.1 How Does It Work?

Let's break down the code shown in Listings 12.2 and 12.3. We begin by importing GDI+-related namespaces in the application: `System`, `System.Drawing`, `System.Drawing.Drawing2D`, and `System.Drawing.Drawing.Imaging`. If we were using Visual Studio .NET, we would simply use the `using` directive followed by the namespace name.

Next we have a `Page_Load` event, which is executed when a Web page is loaded. We create a pen and brush using the `Pen` and `HatchBrush` classes.

```
Pen redPen = new Pen(Color.Red, 3);
HatchBrush brush = new HatchBrush(HatchStyle.Cross,
Color.Red, Color.Yellow);
```

One important limitation of Web applications is Web browser capability. A Web browser can display only certain objects. For example, all graphics objects in a Web browser will be displayed as images. So before a Web browser can display graphics objects, we need to convert them into images that can be displayed by the browser. Our next step, then, is to create a `Bitmap` object. The following line creates a 200×200 `Bitmap` object.

```
Bitmap curBitmap = new Bitmap(200, 200);
```

You already know that the `Graphics` object functions as a canvas and provides members to draw lines, shapes, and images. Now we need to create a `Graphics` object from the bitmap:

```
Graphics g = Graphics.FromImage(curBitmap);
```

Once we have a `Graphics` object, we can draw shapes, lines, and images. In the following code we use the `DrawLine` and `FillRectangle` methods to draw lines and a filled rectangle:

```
g.FillRectangle(brush, 50, 50, 100, 100);
g.DrawLine(Pens.WhiteSmoke, 10, 10, 180, 10);
g.DrawLine(Pens.White, 10, 10, 10, 180);
```

If you don't know how draw and fill methods work, you may want to look again at Chapter 3.

We're almost done. So far we have created `Bitmap` and `Graphics` objects, and we have drawn lines and a rectangle. Because a Web browser can display only images (not pixels), we need to convert the bitmap into an image. The `Save` method of the `Bitmap` object does the trick for us. The following line is responsible for rendering a bitmap and sending it to the browser:

```
curBitmap.Save(Response.OutputStream,
   ImageFormat.Jpeg);
```

Finally, we dispose of the `Bitmap` and `Graphics` objects:

```
curBitmap.Dispose();
g.Dispose();
```

12.2.2 **Understanding the** Save **Method**

The Bitmap class is inherited from the Image class, which defines the Save method. This method saves an image to the specified Stream object in the specified format. For example, in our code the Save method takes the following two arguments: Response.OutputStream and ImageFormat:

```
curBitmap.Save(Response.OutputStream,
  ImageFormat.Jpeg);
```

The Response property of the Page class returns the HttpResponse object associated with the page, which allows us to send HTTP response data to the client and contains information about the response. The OutputStream property of HttpResponse enables binary output to the outgoing HTTP content body. In other words, Page.Response.OutputStream sends the images to the browser in a compatible format. The second parameter is of ImageFormat enumeration type and specifies the format of the image. ImageFormat is discussed in more detail in Chapter 7 (see Table 7.4).

The Save method also allows us to save an image on a local physical hard drive. The following code saves the bitmap on the C:\\ drive.

```
curBitmap.Save("C:\\TempImg.gif",
  ImageFormat.Jpeg);
```

12.3 **Drawing Simple Graphics**

As we discussed in the previous section, from the programming perspective, drawing on the Web is the same as drawing in Windows Forms, except for a few small differences. Drawing on the Web is often called "drawing on the fly" (or "graphics on the fly"). The code in Listing 12.4 draws various graphics objects, including lines, text, rectangles, and an ellipse. We create various pens, brushes, and a 300×300 bitmap. Then we create a Graphics object from this bitmap by calling Graphics.FromImage. Once we have a Graphics object, we can call its methods to draw and fill graphics shapes.

After creating the Graphics object, we set its smoothing mode to AntiAlias, create font and size objects, and call the DrawString, DrawLine, and `DrawEllipse` methods to draw text, lines, and an ellipse, respectively. At this point the bitmap we created contains these objects. The next step is to call the `Save` method and send the image to the browser, which we do with the `Bitmap.Save` method. Finally, we call the `Dispose` method to dispose of various objects.

LISTING 12.4: Drawing graphics objects on the fly

```
// Construct brush and pens
Pen redPen = new Pen(Color.Red, 3);
HatchBrush brush =
 new HatchBrush(HatchStyle.Cross,
 Color.Yellow, Color.Green);
Pen hatchPen = new Pen(brush, 2);
Pen bluePen = new Pen(Color.Blue, 3);
Bitmap curBitmap = new Bitmap(300, 200);
Graphics g = Graphics.FromImage(curBitmap);
g.SmoothingMode = SmoothingMode.AntiAlias;
string testString =
 "Hello GDI+ On the Web";
Font verdana14 = new Font("Verdana", 14);
Font tahoma18 = new Font("Tahoma", 18);
int nChars;
int nLines;
// Call MeasureString to measure a string
SizeF sz = g.MeasureString(testString, verdana14);
string stringDetails =
  "Height: "+sz.Height.ToString()
 + ", Width: "+sz.Width.ToString();
g.DrawString(testString, verdana14,
 Brushes.Wheat, new PointF(40, 70));
g.DrawRectangle(new Pen(Color.Red, 2),
 40.0F, 70.0F, sz.Width, sz.Height);
sz = g.MeasureString("Ellipse", tahoma18,
 new SizeF(0.0F, 100.0F),
 new StringFormat(),
 out nChars, out nLines);
stringDetails =
 "Height: "+sz.Height.ToString()
 + ", Width: "+sz.Width.ToString()
 + ", Lines: "+nLines.ToString()
 + ", Chars: "+nChars.ToString();
 // Draw lines
g.DrawLine(Pens.WhiteSmoke, 10, 20, 180, 20);
g.DrawLine(Pens.White, 20, 10, 20, 180);
// Fill ellipse
g.FillEllipse(brush, 120, 100, 100, 100);
// Draw string
```

```
g.DrawString("Ellipse", tahoma18,
 Brushes.Beige, new PointF(40, 20));
// Draw ellipse
g.DrawEllipse( new Pen(Color.Yellow, 3),
 40, 20, sz.Width, sz.Height);
// Send output to the browser and
// dispose of objects
curBitmap.Save(this.Response.OutputStream,
 ImageFormat.Jpeg);
g.Dispose();
```

For all practical purposes, Listing 12.4 could be a Windows Forms application. The only new code required creates a `Bitmap` object and calls its `Save` method to send output to the browser. We use the `DrawString` method to draw text, the `DrawLine` method to draw lines, and the `DrawRectangle` method to draw rectangles—just as in any other GDI+ application.

Figure 12.10 shows the output from Listing 12.4. The program draws lines, ellipses, and text.

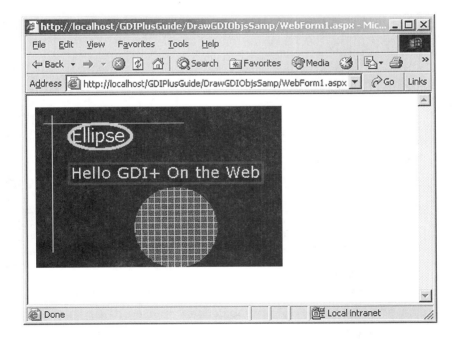

FIGURE 12.10: Drawing various graphics objects

> **NOTE**
>
> For more on the `Graphics` class and its fill and draw methods, see Chapter 3.

12.4 Drawing Images on the Web

The process of drawing images on the Web is slightly different from that of drawing images on Windows Forms. In Windows Forms we create a `Bitmap` object and call the `Graphics.DrawImage` method. Drawing on the Web requires a `Graphics` object. The `Bitmap.Save` method takes care of the rest, as discussed earlier.

To test this, let's create a Web application using Visual Studio .NET and add the code given in Listing 12.5 on the page-load event. This code views an image on the browser. First we create a `Bitmap` object from an image, then we create a `Graphics` object from the image, and then we call the `Save` method of `Bitmap`.

LISTING 12.5: Drawing images on the Web

```
// Create a Bitmap object from a file
Bitmap curBitmap =
 new Bitmap("d:\\white_salvia.jpg");
// Create a Graphics object from Bitmap
Graphics g = Graphics.FromImage(curBitmap);
// Send output to the browser
curBitmap.Save(this.Response.OutputStream,
 ImageFormat.Jpeg);
// Dispose of object
g.Dispose();
```

Notice that we didn't even need to call the `DrawImage` method. Figure 12.11 shows the output from Listing 12.5.

12.4.1 Setting Image Quality

As we discussed in Chapter 3, the `SmoothingMode` and `TextRendering-Hint` properties of the `Graphics` object can be used to set the quality of images and text, respectively. GDI+ cannot draw text directly into a Web

FIGURE 12.11: Drawing an image

application. Like lines, curves, and other graphics shapes, text must also be rendered as an image for display in the browser. All graphics lines, curves, shapes, text, and images are first converted to an image and directed to a browser, so only the SmoothingMode property will be applicable. SmoothingMode has five members: AntiAlias, Default, HighQuality, HighSpeed, and None. The following code snippet sets the smoothing mode of the Graphics object:

```
// Set modes
g.SmoothingMode = SmoothingMode.AntiAlias;
```

12.4.2 **Using** `LinearGardientBrush` **and** `PathGradientBrush`

You can use linear and path gradient brushes in Web applications just as we did in Chapter 4. Listing 12.6 uses LinearGradientBrush and PathGradientBrush to fill a rectangle and a path. First we create a linear gradient brush and a graphics path, and we add two ellipses to the graphics path.

Next we create a path gradient brush, which takes the path as its only parameter, and we set the `CenterColor` property of the path. Then we create `Bitmap` and `Graphics` objects and call `Graphics.FillPath` and `Graphics.FillRectangle`, which fill a path and rectangle, respectively.

As in the previous examples, finally we call the `Bitmap.Save` method and dispose of the objects.

LISTING 12.6: Using `LinearGradientBrush` and `PathGradientBrush`

```
private void Page_Load(object sender,
  System.EventArgs e)
{
 // Create a linear gradient brush
 LinearGradientBrush lgBrush =
  new LinearGradientBrush(
  new Rectangle(0, 0, 10, 10),
  Color.Yellow, Color.Blue,
 LinearGradientMode.ForwardDiagonal);
 // Create a path
 GraphicsPath path = new GraphicsPath();
 path.AddEllipse(50, 50, 150, 150);
 path.AddEllipse(10, 10, 50, 50);
 // Create a path gradient brush
 PathGradientBrush pgBrush =
  new PathGradientBrush(path);
 pgBrush.CenterColor = Color.Red;
 // Create Bitmap and Graphics objects
 Bitmap curBitmap = new Bitmap(500, 300);
 Graphics g = Graphics.FromImage(curBitmap);
 g.SmoothingMode = SmoothingMode.AntiAlias;
 g.FillPath(pgBrush, path);
 g.FillRectangle(lgBrush, 250, 20, 100, 100);
 curBitmap.Save(this.Response.OutputStream,
  ImageFormat.Jpeg);
 g.Dispose();
 }
```

Figure 12.12 shows the output from Listing 12.6.

12.4.3 Drawing Transparent Graphics Objects

The alpha component of a color represents its transparency. Alpha component values vary from 0 to 255, where 0 indicates fully transparent and 255 indicates opaque. Listing 12.7 draws a rectangle, an ellipse, and text on top of an image.

FIGURE 12.12: Using `LinearGradientBrush` and `PathGradientBrush`

LISTING 12.7: Drawing semitransparent objects

```
// Create Bitmap and Graphics objects
Bitmap curBitmap = new Bitmap("c:\\flower13.jpg");
Graphics g = Graphics.FromImage(curBitmap);
g.SmoothingMode = SmoothingMode.AntiAlias;
// Create brushes and pens with alpha values
Color redColor = Color.FromArgb(120, 0, 0, 255);
Pen alphaPen = new Pen(redColor, 10);
SolidBrush alphaBrush =
  new SolidBrush(Color.FromArgb(90, 0, 255, 0));
// Draw a rectangle, an ellipse, and text
g.DrawRectangle(alphaPen, 100, 100, 50, 100);
g.FillEllipse(alphaBrush, 50, 50, 100, 100);
g.DrawString("Alpha String",
  new Font("Tahoma", 30),
  new SolidBrush(Color.FromArgb(150, 160, 0, 0)),
  new PointF(20, 20));
curBitmap.Save(this.Response.OutputStream,
    ImageFormat.Jpeg);
g.Dispose();
```

First we create `Bitmap` and `Graphics` objects and set the `Graphics` smoothing mode. Then we create a color with transparency using the `Color.FromArgb` method, where transparency is the first parameter. Next, using the following code, we create a pen from this semitransparent color, which gives us a semitransparent pen:

```
Color redColor = Color.FromArgb(120, 0, 0, 255);
Pen alphaPen = new Pen(redColor, 10);
```

We also create a semitransparent brush by passing a semitransparent color as a parameter to `SolidBrush`, as follows:

```
SolidBrush alphaBrush =
  new SolidBrush(Color.FromArgb(90, 0, 255, 0));
```

Now to draw transparent shapes, we simply use the transparent brushes and pens. As Figure 12.13 shows, the graphics shapes are semi-transparent.

FIGURE 12.13: Drawing semitransparent objects

12.5 **Drawing a Line Chart**

Charts are useful for representing numeric data in a graphical way. There are several different types of charts, including pie, line, and bar charts. In this section we will learn how to use GDI+ and ASP.NET to draw a line chart from data entered by a user.

A **line chart** is a set of continuous lines. In the example presented in this section, we will read the size of the chart and data points and draw a chart based on the points. Our discussion will focus first on the `ChartComp` component, and then on the client application.

12.5.1 **The `ChartComp` Component**

`ChartComp` is a class that defines the functionality to add points to the chart and draw the chart. The client application (discussed in Section 12.5.2) is a Web application that calls the chart's members to add points to the chart and draw it.

The code for the `ChartComp` class is given in Listing 12.8. The constructor of the class takes the type, color, size, and a page to which this chart belongs. The overloaded `InsertPoint` method adds a point to the array of points, and the `DrawChart` method draws the points stored in the array. `DrawChart` first draws a rectangle, and then it draws points toward the *x*- and *y*-axes.

LISTING 12.8: The `ChartComp` class

```
// Chart component
class ChartComp
{
 public Bitmap curBitmap;
 public ArrayList ptsArrayList =
  new ArrayList();
 public float X0 = 0, Y0 = 0;
 public float chartX, chartY;
 public Color chartColor = Color.Gray;
 // chartType: 1=Line, 2=Pie, 3=Bar.
 // For future use only.
 public int chartType = 1;
 private int Width, Height;
 private Graphics g;
```

continues

```
private Page curPage;
struct ptStructure
{
 public float x;
 public float y;
 public Color clr;
}
// ChartComp constructor
public ChartComp(int cType, Color cColor,
 int cWidth, int cHeight, Page cPage)
{
 Width = cWidth;
 Height = cHeight;
 chartX = cWidth;
 chartY = cHeight;
 curPage = cPage;
 chartType = cType;
 chartColor = cColor;
 curBitmap = new Bitmap(Width, Height);
 g = Graphics.FromImage(curBitmap);
}
// Destructor. Disposes of objects.
~ChartComp()
{
 curBitmap.Dispose();
 g.Dispose();
}
// InsertPoint method. Adds a point
// to the array.
public void InsertPoint(int xPos,
 int yPos, Color clr)
{
 ptStructure pt;
 pt.x = xPos;
 pt.y = yPos;
 pt.clr = clr;
 // Add the point to the array
 ptsArrayList.Add(pt);
}
public void InsertPoint(int position,
 int xPos, int yPos, Color clr)
{
 ptStructure pt;
 pt.x = xPos;
 pt.y = yPos;
 pt.clr = clr;
 // Add the point to the array
 ptsArrayList.Insert(position, pt);
}
```

```
// Draw methods
public void DrawChart()
{
 int i;
 float x, y, x0, y0;
 curPage.Response.ContentType="image/jpeg";
 g.SmoothingMode = SmoothingMode.HighQuality;
 g.FillRectangle(new SolidBrush(chartColor),
  0, 0, Width, Height);
 int chWidth = Width-80;
 int chHeight = Height-80;
 g.DrawRectangle(Pens.Black,
  40, 40, chWidth, chHeight);
 g.DrawString("GDI+ Chart", new Font("arial",14),
  Brushes.Black, Width/3, 10);
 // Draw x- and y-axis line, points, positions
 for(i=0; i<=5; i++)
 {
  x = 40+(i*chWidth)/5;
  y = chHeight+40;
  string str = (X0 + (chartX*i/5)).ToString();
  g.DrawString(str, new Font("Verdana",10),
   Brushes.Blue, x-4, y+10);
  g.DrawLine(Pens.Black, x, y+2, x, y-2);
 }
 for(i=0; i<=5; i++)
 {
  x = 40;
  y = chHeight+40-(i*chHeight/5);
  string str = (Y0 + (chartY*i/5)).ToString();
  g.DrawString(str, new Font("Verdana",10),
   Brushes.Blue, 5, y-6);
  g.DrawLine(Pens.Black, x+2, y, x-2, y);
 }
 // Transform coordinates so that point (0,0)
 // is in the lower left corner
 g.RotateTransform(180);
 g.TranslateTransform(-40, 40);
 g.ScaleTransform(-1, 1);
 g.TranslateTransform(0, -(Height));
 // Draw all points from the array
 ptStructure prevPoint = new ptStructure();
 foreach(ptStructure pt in ptsArrayList)
 {
  x0 = chWidth*(prevPoint.x-X0)/chartX;
  y0 = chHeight*(prevPoint.y-Y0)/chartY;
  x = chWidth*(pt.x-X0)/chartX;
  y = chHeight*(pt.y-Y0)/chartY;
  g.DrawLine(Pens.Black, x0, y0, x, y);
```

continues

```
   g.FillEllipse(new SolidBrush(pt.clr),
    x0-5, y0-5, 10, 10);
   g.FillEllipse(new SolidBrush(pt.clr),
    x-5, y-5, 10, 10);
   prevPoint = pt;
  }
  curBitmap.Save(curPage.Response.OutputStream,
    ImageFormat.Jpeg);
 }
}
```

12.5.2 The Client Application

The client application is a Web page that is used to get input from the user. The main form of the application is shown in Figure 12.14. The user can

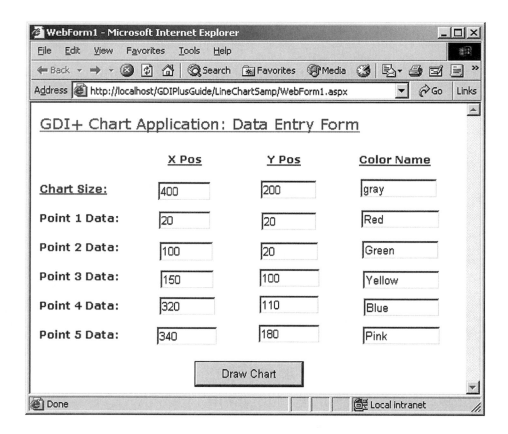

FIGURE 12.14: Entering points on a chart

enter his/her chart size, and values for five points, including the color of each one.

The **Draw Chart** button draws a line chart. Code for the **Draw Chart** button click is given in Listing 12.9, where we create an object of type `ChartComp` and call its `InsertPoint` and `DrawChart` methods. `Insert-Point` adds a point to the chart. `DrawChart` draws a line chart from the first point to the last point entered by the user.

LISTING 12.9: The Draw Chart button click event handler

```
private void Button1_Click(object sender,
  System.EventArgs e)
{
// Get the chart background color
Color clr = Color.FromName(TextBox3.Text);
// Create a ChartComp object
ChartComp chart =
 new ChartComp(1, clr, 400, 300, this.Page);
chart.X0 = 0;
chart.Y0= 0;
chart.chartX = Convert.ToInt16(TextBox1.Text);
chart.chartY = Convert.ToInt16(TextBox2.Text);
// Add points to the chart
chart.InsertPoint(Convert.ToInt16(TextBox4.Text),
 Convert.ToInt16(TextBox5.Text),
 Color.FromName(TextBox6.Text) );
chart.InsertPoint(Convert.ToInt16(TextBox7.Text),
 Convert.ToInt16(TextBox8.Text),
 Color.FromName(TextBox9.Text) );
chart.InsertPoint(Convert.ToInt16(TextBox10.Text),
 Convert.ToInt16(TextBox11.Text),
 Color.FromName(TextBox12.Text) );
chart.InsertPoint(Convert.ToInt16(TextBox13.Text),
 Convert.ToInt16(TextBox14.Text),
 Color.FromName(TextBox15.Text) );
chart.InsertPoint(Convert.ToInt16(TextBox16.Text),
 Convert.ToInt16(TextBox17.Text),
 Color.FromName(TextBox18.Text) );
// Draw chart
chart.DrawChart();
 }
```

Now if you use the data entered in Figure 12.14 and click the **Draw Chart** button, the output will look like Figure 12.15.

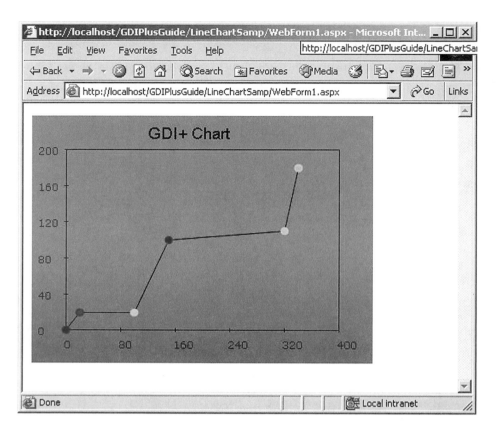

FIGURE 12.15: A line chart in ASP.NET

12.6 Drawing a Pie Chart

Do you remember the pie chart application from Chapter 3 (see Figure 3.43)? Now let's write a similar application using ASP.NET. We will provide both fill and draw options.

We create a Web Forms application using Visual Studio .NET. We add some text and two buttons to the page. The final Web page looks like Figure 12.16. The **Draw Chart** button will draw a pie chart, and the **Fill Chart** button will fill the chart with different colors.

Now we add some variables (see Listing 12.10). Instead of reading values from the user, we use hard-coded values for the valArray and clrArray arrays. The valArray array stores the different portion values of a pie

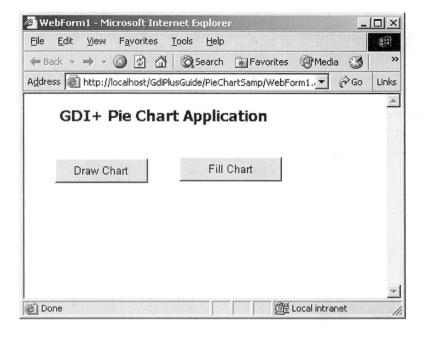

FIGURE 12.16: A pie chart–drawing application in ASP.NET

chart, and `clrArray` stores colors for these portions. If you wish, you can modify the page and add some text boxes to allow users to provide these values at runtime.

LISTING 12.10: User-defined variables

```
// User-defined variables
public Bitmap curBitmap;
private Rectangle rect =
 new Rectangle(250, 150, 200, 200);
public ArrayList sliceList = new ArrayList();
private Color curClr = Color.Black;
int[] valArray = {50, 25, 75, 100, 50};
Color[] clrArray = {Color.Red, Color.Green,
 Color.Yellow, Color.Pink, Color.Aqua};
int total = 0;
```

Now we add a method called `DrawPieChart`. It will both draw and fill the chart. The code for the `DrawPieChart` method is given in Listing 12.11.

We simply read values from the portion and color arrays, and we create SolidBrush and Pen objects, depending on which button is clicked. We create a Bitmap object and set the smoothing mode of the page to Anti-Alias. We also initialize the values of the angle and sweep variables.

We also have a Boolean variable called flMode. If flMode is true, the DrawPieChart method calls FillPie to fill the pie chart; otherwise it calls DrawPie, which draws only the boundaries of the chart. In the end, we save the bitmap, send it to the browser, and dispose of the objects.

LISTING 12.11: The **DrawPieChart** method

```
private void DrawPieChart(bool flMode)
{
// Create Bitmap and Graphics objects
Bitmap curBitmap = new Bitmap(500, 300);
Graphics g = Graphics.FromImage(curBitmap);
g.SmoothingMode = SmoothingMode.AntiAlias;
float angle = 0;
float sweep = 0;
// Total
for (int i=0; i<valArray.Length; i++)
{
 total += valArray[i];
}
// Read color and value from array
// and calculate sweep
for (int i=0; i<valArray.Length; i++)
{
 int val = valArray[i];
 Color clr = clrArray[i];
 sweep = 360f * val / total;
 // If fill mode, fill pie
 if(flMode)
 {
   SolidBrush brush = new SolidBrush(clr);
   g.FillPie(brush, 20.0F, 20.0F, 200,
   200, angle, sweep);
 }
 else // If draw mode, draw pie
 {
   Pen pn = new Pen(clr, 2);
   g.DrawPie(pn, 20.0F, 20.0F, 200,
    200, angle, sweep);
 }
 angle += sweep;
}
```

```
// Send output to the browser
curBitmap.Save(this.Response.OutputStream,
 ImageFormat.Jpeg);
// Dispose of objects
curBitmap.Dispose();
g.Dispose();
 }
```

The **Draw Chart** button click generates the output shown in Figure 12.17 and the **Fill Chart** button click fills in the chart, with output as shown in Figure 12.18.

We call the `DrawPieChart` method from our **Draw Chart** and **Fill Chart** buttons with a single argument—`false` or `true`, respectively—as shown in Listing 12.12.

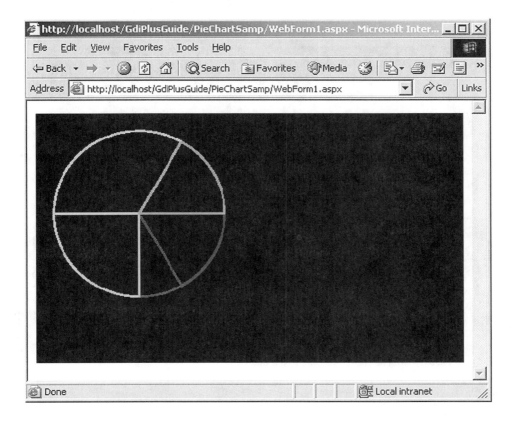

FIGURE 12.17: The Draw Chart button click in action

LISTING 12.12: The Draw Chart and Fill Chart button click handlers

```
private void DrawChart_Click(object sender,
  System.EventArgs e)
{
 DrawPieChart(false);
}
private void FillChart_Click(object sender,
 System.EventArgs e)
{
  DrawPieChart(true);
}
```

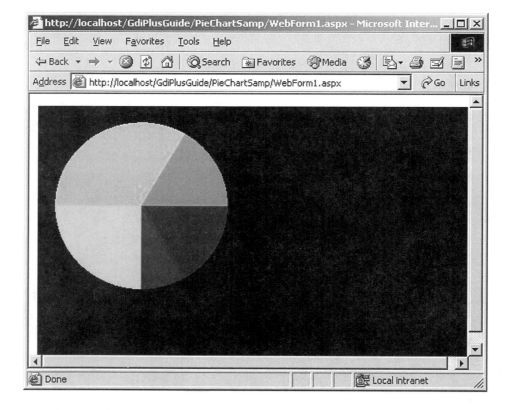

FIGURE 12.18: The Fill Chart button click in action

SUMMARY

In this chapter we discussed how to use GDI+ drawing functionality in Web applications. We started by discussing the basic process of drawing graphics shapes and images on the Web using ASP.NET and GDI+. After that we discussed the drawing process for Web applications, and how it differs from the Windows drawing process.

Next we introduced ASP.NET and how to write a simple ASP.NET application using a text editor or Visual Studio .NET. Then we discussed how to draw simple graphics objects such as lines, curves, rectangles, and images on the Web. After drawing simple graphics objects, you learned how to set the quality and transparency of images.

At the end of the chapter we saw line chart and pie chart applications, as real-world examples of GDI+ on the Web.

Performance is a major factor that developers worry about when dealing with graphics. Chapter 13 is dedicated to GDI+ performance. In it, we will discuss how to optimize GDI+ applications for the best performance.

▪ 13 ▪
GDI+ Best Practices and Performance Techniques

I T MUST BE said that code optimization skill and knowledge of performance techniques are best acquired from the shared experiences of other developers. With the ever expanding capabilities of Internet communication, the best resources are online forums, newsgroups, and sites dedicated to code sharing. A recommended resource for topics covered in this chapter (and indeed throughout this book) is the C# Corner site (http://www.c-sharpcorner.com).

Let's start with an introduction of the basic architecture of drawing (rendering or painting) within Windows Forms using GDI+. By the end of this chapter, you will be armed with GDI+ tips and tricks that make a significant difference in the efficiency of many performance-oriented graphics applications. Note, however, that these tips and tricks may not be applicable for Web applications.

Here are the topics that we will discuss in this chapter:

- Understanding the drawing and rendering process
- How to write paint event handlers for Windows Forms and controls
- Disposing of graphics objects
- The `OnPaintBackground` method
- Drawing performance and the role of variables' scope and type

- Double buffering
- The `SetStyle` method
- Generic tips and tricks for quality and performance

13.1 Understanding the Rendering Process

In previous chapters of this book, you learned how to draw graphics shapes, curves, and images. In all of these cases, the `Graphics` object is responsible for the drawing. When we're drawing graphics objects from within a menu or button click event handler, a call to the `Invalidate` method becomes imperative. If we don't call this method, the form will not paint itself, but if we write the same code on a form's `OnPaint` or paint event handler, there is no need to invalidate the form. In this section we will find out why that's so.

13.1.1 Understanding the Paint Event

Paint event functionality is defined in the `System.Windows.Forms.Control` class, which is the base class for Windows Forms controls such as `Label`, `ListBox`, `DataGrid`, and `TreeView`. A paint event is fired when a control is redrawn. The `Form` class itself is inherited from the `Control` class. Figure 13.1 shows the `Form` class hierarchy.

The `PaintEventArgs` class provides data for the paint event. It provides two read-only properties: `ClipRectangle` and `Graphics`. `ClipRectangle` indicates the rectangle in which to paint, and the `Graphics` property indicates the `Graphics` object associated with the paint event of a particular control (including the form itself). Always be careful when you're dealing with the paint event because it is unpredictable and called automatically.

The `Control` class also provides `OnPaint` methods, which can be overridden in the derived classes to fire the paint event. The signature of the `OnPaint` method is defined as follows:

```
protected virtual void OnPaint( PaintEventArgs e);
```

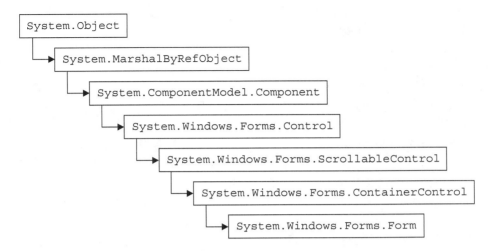

FIGURE 13.1: The Form class hierarchy

As this definition shows, OnPaint takes a PaintEventArgs object as its only argument. The Graphics property of PaintEventArgs is used to get the Graphics object associated with a control—including the form.

13.1.2 Adding a Paint Event Handler to a Form

Adding a paint event handler for any Control-derived class is pretty simple. We write an event handler that has two parameters, of types object and PaintEventArgs:

```
private void MyPaintEventHandler(object sender,
System.Windows.Forms.PaintEventArgs args)
{
}
```

We can give the event handler whatever name we want. After implementing this event handler, we use the parameter args (which is a PaintEventArgs object) to get the Graphics object for the control. The following code delegates the event handler for the Paint event:

```
this.Paint +=
new System.Windows.Forms.PaintEventHandler
(this.MyPaintEventHandler);
```

The following code gives the paint event handler for a form:

```
private void MyPaintEventHandler(object sender,
System.Windows.Forms.PaintEventArgs args)
{
  // Write your code here
}
```

Now we can use the `PaintEventArgs` object to get the `Graphics` object associated with the form and use the `Graphics` object's methods and properties to draw and fill lines, curves, shapes, text, and images. Let's draw a rectangle, an ellipse, and some text on the form, as shown in Listing 13.1.

LISTING 13.1: Using the paint event handler to draw

```
private void MyPaintEventHandler(object sender,
  System.Windows.Forms.PaintEventArgs args)
{
  // Drawing a rectangle
  args.Graphics.DrawRectangle(
    new Pen(Color.Blue, 3),
    new Rectangle(10, 10, 50, 50));
  // Drawing an ellipse
  args.Graphics.FillEllipse(
    Brushes.Red,
    new Rectangle(60, 60, 100, 100));
  // Drawing text
  args.Graphics.DrawString(
  "Text",
  new Font("Verdana", 14),
  new SolidBrush(Color.Green), 200, 200) ;
}
```

Figure 13.2 shows the output from Listing 13.1. Now if the form is covered by another window and the focus returns to the form, the code on the paint event handler will repaint the form.

13.1.3 Adding a Paint Event Handler to Windows Controls

As mentioned earlier, the paint event handler can be added to any Windows control that is inherited from the `Control` class, such as `Button`, `ListBox`, or `DataGrid`. In other words, each Windows control can have a paint event handler and a `Graphics` object, which represents the control as

FIGURE 13.2: Drawing on a form

a drawing canvas. That means we can use a button or a list box as a drawing canvas.

Let's add `DataGrid` and `Button` controls to a form. We will use the button and the data grid as our drawing canvases. Listing 13.2 adds the paint event methods of our `Button1` and `DataGrid1` controls.

LISTING 13.2: Adding a paint event handler for Windows controls

```
// Adding a button's Paint event handler
this.button1.Paint +=
  new System.Windows.Forms.PaintEventHandler
  (this.TheButtonPaintEventHandler);
// Adding a data grid's Paint event handler
this.dataGrid1.Paint +=
  new System.Windows.Forms.PaintEventHandler
  (this.TheDataGridPaintEventHandler);
```

Listing 13.3 gives the code for the `Button` and `DataGrid` paint event handlers. This code is useful when we need to draw graphics shapes on a control itself. For example, a column of a data grid can be used to display images or graphics shapes. In our example we draw an ellipse on these controls, instead of drawing on a form. The `PaintEventArgs.Graphics` object represents the `Graphics` object associated with a particular control. Once you have the `Graphics` object of a control, you are free to call its draw and fill methods.

LISTING 13.3: Drawing on Windows controls

```
private void TheButtonPaintEventHandler(object sender,
  System.Windows.Forms.PaintEventArgs btnArgs)
{
  btnArgs.Graphics.FillEllipse(
    Brushes.Blue,
    10, 10, 100, 100);
}
private void TheDataGridPaintEventHandler(object sender,
  System.Windows.Forms.PaintEventArgs dtGridArgs)
{
  dtGridArgs.Graphics.FillEllipse(
    Brushes.Blue,
    10, 10, 100, 100);
}
```

Figure 13.3 shows the output of Listing 13.3. As you can see, a button or a data grid can function as a drawing canvas. The top left-hand corner of a control is the (0, 0) coordinate of the canvas associated with that control.

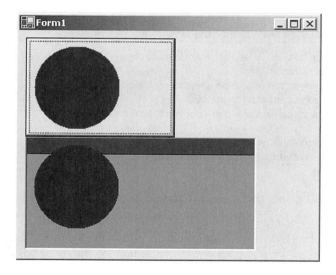

FIGURE 13.3: Drawing on Windows controls

At this stage it is worth pointing out another big advantage that GDI+ has over GDI: the flexibility to have a `Graphics` object associated with a control.

13.1.4 Overriding the `OnPaint` Method of a Form

We have already seen this in previous chapters. We can override the `OnPaint` method by defining it as follows:

```
protected override  void OnPaint( PaintEventArgs args)
{
// Add your drawing code here
}
```

Then we can use the `Graphics` property of `PaintEventArgs` to draw lines, shapes, text, and images. Listing 13.4 draws a few graphics shapes and text on our form's `OnPaint` method. To test this code, create a Windows application and add the code to it.

LISTING 13.4: Using `OnPaint` to draw

```
protected override void OnPaint( PaintEventArgs args )
{
  // Get the Graphics object from
  // PaintEventArgs
  Graphics g = args.Graphics;
  // Draw rectangle
  g.DrawRectangle(
    new Pen(Color.Blue, 3),
    new Rectangle(10, 10, 50, 50));
  // Fill ellipse
  g.FillEllipse(
    Brushes.Red,
    new Rectangle(60, 60, 100, 100));
  // Draw text
  g.DrawString("Text",
    new Font("Verdana", 14),
    new SolidBrush(Color.Green),
    200, 200) ;
}
```

13.1.5 Using Visual Studio .NET to Add the Paint Event Handler

If you are using Visual Studio .NET, the easiest way to add a paint event handler is to use the **Properties** windows of a form or control and add a paint event handler. We have seen examples of this in previous chapters.

13.1.6 Disposing of Graphics Objects

It is usually good programming practice to dispose of objects when you're finished using them. But it may not *always* be the best practice. A Graphics object must always be disposed of if it was created via the CreateGraphics method or other "CreateFrom" methods. If we use a Graphics object on a paint event or the OnPaint method from the PaintEventArgs.Graphics property, we do not have to dispose of it.

> ### ■ NOTE
> Do not dispose of Graphics objects associated with Windows controls such as Button, ListBox, or DataGrid.

If you create objects such as pens and brushes, always dispose of them. Although it is acceptable practice to rely on the garbage collector, doing so may often be at the expense of application performance. Garbage collection can be a costly affair because the garbage collector checks the memory for objects that haven't been disposed of, and this process absorbs processor time. However, the Dispose method of an object tells the garbage collector that the object is finished and ready to be disposed of. Calling the Dispose method eliminates the need to have the garbage collector check memory, and thus saves processor time.

In Web pages, it is always good practice to dispose of objects as soon as they are done being used.

13.1.7 The OnPaintBackground Method

The OnPaintBackground method paints the background of a control. This method is usually overridden in the derived classes to handle the event without attaching a delegate. Calling the OnPaintBackground method calls OnPaintBackground of the base class automatically, so we do not need to call it explicitly.

13.1.8 Scope and Type of Variables and Performance

One of the best programming practices is the efficient use of variables and their scope. Before adding a new variable to a program, think for a second and ask yourself, "Do I *really* need this variable?" If you need a variable, do you really need it right now? The scope of variables and use of complex calculations can easily degrade the performance of your applications. Using global scope for pens, brushes, paths, and other objects may be useful instead of defining variables in the `OnPaint` or `OnPaintBackground` methods.

Let's look at a practical example: Listing 13.5 is written on a form's paint event handler, which creates pens and brushes, and draws rectangles and polygons.

LISTING 13.5: Variables defined in the form's paint event handler

```
private void Form1_Paint(object sender,
  System.Windows.Forms.PaintEventArgs e)
{
  // Create brushes and pens
  HatchBrush hatchBrush =
    new HatchBrush(HatchStyle.HorizontalBrick,
    Color.Red, Color.Blue);
  Pen redPen = new Pen(Color.Red, 2);
  Pen hatchPen = new Pen(hatchBrush, 4);
  SolidBrush brush = new SolidBrush(Color.Green);
  // Create points for curve
  PointF p1 = new PointF(40.0F, 50.0F);
  PointF p2 = new PointF(60.0F, 70.0F);
  PointF p3 = new PointF(80.0F, 34.0F);
  PointF p4 = new PointF(120.0F, 180.0F);
  PointF p5 = new PointF(200.0F, 150.0F);
  PointF[] ptsArray ={ p1, p2, p3, p4, p5 };
  float x = 5.0F, y = 5.0F;
  float width =
    this.ClientRectangle.Width - 100;
  float height =
    this.ClientRectangle.Height - 100;

  Point pt1 = new Point(40, 30);
  Point pt2 = new Point(80, 100);
  Color [] lnColors = {Color.Black, Color.Red};
  LinearGradientBrush lgBrush =
    new LinearGradientBrush
    (pt1, pt2, Color.Red, Color.Green);
  lgBrush.LinearColors = lnColors;
  lgBrush.GammaCorrection = true;

  // Draw objects
```

continues

```
e.Graphics.DrawPolygon(redPen, ptsArray);
e.Graphics.DrawRectangle(hatchPen,
  x, y, width, height);
e.Graphics.FillRectangle(lgBrush,
  200, 200, 200, 200);
// Dispose of objects
lgBrush.Dispose();
brush.Dispose();
hatchPen.Dispose();
redPen.Dispose();
hatchBrush.Dispose();
}
```

In this example we define many variables, all of local scope. Throughout the application, the `redPen`, `hatchBrush`, `hatchPen`, `brush`, and other variables remain the same. Programmatically, it doesn't matter whether we define these variables locally or globally; the choice depends entirely on the application. It may be better to have variables defined with a global scope. If you repaint the form frequently, defining these variables globally may improve performance because time will not be wasted on re-creating the objects for each pass. On the other hand, defining objects globally may consume more resources (memory).

It is also good to avoid lengthy calculations in frequently called routines. Here's an example: Listing 13.6 draws a line in a loop. As you can see, `int x` and `int y` are defined inside the loop.

LISTING 13.6: Defining variables inside a loop

```
for (int i = 0; i < 10000; i++)
{
 Pen bluePen = new Pen(Color.Blue);
 int x = 100;
 int y = 100;
 g.DrawLine(bluePen, 0, 0, x, y);
}
```

We can easily replace the code in Listing 13.6 with Listing 13.7, which is more efficient. If a code statement does the same thing every time a control reaches it inside a loop, it is a good idea to move that statement outside the loop to save processing cycles.

LISTING 13.7: Defining variables outside a loop

```
Pen bluePen = new Pen(Color.Blue);
int x = 100;
int y = 100;
for (int i = 0; i < 10000; i++)
{
  g.DrawLine(bluePen, 0, 0, x, y);
}
```

Sometimes using a floating point data type instead of an integer may affect the quality of a drawing, even though floating point data is costly in terms of resources.

A well-designed and well-coded application also plays a vital role in performance. For example, replacing multiple if statements with a single case statement may improve performance.

13.2 Double Buffering and Flicker-Free Drawing

Do you remember the Web drawing method in Chapter 12? Drawing on the Web works differently from drawing in Windows Forms. On the Web we have many limitations, one of which is no pixelwise drawing support in the Web browser. So our approach in Chapter 12 was to convert our graphics objects into a temporary bitmap image and view the image in a Web browser.

Double buffering is a similar concept. You may have seen one of the frequently asked questions on GDI+ discussion forums: "How do we create flicker-free drawings"? The **double buffering** technique is used to provide faster, smoother drawings by reducing flicker. In this technique, all objects are drawn on an off-screen canvas with the help of a temporary image and a Graphics object. The image is then copied to the control. If the drawing operation is small and includes drawing only simple objects such as rectangles or lines, there is no need for double buffering (it may even degrade performance). If there are many calculations or drawn elements, performance and appearance may be greatly improved through the use of double buffering.

To prove the point, let's write an example. Listing 13.8 gives the code for a drawing method that draws several lines.

LISTING 13.8: The **DrawLines** method

```
private void DrawLines(Graphics g)
{
  float width = ClientRectangle.Width;
  float height = ClientRectangle.Height;
  float partX = width / 1000;
  float partY = height / 1000;
  for (int i = 0; i < 1000; i++)
  {
    g.DrawLine(Pens.Blue,
      0, height - (partY * i),
      partX * i, 0);
    g.DrawLine(Pens.Green,
      0,
      height - (partY * i),
      (width) - partX * i,
      0);
    g.DrawLine(Pens.Red, 0,
      partY * i,
      (width) - partX * i,
      0);
  }
}
```

To test our application, we will call it from a button click. The code for a button click event handler is given in Listing 13.9.

LISTING 13.9: Calling the **DrawLines** method

```
// Create a Graphics object for "this"
Graphics g = this.CreateGraphics();
g.Clear(this.BackColor);
// Draw lines
DrawLines(g);
// Dispose of object
g.Dispose();
```

Figure 13.4 shows the output from Listing 13.9.

Now let's draw the same lines using a `Bitmap` object. We create a temporary `Graphics` object from a temporary image and call its draw and fill methods. Instead of calling `DrawLine` with respect to a form, we call `DrawImage`, which draws the image generated by the `DrawLine` method.

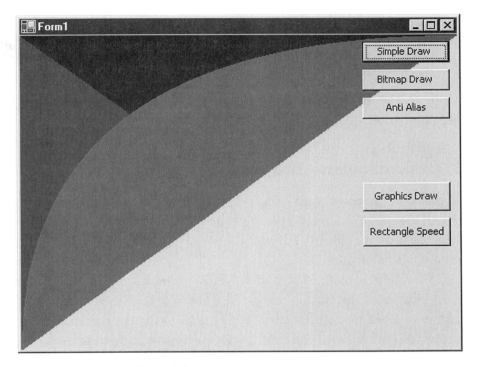

FIGURE 13.4: Drawing lines in a loop

As Listing 13.10 shows, we create a `Bitmap` object in a buffer and send the entire buffer all at once using `DrawImage`. We add the code given in Listing 13.10 on the **Bitmap Draw** button click event handler.

LISTING 13.10: Using double buffering to draw

```
Graphics g = this.CreateGraphics();
g.Clear(this.BackColor);
// Create a Bitmap object with the size of the form
Bitmap curBitmap = new Bitmap(ClientRectangle.Width,
ClientRectangle.Height);
// Create a temporary Graphics object from the bitmap
Graphics g1 = Graphics.FromImage(curBitmap);
// Draw lines on the temporary Graphics object
DrawLines(g1);
// Call DrawImage of Graphics and draw bitmap
g.DrawImage(curBitmap, 0, 0);
// Dispose of objects
g1.Dispose();
curBitmap.Dispose();
g.Dispose();
```

Comparing the two methods given in Listings 13.9 and 13.10 reveals a significant difference in drawing performance. In Listing 13.9, drawing begins as soon as we hit the **Simple Draw** button and continues until it is done. By contrast, when we hit the **Bitmap Draw** button, drawing doesn't start immediately. This method actually draws on an in-memory `Bitmap` object, and when all drawing is done, it displays the bitmap.

13.3 Understanding the `SetStyle` Method

Windows Forms and controls provide built-in support for double buffering, and the `SetStyle` method of the `Control` class plays a vital role in this process. Before we discuss how to use `SetStyle`, let's take a look at this method and its members.

The `SetStyle` method is defined in `System.Windows.Forms.Control`, which sets the specified style of a control. This method takes two arguments. The first argument is of type `ControlStyle` enumeration, and it represents the style of the control. The second argument is `true` if we want to apply the specified style, `false` otherwise. The members of the `ControlStyle` enumeration are described in Table 13.1.

TABLE 13.1: `ControlStyle` members

Member	Description
`AllPaintingInWmPaint`	The `WM_ERASEBKGND` window message is sent to the message queue whenever a control needs to redraw its background. This method tells Windows to ignore the message, reducing flicker. Both `OnPaint` and `OnPaintBackground` are called from the window message `WM_PAINT`. `AllPaintingInWmPaint` should be used only if `UserPaint` is set to `true`.
`CacheText`	Applications can cache text using this option. The control keeps a copy of the text rather than getting it from the handle each time it is needed. This style defaults to `false`.
`ContainerControl`	The control is a container.

TABLE 13.1: ControlStyle members (continued)

Member	Description
DoubleBuffer	This method provides built-in support for double buffering. When it is set to true, drawing is performed in a buffer and displayed only when complete. When using this option, you must also set the UserPaint and AllPaintingInWmPaint bits to true.
EnableNotifyMessage	If true, the OnNotifyMessage method is called for every message sent to the control's WndProc method. This style defaults to false.
FixedHeight	The control has a fixed height.
FixedWidth	The control has a fixed width.
Opaque	The control is drawn opaque, and the background is not painted.
ResizeRedraw	The control is redrawn when it is resized.
Selectable	The control can receive focus.
StandardClick	The control implements standard click behavior.
StandardDoubleClick	The control implements standard double-click behavior. When using this option, you must also set StandardClick to true.
SupportsTransparent-BackColor	The control accepts a Color object with alpha transparency for the background color. The UserPaint bit must be set to true, and the control must be derived from the Control class, like this: this.SetStyle(ControlStyles.UserPaint, true);
UserMouse	The control does its own mouse processing, and mouse events are not handled by the operating system.
UserPaint	The control paints itself rather than having the operating system do it. This option applies to classes derived from Control.

Let's apply the `SetStyle` method to achieve double buffering. Double buffering can be enabled programmatically with the following code:

```
// Activates double buffering
this.SetStyle(ControlStyles.UserPaint, true);
this.SetStyle(ControlStyles.AllPaintingInWmPaint, true);
this.SetStyle(ControlStyles.DoubleBuffer, true);
```

We can also control the redrawing of controls when a control is resized. Setting `ControlStyle.ResizeRedraw` to `true`, as in the code snippet that follows, forces controls to be redrawn every time a control (or a form) is resized.

```
SetStyle(ControlStyles.ResizeRedraw, true);
```

Sometimes we will not want a control to be redrawn when it is resized. In this case we can set `ResizeRedraw` to `false`.

> ■■ **NOTE**
> Many controls, such as `PictureBox`, are double-buffered automatically, which means we don't need to write any additional code when viewing images in a `PictureBox` control.

13.4 **The Quality and Performance of Drawing**

Drawing performance is inversely proportional to drawing quality. GDI+ provides several ways to set the quality of images and text. The `SmoothingMode` and `TextRenderingHint` properties are used to set image and text quality, respectively. The `HighQuality` and `AntiAlias` options provide slow drawing performance and better quality; the `HighSpeed` and `None` options provide poor quality and fast performance. Before using these options, we must decide if we really want to draw anti-aliased objects.

Sometimes anti-aliasing won't affect the quality of a drawing, and it is bad programming practice to use this processor-intensive feature when it is not required. In other cases we might need to set anti-aliasing for just one object out of 50. In these cases it is better to set the anti-alias option for that object only, instead of the entire canvas.

Sections 13.4.1 through 13.4.6 describe some more tips and tricks that may help improve an application's performance.

13.4.1 Repaint Only the Required Area

Avoiding unwanted repainting is a good technique to increase painting performance. GDI+ provides many techniques for painting only required objects. Using regions and clipping rectangles may help in some cases. If you need to draw a single object with anti-aliasing on, just set anti-aliasing for that object instead of for the entire surface (form). Using regions is one of the best techniques for repainting only a required area. For better performance, you should know what area you need to redraw and invalidate only that area, thereby using regions instead of repainting the entire form. See Chapter 6 for details of how to invalidate and clip specific regions.

13.4.2 Use Graphics Paths

Graphics paths may be useful when we need to redraw certain graphics items. For example, suppose we have hundreds of graphics items, including lines, rectangles, images, and text associated with a surface but we need to redraw only the rectangles. We can create a graphics path with all rectangles and just redraw that path, instead of the entire surface.

We may also want to use graphics paths when drawing different shapes, depending on the complexity of the application. For example, Listing 13.11 uses draw methods to draw two lines, two rectangles, and an ellipse. We can write this code on a button or a menu click event handler.

LISTING 13.11: Drawing simple graphics objects

```
Graphics g = this.CreateGraphics();
g.Clear(this.BackColor);
// Create a black pen
Pen blackPen = new Pen(Color.Black, 2);
// Draw objects
g.DrawLine(blackPen, 50, 50, 200, 50);
g.DrawLine(blackPen, 50, 50, 50, 200);
g.DrawRectangle(blackPen, 60, 60, 150, 150);
g.DrawRectangle(blackPen, 70, 70, 100, 100);
g.DrawEllipse(blackPen, 90, 90, 50, 50);
```

continues

```
// Dispose of objects
blackPen.Dispose();
g.Dispose();
```

Listing 13.12 draws the same graphics objects. The only difference is that this code uses a graphics path.

LISTING 13.12: Using a graphics path to draw graphics objects

```
Graphics g = this.CreateGraphics();
g.Clear(this.BackColor);
// Create a black pen
Pen blackPen = new Pen(Color.Black, 2);
// Create a graphics path
GraphicsPath path = new GraphicsPath();
path.AddLine(50, 50, 200, 50);
path.AddLine(50, 50, 50, 200);
path.AddRectangle(new Rectangle(60, 60, 150, 150));
path.AddRectangle(new Rectangle(70, 70, 100, 100));
path.AddEllipse(90, 90, 50, 50);
g.DrawPath(blackPen, path);
// Dispose of objects
blackPen.Dispose();
g.Dispose();
```

Both Listings 13.11 and 13.12 generate the output shown in Figure 13.5. There is no straightforward rule for when to use graphics paths. The choice depends on the complexity of your application.

In the preceding example we saw how to replace multiple drawing statements with a single graphics path drawing statement. But graphics paths have some limitations. For example, we can't draw each element (line, rectangle, or an ellipse) of a graphics path with a separate pen or brush. We have to draw or fill them individually.

13.4.3 **Select Methods Carefully**

Drawing lines and drawing rectangles are probably the most common operations. If you are drawing more than one line or rectangle using the same colors, you should use the DrawLine/DrawLines and DrawRectangle/DrawRectangles methods, respectively. For example, Listing 13.13 draws three rectangles using the same brush.

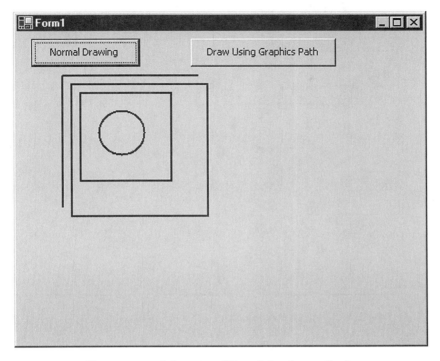

FIGURE 13.5: The same result from two different drawing methods

LISTING 13.13: Using `DrawRectangle` to draw rectangles

```
private void Form1_Paint(object sender,
   System.Windows.Forms.PaintEventArgs e)
{
  Graphics g = e.Graphics;
  // Create a black pen
  Pen blackPen = new Pen(Color.Black, 2);
  // Create a rectangle
  float x = 5.0F, y = 5.0F;
  float width = 100.0F;
  float height = 200.0F;
  Rectangle rect = new Rectangle(20,20, 80, 40);
  // Draw rectangles
  g.DrawRectangle(blackPen, x, y, width, height);
  g.DrawRectangle(blackPen, 60, 80, 140, 50);
  g.DrawRectangle(blackPen, rect);
  // Dispose of object
  blackPen.Dispose();

}
```

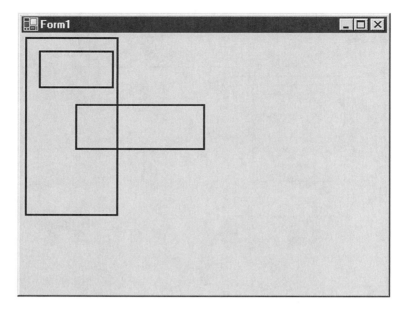

FIGURE 13.6: Using DrawRectangle to draw rectangles

Figure 13.6 shows the output from Listing 13.13. Three rectangles have been drawn.

You can replace the code in Listing 13.13 with Listing 13.14, which uses DrawRectangles to draw the same number of rectangles. Now we use an array of rectangles.

LISTING 13.14: Using DrawRectangles to draw rectangles

```
private void Form1_Paint(object sender,
  System.Windows.Forms.PaintEventArgs e)
{
  Graphics g = e.Graphics;
  // Create a black pen
  Pen blackPen = new Pen(Color.Black, 2);
  RectangleF[] rectArray =
  {
    new RectangleF( 5.0F,  5.0F, 100.0F, 200.0F),
    new RectangleF(20.0F, 20.0F,  80.0F,  40.0F),
    new RectangleF(60.0F, 80.0F, 140.0F,  50.0F)
  };
  g.DrawRectangles(blackPen, rectArray);
  // Dispose of object
  blackPen.Dispose();
}
```

If we run this code, the output looks exactly like Figure 13.6.

13.4.4 Avoid Using Frequently Called Events

It is always good practice to write minimal code on events that are called frequently because that code will be executed whenever the event is called. The Paint event is specifically designed for painting purposes and is called when redrawing is necessary. It is always advisable to write your painting (or redrawing)-related code for this event only. Writing code for other events, such as mouse-move or keyboard events, may cause serious problems or may not invalidate areas as necessary.

13.4.5 Use System Brushes and Pens

You can always create system pens and system brushes with system colors by using the SystemColors class, but for performance reasons it is advisable to use SystemPens and SystemBrushes instead of SystemColors. For example, the following code creates SolidBrush and Pen objects using SystemColors. The brush and pen have the ActiveCaption and ControlDarkDark system colors, respectively.

```
SolidBrush brush =
  (SolidBrush)SystemBrushes.FromSystemColor
  (SystemColors.ActiveCaption);
Pen pn = SystemPens.FromSystemColor
  (SystemColors.ControlDarkDark);
```

We can create the same brush and pen by using the static methods of SystemBrushes and SystemPens, as the following code snippet illustrates:

```
SolidBrush brush =
  (SolidBrush)SystemBrushes.ActiveCaption;
Pen pn = SystemPens.ControlDarkDark;
```

Never dispose of system pens and brushes. Any attempt to do so will result in an unhandled exception. For example, adding the following two lines to the code will throw an exception:

```
pn.Dispose();
brush.Dispose();
```

Listing 13.15 shows the complete code of a form's paint event handler.

LISTING 13.15: Using system pens and brushes

```
private void Form1_Paint(object sender,
  System.Windows.Forms.PaintEventArgs e)
{
  Graphics g = e.Graphics;
  // AVOID
  /*SolidBrush brush =
    (SolidBrush)SystemBrushes.FromSystemColor
    (SystemColors.ActiveCaption);
  Pen pn = SystemPens.FromSystemColor
    (SystemColors.ControlDarkDark);
    */
  SolidBrush brush =
    (SolidBrush)SystemBrushes.ActiveCaption;
  Pen pn = SystemPens.ControlDarkDark;
  g.DrawLine(pn, 20, 20, 20, 100);
  g.DrawLine(pn, 20, 20, 100, 20);
  g.FillRectangle(brush, 30, 30, 50, 50);
  // DON'T
  // pn.Dispose();
  // brush.Dispose();
}
```

Figure 13.7 shows the output from Listing 13.15. The lines and rectangle are drawn with system colors.

13.4.6 Avoid Automatic Scaling of Images

Automatic scaling could result in performance degradation. If possible, avoid automatic scaling. The DrawImage method takes a Bitmap object and a rectangle with upper left corner position and specified width and height. If we pass only the upper left corner position, GDI+ may scale the image, which decreases performance. For example, the code

```
e.Graphics.DrawImage(image, 10, 10;
```

can be replaced with the following code:

```
e.Graphics.DrawImage(image,
10, 10, image.Width,
 image.Height);
```

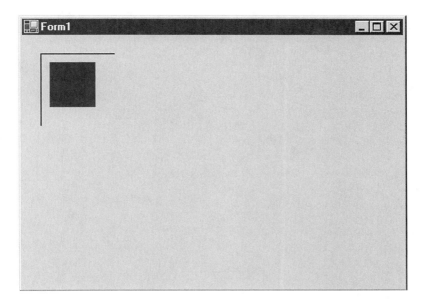

FIGURE 13.7: Using system pens and brushes

SUMMARY

Quality and performance are two basic requirements of all graphics applications. Although an increase in one demands a sacrifice in the other, a good developer will employ good design and coding techniques to provide an optimal solution. In this chapter we discussed some techniques that may be helpful in writing optimal solutions for graphics applications.

We learned about the paint event mechanism and different ways to fire the paint event automatically, as well as manually. We also discussed double buffering, and how it can be achieved with or without the SetStyle method. In addition, we learned a few good programming techniques and covered some topics that may help you implement some good, performance-oriented coding and design practices.

As a GDI developer, you may want to use some of the "cool" techniques of GDI that are not supported by GDI+. Chapter 14 is dedicated to GDI interoperability. In it, we will discuss how you can mix GDI and GDI+ to take advantage of interoperability.

▪ 14 ▪
GDI Interoperability

ALTHOUGH GDI+ IS a vastly improved API, a few features that are appreciated by GDI developers are not available in GDI+, such as raster operations. However, all is not lost. GDI+ interoperability provides a way to interact with GDI in managed applications, which can be used alongside GDI+ to provide the best of both worlds.

This chapter is written particularly for developers who want to use GDI in their managed applications. If you have no interest in GDI, feel free to skip this chapter. It will always be here, should the GDI need arise!

To Learn More about COM and .NET Interoperability

If you know GDI and want to use it in managed applications, this chapter will give you an idea of how to do that. However, COM interoperability is a broad topic. If you want to explore COM interoperability more, some good books are available on the market. One such book is *COM and .NET Interoperability* by Andrew Troelsen (published by APress).

14.1 Using GDI in the Managed Environment

One important feature of the .NET runtime is COM and Win32 interoperability. With runtime interoperability services, developers can use both

COM and Win32 libraries in managed applications. The classes related to these services are defined in the `System.Runtime.InteropServices` namespace.

We can use COM libraries in managed applications by simply adding a reference to the COM library using the **Add Reference** option of VS.NET or the Type Library Importer (`Tlbimp.exe`) .NET tool. Both of these options allow developers to convert a COM library to a .NET assembly, which can then be treated as other .NET assemblies. The graphical user interface (GUI) functionality of Windows is defined in a Win32 library called `Gdi32.dll`. Using Win32 libraries in managed code is a little more difficult than using COM libraries. However, there is nothing to worry about because the `System.Runtime.InteropServices.DllImportAttribute` class allows developers to use functionality defined in unmanaged libraries such as `Gdi32.dll`.

14.1.1 The `DllImportAttribute` Class

The `DllImportAttribute` class allows developers to import Win32 SDK functionality into managed applications. The `DllImportAttribute` constructor is used to create a new instance of the `DllImportAttribute` class with the name of the DLL containing the method to import. For example, the GDI functionality is defined in `Gdi32.dll`. So if we want to use GDI functions in our application, we need to import them using `DllImportAttribute`. The following code imports the `Gdi32.dll` library:

```
[System.Runtime.InteropServices.DllImportAttribute
("gdi32.dll")]
```

After adding this code, we're ready to use the functions defined in the `Gdi32.dll` library in our .NET application.

Now let's take a look at a simple program that uses the `MoveFile` function of Win32 defined in the `KERNEL32.dll` library. The code in Listing 14.1 first imports the library and then calls the `MoveFile` function to move a file from one location to another.

LISTING 14.1: Using the Win32 `MoveFile` function defined in `KERNEL32.dll`

```
[System.Runtime.InteropServices.DllImportAttribute
("KERNEL32.dll")]
```

```
public static extern bool MoveFile
(String src, String dst);

private void Move_Click(object sender,
System.EventArgs e)
{
    MoveFile("C:\\output.jpeg",
        "f:\\NewOutput.jpeg");
}
```

As with KERNEL32.dll, we can import other Win32 libraries to use them in .NET applications. The DllImportAttribute class provides six field members, which are described in Table 14.1.

The CallingConvention enumeration specifies the calling convention required to call methods implemented in unmanaged code. Its members are defined in Table 14.2.

The DllImportAttribute class has two properties: TypeId and Value. TypeId gets a unique identifier for an attribute when the attribute is

TABLE 14.1: DllImportAttribute field members

Method	Description
CallingConvention	Required to call methods implemented in unmanaged code; represented by the CallingConvention enumeration.
CharSet	Controls name mangling and indicates how to marshal String arguments to the method.
EntryPoint	Identifies the name or ordinal of the DLL entry point to be called.
ExactSpelling	Indicates whether the name of the entry point in the unmanaged DLL should be modified to correspond to the CharSet value specified in the CharSet field.
PreserveSig	Specifies that the managed method signature should not be transformed into an unmanaged signature that returns an HRESULT structure, and may have an additional argument (out or retval) for the return value.
SetLastError	Specifies that the callee will call the Win32 API SetLastError method before returning from the named method.

TABLE 14.2: `CallingConvention` members

Member	Description
Cdecl	The caller cleans the stack. This property enables calling functions with `varargs`.
FastCall	For future use.
StdCall	The callee cleans the stack. This is the default convention for calling unmanaged functions from managed code.
ThisCall	The first parameter is the `this` pointer and is stored in the ECX register. Other parameters are pushed onto the stack. This calling convention is used to call methods in classes exported from an unmanaged DLL.
Winapi	Uses the default platform-calling convention. For example, on Windows it's `StdCall`, and on Windows CE it's `Cdecl`.

implemented in the derived class, and `Value` returns the name of the DLL with the entry point.

14.1.2 Using the `BitBlt` Function

One of the most frequently asked questions on discussion forums and newsgroups related to GDI in managed code has to do with the use of `BitBlt`. Is this because developers want to implement sprites and scrolling-type actions in their applications? If you want to use the `BitBlt` function, you are probably aware of what it does. For the uninitiated, however, we should explain that this function performs a bit-block transfer of the color data corresponding to a rectangle of pixels from one device context to another. It is defined as follows:

```
BOOL BitBlt(
  HDC hdcDest,   // handle to destination device context
  int nXDest,    // x-coordinate of destination upper left corner
  int nYDest,    // y-coordinate of destination upper left corner
  int nWidth,    // width of destination rectangle
  int nHeight,   // height of destination rectangle
  HDC hdcSrc,    // handle to source device context
  int nXSrc,     // x-coordinate of source upper left corner
  int nYSrc,     // y-coordinate of source upper left corner
  DWORD dwRop    // raster operation code
);
```

More details of `BitBlt` are available in the GDI SDK documentation. Just type "BitBlt" in MSDN's index to find it.

First we need to import the `BitBlt` method and the `Gdi32.dll` library using the `DllImportAttribute` class.

```
[System.Runtime.InteropServices.DllImportAttribute
("Gdi32.dll")]
public static extern bool BitBlt(
    IntPtr hdcDest,
    int nXDest,
    int nYDest,
    int nWidth,
    int nHeight,
    IntPtr hdcSrc,
    int nXSrc,
    int nYSrc,
    System.Int32 dwRop
);
```

Now we just call `BitBlt`. The code in Listing 14.2 uses the `BitBlt` function. As the function definition shows, we need source and destination device contexts. There is no concept of device context in managed code, but to maintain GDI interoperability, the `Graphics` class's `GetHdc` method is used to create a device context for a `Graphics` object (a surface). `GetHdc` returns an `IntPtr` object.

In Listing 14.2, first we create a `Graphics` object by using `Create-Graphics` and we draw a few graphics items. From this `Graphics` object we create a `Bitmap` object, and we create one more `Graphics` object as the destination surface by using the `FromImage` method of the `Graphics` object. Next we call `BitBlt` with destination and source device contexts as parameters. Finally, we make sure to call `ReleaseHdc`, which releases device context resources. The `Save` method saves a physical copy of the image. We also call the `Dispose` method of `Graphics` objects.

LISTING 14.2: Using the `BitBlt` function

```
private void Form1_Load(object sender,
    System.EventArgs e)
{
    Graphics g1 = this.CreateGraphics();
    Graphics g2 = null;
    try
    {
```

continues

```
            g1.SmoothingMode =
                SmoothingMode.AntiAlias;
            g1.DrawLine(new Pen(Color.Black, 2),
                10, 10, 150, 10);
            g1.DrawLine(new Pen(Color.Black, 2),
                10, 10, 10, 150);
            g1.FillRectangle(Brushes.Blue,
                30, 30, 70, 70);
            g1.FillEllipse(new HatchBrush
                (HatchStyle.DashedDownwardDiagonal,
                Color.Red, Color.Green),
                110, 110, 100, 100 );
            Bitmap curBitmap = new Bitmap(
                this.ClientRectangle.Width,
                this.ClientRectangle.Height, g1);
            g2 = Graphics.FromImage(curBitmap);
            IntPtr hdc1 = g1.GetHdc();
            IntPtr hdc2 = g2.GetHdc();
            BitBlt(hdc2, 0, 0,
                this.ClientRectangle.Width,
                this.ClientRectangle.Height,
                hdc1, 0, 0, 13369376);
            g1.ReleaseHdc(hdc1);
            g2.ReleaseHdc(hdc2);
            curBitmap.Save("f:\\BitBltImg.jpg",
                ImageFormat.Jpeg);
        }
        catch (Exception exp)
        {
            MessageBox.Show(exp.Message.ToString());
        }
        finally
        {
            g2.Dispose();
            g1.Dispose();
        }
    }
```

14.1.3 Using GDI Print Functionality

We discussed .NET printing functionality in Chapter 11, but what about using GDI printing in managed code? One reason for using GDI may be speed and familiarity with GDI or having more control over the printer.

Until now we have been selecting objects such as fonts and lines and then drawing on a page, which is then printed out. Keep in mind that all the fonts you can use within the .NET environment have to be TrueType fonts. Before TrueType came along, there was something called **PCL (Printer Con-**

trol Language), also known as bitmap fonts. So what's the difference?, you may ask. It's simple: A PCL or bitmap font is made up of patterns of dots that represent each letter.

The problem is that a different PCL font was required for *every* size of letter needed, such as 12, 14, and so on. Different PCL fonts were needed even for italic and bold versions! As you can imagine, it was necessary to have lots of PCL fonts to maintain the flexibility we take for granted today.

TrueType fonts, on the other hand, are a lot more flexible. The reason is that the fonts are mathematical representations of each letter rather than a pattern of dots. If I decide I need a Times New Roman font at size 20, the font is simply recalculated rather than just a different pattern of dots being loaded.

What happens if your printer does not support the TrueType font you have selected? The only way to print it is to send what you want to print to the printer as graphics, which can be time-consuming if you're creating large printouts.

The code in Listing 14.3 does a few new things. For one, it uses Win32 APIs to talk directly to the printer, which gives us the best possible speed. Finally, it demonstrates the use of PCL5 commands to draw a box on the page.

Using the code in Listing 14.3, you would be able to create detailed pages consisting of multiple fonts and graphics. The nice thing is that they can all be created by just sending text to the printer rather than using graphics commands.

You may want to change the printer before you test this code. The following line of code specifies the printer:

```
PrintDirect.OpenPrinter("\\\\192.168.1.101\\hp1",
        ref lhPrinter,0);
```

LISTING 14.3: Using GDI print functionality in a managed application

```
// PrintDirect.cs
// Shows how to write data directly to the
// printer using Win32 APIs.
// This code sends Hewlett-Packard PCL5 codes
// to the printer to print
// out a rectangle in the middle of the page.
```

continues

```csharp
using System;
using System.Text;
using System.Runtime.InteropServices;


[StructLayout( LayoutKind.Sequential)]
public struct DOCINFO
{
        [MarshalAs(UnmanagedType.LPWStr)]
            public string pDocName;
        [MarshalAs(UnmanagedType.LPWStr)]
            public string pOutputFile;
        [MarshalAs(UnmanagedType.LPWStr)]
            public string pDataType;
}

public class PrintDirect
{
        [ DllImport( "winspool.drv",
             CharSet=CharSet.Unicode,ExactSpelling=false,
        CallingConvention=CallingConvention.StdCall )]
        public static extern long OpenPrinter(string pPrinterName,
            ref IntPtr phPrinter, int pDefault);

        [ DllImport( "winspool.drv",
             CharSet=CharSet.Unicode,ExactSpelling=false,
        CallingConvention=CallingConvention.StdCall )]
        public static extern long StartDocPrinter(IntPtr hPrinter,
            int Level, ref DOCINFO pDocInfo);

        [ DllImport( "winspool.drv",
             CharSet=CharSet.Unicode,ExactSpelling=true,
        CallingConvention=CallingConvention.StdCall)]
        public static extern long StartPagePrinter(
            IntPtr hPrinter);

        [ DllImport( "winspool.drv",
             CharSet=CharSet.Ansi, ExactSpelling=true,
        CallingConvention=CallingConvention.StdCall)]
        public static extern long WritePrinter(IntPtr hPrinter,
            string data, int buf, ref int pcWritten);

        [ DllImport( "winspool.drv" ,
             CharSet=CharSet.Unicode,ExactSpelling=true,
        CallingConvention=CallingConvention.StdCall)]
        public static extern long EndPagePrinter(IntPtr
            hPrinter);

        [ DllImport( "winspool.drv" ,
```

```
                    CharSet=CharSet.Unicode, ExactSpelling=true,
            CallingConvention=CallingConvention.StdCall)]
            public static extern long EndDocPrinter(IntPtr hPrinter);

            [ DllImport( "winspool.drv",
                    CharSet=CharSet.Unicode,ExactSpelling=true,
            CallingConvention=CallingConvention.StdCall )]
            public static extern long ClosePrinter(IntPtr
                    hPrinter);
}


public class App
{
    public static void Main()
    {
        System.IntPtr lhPrinter =
            new System.IntPtr();
        DOCINFO di = new DOCINFO();
        int pcWritten=0;
        string st1;

        // Text to print with a form-feed character
        st1="This is an example of printing " +
            "directly to a printer\f";
        di.pDocName="my test document";
        di.pDataType="RAW";

        // The "\x1b" means an ASCII escape character
        st1="\x1b*c600a6b0P\f";
        // lhPrinter contains the handle for the printer opened.
        // If lhPrinter is 0, then an error has occurred.
        PrintDirect.OpenPrinter("\\\\192.168.1.101\\hp1",
            ref lhPrinter,0);
        PrintDirect.StartDocPrinter(lhPrinter,1,ref di);
        PrintDirect.StartPagePrinter(lhPrinter);

        try
        {
            // Moves the cursor 900 dots (3 inches at
            // 300 dpi) in from the left margin, and
            // 600 dots (2 inches at 300 dpi) down
            // from the top margin
            st1="\x1b*p900x600Y";
            PrintDirect.WritePrinter(lhPrinter,
                st1, st1.Length, ref pcWritten);

            // Using the print model commands for rectangle
            // dimensions, "600a" specifies a rectangle
```

continues

```
        // with a horizontal size, or width, of 600 dots,
        // and "6b" specifies a vertical
        // size, or height, of 6 dots. "0P" selects the
        // solid black rectangular area fill.
        st1="\x1b*c600a6b0P";
        PrintDirect.WritePrinter(lhPrinter,
            st1, st1.Length, ref pcWritten);

        // Specifies a rectangle with width of
        // 6 dots, height of 600 dots, and a
        // fill pattern of solid black
        st1="\x1b*c6a600b0P";
        PrintDirect.WritePrinter(lhPrinter,
            st1, st1.Length, ref pcWritten);

        // Moves the current cursor position to
        // 900 dots from the left margin and
        // 1200 dots down from the top margin
        st1="\x1b*p900x1200Y";
        PrintDirect.WritePrinter(lhPrinter,
            st1, st1.Length, ref pcWritten);

        // Specifies a rectangle with a width
        // of 606 dots, a height of 6 dots, and a
        // fill pattern of solid black
        st1="\x1b*c606a6b0P";
        PrintDirect.WritePrinter(lhPrinter,
            st1, st1.Length, ref pcWritten);

        // Moves the current cursor position to 1500
        // dots in from the left margin and
        // 600 dots down from the top margin
        st1="\x1b*p1500x600Y";
        PrintDirect.WritePrinter(lhPrinter,
            st1, st1.Length, ref pcWritten);

        // Specifies a rectangle with a width of 6 dots,
        // a height of 600 dots, and a
        // fill pattern of solid black
        st1="\x1b*c6a600b0P";
        PrintDirect.WritePrinter(lhPrinter,
            st1, st1.Length, ref pcWritten);

        // Send a form-feed character to the printer
        st1="\f";
        PrintDirect.WritePrinter(lhPrinter,
            st1, st1.Length, ref pcWritten);
    }
    catch (Exception e)
    {
```

```
            Console.WriteLine(e.Message);
        }

        PrintDirect.EndPagePrinter(lhPrinter);
        PrintDirect.EndDocPrinter(lhPrinter);
        PrintDirect.ClosePrinter(lhPrinter);
    }
}
```

Using this code will enable us to drive a printer at its maximum output rate.

14.2 Cautions for Using GDI in Managed Code

We just saw how we can take advantage of services provided by the .NET runtime, which include the flexibility of mixing GDI with GDI+ and using GDI functionality in managed applications.

14.2.1 No GDI Calls between `GetHdc` and `ReleaseHdc`

GDI+ currently has no support for raster operations. When we use R2_XOR pen operations, we use the `Graphics.GetHdc()` method to get the handle to the device context. During the operation when your application uses the HDC, the GDI+ should not draw anything on the `Graphics` object until the `Graphics.ReleaseHdc` method is called. Every `GetHdc` call must be followed by a call to `ReleaseHdc` on a `Graphics` object, as in the following code snippet:

```
IntPtr hdc1 = g1.GetHdc();
// Do something with hdc1
g1.ReleaseHdc(hdc1);

g2 = Graphics.FromImage(curBitmap);
IntPtr hdc1 = g1.GetHdc();
IntPtr hdc2 = g2.GetHdc();
BitBlt(hdc2, 0, 0,
    this.ClientRectangle.Width,
    this.ClientRectangle.Height,
    hdc1, 0, 0, 13369376);
g2.DrawRectangle(Pens.Red, 40, 40, 200, 200);
g1.ReleaseHdc(hdc1);
g2.ReleaseHdc(hdc2);
```

If we make a GDI+ call after `GetHdc`, the system will throw an "object busy" exception. For example, in the preceding code snippet we make a `DrawRectangle` call after `GetHdc` and before `ReleaseHdc`. As a result we will get an exception saying, "The object is currently in use elsewhere."

14.2.2 Using GDI on a GDI+ Graphics Object Backed by a Bitmap

After a call to `GetHdc`, we can simply call a `Graphics` object from a bitmap that returns a new `HBITMAP` structure. This bitmap does not contain the original image, but rather a **sentinel pattern**, which allows GDI+ to track changes to the bitmap. When `ReleaseHdc` is called, changes are copied back to the original image. This type of device context is not suitable for raster operations because the handle to device context is considered write-only, and raster operations require it to be read-only. This approach may also degrade the performance because creating a new bitmap and saving changes to the original bitmap operations may tie up all your resources.

SUMMARY

With the help of .NET runtime interoperability services, we can use the functionality of the Win32 libraries in managed code. The `DllImportAttribute` class is used to import a Win32 DLL into managed code. In this chapter we saw how to use this class to import `Gdi32.dll` functions in managed code. We also saw how to use printing and `BitBlt` functions in managed code.

GDI+ can also be used to write simple and fun drawing applications. This is what we will discuss in Chapter 15. There you will see how GDI+ can be useful for writing fun applications.

■ 15 ■
Miscellaneous GDI+ Examples

I N THIS CHAPTER we will write some miscellaneous GDI+ samples that you may find useful when writing real-world applications. We will cover the following topics:

- Designing interactive GUI applications
- Writing Windows applications using shaped forms
- Adding custom text in images
- Reading and writing images to and from databases
- Resizing the graphics of a form when the form is resized
- Creating owner-drawn `ListBox` and `ComboBox` controls

15.1 Designing Interactive GUI Applications

In this section we will see some of the Windows Forms control properties that are used in designing interactive Windows GUI applications. Before writing our sample application, we will discuss some common properties of the `Control` class.

15.1.1 Understanding the Control Class

The Control class provides the basic functionality and serves as the base class for Windows forms and controls. Although this class has many properties and methods, we will concentrate on only a few of them.

The ForeColor and BackColor properties determine the foreground and background colors of controls, respectively. Both properties are of type Color, and they implement get and set property options.

The Font property represents the font of the text displayed by a control. The DefaultBackColor, DefaultFont, and DefaultForeColor static properties of the Control class implement the get option only, and they return the default background color, font, and foreground color of a control, respectively.

The BackgroundImage property allows us to both get and set the background image of a control. This property is of type Image. Images with translucent or transparent colors are not supported by Windows Forms as background images.

15.1.2 The Application

Now let's write an application that will use all of the properties we just named.

First we create a Windows application and name it ButtonViewer. Then we add controls (for three buttons, one text box, and one panel) to the form by dragging them from the Visual Studio .NET toolbox. After adding controls to the form, we reposition and resize them, and we change their Text and Name properties. The final form looks like Figure 15.1.

As Figure 15.1 shows, two of the buttons are named **Browse** and **Close**, respectively, and one button has no text. The **Browse** button allows us to browse an image file, and the **Close** button closes the application. The TextBox control displays the file name selected by a click of the **Browse** button. The third button (shown larger and without text in Figure 15.1) displays the image selected by the **Browse** button.

Now let's change the background color, foreground color, styles, and fonts of these controls. To do so, we add code in the form's load event handler, as shown in Listing 15.1. As the code indicates, we set the control's

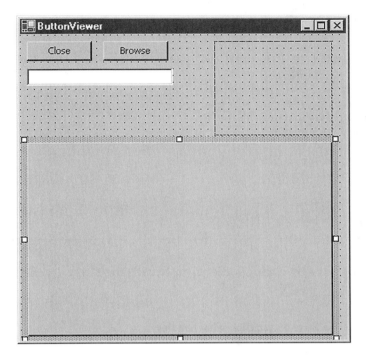

FIGURE 15.1: An interactive GUI application

`BackColor`, `ForeColor`, `FlatStyle`, `BorderStyle`, and `Font` properties. (See Chapter 5 for details on fonts and colors.)

LISTING 15.1: Setting a control's `BackColor`, `ForeColor`, and `Font` properties

```
private void Form2_Load(object sender, System.EventArgs e)
{
  // Button 1
  button1.ForeColor = Color.Yellow;
  button1.BackColor = Color.Maroon;
  button1.FlatStyle = FlatStyle.Flat;
  button1.Font = new Font ("Verdana",
    10, FontStyle.Bold);
  // Close and Browse buttons
  btnClose.ForeColor = Color.Yellow;
  btnClose.BackColor = Color.Black;
  btnClose.FlatStyle = FlatStyle.Flat;
  btnClose.Font = new Font ("Ariel",
    10, FontStyle.Italic);
```

continues

```
btnBrowse.ForeColor = Color.White;
btnBrowse.BackColor = Color.Black;
btnBrowse.FlatStyle = FlatStyle.Flat;
btnBrowse.Font = new Font ("Ariel",
  10, FontStyle.Bold);
// Text box 1
textBox1.BorderStyle = BorderStyle.FixedSingle;
textBox1.BackColor = Color.Blue;
textBox1.ForeColor = Color.Yellow;
textBox1.Font = new Font("Tahoma", 10,
FontStyle.Strikeout|FontStyle.Bold|
  FontStyle.Italic);
// Panel 1
panel1.BorderStyle = BorderStyle.FixedSingle;
panel1.BackColor = Color.Red;
}
```

The **Close** button click handler simply calls the `Form.Close` method, as shown in Listing 15.2.

LISTING 15.2: The Close button click event handler

```
private void btnClose_Click(object sender,
System.EventArgs e)
{
 this.Close();
}
```

The **Browse** button click event handler (see Listing 15.3) uses an `Open-FileDialog` control to browse for an image and sets the selected image as the background image of the button. It also sets the file name as text of the text box control. Finally, it calls the `Invalidate` method to repaint the form.

LISTING 15.3: The Browse button click event handler

```
private void btnBrowse_Click(object sender,
  System.EventArgs e)
{
 OpenFileDialog fdlg = new OpenFileDialog();
 fdlg.Title = "C# Corner Open File Dialog" ;
 fdlg.InitialDirectory = @"c:\" ;
 fdlg.Filter = "Image Files(*.BMP;*.JPG;*.GIF)|" +
  "*.BMP;*.JPG;*.GIF|All files (*.*)|*.*";
 fdlg.FilterIndex = 2 ;
 fdlg.RestoreDirectory = true ;
```

```
if(fdlg.ShowDialog() == DialogResult.OK)
{
  button1.BackgroundImage =
    Image.FromFile(fdlg.FileName) ;
  textBox1.Text = fdlg.FileName;
}
Invalidate();
}
```

15.1.3 Drawing Transparent Controls

How can I draw transparent controls? This is one of the commonly asked questions on discussion forums.

Drawing transparent controls involves two steps. First we set a form's style to enable support for transparent controls. We do this by calling the SetStyle method of the form, passing ControlStyles.SupportTransparentBackColor as the first argument, and setting the second argument (which in turn sets the SupportTransparentBackColor bit) to true. Next we set the control's BackColor property to a transparent color. Either we can use Color.Transparent, or we can create a Color object using an alpha component value less than 255 to provide custom semitransparency. Listing 15.4 sets the background color of controls to transparent.

LISTING 15.4: Setting the background color of controls to transparent

```
/* Code for transparent controls */
this.SetStyle(
ControlStyles.SupportsTransparentBackColor,
true);
button1.BackColor = Color.Transparent;
btnBrowse.BackColor = Color.Transparent;
btnClose.BackColor = Color.Transparent;
panel1.BackColor = Color.FromArgb(70, 0, 0, 255);
```

The output of Listing 15.4 looks like Figure 15.2.

▪▪ **NOTE**

Not all controls support transparent color. For example, if you set the BackColor property of a text box to Color.Transparent, you will get an exception.

FIGURE 15.2: Designing transparent controls

15.2 Drawing Shaped Forms and Windows Controls

Normally, all Windows controls and forms are rectangular, but what if we want to draw them in nonrectangular shapes? We can do this by setting the Region property. The Region property of a form or a control represents that window's **region**, which is a collection of pixels within a form or control where the operating system permits drawing; no portion of a form that lies outside of the window region is displayed. To draw nonrectangular shapes, we trick the system into drawing only the region of a control.

Let's draw a circular form. We can use the GraphicsPath class to draw graphics paths. In this application we'll create a circular form and a circular picture box, which will display an image. To test this application, we follow these simple steps:

We create a Windows application and add a button and a picture box to the form. Then we set the Text property of the button control to "Exit" and write the following line on the button click event handler:

```
this.Close();
```

Next we add a reference to the `System.Drawing.Drawing2D` name-space so that we can use the `GraphicsPath` class:

```
using System.Drawing.Drawing2D;
```

On the form-load event handler, we create a `Bitmap` object from a file and load the bitmap in the picture box as shown in the following code snippet.

```
Image bmp = Bitmap.FromFile("aphoto.jpg");
pictureBox1.Image = bmp;
```

The last step is to set the form and picture box as circular. We can mod-ify the `InitializeComponent` method and add code as in Listing 15.5 at the end of the method, or we can add the code on the form-load event han-dler. We just set the `Region` property of the form and picture box to the region of our `GraphicsPath` object.

LISTING 15.5: Setting a form and picture box control as circular

```
private void Form1_Load(object sender,
System.EventArgs e)
{
 // Create a rectangle
 Rectangle rect = new Rectangle(0,0,100,100);
 // Create a graphics path
 GraphicsPath path = new GraphicsPath();
 // Add an ellipse to the graphics path
 path.AddEllipse(rect);
 // Set the Region property of the picture box
 // by creating a region from the path
 pictureBox1.Region = new Region(path);
 rect.Height += 200;
 rect.Width += 200;
 path.Reset();
 path.AddEllipse(rect);
 this.Region = new Region(path);
 // Create an image from a file and
 // set the picture box's Image property
 Image bmp = Bitmap.FromFile("aphoto.jpg");
 pictureBox1.Image = bmp;
}
```

FIGURE 15.3: Drawing a circular form and Windows controls

When we build and run the application; the output will look like Figure 15.3. Because we have eliminated the normal title bar controls, we must implement an **Exit** button.

15.3 Adding Copyright Information to a Drawn Image

With the popularity of digital cameras and the increase of digital archive Web sites that allow you to buy images, it's handy to be able to add a copyright to your image. Not only that, you can also add text specifying the date and place of the photograph.

In this section we will create an application with support for the display of copyright information on displayed images. First we create a Windows application and add a **File | Open** menu item, a button with text "Add Copyright," and a picture box. The final form looks like Figure 15.4.

After adding the controls, we add a reference to the `System.Drawing.Imaging` namespace to the application. Then we add a class `Image` variable to the application as follows:

```
Image origImage;
```

The **File | Open** menu allows us to browse images and view a thumbnail of a specific image. The code for the menu click event handler is given

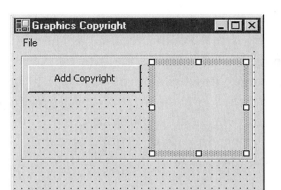

FIGURE 15.4: A graphics copyright application

in Listing 15.6. After reading the name of the image, we create an `Image` object from the file name using the `Image.FromFile` static method. After creating one `Image` object, we create another `Image` object using the `Get-ThumbnailImage` method of the `Image` class. `GetThumbnailImage` returns a thumbnail image. After that we simply set the `Image` property of `Pic-tureBox` to display the image.

LISTING 15.6: Browsing images

```
private void menuItem2_Click(object sender,
  System.EventArgs e)
{
  // Open file dialog
  OpenFileDialog fileDlg = new OpenFileDialog();
  fileDlg.InitialDirectory = "c:\\" ;
  fileDlg.Filter= "All files (*.*)|*.*";
  fileDlg.FilterIndex = 2 ;
  fileDlg.RestoreDirectory = true ;
  if(fileDlg.ShowDialog() == DialogResult.OK)
  {
    // Create image from file
    string fileName = fileDlg.FileName.ToString();
    origImage = Image.FromFile(fileName);
    // Create thumbnail image
    Image thumbNail  =
      origImage.GetThumbnailImage(100, 100,
      null, new IntPtr());
    // View image in picture box
    pictureBox1.Image = thumbNail;
  }
}
```

If we run the application and open a file using the **Open** menu item, the image will be displayed. The output looks like Figure 15.5.

Once the image has been loaded, we click the **Add Copyright** button and let the program do its work. Basically we need to create an image on the fly, add text to the image using the DrawString method, and then save the image. To give the text a different shade, we need to change the color of the pixels that draw the text. In other words, we must change the brightness of the pixels that represent the text to distinguish the text pixels from the image pixels. We increase the values for the red, green, and blue component of the color by 25 to brighten the text pixels. We use the Measure-String method of the Graphics class to set the size and font of the text. (We discussed MeasureString in detail in Chapter 3.)

The maximum value for each of the red, green, and blue components of a color is 255. What happens if these values are already set to 255? Do we still increase their value by 25? No. In that case we cheat and don't touch these pixels. In most cases this approach works because there is always a pixel that is totally different in brightness. One additional thing we could do would be to analyze the image, determine whether it's a dark or bright image, and adjust it accordingly.

To find out which pixels to change, we create a second bitmap that is the same size as the original image. We write "Add Copyright Info" on this image and use it as the pattern for the main image.

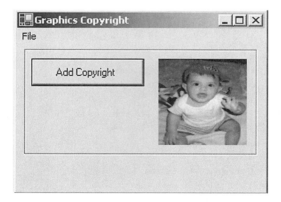

FIGURE 15.5: Thumbnail view of an image

We also want to use the largest font we can to create a big word across the image. Of course, the image can be any size, so we can predict the font size. To do this we create a graphics class based on our pattern image and use the `MeasureString` method until we get a font that fits the graphic, as in Listing 15.7.

LISTING 15.7: Adding the copyright text

```
while(foundfont==false)
{
  Font fc = new Font("Georgia",
    fntSize, System.Drawing.FontStyle.Bold);
  sizeofstring = new SizeF(imgWidth,imgHeight);
  sizeofstring =
    g.MeasureString("Copyright GDI+ Inc.,",fc);
  if (sizeofstring.Width<pattern.Width)
  {
    if (sizeofstring.Height<pattern.Height)
    {
      foundfont=true;
      g.DrawString("Copyright GDI+ Inc.,",
        fc, new SolidBrush(Color.Black),
        1, 15);
    }
  }
  else
    fntSize = fntSize - 1;
}
```

The complete code for the **Add Copyright** button click event handler is given in Listing 15.8. We read the image size and create a `Bitmap` object from the original size of the image. Then we create a `Graphics` object on the fly using this `Bitmap` object. Once the pattern bitmap has been created, all we have to do is loop through all the pixels and if a pixel is black (which means that it's part of the word), we go to the main image and increase its brightness, producing a glasslike effect.

LISTING 15.8: Adding copyright to an image

```
private void button1_Click(object sender,
  System.EventArgs e)
{
  if(origImage == null)
```

continues

```
  {
    MessageBox.Show("Open a file");
    return;
  }
  int imgWidth;
  int imgHeight;
  int fntSize=300;
  int x,y;
  int a,re,gr,bl,x1,y1,z1;
  int size;
  Bitmap pattern;
  SizeF sizeofstring;
  bool foundfont;
  imgWidth = origImage.Width;
  imgHeight = origImage.Height;
  size=imgWidth*imgHeight;
  pattern = new Bitmap(imgWidth,imgHeight);
  Bitmap temp = new Bitmap(origImage);
  Graphics g = Graphics.FromImage(pattern);
  Graphics tempg = Graphics.FromImage(origImage);
  // Find a font size that will fit in the bitmap
  foundfont = false;
  g.Clear(Color.White);
  while(foundfont==false)
  {
    Font fc = new Font("Georgia",
      fntSize, System.Drawing.FontStyle.Bold);
    sizeofstring = new SizeF(imgWidth,imgHeight);
    sizeofstring =
      g.MeasureString("Add Copyright Info",fc);
    if (sizeofstring.Width<pattern.Width)
    {
      if (sizeofstring.Height<pattern.Height)
      {
        foundfont=true;
        g.DrawString("Add Copyright Info",
          fc, new SolidBrush(Color.Black),
          1, 15);
      }
    }
    else
      fntSize = fntSize - 1;
  }
  MessageBox.Show("Creating new graphic",
    "GraphicsCopyright");
  for(x=1;x<pattern.Width;x++)
  {
    for(y=1;y<pattern.Height;y++)//
    {
      if (pattern.GetPixel(x,y).ToArgb()
```

```
            == Color.Black.ToArgb())
        {
        a=temp.GetPixel(x,y).A;
        re=temp.GetPixel(x,y).R;
        gr=temp.GetPixel(x,y).G;
        bl=temp.GetPixel(x,y).B;

        x1=re;
        y1=gr;
        z1=bl;
        if (bl+25<255)
          bl=bl+25;

        if (gr+25<255)
          gr=gr+25;

        if (re+25<255)
          re=re+25;

        if (x1-25>0)
          x1=x1-25;

        if (y1-25>0)
          y1=y1-25;

        if (z1-25>0)
          z1=z1-25;

        tempg.DrawEllipse(new Pen(
          new SolidBrush(Color.Black)),
          x, y+1, 3, 3);
        tempg.DrawEllipse(new Pen(
          new SolidBrush(
          Color.FromArgb(a,x1,y1,z1))),
          x, y, 1, 1);
        }
      }
    }
  MessageBox.Show("Output file is output.jpeg",
  "GraphicsCopyright");
  tempg.Save();
  origImage.Save("output.jpeg",
    ImageFormat.Jpeg);
}
```

Now we can run the application and browse images. When we click the
Add Copyright button, we will get a message when the program is done

FIGURE 15.6: An image after copyright has been added to it

adding text. The result creates what is commonly known as a **watermark** in the image (see Figure 15.6).

15.4 **Reading and Writing Images to and from a Stream or Database**

Sometimes we need to read and write images to and from a stream or database. In this example we will build an application to show how to do this for both streams and databases. We will use Microsoft Access for the database and ADO.NET to read and write data to the database.

Database Programming and ADO.NET

If you are new to database programming and ADO.NET, you may want to look at the ADO.NET section of C# Corner (www.c-sharpcorner.com). Plenty of source code samples and tutorials are available for free. You also might want to check out my book for ADO.NET beginners: *A Programmer's Guide to ADO.NET in C#* (published by APress).

First we need to create a database. We start by creating a new Access database called `AppliedAdoNet.mdb` and adding a table to the database called "Users." The database table schema should look like Figure 15.7. Microsoft Access stores binary large objects (BLOBs) using the OLE object data type.

To make our application a little more interactive and user-friendly, let's create a Windows application and add a text box, three button controls, and a `PictureBox` control. The final form looks like Figure 15.8. As you can probably guess, the **Browse Image** button allows users to browse for bitmap files; the **Save Image** button saves the image to the database; and the **Read Image** button reads the first row of the database table, saves binary data as a bitmap, and displays the image in the picture box.

Before we write code on button clicks, we need to define the following variables:

```
// User-defined variables
private Image curImage = null;
private string curFileName = null;
private string connectionString =
  "Provider=Microsoft.Jet.OLEDB.4.0; " +
  "Data Source=F:\\AppliedAdoNet.mdb" ;
private string savedImageName =
  "F:\\ImageFromDb.BMP";
```

Do not forget to add references to the `System.IO` and `System.Data.OleDb` namespaces:

```
using System.IO;
using System.Data.OleDb;
```

Field Name	Data Type
UserID	AutoNumber
UserName	Text
UserEmail	Text
UserPhoto	OLE Object
UserDescription	Memo

FIGURE 15.7: Users table schema

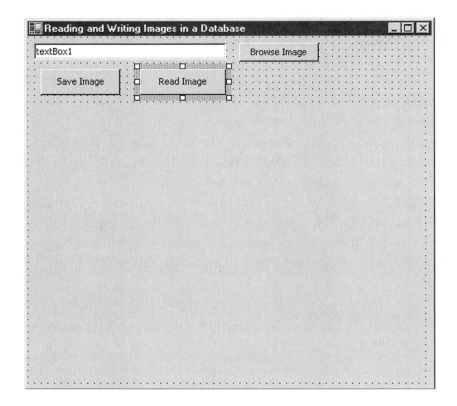

FIGURE 15.8: Reading and writing images in a database form

The stream-related classes are defined in the System.IO namespace. We will use the OLE DB data provider, which is defined in the System.Data.OleDb namespace, to work with our Access database.

The **Browse Image** button click code is given in Listing 15.9, which simply browses bitmap files and saves the file name in curFileName. We can set a filter to access the file formats we want.

LISTING 15.9: The Browse button click event handler

```
private void BrowseBtn_Click(object sender,
  System.EventArgs e)
{
  OpenFileDialog openDlg = new OpenFileDialog();
  openDlg.Filter = "All Bitmap files|*.bmp";
  string filter = openDlg.Filter;
```

```
  openDlg.Title = "Open a Bitmap File";
  if(openDlg.ShowDialog() == DialogResult.OK)
  {
    curFileName = openDlg.FileName;
    textBox1.Text = curFileName;
  }
}
```

The **Save Image** button code given in Listing 15.10 creates a File-Stream object from the bitmap file, opens a connection with the database, adds a new data row, set its values, and saves the row back to the database.

LISTING 15.10: The Save Image button click event handler

```
private void SaveImageBtn_Click(object sender,
  System.EventArgs e)
{
  // Read a bitmap's contents in a stream
  FileStream fs = new FileStream(curFileName,
    FileMode.OpenOrCreate, FileAccess.Read);
  byte[] rawData = new byte[fs.Length];
  fs.Read(rawData, 0,
    System.Convert.ToInt32(fs.Length));
  fs.Close();

  // Construct a SQL string and a connection object
  string sql = "SELECT * FROM Users";
  OleDbConnection conn = new OleDbConnection();
  conn.ConnectionString = connectionString;
  // Open the connection
  if(conn.State != ConnectionState.Open)
    conn.Open();
  // Create a data adapter and data set
  OleDbDataAdapter adapter =
    new OleDbDataAdapter(sql, conn);
  OleDbCommandBuilder cmdBuilder =
    new OleDbCommandBuilder(adapter);
  DataSet ds = new DataSet("Users");
    adapter.MissingSchemaAction =
    MissingSchemaAction.AddWithKey;

  // Fill the data adapter
  adapter.Fill(ds,"Users");

  string userDes =
    "Mahesh Chand is a founder of C# Corner ";
  userDes +=
```

continues

```
        "Author: 1. A Programmer's Guide to ADO.NET;";
    userDes += ", 2. Applied ADO.NET. ";

    // Create a new row
    DataRow row = ds.Tables["Users"].NewRow();
    row["UserName"] = "Mahesh Chand";
    row["UserEmail"] = "mcb@mindcracker.com";
    row["UserDescription"] = userDes;
    row["UserPhoto"] = rawData;
    // Add the row to the collection
    ds.Tables["Users"].Rows.Add(row);
    // Save changes to the database
    adapter.Update(ds, "Users");
    // Clean up connection
    if(conn != null)
    {
      if(conn.State == ConnectionState.Open)
        conn.Close();
      // Dispose of connection
      conn.Dispose();
    }
    MessageBox.Show("Image Saved");
}
```

Once the data has been saved, the next step is to read data from the database table, save it as a bitmap again, and view the bitmap on the form. We can view an image using the Graphics.DrawImage method or using a picture box. Our example uses a picture box.

The code for reading binary data is shown in Listing 15.11. We open a connection, create a data adapter, fill a data set, and get the first row of the Users table. If you want to read all the images, you may want to modify your application or loop through all the rows. Once a row has been read, we retrieve the data stored in the UserPhoto column in a stream and save it as a bitmap file. Later we view that bitmap file in a picture box by setting its Image property to the file name.

LISTING 15.11: Reading images from a database

```
private void ReadImageBtn_Click(object sender,
   System.EventArgs e)
{
   // Construct a SQL string and a connection object
   string sql = "SELECT * FROM Users";
   OleDbConnection conn = new OleDbConnection();
```

```
conn.ConnectionString = connectionString;
// Open the connection
if(conn.State != ConnectionState.Open)
  conn.Open();
// Create a data adapter and data set
OleDbDataAdapter adapter =
  new OleDbDataAdapter(sql, conn);
OleDbCommandBuilder cmdBuilder =
  new OleDbCommandBuilder(adapter);
DataSet ds = new DataSet("Users");
adapter.MissingSchemaAction =
  MissingSchemaAction.AddWithKey;
// Fill the data adapter
adapter.Fill(ds,"Users");

// Get the first row of the table
DataRow row = ds.Tables["Users"].Rows[0];
// Read data in a stream
byte[] rawData = new byte[0];
rawData = (byte[])row["UserPhoto"];
int len = new int();
len = rawData.GetUpperBound(0);
// Save rawData as a bitmap
FileStream fs = new FileStream
(savedImageName, FileMode.OpenOrCreate,
  FileAccess.Write);
fs.Write(rawData, 0, len);
// Close the stream
fs.Close();
// View the image in a picture box
curImage = Image.FromFile(savedImageName);
pictureBox1.Image = curImage;
// Clean up connection
if(conn != null)
{
  if(conn.State == ConnectionState.Open)
    conn.Close();
  // Dispose of connection
  conn.Dispose();
}
}
```

To see the program in action, we select the `MyPhoto.bmp` file by using the **Browse Image** button, and we click the **Save Image** button. When we open the database, we see that a new record has been added to the Users table. When we click on the **Read Image** button, a new `ImageFromDb.bmp` file is added to the current folder. The output is shown in Figure 15.9.

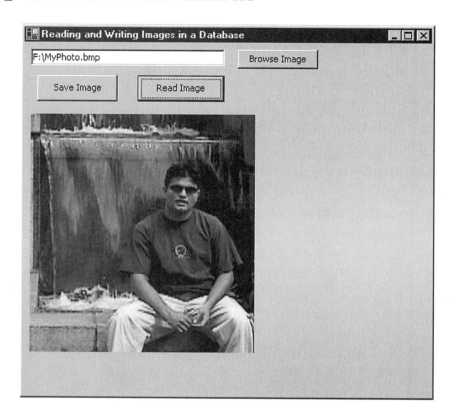

FIGURE 15.9: Displaying a bitmap after reading data from a database

How to Resize Graphics When a Window Is Resized

The `Control` class provides a property called `ClientRectangle` that represents the client area of a control or form. Using this property, we can measure the size of a control or a form, and set its position on the `Paint` event handler or `OnPaint` method. Whenever a user resizes the form, `OnPaint` is called.

15.5 Creating Owner-Drawn List Controls

How to create owner-drawn controls is a frequent topic of discussion forums and newsgroups. In this section we will discuss how an owner-drawn process works for Windows controls and how you can create your own controls.

15.5.1 The `DrawItem` Event

The `DrawItem` event is raised by owner-drawn controls. This event passes an argument of type `DrawItemEventArgs`, which contains data related to the event. The user uses this data to paint a specific item of the control. The properties of the `DrawItemEventArgs` class are given in Table 15.1.

Besides the properties listed in Table 15.1, the `DrawItemEventArgs` class provides two useful methods: `DrawBackground` and `DrawFocusRectangle`. The `DrawBackground` method draws the background of the item when we select an item in a control. The `DrawFocusRectangle` method draws a focus rectangle around the text of an item selected in the control. These methods take no arguments.

15.5.2 The `MeasureItem` Event

The `MeasureItem` event is raised by owner-drawn controls when the size (width and height) of the items in a control is being determined. This event passes an argument of type `MeasureItemEventArgs`,which contains data related to the event. This data is used by the user to paint a specific item of the control. The `MeasureItemEventArgs` class properties are listed in Table 15.2.

TABLE 15.1: `DrawItemEventArgs` properties

Property	Description
BackColor	Background color of the item that is being drawn.
Bounds	Rectangle that represents the bounds of the item being drawn.
Font	Font assigned to the item being drawn.
ForeColor	Foreground color of the item being drawn.
Graphics	Graphics object associated with the item being drawn.
Index	Index value of the item being drawn.
State	State of the item being drawn.

TABLE 15.2: `MeasureItemEventArgs` properties

Property	Description
`Graphics`	`Graphics` object associated with the event.
`Index`	Index of the item participating in the measure-item event. Both get and set.
`ItemHeight`	Height of the item. Both get and set.
`ItemWidth`	Width of the item. Both get and set.

15.5.3 Owner-Drawn `ListBox` Controls

The `ListBox` class represents a list box control in Windows Forms. This class provides two events—`DrawItem` and `MeasureItem`—that participate in owner drawing processes.

Briefly, in **owner-drawn controls** the developer (not the framework) programmatically handles the process of creating controls. One example of an owner-drawn control is a list box in which you can change the color, font, and size of the individual items.

> ■■ NOTE
> The `DrawMode` property of `ListBox` must be set to `DrawMode.Owner-DrawVariable`.

Let's create a Windows application using Visual Studio .NET and add a `ListBox` control by dragging it from the toolbox to the form. We start by drawing a list box with different colors, background color, and size. Then we set the `DrawMode` to `OwnerDrawVariable` using the **Properties** window. Finally, we add the code from Listing 15.12 on `InitializeComponent` after the `ListBox` code. This code sets the `DrawMode` property of `ListBox` and adds `DrawItem` and `MeasureItem` event handlers.

LISTING 15.12: Adding `DrawItem` and `MeasureItem` event handlers

```
this.listBox1.DrawMode =
  System.Windows.Forms.DrawMode.OwnerDrawVariable;
```

```
this.listBox1.MeasureItem +=
  new System.Windows.Forms.MeasureItemEventHandler(
  this.ListBoxMeasureItem);
this.listBox1.DrawItem +=
  new System.Windows.Forms.DrawItemEventHandler(
  this.ListBoxDrawItem);
```

Next we define four arrays to store the text, size, foreground color, and background color, respectively, of a `ListBox` item. We define the following variables in the form class:

```
private string [] textArray = null;
private int [] sizeArray = null;
private Color [] colorArray = null;
private Color [] backColorArray = null;
```

The next step is to initialize these arrays as in Listing 15.13. Our code also binds the text array to the `ListBox` control. You can add this code on the form's constructor after `InitializeComponent` or on the form's load event handler.

LISTING 15.13: Initializing arrays

```
textArray = new String[5]
{
  "Black Item", "Blue Item",
  "Red Item", "Green Item",
  "Yellow Item",
};

colorArray = new Color[5]
{
  Color.Black, Color.Blue,
  Color.Red, Color.Green,
  Color.Yellow,
};

backColorArray = new Color[5]
{
  Color.Gray, Color.LightCyan,
  Color.LightPink, Color.Yellow,
  Color.Black,
};

sizeArray = new int[5]
```

continues

```
{
   12, 14, 16, 18, 20
};

// Bind text array to list box
listBox1.DataSource = textArray;
```

The final step is to write `DrawItem` and `MeasureItem` event handlers. The code for these handlers is given in Listing 15.14. We draw a focus rectangle and background of items, and then we draw text using `DrawString` by passing the color, text, and size after reading from arrays. The `MeasureItem` event handler sets the height of the `ListBox` control items.

> **⬛ NOTE**
> See Chapters 3 and 5 for more about the `DrawString` method.

LISTING 15.14: The `DrawItem` and `MeasureItem` event handlers

```
private void ListBoxDrawItem(object sender,
   DrawItemEventArgs e)
{
   e.DrawFocusRectangle();
   e.DrawBackground();
   // Uncomment this code to set the background
   // color of items
   /*
   e.Graphics.FillRectangle(
      new SolidBrush(backColorArray[e.Index]),
      new Rectangle(e.Bounds.Left, e.Bounds.Top,
      e.Bounds.Right, e.Bounds.Bottom) );
   */
   e.Graphics.DrawString(textArray[e.Index],
      new Font(FontFamily.GenericSansSerif,
      sizeArray[e.Index], FontStyle.Bold),
      new SolidBrush(colorArray[e.Index]),
      e.Bounds);
}

private void ListBoxMeasureItem(object sender,
   MeasureItemEventArgs e)
{
   e.ItemHeight= 24;
}
```

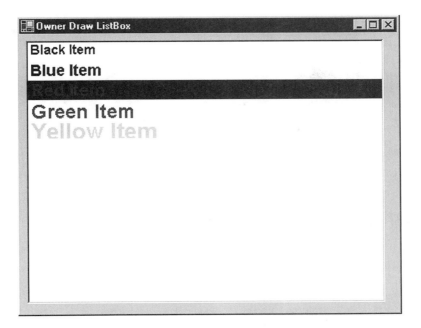

FIGURE 15.10: An owner-drawn ListBox control

If we run the application, the output will look like Figure 15.10.

15.5.4 An Owner-Drawn Image ListBox Control

Sometimes we want to display images in a ListBox control. By applying the method described in the preceding section, we can easily create an owner-drawn ListBox control with images in it. In the previous example we created an array of strings and used DrawString to draw them. This time we create an array of Image objects and call the DrawImage method. First we define an array of Image objects as follows:

```
private Image [] imgArray = null;
```

Then we initialize the image array. We can create an Image object from a file by using the Image.FromFile method. The following code snippet initializes the image array:

```
imgArray = new Image[5]
{
```

```
Image.FromFile("Img1.jpg"),
Image.FromFile("Img2.jpg"),
Image.FromFile("Img3.jpg"),
Image.FromFile("Img4.jpg"),
Image.FromFile("Img5.jpg")
};
```

Next we calculate the sizes of the images and draw them using `Draw-Image` on the `DrawItem` event handler. We can also set the sizes of items on the `MeasureItem` event handler. Listing 15.15 shows how to draw images using the `DrawImage` method.

LISTING 15.15: **DrawItem** and **MeasureItem** event handlers for an image **ListBox** control

```
private void ListBoxDrawItem(object sender,
  DrawItemEventArgs e)
{
  SizeF curImgSize =
    imgArray[e.Index].PhysicalDimension;
  e.Graphics.DrawImage(imgArray[e.Index],
    e.Bounds.X+5 ,
    ( e.Bounds.Bottom + e.Bounds.Top ) /2
      - curImgSize.Height/2);
}
private void ListBoxMeasureItem(object sender,
  MeasureItemEventArgs e)
{
  e.ItemHeight= 150;
}
```

The image listbox application looks like Figure 15.11.

More on Owner-Drawn Controls

Now that you have an idea how the owner drawing process works, you can create owner-drawn menus, combo boxes, and other controls. I recommend that you go to C# Corner and look at the Windows Forms section (http://www.c-sharpcorner.com/WinForms.asp). There you will find hundreds of useful source code samples available for download.

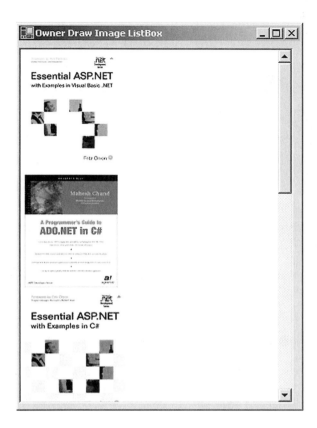

FIGURE 15.11: An owner-drawn ListBox control with images

SUMMARY

GDI+ can be used to write fun applications. In this chapter we covered more practical uses of GDI+ for real-world Windows applications. Topics discussed in this chapter included how to write interactive GUI rectangular and nonrectangular Windows applications, how to add custom text to images, how to read and write images to and from a stream or database, and finally, how to create owner-drawn controls.

A

Exception Handling in .NET

THE HANDLING OF exceptions and errors is critical to the development of reliable and stable applications. You may have noticed that no exception handling was included in the sample applications in this book. There are several reasons for this. First, omitting exception handling code simply makes the source a lot easier to read. Second, you might encounter new objects that we haven't discussed yet. After you read this appendix, you should implement error handling (also known as exception management) in your applications. Efficient exception management allows developers to write reliable and robust code that helps anticipate exceptions and, in doing so, provides an opportunity to present more informative and user-friendly error messages.

If you come from a C++ background, you are probably familiar with techniques such as C++ exception handling, structured exception handling, and MFC exceptions. If you come from a Visual Basic background, you are probably familiar with the On Error statement. Before .NET, every language implemented its own error handling. With .NET, all languages that create managed code share the same error handling mechanism. All .NET-supported languages (C#, VC++.NET, VB.NET, VJ#) enjoy the same rich exception handling.

C++ developers will probably be familiar with the `try...catch` block, which provides structured exception handling. Suspect code is placed within a `try` block, and when an exception occurs, the control is directed to the catch block. We will discuss the try...catch block in more detail in the following sections.

> ■ **NOTE**
> C++ and C# are case-sensitive languages; VB.NET is not, in the sense that no matter what is typed in, the editor automatically corrects the capitalization. In C# and C++, the statement is try...catch; in VB.NET, it is Try...Catch.

A.1 Why Exception Handling?

If you've been writing software for very long, you probably already know why you want to handle exceptions. Have you ever seen a program crash and display a weird message that doesn't make any sense? This is what happens when developers do not handle exceptions properly. Let's look at a simple example. Listing A.1 opens a file named c:\abc.txt.

LISTING A.1: Opening a file

```
using System;
using System.IO;

namespace ListingA1andA2
{
  class Class1
  {
    static void Main(string[] args)
    {
        File.Open("c:\\abc.txt", FileMode.Open);
    }
  }
}
```

What if the file does not exist? We get the error message shown in Figure A.1. We are fortunate that CLR handles so much for us because otherwise this error message could have been a lot worse.

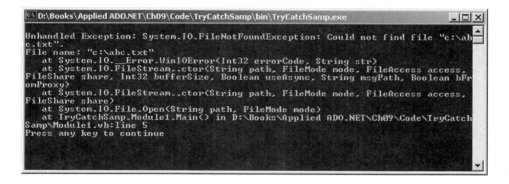

FIGURE A.1: An error generated from Listing A.1

Now let's make a small modification to our program. The new code is shown in Listing A.2. This time we use a simple try...catch block to handle the exception.

LISTING A.2: A simple exception handling block

```csharp
using System;
using System.IO;

namespace ListingA1andA2
{
  class Class1
  {
    static void Main(string[] args)
    {
      try
      {
        File.Open("c:\\abc.txt", FileMode.Open);
      }
      catch (Exception exp)
      {
        Console.WriteLine(exp.Message);
      }
    }
  }
}
```

Figure A.2 shows the output from the modified program. Not only is the exception handled, but also the cause of the exception is reported.

FIGURE A.2: An exception-handled error message

A.2 Understanding the `try...catch` Block

If you come from a Visual Basic background, we recommend that you just forget about unstructured exception handling and learn this new approach using the `try...catch` statement. After you finish reading this appendix, you'll find the structured approach much better!

A.2.1 The `try...catch` Statement

Using the `try...catch` statement is very straightforward. First we decide which code we want the error handler to monitor by placing that code inside the `try` block. When an exception occurs in the encapsulated code, a control goes to the `catch` block that handles the exception. A simple template for a `try...catch` block is shown in Listing A.3.

LISTING A.3: A simple `try...catch` block

```
try
{
  // Place the code that may generate
  // an exception in this block
}
catch ( exception type)
{
  // This code executes when the try block fails and
  // the filter on the catch statement is true.
  // Here you can write your own custom error message
  // or get the message description or other details
  // from the exception class.
}
```

A.2.2 **The** `try...catch...finally` **Statement**

The `try...catch...finally` statement is an extended version of the `try...catch` statement. If an error occurs during execution of any of the code inside the `try` section, the control moves to the `catch` block when the filter condition is `true`. The `finally` block always executes last, just before the error handling block loses scope, regardless of whether an exception has occurred. The `finally` block is the perfect place to close files and dispose of objects. A simple `try...catch...finally` statement is shown in Listing A.4.

LISTING A.4: A simple `try...catch...finally` statement

```
try
{
  // Place the code that may generate
  // an exception in this block
}
catch ( exception type)
{
  // This code executes when the try block fails and
  // the filter on the catch statement is true.
  // Here you can write your own custom error message
  // or get the message description or other details
  // from the exception class.
}
finally
{
  // Release and dispose of objects and
  // other resources here
}
```

Listing A.5 allocates resources at the beginning of the method and releases them inside the `finally` block. Regardless of whether an exception occurs, execution control will pass to the `finally` block and release the resources.

LISTING A.5: Disposing of objects inside the `finally` block

```
private void TestExpBtn_Click(object sender,
  System.EventArgs e)
{
  // Create a Graphics object
```

continues

```
Graphics g = this.CreateGraphics();
g.Clear(this.BackColor);
// Create pens and brushes
Pen redPen = new Pen(Color.Red, 1);
Pen bluePen = new Pen(Color.Blue, 2);
Pen greenPen = new Pen(Color.Green, 3);
SolidBrush greenBrush =
  new SolidBrush(Color.Green);
// Put whatever code you think may cause
// the error within this block
try
{
  // Use the Point structure to draw lines
  Point pt1 = new Point(30, 40);
  Point pt2 = new Point(250, 60);
  g.DrawLine(redPen, pt1, pt2);
  // Draw a rectangle
  Rectangle rect =
    new Rectangle(20,20, 80, 40);
  g.DrawRectangle(bluePen, rect);
  // Create points for curve
  PointF p1 = new PointF(40.0F, 50.0F);
  PointF p2 = new PointF(60.0F, 70.0F);
  PointF p3 = new PointF(80.0F, 34.0F);
  PointF p4 = new PointF(120.0F, 180.0F);
  PointF p5 = new PointF(200.0F, 150.0F);
  PointF p6 = new PointF(350.0F, 250.0F);
  PointF p7 = new PointF(200.0F, 200.0F);
  PointF[] ptsArray =
  {
  p1, p2, p3, p4, p5, p6, p7
  };
  // Draw Bézier curve
  g.DrawBeziers(redPen, ptsArray);
}
catch(Exception exp)
{
  string errMsg = "Message: " + exp.Message;
  errMsg += "Source: "+ exp.Source.ToString();
  errMsg += "TargetSite: "+ exp.TargetSite;
  errMsg += "HelpLink: "
  + exp.HelpLink.ToString();
  errMsg += "StackTrace: "
  + exp.StackTrace.ToString();
  MessageBox.Show(errMsg);
}
finally
{
  // Release resources
```

```
    // Dispose of objects
    redPen.Dispose();
    bluePen.Dispose();
    greenPen.Dispose();
    greenBrush.Dispose();
    g.Dispose();
  }
}
```

A.2.3 Nested `try...catch` Statements

We can provide more specific error handling by nesting `try...catch` blocks. The only case in which we might not want to use nested `try...catch` blocks is when we want to catch different types of exceptions. For example, one block might catch memory-related exceptions; another, I/O-related exceptions; and a third, general exceptions.

Listing A.6 uses nested `try...catch` statements. In this code we create two images. The first image we draw only once, but the second image we draw 15 times at different locations. The first `try...catch` statement covers the entire code with a general exception, and the second `try...catch` statement is specific to the `OutOfMemory` exception. We can use as many `try...catch` blocks as exceptions we want to catch. For example, if our code performs I/O operations, we may want to use the `IOException` class. We can also customize the default message to match the error type.

LISTING A.6: Nesting `try...catch` statements

```
private void NestedMenu_Click(object sender,
  System.EventArgs e)
{
  // Create Graphics object
  Graphics g = this.CreateGraphics();
  g.Clear(this.BackColor);
  try
  {
    // Create an image from a file
    Image curImage = Image.FromFile("roses.jpg");
    // Draw the image
    g.DrawImage(curImage, AutoScrollPosition.X,
      AutoScrollPosition.Y,
      curImage.Width, curImage.Height );
    // Create a second image from a file
    Image smallImage =
      Image.FromFile("smallRoses.gif");
```

continues

```
// Draw the second image many times
int x1, y1, x2, y2, w, h;
x1 = x2 = AutoScrollPosition.X;
   y1 = AutoScrollPosition.Y;
y2 = 300;
w = 20;
h = 20;
// Make a loop to draw second image
// on top of the first image
for(int i=0; i<=15; i++)
{
  try
  {
    // Draw from top left to bottom right
    g.DrawImage(smallImage,
      new Rectangle(x1, y1, w, h),
      0, 0, smallImage.Width,
      smallImage.Height,
      GraphicsUnit.Pixel );
    // Draw from top right to bottom left
    g.DrawImage(smallImage,
      new Rectangle(x2, y2, w, h),
      0, 0, smallImage.Width,
      smallImage.Height,
      GraphicsUnit.Pixel );
    x1 += 20;
    y1 += 20;
    x2 += 20;
    y2 -= 20;
  }
  catch (OutOfMemoryException memExp)
  {
    MessageBox.Show(memExp.Message);
  }
}
}
catch(Exception exp)
{
  MessageBox.Show(exp.Message);
}
finally
{
  // Dispose of objects
  g.Dispose();
}
}
```

A.2.4 **Multiple** `catch` **Statements with a Single** `try` **Statement**

The `try...catch` statement also allows us to use multiple `catch` statements with a single `try` statement, which helps when we're catching multiple types of exceptions and customizing error messages to match the type of error.

Listing A.7 is a modified version of Listing A.6 that uses a `try` statement with two `catch` statements.

LISTING A.7: Using multiple `catch` statements with a single `try` statement

```
private void MultiCatchesMenu_Click(object sender,
  System.EventArgs e)
{
// Create a Graphics object
Graphics g = this.CreateGraphics();
g.Clear(this.BackColor);
try
{
  // Create an image from a file
  Image curImage = Image.FromFile("roses.jpg");
  // Draw image
  g.DrawImage(curImage, AutoScrollPosition.X,
    AutoScrollPosition.Y,
    curImage.Width, curImage.Height );
  // Create a second image from a file
  Image smallImage =
    Image.FromFile("smallRoses.gif");
  // Draw the second image many times
  int x1, y1, x2, y2, w, h;
  x1 = x2 = AutoScrollPosition.X;
  y1 = AutoScrollPosition.Y;
  y2 = 300;
  w = 20;
  h = 20;
  // Make a loop to draw second image
  // on top of the first image
  for(int i=0; i<=15; i++)
  {
    // Draw from top left to bottom right
    g.DrawImage(smallImage,
      new Rectangle(x1, y1, w, h),
      0, 0, smallImage.Width,
      smallImage.Height,
      GraphicsUnit.Pixel );
    // Draw from top right to bottom left
    g.DrawImage(smallImage,
```

continues

```
         new Rectangle(x2, y2, w, h),
         0, 0, smallImage.Width,
         smallImage.Height,
         GraphicsUnit.Pixel );
       x1 += 20;
       y1 += 20;
       x2 += 20;
       y2 -= 20;
    }
  }
  catch (OutOfMemoryException memExp)
  {
    MessageBox.Show(memExp.Message);
  }
  catch(Exception exp)
  {
    MessageBox.Show(exp.Message);
  }
  finally
  {
    // Dispose of objects
    g.Dispose();
  }
}
```

A.3 Understanding Exception Classes

By now you have a basic idea of how to implement structured exception
handling in your code. Now let's take a quick overview of exception-
related classes provided by the .NET Framework library.

A.3.1 The Exception Class: Mother of All Exceptions

The Exception class is the first class we will discuss. It caters to errors that
occur during normal application execution. This is the base class for all
exception classes. In our previous samples, we have already seen how to
use the Exception class. Table A.1 describes its properties.

Listing A.8 uses the Exception class properties to display information
about an exception.

LISTING A.8: Using Exception properties

```
// The error within this block
try
{
```

```
  // Suspect code here
}
catch(Exception exp)
{
  string errMsg = "Message: " + exp.Message;
  errMsg += "Source: "+ exp.Source.ToString();
  errMsg += "TargetSite: "+ exp.TargetSite;
  errMsg += "HelpLink: "
  + exp.HelpLink.ToString();
  errMsg += "StackTrace: "
  + exp.StackTrace.ToString();
  MessageBox.Show(errMsg);
}
finally
{
  // Release resources
  // Dispose of objects
}
```

A.3.2 Other Exception Classes

The .NET Framework class library defines a multitude of exception classes—each designed to handle a specific kind of exception. For example, the IOException error is thrown when an I/O error occurs. All of the classes work in a similar way. If you want to handle I/O-related errors, use

TABLE A.1: Exception properties

Property	Description
HelpLink	Represents the link to the help file associated with an exception. Both get and set.
InnerException	Returns the Exception instance that caused the current exception. Read-only.
Message	Returns the error message that describes the current exception. Read-only.
Source	Indicates the name of the application or object that causes the error. Both get and set.
StackTrace	A string representation of the frames on the call stack at the time the exception occurred. Read-only.
TargetSite	Returns the method that throws the exception. Read-only.

`IOException` instead of `Exception`. This allows your code to respond to a more specific exception. Unlike ADO.NET and other libraries, GDI+ doesn't have any specific exception handling classes.

Some of the common exception handling classes are listed below. The `SystemException` class, which is derived from the `Exception` class, is the base class for system (runtime)-generated errors. The following class hierarchy shows the `SystemException`-derived classes:

```
System.Object
  System.Exception
    System.SystemException
    System.AppDomainUnloadedException
    System.ArgumentException
    System.ArithmeticException
    System.ArrayTypeMismatchException
    System.BadImageFormatException
    System.CannotUnloadAppDomainException
    System.ComponentModel.Design.Serialization
      .CodeDomSerializerException
    System.ComponentModel.LicenseException
    System.ComponentModel.WarningException
    System.Configuration.ConfigurationException
    System.Configuration.Install.InstallException
    System.ContextMarshalException
    System.Data.DataException
    System.Data.DBConcurrencyException
    System.Data.SqlClient.SqlException
    System.Data.SqlTypes.SqlTypeException
    System.Drawing.Printing.InvalidPrinterException
    System.EnterpriseServices.RegistrationException
    System.EnterpriseServices.ServicedComponentException
    System.ExecutionEngineException
    System.FormatException
    System.IndexOutOfRangeException
    System.InvalidCastException
```

```
System.InvalidOperationException
System.InvalidProgramException
System.IO.InternalBufferOverflowException
System.IO.IOException
System.Management.ManagementException
System.MemberAccessException
System.MulticastNotSupportedException
System.NotImplementedException
System.NotSupportedException
System.NullReferenceException
System.OutOfMemoryException
System.RankException
System.Reflection.AmbiguousMatchException
System.Reflection.ReflectionTypeLoadException
System.Resources.MissingManifestResourceException
System.Runtime.InteropServices.ExternalException
System.Runtime.InteropServices
  .InvalidComObjectException
System.Runtime.InteropServices
  .InvalidOleVariantTypeException
System.Runtime.InteropServices
  .MarshalDirectiveException
System.Runtime.InteropServices
  .SafeArrayRankMismatchException
System.Runtime.InteropServices
  .SafeArrayTypeMismatchException
System.Runtime.Remoting.RemotingException
System.Runtime.Remoting.ServerException
System.Runtime.Serialization.SerializationException
System.Security.Cryptography.CryptographicException
System.Security.Policy.PolicyException
System.Security.SecurityException
System.Security.VerificationException
System.Security.XmlSyntaxException
System.ServiceProcess.TimeoutException
```

```
System.StackOverflowException
System.Threading.SynchronizationLockException
System.Threading.ThreadAbortException
System.Threading.ThreadInterruptedException
System.Threading.ThreadStateException
System.TypeInitializationException
System.TypeLoadException
System.TypeUnloadedException
System.UnauthorizedAccessException
System.Web.Services.Protocols.SoapException
System.Xml.Schema.XmlSchemaException
System.Xml.XmlException
System.Xml.XPath.XPathException
System.Xml.Xsl.XsltException
```

As we saw in the class hierarchy, the .NET Framework defines hundreds of exception classes—some of them specific to a particular operation. For example, `OutOfMemoryException` is thrown when there is not enough memory to continue the execution of a program.

The `System.ArithmeticException` class represents arithmetic exceptions that occur in arithmetic, casting, or conversion operations. All of its members are inherited from the `Exception` class. `ArithmeticException` has three derived classes: `DivideByZeroException`, `NotFiniteNumberException`, and `OverflowException`.

`DivideByZeroException` occurs when code tries to divide an integral or decimal value by zero. `NotFiniteNumberException` occurs when a floating point value is positive infinity, negative infinity, or not a number. `OverflowException` occurs when an arithmetic, casting, or conversion operation in a checked context results in an overflow.

`System.Data.DataException` and its derived classes represent exceptions that occur when we're working with data (ADO.NET) components.

`System.IOException` represents an exception that is thrown when an I/O error occurs.

`System.StackOverflowException` represents an exception that is thrown when the stack overflows because too many method calls have been executed.

SUMMARY

This appendix provided a working introduction to structured exception and error handling in .NET. We discussed various exception-related classes that are provided by the .NET Framework. We also discussed how error handling works in .NET and how to use `try..catch` blocks. In addition, we discussed the `Exception` class and its members, as well as other exception-related classes.

Index